BUSINESS ADMINISTRATION
An Introductory Management Approach

BUSINESS
ADMINISTRATION
An Introductory

REVISED EDITION OF

By ARTHUR M. WEIMER

Dean, School of Business, Indiana University

34299

1962

RICHARD D. IRWIN, INC., HOMEWOOD, ILLINOIS

Management Approach

INTRODUCTION TO BUSINESS: A MANAGEMENT APPROACH

REVISED EDITION

First Printing, March, 1962

Library of Congress Catalogue Card No. 62–11280

PRINTED IN THE UNITED STATES OF AMERICA

To My Mother
ANNA L. WEIMER

"The real purpose of books is to trap the mind into doing its own thinking."

—CHRISTOPHER MORLEY

PREFACE

The need for an early revision of this book became clear soon after publication of the first edition. The sheer rapidity of changes in the study of business administration pointed toward such a decision. Even more compelling were the number and variety of suggestions for improvement that came from students and instructors who worked with the first edition. In general they liked the "management approach" but expressed the need for more extensive treatment of many of the topics and the inclusion of additional materials, particularly on decision making, quantitative analysis, and the application of the behavioral sciences to management problems.

Consequently, the revision has been rather extensive. It reflects the growing interest in decision making and decision processes. It recognizes the increasing reliance on quantitative analysis as an aid to decisions, the expanding emphasis on organization behavior, leadership, and related subjects, and the increasing importance of international business administration. The revision also recognizes that students (and their instructors) are bringing more sophisticated backgrounds to the study of business administration.

The extent of the revision would appear to justify a change in the title of the book to *Business Administration: An Introductory Management Approach*. This change of title is intended to suggest a somewhat broader treatment of the subject than typically is found in the more traditional "Introduction to Business" texts.

A need has often been expressed for study materials in the field of business administration which can serve somewhat the same purposes as do texts of the introductory or principles type in the field of economics. I hope that this edition may help to meet this need even more directly than its predecessor. We do not have as yet a "general theory" of business administration to provide a basis for integrating the subject matter. We do find that some help of this type is provided by the management process, decision making, management of resources and operations, and the interactions between the business firm and its environment. These general subjects form the basis for the major sections of this book.

Even so, the organization of the materials presented some difficult problems, not only because of the breadth and complexity of the field, but also because of the diversity of opinion in regard to desirable arrangements for teaching and study purposes. Many instructors prefer to begin with the more general subjects, such as are included in discussions of the business environment in Part Five, and then proceed to subjects related more directly to business firms and their management. Others prefer the type of arrangement that is presented here, which begins with two chapters addressed rather specifically to the student and then proceeds to an "overview" or "preview" as presented in Chapters 3 and 4 (Part One). From these preview chapters the discussions move from business firms and management processes (Part Two) to decision processes and guides (Part Three) to resources and operations (Part Four) to the business environment (Part Five) and finally to emerging problems and opportunities (Part Six).

Instructors who prefer may move from Chapter 4 to Part Five and then back to Part Two. Some instructors may prefer to skip Chapter 4 and return to it prior to the study of Part Five. Such an arrangement is also workable. Some of the materials in Part Three, notably Chapter 14, may be considered too difficult for some students; if so, this chapter may be undertaken later in the course or omitted entirely. The arrangement followed here makes it possible to use Professor E. W. Martin's "Management Decision Simulation" exercise (which is available from the publisher for users of this book) fairly early in the course, if desired, following the study of Chapter 12 .

Professor John D. Long has again produced a highly interesting and stimulating *Workbook* to supplement the text. This edition of the *Workbook* has a number of new features, particularly the easy grading arrangement for the introductory exercise for each chapter. The text materials prove to be much more teachable if the *Workbook* is used in connection with them. This is notably true for such chapters as those included in Part Three on Decision Processes and Guides.

I know that the current edition, like its predecessor, has inadequacies. It is a difficult undertaking to introduce a student (at any level) to the broad field of business administration. There is a tendency to be repetitious in introductory discussions. One is tempted to overemphasize some concepts at the expense of others. There is often a conflict between what one feels should be said from an academic point of view and what "makes sense" in terms of business practice. Even so, I hope the book will prove to be useful.

It would be impossible to acknowledge the assistance of the many instructors, students, and others who have contributed to this revision. Many business school deans and faculty members, as well as faculty members of arts and sciences colleges, made valuable suggestions. Although I undertook the work of writing and recognize, of course, that responsibility for the final product rests with me, I must acknowledge the assistance of at least some of those who contributed to the project. Professor John D. Long worked closely with me in developing the revision and he coordinated the text and workbook materials with great skill. Deans Edward J. Kuntz and John H. Porter, who teach the course in which these materials are used at Indiana University, provided many valuable ideas and suggestions. Dean Porter is also experimenting with some programmed instructional materials that may be available for use with the text. Dean W. George Pinnell again assumed more than his share of administrative work to help me gain much needed time.

As was the case with the first edition, I am especially indebted to Professors John F. Mee and Edward E. Edwards for their valuable criticisms and suggestions in regard to the entire project. Other colleagues were helpful in connection with specific subjects, notably Paul J. Gordon on organization and leadership; Donald H. Sauer on the financial materials and various illustrations; Robert R. Milroy and D. Lyle Dieterle on accounting; E. Wainwright Martin, Jr., on mathematical decision guides; Edgar G. Williams on personnel and organization behavior; L. Leslie Waters on transportation; Howard L. Timms on production; Schuyler F. Otteson on marketing; John P. Lewis and Robert C. Turner on business, governmental, and political conditions; Harold Lusk and Charles Hewitt on the legal system; and Stefan H. Robock on international business administration.

Miss Betty Thickstun and Miss Bonnie Thickstun prepared the manuscript for publication. Miss Betty Thickstun gave additional assistance in the preparation of the index. Other assistance is recognized at various points in the following discussions.

ARTHUR M. WEIMER

Bloomington, Indiana
January, 1962

TABLE OF CONTENTS

PART 1. ORIENTATION

PART 4.   BUSINESS RESOURCES AND OPERATIONS

PART 5. THE BUSINESS ENVIRONMENT

PART 6. EMERGING PROBLEMS AND OPPORTUNITIES

APPENDIXES

INDEXES

part Orientation

SUMMARY OUTLINE

BUSINESS ADMINISTRATION—now one of the more exciting areas of study—may be *approached* in an *introductory* manner from the point of view of the *manager*.

He is the central figure in the business firm—the key social and economic institution of our time. It is managed and operated in a highly dynamic environment.

Business Firms are established as individual *proprietorships, partnerships, corporations,* and other forms.

Firms vary in *size* and engage in many *types* of *work*—manufacturing, trade, finance, service, and others.

The *Decision Makers* in business firms are owners, managers, and business specialists.

The *Management Process* involves establishment of objectives, plans, and controls; organization of resources; and leadership.

Decision Making—a central management responsibility—includes problem and *goal identification* and clarification, development and analysis of *alternatives,* appraisal of most likely alternatives, and *choice.*

Decisions may be guided by financial, accounting, statistical, economic, mathematical, and other considerations.

Business Resources and Operations involve effective utilization of the abilities of people—requiring knowledge of personnel and organization behavior—

as well as other resources including

capital, equipment, knowledge, time, and related aids to productivity, plus the place of business—land, buildings, and location—

in the *production* and *marketing* of goods and services to secure *income.*

The *Business Environment* influences management decisions and in turn is influenced by them, particularly in the areas of

business conditions,
governmental and political conditions,
the legal system,
the enterprise system and competing systems,
and international business administration.

Emerging Problems and Opportunities hold promise for the business community, and for you in managing your future.

OUTLINE FOR CHAPTER 1

THE STUDY OF BUSINESS ADMINISTRATION
is approached here from the viewpoint of the *manager*, the
central figure in the business firm, in order to stress the
interdependence of the many types of activities involved.

Business deals with the economic aspects of life, especially the
production and marketing of goods and services by privately
owned firms in pursuit of profits.

Administration is fundamentally the *direction of affairs*; it includes
decision-making and decision-implementing activities; it is
action oriented.

The business firm is both an economic and a *social institution*,
providing goods and services for sale; it must have public
support for its products in order to gain revenues in excess
of costs, or profits, without which it cannot survive.

The business firm is regulated largely by competition; it is one of
the functions of government to make competition work, or to
provide alternative means of control, if necessary.

Business administration may be studied in terms of career interests,
to improve the world in which we live, or
to satisfy general intellectual curiosity.

The field of business administration is now one of the most
exciting areas of study; largely because of:
increased emphasis on *decision making*,
application of new *statistical* and *mathematical* techniques,
widespread use of the computer,
application of *social and behavior sciences* to the field,
rapid *economic changes* at home and abroad, and
added interest in the role of the business executive and his
community responsibilities.

The study of
business administration is *future oriented;*
teaching and learning methods are similar to those of other
fields, but include also case studies, the incident method,
"the executive game," and other techniques.

THE STUDY OF BUSINESS ADMINISTRATION

He that would govern others, first must be the master of himself.
—MASSINGER

The Student of Business Administration

This book is addressed to you as a student of business administration. You may be a college student or be studying this subject in some other connection. In either event, these discussions are addressed to you on the assumption that you are at an early stage in your career. While you are bound to know something about business from your general experience or from related studies, this book presupposes no special background or basic knowledge. It is designed as an introduction to this broad and challenging subject.

You may approach the study of business administration from many points of view. This book attempts to approach the subject from the point of view of the manager, the central figure in the business firm. By means of a management approach we hope to help you understand the interdependence of the many types of work that are carried on by every business establishment and also to see the interrelationships between the business firm and our society as a whole.

The use of a management or administrative approach to the study of this subject does not mean that we expect every student to become a manager. Some of you will, of course. By contrast some of you will enter other fields such as law, engineering, government, or the sciences. A number of you will become specialists in one or another business field such as finance, personnel administration, accounting, marketing, production, insurance, or transportation. Regardless of your objective in studying this subject, the management approach should help you to develop a basic understanding of the business firm and its administration in a dynamic social, political, and economic environment.

What Is Business?

Like many of those words whose meaning is assumed to be clear, the term "business" almost defies precise definition. Certainly we would agree that the term includes business firms, business executives, business transactions, and many other fairly familiar things. For our purposes we may use a definition prepared by Sir Frederic Hooper:

> By the term "business" we mean the whole complex field of commerce and industry, the basic industries, processing and manufacturing industries, and the network of ancillary services, distribution, banking, insurance, transport, and so on, which serve and interpenetrate the world of business as a whole. Most people who go to work throughout the country do so in some branch of business; all alike are dependent upon its output in goods and services for the fabric of their social life, and in the broadest sense its efficiency determines the whole nation's standard of living. Moreover, in its field most of our children must of necessity seek their opportunities. In short, the operations of business earn the nation its living, and not merely the incomes of a few people: nowhere is success of more material moment and nothing comes closer to us at work or leisure.[1]

Such a definition suggests that we cannot study business by concentrating our attention solely on the business firm, even though it has been called the key social institution of our time.[2] We consider also the management, administration, and operation of the business firm, and the environment or general climate within which business is carried on.

Business deals primarily with the economic aspects of life. It serves the economic needs of our society. Business activities include the production and sale of goods and services, usually by privately owned and operated firms or companies. Various types of business activities, however, are carried on by public and quasi-public agencies.

What Is Business Administration?

Since business deals with economic aspects of life, the basic problems of the economist and the manager or administrator are to a degree similar. Each is concerned with the effective use of resources to achieve desired objectives. The economist, however, is primarily concerned with the economic system or society as a whole while the manager or administrator deals with his particular enterprise, firm, or program. Usually, also, the economist serves in an advisory capacity,

1 Sir Frederic Hooper, *Management Survey* (rev. ed.; New York: Pitman Publishing Corp., 1961), pp. 150–51, by permission.
2 *Ibid.*, p. 158.

while the administrator is a man of action. *The job of the manager or administrator is to get things done.* He may study and consider carefully before arriving at a decision. He may consult economists, lawyers, engineers, and other specialists. Ultimately, however, he has to reach a decision and carry it into effect. Thus, the principal parts of administration are making decisions and implementing them or carrying them out. These two parts of the process are closely interrelated, as we shall see, and it is often difficult to differentiate between them. Recently major emphasis has been placed on decision making in the study of business administration, even to the extent of considering decision making and managing as synonymous.[3]

For our purposes it seems desirable to consider administration to include both decision making and implementation, as a broad range of activities related to the direction of organized effort. As Robert D. Calkins has said:

Administration is fundamentally the direction of affairs. It is purposive action, and to an increasing degree it is informed, rational, and deliberate action. It draws upon the knowledge of the physical sciences and the practical arts; it employs the knowledge and techniques of the social sciences; but it is overwhelmingly concerned with the choice of ends, ways, and means for the attainment of desired results. It is curbed by moral codes and ethical principles; and it is driven by springs of ambition and devotion that largely escape analysis. . . .

The three main elements of administration are the formulation of goals, the choice of ways and means, and the direction of people in some group purpose. These activities may be considered as consisting mainly of two processes: the process of decision-making and the process of execution, or action. The former determines what is to be done and how, while the latter puts decisions into action and oversees the process.[4]

Business administration may be thought of as one aspect of administration in general; it relates primarily to the management of business firms. Typically such firms are privately owned and operated.[5]

Why Do Business Firms Exist?

Basically business firms exist because they do useful work for all of us. They produce and market goods and services in the hope of earn-

[3] See for example, Herbert A. Simon, *The New Science of Management Decision* (New York: Harper & Bros., 1960), p. 1.

[4] Speech given at the annual meeting of the American Association of Collegiate Schools of Business (Milwaukee, Wis.: Marquette University, April, 1955). Reproduced by author's permission.

[5] Some public and quasi-public organizations may be included, as we shall see later.

ing profits. They provide these goods and services at prices that people can afford to pay. Indeed, the history of business indicates that there has been a persistent trend toward the production of better and better goods and services at lower and lower costs.

With few exceptions business firms do their work to the general satisfaction of the public as a whole and in harmony with general social objectives and standards. Otherwise they would not be allowed to exist.

Primarily business firms are involved in helping us all to solve the basic economic problem which may be stated this way: there are not enough goods and services available to enable us to have all of the things that we would like to have. Economists describe this condition as one of limited resources and unlimited wants.

We could get the work of business firms done in other ways. It might be done by government agencies for example, or by the Army. Or it might be done by families or other groups. There is nothing to prevent labor unions from hiring capital and management and engaging in business, for example.

We have found, however, that business firms, large and small, operating within a general framework of laws and regulations are able to provide goods and services for us more efficiently and at lower costs than can be provided by other arrangements. Furthermore, business firms do these things and also help to further our broad social objectives of achieving growth and progress in all aspects of life, pursuing our basic freedoms, and expanding economic opportunity.

To a large degree business firms operate in this way because of competition and because of free markets in which competition can take place. Competition serves as a regulator of business firms. It forces one firm to improve its product or lose its market to another. It forces another firm to develop and introduce a new product, another to raise its wages and salaries in order to attract and hold competent personnel, another to raise dividends, another to buy improved machinery and equipment, and another to lower the prices of its products. It is the responsibility of government to make competition work. In some situations, as in the case of a public utility, competition does not usually provide effective regulation. Then more direct government action is needed to provide for regulation in the public interest.

What Is a Business Firm?

A business firm is an economic unit, entity, or organization. It may in some cases be an informal arrangement of people working together.

But to succeed, some type of formal organization is usually required with some person in charge, who decides what is to be done, by whom, when, where, how, and by what procedures and processes. This is the work of business executives or managers. They may be owners or part owners of the firm, or they may be hired persons who do not have an ownership interest but who have the education, ability, and "know-how" to manage business operations. Regardless of organization, a business firm must provide goods and services—it must produce or market things or services that the public wants and is willing to pay for. It must gain revenues in excess of costs, that is, it must make *profits* if it is to survive. The pursuit of profit is a distinguishing characteristic of the business firm or enterprise. It may pursue a variety of objectives—survival, growth, prestige, or others—but it must operate at a profit.

A business firm is a social organization. People of many different types and abilities are associated together in it for many hours each working day. They make their incomes this way. But they also derive many noneconomic benefits. For example, they may find friends with whom they enjoy being associated. Much of their social life may center around the people with whom they work. They may gain recognition and attain positions of trust. They may develop loyalties to the firm and enjoy being identified with it.

Thus, it is as important to study the relationships between people in a business firm as it is to study the products, the markets, the finances, or the accounts of the firm. The people who work in a firm are all complex persons. Like all of us, the people in business have many and varied objectives in life, interests, likes and dislikes, hopes and fears, successes and failures. Somehow they must work together effectively enough to allow the business firm to meet and if possible to beat the competition of other firms in its field. Getting this done is a primary job of managers at all levels, from president to the supervisor of the smallest part of the work of the firm.

The business firm plays an important role as community citizen. It employs people living in a community. It pays taxes toward the support of schools, police and fire departments, streets and roads, and local services and facilities of many types. Directly or indirectly it may have an important effect on local government and community policies. It also plays an important role in the political life of states, the nation as a whole, and even in international relations. The philosopher Alfred North Whitehead once referred to the "Great Society" as one "in which its men of business think greatly of their functions."

The business firm is being studied increasingly not only by those interested in the field of business administration but by social scientists and others. One recent report states:

> The business firm is one of the dominant institutions of modern life, not only in the United States but throughout much of the world. One may approve of the activities and organization of business, or deplore them, or look on with judicious resignation, but no thoughtful person will deny the *importance* of business in the contemporary world. And the importance of business is a sufficient reason why social scientists should study it.[6]

Why Study Business?

Why should you study business? The answer to this question will vary with your interests, your objectives, and your intellectual curiosity. If you plan to go into business as a career, your answer to the above question probably will be stated in terms of preparing yourself for your future work. Similarly, if you plan to go into the field of law or the government service, you may wish to study business from a career standpoint. Even as a consumer of goods and services of all kinds, or as an investor of your savings, you will find knowledge of business important to you. As a student of economics or of one or another of the social sciences, you will need a working knowledge of business simply because it occupies an important place in American life—or for that matter in the life of any country. As we have indicated, the business firm has been called "the key social institution of our time."

In some cases your interest in this subject may arise from general intellectual curiosity. You may want to know more about business and its administration simply because it is a field that interests you as a student.

All of us have an interest in improving the world in which we live. Thus, we study various subjects in the hope that through better understanding we can help to bring about improvement. The study of business administration is no exception. Many of you will try to find ways of improving the management of business firms or the methods of operating them. Some of you will have a special interest in improving the environment within which business firms carry on their activities.

The ultimate purpose of all study, especially of a scientific sort, is understanding in the sense of explanation and prediction. The field of business administration involves the application of scientific knowl-

---

[6] Robert A. Dahl, Mason Haire, Paul F. Lazarfeld, *Social Science Research on Business: Product and Potential* (New York: Columbia University Press, 1959), preface, by permission.

edge and methods. It is an applied field like engineering, law, or medicine. It is concerned with action. This does not mean that we have no concern with understanding in a scientific sense. We also study to understand, explain, improve, and make better predictions. We need to understand what is known about a subject before we can undertake research to develop new knowledge.

An Exciting Area of Study

Today business administration is one of the more exciting of all areas of study. Our experiences in World War II and in the turbulent years since brought a number of developments that have virtually revolutionized the field of business administration. Our war and post-war experiences fixed attention to an increasing extent on decision making as a central administrative or management activity. Statistical and mathematical techniques have been applied increasingly to the solution of military, governmental, and business problems, aided greatly by the development of the high-speed computer. It may well be that the computer will affect your life and work to an even greater extent than the explosion of the first atomic bomb or the launching of the first space satellite.

The use of "military games" to develop strategic and tactical plans and to train military commanders stimulated the use of similar techniques in the teaching of business administration. This process was aided by the computer. You will have an opportunity to make use of a simple version of the "management game" or "executive simulation exercise" in this course.

The war brought problems of selecting, training, developing, and motivating large numbers of people in a short time. Further, these people had to be organized into effective groups, small and large, civilian and military, at home and abroad. We called on our knowledge of the social and behavioral sciences and on experts in these fields to help solve these problems. Much of this experience was later adapted to business personnel and organizations.

Rapid economic changes in recent years have posed major problems for the owners and managers of business firms. Managers found it necessary to devote increasing attention to the economic, social, and political environment of business at home and abroad. Business has a major stake in the international competition of the U.S.A. and the U.S.S.R. Many business firms have undertaken world-wide activities, in part as a result of this competition.

Other developments also contributed to the emergence of business administration as an exciting area of study. One was the study and use of "game theory" about which we will have more to say later; still another was the "population explosion" and the problems this poses for our society as a whole and for many business firms; and still another was the growing professionalization of management and the efforts of schools of business to improve the education of young people interested in this field.

Professional Management

The professional manager is largely a product of recent years. He may or may not have an ownership interest in his firm. Thus, many young people today may aspire to positions of executive responsibility even though they do not have money or "connections." In an earlier period ownership and management were closely combined and one could not aspire to a managerial position unless he earned or inherited the necessary capital or married the boss's daughter. Then young people with leadership potential typically entered the military or government service or the traditional professions. Today business outranks all fields in the provision of opportunities for potential leaders.

Expanding opportunities in the field of professional management should not cause you to lose sight of the possibilities for establishing and operating your own business firm. The opportunities here are as great as ever. In addition, you may wish to consider the possibilities for a career as a business specialist in such areas as accounting, production, marketing, finance, statistics, business economics, personnel, and related fields. Many mathematicians, physical scientists, engineers, lawyers, and social and behavioral scientists will also find challenging opportunities in business in the years ahead.

The Student as Manager

As a student at an early stage in your career, you are undertaking an important managerial job. You have the job of managing your resources including your energy, your time, your money, and your capacity for growth and development in such a way that you will achieve your study objectives. Learning to manage yourself and your own abilities is the first step in preparing for a full life, a business career, or any other type of career.

In short, administration and management is the center and core of the study of business, but in a broader sense administration is involved in nearly every aspect of your life. You are learning to manage yourself now. Later you will be managing your family, your job, your home, your investments, and many other things. Even though your career objectives are far removed from the business world, you will find a knowledge of business administration helpful to your life and work.

You can also learn a good deal about decision making and the processes of implementing decisions by studying yourself. When you have a decision to make, consider how you go about it. On what basis do you make a final choice? How much information do you collect? Do you seek the advice of others? Once you reach a decision, how is it carried out? Do you do it yourself or through others? Is individual or organized effort involved?

Considering questions like this and relating them to your own experience may help you to see the implications of some of the materials you will be studying. To a degree you can use your own experience and that of your associates as a sort of "laboratory" to help you in studying this subject.

Business and Citizenship

The study of business is essential to understanding and to playing well your role as citizen. During your lifetime you will be called upon to vote on many issues that involve a knowledge of business and of business-community and business-government relationships. Many community activities have important business aspects; and regardless of your day-to-day work, you will undoubtedly become involved as an active participant in the affairs of your local community. You will be called upon to make judgments about state and local government and about federal and even international issues, all of which involve business problems.

As an observer of the American and world scenes, as well as an active participant in various aspects of life, you will need a knowledge of business. In trying to understand the significance of what is going on in the world, as you will throughout your life if you have any intellectual curiosity at all, you will be aided greatly by a knowledge of business principles, processes, and methods.

Education for the Future

What should you learn now in order to prepare yourself for the types of problems you may be facing in 1970 or 1980? The rapidity with which the world is changing and the dynamic character of business in the world make the answer to this question extremely difficult.

Still, if you are to plan any sort of study program, some answers—at least in tentative form—must be found.

This problem of changing conditions was stated rather forcefully by the philosopher, Alfred North Whitehead:

> Our sociological theories, our political philosophy, our practical maxims of business, our political economy, and our doctrines of education, are derived from an unbroken tradition of great thinkers and of practical examples, from the age of Plato in the fifth century before Christ to the end of the last century. The whole of this tradition is warped by the vicious assumption that each generation will substantially live amid the conditions governing the lives of its fathers and will transmit those conditions to mould with equal force the lives of its children. We are living in the first period of human history for which this assumption is false.[7]

This statement suggests that you need to develop the ability to meet new situations as they arise, to adapt to changed conditions, and to solve new and different types of problems. For example, we can study the ways in which people of an earlier period solved the problems with which they were confronted. We cannot accept, however, the specific solutions they found as the solutions to our problems; but we can find help in understanding how they went about finding solutions and which factors they considered to be of major importance. Of course, we can tell by the record of history whether their solutions and decisions were successful.

The development of our ability to solve problems under differing situations, thus, is one of the basic requirements for successful future operations, whether personal or business considerations are involved. In addition, we can anticipate to some extent the general types of problems that may be encountered in the future by a study of the forces that are currently in operation and their relative strength and intensity. These current forces will condition the environment within which your future activities will be carried on and within which business firms will operate. Such changes, naturally, will affect the administration of these firms.

Impact of the Future

The study of business is stimulating because to a large degree this type of study deals with the future. The American economy is highly dynamic. The world as a whole is changing rapidly. Competitive enterprises account in large part for the dynamic nature of our econ-

---

[7] By permission from A. N. Whitehead, *Adventures of Ideas* (New York: Macmillan Co., 1947), p. 117.

omy. Because change is an essential ingredient of our system, we find it impossible to anticipate with any degree of exactness what you and others will have to know fifteen or twenty years from now in order to operate successfully in business or in some other field—even as a private citizen and consumer.

Even though we cannot know with exactness what the future will bring, we are forced, regardless of our wishes, to make estimates and predictions about the future course of events. For example, the choice of a career requires long-range predictions of a high order. It requires you to make some estimate of the future of the American economy and its various divisions. To some degree, it requires you to make an estimate regarding the general trend of world events. Beyond this, you must estimate the potentialities within each specific field that interests you.

Experience—Direct or Indirect

All education is involved in some way with a study of experience. The experience may be gained directly or indirectly, that is, you may learn from your own experience or from the experience of others. All of the materials in textbooks, cases, reports, journals, magazines, and other written sources are based on experience.

We have often been told that "experience is a good teacher." This statement may be true provided we know how to learn from direct experience. For many of us, however, experience is a poor teacher. We make the same mistakes over and over. We do not know how to study, analyze, and evaluate our experience with the objective of avoiding earlier errors.

For some of us the experience of others, as recorded in books and other materials, similarly may be a poor teacher. Learning how to study both direct and indirect experience is one of the most important abilities we can acquire and develop. You can learn how to make experience meaningful by studying your experience as a student. Note your mistakes and errors and plan for correcting them. "Take inventory" of your experience periodically, perhaps at the end of a term, and determine how much progress you have made in correcting deficiencies and in enlarging your areas of strength. Decide what new objectives you should set up and how you should attain them.

The chief advantage of learning from the experience of others, as you do in organized courses or from books, lies in the variety of experience that can be drawn from many individuals and situations. Some people have learned about business largely from their own experience, without the help of recorded experiences of others. Sometimes this approach provides one with an excellent education, indeed. Often though, it leads to a narrow education because of the sheer physical inability of one person to engage in a sufficiently wide range of experience during a single lifetime.

Courses of study and books, thus, may help you to gain experience faster than would be possible by going to work in a business firm. After such studies are completed, work experience in business may be more meaningful and may be converted more rapidly into useful abilities than would be the case otherwise.

Formal Programs of Education

Many types of educational programs have formed the basis for success in the business world. Undergraduate programs of general education in the arts and sciences, as well as combinations of general and specialized programs in schools of business administration or engineering or in other areas have all served as the basis for successful business careers. To an increasing extent both general and specialized programs of undergraduate instruction are now followed by graduate work leading to the Master of Business Administration degree.[8] Also, company training programs have expanded in recent years to supplement academic studies.

To date there does not appear to be a single type of preparation for business administration that is "best." Since many students cannot afford to take the time required for both graduate and undergraduate programs, substantial numbers combine general education in the arts and sciences with study in schools of business administration on the undergraduate level.

Regardless of the program of study followed, you should recognize that a substantial amount of general education is directly applicable in the world of business, as we shall see in the next chapter, and that many business administration subjects may contribute to your general education.

Learning Methods

Without attempting to go into educational psychology or to delve very deeply into the problem of how we learn, we may assume that we

---

[8] For discussions of various programs of education for business, see R. A. Gordon and J. E. Howell, *Higher Education for Business* (New York: Columbia University Press, 1959); and Frank C. Pierson and others, *The Education of American Businessmen* (New York: McGraw-Hill Book Co., Inc., 1959).

learn through one or another of our senses—by seeing, smelling, hearing, feeling, or tasting. These are the only ways available by which experience can be registered in our minds.

Most of our formal course work involves chiefly the senses of sight and hearing. We read books and reports; we listen to lectures and discussions. To some extent the sense of touch may be important, especially as we take notes or write reports. Since this learning process has the advantage of fixing our attention rather firmly on the subject matter at hand, we may note that many of us "learn through the tips of our fingers."

Active participation is important in a learning situation. A lecture is meaningless unless we listen attentively, think with the lecturer, and try to compare his ideas with our own. The same thing is true of books. When we read without attention, no impressions are registered on our minds. When we read attentively—when we really come to grips with what the author has to say—we participate in sharing his thoughts, and as a result we learn.

Learning theory and methods are highly significant for some of the work of business managers. We have more to say about these subjects in Chapter 15.

Instructional Methods

Instructors may use a number of methods in connection with their teaching activities. They may lecture, lead discussions, give written or oral tests and examinations, present demonstrations, criticize oral or written reports, or use other methods. Instructors typically assign readings, problems, papers, and reports to guide your work.

On some occasions you may participate in still other instructional processes. The case method, for example, has been used widely in the field of business administration. This involves the presentation of the pertinent information about a given case (a problem or situation usually taken from actual life), with the student being required to analyze the case and present a suggested solution. Typically, all of the pertinent information is presented as part of the case. The student may be given the problem to be solved or may be asked to identify the problem and then to solve it.

A variation of the case method is the "incident method" of instruction. In the use of this method the student is given an incident or a single situation within a case. The incident requires a decision as to what should be done. The student or students involved ask the instructor the questions necessary to build the required background information on the basis of which a decision can be made and a solution recommended. Proponents of the incident method argue that this more nearly resembles actual business situations than does the case method, since a business manager is usually confronted with an incident and then required to use correspondence, telephone calls, reference books, and other sources in supplying the required information. Since the instructor has the complete case, he serves as a substitute for these sources of information and provides the information requested by the student's questions.

Still another method is often referred to as the "in-basket" technique. A series of letters, memoranda, telegrams, notes on telephone conversations, and the like set forth the problem to be solved, in a manner resembling the materials that might come into the "in basket" on an executive's desk. The student is then asked to solve the problem or problems presented on the basis of the available information. Solutions to cases, incidents, and "in-basket" problems may be required in written or in oral form. The student is usually expected to reach a decision and to prepare himself to defend it. Thus, he gets training in decision making and problem solving.

Other methods may be used as well. Since much business is transacted through small groups of people such as committees, teams, selected company officers, "task forces," and the like, many instructors use the "conference method" of instruction rather extensively. In this method the instructor usually serves as chairman of the conference, although he may assign this task to one of the students. The chairman follows an agenda that is usually announced in advance; and the conference typically centers on one or another problem which may be based on a case, a report, or a directive. The students through deliberations engage in trying to formulate a solution or recommended course of action.

In some instances instructors use such devices as role playing. Students are asked to portray the role of a company president, an investor, a sales manager, a salesman, a customer, the chairman of a company committee, or someone else. Each may be asked to present a report, outline a proposed plan for accomplishing a given purpose, present a recommended solution to a problem, or suggest recommendations for some other course of action. This method gives training not only in problem solving and decision making but also in business practices and methods, since it simulates actual situations.

The traditional methods referred to in the first paragraph of this section are, of course, also used in the teaching of business. Seminars,

FIGURE 1–1

Up the Educational Ladder

ELEMENTARY SCHOOL
ENROLLMENT
OUT OF EVERY 100 CHILDREN 7-13 YEARS OLD:

1910   86.1

1955   99.2

1960   99.4

1965 (Est.)   99.5

HIGH SCHOOL
ENROLLMENT
OUT OF EVERY 100 PERSONS 14-17 YEARS OLD:

1915   20.5

1955   80.3

1960   91.0

1965 (Est.)   92.3

GRADUATES
OUT OF EVERY 100 PERSONS 15 YEARS OLD AND OVER:

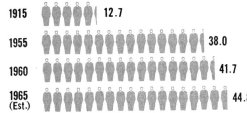

1915   12.7

1955   38.0

1960   41.7

1965 (Est.)   44.8

COLLEGE
ENROLLMENT
OUT OF EVERY 100 PERSONS 18-21 YEARS OLD:

GRADUATES
OUT OF EVERY 100 PERSONS 20 YEARS OLD:

1915   5.4   1915   2.0

1955   32.0   1955   6.6

1960   37.1   1960   7.3

1965 (Est.)   43.4   1965 (Est.)   7.9

NOTE: TWO FIGURES REPRESENT FIVE STUDENTS

lectures, discussions, and demonstrations sometimes work particularly well. Demonstrations may include visits to business firms, tours of plants, motion pictures and slides, and similar presentations of problems, processes, and situations. Seminars are usually associated with graduate study and involve close working relationships between instructor and students, with the latter preparing fairly elaborate seminar reports on assigned topics which may or may not be interrelated. Often a special room is set aside for a seminar with appropriate reference and other working materials readily available to members of the seminar.

The lecture method is used widely. While often condemned, it is an important instructional method and, if well done, has much to recommend it. Typically used for fairly large groups, it is an economical method of instruction. Many instructors are stimulated by large numbers of students and perform more effectively with larger than with smaller classes. Because of large numbers, instructors are justified in preparing lectures very carefully, using attractive charts and illustrations, and putting a lot of energy into their presentations. Also, since lectures are used widely in business, students need to know how to listen to them, to take notes, and to separate major from minor considerations.

There is no one "best" method of instruction. What is best in a given situation depends on the instructor, the subject matter, the students, the learning situation, and related factors. Students should have an opportunity to participate in a wide variety of methods because such participation helps to prepare them for their future work, which will be similarly varied.

"The Executive Game"

As we pointed out earlier, increasing use is being made of the "executive game" or "management decision simulation" exercises in the teaching of business administration. A special game or set of decision simulation exercises has been developed by Professor E. W. Martin, Jr. for use in connection with this book.[9] If you have an opportunity to participate in these exercises, you will see how this method of instruction gives you an introduction to the processes of business decision making and provides you with an understanding of the closely integrated relationships between all parts of a business enterprise or

---

[9] E. W. Martin, Jr., *Management Decision Simulation* (Homewood, Ill.: Richard D. Irwin, Inc., 1960).

program. You will see also the relationships between a business firm, its competitors, the government, and the general environment within which the firm operates. As Professor Martin points out,

Through participation in the Management Decision Simulation you will have the opportunity to engage in decision making in a situation similar to that faced by the top management of a business organization. Thus you can obtain a better understanding of the job of the manager in our competitive economy, while at the same time you can see how the areas of production, marketing, finance, and accounting are related to one another. Although this game is a simplification of the decision-making aspects of the job of top management, company presidents who have participated in similar exercises report that they embody many of the important characteristics of management decision making, and these men have been most enthusiastic concerning the educational benefits to be derived from such synthetic experience.[10]

The Workbook

In addition to the management decision simulation exercises, special provision has been made to help you develop your abilities in problem solving. Professor John D. Long has prepared a student *Workbook* to accompany this text.[11] Its use will help you to apply the discussions in this textbook to specific problems and situations. Problem solving is one of the more important abilities of the business executive. It is also important in many other lines of work or aspects of life. If you have an opportunity to make use of the *Workbook*, you will be able to see how the discussions in the text apply to practical situations. Some of the questions and problems at the end of the various chapters will also help you to do this.

Glossary of Terms

Almost every subject has a special sort of vocabulary. Business administration is no exception although the "language of business" is much closer to our usual language than is the case in many fields. Still, a variety of technical terms and phrases need to be understood. To help you master them we have prepared a "Glossary" which is presented in Appendix I (see pages 663–77). This is a sort of short dictionary covering various terms that are used in this book. Whenever you encounter a term, a phrase, or an expression that you do not understand, look it up in the Glossary. If you follow this practice, especially

---

10 *Ibid.,* p. 1.
11 John D. Long, *Workbook to Accompany Weimer, Business Administration: An Introductory Management Approach* (rev. ed.; Homewood, Ill.: Richard D. Irwin, Inc., 1962).

in the early stages of your study, you will soon acquire a working knowledge of the basic terms used rather widely in the field of business administration.

Sources of Information

Your studies will often carry you far beyond textbooks and readily available materials. You will find it advisable to learn how to use the library and how to make use of the basic references in the field of business administration.[12]

Libraries typically have available a catalogue of books. Such a catalogue usually provides alphabetical listing of books by author, book title, and subject. Each book is identified by a "call number," and this appears both on the back of the book and on the card for the book in the catalogue. The call number places the book in the general library collection and aids the librarian in locating it. In some cases libraries are operated with "open shelves," that is, students may be admitted to the stacks, and then must find the location of books themselves.

Some new developments are occurring in the management of information that we will not go into here. The Navy, for example, has done some pioneering work in making materials of various types more readily available. Many libraries now make available equipment for the easy reproduction of materials, thus reducing the "circulation" of books and other materials.

Most libraries will have available various reference books, including dictionaries, encyclopedias, handbooks, and manuals. Some of the reference materials are published by government agencies and some by private firms. Among the more useful of the government references are the census materials and various yearbooks such as the *Statistical Abstract of the U.S.*

Private reference works of continuing importance are the Standard Statistics Service, Moody's *Manual of Investments*, and various handbooks such as the *Accountant's Handbook, Personnel Handbook*, and the like.

In addition you should be familiar with current publications. The Department of Commerce publishes the monthly *Survey of Current Business* and the Board of Governors of the Federal Reserve System publishes the *Federal Reserve Bulletin*, also on a monthly basis. The Council of Economic Advisors publishes *Economic Indicators* on a

---

[12] A good summary of information about the use of libraries and reference materials is Jennie M. Flexner, *Making Books Work* (New York: Simon & Schuster, Inc., 1943).

monthly basis. These three publications provide excellent summaries of current developments. Current publications such as the *Wall Street Journal, Business Week, Fortune, Nation's Business, Barron's, The Commercial and Financial Chronicle,* and others are also important sources of up-to-date information.

You will find it advisable to get acquainted with these sources of information, not only for assistance in your work as a student but in your later work in business. It would be helpful to your development also if you cultivate the habit of reading regularly the business and financial sections of a daily newspaper and at least one good weekly news magazine, especially one that covers business as well as general news. The rapidity with which business changes makes it almost mandatory to keep in close touch with current developments.

SUMMARY

The study of business administration involves the economic aspects of life, and particularly those related to the production and marketing of goods and services by privately owned firms. Administration is fundamentally the direction of affairs. The business firm is both an economic and a social institution. It undertakes to serve the economic needs of people, and to gain sufficient public support for its products in order to earn revenues in excess of costs, or profits. Without profits it cannot survive. But the business firm is also a place where many people make a living, including employees, managers, and owners; suppliers, investors, customers; and others also have a vital interest in it. Gaining an understanding of people and the relationships among them in a business firm is as important as studying the products, markets, finances, or accounts of the firm.

The business firm is regulated to a considerable extent by competition. Government has as one of its major responsibilities that of making competition work as one form of social control, or to provide other types of control, if necessary.

Business administration often is studied in terms of career interests. But it is being studied increasingly in order to help improve the world in which we live, and in response to growing intellectual curiosity about this field. Indeed, this field is now one of the more exciting of all areas of study. Various factors account for this, including the increased emphasis on decision making as a central management activity, the application of statistical and mathematical techniques to the solution of management problems, the impact of the computer, the expanded use of the social and behavioral sciences in business, the rapid local, national, and international economic changes of recent years, and the growing interest in the role of the business executive and his community responsibilities. Students, business executives, public officials, and others appear to be increasingly aware of the possibility that the great society as Whitehead suggested "is one in which the men of business think greatly of their functions."

QUESTIONS AND PROBLEMS

1. What is your primary objective in studying business administration?
2. Why do we approach the study of business administration from the viewpoint of the manager? Suggest other viewpoints that might be adopted.
3. Explain this statement by Dr. Calkins: "Administration is fundamentally the direction of affairs. It is purposive action, and to an increasing degree it is informed, rational, and deliberate action."
4. What are the principal parts of the administrative process?
5. Why do business firms exist?
6. How can a business firm be both an economic and a social institution?
7. Why must a business firm gain profits? Can you suggest a situation in which a business firm would not need to gain profits?
8. Explain how competition is a regulator of business firms. What types of firms are not regulated by competition? Do business firms have the responsibility for making competition work? Explain.
9. Why has the field of business administration become one of the more exciting of all areas of study?
10. Why do we say that the study of business administration is future oriented?
11. Select a current business publication from those referred to in this chapter and list three types of information that you believe will be particularly helpful to business managers at this time. Justify your selection.
12. Turn to the Glossary at the back of this book. Define the following: business, business administration, business firm, competition.
13. Read the following condensed article from *Reader's Digest* "What Is Profit?" and answer the following questions:
    a) Do you think the article answers the problem raised by the schoolboy: "explain just how there can be a profit which is not taken from the work of someone else?"
    b) Is an economic surplus required for education and cultural development?
    c) Does the pursuit of profit lead to an economic surplus? Explain.

WHAT IS PROFIT?*

Special Request Feature: Norman Strouse, president of J. Walter Thompson Company, one of the world's great advertising agencies, has recommended that this article, originally appearing in the March, 1943, Reader's Digest, be reprinted.
Condensed from a publication of the New York State Economic Council.

FRED I. KENT

A schoolboy, disturbed by the current fashion of speaking disparagingly of the profit system which has formed the basis of the American way of life, wrote to his grandfather asking him to "explain just how there can be a profit which is not taken from the work of someone else." The grandfather, Fred I. Kent, LL.D., was president of the Council of New York University and a former director of the Federal Reserve Board. Dr. Kent replied to his grandson's query as follows:

MY DEAR GRANDSON:

I will answer your question as simply as I can. Profit is the result of enterprise which builds for others as well as for the enterpriser. Let us consider the operation of this fact in a primitive community, say of 100 persons, who obtain the mere necessities of living by working hard all day long.

Our primitive community, dwelling at the foot of a mountain, must have water. There is no water except at a spring near the top of the mountain: therefore, every day all the 100 persons climb to the top of the mountain. It takes them one hour to go up and back. They do this day in and day out, until at last one of them notices that the water from the spring runs down inside the mountain in the same direction that he goes when he comes down. He conceives the idea of digging a trough in the mountainside all the way down to the place where he has his habitation. He goes to work to build a trough. The other 99 people are not even curious about what he is doing.

Then one day this 100th man turns a small part of the water from the spring into his trough and it runs down the mountain into a basin he has fashioned at the bottom. Whereupon he says to the 99 others, who each spend an hour a day fetching their water, that if they will each give him the daily production of 10 minutes of their time, he will give them water from his basin. He will then receive 990 minutes of the time of the other men each day; this arrangement will make it unnecessary for him to work 16 hours a day in order to provide for his necessities. He is making a tremendous profit—but his enterprise has given each of the 99 other people 50 additional minutes each day.

The enterpriser, now having 16 hours a day at his disposal and being naturally curious, spends part of his time watching the water run down the mountain. He sees that it pushes along stones and pieces of wood. So he

* *Reader's Digest,* Vol. LXXVIII, No. 470 (June, 1961). Reproduced by permission.

develops a water wheel; then he notices that it has power and, finally, after many hours of contemplation and work, he makes the water wheel run a mill to grind his corn.

This 100th man then realizes that he has sufficient power to grind corn for the other 99. He says to them, "I will allow you to grind your corn in my mill if you will give me $\frac{1}{10}$ the time you save." They agree, and so the enterpriser now makes an additional profit.

He uses the time paid him by the 99 others to build a better house for himself, to increase his conveniences of living through new benches, openings in his house for light, and better protection from the cold. So it goes on, as this 100th man finds new ways to save the 99 the total expenditure of their time—$\frac{1}{10}$ of which he asks of them in payment for his enterprising.

This 100th man's time finally becomes all his own to use as he sees fit. He does not have to work unless he chooses to. His food and shelter and clothing are provided by others. His mind, however, is ever working, and the other 99 are having more and more time to themselves because of his thinking and planning.

For instance, he notices that one of the 99 makes better shoes than the others. He arranges for this man to spend all his time making shoes, because he can be fed and clothed and sheltered from profits. The other 98 do not now have to make their own shoes. They are charged $\frac{1}{10}$ the time they save. The 99th man is also able to work shorter hours because some of the time that is paid by each of the 98 is allowed to him by the 100th man.

As the days pass, another individual is seen by the 100th man to be making better clothes than any of the others, and it is arranged that his time shall be given entirely to his specialty. And so on.

Through the foresight of the 100th man, a division of labor is created that results in more and more of those in the community doing the things for which they are best fitted. Everyone has a greater amount of time at his disposal. Each becomes interested, except the dullest, in what others are doing and wonders how he can better his own position. The final result is that each person begins to find his proper place in an intelligent community.

But suppose that, when the 100th man had completed his trough down the mountain and said to the other 99, "If you will give me what it takes you 10 minutes to produce, I will let you get your water from my basin," they had turned on him and said, "We are 99 and you are only one. We will take what water we want. You cannot prevent us and we will give you nothing." What would have happened then? The incentive of the most curious mind to build upon his enterprising thoughts would have been taken away. He would have seen that he could gain nothing by solving problems if he still had to use every waking hour to provide his living. There could have been no advancement in the community. Life would have continued to be drudgery to everyone, with opportunity to do no more than work all day long just for a bare living.

But we will say the 99 did not prevent the 100th man from going on with his thinking, and the community prospered. As the children grew up, it was realized that they should be taught the ways of life. There was now sufficient production so that it was possible to take others away from the work of providing for themselves, pay them, and set them to teaching the young.

Similarly, the beauties of nature became apparent. Man tried to fix scenery and animals in drawings—and art was born. From the sounds heard in nature's studio and in the voices of the people, music was developed. And it became possible for those who were proficient in drawing and music to spend all their time at their art, giving of their creations to others in return for a portion of the community's production.

As these developments continued, each member of the community, while giving something from his own accomplishments, became more and more dependent upon the efforts of others. And, unless envy and jealousy and unfair laws intervened to restrict honest enterprisers who benefited all, progress promised to be constant.

Need we say more to prove that there can be profit from enterprise without taking anything from others, that such enterprise adds to the ease of living for everyone?

These principles are as active in a great nation such as the United States as in our imaginary community. Laws that kill incentive and cripple the honest enterpriser hold back progress. True profit is not something to be feared, because it works to the benefit of all.

We must endeavor to build, instead of tearing down what others have built. We must be fair to other men, or the world cannot be fair to us.

Sincerely,

GRANDFATHER

SUGGESTED READINGS

BACH, GEORGE LELAND. *Economics: An Introduction to Analysis and Policy.* 3rd ed. Englewood Cliffs, N.J.: Prentice-Hall, Inc., 1960. Read chap. 1 of this widely used textbook.

BROWNRIGG, WILLIAM. *The Human Enterprise Process.* University, Alabama: University of Alabama Press, 1954. Read chap. 1, entitled "Problems and Concepts," of this stimulating book.

GORDON, ROBERT AARON. *Business Leadership in the Large Corporation.* Berkeley and Los Angeles: University of California Press, 1961. Published in cooperation with the Brookings Institution. Read especially the preface and postscript, pp. v–xvii.

LONG, JOHN D. *Workbook to Accompany Weimer: Business Administration: An Introductory Management Approach,* chap 1. Rev. ed. Homewood, Ill.: Richard D. Irwin, Inc., 1962. This workbook was prepared as an aid in studying this text. Working through the exercises presented should be helpful in gaining an understanding of the text materials.

OUTLINE FOR CHAPTER 2

The BASIC ABILITIES OF THE MANAGER
are also required in many other lines of work.
They include the ability to
recognize and solve problems,
work with people,
communicate ideas,
organize activities and resources,
work hard—and like it, and
memorize—names, faces, relevant facts.
Such basic abilities may be developed through study of English,
speech, science and the scientific method, economics, the
social and behavioral sciences, quantitative analysis, and
related subjects. Also of importance are *creative thinking, straight thinking, innovation,* and *problem solving.*

Generalizations from experience—
laws,
principles,
theories, and
hypotheses
are important to student and manager alike.
Management may be studied as a *science* or as an *art.*
Leadership abilities, while hard to identify and define, are
important to successful management.
Personal qualities of management leaders vary widely,
but may include high standards of values, conduct,
workmanship; dedication to work and achievement
of objectives; fairness and honesty in dealings
with others; willingness to compete; courage
and spiritual depth; balanced viewpoint; and
mature judgment.

BASIC ABILITIES
OF THE MANAGER

The Manager's Work

As we pointed out in the first chapter, the business manager is concerned with the direction of affairs, and more specifically, with economic affairs. He makes decisions and he also implements decisions. He determines objectives and policies but also undertakes to achieve them. His job involves actions based on thought and analysis.

The manager works with people. Essentially his job is that of getting things done through people. He must get things done efficiently, since his resources usually are limited. He attempts to get ordinary people to do the work of superior people. He must provide for the production of goods or services that will meet the needs of people, and meet them at competitive prices. He sets objectives, plans for their achievement, organizes people and material resources, controls activities, and provides leadership for his organization. He must be able to operate at a profit in order for his firm to survive or grow or pursue any other objective.

The manager is concerned with current affairs and also with their background and the directions toward which they may lead. He tries to understand the political, social, and governmental as well as the economic environment in which he works, its background, and its directions of movement.

Yet, distinctive as this outline of managerial duties appears to be, many other lines of work have very similar requirements. Nearly all of us work with people to a greater or lesser extent. For example, military officers and government administrators work through people. Everyone has to make decisions of varying degrees of importance. Almost all lines of work require an understanding of the environment in which the activity is carried on. This suggests that at least some of the abilities that are needed by a business manager are likely to be the product of general education. It suggests also that a number of abilities are useful in a variety of occupations. Dr. Theodore O. Yntema has referred to abilities of this type as the "transferable skills of the manager."[1]

There are, of course, distinctive elements in the manager's job and we consider them later. Directing economic affairs, pursuing profits, getting business operations and activities done through others, understanding business and economic activities, recognizing the financial implications of decisions and problems, and related activities are, at least to a degree, distinctive. The work of the business manager is distinctive also because he operates within a strict discipline of financial relationships: income must exceed expenditures or failure will result. The manager operates also under the discipline of competition. Other firms are trying constantly to beat him in the competition for income. Further, he operates under the restraints imposed by government regulations, taxes, and business customs. He is also affected by the attitudes of the public generally, and those of his customers and investors in particular.

The Transferable Skills of the Manager

As we mentioned, Dr. Theodore O. Yntema has outlined a number of "transferable skills of a manager," those abilities required of various types of managers, but required of those in many other lines of work as well. He says,

In almost any kind of career we have to (1) recognize and solve problems—that is, we have to use the scientific method, which in its essentials is universally the same; (2) work with people—and to do this well, we have to understand them, size them up, motivate them, lead them, follow them, cooperate with them, love them, and be loved by them; (3) communicate our ideas to other people and receive communication from them; (4) organize—we have to organize our own activities and the activities of others for whom we are responsible; (5) work hard at the job—keep on working—and like it; and (6) learn to memorize faces, names, and facts important to our jobs.[2]

In the first chapter we referred to some of the relationships between your work as a student and the work of a manager. It may be advisable to consider some of these relationships further and to review some of the types of study programs that will contribute to your development

---

1 Theodore O. Yntema, "The Transferable Skills of a Manager," *Journal of the Academy of Management*, Vol. III, No. 2 (August, 1960).
2 *Ibid.*, p. 80.

as a potential manager or that will be helpful in pursuing some other career.

Memory

As suggested in the first chapter, we learn largely through our senses. Unfortunately we still need to know a great deal more about the learning process in order to understand it. Certainly we can agree with Yntema when he says, "one cannot operate with an empty head." Each of us needs to master certain basic information, concepts, and relationships. We need to train our memories to remember events, names, and faces and to retain other information. You can begin doing this now. Not only will your courses require some memory, but your relationships with students and instructors will provide numerous opportunities to train your memory for names, faces, and events. The returns are significant, as Yntema points out, ". . . many a man, by memory of events and faces and names, has gone far beyond his competitors, who, in analytical capacity, outrank him."

Persistent Effort

There is little question about the importance of persistent effort and of industrious application to the task at hand. The problem is how to acquire this ability. It is largely a matter of self-discipline and your experience to date may have given you only limited opportunity to develop this type of self-discipline. The manager needs this ability himself and the capacity to recognize it in others.

Persistent effort by itself, of course, can be dangerous, if the wrong goals are being pursued or if they are being pursued by the wrong methods. There is an old cross-classification relating to those who possess varying degrees of capacity and persistency. This classification may have had its origin in the German general staff. It goes like this:

The brilliant and lazy make good staff officers, that is, advisers and experts but without responsibility for action. The brilliant and industrious make excellent managers and line operators; they get the right things done. Those who are lazy and have limited ability make up the bulk of the workers on assigned tasks. Those who are industrious but have limited ability must be eliminated from any organization as soon as possible, otherwise they will soon wreck it.

Communication

The ability to communicate—to transmit facts and ideas clearly and effectively—is essential in nearly all aspects of life and all types of work. It is especially important in the field of business administration since communication is one of the major links in the processes of decision making and implementing.

The preparation of this book is largely a problem in communication. Information and ideas must be presented to you in such a way that you can understand them. This requires not only clarity of expression but also a proper order of presentation and an indication of the relationships between the topics covered. It would be desirable also if the materials in the book stimulated your interest in the subject.

Communication, of course, is a two-way street. We cannot communicate the ideas in this book effectively unless you are able to read. You may believe that you know how to read now and to a degree doubtless you do. It must be recognized, however, that relatively few students, especially those who are just beginning their college or university careers, really know how to read. By this we mean the ability to read with such intensity that you extract the full meaning and every possible shade of meaning from what is being read. When you get a letter from home or from a close friend, you give it your complete attention. You may read and reread it many times to be sure that you get its full meaning and understand exactly what the writer wished to convey. You should learn to read important study materials this way.

Business processes are carried on largely by written materials—by letters, reports, accounts, statements, memoranda, telegrams, cables, contracts, policy statements, outlines of proposed programs, directions for carrying out jobs, and many others. Your ability to read in the manner in which we are using the term is a basic tool if you are to succeed as a student or in a business career, or in almost any other type of career.

You will find it advisable to work hard in developing this ability in connection with all of your studies. On the college and university level we usually do not provide formal courses in reading, but some clinical work and remedial courses often are available. In some schools courses are offered in "rapid reading," and if your reading ability is limited, by all means take advantage of such opportunities.

If you care to pursue this topic further, we suggest that you refer to a very interesting book written by Mortimer Adler entitled, *How to Read a Book*.[3] He says, for example:

If we consider men and women generally, and apart from their professions or occupations, there is only one situation I can think of in which they almost pull themselves up by their bootstraps, making an effort to read better than they usually do. When they are in love and are reading a

---

[3] Mortimer Adler, *How to Read a Book* (New York: Simon & Schuster, Inc., 1950), p. 14.

love letter, they read for all they are worth. They read every word three ways; they read between the lines and in the margins; they read the whole in terms of the parts, and each part in terms of the whole; they grow sensitive to context and ambiguity, to insinuation and implication; they perceive the color of words, the odor of phrases, and the weight of sentences. They may even take the punctuation into account. Then, if never before or after, they read.

Written and Oral Expression

Your future success as a student or in your chosen career will depend greatly on your *ability to write*. We do not mean simply the ability to put letters or words on paper. We mean the capacity to write exactly what you mean, giving the right shade of meaning to your written statements so that whoever reads them will understand precisely what you intended to say. You will undoubtedly work on the development of your writing ability throughout your entire career. It is not an easy thing to learn. You may also take courses in English composition and report writing, and these will help you to develop skill in writing. The study of languages other than English can be helpful in

FIGURE 2–1

"Brinkley, my son feels it's time he went to work. See if you can get him a job with one of our competitors."

From the *Wall Street Journal,* November 21, 1961.

this connection. At the end of this chapter we present an excerpt from Benjamin Franklin's autobiography which outlines the methods he used to improve his ability to write clearly. Similar exercises will be as valuable to you as they were to him.

Oral expression is as important in business as written expression. You may already have developed this ability to some degree. But can you talk to a group, small or large, and in a short time "put over" your ideas so that your listeners know exactly what you intend to say? Can you "think on your feet," that is, can you talk from notes or without notes and present your ideas in a clear and interesting manner? Or will you always be sentenced to reading a prepared statement in connection with any future conferences or meetings in which you may be involved?

Business activities are not only conducted by means of written reports of various kinds but by conferences, meetings, discussions, and conversations. You may participate in conventions attended by thousands, or in committee meetings attended by four or five people. You may attend board meetings, staff meetings, sales promotions, and many other kinds of meetings. You can easily see how important your ability to speak effectively will be to you in almost any type of career you may choose to follow.

We do not suggest that it is necessary for you to become an orator, but rather that you develop the capacity to present your ideas effectively in almost any kind of situation. You may find it advisable to enroll in courses in speech. By careful application and attention in your day-to-day conversations and meetings you can do much to develop your ability along this line.

Closely related to the ability to talk is the ability *to listen*. This is similar in many respects to the ability to read. In one situation you may become informed by reading and in another by listening. You will find no classes available which will help you to become a good listener, but by careful application you can do much to develop your own abilities. Such processes as paying close attention in classes, taking notes, listening carefully in private conversations, and reviewing after a meeting or discussion the highlights and most important items that were covered will all help you to become a better listener. The ability to listen is often overlooked in our education programs.

Working with People

While the business manager works with things, his primary duties involve work with people. As we have suggested, this is also true of many other lines of work. The business firm is a social as well as an economic institution. Business firms are made up of people, organized into a team effort. The manager should be able to understand and work with the people in his organization, individually and in groups. He needs the capacity to lead them, direct them and co-ordinate their efforts. This requires that he be able to appeal to them and motivate them so that they will follow his plans and directions. The manager also works with people who are his superiors, the owners and directors of the enterprise he is managing. Of course, the manager may be the sole owner, in which case this relationship will not exist, or he may be a partial owner as in the case of a partnership. More frequently he will work with a board of directors who represent the owners, that is, the stockholders of the corporation. (These types of business entities will be discussed in Chapter 5.)

The manager will also work with people outside the firm—customers, suppliers, bankers, investors, government officials who have regulatory or other relationships with the firm, union officials, competitors, trade association officials, the press, politicians, and many others. Working with such a wide diversity of people requires an understanding of their likes and dislikes, their motives, their aims and aspirations, their fears and frustrations, and many related factors.

To quote again from Yntema:

To work with people well we have to understand them—how they act and react, and, insofar as possible, why they react as they do. We have to size them up—their demonstrated and especially their potential abilities. We have to learn to take orders, to give orders, to join with colleagues in common effort, to touch base with interested parties, to motivate people to the action we want, to lead and to follow, to trust those who can be trusted, and to rely on those who can be relied on. If you know how to win friends and influence people, I will give you long odds on your success in almost any field.[4]

Learning how to work with people is a lifetime job. The extracurricular activities of most college campuses often provide a training ground. Studies of literature often are helpful as are studies of history, philosophy, and especially the social and behavioral sciences.

Behavioral Sciences

Your knowledge of people and how to work with them will be increased by studies of the behavioral sciences—psychology, sociology, and cultural anthropology. Indeed, many schools of business admin-

---

4 Yntema, *op. cit.*, p. 82.

istration are now making special efforts to assure that all of their students develop a basic familiarity with the work of these fields. As one writer has pointed out: "There is, of course, a close logical relationship between the study of business and the behavioral sciences. Indeed, the study of business *is* a behavioral science, studying a sample of behavior in a particular context."[5]

The behavioral sciences are concerned both with individual and group behavior. They are related to business administration in a variety of practical ways ranging from the selection and training of personnel to communication, motivation, leadership, small and large group organization, group processes and structures, organization theory, formal and informal organizations, goals and satisfactions, individual and group decision making, consumer motivation, motivation research, roles and role playing, and various related subjects. We mention these here, not with a view to considering them further at this point but to suggest to you the types of subjects in the behavioral sciences that are particularly relevant to the work of the business manager and to encourage you to pursue studies of this type if you have an opportunity to do so.

Organizing Ability

We shall be studying organizations and the processes of organizing resources to achieve desired results at various points in these discussions, particularly in Chapter 9. You should recognize at an early stage, however, that the ability to organize is applicable to almost every aspect of life. It is important to you as a student, as we pointed out in the preceding chapter. It is important in our personal lives and it is difficult to think of a successful career in any field that is not based in part at least on the ability to organize. Dr. Yntema has stated this concept so clearly that we quote his statement here.

In every aspect of life we try to utilize scarce resources to achieve, in the best possible way, some given end. Here is a process universal in our experience—a process susceptible to analysis and generalization. It involves such basic ideas as classification, order, and rational planning. In the life of an individual it means planning his activities, budgeting his time among them, and meeting deadlines. In group activities it involves defining jobs, assigning responsibilities, and developing means for co-ordination and supervision.[6]

---

5 Robert A. Dahl, Mason Haire, Paul F. Lazarfeld, *Social Science Research on Business: Product and Potential* (New York: Columbia University Press, 1959), p. 47.

6 *Ibid.*, p. 83.

The ability to organize, of course, is among the more important prerequisites for successful management. Organization involves team effort, the establishment of proper relationships between people and between people and things. Quality of organization is often the difference between the success or failure of a business firm, or of any agency or group.

You will have an opportunity to learn more about organization in your future studies. Your concepts regarding the organization of our society as a whole may be developed through the study of political science, history, and especially economics. You will find it helpful to relate such studies to your own problems as well as to those of business firms or other organizations.

Economics

Economics is often referred to as the "mother science" of business administration. It involves the study of the principles explaining the allocation of scarce resources to maximum advantage in the attainment of desired ends or objectives. Economics is concerned generally with the problems of the community or society as a whole and with the effective organization of the resources of society in achieving its goals. There are several applied areas of economics, however, such as managerial economics, for example, which relate to the problems of effectively organizing and allocating the resources of the business firm in the attainment of its objectives. Thus, the subject matter of managerial or business economics is closely related to the study of business management and administration. Courses in "Principles of Economics" or in economic theory are especially helpful in developing an understanding of our society as a whole. The manager needs to know and understand the environment of which the business firm forms a part.

In our society we enjoy a wide latitude of choice as to our goals or objectives. We can spend our nontaxable income largely as we wish. In the process, we indicate our preferences for various things. Economics is concerned with the methods by which we indicate our preferences and with the effective utilization of resources to satisfy such preferences. As Professor Samuelson points out:

Any society, whether it consists of a totally collectivized communistic state, a tribe of South Sea Islanders, a capitalistic industrial nation, a Swiss Family Robinson or Robinson Crusoe—or, one might almost add, a colony of bees—must somehow meet three fundamental economic problems.

1. *What* commodities shall be produced and in what quantities? That is, how much and which of alternative goods and services shall be produced?
2. *How* shall goods be produced? That is, by whom and with what resources and in what technological manner are they to be produced?
3. *For whom* are goods to be produced? That is, who is to enjoy and get the benefit of the goods and services provided? Or to put the same thing in another way: How is the total national product to be *distributed* among different individuals and families?[7]

Of course, these problems would not exist if there were no scarcities, if we could have all of what we wanted for the taking. But such is not the case. People throughout the world are concerned with scarcities, with the effective use of scarce resources to satisfy competing ends. The people in one society may define their objectives quite differently from those in others and their choices of ways of achieving such objectives may vary greatly. Within the confines of a given set of cultural patterns and legal and governmental arrangements, however, the economist undertakes to understand and explain how the basic economic problems may be met, and met in such a manner as to avoid "booms and busts," inflation and deflation, and a host of other problems.

As we have pointed out, business firms are engaged largely in helping all of us in the solution of economic problems. Such firms produce goods and services for sale. Each firm has its own set of economic problems, which to a degree at least mirror the more general economic problems of the society as a whole. Thus, an understanding of economics is basic to the study of business administration. A number of elementary economic concepts are introduced in our discussions here. You will probably take one or more courses in economics and such studies should help you greatly in understanding the economic problems of our society as a whole and of business firms as well.

The Scientific Method

Much has been said and written about the scientific method. Too often we assume that unless we are students of science we have little interest in the scientific method. In fact, the scientific method has almost universal applicability. For example, Yntema explains:

The scientific method is not the prerogative of the physical, the biological, or the social sciences. Science and the scientific method are not the same thing. A science is a body of systematic, ordered knowledge. The scientific

---

[7] Paul A. Samuelson, *Economics: An Introductory Analysis* (5th ed.; New York: McGraw-Hill Book Co., Inc., 1961), pp. 16–17.

method is *the process of seeing and solving problems* . . . I believe that the scientific method (including perception) can be learned by competent students. I believe, moreover, that such learning should be one of the prime objectives of liberal and professional education. I think there should be more room in the curriculum for invention, creative thinking, and the specification of hypotheses. . . . It [the scientific method] involves observation, the detection of similarities and dissimilarities in phenomena, the tentative specification of categories and relationships based on observation and on deduction from prior discoveries, and the testing of such tentative hypotheses by experiment and experience.[8]

In short, the scientific method includes the collection of observations or facts, the classification of such data, analysis, and, to the extent possible, generalizations based on such study. The scientific method may be contrasted with the method of authority. When we trust authority—governmental, religious, or other authority—to tell us what to think or believe, our knowledge is limited by the capacity of the authority involved. Such authority may resent new ideas, or new solutions to problems and prohibit their introduction. By contrast the scientific method rejects authority as a basis of knowledge; the scientific method stresses direct observation of happenings or occurrences and, through analysis, the development of a solution to a problem or the explanation of an event.

While the scientific method has been used most widely in the physical and biological sciences, its application to the social and behavioral sciences, to business administration, and other applied fields has expanded rapidly in recent years.

You will find it advantageous, however, to have some experience with at least one of the laboratory sciences. Such experience will add to your understanding and appreciation of the scientific method. In the social sciences and in business administration it is seldom possible to hold conditions constant as in the laboratory. Experiments cannot be repeated exactly in the social sciences or in business studies. Indeed, even talking about problems often changes them to a degree. Despite the difficulties in applying the scientific method to fields involving the decisions and actions of human beings, considerable progress has resulted from its more widespread use.

The increased use of the scientific method in the world of business has brought rapid progress, not only in terms of new products and processes, but also through improved methods of organizing men and materials, better relationships between people working together in

---

[8] Yntema, *op. cit.*, pp. 79–80. Italics added.

group efforts, more effective control methods, and greatly improved planning procedures and programs.

Throughout this course of study we will attempt to give you some basic experience in using and applying the scientific method to the solution of various problems related to business administration. Development of the ability to understand and use the scientific method should be one of your primary objectives as a student.

Quantitative Analysis

The application of the scientific method to the field of business administration has been facilitated by the high-speed computer. The computer has made it possible to apply elaborate quantitative analysis economically to the solution of business problems.

Of course, business has always involved the use of quantitative methods to a degree. One of the distinctive features of the field of business administration is the extent to which information and values can be quantified. As a minimum, a knowledge of arithmetic and the essentials of accounting has always been necessary to those engaged in business. Indeed, numbers have been and continue to be a large part of the language of business. Prices, markups, wage rates, dividends, salaries, bonuses, costs, valuations, profits, and many other things are usually stated in terms of numbers. Quantitative relationships, thus, have always been widely used in business.

In recent years, however, mathematics and statistics have been applied increasingly in business analysis, particularly since the high-speed computer has made it possible to do this economically. In addition, machines have been used to a greater extent in accounting work. Accounting techniques have become more sophisticated as greater use has been made of mathematical methods and statistical concepts. The combination of mathematics, statistics, economics, and accounting has brought new dimensions to the quantitative analysis of business processes, activities, and problems. Thus, the manager has had to learn how to use quantitative methods to a greater extent than a decade ago.

The increasing use of quantitative methods and the scientific method in attacking managerial problems and in redefining business concepts suggests that you should include mathematics beyond basic levels in your study programs. It would be desirable also to study statistical methods and concepts, as well as to develop a broad understanding of accounting principles. In addition, you may find it advisable to gain a basic familiarity with the high-speed computer and at least some of its uses.

Creative Thinking

Another development resulting from the application of the scientific method to business administration is the increased emphasis placed on "creative thinking." Many company programs for management development now place substantial emphasis on this area.

The effective use of the scientific method requires imagination, the ability to develop new concepts and insights. Similiarly, successful management requires imagination, that is, the ability to see new problems and to develop new solutions to old problems. Planning, one of the basic elements in the management process, requires substantial imagination and creative ability. Many business decisions result from the development of new ideas and concepts rather than from the application of standard procedures and practices.

As we shall see, management may be thought of both as a science and an art. The creative side of management requires some measure of artistic ability. Basically, the manager, particularly if he operates beyond the primary levels of supervision, is an *artist* rather than an *artisan*.

In his work the artisan, for example, the carpenter, learns a process or procedure and then applies it over and over again to the problems or pieces of work that come his way. Even some professional activities resemble the work of the artisan, although they may, and should, include creative elements. By contrast the artist's work is primarily creative. Its success depends on new ideas, insights, and concepts. It is not repetitious, at least in the same way as is the work of the artisan. Of course, the artist may use specific procedures in painting a picture or writing a book or developing a musical composition, but the essential element is the new idea, insight, or concept that is being expressed.[9]

Development of Creative Thinking Ability

The extent to which the ability to think creatively can be developed is not known. Some basic abilities to use imagination must be present, but we vary greatly in the extent to which we have such abilities.

Some writers contend that the process of getting and developing new ideas and thoughts can be learned—that it is something more than a hit-and-miss matter. James Webb Young has referred to this

---

[9] See, for example, David McCord Wright, *Democracy and Progress* (New York: Macmillan Co., 1948), p. 23.

as "a technique for producing ideas."[10] Professor John F. Mee has summarized the steps involved in creative thinking as, first, selection and definition of the problem; second, exploration and preparation; third, the development of hypotheses or partial solutions; fourth, the incubation stage, sometimes called "unconscious cerebration"; fifth, illumination, or the appearance of the idea; and, finally, verification and application.[11] Note the similarity of these steps to Yntema's characterization of the scientific method.

Creative thinking requires an attitude of mind that is receptive to new ideas and thoughts. Often ideas are the result of combinations of existing facts, ideas, or concepts. Some business firms and other groups have used "brainstorming" sessions as an approach to the stimulation of ideas. In this process, all possible combinations of existing facts, concepts, and ideas are brought out. Some are wild and impractical but often they lead to a solution to the problem by hitting on the right idea. Thinking about a problem over a period of time frequently results in the appearance of an idea when it is least expected.

As has been suggested, the creative thinking process is a part of the scientific method. Both the processes of induction and deduction are involved. Induction is the process of reasoning from facts that have been collected and assembled in order to arrive at a general hypothesis or theory which can then be tested. Deduction involves reasoning from general principles or laws to specific adaptations or conclusions.

Three main levels of thinking have been identified by Professor B. H. Jarman. These are the habit level, the problem-solving level, and the creative or insight level.[12] The habit level is of a routine type and usually involves the following of standardized procedures or methods. It relies on habit patterns, memory, or formulas. No originality is involved.

Thinking on the problem-solving level is of a higher order. It depends on logic and selection among alternatives. For example, a problem is identified. Related facts are analyzed and evaluated. Presumably all of the necessary facts are available. Alternative solutions are set up, and a selection of the one offering greatest chance for success is made.

Thinking on the creative or insight level requires the mind to op-

---

[10] James Webb Young, *A Technique for Producing Ideas* (7th ed.; Chicago: Advertising Publications, Inc., 1952). See also Alex F. Osborn, *Applied Imagination* (New York: Charles Scribner's Sons, 1953).

[11] John F. Mee, "The Creative Thinking Process," *Indiana Business Review*, Vol. XXXI (February, 1956), pp. 4–9.

[12] B. H. Jarman, "Can Executives Be Taught to Think?" *Advanced Management*, Vol. XIX (January, 1954), pp. 5–8.

erate more imaginatively. Many facts may not be known. Only partial knowledge regarding a situation or problem typically is available. Most business decisions are made under such limitations. A new idea or approach or method often must be found to arrive at a decision. This may come from analysis, attempts at forced relationships, free association of ideas, or from prolonged effort and thought.

As suggested, some people have greater capacity for creative thought than others. Even limited capacity in this area can be developed by practice and application. You can improve your abilities along this line by studies that stimulate your imagination, such as literature or history. You should attempt also to develop an inquisitive frame of mind. Raise questions about your studies, your personal problems, or your work, such as these: Are there better ways of doing this? Are there alternative solutions? Would assuming the opposite throw light on the situation? What is a substitute for a given item or method? Can two or more things be combined to advantage?

Business depends greatly on innovations, on new ideas, new concepts, improved methods, and better products. The development of your ability to produce ideas—to think creatively—should be one of your major objectives as a student.

Straight Thinking

Not only is it important for the manager to think creatively, he must also be able to "think straight," to see problems clearly, to avoid errors in reaching conclusions, to use "common sense," although we are not always sure just what this means. It is as easy for a manager as for any of us to follow good information to an erroneous conclusion.

A few examples may indicate what we mean. We may assume, for example, that "facts" are true, when they are not or are only partially true. Sometimes information that supplies "facts" for business decisions is taken from biased sources, or presents only one side of the picture, or overstates a position. Statements that include such words as "always," "every," "never," and the like should be considered with care. There is a famous statement to the effect that all generalizations are false, including this one.

In the business world things are often relatively true rather than absolutely true or absolutely false. Often facts are only partial facts. Also, we may be misled by one partial fact into assuming that something else follows. For example, a manager may read in a newspaper that there is a flu epidemic in the town where one of his plants or stores is located. He may assume that this means curtailed operations because of the probable illness of employees. He may find on more careful investigation, however, that the newspaper was stretching a point to call this an "epidemic," that those who are ill are largely children attending one particular school, and that the health authorities do not expect the illness to spread widely among the people in the town.

Often it is tempting to reason from a limited number of cases. Three people on a production line are reported to have had accidents in the past day. The manager of the plant may assume that this means some special hazard has developed, when in fact he may find on investigation that the workers who were injured had removed a safety device because they felt it interfered with their freedom of movement.

Similarly, we often reason from our own experience to general conclusions that are not warranted. Because we don't like oatmeal, for example, we may assume that a new oat cereal just put on the market will not sell, when in fact, it may sell very well. Many businessmen have gone bankrupt because they assumed the buying public would like the same products as those preferred by these businessmen or the members of their families.

Sometimes we make errors in reasoning by analogy. We tend to assume that because one proposition is true a reasonably like proposition is also true. For example, it was assumed that because the case method of instruction works well at the graduate level it will also work well on the undergraduate level. Undergraduates, however, may not have the necessary background for the cases or may require special assistance in using this method. Sometimes managers assume that because a certain type of organization works in one plant it will also work in another. This may be true, but it is not necessarily so. More careful investigation may be needed to be reasonably sure.

Often we want something to be true so much that we fail to exercise careful judgment. You may want a good grade in a course so much that you assume your work is good, without checking with the instructor. Or a manager may want high morale in his firm so much, that he assumes it exists. A healthly skepticism is a good defense against errors that result from wishful thinking.

In some cases we tend to make the familiar error of assuming that because something happened before an event, it is the cause of the event. For example, it may be concluded by sports fans that because the basketball team was delayed as a result of airplane trouble, they lost the game. This might have been the reason, or a reason, but it is not necessarily the explanation of losing the game. Or a manager fails to attend a union-management conference; later a strike breaks out; some may assume that the strike was due to the failure of the manager to attend the conference. It may have had nothing to do with the result. This type of thinking is often referred to as *post hoc ergo propter hoc*, which in Latin means, "before this, therefore the cause of this." This type of error in logic is made often.

A related one is reasoning from a general proposition to a specific conclusion without taking all of the necessary intermediate steps. There is a famous logical syllogism that is stated this way:

> All men are mortal. (major premise)
> Socrates is a man. (minor premise)
> Therefore, Socrates is mortal. (conclusion)

No one can argue with the logic in this statement. But suppose we change it this way:

> All men are mortal.
> Socrates is mortal.
> Therefore, Socrates is a man.

Such a conclusion, of course, is not warranted. Socrates might be a dog or a horse. Simply because he is mortal does not mean that he is a man. This is called in logic the "undistributed middle," that is, failure to include the minor premise in the major premise. Often if we set down the premises involved in a line of thought we can avoid errors of the type illustrated here. We can examine the validity of the major premise, the minor premise, determine proper relationships between them, and then move to a conclusion if it is warranted.[13]

Sometimes we tend to assume that what is true of a part must also be true of the whole, and as a result, reach unsound conclusions. For example, a manager may assume that because the people in one city like daylight saving time, people in all cities will like it. Of course, this may not be true of a rural community.

We could multiply illustrations. Those mentioned above should suggest, however, that the ability to think straight is one of the important abilities of the manager.

Generalizations from Experience

The successful manager usually has the ability to generalize from experience, to develop general ideas or concepts that may be applied to many areas of his work. The use of the scientific method (either used

---

13 See G. Lee Bach, *Economics* (3rd ed.; Englewood Cliffs, N.J.: Prentice-Hall, Inc., 1960), pp. 70–75.

in a formal or informal manner) will help him to do this. This method helps us not only to develop new knowledge but also to establish generalizations based on studies of experience which may have broad applicability. Such generalizations may be stated in the form of "laws" or principles." A law is a generalization based on studies of experience that applies almost universally. For example, we refer to the "law of gravity."

A "principle" is a generalization that has widespread application, but not to the universal extent of a law. Thus, we refer to the "principle" of diminishing utility—that the satisfaction derived from goods or services diminishes as more units are added. For example, the first cup of coffee may give great satisfaction, that is have "high utility" to use an economics expression, but each succeeding cup will tend to bring somewhat less satisfaction than the preceding one.

In the field of business administration we have few "laws" in the sense in which we are using the term here. Business is more closely related to the social than to the physical sciences and generalizations of universal or nearly universal validity are not very common, if, indeed, any exist at all. This is because the study of business is basically a study of people, individually and especially in groups. We have developed some general principles that help us to understand and explain individual and group behavior, but few, if any, laws.

If we develop our studies of experience to the point where we appear to be able to generalize fairly widely—but still with some uncertainty—we usually refer to this type of generalization as a "theory." Thus a theory could turn into a principle if we could demonstrate by additional experience and study that it had the necessary general applicability. On the other hand, the theory might turn out to be incorrect, in which case it would have to be abandoned.

Sometimes a preliminary and tentative estimate is made of the results that may be derived from a body of experience. We usually refer to such an estimate or tentative generalization as a "hypothesis." With additional testing and experimentation a hypothesis may develop into a theory or principle.

As we have suggested, a large number of successful managers have the ability to generalize from their experience and the experience of others. While many of them would not recognize that they make use of hypotheses, theories, and principles in their work, the fact remains that they do and that the ability to think in such terms has widespread importance in business administration.

In many of your studies you will have an opportunity to develop your ability to think in terms of generalizations from experience. You will study currently accepted theories and principles. For example, you will undoubtedly study principles of economics, principles of accounting, statistical principles, and principles and theories in other fields. Insofar as possible we follow a "principles approach" in these discussions in the belief that it is more practical for you to gain an understanding of principles that have fairly widespread applicability than to learn a series of techniques and detailed procedures. It will be important for you to develop the ability to generalize, to think in terms of theories and principles, whether you enter the field of business administration or go into some other line of work.

Management as Science and Art

As we have suggested, management may be studied both as a science and an art. Management as a science involves the application of the scientific method to the processes of management. As a science, management includes the orderly application of pertinent information to specific management problems and the objective evaluation of results.

Examples of the types of problems in which the scientific method may be used include determining a layout for a plant, production scheduling, selecting and evaluating personnel, controlling costs, improving group behavior, analyzing markets, determining sales territories, controlling inventory, determining consumer preferences, and many others. Historically, scientific management arose from time and motion studies and other analyses related to improving efficiency in production. Scientific management has made important contributions to progress in production and it has also helped to improve the marketing and the financing of goods and services.

Important as the contributions of scientific management have been, the *art of management* has also played a vital role in the progress of business administration. In a sense management as an art begins where management as a science stops. After all of the data have been gathered, evaluated, and analyzed, it is essential that decisions be made. Sometimes scientific studies point clearly to a decision, but often this is not the case. Then management has to make decisions—to come up with the best possible answers—based on a "feel" of the situation, on experience with other similar situations, on the many intangible factors that are almost always involved in a business decision, on strategic factors, and on "hunches" or intelligent guesses. Such decisions almost always reflect value judgments, including such things as the desire to attain the firm's objectives, the personal philosophy of the manager, market conditions, dollars and cents factors such as returns and costs, and the like. The art of management involves the willingness to take action, to make decisions even when all desirable information is unavailable, to assume responsibility for going ahead at one time rather than another, and to select among many alternatives the route that will be followed toward an objective.

Management as an art has been broken down into such classes as the art of knowing when, the art of knowing how, and the art of using power. These are all a part of the process of exercising leadership. Management is one form of exercising power, not only with respect to energy but especially in relationships between people. Thus, a good manager knows the difference between power *over* people, power *with* people, and power *through* people.

Leadership Abilities

The exercise of leadership is one of the important aspects of management as an art. Leadership is such an intangible set of qualities that we find difficulty in generalizing about it. One way of defining the leadership role of the manager is in terms of the capacity to enable ordinary people somehow to do the work of superior people.

This provides a general description of the leadership job of management. We must recognize, however, that different managers undertake to do their jobs in various ways. One manager may rely on his personal traits and characteristics to inspire, motivate, and stimulate his followers. Another may rely on superior knowledge and judgment; another on his ability to develop mutual confidence between himself and his followers. Still another may rely on his reputation for past success.

Many intangible factors are involved in leadership. Why does one boy more or less automatically become captain of the ball team? Why does one politician command wider support than another? How does one business executive manage to weld together an organization when others have failed in the job? Various attempts have been made to provide answers to these questions. We discuss them later in Chapter 9.

Although some qualities and abilities may be characteristic of many leaders, whether in business, government, military service or other fields, we have not as yet been able to determine specifically what they are. Studies and research should throw more light on this interesting field as time goes on. Because of our lack of knowledge, it is difficult to "teach" leadership or to develop such leadership qualities as one may have. You may have opportunity in working with student organizations to develop leadership abilities. Studies that will increase your knowledge of people—the social sciences, literature, behavioral studies, and others—may be especially helpful in developing leadership abilities.

Personal Qualities of the Manager

The successful manager like the successful person in almost any career, needs personal standards of values and conduct that serve as guides to his activities. Honesty in dealings of all types is of primary importance. Basic honesty does not appear to be something that can be taught, or it is taught gradually as one becomes aware of the standards of the culture in which he grows up. To a large extent, the development of standards of honesty and integrity is something that you must accomplish yourself.

Fairness in dealing with others is closely related to honesty. The application of the "Golden Rule"—to treat others as we would have them treat us—is a basic guide. Business executives follow this standard more generally than is commonly believed.

High standards of workmanship, dedication to work, and perseverance (as we suggested above) are all important qualities. The development of sound standards of workmanship requires that you be as critical of your own work as of the work of others. As has been pointed out, "The trouble with most of us is that we would rather be ruined by praise than saved by criticism."[14]

Most successful people including business executives appear to be competitive. They welcome competition, enjoy matching abilities and wits with competitors, and get great satisfaction from winning. They are not always good losers. They want to win so much that they are unlikely to accept anything short of beating the competition. They are willing to pay a big price to win. They welcome tests of ability, opportunities to excel, and live by the concept that there are "no excuses" in business for failure in competition or inability to attain established objectives. They have the determination to carry through their programs to attain desired results.

Often people of this type have courage in a high degree. This is a difficult quality to define but we recognize its essentials in terms of dedication to achievement, willingness to sacrifice in order to attain objectives, and the moral, spiritual, or physical stamina necessary to such sacrifices. Often loyalty to principle, objectives, friends, and as-

---

14 Quoted in *Coronet*, January, 1961, p. 112 (from General Features Corporation).

sociates is a closely related characteristic. Whether qualities of this type can be taught is far from clear.

An inquisitive point of view, interest in new things and ideas, is characteristic of many good managers. This quality can be developed in part by learning to use the scientific method, as we indicated above. Friendliness and a genuine interest in others is another quality often found in good managers. Each of us wants to feel important. Managers often are able to get ordinary people to do extraordinary things by taking a real interest in them and "believing" in them. Coaches of athletic teams often have this ability.

A balanced point of view in regard to issues about which there may be major disagreement is often found in successful managers. The capacity to make well-considered judgments, to resist panic and pressure, and to think carefully through knotty problems and issues is highly important in management and in nearly all lines of work.

The good manager knows how to make effective use of his personal as well as his business resources. Your own personal resources and abilities represent certain forms of power, and in a sense you are the manager of these types of power. There is sheer physical power which we may possess in greater or lesser degree. There is mental power, the ability to think creatively, to develop new ideas, new approaches to problems, and new methods of adapting to situations. The power of personality is a significant personal resource. The ability to get along with others, to influence them, and to impress them are all parts of personal power. A pretty girl has power because of her beauty and personality. An effective speaker has power. The ability to persuade others and to sell ideas and things is a form of power. The capacity to lead, to attract followers is of vital importance in many lines of work.

Spiritual depth is an important source of power, including the ability to meet and face difficult situations, the courage to meet reverses, loyalty to friends, devotion to principle, and the pursuit of truth.

Our emotions are a form of power if properly managed. Emotional "drive" often carries one farther than he could go by sheer physical or mental strength. Our emotions are complicated things, and the better we understand them the more we are likely to be able to manage them to our own best interests and those of others.

Some people have many abilities and talents, many forms and types of power, at their command. Often they lose out in competition with others who may have less native ability but who are more competent managers of the abilities at their disposal.

In the selection of our personal objectives we must face up to the question of whether superior abilities and training give us greater rights, bigger claims on the world, or whether they constitute heavier responsibilities to it. Usually if the responsibilities are accepted, the rewards will follow as a matter of course. But we must recognize that the big rewards are likely to be the personal satisfactions that come from real achievements rather than money, prestige, or power. Thus, good workmanship in the pursuit of sound objectives, the means rather than the things usually thought of as ends, may ultimately prove to be the ends themselves. This is not only the case with respect to individuals but to an important degree it is true of our economic and social system as well.

This discussion suggests that your instructors can impart knowledge, but that they can impart wisdom only to a limited degree, if at all. You may attain wisdom only through your own efforts. The attainment of wisdom may well be set up as one of your major personal objectives in life. Successful managers and successful persons in most other careers have usually become wise as well as knowledgeable.

SUMMARY

The basic abilities of the manager, while distinctive to a degree, are also required in many other lines of work. As outlined by Dr. Yntema, these abilities, referred to as the "transferable skills" of the manager, include the ability (1) to recognize and solve problems, making use of the scientific method; (2) to work with people, understanding them, co-operating with them, motivating them, leading them, and following them; (3) to communicate thoughts and ideas and receive communication from others; (4) to organize our abilities and those of others for whom we are responsible; (5) to work hard—and like it; and (6) to learn to memorize names, faces, and significant facts.

These abilities may be developed through the study of various subjects including English, speech, science and the scientific method, economics, the behavioral sciences, mathematics, and quantitative analysis, as well as related areas. Development of the ability to think creatively, to innovate, and to think straight are also important to the student and to the manager.

The work of the manager is often facilitated by the ability to develop generalizations from experience, including laws, principles, theories, and hypotheses.

Management may be studied as a science or as an art. As a science it includes the application of the scientific method to the solution of problems, the orderly application of pertinent information and the objective evaluation of results. Management as an art goes beyond definite information, involves judgment, intuitive reactions, and leadership abilities.

Personal qualities of management leaders vary greatly. Typically these include high value standards, as well as high standards of workmanship and conduct. Successful managers have the ability to accept and carry responsibility. Dedication to achievement of objectives often is found as a quality of successful managers. Many are competitive, they have the capacity to attract others to them and to motivate them. Often they have courage in a high degree as well as loyalty to their organizations, associates, and friends. Many have spiritual depth. Often successful managers are those with a balanced viewpoint, and ability to think objectively and impersonally; they usually have maturity of judgment.

QUESTIONS AND PROBLEMS

1. The following quotation from Benjamin Franklin's autobiography indicates how he attempted to improve his writing ability.

   "About this time I met with an odd volume of the 'Spectator.' It was the third. I had never before seen any of them. I bought it, read it over and over, and was much delighted with it. I thought the writing excellent and wished if possible to imitate it. With that view, I took some of the papers, and making short hints of the sentiment in each sentence, laid them by a few days, and then without looking at the book, tried to complete the papers again by expressing each hinted sentiment at length and as fully as it had been expressed before, in any suitable words that should occur to me. Then I compared my 'Spectator' with the original, discovered some of my faults, and corrected them. But I found I wanted a stock of words or a readiness in recollecting and using them, which I thought I should have acquired before that time if I had gone on making verses; since the continual search for words of the same import but of different length to suit the measure, or of different sound for the rhyme would have laid me under a constant necessity of searching for variety, and also have tended to fix that variety in my mind, and make me master of it. Therefore I took some of the tales in the 'Spectator' and turned them into verse, and after a time, when I had pretty well forgotten the prose, turned them back again. I also sometimes jumbled my collections of hints into confusion, and after some weeks endeavored to reduce them into the best order before I began to form the full sentences and complete the paper. This was to teach me method in the arrangement of the thoughts. By comparing my work afterwards with the original I discovered many faults and corrected them; but I sometimes had the pleasure of fancying that in certain particulars of small import I had been lucky enough to improve the method or the language, and this encouraged me to think that I might possibly in time come to be a tolerable English writer, of which I was extremely ambitious."

Select a paragraph from this chapter and rewrite it in your own words following the general procedure suggested in this quotation.

2. What does Dr. Yntema consider to be the transferable skills of the manager? Do you agree with his list? Could you add others to it?

3. How does the scientific method differ from the use of authority? Present an outline of a situation in which you made use of the scientific method, either consciously or by chance.

4. To what extent is there a relationship between the scientific method and creative thinking?

5. Why is the study of economics important to the student of business administration?

6. Explain the growing importance of mathematics and quantitative analysis for the student of business administration.

7. Differentiate between management as a science and as an art.

8. How does the work of the artisan differ from the work of the artist? Which does management resemble most closely? Explain.

9. Give an illustration of a generalization from experience that may be classified as a law. Present another that may be classified as a theory.

10. Explain the difference between a theory and a hypothesis.

11. Do you think it would be possible for two managers faced with an identical problem and provided with identical information to reach different decisions? Explain.

12. From among your acquaintances choose one whom you regard as a leader. Which of his abilities tend to make him a leader? Explain.

13. Comment on the following statement:
"Almost all of the economic needs of the American people are met through the operations of business organizations. The individual business enterprise attains and maintains economic success only by meeting an economic need of the people in a manner which pleases them.
"The student of business must then learn a great deal about people, the things that they need, and the ways in which business can serve their needs in a manner that will please them. This is just another way of saying that the study of business is a study of people and of the economic processes that serve them. This is, of course, a large order because people and their needs and wants are very complex and they are always going through processes of change." (The late Fred T. Greene, formerly President, Federal Home Loan Bank of Indianapolis)

14. Using the Glossary define: Administration, innovation, deduction, leadership, profit and loss system, analysis, negative leadership, motivating, communication.

SUGGESTED READINGS

ADLER, MORTIMER. *How to Read A Book.* New York: Simon & Schuster, Inc., 1950. You will find the following chapters of special interest: chap.

i, "To the Average Reader"; chap. ii, "The Reading of Reading"; and chap. iii, "Reading Is Learning."

LONG, JOHN D. *Workbook to Accompany Weimer: Business Administration: An Introductory Management Approach,* chap. 2. Rev. ed. Homewood, Ill.: Richard D. Irwin, Inc., 1962.

OSBORNE, ALEX F. *Applied Imagination.* Rev. ed. New York: Charles Scribner's Sons, 1957. This is a stimulating book. Read especially chap. i, "The all-importance of imagination," and chap. viii, "Creative and non-creative forms of imagination."

YNTEMA, THEODORE O. "The Transferable Skills of the Manager," *Journal of the Academy of Management,* Vol. III, No. 2 (August, 1960).

YOUNG, JAMES WEBB. *A Technique for Producing Ideas.* 7th ed. Chicago: Advertising Publications, Inc., 1952. You can read this short book rather quickly and you will find it very useful in stimulating your interest in creative thinking.

OUTLINE FOR CHAPTER 3

The study of THE MANAGER AND THE BUSINESS FIRM is complicated because of the absence of a "general theory." Hence, other bases for organizing studies are used, including
    the business firm,
    the management process,
    decision making and decision guides, and
    business resources and operations.
    (Environmental influences are considered later.)
The early history of the DuPont Company illustrates types of management—from Caesar to group management, and the evolution of various management methods.
    Some *conclusions* based on this company's early history include:
        A variety of management methods may succeed, if adapted to abilities and requirements.
        Many business problems can be subjected to study and analysis.
        Objectives guide managers, indicate priorities, set standards.
        Financial standards and controls are valuable management guides.
        The training and development of managers is important, creating an "executive life line."
    Knowledge of business principles is more important to managers than operating details.
    Special importance may be attributed to:
        flexibility and adaptability of operations,
        well-being of people in the organization,
        low-cost, high-volume operations,
        research and experimentation, and
        environmental factors.

THE MANAGER AND
THE BUSINESS FIRM

It is not from the benevolence of the butcher, the brewer, or the baker that we expect our dinner but from their regard to their own interest.

—ADAM SMITH

Lack of a "General Theory"

We do not have available as yet a "general theory" of business administration. There is not a well-defined body of principles or theories that we can present to you as a means of explaining this broad field.

Business activity, of course, has been carried on since the early stages of our civilization. We have some general guides to the conduct of business activity as a result of this long experience. But while the experience has been long, it has also been highly diverse. For every generalization it is possible to find exceptions—usually more than a few exceptions—and we seem to be confronted with a large mass of experience from which it is possible to develop few valid generalizations.

We suggested in our earlier discussions that we would make use of a "management approach" to our study of this subject, since the manager is the central figure in the business firm and represents one method of integrating and bringing together a variety of information and concepts.

We might use the business firm as the central point of our discussions. To a degree we do this, since it is necessary to discuss the main characteristics of business firms, how they are established, the principal types of firms, and the kinds of work they do. We cover these subjects in Chapters 5 and 6.

All business firms, however, are managed in one way or another. Even though they may be of many different sizes and types, and engage in a variety of activities, their managers all face certain basic problems and perform certain functions. We group these problems around the determination of objectives and the use of resources by means of appropriate planning, organization, and controls to achieve these objectives. The organizations require direction, co-ordination, and leadership. We consider these topics in Chapters 7, 8, and 9.

The Management Process

The division of the manager's work into such functions or stages as planning, organizing, and controlling, often with the addition of leadership (including direction and motivation) is frequently referred to as "the management process." The stages have been variously identified. One of the more widely used is referred to by the initials of the words involved: "POSDCORB"—planning, organizing, staffing, directing, co-ordinating, reporting, and budgeting. Regardless of how divided, there is widespread use of the concept of a management process in explaining the manager's work.

All managers engage in these activities to a greater or lesser extent. We make use of the management process plus a consideration of objectives as the basis of a part of our discussions in Part 2. We do this, however, not in the belief that this provides the basis of a "general theory" of management but because it gives us a convenient basis for introducing you to the functions of the manager in operating the business firm.

As Ernest Dale has aptly said:

We all know of the universals of management which all managers engage in to a greater or lesser extent—POSDCORB—planning, organizing, staffing, directing, coordinating, reporting, and budgeting. But we may say that Sewell Avery of Montgomery Ward, Frederick Donner of GM, Charles Luckman as head of Lever a few years ago, Sir Jehangir Ghandi of Tata Steel in India, Mikoyan of Russian foreign trading, the small-town merchant with a few employees, and the cardinal in charge of administration in the Roman Catholic Church all posdcorb—but what a world of difference in the way they do it, both in aim and method! Only an empirical study could uncover the differences and similarities.[1]

In much the same vein the authors of a leading textbook in *Principles of Management* say this:

Since the organization of human beings for the attainment of a common objective is as old as civilization itself, one would expect that, of all sciences, the science of management would be the most advanced. Despite the increasing complexity of modern civilization, however, and the recognized need for effective coordination, only the beginnings of such a science

---

[1] Ernest Dale, *The Great Organizers* (New York: McGraw-Hill Book Co., Inc., 1960), p. 10.

have been developed; many principles of management remain relatively unexplored, and there are doubtless others as yet unrecognized.[2]

Efforts to develop general principles of management date back to ancient times. Of the more recent writers the works of Henri Fayol, Lyndall Urwick, Chester I. Barnard, V. A. Graicunas, Alvin Brown, Ralph C. Davis, and others have been given widespread attention by the business community and by students of business administration.[3] Such writers have stressed among other things the importance of specialization, the relationships between responsibility and authority, the principle of "unity of command" (each person has one boss only), unity of direction (one head and one plan for each activity), and the concept of "span of control," that is, one person can supervise effectively only five or six people. Other "general principles" often referred to include subordination of individual interest to that of the organization; discipline (respect for agreements and authority); order—"a place for everything and everything in its place"; the "scalar" principle, that is, a chain of command or "chain of superiors" from lowest to highest ranks but which may be short-circuited if necessary.

You will be encountering some of these concepts in our later discussions. To date, however, they do not provide us with a "general theory" for our guidance in the study of this subject. In some cases general principles of the type outlined above are greatly modified in dealing with specific problem situations.

Decision Making

Attention has centered in recent years on the *decision-making* activities of managers. Decision making is certainly one of the exciting aspects of the manager's work. Some students of the subject consider decision making as virtually synonymous with management.

For example, Professor Herbert A. Simon takes this position:

In treating decision making as synonymous with managing, I shall be referring not merely to the final act of choice among alternatives, but rather to the whole process of decision. Decision making comprises three principal phases: finding occasion for making a decision; finding possible courses of action; and choosing among courses of action. These three

---

2 Harold Koontz, and Cyril O'Donnell, *Principles of Management* (2nd ed.; New York: McGraw-Hill Book Co., Inc., 1959), p. 3.

3 *Ibid.*, chap. 2. You may also wish to refer to some of the following: Henri Fayol, *General and Industrial Management* (New York: Pitman Publ. Corp., 1949); L. Urwick, *The Elements of Administration* (New York: Harper & Bros., 1944); C. I. Barnard, *The Functions of the Executive* (Cambridge, Mass.: Harvard Univ. Press, 1938); and R. C. Davis, *The Fundamentals of Top Management* (New York: Harper & Bros., 1952).

activities account for quite different fractions of the time budget of executives. The fractions vary greatly from one organization level to another and from one executive to another, but we can make some generalizations about them even from casual observation. Executives spend a large fraction of their time surveying the economic, technical, political and social environment to identify new conditions that call for new action. They probably spend an even larger fraction of their time, individually or with associates, seeking to invent, design, and develop possible courses of action for handling situations where a decision is needed. They spend a small fraction of their time in choosing among alternative actions already developed to meet an identified problem and already analyzed for their consequences. The three fractions, added together, account for most of what executives do.[4]

In our discussions we recognize the importance of decision making and make use of this subject as one of our bases for the organization of the topics we undertake to cover. Part 3 of our discussions deals with decision making and decision guides, including Chapters 10 through 14 inclusive. Although decision making is emphasized we also recognize that many of the activities of managers are concerned with *making decisions work*. Once a decision is made the required actions and operations usually do not take place automatically. In addition to decision making, managers are concerned with exercising leadership, motivating the members of their organizations, exercising authority in a manner that will prove to be effective, attracting competent people to the firm, developing loyalties to the firm, winning customers and the support of bankers and investors, and co-ordinating a wide variety of activities.

Nevertheless, the decision-making activities of management are highly important. Decisions may be made entirely on the basis of intuition and indeed a number of business decisions are made in this way. Since no one can foretell the future, a manager who somehow is able to come up with the right decisions will succeed even though he does not try to make use of a variety of information or complicated techniques of analysis. Some managers base their decisions largely on the opinions of their associates or on what they read in newspapers or business journals. Increasingly, however, emphasis has been placed on *rational* decision making—that is, on trying to use the best possible information and the most appropriate means for analyzing such information to provide guides to decisions.

The decisions of managers—particularly if they are to be rational

---

4 Herbert A. Simon, *The New Science of Management Decision* (New York: Harper & Bros., 1960), pp. 1–2.

decisions—are guided by a variety of considerations. Thus, there are financial guides to decisions. It is difficult to think of a business decision that does not have some kind of financial implication. Money is the least specialized resource of the business firm. Business success and failure are both measured in financial terms. We consider these and related topics in Chapter 11.

The financial transactions of a business firm are recorded, analyzed, and reported by means of accounting processes and procedures. Hence, the manager typically has available a variety of accounting reports and analyses to guide him in trying to solve decision problems. Accounting enables the manager to view the firm as an *entity* separate from its owners, managers, or other personnel. Income and expense statements and balance sheets are among the oldest of the manager's decision guides. The "balance sheet equation"—assets (things of value that are owned) equal liabilities (obligations owed to others) plus the owner's equity or proprietorship interest—is a fundamental concept. The balance sheet equation provides a basic set of relationships of major significance to business administration. We discuss various accounting guides to decision in Chapter 12.

Most managers have a variety of statistical information available to them. It may result from the operations of the firm and be available from the firm's records or come from other sources. The analysis of such information often makes valuable decision guides available to the manager. Statistical methods provide one important body of concepts for applying the scientific method to the solution of decision problems.

The business firm is an economic institution—along with being a social and, to a degree, a political unit. Its managers use scarce and often expensive resources to attain their objectives. Thus, the manager deals with essentially economic problems. Hence, economic analysis often provides a number of useful guides to management decisions, notably with reference to costs, revenues, and operating levels. The "theory of the firm" developed by economists provides us with a valuable set of concepts for understanding the work of managers. We give this subject further attention in Chapter 13.[5]

As we suggested in our earlier discussions mathematics has been applied increasingly to the solution of management decision problems.

---

[5] An advanced but very illuminating book by Kenneth E. Boulding and W. Allen Spivey, *Linear Programming and the Theory of the Firm* (New York: Macmillan Co., 1960) should be noted here. You may wish to refer to it as you move on to more advanced studies.

This has been especially true since the computer has come into widespread use. Additional guides to management decisions are often available from the use of such mathematical applications as linear programing, game theory, and other related areas, as we will see in Chapter 14.

Resources and Operations

Management processes and decision making would be rather abstract matters if they were not applied to the utilization of the firm's resources in production and marketing *operations* in the creation and sale of goods and services in order to secure *income*. Thus, to understand the work of the manager of the business firm we need to know something about the human and nonhuman, and the tangible and intangible resources that he uses in attempting to achieve established objectives. Some resources are owed, others may be borrowed or leased. Some resources have a long life, others a short one.

Human resources, however, are distinctive because of the complexity of people. To organize people with diverse backgrounds, interests, and aspirations into productive teams, to motivate them to put forth their best efforts, to develop their capacities, and to help them derive satisfactions from their work presents management with highly complicated problems. A knowledge of how people behave, individually and in groups of various sizes, is of growing importance to managers. We consider these topics at greater length in Chapter 15.

If people are to be productive in a business or economic sense, they usually need things to work with—tools, machines, equipment. They need a location—a place of business. They need knowledge, know-how, ideas, and time. Managers need to know how to bring together the best combinations of people, machines, and other resources, to locate them at desirable places, and to co-ordinate their efforts. On the average our business firms invest between $15,000 and $20,000 per worker in machinery, plant, and equipment resources of various types. As automation advances and as new sources of energy come into wider use, such investments will tend to expand even more. We consider these and related topics in Chapters 16 and 17.

The resources that are assembled by the manager are used to create things of value, usually referred to as goods and services. By things of value we mean goods and services that people want and are willing to pay for. The processes of creating things of value—including not only manufacturing activities but also transportation, communication, making things available at convenient times and places, and the provision of personal services—usually are referred to as *production*. We should note that a bank engages in production activities, just as a manufacturing firm does. Most business managers usually will be involved in some degree with production. This subject is discussed in Chapter 18.

FIGURE 3–1

"OK, so my mistakes cost the company $395,000. For goodness sake, I said I was sorry!"

From the *Wall Street Journal*, October 31, 1961.

Once produced, goods and services are marketed, that is, transferred to users, in return for payments to the firm. Of course, goods may be held in inventory for a time, but ultimately they are intended for sale. Personal services may be thought of as being marketed in somewhat the same way as goods. *Marketing* includes a variety of activities ranging from advertising, sales promotion, and sales management to demand analysis and market research. We discuss these topics in Chapter 19, which concludes Part 4 of this book.

We should note that *business firms do not operate in a vacuum*. Their environment often has a controlling effect on managers and on management decisions. Managers may adapt to their environment or attempt to change it. In Chapter 4 we consider some of the major environmental factors that affect business firms and their managers;

we cover these topics in greater detail in Part 5. In Part 6 we consider some potential trends of development that may hold significance for business managers and for you in the years ahead.

Some Comparisons—The DuPont Company

Now that we have previewed in an outline fashion the general range of our discussions in the next three sections of the book, suppose we make some comparisons between various types of managements and also review a little history.

One way of classifying types of managers or managements is by setting up a range from a one-man, autocratic, or what has been called a "Caesar" type to the other extreme of a management team, with a number of top managers participating in the major decisions and operations. Of course, there may be varying combinations between these extremes. An interesting illustration of these ranges of management types is provided by the history of the DuPont Company. We review this company's history here briefly as an illustration of various management methods and as an example of how this famous company came to grips with some of its problems.

Ernest Dale presents a highly interesting history of the DuPont organization in his book, *The Great Organizers.*[6] He points out that the beginnings of systematic management at DuPont may be traced to the necessity of solving problems of succession that arose when General Henry DuPont died. The General represented a Caesar type of management. Dale defines this type of management as follows:

"Caesar management" may be said to be a comparative term in administration. The founder of a business may be likened to the founder of any organization—political, social, religious, or educational. These "Caesars" are usually unique in their talents applied at their particular time and opportunity; they create original organizations, difficult to explain, impossible to teach or to imitate. Their successors may be compared to "kings" who need to use a systematic administrative approach in order to survive.[7]

General Henry DuPont brought his company to a leadership position in the powder-making industry. He was the son of the company's founder and when he took over the company it was a half-million dollars in debt. He reorganized the company, introduced the most modern machinery, reduced costs in order to improve the company's competitive position, reorganized marketing activities, setting up agents in all parts of the country, imposed careful accounting systems, insisted on prompt payment, and emphasized service to customers.

---

6 Dale, *op. cit.*
7 *Ibid.*, p. 32.

As Ernest Dale points out:

The General's method of management was one-man control. For almost forty years he made all the major decisions and many minor ones. He determined the distribution of profits, at times putting as much as half of the total profits back into the company, and he enforced a large rate of savings among his partners. . . . At meetings with department heads he received information in answer to his questions but gave little or none in return. . . . The General personally supervised the company's several hundred selling agents and initially traveled all over the country to keep in touch with them. Even each worker had access to his office and could consult "Mr. Henry" on any problem. . . . He wrote all the checks and signed all the contracts; he received and distributed the mail. He personally answered all letters addressed to him. He probably wrote over a quarter of a million letters in his almost forty years of tenure, writing with a quill (even when steel pens were available), using candlelight (even when coal-oil lamps, gaslight and electric light existed), blotting the pages with sand, and taking the low-burned candles homes. . . . General DuPont was thus engrossed in thousands of details, yet he did not lose sight of the firm's over-all goals. Though the modern administrator might argue that success could not be gained in this way, the General proved that it could be.[8]

The General's successor was not able to manage in this way. Despite incorporation of the business in 1899 and some attempts at delegation, Eugene DuPont was unable to carry the administrative or physical burdens and died in 1902 at the age of sixty-one. The survivors were discouraged, decided to sell the business, but the youngest partner Alfred I. DuPont disagreed, offered to buy the business and did so with the aid of his cousin T. Coleman DuPont and another cousin Pierre Samuel DuPont. They took over the firm for $2,100 cash and $12 million in notes, reincorporated, and gradually introduced systematic management.

Systematic Management at DuPont

The early beginnings of systematic management may be traced to Lammont DuPont, Sr., who had started the manufacture of dynamite in the Repauno Chemical Company which he had set up (in opposition to the General's judgment). He had developed systematic approaches to the solution of many of the problems of the Repauno Chemical Company and it was the men of this company that supplied the required executive talent for the three cousins who had taken over the DuPont Company.

Lammont DuPont stressed experimentation, permitted rather widespread participation in decision making, refused to follow conventional or authoritarian methods, made use of deductive reasoning and

---

8 *Ibid.*, pp. 33–35.

logic, tested hypotheses, and in general followed a pattern of nonconformity in his management methods. He was killed in an explosion at the age of fifty-three. He was succeeded by William DuPont, who subsequently resigned, and a man from outside the family, J. Amory Haskell, was brought in as president of the company.

Although Haskell was only in his early thirties, he had been head of a coal and iron company, which had enjoyed great success. He brought in H. M. Barksdale as general manager. These two men introduced a number of systematic methods of management into the company. They stressed low prices and large volume. They set up a sales manager, made use of systematic reports of sales personnel, mechanized operations wherever possible, brought in scientists and technically trained people, and established an experimental laboratory. When Haskell left the company, Barksdale took over and had a major influence on its development in subsequent years. He stressed opportunity for individual development for his personnel, and paid special attention to training. He advocated decentralization in order to provide management opportunities for young men.

Uniformity of objectives among the various divisions of the company was stressed; best practice was determined, written up, and made use of throughout the company. Accidents were common; statistical studies were made of accident experience and on this basis safety measures were introduced. Other problems were similarly subjected to systematic study and analysis; abstract models ("engines for thinking") were utilized in some of these studies. Expenses were studied with care; comparisons between various operations were developed; customer complaints were evaluated. A system of departmental charts and reports was established. Wages were studied; an employee bonus system was set up; a new system of accounting was introduced; labor costs and other expenditures including administrative expenses were subjected to rigorous analysis.

In 1912 a paper was prepared setting forth the four major principles of "Scientific Management in Powder Making." These were summarized as follows: "1. Find the best way to do a thing. 2. Make this way standard as to both method and time. 3. Teach employees how to reach the standard. 4. Give them the right incentive to do it."[9]

Adaptive Management

In 1903 a DuPont executive committee had been set up to assure the careful formulation of objectives and co-ordination of controls

---

[9] *Ibid.*, pp. 44–45.

throughout the company and its various subsidiaries and branches (various amalgamations with other powder companies had occurred as time went on). This committee provided for group decision making by the top managers of the various divisions of the company. It gradually became the major means for reaching decisions, with the president of the company recommending programs and policies to this group. At about this time a company-wide operating manual was developed (the DuPont "bible"). A central sales board was set up as well as a research department and subsequently a development department, a major DuPont innovation.

After losing an antitrust suit in 1907 followed by a dissolution order in 1912 the company was divided into three parts. The principal owners and managers recognized that they could no longer expand in the powder field and began diversification into other lines. Heavy losses were incurred in some of the early attempts to diversify. As a result organization studies were made and various criteria developed to serve as management guides. Among these were first, co-ordination of related effort and segregation of unrelated effort; second, undivided responsibility, with the best available person placed in charge of an operation and held entirely responsible for results; third, clearly defined superior-subordinate relationships; fourth, utilization of centralized staff services to achieve economies of operations.

A fifth criterion was of major importance: evaluating a unit's performance on the basis of *rate of return*. To achieve this the Executive Committee operated somewhat like a banker in appraising a loan of funds and determining the effectiveness of their use. The sixth major criterion also was significant: ultimate control by *group management*. This was accomplished by establishing an Executive Committee of the Board of Directors, all members being divorced from the departments of the company.

The older executive committee had been made up of top managers. This arrangement had failed to provide the breadth of view required for success; each manager was also operating a department or division of the company, hence, decisions tended to be compromises between them rather than the result of careful evaluation of what would be in the best interests of the firm as a whole. The new Executive Committee drawn from the Board was set up to assure a company-wide point of view.

Other criteria that were developed included the requirement of a knowledge of general business principles as a requisite for each general manager rather than a knowledge of operating details; recognition that there might be several ways of doing things without loss of operating efficiency, hence, avoiding undue bickering among managers or undue standardization throughout the company; emphasis on adaptability to change; and the concept of an "ideal" set of conditions for the management of the company which were spelled out as follows:

"The ideal condition is one in which every unit or group is so coordinated and controlled that each functions to the best advantage with respect to its own work and the work of the whole company. . . . Each unit should be so organized as to contribute to total organic unity."[10]

These general principles helped to guide DuPont's rapid growth throughout the first quarter of this century. Perhaps of major importance to this growth was *group management of a highly sophisticated type* which took a broad (almost philosophical) approach to management problems that was rationalist and pragmatic. Adaptability to change and flexibility of operations were emphasized. Beyond this a major factor in the success of this company was the emphasis on the *training and development of top management personnel.* Such men were carefully selected, subjected to a variety of experience, and usually achieved top positions only after a fairly long period of association with the company; even so the top executives tended to be in the middle rather than in the older age groups.[11]

Evaluation

All of this happened prior to the end of the first quarter of this century. The company, of course, is still of major importance in our economy. Its earlier history, however, presents us with an interesting and enlightening set of experiences which include a variety of management methods.

We may be impressed by a number of things in this summary review of a "case history" of the management of an important business firm, but for our purposes the following appear to be significant:

1. A firm may be managed in a number of ways, ranging from "Caesar-" type management to group management, either made up of top executives or members of the board of directors. Each type of management may fit well the requirements of an organization at a given time. There would probably not have been need for group man-

---

[10] *Ibid.,* p. 61, quoted from a company report.

[11] Among the important men in the company during its rapid growth in the early days of this century were Coleman DuPont, Pierre S. DuPont, Alfred I. DuPont, Irénée DuPont, Lammont DuPont, Walter S. Carpenter, Jr., John J. Raskob, and Donaldson Brown.

agement at the time the General ran the company, but clearly he would have had difficulty managing the far flung DuPont empire that emerged later. Similarly, the General's successor might have succeeded had he not tried to follow the General's example and had adopted management methods that more nearly fitted his capacities.

2. Many business problems can be solved by careful study and analysis. A rational and inquiring approach to management problems often yields dividends as Lammont DuPont, Sr., demonstrated. To subject problems to study and analysis, however, the necessary data must be available, and this means that provision must be made for accounting and reporting systems. Models or "engines for thinking" are helpful in management studies; those used by the DuPonts were forerunners of those now used by managers that result from the application of economic, statistical, and mathematical analysis to decision problems.

3. Objectives are vital to good management; the careful establishment of objectives indicates the relative importance of programs and helps to guide management decisions. Major objectives dare not be lost sight of by the pursuit of minor objectives or those related to a part of the enterprise rather than the whole. This was illustrated by the breakdown of the early executive committee of the DuPont organization since it tended to develop conflicts between the over-all objectives of the company and the objectives of the various departments.

4. Financial controls and standards are important to management. Until the "rate-of-return" criterion was adopted by DuPont, severe losses had been incurred. By evaluating performance on a rate-of-return basis, the executive committee was able to avoid the emergence of very many situations that were unprofitable.

5. Men who are to assume major management responsibilities must be carefully trained, given opportunity to develop, and moved into positions of authority as they are ready. The "executive lifeline" at DuPont became a long one after programs were developed to assure that men would be carefully trained, provided with broad experience, and given opportunity to advance. DuPont men were much in demand not only to meet the requirements of their own company but also of others. DuPont men largely ran General Motors for a time. DuPont men usually followed DuPont money. Whenever an investment by DuPont was made, men who had been trained in the company usually were put in charge.

6. In the training and development of managers general business

principles are more important than details of operations. To quote from a DuPont report:

The objection has been advanced that some of the grand divisions are too large and too diversified to be under the control of one individual. The answer is that the controlling individual need not know every detail of the business, but requires only a good mind, sound judgment and knowledge of general business principles. He will never have occasion at one time to need to know all conditions—what he will have to do will be to examine the facts affecting certain portions of his domain and make his decisions accordingly. It is no more impossible to find such a man than it is impossible to select a man for Justice of the Supreme Court on the ground that no one can have knowledge of all the cases that are likely to come before him.[12]

(As a student of business administration this statement should have special significance for you.)

7. Business organizations work best if they are reasonably flexible and adaptable to changing requirements. The changes that took place during the history of the DuPont company certainly illustrate the need for adaptability. As problems changed, management changed to meet them. Unless this had happened, the company's history undoubtedly would have been quite different.

8. The people in an organization need to be given incentives, provided with growth opportunities, protected against accidents and other hazards, made an integral part of the organization. From the General's concern about the problems of his workers, through the efforts of later managers to reduce accidents, to the development of bonus systems of payment well in advance of most companies, the history of DuPont emphasizes the importance of the well-being of the people in the organization.

9. Low-cost, high-volume operations help to achieve success. DuPont adopted this formula early. To achieve it, however, requires the use of the best possible machinery to supplement the efforts of workers, the careful control of costs, efficient production methods, and systematic evaluation of markets through reports of sales personnel and studies of customer needs and requirements. The history of DuPont illustrates these conclusions at a number of points.

10. Research, experimentation, and development work are important to the success of a firm. A willingness to try new things, to experiment with products and processes, to innovate, to follow facts rather

---

12 Dale, *op. cit.*, p. 60.

than opinion, to make use of the scientific method—all these were characteristic of DuPont from the time of Lammont, Sr., on.

11. Environmental factors are important, in some cases controlling. One of the major factors in the decision of the DuPont management to diversify was the loss of the antitrust suit in 1907 and the dissolution order of 1912. The first World War had a significant impact on the growth of the company; conversion to peacetime conditions after the war posed special problems. Thus, even a very large company like DuPont is affected greatly by what is going on in the business environment. Consequently, managers need to study and analyze their environment with care, anticipating in so far as possible potential economic, political, or social changes and developing programs to meet them. (We discuss this point at greater length in the next chapter.)

12. Management is both a science and an art, as we pointed out in the preceding chapter. While some aspects of management can be subjected to careful study and analysis, others cannot. The General exemplified primarily the art in contrast to the science of management; the group management of a later period came closer to exemplifying management as a science. Even so, these contrasts should not be overstressed. The General drew on his experience and studied it, even though this was largely an informal process; the group managers of a later day practiced the art as well as the science of management. Their emphasis on flexibility, recognition that several types of methods might be equally effective in achieving desired results, their philosophical and sophisticated viewpoint are all illustrative of management as an art.

SUMMARY

A "general theory" of business administration is not as yet available as a guide to the study of this subject. The study of the business firm provides one method for integrating a variety of concepts. Business firms have to be managed, and the work of the manager—often divided into functions or "the management process"—gives us another center around which to develop our discussions. Decision making and various decision guides give us another means for bringing together a variety of subjects, whether or not decision making is considered as synonymous with management. Various financial, accounting, statistical, economic, and applied mathematics guides are available to help managers solve decision problems. Another important group of topics centers around business resources and operations, including both human and nonhuman resources, and production and marketing operations.

The early history of the DuPont Company provides an interesting series of illustrations of various types of management and the evolution of a number of modern management methods and concepts. From this history we are able to draw several conclusions that may be helpful later on; notably, the diversity of ways in which a firm may be managed; the value of careful study and analysis in the solution of business problems; the importance of objectives; the significance of financial controls and standards; the value of an "executive lifeline"; priority of general business principles over a knowledge of operating details; importance of flexibility and adaptability, the well-being of the people in an organization, low-cost, high-volume operations, research and experimentation, and environmental factors; and the recognition that management is both an art and a science.

QUESTIONS AND PROBLEMS

1. Why does the absence of a "general theory" of business administration complicate our problems of studying this field?
2. What is meant by the "management process"? Does this provide a means for organizing our studies?
3. What do the initials POSDCORB stand for?
4. Do you think "decision making" may be considered as synonymous with "management"? Why or why not?
5. What is meant by the statement: "many of the activities of managers are concerned with making decisions work"?
6. What is the "balance sheet equation"?
7. Identify the major types of business resources.
8. Why do our business firms invest on the average between $15,000 and $20,000 per worker in machinery, plant, and equipment resources of various types?
9. What is meant by "production"? By "marketing"? Does a bank engage in production? Explain.
10. What is meant by "Caesar management"? Can you give an illustration from your own experience?
11. How does group management contrast with Caesar management?
12. Why did the work of the early executive committee of the DuPont organization tend to break down? How was this situation remedied later?
13. If you were evaluating the significance of the early history of the DuPont Company would you agree with the conclusions set forth in the above discussion? To which conclusions would you take particular exception? Explain.

SUGGESTED READINGS

DALE, ERNEST. *The Great Organizers.* New York: McGraw-Hill Book Co., Inc., 1960. Read chap. 1, "Some Foundations of Organization Theory," and chap. 2, "DuPont: Pioneer in Systematic Organization and Management." This is a very stimulating book and you may wish to read other parts of it as well. We have additional assignments in it later.

KOONTZ, HAROLD, and O'CONNELL, CYRIL. *Principles of Management.* 2nd ed. New York: McGraw-Hill Book Co., Inc., 1959. This is a widely used textbook in this field. Read chap. 1, "The Present Pattern of Management," and chap. 2, "The Development of a Theory of Management."

LONG, JOHN D. *Workbook to Accompany Weimer: Business Administration: An Introductory Management Approach,* chap. 3. Rev. ed. Homewood, Ill.: Richard D. Irwin, Inc., 1962.

SIMON, HERBERT A. *The New Science of Management Decision.* New York: Harper & Bros., 1960. Read pages 1–8 inclusive, "The Executive as Decision Maker," in this interesting and important volume.

OUTLINE FOR CHAPTER 4

The study of THE MANAGER AND THE BUSINESS ENVIRONMENT provides for a consideration of "external" in contrast to "internal" factors affecting management decisions. The line between them, however, is difficult to draw.

The manager tries to determine when he should
  (1) *adapt* his operations to economic, social, or political trends;
  (2) *move contrary* to such trends; or
  (3) *undertake to change* the environment.

The *character* of the environment is determined in large part by
  billions of decisions by
  millions of people registered in
  markets and political elections; and by
  historical, cultural, and institutional changes.

Divisions of the business environment include
  business and economic conditions,
  government and political conditions,
  the legal system,
  the enterprise system and competing systems, and
  international business administration.

Background factors of importance include
  characteristics of the American economy,
  social and business objectives, and
  historical forces.

Emerging trends likely to affect managers are numerous and varied; important issues likely to affect emerging trends are
      war and peace,
      progress versus security, and
      equality versus excellence.

THE MANAGER AND THE
BUSINESS ENVIRONMENT

*Not in vain the distance beacons. Forward, forward let us range,
Let the great world spin forever down the ringing grooves of
change.*

—TENNYSON
(Locksley Hall)

Importance of the Business Environment

In the preceding chapter we outlined some of the activities of the manager in administering the programs of the business firm and told you in general how Part 2, Part 3, and Part 4 of this book are organized. We stressed those aspects of the manager's work that relate to his major functions, decisions, and operations in utilizing the resources of the firm in achieving its objectives. Our attention centered primarily on the firm as a going concern.

The manager's work, of course, is influenced not only by the "internal" operations of the firm, but also by many "external" or environmental factors as well. It is far from easy to draw a line between the firm and its environment. Loyal customers may be almost a part of the firm, even though they are also a part of its market. Employees of the firm are influenced greatly by their life outside the firm as well as by their work in it. Investors may be balancing the opportunities offered by the firm against those that may be offered by competitors.

Because of the difficulty of drawing a line between the firm and its environment, we make some arbitrary divisions in order to facilitate our consideration of the subjects related to the manager and the business environment. In this chapter we outline briefly some of the topics that are considered at greater length in Part 5, which covers such subjects as business conditions, government and political conditions, the legal system, the system of enterprise and democracy as well as major competing systems, and international business administration. In this chapter, we also consider several general background topics that may be helpful to you, including some observations on social and business objectives and a few historical viewpoints. In addition, we anticipate several of the topics covered in Part 6 in which we consider emerging problems and opportunities that may be important to executives in the future or to you in managing your future.

The Manager and the Pilot

The influence of environmental factors on the business manager may be compared to the influence of the weather on the airplane pilot. A good pilot finds out all he can about weather conditions before he undertakes a flight. He may decide to cancel his flight on the basis of weather reports; he may plan his course so as to avoid thunderstorms along the way; or he may plan to fly at a certain altitude because of the direction or velocity of winds at that level.

Similarly the general economic, political, and social weather will influence the decisions of the business manager. He may try to take advantage of favorable developments in the market for his product just as the airplane pilot takes advantage of favorable winds. The manager may decide to drop a product line because of unfavorable conditions just as the pilot may decide to fly around a thunderstorm. The manager may decide to enter the international field because of favorable competitive conditions just as the pilot may decide to fly at an altitude that has favorable winds.

Like the pilot, the manager is subject to certain "rules of the game." He must conform to established laws and practices in the conduct of his business just as the pilot must conform to orders from control towers or to established flying patterns (see Figure 4–1).

Our analogy, however, is not entirely complete. An airplane pilot will not take off in the face of bad weather. To do so might be suicide. In some cases, however, a manager may decide to move contrary to the general economic climate—to "buck a trend"—because he believes he may gain advantages over his competitors in this way. Since his competitors may reduce their operations, he may be able to take advantage of this situation. He does so at considerable risk in most such situations, but we should note that the manager's decisions are not as clearly indicated by environmental factors as those of the pilot.

In addition, the business manager has to some extent *an opportunity to change his environment.* Through his trade association, for example, he may be able to secure legislation that is favorable to his line of business. By working through his elected representatives in government he may obtain favorable laws or prevent the establishment of unfavorable regulations. He may be able to institute advertising and

FIGURE 4–1

Environmental Influences

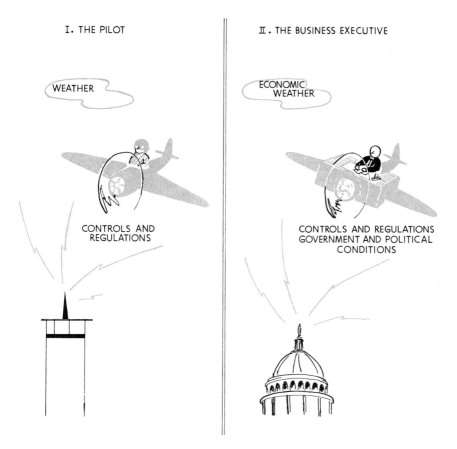

sales policies that will cause a change in the market in which he is operating.

Thus, he tries to determine (1) when he should adapt his operations to the economic, social, and political environment, (2) when he may move contrary to established trends, and (3) when he may undertake to change the environment to a greater or lesser degree. The more accurately he is able to anticipate changes in his environment or "weather," the more successful he is likely to be.

Determining Environmental Trends

The manager studies his environment almost constantly in order to understand in so far as possible the forces that are at work. In his day-to-day activities he usually reads widely, including in his reading current newspapers and magazines as well as publications in the business field generally or in his particular line of business. He talks with many people—other businessmen, customers, suppliers, labor leaders, politicians, government officials, people he meets on social occasions, taxi drivers, barbers, and people he meets on trains or planes—in the hope of developing an understanding of what is going on around him. He needs a "feel" of the general climate in which he is trying to manage his firm.

Some firms employ business economists, lawyers, sociologists, social psychologists, and others to help their managers understand changes and potential changes in environmental conditions. Often specialists in market analysis or in public opinion analysis are used as well.

The manager tries through his own efforts or with the help of others to *anticipate* developments, to project, predict, or postulate the changes that may lie ahead. In so far as future changes in the environment can be anticipated, decisions may be made within a smaller margin of error.

In our type of society the economic, social, and political climate is determined to a large extent by billions of decisions made by millions of individuals and families, business executives, farmers, government officials, labor leaders, and others. These decisions are registered either (1) in markets or (2) through political elections.

Our system of generally competitive markets enables each of us through decisions to buy or not to buy, or to buy more or less, to help determine what will be produced, how much, and for whom. Such decisions have an important bearing on whether business activity will expand or decline. Our individual decisions may be influenced by business firms through their advertising and sales programs, or by government regulations or programs, but ultimately each of us plays a role in determining the character of the economic "weather" in which business firms of all types will operate.

Similarly, we register our decisions about candidates for office and about public issues through our votes. These votes help to determine the kind of government we have and thus the kind of political and governmental environment in which business firms must operate. Thus, through our "dollar votes" or our political votes each of us exercises some influence in determining our general economic and political environment.

In different parts of the world, of course, the extent to which decisions can be registered in markets or in political elections varies widely.

Competitive markets play a much smaller role in the Communist bloc countries than in the Western world. Political elections are seldom held in countries ruled by dictators.

We should note also that there are some areas in which we seldom make conscious decisions. These are the areas of *accepted ways of doing things*. Sometimes these are referred to as "institutional" or "cultural" arrangements. Customs and traditions are important in this connection. A good illustration is provided by language. No legislature decided that we would use the word "book" to designate the kind of thing you are now reading. Indeed, in other countries other words are used to designate a book.

A distinguished anthropologist, for example, makes this statement:

The essential aroma of each culture or subculture may be caught as a fragrance of language. . . . Although one could press this point of view too far, there is *something* significant in the lists of words from each European language that have become widely current in other languages. From English: gentleman, fair play, week end, sport. From French: *liaison, maitresse, cuisine*. From Italian: *diva, bravo, bel canto*. From German: *Weltschmerz, Sehnsucht, Weltanschauaung*, and *Gemutlichkeit*.[1]

We almost never make conscious decisions about a number of things. We follow accepted ways and established practices. Men are not likely to decide to wear women's clothing, for example. Women are not likely to decide to rise when men enter a room. Here we eat with knives, forks, and spoons rather than chopsticks; we hold our forks differently from the people in Europe; we seldom wear sport clothes to business conferences. Illustrations of cultural factors could be multiplied.

We are trying to point out that there are a great many elements in our environment and in the environment of business which result from our general cultural heritage. We cannot change them even if we wished to do so, or we can change them only gradually over a long period of time. They are products of historical developments and gradual adaptations over long periods of time.

The writer previously quoted also makes this significant statement:

Perhaps the most important implication of culture for action is the profound truth that you can never start with a clean slate as far as human beings are concerned. Every person is born into a world defined by already existing culture patterns. Just as an individual who has lost his memory is no longer normal so the idea of a society's becoming completely emanci-

---

[1] Clyde Kluckhohn, *Mirror for Man* (Greenwich, Conn.: Fawcett Publications, Inc., 1960), pp. 118–19.

pated from its past culture is inconceivable. . . . Since every culture has organization as well as content, administrators and lawmakers should know that one cannot isolate a custom to abolish or modify it. The most obvious example of failure caused by neglect of this principle was the Eighteenth Amendment.[2]

Major Topics for Consideration

As we suggested above, we have divided the business environment into several broad topics as the basis for our discussions. These topics are considered at greater length in Part 5 of this book.

The first broad topic is "business conditions." The manager is concerned almost constantly with potential changes in general business and economic conditions or in his industry or line of business. For example, if business conditions are favorable, his programs may be quite different from those he would follow in a period of recession.

The main indicators of business conditions include: (1) employment and unemployment, (2) incomes, (3) prices and price levels, (4) financial information, (5) consumer spending, (6) government spending, (7) business spending for plant and equipment, (8) inventory changes, and (9) gross national product and income.

The American economy produced over $500 billion of goods and services in 1960. This is the gross national product (often designated by the letters GNP). GNP is the sum of the values of all final goods and services produced in the economy in a year. It includes every type of product, any good or service, to which a market value can be assigned. We discuss various indicators of business activity and other subjects related to business conditions in Chapter 20.

The manager's decisions are influenced to a significant extent by political and governmental conditions and programs. These conditions and programs constitute another broad topic. The manager's decisions usually will take into account community and general public attitudes. He may try to influence legislative programs through the work of his trade association, Chambers of Commerce, or political parties. He may undertake community and public relations programs in an effort to improve the general climate in which his firm operates. For the most part, however, his job is one of adapting operations to governmental and community conditions as they exist or are likely to exist in the future.

Probably the most important impact of government on business firms is in the area of taxes. A great many business decisions are affected by taxes, and in a large number of cases taxes may exercise a

---

[2] *Ibid.*, p. 37.

determining influence. Business managers thus must administer their tax liabilities with great care.

Incidentally we should note that one of the strengths of our two-party system comes from the wide representation of interests of all types in each party. The differences are of degree rather than kind. This makes it possible for the elected candidates of either party to represent all parts of our society. Thus, our system of "legalized revolutions" through political elections has a better chance of working than if one party represented a "right" and the other a "left" position. We discuss governmental and political aspects of the business environment in Chapter 21.

Business firms are operated within a general *system of law* and accepted standards of conduct and practice. Our system of common law has important roots in the history of trade, negotiation, and commerce. Our system of private property and contract rests on the common law. Thus, the business manager needs to be familiar with our legal system, to know how best to conduct operations in relation to it, and to recognize when he needs legal counsel to help him reach sound decisions. We consider this subject in Chapter 22.

As we have suggested, the business firm is a social as well as an economic institution, in fact, the key social institution of our time. It is a unit in a complex society and must be managed in a way that recognizes the objectives, standards, mores, and customs of our society. Many of the relationships between a business firm and our society as a whole center in the *enterprise system*, which in connection with our democratic form of government provides the basic framework of our society. The manager needs an understanding of this system if he is to carry on his operations with success. He needs also an understanding of other competing systems, notably communism and socialism. These topics form the basis of our discussion in Chapter 23.

The international business operations of American firms are growing in importance. Thus, the managers of many companies are concerned increasingly with the international environment, both with respect to the conduct of business activities abroad and because of the growing impact of international developments on the business climate at home. We consider this subject in Chapter 24.

Characteristics of the American Economy

So much for the organization of Part 5. We mentioned in the first section of this chapter that we would also look at several general background topics. The first such topic pertains to major characteristics of the American economy.

As we have suggested the environment within which business firms operate is as broad as the entire world. Many firms carry on world-wide operations, serving both domestic and international markets.

The American economy, of course, continues as the major factor in the environment of most firms in this country. Our economy has a number of important characteristics that are recognized by managers and that are important to all of us. First, *the American economy is very big*. It is big in terms of people with a population of some 180 million persons in 1960. It is big in terms of resources. It is big as measured by productive capacity. Output per man hour in this country is substantially higher than in any other country of the world. As a result, the typical citizen of this country enjoys a standard of living that is several times higher than the average of the 2.5–3 billion people that currently inhabit the earth.

Second, *the American economy is competitive*. People compete for jobs. Business firms compete for markets. Students compete for grades. The competitive character of the economy keeps business managers

FIGURE 4–2

Disposable Income, 1880 and 1960
(In 1960 Dollars)

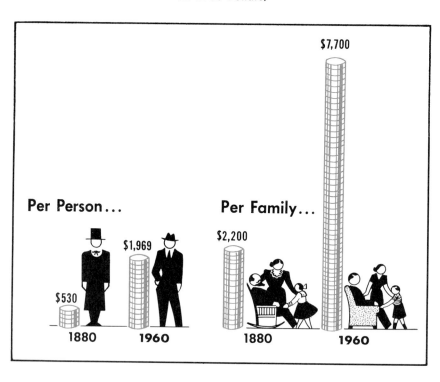

looking for new and better products and for new and better ways to turn out their products at lower and lower costs. Despite concern over the decline of competition, the growing diversity of the economy and the rate at which new products are being introduced suggests that it will remain competitive for some time.

Third, *the American economy is made up largely of private enterprises.* A very large proportion of total output is privately produced. Only about an eighth is produced by government. However, our economic system is one that operates within a framework of laws and regulations, some of which impose rather strict limits on individual firms.

Often we hear the term "laissez faire" (a French term literally meaning "let people do [or make] what they choose") used to designate a situation in which business firms are free to compete in whatever manner they choose and virtually without regulation. It is doubtful, however, that a system of laissez faire was ever intended as one in which the government did nothing. Basically, government has always been responsible for making the system workable. Competition is itself a form of social control. In some situations competition controls with a minimum of regulation or restriction; in others it may be necessary to impose substantial controls or to rely on direct government action rather than competition.

Fourth, *the American economy is one in which the gains have been widely distributed.* The share of total income going to property has tended to decline relative to the share going to the people who are employed. For example, in 1880 profits, interest, and rent represented around a fourth of total income; in 1940 about a fifth; and currently around a sixth.

Fifth, *the American economy is capitalistic.* This does not mean that it is run by capitalists but rather that capital may be owned privately and used extensively in production processes. A large amount of machinery and equipment is used per worker, and as a result output per hour of labor is very high. As we have pointed out, an investment of between $15,000 and $20,000 per man is required for our economy to operate as it does currently. In some industries this investment runs as high as $50,000, in some over $100,000, while in others—notably trading enterprises—it is substantially lower.

Objectives of Our Society

American business firms operate in an economy that is dynamic and progressive. Indeed, progress may be considered one of the major objectives of our society. Progress is characterized not only by increasingly higher incomes and better living conditions but by greater equality of economic opportunity, and the improvement of the cultural standards of people generally. As Professor Wright has said: "Not the ending of competitive acquisition should be our goal but the competitive acquisition of nobler things in a nobler way."[3]

The American economy reflects the attitudes, ideals, objectives, and characteristics of the people who work in it. The characteristic which distinguishes the American economy in comparison to other economies of the world is its capacity for *growth and progress*. While growth is sometimes interrupted and the pattern of growth is irregular, it comes close to being a continuous process when viewed over long periods of time.

Growth results from the positive actions of individuals in every walk of life. For an economy to grow, however, certain conditions must be present. Human and material resources, as well as the resources of time, knowledge, and ideas, are basic, but in addition there must be a climate that is conducive to growth.

Such a climate must include a substantial amount of individual freedom, not only economic freedom but freedom to make choices in all areas of life. No one tells us which church we must attend, the political party we must support, the career we must follow, the person we must marry, the automobile we must buy, the place we must live, or the way we must spend our incomes.

Such a wide latitude of choice inevitably leads to change. Dynamic and changing conditions are conducive to economic growth and progress. Changing conditions allow for experimentation; the development of new ideas, processes, and products; substitution of new equipment for old; introduction of new designs and models; and changes in the tastes and preferences of the people generally.

In addition the *will* to grow, to improve, and to make the world a better place to live appears to be an essential ingredient of progress. Americans have had this will to grow and to make progress throughout our history. It is the product of many forces, including the restlessness and desire for change that probably came from our immigrant ancestors, the scarcity of tradition and binding customs, the lack of a rigid social system, the belief in the individual and his capacity for development, the generally accepted goal of increasing equality of economic opportunity, and the maintenance of conditions which allow

---

[3] David McCord Wright, *Democracy and Progress* (New York: Macmillan Co., 1948), pp. 24–25.

each person to progress as far as his ability, energy, drive, and luck may carry him.

The will to progress is also the product of our competitive business system. This competitive system puts a premium on the new and better product. Growth and progress have been fostered by a democratic form of government which protects us against special privilege, monopoly, and the intrenched positions of any group or class.

An understanding of the objectives of our economy and our system —growth and progress in all desirable aspects of life and the maintenance and improvement of the conditions that make such progress possible—is basic to an understanding of the work of business firms and the people who manage them.

The maintenance and expansion of the basic freedoms that are essential to growth and progress is one of the major objectives of our society. Thus, to a degree at least, *the means become the ends.* Preservation of the freedom of the individual and of the conditions, or improvement of them, which enable him to develop his capacities to the fullest extent must be considered a major goal of American society— and business firms are expected to help achieve this goal.

Prosperity and full employment are often mentioned as primary objectives of our economy. We do pursue these objectives and develop governmental and business policies that will further them. We try to develop such policies, however, in a manner which will not make it necessary to sacrifice our basic freedoms.

Social and Business Objectives

As we have noted, the objectives of individual business firms may be quite varied. Many want to grow and progress. A few prefer to maintain a stated size. Nearly all try to provide a good return to owners and investors and to pay wages and salaries that are high enough to hold and attract competent personnel. Most of them try to maximize profits in the long run. Many firms try to market their products at prices that are as low as possible in order to meet and if possible to beat their competitors. A considerable number of business firms try to be good citizens in the broader sense of the term. In some cases they try to pursue policies and objectives that will support the general objectives and purposes of their local communities and the economy as a whole. In other cases such objectives are incidental to the achievement of more specific goals of individual companies.

By pursuing their own interests, however, we have found that in our competitive type of society the owners and managers of business firms usually tend to serve the long-term objectives of the entire community. This is especially true when business executives give careful consideration to such objectives as maximizing their profits or competitive position over the long run rather than in terms of short-run periods only.

To illustrate the relationship between the objectives of an individual firm and those of the general community, we may borrow an illustration from another field. In this country we take pride in our free press and in maintaining freedom of expression. What is the general objective of maintaining a free press? Basically it is to disseminate the truth. We achieve this objective, however, not by limiting each publication to presenting only the truth but by allowing it to publish whatever it pleases. To limit publication would defeat the ultimate purpose.

Similarly, by allowing business firms to pursue their individual objectives, within the general framework of our laws and regulations, they tend to serve the best interests of the community as a whole. In other words, if a business firm wishes to maximize its profits over the long run, to preserve and augment its capital investment, to provide employment for people in the community, to earn fair returns for its owners or pursue any other similar objective, it accomplishes these things by providing goods and services that the people want and by providing them at as low a cost as possible. Of course, there may be cases of business firms which pursue monopolistic or related objectives and must be subjected to special regulation. So long as business firms meet the tests of competition within the framework of our laws and regulations, they serve purposes that are useful to all of us.

In short, business firms in the pursuit of their own objectives—including profit maximizing in the long run—contribute to the achievement of the basic objectives of our society as a whole. This is a primary condition of the existence of business firms and of the private business system. As we have pointed out, it is the function of government to make competition work, to maintain conditions that make the system workable. In some cases this means encouraging competition, in others, supplementing or supplanting it. Democracy and enterprise go hand in hand. Each is essential to the other.

Historical Forces

Since the environment of business is a product of historical forces, the manager needs some knowledge of historical processes. This does not mean that he should have a detailed knowledge of history but rather that he needs some "historical sense," an awareness of the forces operating over time which have shaped the current environment and those which are likely to influence it in the future.

For example, the Industrial Revolution represents one of the forces with which the business manager needs to be familiar. The Industrial Revolution in turn was largely the product of a broader set of historical forces, most of which arose in the Renaissance period of history. Out of it came a rebirth of interest in natural science, technology, and the solution of the problems of this world in contrast to the "other worldliness" which characterized the medieval period of history. The rise of national states grew out of the same set of forces. Whether internationalism will represent a further development in the process remains to be seen.

Another historical force of importance to the business manager in this country is the American frontier. While the physical frontier has long since disappeared, the influence of the frontier on American life continues to be great. The idea of progress, the belief in the capacity of individuals for improvement, and the "pursuit of nobler things in a nobler way" are the products of historical forces of significance in understanding modern American society.

There are many other types of forces, of course, including urbanism, capitalism, the competitive spirit, socialism, agrarianism, science, technology, and others. It is not our purpose here to undertake a discussion of them but rather to mention their importance as a basis for understanding the business environment now and in the future. Courses in history, economic history, and business history will help you to gain such understanding.

In trying to understand other parts of the world, of course, a background in the history and cultural development of such areas can be most helpful. The development of international business operations has placed a premium on knowledge of this type.

It is important for us to recognize also that business has played an important role in the history of civilization. The philosopher, Alfred North Whitehead, pointed out that commerce was the beginning of civilization since it involved relationships between people on the basis of persuasion rather than on the basis of force. Business has stimulated a spirit of adventure and has been stimulated by it in turn. There were business motives back of many of the early explorations including the adventures of Marco Polo, Columbus, Magellan, and others. There is little doubt also that the exchange of goods and services has led throughout history to an exchange of ideas. While few businessmen have achieved historic significance as individuals, business as a whole has played a significant role in creating the present environment in which we live.

As Miriam Beard has said:

They [the businessmen] have not sacrificed others like tyrants or themselves like saints; through the stormiest ages they were the carriers of morality, the representatives of thrift, temperance, reticence, hard work, domesticity and other qualities which wearied, instead of thrilling readers. Few really horrid crimes, without rational motive, may be imputed to businessmen. Seldom have they put out the eyes of competitors with hot irons or burned rival salesmen at the stake . . . or murdered bankers just for fun, or thrown away monopolies for love.[4]

In more recent years the study of *business history* has assumed increasing importance in the education of future business managers. The history of business firms studied in relationship to the environment in which their operations were carried on can be a valuable aid to present and future managers. The successes or failures of management at earlier periods may contribute to an understanding of present problems even if they are different in type, scope, or in terms of the forces at work. A knowledge of what led to good or bad decisions in earlier periods may be highly useful to present managers in making current or future decisions.

Uses of History

Since we have stated that management is future oriented, you may wonder why we are emphasizing the importance of history and the study of historical forces in understanding the environment of business. There are several reasons. The present is obviously a product of the past—either the remote or the recent past. The major forces, those which have persisted for a long time, may well continue into the future and thus help to shape the environment of business. History, thus, may be a valuable guide to the manager in understanding that phase of the environment which changes very slowly and about which we make few conscious decisions—what we referred to above as "cultural" or "institutional" factors in the business environment.

History seldom repeats itself very closely, but a knowledge of how people in previous civilizations came to grips with their problems provides us with a background for attacking our own problems or those

---

[4] By permission from Miriam Beard, *A History of the Business Man* (New York: Macmillan Co., 1938), p. 2.

we may encounter in the future.[5] It is interesting to note that each generation undertakes to rewrite history in order to make it more meaningful to the solution of current problems. Thus, history may be thought of in a dynamic rather than a static sense, as a way of looking at our problems in perspective, and as an aid to decision making in our private or business lives.

Of interest in this connection is an observation by Herbert J. Muller in his book, *The Uses of the Past:*

Up to a point, all this implies something like Croce's principle, that true history is always contemporary history—history "for the occasion," of what is alive for us. The past has no meaningful existence except as it exists for us, as it is given meaning by us. In piety and justice we try to see it as it was, or as it seemed to the men who lived it, but even this poetic interest is not disinterested; in our contemplation of the drama we see what is most pertinent for our own hopes and fears. Hence the past keeps changing with the present. Every age has to rewrite its history, re-create the past; in every age a different Christ dies on the Cross, and is resurrected to a different end. Today the Peloponnesian War and the decline of the Roman Empire have a special significance for us that they could not have had for the Middle Ages or the Renaissance; by the same token, they will have a different significance for a Hindu or Chinese than for a Western historian. Our task is to create a "usable past" for our own living purposes.[6]

Emerging Trends

Part 6 of this book deals with emerging trends that may bring both problems and opportunities to business managers and to you in planning your future. Among the topics considered in Part 6 are those dealing with changing relationships between owners and managers of business firms, the large corporation controversy, management by machines, research, economic growth, industrial relations, fear of war, fear of depressions, fear of inflation, changing cultural and educational standards, and others.

There are several sets of issues with which all of us, including business managers, are concerned. How these issues are resolved will influence many emerging trends. They are the issues related to war and peace, progress and security, and equality and excellence.

The twentieth century has been marked by wars—cold and hot. Large portions of our incomes have gone to pay for wars, past and present, and perhaps future. Tax rates have been high for business

---

5 Incidentally, the study of literature from a problem-solving standpoint may be helpful to you in developing an understanding of many types of personal problems.

6 By permission from Herbert J. Muller, *The Uses of the Past* (New York: Oxford University Press, 1952), p. 33.

firms and individuals. Inflationary pressures have been generated. The defense industry in this country has become a significant sector of our economy.

Business managers have had to live with the forces generated by the problems of war and peace. Every manager today keeps one eye on the international stage because of its potential impact on his operations. If he is in a defense or defense-related business, the relationships are very close. Even if he is in a business far removed from defense, he knows that his best-laid plans may be changed by a sudden outbreak of a hot war, or intensification or relaxation of cold war, or the possibility that peace might "break out," the imposition of new taxes to pay for old wars or prepare for future ones, changes in the programs of stockpiling of strategic materials, and many others.

International conditions affect greatly the movement of capital between countries, the movement of people and goods, the exchange of knowledge and information, and the division of labor between the various parts of the world. All business firms are affected by these conditions, and not only those engaged in international business activities.

The problems of managers operating under these conditions contrast sharply with the problems of the managers who operated at the turn of the century. At that time there was a very small standing army. Capital, goods, and people could move freely between most parts of the world. The price level was generally stable; there was no income tax, and the national debt was very small.

American business managers have been spared to some degree the full impact of unsettled international relations. We have in this country a large free-trade area in which people, goods, and capital can move freely. We are relatively less dependent than many other countries on the resources available only in other parts of the world. Despite these advantages the issues related to war and peace have had and will continue to have a major impact on the environment of business and hence on the problems of business managers.

Progress versus Security

The broad issue of progress versus security is almost as old as history itself. In the past two generations, however, this issue has been especially important. It has centered to a considerable extent in the problems of economic stability and instability. Sometimes the issue includes also the broader implication of control versus freedom in economic affairs. As David McCord Wright has pointed out:

At the present time there is a deeply seated, though largely unconscious, conflict between two basically different concepts of social betterment. One group looks upon the matter as the achievement of a fixed ideal static pattern of technical and social organization. Once this ideal is reached, or closely approximated, it needs only be repeated endlessly thereafter. The other group looks upon life as a continual development. While usually admitting certain eternal values, it does not relate them to any fixed static cultural pattern. And the eternal values themselves are related more to the manner than to the direction of change. Emphasis shifts from an ideal final aim to an ideal process of variation.

In times of great and disastrous disturbance men are attracted to the ideal of the static pattern. Somewhere, they think, we must find permanence. The static pattern has, therefore, a special appeal for the weary, the bewildered, and the intellectually immature. It is from such elements as these that the authoritarian state has so often taken its birth. But when men are less hungry and less frightened they have time to be tolerant. When they are more vigorous they are less content with the endless repetition of a single form of creation. And when they are intellectually mature the prospect of change becomes less horrifying. Under these circumstances the ideal of continued development tends to gain.[7]

A dynamic and progressive economy tends also to be an unstable one. If people are free to innovate and to pursue new projects and adventures, they are likely to create instabilities. If the instabilities become so great that large numbers of people are thrown out of work or savings are lost or many business firms fail, popular demands for security and stability may result in very rigid controls such as limiting the introduction of new inventions or the licensing of investment. As a result the dynamic qualities of the economy may be smothered or legislated into a state of suspension.

Our system requires a great deal of freedom to innovate in order to maintain its dynamic qualities; hence, business has a big stake in avoiding major depressions and dislocations in the economy in order that the essential nature of the system may be preserved.

Equality versus Excellence

In our society there tends to be a conflict between excellence and equality. As John W. Gardner, president of the Carnegie Corporation, points out, we emphasize individual performance but at the same time put restraints on it, first, through our emphasis on equalitarianism, and second, by such hereditary stratification of our society as still persists.[8]

---

7 Wright, *op. cit.*, pp. 21–22.
8 John W. Gardner, *Excellence* (New York: Harper & Bros., 1961), p. 27.

Hereditary stratification has been a problem only of degree; it is unlikely to be a major problem in the future—although tendencies toward privilege, hereditary protections, and favoritism are always dangers both to equality and excellence. Further, tendencies toward the recognition of seniority in many of our organizations represents a closely related danger.

Of greater importance, however, is the conflict between excellence and equality. Major restraints on excellence appear to arise from our tendency to stress equality—to emphasize values related to equality in preference to those related to excellence. Yet both sets of values are important for our type of society. In all probability conflicts between these two types of value cannot be resolved; we must live with both.

Gardner aptly points out:

No democracy can function effectively until it has gone a long way toward dissolving systems of hereditary stratification. This is presumably true of any democracy, but overwhelmingly true of the urbanized, industrial democracy with which we are familiar. On the other hand, no democracy can give itself over to extreme emphasis on individual performance and still remain a democracy—or to extreme equalitarianism and still retain its vitality.[9]

Excellence of performance in any field requires a sorting out process, which many regard as undemocratic. By its very definition, however, excellence demands a sorting out of the more competent from the less competent. The process is sometimes painful; it creates frustrations and heartbreaks, but the pursuit of excellence demands it.

By the very nature of their positions, business managers are leaders. They represent, in their respective fields, various degrees of excellence. They have been "sorted out" in many cases; in some, of course, they may have inherited their positions. In any event they are faced with many of the problems of leaders in all fields. In a democratic society this imposes some special obligations: to excel and at the same time to keep open avenues of opportunity for others to excel, and to help assure that the opportunities to excel will not be denied to persons of ability who are willing to pursue excellence.

As David McCord Wright has pointed out:

... Democracy imposes upon the leader and the superior man a peculiarly difficult task and demands of the lead also a higher achievement. The democratic hero, if one may use the term, must have a higher character than the authoritarian hero. Democracy, properly understood, does not require that he surrender his values, but it limits his way of enforcing

---

[9] *Ibid.*, pp. 28–29.

them. To say that he must suffer fools gladly is too emphatic; but suffer fools to some extent, he must.[10]

Business managers will play a significant role in determining how we work out an acceptable balance between equality and excellence. They have the problems of leading without using authoritarian methods, of protecting the weak against injury, of expanding equality of economic opportunity, and yet of pursuing excellence in performance. Although leaders in other fields also face problems of much the same type, the business manager currently appears to be under particular public pressures to work toward acceptable solutions.

SUMMARY

The business environment represents another set of factors that influence the decisions and operations of managers, in addition to those considered in the preceding chapter. The manager generally has three major sets of alternatives with respect to environmental changes: (1) to move with anticipated trends, (2) to move contrary to them, or (3) to undertake to change his environment to a greater or lesser extent.

The character of the business environment is determined to a considerable extent by billions of decisions by millions of people registered primarily in markets or political elections. In addition, however, historical, cultural, and institutional factors play a large part in shaping the business environment.

The following divisions of the business environment were considered briefly in this chapter: business conditions, governmental and political conditions, the legal system, the enterprise system and competing systems, and international business administration and conditions. Each of these topics is considered further in Part 5 of this book.

As the basis for developing a broader background for understanding the business environment several subjects were considered, notably the major characteristics of the American economy, objectives of our society, social and business objectives, and various historical forces.

Several emerging trends are likely to affect the business environment in the future. These are considered in Part 6. Important issues that are likely to influence future trends of development are those related to war and peace, progress and security, and equality and excellence.

---

10 Wright, *op. cit.*, p. 28.

QUESTIONS AND PROBLEMS

1. Why is it difficult to draw a line between the business firm and its environment?

2. Outline a situation in which environmental factors would play a dominant part in shaping the decisions of a manager. A situation in which "internal" factors would be dominant.

3. What are the three principal types of alternatives open to a manager with respect to major environmental trends?

4. The manager of a chain of retail stores encounters a period of declining employment in the communities in which his stores are located. He decides to step up his advertising and sales promotion programs believing that he can capture a larger share of a declining market. Under what conditions would you consider this is a wise decision?

5. Give an illustration of two important cultural factors that have helped to shape our present-day business environment.

6. Do you think that markets or political elections play the dominant role in shaping the business environment currently?

7. List and define four of the principal indicators of business conditions.

8. What is meant by gross national product? Is this an important indicator of business activity? Why or why not?

9. Outline the principal characteristics of the American economy. If you were to pick one of these characteristics as being most important, which would it be? Justify your selection.

10. Do you think that business firms can pursue their private objectives and still serve the objectives of our society? Explain why or why not.

11. What is meant by the following statement, which was quoted in this chapter? "The past has no meaningful existence except as it exists for us, as it is given meaning by us . . . hence, the past keeps changing with the present."

12. How does the threat of war influence the business environment?

13. How could the desire for security interfere with progress?

14. Do you think we should place greater emphasis on equality or excellence?

15. Comment on the following statement made by John A. Barr, Chairman and President, Montgomery Ward & Company, in a letter to the author discussing current programs of business schools designed to prepare young men and women for the business world of the future: "The main point to be stressed, in my opinion, is the development of intellectual curiosity, and a general thirst for knowledge and learning which will lead to the development and maintenance of a broad cultural base. Interest in, and an understanding of, the economic, social, and political developments of the world about him are most essential to real success as a businessman."

SUGGESTED READINGS

KLUCKHOHN, CLYDE. *Mirror for Man.* Greenwich, Conn.: Fawcett Publications, Inc., 1960. This interesting book is available in a "paperback" edition as a Premier Reprint. It is written in a popular manner and you may wish to read all of it; at least read the first chapter entitled, "Queer Customs, Potsherds, and Skulls."

LONG, JOHN D. *Workbook to Accompany Weimer: Business Administration: An Introductory Management Approach,* chap. 4. Rev. ed. Homewood, Ill.: Richard D. Irwin, Inc., 1962.

MULLER, HERBERT F. *The Uses of the Past.* New York: Oxford University Press, 1952. Published as a Galaxy book, 1957. This book represents a series of studies of former societies and contains a number of interesting insights into the significance of the study of history. You may be especially interested in chap. ii, "The Nature of History."

WRIGHT, DAVID McCORD. *Democracy and Progress.* New York: Macmillan Co., 1948. This is one of the important books published since the end of World War II. Refer especially to pages xiii to xvii, chap. i, "Science, Democracy and Capitalism," and chap. vi, "Progress and Instability."

part Business
Firms and
 Their
Management

6

SUMMARY OUTLINE

BUSINESS ADMINISTRATION—now one of the more exciting areas of study—may be *approached* in an *introductory* manner from the point of view of the *manager*.

He is the central figure in the business firm—the key social and economic institution of our time. It is managed and operated in a highly dynamic environment.

Business Firms are established as individual *proprietorships, partnerships, corporations,* and other forms.

Firms vary in *size* and engage in many *types* of *work*—manufacturing, trade, finance, service, and others.

The *Decision Makers* in business firms are owners, managers, and business specialists.

The *Management Process* involves establishment of objectives, plans, and controls; organization of resources; and leadership.

Decision Making—a central management responsibility—includes problem and *goal identification* and clarification, development and analysis of *alternatives*, appraisal of most likely alternatives, and *choice*.

Decisions may be guided by financial, accounting, statistical, economic, mathematical, and other considerations.

Business Resources and Operations involve effective utilization of the abilities of people—requiring knowledge of personnel and organization behavior—

as well as other resources including

capital, equipment, knowledge, time, and related aids to productivity, plus the place of business—land, buildings, and location—

in the *production and marketing* of goods and services to secure *income*.

The *Business Environment* influences management decisions and in turn is influenced by them, particularly in the areas of

business conditions,
governmental and political conditions,
the legal system,
the enterprise system and competing systems,
and international business administration.

Emerging Problems and Opportunities hold promise for the business community, and for you in managing your future.

OUTLINE FOR CHAPTER 5

ESTABLISHING BUSINESS FIRMS

 requires decisions that may be based on
  hunches, intuition, or on careful analysis of information, projections, and predictions.

 Value judgments and decisions are made—choices among
  alternatives.

The *right to make decisions* is essential to a profit-and-loss system, as is the "bundle of rights" of *private property*, which
  provides authority to establish and operate business firms.

A business firm may be started with little advance planning,
 or after careful consideration of chances for success and
  failure, including such factors as
   risk-cost-return relationships,
   the competitive situation,
   availability of resources, and
   special arrangements required.

Choice of *business entities* includes
 individual proprietorship,
 partnership,
 corporation, or
 other forms,
  each of which has advantages and disadvantages.

The *large corporation* is a powerful force in our society and
 as such is often subject to favorable and unfavorable
  criticism.

ESTABLISHING BUSINESS FIRMS

A wise man will make more opportunities than he finds.

—BACON

Business Firms and Their Management

Having finished the introductory section of our discussions, we turn now to a consideration of business firms and their management. These topics are the subject matter of this section of the book, including Chapters 5 through 9.

In this chapter we are concerned with the functions of the business firm, the significance of the right to make decisions including decisions to establish and operate business firms, opportunity costs, and the basis of the authority to operate business firms in our profit-and-loss system. We turn our attention then to various decisions related to the establishment of business firms and to the alternatives open as to the ownership and legal framework of business firms.

In the following chapter we consider some of the factors that influence the size of business firms and the various fields of activity in which American business firms are engaged. These materials are followed in succeeding chapters by discussions of the principal decision makers in business firms; business objectives, plans, and controls; and organization and leadership.

Functions of the Business Firm

As we have pointed out, the study of business is primarily a study of people. Business firms are social as well as economic institutions. They are made up of people. Thus, one of the principal functions of business firms is that of providing employment and career opportunities for the vast majority of our citizens. Not the least of these are the opportunities for starting new firms or the management and ownership of existing firms.

The business firms in this country currently provide employment for over fifty million people. If we include agriculture, which is tending to become a business activity to an increasing extent, only governmental and institutional employment remain outside the business field. In the years ahead business firms will attempt to provide more and more employment and career opportunities for our expanding population.

As we have seen, business firms perform the major function of providing goods and services for all of us. They do this in as efficient a manner as possible in order to meet the competition of other firms and in order to gain revenues in excess of costs.

In addition, as we have pointed out, business firms help us to achieve our major objectives—not only improving our standards of living and general well-being but also achieving progress in all desirable aspects of life.

Thus, the business firm exists to serve the needs of our society as a whole and also the needs of individuals by providing, on the one hand, a large proportion of the goods and services which they need and, on the other, many of the business and career opportunities that will enable them to develop their abilities to the fullest possible extent.

Right to Make Decisions

An essential element in our economic, political, and social system is the right of the individual to make decisions that range over a wide latitude of activities, including the establishment of business firms. Individualism as we understand it means that the individual citizen has the right to decide major issues for himself. He can choose his occupation among many alternatives. He may decide to go into business for himself or to work for someone else. He may spend his money as he chooses, subject to certain limitations on the purchase of harmful drugs, or he may spend his money or save it. He may choose freely among the candidates for public office. He may choose his friends and associates. He may join a church or not as he chooses, or join or not join various other organizations.

Some decisions are not open, however. For example, one must choose to pay his taxes or incur heavy penalties. Similarly, one may not choose to engage in criminal acts or to slander or libel others without incurring penalties. In most states one may not drive a car without a license or permit. Also, one may be required to join a union under certain conditions.

The right of the individual to decide major issues for himself is essential to a free society. As Henry C. Simons has said:

A free society must be organized largely through voluntary associations. Freedom to associate or to dissociate, to belong or not to belong, especially in economic activities, is an essential liberty—and will remain so, short of the millennial "economy of abundance." Man will continue indefinitely to be occupied, even in the richest nations, mainly with "making a living"; and his other liberties are unlikely to be or to remain larger than the liberty he enjoys in such central activity.

Freedom of association, of course, implies also coercive association, that is, strong government and an elaborate, stable, confining structure of law. Liberals exalt the "rule of the law" and hold that, as the antithesis of the rule of men or authority, it is attainable only within an economy of (largely) voluntary association.

Freedom to belong or not to belong also implies multitudes of similar associations among which one may choose and move, as worker, as investor, as consumer, etc. Likewise it implies effective freedom to initiate new associations, that is, free enterprise.[1]

We must recognize that the decisions of some people are more important than those of others. The decisions of the president of a large corporation have greater impact and affect many more people than the decisions of a worker in one of his plants. The right to make the major decisions rests on capacity—economic, political, or other power —to assume the responsibility for decisions affecting large groups of people or large blocks of resources. What we try to guard against in our system, through wide dispersion of various forms of power, is the ability of any person or group to deny the right of decision making to others, to prevent their entry into business, to establish self-perpetuating authorities, or to establish and maintain economic monopolies— that is, the control of the supply of goods and services.

Freedom to Start a Business

One of the important characteristics of the American system is the freedom we enjoy to start a business. No one needs to ask permission of an entrenched group. There is no licensing of investment. For most small businesses no government permission of any kind is required. Only in some cases are licenses or other permissions necessary.

Critics of the American system sometimes object to this general freedom to start new businesses. They argue that if sufficient production is available from existing firms to meet requirements, no new firms should be started until greater output is needed. This point of view fails to recognize the benefits of competition. It assumes that the new firm would be no more efficient than those that are now operating.

---

[1] Henry C. Simons, *Economic Policy for a Free Society* (Chicago: University of Chicago Press, 1948), pp. 3–4.

In fact, of course, many new firms are established because their founders believe that a new process or method is available which will enable them to compete to advantage with existing firms. Only in this way is the consumer assured that he will receive the greatest possible value per dollar of expenditure.

Thus, the freedom to enter business is basic to our system. It is essential to the maintenance of competition. It is true that many new firms fail because they are unable to meet the competition of established firms, or because of mismanagement, or lack of capital, or for other reasons. But the enterprise system in order to provide freedom of opportunity to succeed also must *maintain the freedom to fail.* Some failures are almost inevitable when there is widespread opportunity to start business firms. The failure of business firms involves their owners in losses. But such losses are more than made up by the gain to consumers that competition generates.

Critics of the enterprise system sometimes question whether the freedom to start a new business really exists on a widespread basis. It is contended that the capital required in many lines of business is now so great that only the wealthy can afford to start new firms.

This argument has some validity, especially in industries that require large amounts of machinery and equipment like the steel industry or the automobile industry. Even here, however, a new idea may enable a man of modest means to bring together the required capital through the sale of securities to the public. The ill-fated case of Mr. Tucker who planned to start a new automobile company shortly after World War II is pertinent here. He was able to sell a substantial amount of stock to the public by promising to bring out a new type of automobile using a revolutionary type of front-wheel drive. Unfortunately for those who bought stock, he proved to be in error but the case does illustrate the fact that it is often the *idea* rather than the money available that is important in starting a new business since the idea may be sufficiently appealing to call forth required capital and other resources.

We should note also, that in many lines of business, especially in the service fields, the capital requirements are usually modest. In all probability this is the area in which most new business firms will be established in the next ten years.

Authority to Operate Business Firms

We have pointed out that our people enjoyed broad freedom to go into business for themselves—to start new enterprises or to buy interests in established firms. Essentially, this means that you (or others) can arrive at your own decision to start a business. But, of course, one needs more than the desire to do this. It usually takes some money, time, energy, and often the assistance of others to get started in business. In short, one must have the capacity to back up his decision to go into business, and this capacity usually involves control over economic resources of some type.

Except for personal abilities, which may be used to create a marketable product, control over economic resources rests on the right of property. In our system private individuals enjoy the right to own things—both *things real* and *things personal* as the lawyers put it—that is, both real property which is fixed in location, such as land, houses, plants, and stores, and personal or typically movable property, such as clothing, furniture, automobiles, goods in process, and the like.

Our government protects us in the ownership of property. The authority to acquire, hold, improve, develop, manage, lease, use, or borrow against property is one of the foundations of our business system. A business firm is a property. Someone owns it. The firm can be bought and sold or used as security for a loan. Thus, authority to operate a business firm rests on the right of private property which in turn rests on public approval.

In a more general sense we must recognize that the right of private property rests on the will of the people at large. We may think of it as a "bundle of rights" which are more or less constantly undergoing review and redefinition. We support private property because we believe that all of us benefit from such an arrangement. If this were not true, it would be possible to change our laws in such a way that no private ownership of property, or of various types of property, or of business firms would be allowed. To a considerable degree, of course, this is what has happened in Russia and in some other countries of the world.

So in a final analysis, we enjoy the right to establish, own, and operate business firms because our people believe that this is a good arrangements for providing the goods and services that they want at reasonable cost. They believe also that this arrangement provides maximum economic opportunities for the people of the country either as owners, managers, or employees of business firms.

One of the problems currently facing the business community is that of expanding employment to provide opportunities for a rapidly growing population and at the same time taking advantage of the savings resulting from automation and related production methods.

To employ people at the cost of efficiency would result in higher prices for goods and services and, of course, would remove a major benefit of competition.

A Profit-and-Loss System

The right to establish, own, and operate a business firm carries with it major responsibilities. One of the more important of these is the *assumption of the risks* that go with business. The owner of a firm may spend several thousand dollars to buy merchandise that he hopes to sell at a profit. But some other firm may provide the goods at a lower price, or some other development may occur which results in a loss in the sale of the merchandise. This loss the owner of the firm must assume.

Similarly, he may hire several employees at an agreed-on salary of, say, $500 per month. He must pay these people at this rate. He has contracted to do so, and he assumes the risk that they will be worth this much to him in terms of their productivity and that his business will earn enough to pay these salaries. If he does not, they can take legal action against him for their unpaid salaries.

Thus, the owner of a business gets his income as a *residual*—as a profit, or in some cases a loss—after he has fulfilled the *contractual* obligations involved in paying his employees, paying interest on borrowed funds, or paying rent on his place of business. He earns this residual return by assuming the risks that are involved. Remember that ours is a *profit-and-loss* and not simply a profit system. Or we might refer to it as a *"quest-for-profit"* system.

Opportunity Costs

The establishment of a business firm not only requires the assumption of various risks but also the responsibility for costs. Such costs may be of many types. Of primary importance for us at this stage of our discussions, however, are alternative or opportunity costs. Fundamentally every decision represents a choice among alternatives; thus, deciding to start a business costs the selection of an alternative line of action and the returns that might have resulted from such an alternative line of action.

We might illustrate this concept in terms that are more closely related to your own experience. Suppose you have a choice between preparing for a class in history or a class in mathematics. Because of time limitations, you can only prepare for one. Thus, the cost of preparing for one of the classes is the loss of preparation for the other.

You might decide to prepare for both classes on a limited basis. Then the cost incurred is the loss of adequate preparation for either. Similarly, the cost of setting up your own business is the career you might have pursued by working for another establishment. Further, the cost of starting one type of business is the loss of the opportunity to set up another.

Katherine Edelman states this concept very well in "After Decision,"

> Why must decision ever leave
> A haunting thought behind,
> A wondering look to what we might
> On other pathway find?
>
> Why must the final word awake
> A strange, far sense of loss;
> A thought of hidden steppingstones
> That we will never cross?[2]

We stress this concept here because of the difficulties involved in most decisions to start a business firm. It is also, of course, a factor in other business decisions, as we shall see.

Starting a Business Firm

Many people have thought about starting a business firm. Some go ahead. Others do not. Why is this? It is not a difficult job to set up a business firm. Almost anyone can start a small store, undertake a simple manufacturing process, provide a new service or an old service in a different way, or undertake other lines of business activity on an independent and self-employed basis. Each year some 350,000 to 400,000 new business firms are set up. We should also note that each year 300,000 to 350,000 go out of business. (These figures exclude agriculture and professional services.) Some new firms fail; in 1960 for example failures totaled 15,445 and this was the highest number of failures in 27 years. Some new firms are merged with others, and some are discontinued, even though successful in varying degrees. Of course, many plans for starting firms never get off the ground.

Some business firms are started with little or no analysis of possible costs and returns. In other cases the chances of success and the degree of success that may be obtained relative to the risks and costs involved are considered with care. In some cases objectives are spelled out, for example, desired profit levels, rate of growth, desired rate of return on

---

2 Katherine Edelman, "After Decision," *Saturday Evening Post,* September 27, 1958, by permission.

FIGURE 5–1

Nonfarm Business Enterprises, 1900 and 1960

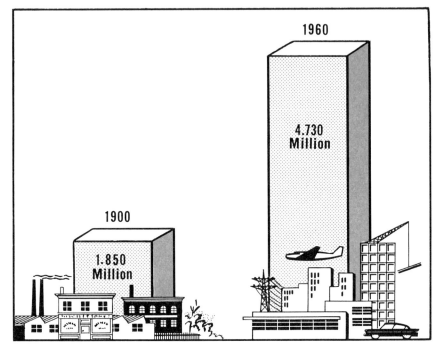

investment, position in the industry, recognitions that may be won, or others.

Most people who consider the establishment of a business firm are already employed. Some of them have good jobs drawing excellent salaries. They are unlikely to start a business of their own if income prospects are not good enough to maintain their incomes at or near present levels. Some people, however, have a strong urge to engage in independent operations. They want to be their own bosses, and they want freedom from the restrictions involved in working for others. Most of these people recognize that at least in the early stage of a new firm's development and often for a long time thereafter they will have to work much harder and probably enjoy much less leisure than in a regular job situation. But they prefer to get their "kicks" or satisfactions from life through building a business, even if this re-quires sixteen hours of work a day plus the acceptance of major responsibilities and risks.

Establishing a business firm usually involves getting control of resources of various types. These may include money or capital, man power, materials both tangible and intangible, know-how, and ideas, plus time. In some cases a limited reserve of money, enough to support a man and his family for a few months during the beginning phases of the firm, may be adequate. In other cases very large amounts of capital may be needed, and it may be necessary to hire many people. If a man and the members of his family are to do most of the work and if they have among them the necessary know-how, the process of starting a firm is much simpler than if a number of people with special abilities and qualifications must be hired and paid over a fairly long period of time before products are ready for the market.

Sometimes the starting of a new firm depends on the potential success of a new idea. It may be possible to patent the idea, but this may require complicated legal procedures. Or the idea may not be patentable and may be protected only by secret production or marketing processes carried on by the firm itself.

In some cases the starting of a business firm depends on securing governmental permission of one kind or another in the form of licenses or charters. This is not true in all cases, of course, but in some cases such as financial institutions, for example, special governmental permission must always be secured before operations can begin. It would not be possible for you to set up a bank just because you wanted to. Engaging in the banking business requires that a special charter be secured from state or national authorities. The same thing is true of insurance companies, savings and loan associations, and most other financial institutions. In the real estate field brokers and salesmen must be licensed in most states. This is also true in the field of insurance. Some cities require businesses of many types to secure certain local permits before beginning operations.

Those who are cautious about starting a business try to estimate its potential. Such questions as the following may be considered: What kinds of earnings on original investment may be possible or probable? How big is the present and prospective market? How rapidly can the firm grow? How rapidly should it grow? How strong is competition now and how strong will it be in the future?

In addition, general business conditions may govern a decision as to whether to start a firm or if started whether to keep it going. If business appears to be entering a slump, a new firm may have less of a chance to survive than one that has been in operation for some time.

It would be impossible for us to list all of the factors that might influence a decision to start or not to start a business firm. Once a decision to start an enterprise is made, whether on a hunch or on an intuitive basis or after careful analysis, it is necessary to determine the form of ownership or the type of legal entity that will be set up.

Types of Business Entities

Most of the types of business entities which operate today have had a long history. The individual proprietorship or independent business goes far back into ancient history. Similarly partnerships in various forms have been common for many centuries. Even the basic principles of the corporation were used by the Romans. During the middle ages the merchant guild and craft guild system developed, and to some extent these provide an early prototype of such business associations like the modern chamber of commerce. As nationalism emerged, the kings of various countries provided special charters which typically granted monopolies for operations in some specific part of the world or in some particular line of business. Many of the charters granted for the early development of the North American continent were of this type. (In a legal sense partnerships and individual proprietorships are not considered entities but for business purposes and accounting purposes this concept is useful.)

Joint ventures were established at an early date to spread the risk of sea voyages. Similarly, charters were granted to churches, municipalities, and charitable organizations at an early date, and these forms continue to the present time.

In the United States after the American Revolution, corporations were first used largely to operate toll roads and toll bridges and other types of business which typically provided some form of monopolistic power. As early as 1811 general incorporation statutes were passed which set up procedures for the establishment of business corporations and provided that those who complied with the requirements as laid down in the statute would be granted corporation charters.[3]

After 1830 statutes generally were passed in the various states providing for limited liability for the stockholders of corporations, and by 1860 this principle was generally accepted. Under this principle the stockholders could lose only the funds invested in the corporation in the event of the failure of the firm.[4]

Today the three principal types of business ownership are the

---

[3] Harold F. Lusk, *Business Law: Principles and Cases* (6th ed.; Homewood, Ill.: Richard D. Irwin, Inc., 1959), p. 462.

[4] Ross M. Robertson, *History of the American Economy* (New York: Harcourt Brace & Co., Inc., 1955), pp. 213–14.

individual proprietorship, the partnership, and the corporation. There are syndicates or joint ventures which are typically forms used for specific programs rather than for the purpose of carrying on business activities over a period of time. The joint-stock company is not generally used, although it was one of the forerunners of the modern corporation. Also, the common law or Massachusetts Trust is used to some extent. There are, of course, various types of mutual organizations such as co-operatives, mutual insurance companies, mutual savings banks, savings and loan associations, and others. Typically these entities operate under the corporation form but have special arrangements as to ownership which allow for a spreading of ownership among those with a mutuality of interest. Thus, in a savings and loan association the savers are the owners, but not in the same sense as the stockholders of a corporation. They are "members" and vote as individuals rather than in terms of the size of their savings accounts.

There are also "corporations not for profit," such as foundations and charitable, educational, or religious bodies. Most states have passed general acts providing for the establishment of such entities as well as of business corporations for profit. There are also government corporations.

Distribution of Business Firms in the United States

Of nearly five million business firms in the United States, approximately 82 per cent are individual proprietorships, about 9 per cent are partnerships, and 9 per cent are corporations. In terms of the volume of business transacted, however, the corporations are clearly predominant, accounting for 73 per cent of total volume. Individual proprietorships account for about 18 per cent, and partnerships for approximately 9 per cent. Individual proprietorships predominate in the retail and service fields; corporations in mining and manufacturing (see Figure 5–2).

Factors Influencing Types of Ownership and Legal Framework

Whether a particular business will be set up in one manner or another depends on a variety of considerations. Among these are the following:

1. Ease of organization. While the individual proprietorship and partnership are easier to set up than the corporation, it does not always follow that ease of organization will lead to the best decision. Still, it is a factor that will be given consideration at the time a firm is organized.

FIGURE 5-2

Comparison of the Number of Business Firms by Type of
Ownership and Volume of Business Transacted

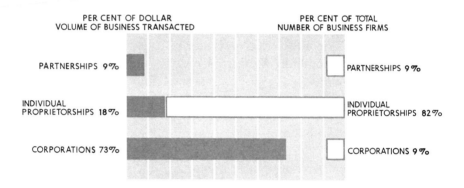

2. Ease or difficulty of raising money. In some cases the founders of a business firm will have adequate funds to begin operations; in others it will be necessary to bring in outside capital. The decision as to the form of organization selected may be influenced greatly by this factor.

3. Liability for debts. This consideration is closely related to the problem of raising the necessary funds. It is related also to the role of the owners in the operation of the firm. Often the desire to limit liability for debts will result in the selection of the corporate form of organization, even though other factors might indicate another organization form.

4. Definition of management authority. Usually no problems of this type are involved in the individual proprietorship. Such problems may be of major importance in connection with partnerships or corporations.

5. Transfer of ownership. While a business firm can be sold in its entirety, some advantages may be gained if ownership can be divided into shares which can be bought and sold. The corporation offers this advantage especially. Also, there are sometimes extremely difficult problems of continuing a firm after the death or incapacity of one or more of the owners, especially in cases of individual proprietorships and partnerships.

6. Possibilities of expansion. Some business firms give little attention to the possibilities of growth and expansion at the time they are established; others plan for expansion and consider the factors that

may aid or impede growth in selecting the form of organization that will be set up.

7. Geographical area of operations. A business firm may plan to operate largely in a single neighborhood or community, for example, a local drugstore, or it may operate on a national or even an international basis. Factors of this type may influence the form of organization and ownership that is selected.

8. Change of operation. After a business firm is set up, it may be desirable to change its products, its markets, its size, the scope of its activities, and many other things. Change can usually be accomplished more easily in an individual proprietorship than in other types of firms. Other considerations, of course, may outweigh this particular advantage.

9. Government control. Different types of business firms are subject to varying degrees of government control. Some are rather closely regulated; others are not. Typically those subject to greatest control will find the corporate form of organization more advantageous to their operations with respect to government control.

10. Taxes. Individual proprietorships and partnerships are not taxed directly; their owners pay taxes as individuals. Corporations are taxed directly, hence, are at a disadvantage in this respect. However, as the result of recent tax law changes some small corporations can elect to be taxed as partnerships. Other considerations may be more important in determining the form of organization, but the tax factor bulks large in many decisions of this type.

The Individual Proprietorship

The most widely used form of business organization and ownership is the individual proprietorship. It is the simplest and also the oldest organizational form. Basically it is a business owned and typically operated by one person, although the owner may, of course, employ managers, specialists, and others to help him. It has the advantage of being easy to form, simple to operate, and easy to dissolve. It is found most frequently in the small retail field, in the service trades, and in agriculture and the professions. No legal formalities are necessary to set up a business as an individual proprietorship. Of course, in areas where laws require permits or licenses it is necessary to comply with such regulations. In general anyone who has the capacity to enter into contracts is free to set up an individual proprietorship and to carry on any legal form of business activity.

The individual proprietorship has the advantage of concentrating authority in a single person, and hence he makes all decisions and is solely responsible for the results of such decisions. Consequently, his policies may be higher flexible. He can adapt his operations rapidly to changes in business conditions or to the actions of his competitors. If the individual proprietor has any special abilities or know-how, he need not share them with anyone else. In the case of the individual proprietorship the business itself is not taxed since the taxes are levied against the owner rather than the business as such.

While this form of organization has many advantages, there are also some important disadvantages, such as limited capacity to raise capital, limited assistance from others, complete liability for debts, and the difficulty of continuing the business after the death or disability of the proprietor. It is apparent that only the unusual individual of substantial resources could operate a large-scale enterprise on an individual proprietorship basis. Thus, the individual proprietorship is found largely in the small business area.

The Partnership

Two general types of partnerships are normally found in business operations—the general partnership and the limited partnership. A general partnership is an organization including two or more persons who carry on the activities of a business firm as co-owners. While no more formal legal requirements are necessary for the establishment of a partnership than are involved in the establishment of an individual proprietorship, most partnership agreements are based on a written contract that is carefully drawn up at the time the enterprise is established. Partnerships are often found in small business enterprises where various individuals pool their abilities and resources. For example, one partner may specialize in production, another in sales.

While the partnership has most of the advantages of the individual proprietorship plus the advantage of pooling the abilities and resources of two or more persons, it also has the disadvantage of typically being dissolved upon the death or incapacity of one of the partners. There is no limitation of liability for debts since each partner is personally liable for all debts of the business, and actions taken by one partner are binding on the others. It is obvious that the partnership does not have the same flexibility of operations as the individual proprietorship, although substantial flexibility may be maintained. Division of authority, however, is certainly one of the main disadvantages of this form of business organization, along with the unlimited liability of the partners and the difficulty of arranging for the continuity of operations upon the death or disability of one of the partners.

The limited partnership is an arrangement under which one or more of the partners may enjoy limitation of liability for the debts of the organization. Limited partnerships must be authorized under a state statute. While this arrangement has the advantage of attracting capital into the business, there are some definite legal limitations involved since due notice must be given in regard to the limited arrangement whenever a firm does business in another state than the one in which it resides.

The Corporation

The most important form of business organization in terms of funds invested or value of products created is the corporation. The corporation is formally organized under the laws of one or another state, depending on the wishes of those who set it up. There is provision also for some federally chartered organizations. A charter is issued which states the purposes of the business, the manner of organization, and the general limitations within which the corporation may operate. It is recognized as a "legal person" separate from its owners. It may sue and be sued as a legal person. It may engage in business under its own name and own or lease property as required to carry out its activities. The owners' interests are represented by shares of stock, and these may be transferred from one person to another without the necessity of obtaining the permission of other stockholders. (In partnerships by contrast, permission of other partners is usually required when an interest is transferred.) The corporation's life is not related to the lives of its owners, and its debts do not become the individual obligations of its owners. As Chief Justice Marshall said in the celebrated Dartmouth College case of 1819: "A corporation is an artificial being, invisible, intangible and existing only in contemplation of law. Being the mere creature of law it possesses only those properties which the charter of its creation confers upon it either expressly or as incidental to its very existence."

A corporation enables many persons to pool their resources for a common purpose without becoming involved in liabilities for amounts greater than those invested. It allows for the concentration of large amounts of capital and permits relatively easy transfer of the ownership of shares.

Management is usually determined by principal stockholders

through the board of directors. Professional managers may be hired to carry on the affairs of the business. The corporation's officers and managers are responsible to the board of directors which, in turn, is responsible to the stockholders. Periodic reports are required. Provision is made for the election of directors at stated times.

It is obvious that the processes of forming a corporation are much more complex than in the case of other forms of business organization. Business transactions are usually carried out on a relatively formal basis. Corporations are taxed separately from their owners, and, consequently, double taxation is involved when dividends are paid to stockholders since they, in turn, must pay taxes on such income.

Stockholders may be of two general types—common and preferred. Common stockholders have no preference of any kind, while the preferred stockholders enjoy some kind of preference such as the payment of a stated rate of return prior to the payment of dividends to common stockholders, or being treated in a preferred manner in case the firm is liquidated. Bond holders are creditors rather than owners of the business. They loan money to the business, and the bonds are evidence of indebtedness rather than of ownership.

The Small Business Corporation

An act of Congress passed in 1958 made special provisions for smaller business corporations whereby they could be taxed as partnerships. Corporations set up in this way are known by various names such as an "Electing Corporation," a "Tax Option Corporation," a "Subchapter S Corporation," but most frequently a "Small Business Corporation."[5] There are still some uncertainties regarding the interpretation of the act that made provision for this arrangement. In general it permits such a corporation to enjoy the advantages of limited liability and permanence of operations but also to avoid possible tax disadvantages. The main legal requirements of a small business corporation of this type are the following: it cannot have more than ten shareholders; all shareholders must be individuals or estates; no shareholder can be a nonresident alien; the corporation can have only one class of stock; it may not get more than 80 per cent of gross receipts from outside the United States; all shareholders must have consented to becoming a small business corporation; and not more than 20 per cent of gross receipts may come from so-called "personal holding com-

---

5 Robert R. Milroy, "The Small Business Corporation: Proceed with Caution," *Business Horizons*, Summer, 1960, pp. 97–109.

pany income" (rents, royalties, interest, dividends, sales, or exchanges of stock or securities).

As a general evaluation of the small business corporation, Professor Milroy points out, "There is not much sense in organizing a business in a form that will minimize taxes if doing so stifles its ability to take advantage of profitable growth opportunities or limits the owner's ability to dispose advantageously of an interest."[6]

The Syndicate

The syndicate or joint venture usually is formed for the purpose of carrying out a specific program and, consequently, is relatively temporary in nature. A syndicate resembles a type of partnership, although the "partners" may be corporations. It may be used in the sale of securities, as when several security firms come together to handle a particular issue that is too large for any one of them alone. Upon the sale of the stock issue or other securities which may be involved, the syndicate is dissolved. Syndicates have been used for large undertakings such as the San Francisco-Oakland Bay Bridge, other large construction projects, or for other activities that require the pooling of large blocks of resources for limited periods of time. Joint ventures have regained popularity in recent years.

The Joint-Stock Company

The joint-stock company, while not generally in use today, represents an interesting business form which stands somewhere between the partnership and the modern corporation. Like the corporation, shares which represent ownership rights are issued, and these shares may be transferred from one person to another; but those who participate do not enjoy the limited liability feature which is such an important characteristic of the modern corporation. The joint-stock company, however, unlike the partnership does not involve mutual responsibility for all actions since the shareholders elect a board of managers who have the authority to transact business for the entire organization.

Common Law or Massachusetts Trust

This type of entity, often referred to as the "Massachusetts Trust" because of its development largely in that state, provides a legal arrangement in which the interested party or parties place legal title

---

6 *Ibid.*, p. 99.

of the property of the business in the hands of a trustee or trustees. The trustees have the power to act for all of the interested parties and to engage in business for them. The owners hold certificates of interest. Certificate holders, however, have no voice in the management of the trust. Typically the participants enjoy limited liability, and it is possible in most cases to transfer interest from one person to another. Matters of this type often depend on state regulations. One of the main difficulties of this type of organization is that the general trust agreement originally set up may be difficult to alter, as required by changing business conditions.

Other Types of Entities

The types of entities we have discussed above are usually involved in business activities. We should mention also the corporation not for profit which is ordinarily used for churches, educational institutions, foundations, and other similar types of activity.

There are, of course, many other establishments of importance in our economy. One of these is the labor union which is a mutual association of persons who are joined together for a common purpose. Officials are elected and typically vested with considerable power to carry on business for the membership. The labor union can and does enter into contracts, but typically these contracts are not enforceable in the courts. This represents one of the principal problems in the modern business world since individual proprietorships, partnerships, and corporations can sue and be sued in the court and are forced to live up to the terms of the contracts into which they enter.

Similarly, such establishments as chambers of commerce and association of commerce or mutual benefit societies such as alumni associations of schools and universities, or parent-teacher associations, or groups of various kinds typically have a most informal sort of arrangement and have a very limited legal status. In some cases, of course, they do take out charters as corporations not for profit and thus attain a more definite status.

The Large Corporation Controversy

The major role of the large corporation in our economy has led many to raise questions in regard to it. While it is generally granted that our large corporations operate efficiently, it is also contended that they wield too much power—or more specifically, that their managers wield too much power. Just how much is "too much," of course, is difficult to define. It is claimed, however, that because of widespread distribution of stock ownership, managers are able to do as they wish in running the corporation without regard to the desires of the owners. Much the same type of charge has from time to time been made against civil service officials in government who acquire and hold substantial power without being directly responsible to the electorate as is the case when appointments to such posts are made by elected officials.

It is often said also that because of their large size corporations can dominate markets, virtually eliminating competition and giving the buying public only those goods and services that bring greatest profit, rather than what the public really wants. Also, it is claimed that through advertising programs people are "brainwashed," and made to want what the large corporations prefer to sell. In addition, it is argued that the quest for profit is not a "proper" motivating force for the corporation, or if profits are acceptable in general, the maximizing of profits is not desirable.[7]

Those who make charges of this type often suggest that corporations should be brought under some direct form of government regulation rather than relying on competition as a regulator, or some go so far as to suggest that large corporations should be broken up into smaller private units or be socialized and made agencies of the government.

We will be considering some of these and related topics at various points in our discussions. We should note here that professional managers, that is, nonowner managers, are usually quite responsive to the wishes of owners, even when ownership is splintered. Sale of stock by a number of dissatisfied owners brings declines in the prices of the stock, reflects on the success of the corporation, and in some cases sets the stage for a few persons to acquire large blocks of stock and then to dismiss the present management, substituting managers more acceptable to owners. Thus, professional managers usually watch the prices of the corporation's stock rather closely. Such prices reflect in part what owners think of management.

We should note also that many directors of corporations actively represent stockholders interests and reflect stockholder viewpoints in dealing with hired or professional managers. In some cases there are active "proxy fights" to win positions on boards of directors in order to make certain that the interests of specific owners will be represented.

In a final analysis, owners can always dislodge professional man-

---

[7] See, for example, Edward S. Mason, *The Corporation in Modern Society* (Cambridge, Mass.: Harvard University Press, 1959), especially the introduction.

agers. In some cases this may take time, but even minor stock interests can proceed through the courts to protect their positions. Managers must act in the best interests of a majority of the ownership over a period of time or lose their positions.

In some cases, of course, managers are given options to buy stock at stated prices and thus reap rewards as owners for good managerial programs. When this happens the manager becomes in part at least an owner-manager and his status changes from that of a purely hired manager. He may, of course, purchase stock at any time but the stock option arrangement may encourage him to do so.

The profit issue is the subject of perennial debate, even in the case of the individual proprietorship, partnership, and small corporation. We will say more about this issue in our discussion of business objectives in Chapter 8. We should note here that the quest for profits is the main driving force of business, whether attempts are made to maximize profits or to achieve "satisfactory" or other profit levels. But the assumption that profits are somehow "automatic," and that their levels can be determined in advance by management or owners assumes monopoly positions for business firms that overlooks the regulative force of competition, even for very large units.

Do big corporations eliminate or reduce competition? This depends considerably on the field involved and on the extent to which a given corporation can control the supply of a commodity on the market and hence its price. Our public utilities can do this, and, of course, they are much more directly regulated than are other types of business.

The extent of competition, even among a few large producers such as the major automobile companies, is much greater than is often suspected. The case of the compact car is of special interest in this connection. Competition from foreign cars, followed by competition from a few "minor" domestic companies soon brought vast changes in products.

This discussion is not intended to suggest that there is no ground for some of the charges often made against large corporations. We intend to suggest that the questions raised about the large corporation are far from simple, that there are two (and sometimes more) sides to nearly all of them, and that careful study is essential to an understanding of these issues.

In a final analysis it is the job of government to regulate business activity, either through competition or in other ways. When competition cannot be made to work, other forms of regulation must be used. Government has the main responsibility for devising rules that will make business firms, large or small, serve the best interests of our people. In some cases this means making competition work better, in others direct regulation, in still others (the post office, for example) government ownership and operation.

SUMMARY

The establishment of a business firm involves a number of basic decisions—choices among numerous alternatives. Such decisions may be made on the basis of intuition or hunches, or they may be based on careful analysis of pertinent information. The choices made require the giving up of other alternatives; that is, the application of the principle of opportunity costs. This principle helps us toward an understanding of many management decisions.

The right to make decisions is basic to our type of society and is essential to a system of democracy and enterprise. The freedom to start a business is one of the important liberties in our system. The authority to own and operate a business firm rests on the "bundle of rights" of private property, which is a basic element in our system. It is important to recognize that ours is a *profit-and-loss* system.

A business firm may be started with little advance planning or after a careful consideration of pertinent cost-risk-return relationships; the resources available or that can be made available; government approvals that may be required; possible intensity of competition; potential growth that may be achieved; and related factors. Decisions as to the form of ownership involve choices among the individual proprietorship, partnership, corporation, or other less widely used forms. Each has a number of advantages and disadvantages related to ease of establishment, ease or difficulty of raising required funds, liability for debts, continuity of operations, government controls, and taxes.

The large corporation plays a significant role in our society. It is sometimes charged that the managers of large corporations wield too much power. There are two or more sides, however, to the controversy over the large corporation.

QUESTIONS AND PROBLEMS

1. What do you believe to be the most difficult decision you have ever made? Which choices among alternatives were open to you?
2. Explain why the right of the individual to make decisions for himself is a basic characteristic of a free society.
3. Henry C. Simons said, "A free society must be organized largely through voluntary associations." What is meant by this statement? Do you agree with it?

FIGURE 5-3

A. T. & T. Goes to Chicago and Outdraws Sox

Meeting Has Record Crowd—Ball Game Runs Second

By GENE SMITH
Special to The New York Times.

CHICAGO, April 19—From the four corners of the land they came—some 20,000 strong —to the annual meeting here today of American Telephone & Telegraph Company.

The turnout of stockholders was by far the largest ever to attend any corporate meeting, well exceeding the previous record attendance of 11,900 at A. T. & T.'s 1959 annual meeting in the Kingsbridge Armory in the Bronx, New York City. This year, for the first time, the Bell System decided to hold its stockholder session outside of metropolitan New York. The move west, to a more central location, apparently acted as a magnet drawing stockholders from all directions.

The meeting, in fact, attracted a bigger throng than the home opening game of the Chicago White Sox yesterday. The Sox played the Washington Senators here to a crowd of 16,637.

To the assembled stockholders, the giant utility made a striking promise—to "deliver the first of several experimental satellites by Christmas" if Government authorization were received promptly.

Frederick R. Kappel, president of A. T. & T., told a press conference prior to the meeting that "if we knew this afternoon the exact type of rocket and launcher that would be used we could get the first satellite ready by Christmas."

In his prepared remarks, Mr. Kappel drew the applause of the crowd when he said, "I for one would dearly like to see this country the unquestioned leader in space communications and I am sure I am not alone in that wish.

"None of us wants the United States to come in second again," he went on. "To accomplish the results we all hope for, it is essential to move ahead without delay."

Mr. Kappel asserted again his company's contention that its proposals for a satellite communications system were patterned after existing regulations and that the company did not seek a communications monopoly. He also said that much of the equipment used in the proposed satellite systems would be obtained from other companies on a competitive bidding basis, and that the rockets and launching services would be obtained from other companies, with the launchings under Government supervision.

"We can move quickly," the president said. "The system we propose calls for a number of satellites orbiting a few thousand miles in space. Each would contain equipment to receive, amplify and retransmit communications signals. Continuous service to Europe could be provided with from twenty to twenty-five such satellites, and world-wide service with about fifty. We are confident that in a very few years—three or four, or maybe even less—we could have a full-scale system in operation. But the immediate need is this: It is to get a bird [satellite] in the air for testing at the earliest possible moment."

Mr. Kappel also sought to end rumors that Bell planned to "spin off" Western Electric, its manufacturing arm. He noted that such reports had caused the few shares of Western Electric that are publicly held to rise very steeply. Bell owns 99.82 per cent of Western Electric's stock.

"I wish to say on behalf of your board, and with all possible emphasis, that the company has no intention of spinning off Western Electric either now, in the near future, the distant future or a any time whatsoever."

This was the first A. T. and T. meeting that had ever been held outside of New York City. Sunny skies and a fifty-six-degree temperature brought out even more stockholders than the company had expected. Tables for serving the box lunches and seats for about 18,000 had been set up in huge McCormick Place Exposition Hall on the shore of Lake Michigan.

The first stockholders began arriving at 8:30 A. M. The box lunches were served at 11 and ran out soon after noon. Tickets to a cafeteria in the building were given to those who did not get their box lunches. The meeting lasted 4 hours and 27 minutes, which was shorter than usual for A. T. & T.

On the agenda was a management proposal authorizing the issuance of 15,000,000 additional shares of stock to be used for the employes' stock plan and the re-election of seventeen directors and the auditing concern. A stockholder proposal calling for a secret ballot was also on the agenda.

Ballot Move Defeated

The vote for the employes' stock plan was approved by 98.01 per cent of the eligible 223,838,761 shares. Directors were re-elected by an 81.16 per cent margin and auditors retained by 81.22 per cent. The secret ballot proposal was voted down by 94.77 per cent of the shares. It received 9,449,762 favorable votes.

In answer to the woman stockholder, who co-sponsored the secret ballot resolution, Mr. Kappel said that management's opposition was "only too obvious."

Such a proposal, he went on, "would actually deprive stockholders of many rights they now enjoy." Chief among these he listed would be destruction of the right-of-stockholders to challenge elections; inability of the company to show in court how certain things were voted and the right to change votes after meetings began.

He also denied that any pressure was ever brought to bear on employes, forcing them to vote as the company might want.

In his press conference, Mr. Kappel said that he was "hopeful but doubtful" that anything would be done to repeal the excise tax on telephone service.

4. Suppose you have $100, that you are interested in buying a share of stock in Company A and Company B, but the shares of each are priced at $100. You decide to buy a share of Company A's stock. What is the alternative cost of this stock? Explain.

5. How can we justify starting a new firm to manufacture TV sets when it appears that existing firms are meeting the demand?

6. Should we require all who want to start a new business to pass a standard government test? Why or why not?

7. Do you agree that the authority to establish and operate a business firm rests on the right or the "bundle of rights" of private property? Explain why or why not.

8. Does the right of private property depend on the will of the people at large or does it rest on some other base? Explain.

9. If we assumed that all business firms were guaranteed against failure by the federal government, how would this change our system? Is the freedom to fail necessary to the freedom to succeed?

10. If you had an opportunity to start a business firm which of the various factors that might be involved would you give greatest consideration? Justify your answer.

11. Do you think you will go into business for yourself if you have an opportunity to do so? Why or why not?

12. Present an idea for a new business and indicate how you might go about putting it into effect.

13. On what basis would you decide whether a business firm should be incorporated?

14. What are the chief disadvantages and advantages of the individual proprietorship? The partnership? The corporation?

15. Is the "small business corporation" a significant development? Why or why not?

16. Do you think the managers of large corporations exercise too much or too little power in our society? Explain.

17. What do you think is significant about the accompanying news story (Figure 5–3), "A.T.&T. Goes to Chicago and Outdraws Sox"?

SUGGESTED READINGS

LONG, JOHN D. *Workbook to Accompany Weimer: Business Administration: An Introductory Management Approach,* chap. 5. Rev. ed. Homewood, Ill.: Richard D. Irwin, Inc., 1962.

LUSK, HAROLD F. *Business Law: Principles and Cases.* 6th ed. Homewood, Ill.: Richard D. Irwin, Inc., 1959. See especially chap. xix, "Partnerships," and xxiii, "Nature and Incorporation."

MASON, EDWARD S. *The Corporation in Modern Society.* Cambridge, Mass.: Harvard University Press, 1959. See, especially, the introduction.

MILROY, ROBERT R. "The Small Business Corporation: Proceed with Caution," *Business Horizons,* Summer, 1960, pp. 97–109.

OUTLINE FOR CHAPTER 6

TYPES OF BUSINESS FIRMS
  depend on method of classification with
    form of entity,
    size, and
    type of work
  considered most important.
    Classes by *size* include
      small,
      medium, and
      large.
    Firms grow because of
      favorable conditions,
      good management,
      specialization,
      desire for expansion,
      research programs, and
      other reasons.
    Growth may be accomplished by means of
      new products, resulting from
        research and development or the
        purchase of other firms or products; and by
      expanding markets for existing products.
        Expansion may be
          vertical or
          horizontal.
    Extent of growth is determined in part by best or optimum
    size of the business firm.
    Classes of firms by *type of work* include:
      manufacturing;
      mining;
      contract construction;
      transportation and public utilities;
      wholesale and retail trade;
      finance, insurance, and real estate; and
      service and miscellaneous activities.

TYPES OF BUSINESS FIRMS

There is a lot of difference in pioneering for gold and pioneering for spinach.

—WILL ROGERS

Methods of Classification

One approach to the study of any subject is to break it down into classes or subdivisions so that we can consider each part individually. Suppose, for example, that you were going to study the broad field of sports. While there are many things that are common to all sports, you would undoubtedly find it helpful to divide the field into such subdivisions as football, basketball, baseball, track, swimming, golf, tennis, and others. Our understanding of the entire field would be increased even by the knowledge that these various subdivisions existed.

Much the same thing may be said about the broad field of business. There are many advantages to dividing it into parts. We can see the relationships of the parts and their relative importance in our economic system.

Unfortunately, there is no single way to make divisions. Even if we limit our attention to types of business firms, as we shall do in this chapter, we will find it advisable to use several methods of classification.

We may divide business firms into groups according to size—large, small, and medium-sized firms being the classes most frequently used. Or we may divide them according to the type of work they do. In this connection we may use the system set up by the Department of Commerce to classify employment. In this system, the first major division is made between agricultural and nonagricultural employment. The nonagricultural sector is then divided into such groups as manufacturing, wholesale and retail trade, finance, and the like.

As we have already seen, business firms may be classified according to type of ownership, the main classes being (1) individual proprietorships, (2) partnerships, (3) corporations, and (4) other less frequently used forms.

Another useful method of classification is by area or region served; for example, local, regional, national, and international enterprises. Still another method provides for classification by age. Here the main groups are new enterprises and older or more firmly established business organizations.

In some cases we may find it useful to distinguish firms as to their degree of integration either "horizontal" as in the case of a chain store or "vertical," that is, the extent to which they engage in activities that cover different stages of the production process ranging from mine, forest, and farm products through manufacturing, wholesaling, and retailing with final sale to ultimate consumers.

We might also classify establishments according to the degree to which they are subject to government regulation. At one extreme we find the publicly owned entity such as a municipally owned water works, a national park, or a state forest preserve. At the other are firms which encounter a minimum of direct government regulation with respect to their operations, with competition the main regulator. Between are varying degrees of regulation ranging from control of establishment to regulation of earnings.

We must recognize that all systems of classification are somewhat arbitrary, whether we are trying to classify business firms or other things. We could spend many hours arguing about the soundness of any system of classification, and we could divide and subdivide the classes to such an extent that the result would become almost meaningless.

Our main purposes in setting up various classes of business firms are to help us study them and to understand their operations. For the purposes of our discussions in this chapter we will center our attention on (1) the size of business firms and (2) the types of work in which they may engage.

The Problem of Size

Of the nearly five million business firms in this country a very large proportion, perhaps over four million, are of relatively small size. They produce only about a fifth of the total output of all business and employ about a third of the workers in business exclusive of agriculture. There are nearly five million farms in the country. Of these only a few are of large size. While farms are not usually considered to be business firms, they have important business aspects.

In recent years the number of business firms has been growing more rapidly than the population of the country, with thousands being started each year.

Why do some firms attain large size while others do not? How important is the size of a business unit? Is there a "best" size for a firm? Are the very large enterprises like American Telephone and Telegraph, Standard Oil of New Jersey, U.S. Steel, General Motors, Pennsylvania Railroad, General Electric, Prudential Life Insurance Company, or others destined to become larger and larger? Does this mean that small business enterprises will become less important in our system? Are the management problems of small business and large business different?

Larger business firms enjoy a number of advantages, it is true, but we should note that smaller firms also have their advantages. The fact that growth has occurred usually indicates that a firm has enjoyed some success in the past. Growth does not usually come from sheer luck or the general trend of events. Once a firm attains some size, however, this in itself is no assurance of continued success. Changes in management, market conditions, competition, consumer preferences, and related developments can cause trouble even for the large and well-established firm.

Typically, the larger firms enjoy the advantage of *specialization*. It is possible by virtue of their size to employ specialized machinery and personnel. Processes can be subdivided sufficiently to gain the maximum advantage of division of labor and specialization.

Often larger firms are able to buy the materials that they need in quantity and thus gain an advantage over firms of smaller size. Similarly they may be able to raise funds on favorable terms because of established reputations and credit positions. Most small firms do not undertake to sell their stock to the general public, although this practice is expanding, or to float bond issues in the general securities market.

By virtue of their size and strength, larger firms usually can compete to advantage for the most competent executive abilities and the best business specialists. High salaries, bonuses, profit participation arrangements, retirement programs, and the like are often used by large firms to attract and hold those with excellent managerial abilities. Often the larger firm is able to use management ability more advantageously than the small firm. Much the same thing may be said of business specialists.

Of major importance to larger firms is their ability to conduct extensive research and development programs. Such programs are often very expensive, and the amount of money being spent in this area is increasing year by year.

In some lines, as we have suggested, it is necessary for a firm to begin operations on a substantial scale. It is impossible to start on a modest basis and grow gradually because of the large amount of machinery, equipment, or land and buildings required. Examples include railroads, automobile manufacturing, and steel production.

Why Do Firms Grow?

Firms may grow in part because of the advantages of size as outlined above. Thus, growth may be due to competent management, the availability of outstanding business specialists, the economies resulting from specialization and division of labor, quantity buying, favorable financing terms, and research and development programs.

They may grow because of a highly favorable market or competitive situation. A firm may be in an expanding industry and grow as the entire industry advances. Some firms grow because they want to—growth is a primary objective of owners and managers. In some cases growth may be almost accidental, occurring because of unusually favorable circumstances. Growth may be the result of a favorable governmental climate or because of special concessions, subsidies, or protections as to taxes or market competition; for example, tariffs and the like.

Growth may take place when owners and managers plan for it, set up rates of growth as objectives to be achieved, and organize their operations in a manner that makes growth possible. Growth may be used as a motivating force, as a means of stimulating workers at all levels of the organization to do their best.

Some firms, of course, do not wish to grow, preferring a smaller and perhaps more "comfortable" size. In a few cases growth may occur even if the owners and managers of a firm would prefer not to have it. For example, a retired business man bought a small hardware store in a resort community in order to have a convenient place to visit with his friends. He tried to discourage trade by not ordering popular items, but in spite of himself the store grew as the community expanded and the hardware store owner had to hire a manager in order to accomplish his main objective, which was simply to have a convenient place to visit with his friends. Of course, managers usually cannot achieve growth if general business or industry conditions are highly unfavorable. But even in declining industries, some firms enjoy growth chiefly because they are well managed.

How Do Firms Grow?

Some firms grow by adding products; others by expanding markets for present products. Some grow as the result of their research and development programs. Often firms grow by buying control of other firms either in the same or related fields or in others. In some cases firms finance growth by retaining earnings, that is, "plowing back" earnings into the business rather than paying out earnings to owners; in other cases by attracting additional investments from outside the business.

Growth may be the result of "horizontal" combination—that is, the addition of firms or plants that are operating at the same general level of the production or marketing process. A good example of horizontal combination is the chain store, as we suggested above. A chain of stores in contrast to a single store gains the advantages of large-scale buying, financing, and advertising; executive ability can be used with great efficiency; advanced merchandising methods can be used for all units.

Some enterprises grow by "vertical combination," that is, by integrating various steps of the production and marketing process. For example, the Ford Motor Company owns and operates its own steel plants, steamships, assembling plants, and distribution plants. In some instances it controls all of the processes involved in bringing raw materials from their original sources through various stages of production and into the hands of automobile dealers. Vertical combinations of this type assure control of raw materials, quality of materials used, and delivery of materials as needed. Typically, smaller inventories are required at various stages of the production and marketing processes.

In recent years combinations and mergers have often been undertaken for the purpose of securing product diversification, rather than for horizontal or vertical integration. Reasons for diversification include the desire to link together a company with an uneven sales pattern with one that has a more stable pattern. In this way it is hoped that a cushion may be provided in periods of recession. Sometimes companies in declining industries try to shift their capital into new growth lines.[1] The railroads, for example, might be more prosperous today if they had shifted at least to a degree into the airline business.

---

1 See, Dexter M. Keezer and Associates, *New Forces in American Business* (New York: McGraw-Hill Book Co., Inc., 1959), pp. 170–71.

It should be recognized, however, that regardless of the ways available by which a business firm can expand, growth may be facilitated if owners and managers set it up as one of their primary objectives. Firms grow because they want to, or because conditions in terms of markets, competition, and governmental and political conditions are favorable, or because the best methods of growth are adopted—expanding existing products, adding new products, supporting research and development programs, buying control of other firms in order to gain the advantage of horizontal or vertical combination, or for other reasons. Effective management is often the key to growth.

The business climate, of course, is important. Independent business firms could hardly be expected to grow in a socialistic state regardless of the ability, industry, and determination of managers.

What Is "Best" Size?

Theoretically there should be a "best," or what is called an "optimum," size for each business firm. Despite the advantages of larger size outlined above, size itself develops some disadvantages. Operations cannot be changed easily. Management may grow more and more remote from problem situations. New programs cannot be started quickly, and old programs cannot be changed rapidly. The larger firm may suffer from bureaucratic tendencies—people in it follow policies simply because they are policies and not because of the reasons underlying them. Even management personnel may in some cases tend to operate in a stereotyped or bureaucratic manner just because of the large size of the firm.

By contrast, a smaller firm may adapt quickly to changed conditions. Programs may be altered without going through a long series of discussions and decisions. Policies tend to be more flexible than in the case of large operations. Smaller firms may have tax advantages. In case earnings are less than $25,000 per year the federal corporate tax rate is lower than for firms with higher incomes. In some cases, however, the costs of defending their tax position may offset the tax rate advantage. As we noted in the preceding chapter a small business corporation can elect, under certain conditions, to be treated for tax purposes as a partnership.

Ownership and management are more frequently combined in smaller firms. Consequently, the motivations toward success may be stronger. Risks may be assumed more willingly, and competition may be a more definite stimulus than for larger firms.

Beyond certain points, firms become less efficient as they grow in size. Typically those companies that use large amounts of machines relative to labor can efficiently attain greater size than those which use large amounts of labor relative to capital. An example is the tobacco industry. Cigarette production requires large amounts of capital—plants, machines, and equipment—relative to the labor required. Here large organizations are typical. In cigar making the reverse is true, and firms are typically smaller in size.

Decentralization

Some firms have been able to combine various of the benefits of large- and smaller-scale operations through decentralization. General Electric is an interesting case in point. This giant corporation with around a quarter of a million employees has been divided into more than a hundred largely independent units. Such units are sometimes called "profit centers." Each operates within broad corporate policy limits, but with a substantial amount of independence for each unit. Other companies have been adopting similar arrangements to an increasing extent in recent years.

Ralph J. Cordiner, president of the General Electric Company made this interesting statement regarding the size of business firms:

The economy of the United States, and its position as a world power, make large enterprises both an irreversible fact and an actual necessity for economic and national security reasons. Any attendant perils lie not in bigness itself, but in the way the energies of large organizations are organized and managed. Centralized administration of large institutions of any kind can lead to irresponsibility, short-sightedness, inefficiency, and the abuse of power—but this need not happen under wise and self-disciplined guidance. Responsible decentralization—as a philosophy—makes it possible to provide at once the big results that come from big enterprises, with the human freedom that comes from respecting the competence and dignity of every individual in the enterprise.[2]

Experimentation with various types of arrangements for decentralizing the operations of large corporations is going on continuously. Current trends suggest that further decentralization will take place in the years ahead.

Relationships between Larger and Smaller Firms

Larger and smaller firms compete against each other, of course. They also do a lot of business with each other. Large firms often rely on smaller firms for various production and marketing work. Subcon-

---

[2] Ralph J. Cordiner, *New Frontiers for Professional Managers* (New York: McGraw-Hill Book Co., Inc., 1956), p. 79, by permission.

tracts and various other arrangements are used, as well as the direct purchase and sale of goods and services. General Motors, for example, typically uses a large number of smaller firms as suppliers. In one year this company paid out over $6 billion to some 26,000 suppliers, nearly two thirds of which employed fewer than 100 people. According to a recent report, the DuPont Company distributes only about 10 per cent of its volume to ultimate consumers; the other 90 per cent goes to around 75,000 smaller firms which carry on further processing, convert, and finally sell the products. This company counts heavily on some 30,000 smaller firms for services and raw materials.[3]

Thus, we should recognize that the relationships between larger and smaller business firms often are complex. Much more is involved than competitive processes. Certainly we should not assume that big companies only do business with other big companies and small firms only with small ones.

Types of Work

As we suggested above, business firms may be classified according to the types of work they do as well as in other ways. All firms are engaged in providing goods and services for their customers. Thus, we might begin by dividing firms according to whether they produce goods or services, although this division is not necessarily a clear-cut one. Firms primarily engaged in producing goods include those involved in the extraction of basic materials from mine, field, forest, or water; those engaged in processing materials, that is, changing their form; and those providing for the distribution of goods to intermediate or final users.

Firms that provide services do such a variety of things that it is difficult to divide them into classes. Among the types of services are recreation, entertainment, personal care such as beauty and barber shops, some advisory services, repair and maintenance, cleaning and dyeing, and others.

It is difficult, however, to make sharp divisions with respect to either goods or services and as we have already suggested, no single classification appears to meet all requirements. Consequently, we will make use of a system that has been developed by the Department of Commerce for grouping types of employment. This system is now in fairly general use by business and by government agencies. While it has disadvantages, it provides us with ready access to many types of informa-

---

3 See Keezer, *op. cit.*, pp. 164–66.

tion such as that which appears in the *Survey of Current Business* and in other government publications.

In this system a primary division is made between agricultural and nonagricultural employment. Then the nonagricultural or essentially business employment is subdivided into these classes: (1) manufacturing; (2) mining; (3) contract construction; (4) transportation and public utilities; (5) wholesale and retail trade; (6) finance, insurance, and

FIGURE 6–1

Types of Business Firms

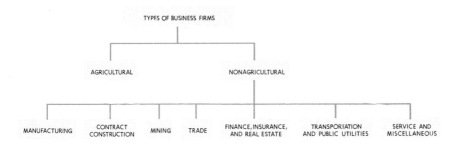

real estate and (7) service and miscellaneous activities. We will consider each of these groups briefly, beginning our discussions with the field of agriculture since it also has important business aspects.

Business Aspects of Agriculture

Agriculture includes many types of activities ranging from such highly intensive crops as citrus fruits, vegetables, cotton, and tobacco to extensive activities such as ranching in which a section of land (a square mile, 640 acres) is required to support a small number of cattle.

As recently as a hundred years ago agricultural activity accounted for over half of the employment in the country. Today only about 10 per cent of those gainfully employed are in this field. Similarly, the number of farms has tended to decline as more and more mechanization has taken place. The increased use of machines tends to increase the size of the farm that can be operated efficiently. Today there are less than five million farms in the country in contrast to nearly six and a half million in 1940.

The trends toward increased mechanization and larger farm units have caused the farm to take on many of the characteristics of the business enterprise. While there are still many small farms and while some of them are operated fairly efficiently, the major current trends suggest that farms will continue to increase in average size and to require relatively larger investments in land and equipment in the years ahead. Thus managerial ability will tend to play an increasing role in this field.

These trends have sometimes been referred to as an "agricultural revolution." Certainly the rapidity of changes in this field since World War II indicates that American agriculture is undergoing many significant changes and the end result may well be revolutionary in character.

You have undoubtedly read and heard about the "farm problem" in this country and about various programs for attempting to solve it. It has been virtually impossible to avoid substantial government programs in agriculture in part because of the impact of war and in part because of the peculiar nature of the markets for farm products.

During World War II, for example, many farms in Europe and in other areas covered by armed conflict were out of production. It became necessary to turn out more farm products in this country to support our allies, and as a result marginal land was brought into use.

After the end of the war the readjustment to more normal world production conditions made it difficult and in some cases impossible for the marginal farms to operate successfully. These are farms with high production costs relative to output, arising from poor land or other conditions. However, unlike business firms under similar conditions, the marginal farms did not tend to reduce output as prices dropped and thus re-establish a balance in the market. Because of heavy fixed costs, that is, costs which must be met regardless of market conditions including taxes, interest on mortgages, payments on machinery, and the like, many farmers simply produced more when prices went down. This, in turn, tended to force market prices lower and to create problems for all farmers rather than just for the marginal ones. Consequently, production quotas were set up and attempts were made to maintain a definite relationship between the prices which farmers had to pay for things they bought and the prices they received for the things they sold. Some land was kept out of production by the use of "soil banks" and various conservation programs.

Despite these efforts the "farm problem" persists. It may be that the trend toward capitalistic agriculture including larger farm units, greater use of machinery, improved crops, better fertilizers, and, above all, *more effective management* will ultimately provide a solution to the whole range of difficulties usually included under the term "the farm problem." Indeed, it is possible that the corporate form of organization may become more important in the farm field and that managerial improvements will contribute greatly to the solution of problems in this area in future years. Thus, the agricultural field may present a number of opportunities for young people with managerial ability. Often the fields with the greatest problems are also the areas of greatest opportunity.

Manufacturing

The business firms in the manufacturing field are involved principally with changing the form of things. Raw materials are processed or partially processed; then partially processed materials are processed further, or various parts are assembled. The stages in manufacturing that begin with raw materials and continue until a product is ready for ultimate use are many and varied. In some cases firms limit their activities to one stage of the process; in others they cover many stages of manufacturing and may also include original procurement as well as final distribution. Often a single firm will manufacture a variety of products covering various stages of production as well as finally processed goods.

One of the dramatic developments of modern times is the application of machine methods to manufacturing. The transition from handicraft methods, that is, the use of simple hand tools, to large-scale manufacturing processes with the use of machines to do an increasing amount of work is often referred to as the "Industrial Revolution." While the early stages of this process in the late eighteenth and early nineteenth centuries are usually identified historically with the term "Industrial Revolution" we should recognize that the process has not stopped and that indeed the trends toward automation, use of atomic power, and related developments coupled with improved managerial methods may bring even more revolutionary changes in the years ahead.

The U.S. Department of Commerce subdivides the broad field of manufacturing into a number of areas. These are set forth in the *Census of Manufactures* and the *Survey of Current Business.* A primary division is made between durable goods and nondurable goods industries. In the durable goods field are included lumber and wood products; furniture and fixtures; stone; clay and glass products; primary metal industries including blast furnaces and primary smelting and refining processes; fabricated metals; machinery; electrical machinery; transportation equipment including the automobile, aircraft, ship and boat building, and railway equipment industries; instruments; ordnance (that is military weapons); and others.

The nondurables include food and related products; tobacco manufactures; textile-mill products, apparel (clothing), and other finished textile products; paper and allied products; printing, publishing, and allied industries; chemicals; products of petroleum and coal; rubber; and leather and leather products.

We list these many types of manufacturing not with the thought that you will commit them to memory but rather to give you an understanding of the diversity of industries and products that are involved in the broad field of manufacturing.

The field of manufacturing accounts for about a third of the non-agricultural employment in the country. The area of durable goods provides employment for nearly three fifths of the total in manufacturing, and nondurables the remainder. The proportion of people employed in manufacturing has not tended to rise in recent years and this area may become of relatively less importance. The rate of change in this direction, however, may not be as marked as it has been in recent years.

Mining

Business firms engaged in mining are concerned with separating basic materials from the earth. The principal fields of mining, according to the Department of Commerce classification, are: (1) metal; (2) coal, including the anthracite and bituminous divisions; (3) crude petroleum and natural gas production; and (4) nonmetallic mining and quarrying.

Like manufacturing, mining has gone through revolutionary changes in the application of more and more machinery to the processes involved. Even coal mining which for many years was almost a handicraft process, has been largely mechanized. It may be that in future years the mining processes in this field will be altered greatly, with the coal burned in the mine and the resulting energy transmitted to users in other forms. Mining firms employ less than 2 per cent of the work force. The importance of this field in terms of the investment represented or the value of the goods produced is much greater than this percentage would indicate. In many instances, and this is notably true in the petroleum industry, the mining phases of production are integrated with manufacturing, and sometimes with distribution activities as well.

Prospecting for metals and oil represents one of the dramatic chapters in our economic history. And such prospecting, some by individuals, some by business firms, still goes on. The most recent chapters are being written in uranium prospecting and in off-shore oil drilling.

Often we hear discussions of the likelihood that many of our basic resources will be exhausted if current rates of extracting materials from the earth are maintained. Thus, it is sometimes argued that mining activities of all types must be closely regulated to conserve future supplies of raw materials.

FIGURE 6–2

Percentage of Total Nonagricultural Wage
and Salary Workers by Industry

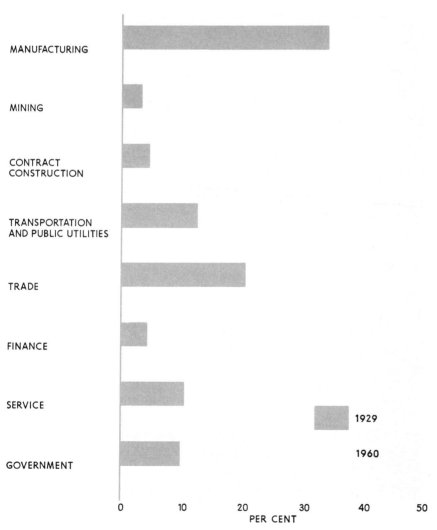

Such arguments fail to consider the potentialities of invention and technological advance. We now know that atomic energy may provide some of the power of the future that might otherwise have had to come from coal and petroleum. Other sources of energy also may be released and stored, such as the energy from the sun. Sea water is another possible source of raw materials in the future. Indeed by atomic fusion rather than fission a cubic mile of sea water is estimated to contain enough basic materials to supply all of the energy needed for industry for a year.

Construction

The construction industry is a big one, employing nearly 2.8 million persons, or around 5 per cent of all wage and salary workers. It contains a wide variety of business units ranging in size from very small firms to those of substantial size.

In a sense construction is a type of manufacturing, but since the work must be done ultimately at the building site rather than in plants it typically is separated from what we usually term manufacturing industries. We should note that more and more factory production is taking place in the building field with numerous parts and components of buildings being manufactured in plants and then transported to sites for assembly. The rise of the prefabricated housing industry in the postwar years is a case in point.

The two big divisions of the construction field are private and public building activities. The main subdivisions of the private field include residential; industrial; commercial; religious, educational, hospital, and institutional buildings; farm construction; public-utility construction; and others.

In the public field many of the same classes are found plus military construction, highways, sewer and water projects, conservation and development programs, and miscellaneous public-service enterprises.

Private construction projects typically involve three or more times as much dollar volume as do public projects, although this proportion changes greatly in wartime or in other emergency periods. Firms engaged in construction of course, may work on both public and private contracts. Many building firms are small, engaging in specialized work which may be secured under subcontracts from larger organizations.

Transportation and Public Utilities

Organizations engaged in the broad field of transportation and public utilities employ about 6 per cent of the gainfully employed in the country. Thus, while these organizations do not provide work for a large percentage of the people, their activities are of key importance to the operation of the economic system as a whole.

Organizations engaged in transportation include both private firms and public agencies, the latter being concentrated in the provision of local community transportation to a large extent. Railroads; airlines; trucking firms; bus companies; river, lake, and ocean shipping organizations; pipelines; rent-a-car firms; and taxi companies are all included in this area of work.

In the public-utility division of this area are included telephone and telegraph companies, with the American Telephone and Telegraph Company (A. T. & T.) the dominant firm, television and radio companies, gas and electric utilities, and related organizations. In many instances water companies, sewage disposal plants, and the like are municipally owned, and those working in such organizations are included in public employment.

In nearly all cases transportation and public-utility organizations operate on the basis of governmentally issued permits or licenses to do business. Such agencies as the Interstate Commerce Commission of the federal government, the Federal Communications Commission, the Federal Power Commission, and the Civil Aeronautics Administration play a vital role in this field.

While competition is a strong force in this area, for example, the competition between railroads and airlines, it does not operate as directly as in many other fields. This is why permits and licenses typically are required as the basis for doing business. Often rates are fixed by public and quasi-public bodies, and earnings are controlled as a result. Thus, this general group of organizations has peculiar sets of problems, although the management processes and the types of business specialists required are not substantially different from those required by other business firms. Usually large initial investments are characteristic of these organizations. The services they render are of key importance to the public.

The question of public versus private ownership of public-utility organizations has been debated for many years. On the one side it is argued that when detailed regulations are required in an area which does not fit the usual competitive pattern, the activity might as well be socialized. The other side of the argument emphasizes the advantages of private ownership even under detailed regulations.

One writer has suggested that under emergency or experimental conditions public ownership may be justified but that once the emergency has passed or the early experimentation has been completed, sale to private firms is desirable.[4] Public housing programs and the development of private uses of atomic energy are cases in point here.

Trade or Marketing

Around 17 per cent of the total employment in this country is found in trade. The field of trade or "marketing" or "distribution," as it is often called in business discussions, includes both wholesale and retail branches. The field is generally considered to include the processes of transferring products from the mining and manufacturing stages of production to various levels of consumers. Thus, in one situation such as automobile parts the consumer might be an assembly plant; in another such as cigarettes the consumer would be the final user of the product.

Wholesalers may be thought of as the first of a number of businesses that handle goods after the manufacturing stage as they proceed toward the ultimate consumer. Thus, manufacturers' sales offices and branches, and petroleum bulk stations and terminals fall into the wholesale group as do agents and brokers and a group called "service and limited-functions wholesalers."

The average size of firms in the wholesale field is relatively small in comparison to the average size of manufacturing companies. Also, requirements for machinery and heavy capital investments typically are not as great as in manufacturing.

The wholesaler usually operates between the manufacturer and the retailer, anticipating demands, buying in relatively large quantities, providing for sale in desired amounts, and storing goods as required. Since wholesalers usually serve independent rather than chain stores, they may provide special services for their customers such as extending credit, aiding with advertising and promotion programs, and the like.

The trend toward chain operations in the retail field and distribution directly by manufacturers in some lines has tended to reduce the relative importance of wholesalers. However, they still play an important role in the business community and undoubtedly will continue to do so.

Retail stores include many types. The Department of Commerce divides them according to the kinds of products they sell, distinguish-

---

4 H. L. Simons, *Economic Policy for a Free Society* (Chicago: University of Chicago Press, 1948), pp. 30–31.

ing general merchandise stores, food and liquor stores, automotive and accessories dealers, apparel stores, eating and drinking places, filling stations, furniture and household appliance stores, lumber dealers, drugstores, hardware stores, and others.

Retail establishments cover a wide range of firms from large department stores to small specialty shops. The rise of chain stores, the rapid development of outlying shopping centers, the growth of supermarkets, and the streamlining of many merchandising operations have all been important trends in retailing during the postwar years. These trends are providing us with a system of mass distribution that parallels in large degree our mass-production processes.

The average size of the business firm in the retail field is relatively small, hence nearly half of the firms in the country are found in this area. Of these about half are very small and account for only about a tenth of retail sales. Thus, this is an area in which many small businesses are found, but it includes also such companies as the A & P Tea Company; Marshall Field & Company; Macy's; Gimbels; Kroger Stores; Sears, Roebuck & Company; Montgomery Ward & Company; Woolworth; Kresge; and other firms of large size.

Finance, Insurance, and Real Estate

The business firms engaged in this broad area of work include commercial banks, savings banks, savings and loan associations, mortgage companies, finance companies, investment houses, security dealers and brokers, insurance companies and agencies, real estate brokers and property managers, and others. In addition there are pension funds, mutual funds and other organizations. A series of public and quasi-public agencies play important roles, including the Federal Reserve System, the Federal Home Loan Bank System, the U.S. Treasury Department, the International Bank for Reconstruction and Development, the Federal Housing Administration, and others. Only about 3.5 per cent of the total employment is found in the private areas of these fields. Nevertheless, they occupy key positions in the business world being concerned with savings, capital formation, and investment as well as with real property which constitutes a large portion of our national wealth.

The financial institutions of the country bring together savings and provide appropriate uses for these savings. Because of their key importance in our economic system, many financial institutions may be established only under special government charter, some being chartered by the federal government and some by state governments. For example, national banks hold their authority to operate from the federal government and state banks from the states in which they are established.

Commercial banks whether organized under national or state charter range in size from small institutions serving local communities to giant financial organizations operating on an international basis. In some states "branch banking" is allowed, that is, a bank may establish branches which may be located at a number of points to serve local needs. Each branch, of course, is operated as a part of the total institution. In other states the "unit bank" system prevails. This means that each bank operates as a single unit, without branches.

Commercial banks accept demand and savings deposits. Demand deposits form the basis for checking accounts and large volumes of funds are transferred from one account to another, and from one bank to another, each day. Demand deposits also form the basis for short-term (usually less than a year) loans. Savings accounts are not subject to checking privileges, and they usually do not turn over as rapidly as checking accounts. Deposits of all nationally chartered banks and qualified state banks are insured up to $10,000 per account by the Federal Deposit Insurance Corporation.

Commercial banks are tied together through the Federal Reserve System, which is a regional reserve banking arrangement operating through twelve regional banks with their activities co-ordinated by the Board of Governors in Washington. This system is quasi-public in that the member banks own the stock of the reserve banks, elect their officers, and the system has generally been largely independent of politics. The Board of Governors supervises the Federal Reserve banks and thus plays a vital role in the economic life of the country.

Savings banks contrast with commercial banks in that they specialize in longer-term loans such as real estate mortgages, municipal bonds, and the like. Most of the savings banks in this country are organized on a mutual rather than a stock basis and they are concentrated largely in the New England and Middle Atlantic states.

Savings and loan associations specialize in home mortgage financing but may lend also to a limited extent on real estate used by business firms and other organizations such as churches. These institutions also may be organized on a national (federal) or state basis. They are also referred to as building and loan associations, homestead associations, and co-operative banks. They may be organized on a mutual or stock basis, with the former predominant. There is also a central banking system called the "Federal Home Loan Bank System," to serve these institutions. Deposits in qualified institutions are insured up to $10,000 per account by the Federal Savings and Loan Insurance Corporation.

Investment bankers play an important role in underwriting and marketing the securities of business firms and thus helping them to finance their operations. The various security exchanges, ranging from the large New York Stock Exchange and the American Stock Exchange to small local exchanges and "over-the-counter" arrangements, serve a vital purpose in bringing savings to business firms and in facilitating the sale and purchase of corporate securities. Over-the-counter arrangements refer to trading that takes place largely between security dealers in contrast to a central exchange.

Insurance companies may be thought of as financial institutions since they play an important role in the mortgage and investment markets. In addition they provide the specific services of spreading or pooling risks and hazards to life and property. The major forms of insurance are life, property, casualty, and marine protections. Business firms, as well as individuals rely heavily on the services of insurance companies. In recent years protections against accidents and illness have developed into important forms of insurance, and the growth of annuities and pension plans has expanded the role of many insurance companies.

Firms engaged in the field of real estate typically are brokerage or property management organizations. Brokers sell and lease properties for owners and in some cases manage properties as well.

Some real estate firms operate largely on a local basis. Typically these are in the field of residential real estate. Real estate firms in the commercial and industrial fields more frequently operate on a regional or national and in some cases on an international basis.

Frequently real estate firms serve as investment counselors in the real property field. Often they manage properties for small or large investors, arranging for leases, maintenance and repair, taxes, insurance, and related activities. Thus, they perform an important stewardship function in this field.

Real estate firms usually are of small size, especially in the residential field. This is an easy field to enter, usually the only requirement being to pass an examination and to secure the listing of properties for sale.

In some cases real estate firms attain fairly large size, typically dealing in large projects, assembling land for investors and developers, or representing financial institutions in mortgage or property management work.

Service Industries

The broad group of businesses classified in the service field include hotels; cleaning and dyeing plants; laundries; barber and beauty shops; places of entertainment and amusement; automobile repair and service establishments; other repair shops such as shoe, watch, radio and TV, and others; business services including credit and collection agencies; advertising agencies; and small custom shops such as printing establishments, and others. In short, service industries include a wide variety of activities; the firms tend toward small size on the average, although some, such as theater chains and the like, are of substantial size; and markets typically are limited in scope. We should note that professional services are not included in this group. Over 10 per cent of all employed persons are engaged in service industries.

Many of the firms in this field are small, individually owned and operated enterprises. The role they play, however, is important in that they provide vital services for other business firms, individuals, and families.

SUMMARY

Business firms may be classified in many ways: by size, type of economic activity, form of ownership, area of operation, degree of regulation, and others. Emphasis here is placed on size and type of work; form of ownership was covered in the preceding chapter.

The extent to which a firm will expand depends on a number of factors, including favorable conditions, quality of management, degree of competition, research and development programs, and others. Larger firms enjoy the advantages of specialization, large-scale purchase of materials, and the ability to conduct research and development programs. Firms may grow by adding products or expanding markets for present products. They may develop new products through research and development programs or by expanding existing product lines. Sometimes other firms are purchased in order to provide for expansion. Business firms may expand horizontally, adding firms or plants at the same general level of production or marketing, or they may expand vertically by adding various steps in the process of bringing goods from mine or forest through the various stages of manufacturing and marketing.

Theoretically, there is a best or optimum size for a business firm. As firms expand, they encounter certain problems of size, they lose flexibility in their operations, and often suffer from bureaucratic tendencies. In some cases problems of this type can be solved by decentralization, thus, in effect, dividing a business firm into a number of more or less autonomous parts.

The types of work which business firms carry on may be classified in accordance with a system developed by the Department of Commerce which includes the following groups: (1) manufacturing; (2) mining; (3) contract construction; (4) transportation and public utilities; (5) wholesale and retail trade; (6) finance, insurance, and real estate; and (7) service and miscellaneous activities.

QUESTIONS AND PROBLEMS

1. Why do some firms attain large size while others do not?
2. Do you believe that research and development programs will be a major factor in the future growth of business firms? Explain.
3. How important is good management to business growth? Could a firm enjoy growth without good management? Explain. Could a firm fail to grow even with good management? Explain.
4. Differentiate between "horizontal" and "vertical" expansion. Can you give illustrations?
5. Is it possible for a firm to become too large? Explain.
6. Classify business firms in terms of the types of work they do. Develop an alternative classification.
7. Why are many farms taking on the characteristics of business enterprises? Do you think this trend will continue? Why or why not?
8. Why has competition failed to work satisfactorily in the agricultural field?
9. Distinguish between durable goods and nondurable goods industries. Give examples.
10. Do you think that mining activities should be regulated in order to conserve future supplies of raw materials? Why or why not?
11. How does the construction industry differ from manufacturing?
12. Why are firms in the transportation and public-utility field regulated to a greater extent than those in wholesale and retail trade?
13. Distinguish between wholesaling and retailing.
14. What are the principal types of financial institutions in this country?
15. Present at least six examples of firms in service industries.
16. Read the following "Profile" of the H. H. Hicks Company and answer these questions:

    a) Are there shopping services which the company might add?

b) Do you think the trend toward branch stores in suburban shopping centers will continue?

c) Will department stores like this one tend to gain a relatively larger proportion of retail sales? Why or why not?

H. H. HICKS COMPANY: PROFILE*

H. H. Hicks Company of Middletown, a merchandising institution established in 1876, is located in the downtown area of a city of 32,000 people. Listed as a junior department store by the National Retail Merchants Association, it is one of seven departmentalized retail stores in the Middletown shopping district. The Hicks Company is an independent establishment, i.e., one which has no ownership affiliation with other department stores. It is a locally owned and operated corporation which has been under the management of its present owners since 1950.

The company carries a wide range of merchandise, including specialty, convenience, and shopping goods, of which shopping goods are by far the most important class of goods sold. The sale of women's ready-to-wear and accessories, piece goods, and domestics is of greater relative importance in junior-type department stores than in larger stores.

The store occupies a brick and stone building located on the north side of the court-house square. It operates all four floors of this building and utilizes approximately 50,000 square feet of selling and counter space. In its central location it provides easy access to all downtown shoppers.

There are 23 separately departmentalized units in the store. These departments have been further subdivided into 73 different categories which clearly distinguish between product lines and allow for a wide range of product differentiation. The shoe department at Hicks is of such size as to require a special manager, as compared to the other departments which are in the charge of chief salesclerks. Approximately 65 sales personnel are employed during the peak sales periods. Since department store sales are subject to seasonal variations, this figure varies from month to month.

The buying function is handled by seven buyers who purchase a majority of the store's stock. Their ability to select from many offerings just what will sell best and to determine the most economic quantities to be bought at a given time is a prime test of their efficiency and the measure of their value to the store. The store also depends upon its resident buying office in New York City for market information and as a supplement to its buying operations. This buying office represents retailers in the same kind of business, and because of this fact they are able to render many services at a relatively small cost. By means of a force of experts constantly in touch with developments in the manufacturing area, the resident buying office is able to help keep its clients in touch with the best sources of supply. Style bulletins are sent to its member stores at regular intervals and, in general, the office acts as their representative in the market.

Hicks maintains a fairly complete line of customer services to facilitate congenial consumer relationships and consolidate its position among its

---

*Report prepared by Richard Oliker, Graduate School of Business, Indiana University.

departmentalized competitors in Middletown. Store-owned and operated trucks make daily deliveries to a large consuming area. The store also offers a complete interior decorating service to the community. An interior decorator from the store will visit the home or office, offer suggestions, purchase and install the required materials and furnishings at no extra cost above the cost of the required labor and the materials used. The store has also established a complete brides' service which is capable of handling the arrangements for a wedding of any size.

In line with its shopping services, Hicks also provides the standard financial services to all of its customers. Installment purchase plans are available on all consumer durables, as well as the usual 30-day charge accounts, and budget accounts.

Hicks makes regular use of newspapers within the trading area to advertise its shopping potentialities. Frequent radio announcements inform the public as to special sales and bargains. All new mothers in the trading district receive a complimentary book on baby care which also advertises nursery supplies carried by the store. None of the department stores in the Middletown area make use of television advertising because of its relatively greater cost.

Indications as to the exact number of department stores in the United States vary considerably. This is due in large part to the difference of opinion as to what constitutes a true department store. Size, sales volume, and location have all been used as criteria to determine whether an establishment is or is not a department store.

The Bureau of the Census has developed a definition which would seem to be the most appropriate.

Department stores are retail stores carrying a general line of apparel, such as coats, suits, dresses, and furnishings: home furnishings, such as furniture, floor coverings, curtains, draperies, linen, major household appliances, and housewares such as table and kitchen appliances, dishes, and utensils. These and other merchandise lines are normally arranged in separate sections or departments with the accounting on a departmentalized basis. The departments and functions are integrated under a single management. Establishments included must normally employ 25 or more persons.

In its highly competitive industry—that of retail merchandising—the department store has averaged only approximately 7 per cent of total national retail sales in the past thirty years. In the period following World War II, department stores have tended to decline in sales volume importance, relative to the total retail trade structure. The principal reason for this relative decline is that consumer expenditures for the goods commonly handled by department stores have not increased in the same proportion as other categories of expenditures in retail stores.

With its quantity buying, specialization of personnel, convenience to the customer, and prestige of size, the modern department store is in a strong position to compete with other types of retail establishments on an equal footing. However, its high cost of operation, due primarily to the large amounts which must be spent for the special services it offers, and the problems it encounters in the training and maintaining of a skilled selling force have caused the department store to resort to several developments in an effort to maintain its competitive position in retail trade.

First, the development of department-store chains has been accomplished in order to obtain the economies inherent in large-scale institutions. Independent department stores, like H. H. Hicks, endeavor to accomplish these same desired results through co-operative buying associations, and still retain their independence. Secondly, efforts have been made to widen the public appeal of department stores by the institution of bargain basements and exclusive shops. In this way the department store hopes to induce patronage from all income levels. Thirdly, branch stores have been established in suburban shopping areas. This trend has been the result of the increasing importance of suburban shopping centers in retail trade and the congested traffic conditions in metropolitan districts.

When considered from another point of view, the department store has developed a permanent place in the American shopping scene. Although the suburban shopping center and the discount house have made recent inroads into markets which were formerly the exclusive property of the department store, it remains a high-prestige institution which attracts shopping traffic to the metropolitan shopping district. Their wide range of merchandise and customer services place them in a position to lead the other types of retailing institutions in setting the general trading tone of the community.

SUGGESTED READINGS

Long, John D. *Workbook to Accompany Weimer: Business Administration: An Introductory Management Approach,* chap. 6. Rev. ed., Homewood, Ill.: Richard D. Irwin, Inc., 1962.

Keezer, Dexter M. and Associates, *New Forces in American Business.* New York: McGraw-Hill Book Co., Inc., 1959. See especially chap 2, "Prospects for Sustaining a High Level of Business Investment."

Survey of Current Business, Washington, D.C.: U.S. Department of Commerce. Look over a current issue of this important publication and note the reports set forth in regard to the current work of various types of business firms.

OUTLINE FOR CHAPTER 7

THE DECISION MAKERS IN BUSINESS FIRMS include
    owners,
    managers, and
    specialists
      who are selected by
        themselves as owners or
        by representatives of owners.
  Principal decisions are made by
    owners, boards of directors, and
    top managers, such as
      president,
      owner,
      principal partners,
      executive vice-president,
      other vice-presidents, and
      committees or other special groups.
  Supporting decisions are made by
    operating or "middle" managers and
    specialists.
  Decision makers, if successful, are well compensated
  because of
    their scarcity,
    risks incurred, and
    heavy pressures and demands.
  Some managers may be classified as "organization men" but
    the diversity of interests,
    the variety of firms, and
    competition
      make for lack of conformity.
  Popular estimates of business executives vary greatly—with
  relatively few winning widespread popularity.

THE DECISION MAKERS
IN BUSINESS FIRMS

No other touchstone can test the heart of a man, the temper
Of his mind and spirit, till he be tried in the practice of
Authority and rule.

—SOPHOCLES
(Creon in Antigone)

Leaders as Decision Makers

In this chapter we consider the people who play the major roles in
the drama of business firms—the major decision makers. These are
the men and women who by virtue of their ownership, their managerial ability, or their specialized professional competence exercise
the leadership of business firms or major divisions of firms. They determine the objectives that will be pursued, the methods by which the
objectives will be attained, the various resources or combinations of
resources that will be used in their operations, and the ways in which
they will adapt operations to the general economic and social environment in which business is carried on.

Decision making has come to be thought of as almost synonymous
with management. Certainly decision making represents one of the
more dramatic and interesting aspects of the manager's work. But he
carries on many other significant activities as well, many of which (1)
capitalize on good decisions, (2) make questionable decisions work, or
(3) prevent bad decisions from leading to disastrous results. For example, the ability of a manager to develop loyalty to the organization,
to motivate his associates and assistants, to develop team effort, and to
direct complicated operations are all matters of importance to the success of the firm. Often these types of abilities and activities are referred
to as "leadership." This is a term that is hard to define, as we shall see
in Chapter 9. Leadership typically includes the ability to influence
followers to an extent beyond the making of decisions. Usually decision making will be interrelated, and it will also be interrelated with
other management functions.

We should note also that the leaders and principal executives, while major decision makers in the firm, are not by any means the *sole* decision makers on matters affecting the programs of the business firm. For example, the decision of a banker not to lend money to the firm, or not to lend it on the terms desired, may set definite limits on the decisions that the owners and managers can make. The decision of a labor leader to call a strike may cancel out many plans that have been made and severely restrict the decision-making ability of the firm's executives for some time. The decisions of a government regulatory agency or taxing authority may impose limits on a firm's operations. The decisions of a competitor may be controlling, for example, his decision to offer easy credit terms may require that a like decision be made by a firm's executives. Decisions of specialists to accept or not to accept employment with the firm may determine the future of some of its programs. And, of course, decisions of potential customers to buy or not to buy the firm's products, or to buy greater or lesser quantities are likely to determine the degree of success it may enjoy.

We have a tendency to think of the major executives of the firm as having wide decision-making latitude. This may be the case. It is important to note, however, that many other decision makers, within and outside the firm, also play important roles. The decisions of these other decision makers may establish severe limitations on the latitude of the decisions that the firm's executives may make. To some extent, of course, the firm's executives may influence the decisions of others. Lower prices may influence the decisions of customers; higher salary offers may attract more of the specialists needed, good management may influence the banker, and so on.

In this chapter, however, our attention centers chiefly on the executives in the firm, on who they are, the roles they play, and their relative importance in more or less typical situations.

Owners and Managers

As we have suggested, the owners of business firms are among the major decision makers. The extent to which owners dominate the decisions that are made depends somewhat on the relationships between owners, managers, and specialists in the firm and on the extent to which the business is regulated by government.

For example, in an individual proprietorship all of the decisions are likely to be made by the owner, who in the typical situation is also the manager. In a partnership, decisions are likely to be made largely by the principal owners—the partners. Often one of them will become the principal decision maker. In some cases when partnerships attain relatively large size some decisions may be delegated to hired managers.

In the typical corporate organization both owners and managers are likely to play important roles in making decisions. In some cases, usually the smaller and closely held corporations, ownership and management may largely be merged and the situation may differ little from that of the individual proprietorship or the partnership. ("Closely held" is a term used to indicate that the stock is owned by only a few people and is not usually bought and sold, that is, "traded" in financial terms.)

At the other extreme are very large corporations with widely dispersed ownership. In such cases professional managers may occupy major decision-making roles. Even in such cases managers are accountable to the owners, that is, the stockholders, and if they should carry out policies that a large number of stockholders considered detrimental to their best interests, the managers could, of course, be fired and replaced. Also, if managers followed policies that caused the company to fail, they would be replaced through reorganization.

It is sometimes contended that in cases of widespread or "splintered" ownership, managers are able to make major decisions with little regard for the opinions of owners. As we have pointed out, however, owners who are dissatisfied with management will sell their stock, drive down stock prices, and make it relatively easy for a few people to buy enough stock to exercise control and replace current managers by new personnel. Even a relatively small decline in stock prices (relative to prices of other stock) often is a signal to managers that owners are dissatisfied.

In the typical corporation the owners, acting through the board of directors, will establish basic objectives and broad operating policies for the managers and specialists to carry out. Managers such as the president of the company and the executive vice-president may also have ownership interests, but even if they have none, they are usually members of the board of directors or meet with the board.

Business specialists in such fields as production, marketing, finance, accounting, advertising, purchasing, personnel, real estate, transportation, insurance, public relations, and other areas also play important roles as decision makers. Typically their decisions are made within the framework of the more general decisions as to objectives and basic policies established by owners and those with general managerial responsibilities. Even so, the decisions of specialists often are highly important to the success of an enterprise. Usually such decisions involve both detailed knowledge of a specialized field of business as well as the general purposes and policies of the enterprise.

How Are Business Leaders Selected?

To some extent business leaders select themselves. For example if you set up an individual proprietorship or go into a partnership, you become a business decision maker by virtue of your decision to go into business. Much the same thing may be said of the people who are the original incorporators of a firm that is established as a corporation.

After the business has been operating for a time, there may be changes in the original decision makers who largely selected themselves. An individual proprietor may hire a manager whom he selects to relieve him of a part of the managerial responsibility of the firm. A partnership with two original partners may add a third or a fourth, who will be selected by the original partners. An investor may buy a controlling interest in a going corporation and thus become a major decision maker, having selected himself. Or one of the original incorporators of a firm may sell his interests and then substitute another person for himself as a result.

In some cases because of retirement or dissatisfaction, some of the original members of a board of directors of a corporation may be replaced by new members. In such cases they are elected by the stockholders, although the persons proposed for membership often are selected by the other board members.

Of course, you have heard of "proxy fights." Such situations occur when membership on a board of directors is contested, with two or more candidates trying for the same post. Stockholders are provided "proxies," that is, voting rights which they transfer to someone else to cast for them in lieu of being present at the meetings in person. Attempts are made by the contestants for a board position to secure as many proxies as possible. Sometimes control of a corporation hinges on the outcome of a proxy battle.

The officers of a corporation are selected by the board of directors. Typically these include a president, an executive vice-president, vice-presidents for various divisions of the company, a secretary, a controller (or comptroller), and assistant vice-presidents or other officers, depending on the organization and size of the company. In some cases the board of directors designates only the principal officers, such as the president and executive vice-president, and approves the selection of other officers by these top executives.

The specialists in a firm often occupy top executive positions, but in such cases they take on general managerial rather than special responsibilities. In their role as specialists they are usually selected by the officers for the specific assignments they are to fill. Those who fill top positions as specialists such as director of research and development, chief accountant, director of sales training, and the like may be selected by the president or executive vice-president. Typically such officers have managerial responsibilities as well as functioning as specialists. They may be secured from personnel already working for the firm or from outside sources.

The director of personnel in most companies is typically concerned with the selection of personnel below the top officer level. He works with top officers in the selection of assistant officers and specialists. There are wide variations from company to company in this respect.

Some companies operate management development programs for the purpose of preparing people for general or special managerial responsibility. In other cases, key personnel are selected to attend executive development programs sponsored by a university or a trade association. Usually the purpose of such programs is to prepare lower level executives and specialists for general managerial responsibilities.

In some cases management consulting firms help to spot potential executives for a firm, and the placement bureaus or offices of universities frequently play a similar role with respect to the alumni of their schools.

In a broad sense the public exercises a controlling influence over the selection of the leaders and major decision makers in business. While a man may select himself as a leader by buying a business firm or an interest in one, he will not remain in this position long if the public fails to buy the goods and services he attempts to sell or prefers to buy them from his competitors. Or if he pursues practices which offend the public, laws may be enacted which will put him out of business or regulate his activities rather closely.

The Board of Directors

The board of directors is the principal governing body of a corporation. It varies in size from normally a minimum of three to as many as fifteen or more members. Typically it includes the principal owners, that is, stockholders, or people who represent them, and the chief executive officer or officers. Sometimes "public interest" directors are included, that is, people who are believed to represent the viewpoint of the public at large. In some cases board members are selected to represent principal customers, or interested financial institutions, such as banks or principal suppliers of important goods or services.

Frequently, the chief legal counsel of the firm will be a member of the board, although the desirability of this arrangement is often debated. Similarly, other specialists such as the controller, the financial vice-president, or the sales manager may be included.

In an individual proprietorship the owner typically is his own board of directors, although he may arrange for certain advisers to meet with him periodically. Much the same thing may be said of a partnership since the principal partners are, in effect, the board.

A board of directors is usually organized with a chairman and a secretary. Typically an agenda is prepared, and careful minutes of the meetings are kept. Formal reports to regulative agencies, if any, are generally cleared by the board and are made a part of the minutes of proceedings.

As we have indicated, the board of directors in the case of a corporation or the proprietor or partners in the case of noncorporate organizations determine objectives and major policies for the operation of the firm. Obviously, the interests, personal objectives, and attitudes of the board members or their equivalent in other firms will have an important bearing on the determination of objectives and policies. Consequently, there is some merit in having people of different types and interests as members of a board. Too great a diversity, however, often leads to problems.

Many boards tend to be self-perpetuating, and this often leads to the following of established patterns and policies with resistance to the making of major changes so long as the firm is operating on a basis that is satisfactory to the board. In other cases the board of directors is the main stimulating force in a firm, establishing rates of growth and other standards of performance that tax the best efforts of the managers and their assistants.

The President

Typically the president is the chief executive officer of a corporation, although in some cases the executive vice-president or the chairman of the board may serve in this capacity. In such cases the president may have other business interests or may be advanced in age or for some other reason be unable to give full time to the business. Sometimes the offices of president and chairman of the board are combined.

When the president is the chief executive officer, he carries the major management responsibility for achieving the objectives of the firm.

He serves as a connecting link between the board of directors on which he usually serves and the management personnel of the firm. Thus his position is a powerful one since he may interpret management to the board and interpret the wishes of the board to management.

While he may have started his business career as a specialist in one or another field, his duties and his authority as president are as wide as the business firm's activities and those related to them. To borrow a military analogy he is a "general" officer, not a colonel or lieutenant colonel.

The success or failure of many firms is determined to a large extent by the president, by his leadership qualities, his organizing ability, his power to motivate his associates and subordinates, his capacity to plan or to bring together people who can do this for him, and his ability to control all phases of the organization in accordance with established plans and policies. He is the symbol of the company in public and industry meetings; his personality and reputation tend to be identified with that of the company; he is the chief public and community relations officer, even though the firm may have a department for this function; his integrity or lack of it will have a major bearing on the credit standing of the firm; and his reputation as a manager and business leader will determine in large degree the type of persons he is able to attract into his organization.

The Executive Vice-President

As we indicated above, the executive vice-president serves as the chief executive officer in some firms. In such cases the above discussion about the president would be pertinent to the executive vice-president, since this discussion was concerned with the chief executive officer, regardless of the title by which he might be designated; for example, managing officer, managing partner, owner, and others.

Typically, the executive vice-president is second in command to the president of the company. In some cases he is called the senior vice-president, or in smaller firms there may be only one vice-president and this title will indicate that he is second in command. Regardless of how designated by title, the second in command usually serves in place of the president when required to do so by the president's absence. The executive vice-president may also have specifically designated duties such as being chairman of major management committees. He may serve as the "inside" man in the organization if the president's chief work is with "outside" persons and groups. In some cases the executive vice-president combines this function with heading a key department or serving as the principal financial, planning or control officer. Typically, his range of operations is as broad as those of the president. Often he is in the process of developing his abilities so that he may succeed the president when required to do so.

In some company organizations the president is responsible chiefly for the interpretation of broad objectives and policies and for developing the general framework of the programs required to carry them out. In such cases the executive vice-president is largely responsible for carrying the president's decisions and programs into effect.[1]

The executive vice-president is often expected to suggest changes in policies or organization to the president, to see that the executives under his direction carry out their programs, to co-ordinate the work of various departments in the organization, to serve as a central clearing officer for the various departments, and to aid in promoting satisfactory customer, investor, and public relations.

Other Vice-Presidents

A firm may have one or more vice-presidents in addition to an executive vice-president. A typical situation is one in which there is a vice-president for production and another for marketing or sales, although various combinations exist. In some cases the controller or treasurer is also a vice-president. In other cases there may be vice-presidents for personnel, public and community relations, research are development, and other activities.

When a vice-president is in charge of a major division of a firm, he functions both as a manager of his division and as a general company officer. He is responsible for achieving the objectives set for his own division and also has general responsibility to the executive vice-president and the president for helping to achieve major company objectives.

Vice-presidents often start as specialists in one or another division of the company and move up in the organization to the top position in the division. Sometimes, of course, they are brought in from other companies or from government agencies or from other organizations such as the military establishment.

In some cases vice-presidents are "line" executives; that is, they operate in a direct line of authority between the president and subordinates. In other cases they are "staff" vice-presidents; that is, they serve

---

[1] See *Research Report No. 20*, Ernest Dale, *Planning and Developing the Company Organization Structure* (New York: American Management Association, 1952), pp. 172–74.

primarily as advisers to the president or executive vice-president. Examples of line executives include vice-presidents for sales or marketing, or for production or manufacturing. Examples of vice-presidents in staff capacities include those responsible for market research, for public relations, for research and development, or other areas.

Group Decision Making

In many business organizations arrangements are established for the making of decisions by groups of executives or for the preparation of recommendations by groups of executives to the board of directors which also serves as an example of group decision making. One of the most frequently used organization devices for this purpose is the committee.

The board of directors may have standing or special committees made up of its members for various purposes. There may be a management advisory committee or an executive committee typically made up of the president and other executives reporting directly to the president. Often a financial committee is established including the treasurer or vice-president for finance, the controller, the economist or economic adviser, and other major accounting and financial representatives.

Other committees frequently found in company organizations are committees for manufacturing, marketing and sales, human relations, research, retirement programs, review programs, and others. Some committees have only the authority to recommend and report to one or another of the top officers of the company. In some cases approval by the appropriate officer puts recommendations into action and the committee has the further responsibility of checking on such programs and the results that are achieved. Thus there may be *advisory* and *operating* committees.

In some cases "task forces" are organized for specific assignments, either for the purpose of studying and reporting in which case they resemble advisory committees, or to carry out assignments. Usually task forces are set up for a special effort covering a limited period of time. Committees are often used to facilitate communications between departments and to co-ordinate the work of the various departments as well as to gain the stimulus that often comes from group thinking and deliberation. Of course committees can be ineffective devices in some cases. They have sometimes been called "organized methods for wasting time." The success of committee operations depends largely on the character and capacity of the committee chairman and also on

FIGURE 7–1

"We've been through the winter slump, the spring soft-spot, and the summer drop-off. . . . I wonder what's ahead!"

Source: *Wall Street Journal* (by permission of Cartoon Features Syndicate).

the ways in which top officers in the organization make use of the committee.

Operating or "Middle Management"

The chief executive officer and other members of the top-management group cannot do all of the managing that is necessary in larger business firms. Consequently, in firms of this type there are usually operating managers or a "middle" management group. Typically, this group is made up of people who are in charge of specific units within the organization. In some cases they may be specialists, as would usually be the case of the manager of a sales training department or the media division of the advertising department which in turn might be run by a middle manager under the general direction of the marketing manager.

The general principle involved in the delegation of authority and responsibility to operating or middle managers is well exemplified by the way in which Moses set up his administrative organization. This is explained in the Bible in Exodus 18:13–26:

> Moses sat to judge the people; and the people stood about Moses from the morning unto the evening. And when Moses' father-in-law saw all that he did . . . he said unto him: "The thing that thou doest is not good. Thou wilt surely wear away, both thou and this people with thee; for the thing is too heavy for thee—thou art not able to perform it thyself alone.
>
> "Hearken now unto my voice . . . Be thou for the people Godward, and bring thou the causes unto God. [Then] thou shalt teach [the people] the statutes and the laws, and shalt show them the way wherein they must walk, and the work that they must do.
>
> "Moreover thou shalt provide out of all the people able men, such as fear God, men of truth, hating unjust gain; and place such over them, to be rulers of thousands, rulers of hundreds, rulers of fifties, and rulers of tens; and let them judge the people at all seasons. And it shall be that every great matter they shall bring unto thee, but every small matter they shall judge themselves. So shall it be easier for theyself, and they shall bear the burden with thee. If thou shalt do this thing . . . then thou shalt be able to endure, and all this people shall go to their place in peace."
>
> So . . . Moses chose able men out of all Israel, and made them heads over the people, rulers of thousands, rulers of hundreds, rulers of fifties, and rulers of tens. And they judged the people at all seasons; the hard causes they brought unto Moses, but every small matter they judged themselves.

Unit Managers, Supervisors, and Foremen

At the lower end of the management organization are those who supervise workers of various types who have no managerial responsibility. In some cases this level of managerial work is done by foremen. Sometimes supervisors are used for this purpose, or a supervisor may direct the work of several foremen. There has been some experimentation with these arrangements by various business firms. General Electric, for example, has established "unit managers" at this management level. In such an arrangement a substantial number—often 50 to 100 workers—report to the unit manager and the more traditional supervisors and foremen are eliminated. Whether the use of unit managers will expand remains to be seen. There is a growing recognition, however, that the number of workers who can be supervised (the span of control) is greater than formerly was believed possible.

Specialists

The other big group of decision makers in a company is the special-ists. As we indicated above, there is a difference between "line" and 'staff" functions. The term "staff" comes from military organization and broadly refers to the nonfighting element as distinct from the "line" or fighting forces.

Originally, staff officers were set up to help the commander-in-chief with his planning. The staff developed, however, not only as an ad-visory group but also as interpreters of the commander's orders to sub-ordinates and as control officers to make certain orders were carried out.[2] As time went on "staff assistants" or general staff officers were distinguished from staff specialists or technical and administrative staff officers.

In business firms much the same type of distinction has grown up. There is the staff assistant such as the "assistant to the president" or "assistant to" some other major officer. Then there is the specialist as such whose work requires specialized knowledge, training, experi-ence, and know-how. Examples of specialists include experts in per-sonnel, purchasing, accounting, and law. Increasingly, business firms make use of such specialists as physical or biological scientists, econo-mists, mathematicians, behavioral scientists, and other highly special-ized experts. Specialists may also carry management responsibilities as in the case of the personnel director, director of purchasing, chief ac-countant, or the legal counsel.

Even a small business needs technical assistance—someone to keep books, prepare tax returns, draw up contracts, estimate market poten-tials, make reports to various supervisory agencies, and related activi-ties. When a business is small such as a one-man grocery store or a small manufacturing plant, the services of outside specialists such as lawyers, accountants, and management consultants are usually secured on a part-time basis. As a business firm grows larger, it will typically employ its own specialists on a full-time basis, as well as making use of outside specialists.

In some cases a specialist, for example, the director of personnel or the chief accountant, will serve general officers and the heads of vari-ous departments in an advisory or staff capacity but will also have line authority with respect to his department or division. In other cases a specialist serves entirely in an advisory capacity, summarizing data, preparing reports, providing operating information, making estimates

---

2 *Ibid.*, pp. 66–67.

and projections, and performing similar tasks for one or another of the general officers.

Sometimes specialists exercise a great deal of influence even though they do not have line authority. This may be due to the personal abilities of the specialists themselves or to their interpretations of information, to their technical competence, or through the reputations they achieve for providing valuable advice. In some cases, as we have indicated above, they may be made vice-presidents. They may serve on influential committees. In some instances they are made members of the board or because of their close working relationships with top officers, they may be able to command authority over others down the line in the organization simply because of the types of work they do and the work relationships which they enjoy. In some instances they acquire authority by default of other officers. In any event the specialists in the business firm or outside consultants to the firm often occupy important positions as decision makers in the company.

The Use of Specialists

The general officers of a firm need a basic understanding of the work of specialists and know what they may be called upon to do. This is one reason why business schools typically require all of their students to become familiar with such fields as accounting, statistics, business law, finance, marketing, production, and economics, as well as management and administration. To an increasing extent such schools are also insisting that students have a basic knowledge of mathematics, the social and behavioral sciences, and related fields. Business firms are using specialists in such areas to an increasing extent as we have seen.

Even though a student does not become a specialist in one or another field, he needs sufficient knowledge of these fields to enable him to direct specialists in such areas effectively. Without such knowledge it would be difficult for him to arrive at a position of general managerial responsibility, or if he reaches such a position to discharge the duties of the office successfully. The effectiveness with which specialists are used is often a determining factor in the success of a business firm.

Compensation of Decision Makers

The compensation of the leaders and decision makers in business firms may be in the form of salaries, dividends on stock, earnings of partners or individual proprietors, sale of ownership interests in whole or in part, stock options, "fringe benefits" such as insurance, medical, and hospital benefits, retirement income, and others.

Noneconomic returns often are important as well. Many business executives derive a tremendous amount of pleasure from their work. This is the dominant factor in their lives and the economic gains are, at least to a degree, incidental. As Dale and Urwick point out:

> Taxes and social changes have made the accumulation of great wealth much more difficult than it was two or even one generation ago. Hence the power and pleasure derived from great wealth have lessened. Gone are the days when Andrew Carnegie drew an annual salary of $23 million from the presidency of the Carnegie Illinois Steel Corporation and all of it was take-home pay. The present president of that corporation, doing in many ways a more difficult job, is fortunate to retain $1/10$ of 1 per cent of the equivalent (in purchasing power). Hence it is not surprising that with the decline of financial rewards which made possible the exercise of many kinds of personal power, businessmen seek substitutes. One of these surely is the retention of decision-making power within the corporation.[3]

These authors also refer to a statement by the English novelist Arnold Bennett, who made the following observation as long ago as 1912.

> Recounting a visit to the highly successful president of a great insurance corporation, the late Arnold Bennett wrote: " 'And what do you do with yourself in the evening?' I inquired. He seemed a little disconcerted by this perhaps unaccustomed bluntness. 'Oh,' he said casually, 'I read insurance literature.' . . . The rough, broad difference between the American and the European business man is that the latter is anxious to leave his work, while the former is anxious to get to it. The attitude of the American business man toward his business is pre-eminently the attitude of an artist . . . He loves his business . . . He does not look forward to living in the evening; he lives most intensely when he is in the midst of his organisation . . . Watch American business men together, and if you are a European you will clearly perceive that they are devotees . . . They are cemented by one religion—and it is not golf. For them the journey 'home' is often not the evening journey, but the morning journey. Call this a hard saying if you choose: it is true. Could a man be happy long away from a hobby so entrancing, a toy so intricate and marvellous, a setting so splendid?" (Arnold Bennett, *Those United States* [London: Martin Secker, 1912], pp. 119–22.)[4]

Usually the owners are compensated through return on their investments. For example, the president of a small corporation may own a third of its stock. Usually he would be paid a salary for his services as president and also receive dividends on his stock. In addition the company might make payments into a pension plan for his benefit,

---

3 Ernest Dale and Lyndall F. Urwick, *Staff in Organization* (New York: McGraw-Hill Book Co., Inc., 1960), p. 47.
4 *Ibid.*, pp. 42–43.

pay for a certain amount of group insurance and for medical and hospital benefits. The partner in an enterprise might be compensated in much the same manner if he worked on a full-time basis. If he worked on a part-time basis his salary typically would be adjusted accordingly. The owner of an individual proprietorship might have his personal affairs so closely interrelated with the business that separation would be difficult. He might draw a regular amount weekly or monthly or he might adjust what he took out of the business to its volume.

Often it is difficult to secure exact information about the compensation of officers of corporations because fringe benefits are hard to evaluate. Also, officers may have options to buy company stock at fixed prices, be paid bonuses varying with business volume, or compensated in other ways. Even such things as excellent offices and working conditions may constitute an indirect form of income.

Taxes, of course, take a big portion of the salaries of executives due to the progressive nature of our income tax rates. For example, a salary of $150,000 would mean (at 1961 tax rates) an after-tax income of around $60,000.

Principal officers of corporations (and in some cases middle managers and others as well) are sometimes given stock options. This means that in addition to salary and bonuses corporate executives are given the right to purchase company stock at a predetermined price. If the stock appreciates in value within the option period, the executive may exercise his option and hold the stock for a required period and then sell it. Gains are usually taxed on a "capital-gain" basis. Capital gain resulting from the sale of investments (such as stock) typically held longer than six months is taxed more favorably than ordinary income, such as salary.

Owners of individual proprietorships, partnerships, and small corporations sometimes sell their business firms and thus qualify for capital gain treatment on the appreciation in value of the firm. The desire for income taxed on a capital-gain basis often explains why owners of smaller enterprises are willing to sell their firms to larger companies. It is interesting to speculate about what might happen if owners of small business firms were given more liberal tax treatment than at present. Many who now aspire to executive positions in larger companies might then prefer to set up their own enterprises or to become part owners of smaller firms.

Sometimes people wonder why anyone should be paid an amount in excess of, say $25,000 per year, arguing that it is difficult to "earn" that much. The answer, of course, rests on the relative scarcity of people with the ability to manage and operate large organizations and on the tremendous effort they are required to put forward. Except for vacations now and then, most corporation presidents or other chief executive officers put in many fourteen- and sixteen-hour days per week, must be available on call at all times, have few week ends free, must operate under the pressure of many demands on their time, and, of course, must conduct themselves in a manner befitting their positions.

Their responsibilities to stockholders and other investors, to the managerial and nonmanagerial personnel in the firm, to customers, to the community at large, to regulatory agencies, and others is very great. A single mistake, sometimes even of a minor kind, may mean the difference between success and failure for a period of time, or even for all time.

It should not be assumed from this discussion that all of the "big money" is made in the big companies. The owners of many small companies frequently fare very well, and, of course, their returns should be great in view of the heavy risks that many of them are called upon to assume. Salaries of the chief executive officers of smaller companies often fall in the range of $25,000 to $50,000 or higher. In addition, they derive the benefit of building up a business firm in which they have important ownership rights which may be subject only to capital gains taxes whenever they wish to dispose of them.

Thus, you should consider seriously the possibilities of working for small companies, especially when there are opportunities for acquiring ownership interests. There are many advantages to acquiring ownership, not the least of which is the tax factor, but in addition ownership protects the professional manager against the whims of those who may employ him simply on a "hired-hand" basis.

In addition, the acquisition of ownership in a small enterprise or a large business, in an industry with growth potential, provides the possibility of participating in rising values resulting from general industry expansion as well as from good management and administration.

The "Company or Organization Man"

The charge is sometimes made against business organizations that they force a certain pattern of thinking on their management personnel, particularly middle management, and demand almost blind loyalty to the company. Thus, it is claimed that independent thinking is limited, that the successful executive must be or become an "organization man" or a "company man." Along the same line it is contended that group decision making has largely replaced individual decision making and that the present-day executive is forced to conform to the standards of the group in which he works and to adjust his thinking to theirs.[5]

To a degree, of course, these charges are true. They are true also of establishments other than business firms. The armed services, for example, allow for very little deviation from "doctrine" or established policy. Much the same is true of government agencies, universities and colleges, and other establishments. Indeed, loyalties to such establishments may be stronger than to business firms.

There is a tendency for each of us to give loyalty to a business firm or to other enterprises with which we are associated. Such loyalty, however, need not blind us to faults that need correcting or to policies that are in error. Blind loyalty is likely to do the enterprise a disservice rather than a service.

It would be difficult to determine whether present-day business firms bring about greater conformity of thinking than did those of a generation ago. Often it is assumed that because some of them are larger more conformity follows as a logical result. We should recognize that much depends on top management. In some cases the top managers prefer "yes men" and conformists. Others encourage nonconformity; they stress the importance of innovations and new ideas; and they try by example to prevent their subordinates from stifling initiative and ideas. The decentralization of many larger firms that we mentioned briefly in the preceding chapter is one type of effort to move in this direction.

The tendency toward the development of "company" or "organization" men is one of the problems of bureaucracy, whether in private business firms, government agencies, or other establishments. It is important that it be recognized and if possible, controlled. Some uniformity of action is essential to the effective operation of an enterprise but blind loyalty and conformity may defeat rather than serve the purposes of the organization.

One of the main safeguards against the attributes usually associated with the "organization man" is competition. Doing things the way another firm does them gives no competitive advantage. Conformity of thought seldom produces the new idea that will enable a business

---

[5] See for example William H. Whyte, Jr., *The Organization Man* (Garden City, N.Y.: Doubleday & Co., Inc., 1956). See also our discussions in Chapter 25.

firm to move ahead of its competitors. Blind loyalty may prevent the weeding out of inefficient personnel or practices and thus result in lack of efficiency and high costs. Thus, competition and the necessity of making profits impose a discipline on top management that may prevent turning subordinates into company or organization men.

One of the main advantages that we may have against Russian communism in the long run is the widespread dispersion of power and decision making that prevails in our society. Russian thought stresses conformity of thought and action. The communist may well be the extreme example of "the organization man."

Public Estimates of the Business Executive

Public estimates of the principal executives in business firms range from respect to virtual contempt. The great depression of the 'thirties caused business executives to lose much of the esteem in which they were often held earlier; their performance in World II and thereafter helped to recapture some of their lost prestige. Even so, there are many in our society today who hold business executives in low regard. You may have been exposed to popular versions of the business manager in the movies, plays, or novels that reflect such viewpoints. He may be portrayed as a profit-mad seeker after economic power, a domineering figure with little or no regard for those under his direction, an "organization man" carefully patterning his behavior after other managers, top or middle, a behind-the-scenes controller of politicians, a "fixer" involved in graft and the corruption of public officials and in other related ways.

Most of such characterizations are far from reality. A few extreme cases may be found but they are not characteristic of the typical business executive. We should recognize that our business executives are a highly diverse group. They differ in education, age, ability, personal goals and philosophies, and in many other ways.

Even so, it is often difficult to understand why business executives are not held in higher regard by various people. One explanation may be the mistrust of power that is typical of our thinking. Yet, politicians and statesmen often wield much more power than business executives but often are held in high regard.

There is in our society also a tendency to glorify the "little fellow." We appear to admire the common soldier who "knows better" than his officers, and who by disobeying orders and by his own courage and ingenuity wins the key strong point that turns the tide of battle and the war. We respect generals but secretly think wars are won in spite of rather than because of them. Much the same type of thinking may be reflected in our attitudes toward business executives and those they direct. The salesman who gets the big order by disregarding company policy tends to be preferred in popular opinion to the executive who assigned the salesman to his territory.

These considerations, however, do not seem to apply to the small business man. Although he is seldom cast in the role of hero in the popular mind, he tends to be more popular than the big business executive. George Romney of American Motors seem to have struck the popular fancy by "taking on" the "Big Three" in the automobile industry. He is not thought of as a small business man, however. In his time Henry Ford was popular, probably reflecting public reaction to his bonus to car buyers (which Romney later copied), the first $5 a day wage paid in this country, and his suspicion of "Wall Street."

Popular reaction typically is "against" Wall Street, again a set of attitudes that is not easy to explain. If we could explain these attitudes, we might understand more about the popular opinion of business and business executives generally. In part it is undoubtedly a suspicion or fear of power, in part lack of understanding, in part jealousy; but it is also distrust, as for example, what Wall Street is doing with "other people's money."

Even if we cannot explain many of these general attitudes, we should recognize that they exist. We need a more general understanding of business administration and management, the role and responsibilities of business executives and the contributions that they make (regardless of their motivations) to our society. But how this may be accomplished is far from clear.

SUMMARY

The principal leaders of business firms include owners, managers, and specialists. Owners and managers are the major decision makers in the firm but by no means the sole decision makers; bankers, customers, government officials, labor leaders, and others may play important roles in affecting the programs of a firm.

In some cases ownership and management are combined; in others separated to a greater or lesser degree. Management ranges from top policy making to operating or "middle" management to supervisors, unit managers, and in some cases foremen. Business specialists include experts in production, finance, marketing, personnel, accounting, research, law, and other fields. In most cases specialists operate in a staff capacity, but they may hold line positions as well.

The principal executives and decision makers in business firms may select themselves or be selected by others; for example, the board of directors or the proprietor or partners ordinarily select those who are to hold top-management positions, and they in turn select "middle" managers, who may select supervisors and others. Major objectives and broad policies usually are determined by the board of directors in the case of corporations, or by those who correspond to the board in other types of establishments.

The chief executive officer is usually the company president, the owner, the principal partner, or in some cases he is the chairman of the board, or the executive vice-president. Typically there will be a second in command, such as the executive or senior vice-president, various heads of divisions who may be vice-presidents, and operating managers for smaller units in the firm. In some cases division heads and operating managers are specialists. Typically specialists influence decisions through operating or top management; in some cases they make decisions directly. Group decision making has tended to increase in importance.

The controversy over the "company" or "organization" man has stimulated widespread interest. While true in some cases, such designations often fail to recognize the variety of abilities and interests of managers, the diversity of the business firms they serve, and the impact of competition. Public estimates of business executives cover a wide range. Business executives may gain increased esteem through improved performance and a more widespread understanding of the range and significance of their work.

QUESTIONS AND PROBLEMS

1. Outline a situation in which the owner of an individual proprietorship would not be the principal decision maker.
2. Indicate the major differences between the decision making responsibilities of the principal executives in the small, closely held corporation operating on a local basis, and those in the large corporation operating on a national or multinational basis.
3. Is a business leader typically a decision maker? Is a decision maker a leader?
4. Explain what is meant by the statement: "To some extent leaders in business select themselves."
5. How is the president of a corporation selected? Suppose you wanted to become a member of the board of directors of a corporation, how might you go about it?
6. In a large corporation, who is likely to be responsible for the selection of the executive vice-president?
7. What is meant by the statement that boards of directors tend to be self-perpetuating?

8. List the principal responsibilities of a typical company president.

9. How may the responsibilities of the president differ from those of the executive vice-president?

10. What is meant by group decision making?

11. Indicate some of the ways in which business specialists may influence the major decisions of a company. Are specialists likely to increase or decrease in importance in the management and operation of business firms?

12. On what basis can a salary of $100,000 per year for a company president be justified? How do you account for the fact that some company presidents receive more income than the President of the United States?

13. In the following quotation from the novel *Cash McCall,* do you think Mr. Hawley through his character, Cash McCall, has described accurately the attitudes of businessmen generally toward their companies? Or do you think Mr. Hawley overstated the situation?

> "When I was in India I lived for a while in a little village in Rajputana. I asked a group of people who owned their temple. They were horror-stricken at the idea of my imagining that anyone could *own* a temple. I think that's more or less the way my father felt. I'm sure he never thought of the plant as something that anyone *owned*. It was an institution—"
>
> "*His* temple," she suggested.
>
> "That's it," Cash said.
>
> . . . Cash went on . . . "There's no place in the temple for the nonbelievers. Every religion has a curse for the infidels—and this one does, too. My father shouted it at me once. I'll never forget it." Cash paused, a bitter smile quickly softening to tolerance. "He accused me of not being a *company man*—and he said it as if he'd just looked into my soul and seen all the devils of hell writhing around in there." (Cameron Hawley, *Cash McCall,* Boston: Houghton Mifflin Co., 1955, p. 353.)

SUGGESTED READINGS

DALE, ERNEST. *The Great Organizer.* New York: McGraw-Hill Book Co., Inc., 1960. We quoted extensively from this highly stimulating book in Chapter 3. Read chaps. 3 and 4.

KAPPEL, FREDERICK R. *Vitality in a Business Enterprise.* New York: McGraw-Hill Book Co., Inc., 1960. Read the last chapter entitled "The Spark of Individuality," beginning on p. 69 of this interesting short book by the president of the American Telephone and Telegraph Company. This book presents a series of lectures at the Graduate School of Business of Columbia University.

LONG, JOHN D. *Workbook to Accompany Weimer: Business Administration: An Introductory Management Approach,* chap. 7. Rev. ed. Homewood, Ill.: Richard D. Irwin, Inc., 1962.

WHYTE, WILLIAM H., JR. *The Organization Man.* Garden City, N.Y.: Doubleday & Co., Inc., 1956. Read chapter one, the introduction to this controversial and interesting book—more if you like.

OUTLINE FOR CHAPTER 8

The establishment of OBJECTIVES, PLANS, AND CONTROLS ranks among the major functions of management.

Controversies over objectives center around profit—whether maximized or not in the short- or long-run; relationships between service and profit objectives, between public and private objectives.

Profits are the primary measure of a firm's success and an essential to survival, growth, or attainment of a prestige position.

Objectives stated in terms of share of market, return on investment (total or equity), and position in the industry are closely related to profits.

Objectives form basic *management decision guides*—but same objectives may be variously interpreted or lead to a variety of programs.

Policies are related to objectives and serve as continuing guides or a framework for decisions.

Plans represent the most plausible alternatives for achieving objectives; they relate to the future and to programs of action; they are "blueprints" for achieving objectives.

Plans may be *primary* or *supporting*, simple or complex; *budgets* often serve as plans; market factors often are controlling in development of plans; time and timing are also important.

Controls are closely related to plans; plans indicate reasonable hopes, review and control processes indicate extent of realization. Controls relate to past performance but are *future* oriented.

Major steps in control processes are establishment of standards, appraisal of performance, and correction of deviations.

OBJECTIVES, PLANS, AND CONTROLS

Defining the situation always requires a decision on objectives, that is, on values and their relationship. . . .

— PETER F. DRUCKER

Relationships between Objectives, Plans, and Controls

In this chapter we discuss various objectives of business firms and also consider their uses as guides to further decisions and operations. The achievement of objectives typically involves as a first step or stage management *planning,* which is also discussed in this chapter. Closely related is the subject of *controls* which we also consider here. The *organization* of resources including men, machines, materials, and money, and the direction and leadership of organizations are discussed in the following chapter.

Sometimes it is helpful to think in terms of decision implementing in contrast to decision making, and we have made use of this distinction in our earlier discussions. The interrelationships between decisions and actions often are very close. It may be helpful to think in terms of decisions as to objectives, basic plans, and organizational matters as *primary* or major decisions, with others as *supporting* decisions.

Management *plans* narrow the range of choice to a particular line of action that is then worked out in some detail. Managers often lay down *policies* which may be thought of as standing guides to related decisions. Policies in turn may be supplemented by "standard operating procedures," by detailed instructions and procedural manuals that spell out carefully the types of decisions and operations that are expected under given conditions.

Controls determine the extent to which objectives are being realized, and are closely related to plans. If plans may be thought of as reasonable hopes, review and control processes indicate the extent to which such hopes have been realized.

Controversy over Objectives

Traditionally it has been assumed that the primary or major objective of the business firm was to maximize profit. More recently the concept of maximizing profits *in the long run* has been given greater emphasis. With the emergence of business firms of larger size, we recognize that their managers have difficult political and public relations problems as well as problems of securing and maximizing income. In some cases short-term profits are foregone because they might invite regulation or public criticism which in the longer run would tend to reduce profits. An illustration is provided by the automobile industry immediately after World War II. Cars were in short supply. Demands were strong. The automobile companies probably could have put much higher prices on their cars than they did and still have sold all they could produce. To do so, however, might have invited price control and created unfavorable public opinion. Hence the automobile companies priced their cars at levels that would yield a "reasonable profit," rather than a maximum profit in the short run. By so doing they probably maximized profits in the long run.

In some cases it is contended that business executives do not attempt to maximize profits or anything else. Professor Simon suggests that they "satisfice," that is aim for what is "good enough" under the circumstances. He points out, for example:

In most psychological theories the motive to act stems from *drives,* and action terminates when the drive is satisfied. Moreover, the conditions for satisfying a drive are not necessarily fixed, but may be specified by an aspiration level that itself adjusts upward or downward on the basis of experience.

If we seek to explain business behavior in terms of this theory, we must expect the firm's goals to be not maximizing profit, but attaining a certain level of profit, holding a certain share of the market or a certain level of sales. Firms would try to "satisfice" rather than to maximize.[1]

There may be a relationship, however, between "satisficing" at one time or in connection with one aspect of a firm's activities and maximizing over the longer run or in terms of the totality of the firm's programs. For example, a firm entering the international field for the first time might be willing to accept a lower rate of profit on domestic operations for a period in order that resources may be shifted to inter-

[1] Herbert A. Simon, "Theories of Decision-Making in Economics and Behavioral Science," *American Economic Review,* Vol. XLIX, No. 3 (June, 1959), pp. 262–63.

national operations. For the longer run, however, its managers may be aiming at total profit maximization.

In any event, we should recognize that the determination of objectives for a business firm may be a fairly complicated matter. Some firms aim at *maximizing* return on total investment, others return on owners' investment, some aim at achieving what is considered a *desirable* or sustainable rate of return either on total investment or owners' investment. Some stress the share of the market they wish to capture or the sales volume they hope to reach. Others emphasize rates of growth. All of these have some connection with profit maximizing over the longer run.

A business firm must have income—revenues in excess of costs (or profit)—if it is to survive at all. Typically it needs profits beyond minimal levels if it is to grow or to attain a prestige position.

Definition of objectives, of course, does not stop with the establishment of general, over-all objectives for the firm. Objectives need to be defined in terms of time, say, the year ahead, three years ahead, five years ahead, or longer; objectives are required for specific aspects of the firm's operations, such as sales volume or production costs, or for a product division or a territory. Also objectives often are redefined from time to time.

For example, the managers of a business firm may find it necessary over a period of time to decide which line of business they want to be in. The original line of business may be encountering heavy competition or the managers may see growing opportunities in new lines. They may decide to shift emphasis by adding product lines or in some cases to move into an entirely new area.

Similarly, over a period of time the limitations which bound the actions of the managers of a firm may change. Government regulations may be altered; the competitive situation may change; or new methods may make it possible to undertake operations that were previously impossible.

In some cases managers tend to stress "public relations" objectives, that is, the types of goals that may have a wide public appeal. In other cases operational objectives, those that relate to such things as gaining a given share of the market or attaining a certain rate of return on investment, will be emphasized. In a final analysis, of course, all such goals are related to long-run profit maximization.

Some business managers differentiate between short-term, operational, and perpetual objectives. Such distinctions may be helpful but divisions on this basis are difficult to make.

Attitudes toward Profits

Many contend that the pursuit of private profit on the part of the owners and managers of business firms is a bad thing. Others argue that only by the pursuit of profit can business executives have a standard by which to judge the performance of their firms. Otherwise, the decisions of executives would tend to be made on the basis of personal preferences or in terms of concepts that are subject to a variety of interpretations rather than on the basis of rational analysis.

Viewpoints differ widely. Some stress profits as a means to an end. J. Irwin Miller, chairman of the board of Cummins Engine Company, says: "Profits are the means, an instrument society uses to get a corporation to do things for it, not an end in themselves."[2]

James F. Lincoln, president of the Lincoln Electric Company, states his position as follows: "The primary goal of any organization to be successful continuously must be to make a better and better product at a lower and lower price. Profit will and must be a by-product of service only."[3]

Some argue that the making of a profit is not necessarily an indication that society is being benefited. Such arguments typically establish some other standard for measuring performance than public acceptance, as reflected in markets or through elections.

A good summary statement on the profit issue has been made by Joel Dean: "A business firm is an organization designed to make profits, and profits are the primary measure of its success. Social criteria of business performance usually relate to quality of products, rate of progress, and behavior of prices. But these are tests of the desirability of the whole profit system. Within that system, profits are the acid test of the individual firm's performance."[4]

The argument over whether service or profit is a primary objective of the business firm depends a good deal on one's point of view. For example, one may view the firm from outside or inside; thus, customers are primarily interested in service, and support a firm if they believe they are securing good values; employees are concerned with their own incomes and hence are indirectly concerned with profits; stockholders are directly interested in profits. One of the primary

---

2 See *Life*, June 25, 1957, p. 162.

3 James F. Lincoln, *Incentive Management* (Cleveland: Lincoln Electric Co., 1951), pp. 14–15.

4 Joel Dean, *Managerial Economics* (Englewood Cliffs, N.J.: Prentice-Hall, Inc., 1951), p. 3.

functions of management is to co-ordinate such a variety of interests and yet to try to maximize profits in the long run. Basically the owners and managers of a business firm exchange services to society for profits.

Public and Private Objectives

Undoubtedly there must be some identity of private and public objectives if business firms are to continue to function in our society. If business firms do not provide the public with the goods and services it wants, they will soon fail. Thus, selfish interest tends to dictate that the owners and managers of business enterprises set objectives that will be supported by their customers, employees, and the public at large, as well as their stockholders and managers.

It is sometimes argued that business firms give the public, not what the public wants, but whatever will gain the greatest profit. This might be possible for short periods or in cases where firms had a monopoly position or a protected market. Competition from other firms at home and abroad, however, would soon result in serving the public's preferences; or in monopoly cases, public opinion would soon bring regulations that would force the firms involved to serve the wishes of the public.

To a degree, at least, the owners and managers of business firms resemble politicians. They must have an awareness of what the people as a whole are striving for and what they hope to achieve. Both business executives and politicians typically have *survival* as a basic goal. The politician wants to be elected and after election to stay in office. The business executive wants to establish a firm or attain a position of responsibility in one and then to keep it in business. Business executives that set for their firms the goal of survival and continuous existence over long periods of time must be aware of the changing tastes and preferences of consumers and the long-term hopes and objectives of the public at large. This is also essential if their firms are to grow or to attain a *prestige* position.

We should note that profits are defined by society at large. We set up rules governing the conduct of business and thus define the limits within which profits may be pursued. We establish tax laws that define "net profit after taxes." Thus, we make use of profits as incentives but we define these incentives rather carefully.

Our society expects business firms to help raise living and cultural standards. While business firms may not pursue such objectives directly, competition forces them to develop new products, methods, and processes almost constantly. Thus, they make substantial contributions to the improvement of our living and cultural standards, even though this may be done incidentally to the pursuit of profits.

In addition, we expect business firms to increase the economic opportunities that are available to our people. More and better jobs and greater opportunities for advancement are expected of our enterprises by the public generally. Again, business owners and managers may not be pursuing such objectives directly, but many will find it in their best interest as a result of competition to offer good job opportunities at favorable salaries. Otherwise a firm would be likely to lose its best people to its competitors. Thus, the pursuit of profits over the long run tends to result in the expansion of economic opportunities throughout our business system.

Unless business firms show the public what is possible in terms of new goods and services, the public may not be aware of the inadequacies of present products. And unless a business firm brings out better products and services, it will undoubtedly lose out in its competition with other firms. If all business firms failed to improve the standards of their goods and services, the public might turn to the government for the provision of such goods and services. Competition between business firms, thus, is one of the greatest assurances we have of progress in material standards and also in cultural standards. In order for a society to improve its culture it must have an economic surplus, an ability to support some portion of its people in cultural activities. The greater our economic progress, the greater the support that can be made available for our cultural development.

Types of Objectives

As we have suggested, profit maximization is the over-all goal of most business firms. Whether profits are pursued directly or as a means for achieving some other objective, the business firm must have income—net income (revenues in excess of costs) if it is to (1) survive, (2) grow, or (3) attain a prestige position. These three objectives or types of objectives help us to understand the management of business firms. While the objectives of business firms may be as varied as the firms themselves, or may vary for the same firm over a period of time, these three—survival, growth, and prestige or recognition—may be considered for our purposes as typical. These, of course, are general or major objectives. They may be expressed in various ways or subdivided to fit particular parts of a firm's program. In turn general objectives may be supplemented by specific or supporting objectives.

By objectives related to *survival* we may include the maintenance of a firm's competitive position, the earning of returns sufficient to hold its position or to keep it from deteriorating, building of reserve strength, protection against legislation that may favor its competitors, and the like. In short, business owners and managers who are concerned primarily with survival, and this probably is a basic objective of most firms, will pursue those forms of power, usually economic or political, which are most likely to assure this result.

As we have suggested, a second general objective appears to be *growth*. While some firms prefer to maintain a stated size or to avoid growth because of the problems it brings, growth appears to be pursued by a considerable majority of business firms. It may be pursued in several ways. Size is one way of measuring growth, but there are others, including the capturing of a larger percentage of the market, increased earnings on owners' investment, and the like. In a sense we might say that growth is an element in survival. Failure to grow—or at least to expand as rapidly as the industry or as the general economic system is expanding—causes a firm to decline in relative importance.

Objectives related to *recognition* or *prestige* may include both economic and noneconomic connotations. For example, the development of a prestige position for a firm may assure survival and aid growth, but prestige and recognition may be pursued in their own right (see Figure 8-1).

Many firms strive to develop a desirable "image" or "corporate personality." This may help to provide special advantages over competitors. It may be easier to attract competent personnel or to borrow funds. The public may tend to favor the products of a firm with a favorable image over those of other firms. The attainment of the number one position in an industry, for example, has major advertising and promotional value, even though it may sometimes be achieved by incurring costs in other lines. You are familiar with the newspaper stories which report the production levels of various types of General Motors, Chrysler, Ford, or other automobiles. In some respects these comparisons are reported almost as dramatically as scores of baseball games.

Some firms spend huge sums to assure identification with a particular market. Others stress ideas; for example, General Electric's slogan, "Progress is our most important product."

Especially in the years since World War II the owners and managers of business firms have tended to consider community relationships when determining company objectives. Many of them have wanted their firms to be known as "good citizens" and have in numerous cases made significant monetary contributions to local community activities and have provided the time of executives to serve on local, state, or national commissions or boards. The "image" concept has often been important in such cases.

FIGURE 8–1

Management by Objectives

Examples of Objectives

It is difficult to generalize about the objectives of business firms. As suggested above, they may be stated in terms of a desired rate of return on investment, a predetermined rate of growth, capturing a percentage of the market, accomplishing specific cost reductions, the addition of new products, or others. All bear some relationship, however, to the financial condition of the firm and to long-run profits. Sometimes sheer survival will make it necessary to stress liquidity in the short run, in order to avoid failure to meet interest or loan payments when due. In some cases return on total investment (owners' plus borrowed capital) is stressed, in others return on equity (owners') investment only. Expanding sales may be stated as a target but this usually has some implications for total and for net revenue.

At the risk of oversimplification we may outline some of the relationships between various types of objectives as follows:

I. Survival
   1. Attaining a desired liquidity position
   2. Reduction of borrowed funds
   3. Reducing costs
   4. Holding a given market position
   5. Meeting competition
   6. Providing for continuing leadership
   7. Protection against adverse legislation
   8. Maintenance of reserve strength
   9. Defense against tax increases
   10. Maintenance of community role and image
   11. Minimizing risks

II. Growth
   1. Expansion of return on investment
   2. Making plant additions and improvements
   3. Increasing output
   4. Gaining larger share of market
   5. Expansion of executive and other personnel
   6. Increasing expenditures for research and development
   7. Expansion of equity or borrowed funds
   8. Gaining a more favorable tax position
   9. Improving the product mix
   10. Holding or reducing costs
   11. Gaining special regulatory treatment

III. Prestige and recognition
   1. Achievement of outstanding position in industry
   2. Getting and keeping top-quality executive and other personnel
   3. Addition of new and appealing products
   4. Aiming at stable growth rates
   5. Paying dividends regularly
   6. Special provision for "fringe benefits"
   7. Heavy participation in community and public affairs
   8. Improving quality, reducing costs, and prices
   9. Establishment of special grants and awards
   10. Emphasis on "service" role

In some cases the long-range objectives of a business firm tend to be stated in general terms, the shorter-range objectives in more specific terms. Or the over-all objectives of the firm will be stated in general terms, but those for specific departments and divisions will be defined more precisely.

Business objectives are more often than not stated in terms of financial goals. Thus, they can be quantified and related to all aspects of a firm's operations.

Changes in Objectives

The objectives of a business firm may change over time. This may happen quickly as a result of a change of ownership or top management, or it may be a gradual process that may scarcely be recognized. As the owners of a firm grow older and more conservative they may "pull in their horns" and pursue objectives of a more limited type than was originally the case.

A business firm may be content with a sales volume of $500,000 per year for a time, but its owners may decide that unless sales are raised by 50 per cent or 100 per cent their interests can best be served by shifting their investments to another line of business activity. Thus, the alternatives open in competing lines may lead to changes in the objectives of a specific business firm. A new manager may decide to do a better job than his predecessor, and this may bring changes in company objectives.

Sometimes general business conditions bring changes in objectives. A rapid expansion of the entire economy may cause firms to advance the targets that they hope to reach. Or a slowing down in the general levels of business activity may have the opposite effect.

Actions of competitors may bring changes in the objectives of a firm. There is in business somewhat the same desire to "keep up with the Joneses" that is apparent in competition between families. Sometimes the actions of competitors bring emotional reactions on the part of managers that cause rapid changes in objectives or the pursuit of goals that more careful consideration would indicate were impossible to attain.

Great political changes such as the outbreak of war, sudden changes in international relations, or major changes in government policies may all bring changes in business objectives. Also, either sudden or gradual changes in public attitudes may have a similar effect.

Objectives as Management Decision Guides

Objectives not only define goals, they serve also as the basis for a value system that helps managers to determine the relative importance of various parts of a firm's activities and establish priorities between them. This value system provides the basis for establishing standards against which to measure performance. It serves as a guide to decisions at various levels of operation. The use of objectives as management standards and guides to management is sometimes referred to as "management by objectives," a phrase usually attributed to Peter Drucker.

Even if long-run profits are the central objective of all firms, their value systems will differ. Some may stress security against unfavorable economic developments. For example, the top managers of Montgomery Ward and Company expected a major depression after the war. Hence, expansion was avoided and the assets of the company were shifted to a considerable extent into cash and other assets that could be turned quickly into cash. By contrast, Sears, Roebuck and Company stressed growth during the postwar period. They opened stores rapidly, expanded operations, and greatly increased their earnings. Here we have an interesting illustration of the program of two large companies in the same line of business pursuing contrasting objectives. Thus, their value systems contrasted sharply as did their programs of operation even though both hoped to maximize profits.

The objectives of a firm will have a direct bearing on location or locations, organizational structure, planning activities, personnel hired, training programs, emphasis given to research and development activities, methods of paying employees, dividend policies, fringe benefits, and a host of other things. Drucker suggests that there are eight areas in which objectives of performance and result should be set: "Market standing; innovation; productivity; physical and financial resources; profitability; manager performance and development; worker performance and attitude; public responsibility."[5]

Management by objectives usually leads to "hard headed" decisions that reflect means-end, input-output, cost-risk-return relationships. When objectives, both general and supporting or specific, are less precisely defined decisions will reflect a value system that is more difficult to interpret.

Objectives and Policies

The term "policy" has a variety of meanings. In some cases it has an ethical connotation; business policy is related to public policy or to value standards of individuals and social groups. Such expressions as, "This is contrary to public policy," or "Business and public policy are in conflict on this point," suggest this connotation.

Individuals often follow policies they have been taught to respect, such as, "Honesty is the best policy," or "Punctuality is sound policy," and the like. In this sense, policies become guides to personal deci-

---

[5] Peter F. Drucker, *The Practice of Management* (New York: Harper & Bros., 1954), p. 63.

sions; they are often used in this sense in the business world. We hear the top management of a business firm referred to as the "policy-making group." This suggests that they lay down general guide lines for decisions throughout the organization.

Sometimes policies and objectives tend to be confused. A business firm may pursue a policy for such a long time that it virtually becomes an objective. For example, a policy of meeting the prices of competitors may be so strong as to become an objective and to subordinate other objectives to it. For our purposes we will consider objectives as goals and policies as guide lines for decisions.

Examples of policies include hiring from within, "plowing back," that is, retaining in the firm and not paying out in dividends, a certain percentage of earnings, spending a certain percentage of sales volume for research and development, and hiring in so far as possible from the local community. Of course, there are many others. Some policies might often be referred to as "working policies," since they relate to very specific operations such as rules governing sick leaves, maintaining central file systems, and others.

Once policies are determined, a number of decisions become more highly standardized than would be the case otherwise. In a sense policies may be thought of as "continuing plans," in that the policies make it unnecessary to start over every time a new problem arises. Old decisions (established policies) govern new decisions that come under their guidance.

Policies are not always spelled out in specific terms. Managers and supervisors below the policy-forming levels often find it necessary to interpret policies. As a result there are sometimes wide differences between the policy that was intended by top management and the actual policy that is followed. Often policies are reviewed from time to time in order to assure that they are working as intended.

In some cases policies are followed for such a long time that they become a part of the thinking of those who apply them. Such policies are hard to change since they acquire a sort of institutional status. In some cases policies evolve from practice and experience and are never established in any formal sense. These policies are extremely difficult to change and are likely to become rather specific guides to decisions.

Objectives and Plans

If we think of objectives as goals, either primary or supporting, then plans may be considered as the first, or at least one of the early steps in undertaking to achieve objectives. For example, we may have for our objective the sale of 25,000 copies of a book. To do this will require a plan, a sort of blueprint for getting this done. Shall we try to sell on a national or a more restricted basis? Shall we try to sell books by means of direct mail, through book stores, or salesmen? Will advertising be used, and if so, how much and in what forms? Many other questions might be raised. A plan would involve the determination of a few of the more promising lines of action, the selection of what is considered the best of these, and then the laying out of a specific program for getting the job done.

Simons says, "The psychological processes involved in planning consist in selecting general criteria of choice, and then particularizing them by application to specific situations."[6] He points out, also, that

FIGURE 8–2

"Lemme see those plans again, Hank!"

Source: *Saturday Evening Post*, May 6, 1961.

---

[6] Herbert A. Simon, *Administrative Behavior* (rev. ed.; New York: Macmillan Co., 1957), p. 99.

the planning procedure tends to be a *compromise* with only the most promising (or "plausible") alternatives worked out in detail.

The criteria of choice are usually provided by the objectives that are to be achieved, the resources available, time limits, environmental conditions, and cost-risk-return relationships. The selection of a plan is a projection, prediction, or postulate of future developments. The selection of one plan, of course, means the exclusion of others, and hence the principle of "opportunity costs," is of major importance in the planning process.[7]

Not only are plans concerned with the future, they are related to programs of action. As we have indicated, a manager is not concerned with the study of a problem from an academic standpoint. He studies a problem in order to take action in regard to it. If he is unable to develop a plan that is based on the knowledge available, he must proceed without adequate knowledge, trusting his best estimate of the situation to carry him through.

In planning managers are concerned primarily with *people*. Other things, materials, the place of business, money, time, and the like are also involved, but it is the people, the relationships between them, and the ways in which people use the resources available that finally count in determining the success or failure of a management program.

Steps in Management Planning

The process of management planning is similar to planning in other fields. If you are taking a vacation trip, you decide first where you want to go, that is, you determine your objective, and then lay out a plan to get there. You will have to decide whether to travel by car, plane, train, or boat; whether you are going to travel at a leisurely pace or get to your destination as rapidly as possible; whether others will be included in the trip; how long you are going to be away; how much money you will budget for this purpose; and decide other related matters in advance of beginning your trip.

This is a simple illustration of the planning process. Similarly, the manager of a business firm or of one or another division of a firm develops plans in order to accomplish the objectives that have been established. As we have suggested planning always involves the selection of a line of action among various alternatives.

A management plan may be simple or complex; it may be of short or long duration; it may be designed to achieve a primary or a sup-

---

[7] See our discussion of opportunity costs in Chapter 5.

porting objective. In short, a management plan is a blueprint or a "road map" indicating how a management objective is to be achieved. It is a *program of action* since its ultimate purpose is to achieve an objective. A plan is developed in order to reduce or to anticipate risks, to specify some choices in advance of action, to specify delegation of authority, and related purposes.

The development of a plan may be illustrated by a series of questions.[8] First, "What is to be done?" Stated in another way, this question means that the objective has to be defined carefully before a plan can be made. Then certain lines of action will be selected which are designed to achieve the objective or the desired results.

Second, "Where is the action to take place?" For example, it is necessary to determine whether the program involves a single location or a number of locations, whether available plant facilities will be adequate, whether special transportation or communication problems may be involved, and related problems.

Third, "When is the action to take place?" Specific problems of timing are often involved in management, and the necessity of action in a short time may require quite a different plan than would result if no time pressures were present. Also, it is necessary to decide whether special scheduling problems have to be considered; that is, whether one line of action has to precede another or whether several programs can be carried forward simultaneously.

Fourth, "Who will carry the plan into effect?" It is necessary to consider the special abilities that may be required, the training or retraining programs that may be needed for the personnel who will be involved in the process, the additional people who may need to be hired, or the possibility of transferring personnel from another phase of the operation to the program under consideration.

Fifth, "How will the action be carried out?" This question, of course, is a very broad one and includes the determination of the specific methods which will be followed in carrying out the action. For example, it is necessary to determine how the available people, materials, and know-how will be organized or put together to best advantage. The division of the total effort will have to be decided.

Costs are always an important factor. Relationships between costs and estimated *returns* and between costs and possible *risks* are almost always considered in advance. Specific problems and arrangements must be considered, such as whether certain contracts will have to be

---

8 See, for example, George R. Terry, *Principles of Management* (3rd ed.; Homewood, Ill.: Richard D. Irwin, Inc., 1960), p. 131.

negotiated in advance, or whether the permission of a regulating authority is necessary.

A manager considers a plan as a general strategy that he will follow. He may also try to estimate in advance the actions that are likely to be taken by competitors, or the effect of the plan that is being developed on the programs of competitors. Every management plan tries to anticipate as many problems as possible and to develop solutions in advance. Basic questions in planning center around objectives, the resources available, and the methods and the procedures that may be used to advantage in the attainment of the objectives.

The plan of campaign of a military commander differs only in degree from a management plan. The military commander has an objective. He has certain resources of men, materials, equipment, and know-how available to him, and he makes use of the most effective technical and strategic methods for employing these resources in attaining his objective. You have undoubtedly heard or read about military campaigns in which a military commander shifted from plan "A" to plan "B." Typically a military commander sets up alternative plans for achieving his objectives and changes the plan as required to meet the situation in which the action is taking place. Typically there is a plan for attack, a plan for holding operations, and a plan for retreat involved in each military action that is undertaken. There may also be modifications of each of these broad plans.

Advantages of Planning

Planning by business managers, military commanders, or the directors of other organizations forces careful advance consideration of the operations or the action that lies ahead. Thus, requirements in terms of man power, materials, machinery, equipment, money, space, legal arrangements, insurance, government regulations, community and public relations, sales effort, market potentials, competitive position, and the like are anticipated in so far as possible in advance as a result of careful planning. As we have indicated, potential problems are anticipated as well, and in so far as possible, solutions or alternative solutions are worked out in advance. The necessity of synchronizing certain phases of the operation is considered, and time sequences for various phases of programs are worked out. Similarly, methods of organization are laid out in advance and relationships between parts of the organization are planned.

Some business managers do not undertake to establish *formal* plans and may not be aware of the extent to which they are developing plans in advance. This was especially true in earlier periods of our history when business operations were less complicated than is typical today. Management planning has been given increasing attention, however, in recent years.

Types of Plans

Just as we distinguished between primary or basic and supporting objectives, we may differentiate between primary and supporting plans. The primary or basic or master plans may be related to primary objectives and supporting plans to supporting objectives, but this is not necessarily the case. Lines of distinction are not easy to draw. A plan designed to support a primary objective may also help in the achievement of a supporting objective.

It is important for us to recognize, however, that a "master plan" may have many parts, each of which is intended to support the master or primary plan in some way. Plans may be divided and subdivided as necessary to develop blueprints for the actions that are decided upon.

To return to our previous illustration, we may have developed a master plan for the sale of 25,000 books. In all probability, however, it will be necessary to develop specific plans for selling 1,000 or even 100 books.

Plans may be classified in other ways than breadth; for example, there are single use and standing plans.[9] Plans may pertain to specific functions and operations such as marketing, production, and financial programs.

Marketing plans often control other aspects of planning since sales estimates frequently are the first step in developing plans for an ensuing period of operations. Plans are used to indicate probable costs of securing necessary resources and using them in operations. For example, plans may be developed for personnel procurement, training and development programs, employee compensation, equipment purchases and replacement, establishing new locations, expanding existing space, research and development programs, production programs and schedules, maintenance of buildings and equipment, and for many other aspects of a business firm's operations.

Budgets as Plans

Since business objectives and the cost of achieving them usually are stated in financial terms, many plans are of a financial nature. In large

---

[9] See Preston P. LeBriton and Dale A. Henning, *Planning Theory* (Englewood Cliffs, N.J.: Prentice-Hall, Inc., 1961), p. 9.

corporations the finance committee often has the primary responsibility for the development of over-all or master plans. The financial *budget* probably is the most widely used type of management plan. We discuss this subject in greater detail in Chapter 12. We should note here, however, that a budget is a financial plan which forecasts probable income from the anticipated income sources, probable expenses by major items of expense, and the anticipated profit that may be earned at the end of a period, usually a year hence. A budget usually is broken down to show estimates for subdivisions of a firm's operations, with all parts carefully interrelated. At the end of a period of operations budgets are compared with actual results and thus serve also as a *control* device. Good planning arrangements typically make provision for controls through review and appraisal of performance and comparison with plans.

Budgets have formed the basis for constructing models to show the interrelationships between the various parts of a firm's anticipated incomes, costs, and profits. Some models may become very complex, based on complicated sets of mathematical relationships. The computer, of course, has made possible the use of much more complicated models for management-planning purposes than were possible prior to its use.

Various *formulas* are sometimes developed to reflect basic relationships between the various divisions of a firm's operations. They are often of substantial assistance in managerial planning. For example, the so-called "Dupont formula" has been used widely for planning and related purposes.[10] We consider this and related topics at greater length later in our discussions.

Marketing and Production Factors in Planning

As we suggested above, many business plans begin with a consideration of current and potential markets. Studies and analyses are made of the market potential for the product or products in which the firm deals or plans to deal. The position of present and prospective competitors is analyzed along with potential strengths and weaknesses of such competitors. Efforts are made to determine how many units of a product can be sold and under what conditions.

For example, suppose a company is considering the desirability of introducing a new breakfast cereal. Present products will be studied in terms of their relative success, price ranges, extent of advertising

---

[10] T. C. Davis, "How the Dupont Organization Appraises Its Performance," *Financial Management Series No. 94* (New York: American Management Assn., 1950).

support, and market position. Consumer surveys may be conducted to determine likes and dislikes relative to current products and to find out whether a new cereal might be welcomed. On the basis of such studies it may be possible to determine the character of a new cereal that might be marketed, the price at which it would have to be sold to attain a certain volume, and the share of the market that might be captured. Information of this type would provide the basis for determining whether the managers of this firm wished to carry their plans further.

If the prospects appear to be encouraging, studies will be made to determine whether the new breakfast cereal can be produced at costs that will provide at least a reasonable opportunity to gain revenues in excess of costs. Does the firm have the facilities, manpower, and know-how required or can these be obtained at costs that are favorable relative to sales prices? Distribution channels will be studied; advertising budgets estimated. Analyses of this type will proceed to a determination of the financing that will be necessary to secure the equipment, personnel, materials, and other resources necessary to proceed.

Thus, management planning encompasses every aspect of a business firm's operations. Even after a product has been introduced and enjoyed some success, further planning will be required to determine whether the product may be changed so as to capture more of the market, production problems related to such decisions, and the financial feasibility of proceeding with such plans.

Time Factors

Plans almost always are confined to definite *time limits*. A given objective usually is stated as applying to a specific time period and plans are made to fit such limitations. As you have often heard, "Time is money," and this is especially true in business. Because time is money, and cannot be recaptured, careful planning often pays big dividends.

Beyond general time limits, certain operations must coincide in time; one item is needed in advance of another; goods must be moved from warehouses to stores before they can be sold; people must be trained before they can fill certain jobs; and numerous other illustrations could be added.

Planning is concerned not only with time but *timing*. A new product is scheduled for the market in the spring rather than the fall because this is considered to be the best time for its appearance; or a new product is rescheduled to make its appearance earlier because a competitor is bringing out a similar product and it is considered desirable to beat him to the market.

Major Characteristics of Planning

Planning is one of the creative parts of the manager's job. It requires imagination and vision. The manager tries to project his program into the future, in short, to estimate what must be done, when, where, how, and by whom.

Frequently, it is impossible to anticipate all of the kinds of problems that may develop. That is why alternative plans are often made or why it is necessary to modify original plans as a program is carried forward. Since planning deals with the future, predictions or postulates as to future developments are set up, making use of as much knowledge and information as can be made available. Current trends of development are considered, past experience is studied, available information is analyzed, and past performance of various elements in the organization are considered.

As the authors of one well-known book in the field have pointed out, "Planning is to a large extent the job of making things happen that would not otherwise occur."[11] Planning also helps to make things happen in proper sequence as we have suggested.

Some of the essential characteristics of management planning are included in the following list:

1. Objectives are paramount. Plans that neglect consideration of objectives might as well not be made. Indeed, it is impossible to plan without reference to objectives.
2. To be effective, plans must be readily understandable by all who have responsibility for carrying them out.
3. Plans should be flexible. Business conditions, competition, governmental regulations, and other factors often change rapidly, hence flexibility is essential.
4. Planning deals with the future, hence always involves forecasts or postulates as to the future.
5. Time is an essential element of all planning processes.
6. Plans must be worked out within given cost, return, and risk limitations as well as the limits of available or obtainable resources.
7. Planning typically involves *organized* effort and action.
8. Good management plans include provisions for adequate control.
9. The planning process is continuous.

In summary, plans deal with the possible, with what can be done with the resources available in given time limits and under anticipated competitive and regulatory conditions. Plans are used to aid in the

---

11 Harold Koontz and Cyril O'Donnell, *Principles of Management* (New York: McGraw-Hill Book Co., Inc., 1955), p. 429.

accomplishment of a business firm's objectives at every stage and level of its operations. We will refer to management planning frequently in ensuing discussions of various resources and their uses, marketing and production activities, the management of income, and the adaptations of operations to the environment of the firm.

Review and Control

As we have suggested the processes of planning and control often are closely interrelated. Plans indicate reasonable hopes, review and control processes indicate the extent to which the hopes were realized. Plans are often developed in such a way as to facilitate reporting on operations, review of performance, and control of operations in accordance with plans, or if necessary the modification of plans, or the objectives they are intended to achieve. Control is a process of determining through observation, measurement, reporting, and analysis whether the organization is carrying out operations in accordance with plans and whether standards of performance are being met.

To illustrate the management process of controlling, we may use a football analogy. After a game has started, the coach may find that the center is not performing satisfactorily and will send in a substitute. Or an assistant coach may report that a halfback is not discharging a blocking assignment. The coach may take the halfback out of play briefly and try to explain the errors.

It must be recognized that no manager can control past actions. By means of reviews and controls of various types, however, the manager knows whether operations have proceeded in accordance with plans, and if they have not, he undertakes to change them so that they will conform to established plans in the future. Thus, *control is forward looking* in the same manner that managerial planning and organizing are forward looking.

In some cases controls will indicate that a plan is not workable and must be changed. They may indicate also that a particular objective is not attainable within the resources available to management. Thus, controls aid in the process of establishing objectives, of developing plans, and of organizing the effort of the firm.

Steps in the Control Process

As Koontz and O'Donnell have pointed out, three steps are involved in the control process. "1. The establishment of standards. 2. The ap-appraisal of performance. 3. The correction of deviations."[12]

---

12 *Ibid.,* p. 550.

The standards, of course, are basically the objectives of the company's program. Objectives, however, must be translated into operational and measurable terms, that is, into standards in order to serve

FIGURE 8–3

"And *I* thought *you* were looking after the vacation schedule."

Source: *Wall Street Journal* (by permission of Cartoon Features Syndicate).

control purposes. Standards may be quantitative or qualitative. They may be stated in such terms as costs, rates of return on investment, profits, relationships between sales and inventories, and in other ways. On the other hand, standards may be of a very general type, such as the desire for a spirit of co-operation among the members of an organization, or high morale, or good public relations, any of which are very difficult of measurement because of the inability of establishing standards that are very precise. Nevertheless, managers must undertake to measure them in whatever manner is available, even though these may require very rough approximations at times. One of the more important control devices is the budget as we suggested in our discussions earlier in this chapter. The budget may be of a financial type, or there may be budgets for space, personnel, equipment, or others. They represent anticipated results of operations. Financial budgets are probably used more widely than any others by business managers.

Appraisal of performance, of course, means the comparison of operations with the standards that have been established. Cost standards are frequently developed by the accounting department of a firm. Quotas may be set up for the sales force. Performance is measured against standards of this kind. Quantitative measures are very helpful in making appraisals of performance because of their rather precise character.

Correcting deviations, the third phase of the control process, involves a review of management decisions. A manager may decide that the standards are not proper and that new ones need to be developed, or he may decide that goals are unattainable or that the established goals are too easy to attain. If he determines that the standards are fair and that appraisals are accurate, action must be taken to bring operations into line with the established plans and standards. This may require disciplinary action, the retraining of employees, the firing of some employees and the hiring of others, the use of better materials, the installation of improved machinery and equipment, or many other possible lines of action.

Most managers undertake to find strategic control points in order to expedite the process of carrying out operations in accordance with plans. These strategic control points will vary widely with the kind of firm and with the type of operations that may be involved. Usually, however, they center at points where information can be secured and corrections can be made at least cost, both in terms of efforts and consequences.

SUMMARY

Business objectives center around profits. For most business firms, profit maximization in the long run represents the primary objective, and profits are the primary measure of their success.

Controversies over profits include the following: (1) whether profits are maximized or if "reasonable" profits are often the goal, or as Simon suggests, "satisficing" rather than maximizing; (2) whether service or profit objectives should be paramount; and (3) whether private pursuit of profit serves the public interest; plus others.

The attainment of such objectives as survival, growth, or the achievement of a prestige position depends on the firm's ability to make profits, at least over the long run. Often objectives are stated in terms of achieving sales that represent a certain percentage of the market, or of making a stated return on investment, either owners' or equity investment, or total investment, including borrowed funds. Sometimes the attainment of a certain position in an industry is set up as an objective. In general, these are alternative ways of stating profit objectives and are closely related to profit maximizing in the long run.

Objectives, regardless of how stated, serve as major guides to management decisions. The concept of "management by objectives" is widely accepted. The same objectives may be variously interpreted or may call forth different types of programs in different firms, as for example, the contrast between the programs of Montgomery Ward and Sears, Roebuck following World War II.

Policies are typically based on objectives and serve as continuing or standing guides to supporting decisions. Thus, certain old decisions may be thought of as established policies which in turn govern new decisions.

Plans may be thought of as the most plausible of the various alternatives available for achieving objectives. Selection of plans depends on the objectives desired, resources available, time limits, and cost-risk-return relationships. Plans may be primary or supporting in nature, relate to the entire operation of a firm or to a specific part. Plans are future oriented and typically relate to programs of action. They may be thought of as blueprints or "roadmaps" leading toward objectives. Management planning often begins with a determination of market potential and the competitive position of the firm. Often budgets are used as a major planning device.

Controls are closely related to plans; for example, a budget may be used both for planning and control purposes. If plans indicate reasonable hopes, review and control processes indicate the extent to which such hopes have been realized. The major steps in the control process include (1) the establishment of standards, (2) appraisal of performance in the light of such standards, and (3) making corrections and adjustments in standards or programs of performance as required.

QUESTIONS AND PROBLEMS

1. Do business firms try to maximize profits? Do you think profit maximization is a desirable objective of business firms?

2. What does Professor Simon mean by suggesting that firms try to "satisfice" rather than maximize?

3. Comment on this statement by Joel Dean: "A business firm is an organization designed to make profits, and profits are the primary measure of its success."

4. Compare and contrast such objectives as survival, growth, and attainment of a prestige position. Are such objectives interrelated? Does their achievement depend on the making of profits?

5. Are the objectives of a business firm likely to change over time? Give examples.

6. Explain how business objectives serve as management decision guides. What is meant by the phrase "management by objectives?"

7. Give examples of management policies. How are policies related to objectives? To supporting decisions?

8. To what extent are plans related to objectives?

9. Explain this statement: ". . . the planning procedure tends to be a *compromise* with only the most promising (or 'plausible') alternatives worked out in detail."

10. Assume that you are assigned the task of planning a meeting for alumni after the homecoming game. Outline the major steps you would take in developing your plan.

11. Explain how budgets may be used as plans.

12. Why do many business plans often begin with a consideration of current and potential markets?

13. What is meant by the statement: "The planning process is continuous."

14. Explain how controls are related to plans.

15. What are the major steps in the control and review process.

16. In connection with the planning steps you established in your answer to question 10 above, indicate how you might set up controls for this meeting.

SUGGESTED READINGS

DEAN, JOEL. *Managerial Economics*. Englewood Cliffs, N.J.: Prentice-Hall, Inc., 1951. Read pages 3–12 dealing with the nature of profits.

DRUCKER, PETER F. *The Practice of Management*. New York: Harper & Bros., 1954. Read especially chap. 7, "The Objectives of Business," and chap. 11, "Management by Objectives and Self Control," of this widely used book.

LONG, JOHN D. *Workbook to Accompany Weimer: Business Administration: An Introductory Management Approach,* chap. 8. Rev. ed. Homewood, Ill., Richard D. Irwin, Inc., 1962.

OUTLINE FOR CHAPTER 9

ORGANIZATION AND LEADERSHIP are among the major functions of the manager.

Organization is undertaken to achieve the objectives of the firm through effective use of human and nonhuman resources.

Organization usually makes provision for
  division of work,
  structuring of authority and decision-making, and
  developing sound working relationships among the people involved.

Division of work provides for
    specialization,
    economy of effort, and
    efficiency of input-output ratios.

Organization structure usually is based on authority relationships; formal or official framework often is set forth in organization charts based on several models, such as
      line, line and staff,
      and line, staff, and functional arrangements.

"Informal" organization often is revealed through analysis of organization behavior, including
        small-group behavior, large-group behavior,
        group dynamics, effects of roles,
        motivations, conflicts, "inside" and
          "outside" relationships.

The manager directs and co-ordinates activities of members of the organization through a variety of methods.

Leadership relates to all phases of the manager's role.
  Variation found in type and degree as between
      critical and routine decisions,
      institutional and interpersonal leadership.

Theories and explanations of leadership include those related to
        traits, situations,
        leader-follower relations,
        human relations,
        management by objectives, and others.

All involve power-influence relationships and ability to adapt to change.

ORGANIZATION AND LEADERSHIP

Socially as well as individually organization is essential to growth; beyond a certain point there cannot be further growth without further organization.

—HERBERT SPENCER

Relation of Plans to Organization

In the preceding chapter we considered business objectives, plans, and controls, pointing out that objectives defined goals, plans indicated programs for their achievement, and controls measured the degree of success in attaining established goals and indicated required adjustments. We suggested that policies might be thought of as established guides to management decisions, or as general decisions that set the outside boundaries for subsequent decisions. We move on now to consider the organization of resources that may be required to attain established objectives. Of course, in a small business firm it is often possible to proceed with virtually no systematic organization at all; for most business enterprises, however, the organization of the available resources or those that can be made available is given careful consideration.

In a sense, organizations are extensions of plans. We must be concerned with the establishment of a plan for organization before we can develop a fully staffed and operating enterprise. Plans indicate the types and amounts of resources that are likely to be needed to reach established goals as well as the general nature, size, and type of organization that may be required. After an organization is once set up, of course, it tends to limit the kinds of plans that may be made, since it is often easier to start *de novo* than to adapt from an existing and operating enterprise. The establishment of one organization is accomplished at the expense of others that might have been set up. This is another illustration of the principle of "opportunity costs."

Organizations and Teams

Organizations are not completely new to you since you have been a part of several. For example, a family is a type of organization, as are clubs, teams, and student groups. Some business firms, especially smaller ones, may be organized on a basis that is little more formal than that of a club or team. As firms grow larger, however, working relationships between members of the organization are needed, as well as arrangements for co-ordinating decisions and for dividing and assigning the work. The larger the business firm, the more complex its organizational arrangements tend to become. In large firms problems of bureaucracy often appear since their organizations tend to become formal and relatively inflexible.

Organization may be illustrated by a team, for example, a football team. The members of the team are assigned specific duties; their decisions are controlled in the interest of a unified effort; authority and responsibility are carefully assigned. The captain or quarterback has authority to select plays, and the members of the team accept his decisions. Plays are worked out in advance and each member of the team has an assignment which is co-ordinated with that of the others. Specialization is possible; one member of the team may develop his passing ability, another blocking, another kicking, and so on. The coach supervises and controls activity by spotting and correcting errors, substituting players, and making changes in the pattern of play. He may delegate greater or lesser authority to the captain or quarterback.

As a result of organized action, a football team is much more effective than would be the case if each of the eleven members of the team followed his own decisions and inclinations. This illustration suggests several important characteristics of organizations. Team effort takes from the individual a part of his freedom to make decisions and requires him to conform to decisions of the organization. Organizational decisions are concentrated in so far as possible, with authority centered in the coach, captain, or quarterback. Members of the team accept this authority. Training and practice develop habit and thought patterns that bring desired responses. Loyalty to the team effort is developed. Work assignments are made, specialization is made possible, proficiency in particular tasks can be developed. Patterns of play are designed in advance to co-ordinate efforts.

We may adapt many of these concepts to business organizations. Managers have the task of planning and designing the organizations, staffing them and securing the necessary people and other resources to make them into "going concerns." They also have important jobs of determining authority and responsibility relationships, developing loyalties, dividing and co-ordinating efforts, and doing many related things, as we shall see.

A good general definition of organization has been provided by Ernest Dale. He says, " 'Organization,' as used by organization specialists, may be defined as a method of breaking down broad and overwhelming tasks into manageable and pinpointed responsibilities and at the same time insuring coordination of the work."[1]

Purpose of Organization

From the standpoint of the business manager the main reason for establishing an organization is to achieve the objectives of the firm. This requires that he maximize in so far as possible the efforts of the people who make it up; that is, to increase their productivity or output per man-hour or dollar's worth of income relative to dollar's worth of cost. As we have seen, the eleven men on a football team operating in an organized manner have a great deal more power than eleven unorganized individuals. The same thing is true of business organizations, or for that matter of political organizations or organizations in other areas. Thus, the manager of a business firm in effect is creating power, and will create greater or lesser degrees of power, depending upon the effectiveness with which he organizes his work force and the equipment, materials, and other things with which the members of the organization work.

The ways in which a manager will undertake to maximize the efforts of his organization will vary with the personnel in it, the specific objective that is to be achieved, the time available, and the place or places within which the operation is to take place. No single organizational plan is best. In some cases division of work will be stressed, in others the roles of people in the firm. Sometimes work will be organized around people rather than people being filled into work assignments.

When carried out effectively, good organization results in careful division of work, definition of authority, the fixing of responsibility, and balanced and co-ordinated effort. Thus, a good organization will take advantage of the special capacities, interests, personal character-

---

[1] Ernest Dale, *The Great Organizers* (New York: McGraw-Hill Book Co., Inc., 1960), p. 2.

istics, and special talents represented by the people in it. Advantage will also be taken of the material resources available and any special strategic advantages that may be enjoyed.

Resource Organization

Organization involves all of the resources that are available for use or can be made available for use by a business firm in attempting to attain its objectives. The least specialized resource in the sense that it can be used for the widest variety of purposes is money. As we have suggested, financial considerations bulk large in most business decisions; the general nature of money as a resource is one reason why this is the case. Money is expended in order to hire people, and to buy or rent space, equipment, machines, land, materials, and other resources. All of these resources, human and nonhuman, must be put together in some manner. In some cases one man may arrange everything on an informal basis, even in fairly sizable enterprises. As we pointed out in Chapter 3, this is sometimes called "Caesar organization," since one strong man, often the founder of the firm, runs everything.[2] Sometimes such arrangements work out fairly well. Usually, however, as firms attain larger size, more formal organizational arrangements are necessary. Typically organization makes provision for the following:

1. Division of work.
2. Structuring of authority and decision making.
3. Developing sound working relationships among the people involved.

In terms of division of work, the kinds of equipment, space, machines, and other physical resources that are available or can be made available often are of major importance. Their location may be controlling in regard to how geographic divisions of the firm's operations may be made. The type of equipment may dictate the backgrounds and training of some of the people who will be hired, or the special training programs that may have to be established. As we shall see in Chapter 16 the types of equipment, machines, and other aids to productivity provided by a firm add greatly to its efficiency and have an important bearing on its successful operation. Similarly in Chapter 17 we give additional attention to factors of location and the work place.

In addition, the types of work involved, whether largely manufacturing, retailing, or service activities, may have an important bearing on the way work is divided for organizational purposes. Some types of work require more detailed supervision than others, for example.

---

[2] See for example, *ibid.*, p. 11.

Important as these considerations may be, most organizational problems tend to center around *people* and the relationships among them. Authority relationships need to be defined and understood. Typically, a hierarchy of decisions, ranging from the critical to the routine, must be established. The decisions and efforts of people in the organization require direction and co-ordination. To accomplish these things and others related to them the organization is often given a formal structure, which shows who reports to whom, and who has responsibility for what decisions. This provides a structure and a sort of legal framework for the organization.

People typically, however, do not usually fit themselves into neat patterns as indicated in formal organization structures (often set forth in organization charts). The behavior of people in an organization may not conform to what is expected by the organization plan, or may conform only in part. In some cases people may develop working relationships among themselves. The people in a firm usually have many loyalties outside the firm to family, friends, and other organizations. Factors of this type emphasize what we have stressed at many points: a business firm is a social (and to a degree a political), as well as an economic, institution. Managers must consider matters of this type in developing organization arrangements.

In addition, we should stress again that business firms do not operate in a vacuum. They are influenced by their environment in many ways, not the least of which is the impact of environment on organization arrangements. Degree of regulation or competition often is important. A unionized plant may be organized somewhat differently from one that is not unionized. A firm operating on a world-wide basis may have a different organization from one that operates entirely in this country. A multinational firm does business under varying political and economic systems. And many other illustrations might be added.

Division of Work

The achievement of most business objectives requires effort of one type or another. Such effort is most likely to be successful if it is organized, and one way to do this is to break down the effort into parts, develop working arrangements among these parts, assign people to specific efforts, and co-ordinate the whole effort. This may be done very informally as in the case of several people trying to move some heavy object such as a piano. It is done more carefully if a team is organized with certain workers specializing in one type of assignment and others in different types. In a large business firm work divisions typically are made with great care.

Division of work has a number of advantages. The people in a specific assignment can learn how to do it well. Specialized machines may be developed to do specific jobs. Division of work leads to economy of effort and to efficiency of input-output relationships.

The work of a business firm may be organized around: (1) basic functions, such as production or marketing; (2) products, for example a refrigerator division, a television division, and others; (3) locations, such as plants located in different cities; (4) markets, with division into regional, state, and local areas or by clientele; or (5) processes, for example, stages in manufacturing.[3] Various combinations of the foregoing divisions may also be used. In some situations, typically smaller companies, the organization may be built around the interests and abilities of key personnel. This tends to result in a less formal type of organizational structure, but may be effective until the firm attains larger size. Military organizations are highly formalized structures. Political organizations typically are somewhat less formal than business or military organizations. Government agencies, however, more nearly resemble business firms in organizational arrangements, although differences in purpose often bring about some variation.

Organization Structure

As we suggested, it is not enough in most situations to divide the work; relationships as to authority for decisions also are essential. In small organizations this may be done by requiring the production manager and marketing manager to report to the president or executive vice-president, with production superintendents or department managers reporting to the production manager, and supervisors to them; in turn the sales, advertising, and market research managers would report to the marketing manager. In larger organizations the arrangements tend to be more complicated. This is especially true of the large multiproduct, multinational enterprises.

Whether the firm is large or small, however, some sort of structure usually is necessary. It may vary greatly from firm to firm. While some general principles of organization structure have been worked out, business firms are highly dynamic establishments and their organization structures often are highly varied, rather than conforming to standard patterns. For example, there is the "unity of command"

---

[3] Ernest Dale, *Planning and Developing the Company Organization Structure*, Research Report No. 20 (New York: American Management Association, 1952), p. 25.

principle, that each man should have only one person to whom to report. This works in some situations, does not in others. "Span of control" is often emphasized. Generally this means that no more than five or six persons report to one superior. Again there are wide variations; indeed, the trend seems to be in the direction of a much wider span of control. The "scalar" principle is often stressed. This means that subordinates communicate with top executives only through their superiors. For example, the market research manager would report to the president only through the marketing manager. But the following of the scalar principle often leads to highly rigid operations.

Organizational structure usually is based on authority relationships. Usually a hierarchy of decisions is created, with top managers having the broadest latitude and middle managers and supervisors making decisions in a more restricted framework. Orders resulting from decisions are communicated, usually through regular "channels," that is, from superior to subordinate, who in turn has accountability and responsibility for reporting back the results.

Organization structures are illustrated by "organization charts," which usually indicate by relative position the authority relationships that exist, as well as reflecting some types of work divisions. An organization chart may be thought of as a map outlining the main features of an organization's structure. Several types are illustrated in the following discussion.

Organization structure helps to assure that different parts of the organization will not be making decisions that are in conflict, that all decisions and actions will dovetail together so that resources will be used effectively and in accordance with plans designed to achieve the desired results. The structure of an organization also provides an official framework as we have suggested. It indicates the points at which authority and responsibility reside. If conflicts arise, a sound organizational structure often helps to resolve them.

Effective organization structures usually have some flexibility, more than is apparent from a review of organization charts or organization manuals. Such flexibility is often indicated by the extent to which an organization structure can accommodate the "informal" organizations which often grow up around it, as we shall see.

Organization Types and Patterns

Various organization types and patterns may be distinguished. We outline several of those rather generally found in business firms in the following discussion. It should be noted, however, that many variations from these types may be found. Perhaps the type of organization most widely encountered is the "line" type. In this type of arrangement the chief executive directs his assistants who may have responsibility for certain specific phases of the operation, and each assistant, in turn, directs others who are responsible to him. Figure 9–1 illustrates this type of organization. It is a relatively simple arrangement. There are no questions regarding the "chain of command," and each person understands exactly to whom he is responsible for the performance of the duties which have been assigned to him.

FIGURE 9–1

Illustrative Line Organization

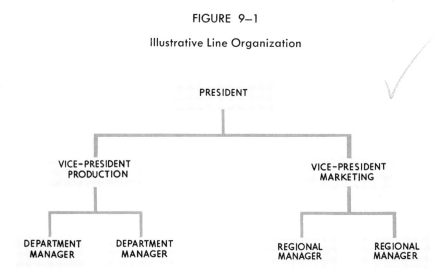

A *line and staff* organization represents a combination of line relationships plus advisory or technical relationships. Direct lines of authority are laid down, but provision is made for "staff" assignments which are advisory or technical in nature. A legal counsel or a public relations counsel may function in this capacity and be on the staff of the chief executive, while at the same time there will be a manager for sales or marketing and a manager of production, who are in a line relationship to the chief executive officer. It is often helpful to distinguish between a function and the person or department responsible for that function. An illustration of this type of organization is presented in Figure 9–2.

Some business firms make use of "functional" relationships as well as those described in "line" and in "line and staff" arrangements. In functional arrangements staff personnel have program authority, for example, supervision of programs for research and development, or

FIGURE 9-2

Illustrative Line and Staff Organization

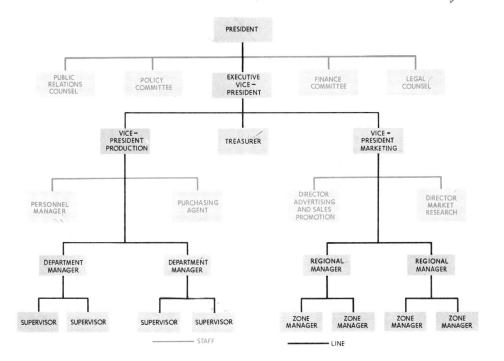

personnel, or other programs of a specialized nature. A division manager makes use of personnel; the activities of the personnel manager may be co-ordinated in part by the vice-president for personnel and in part by the division manager. This type of arrangement is illustrated in Figure 9-3. It makes provision for special emphasis on a particular function, for example in Figure 9-3 on personnel and research. In the case of personnel, for example, national contracts with unions may require careful central co-ordination and direction of a type that could not ordinarily be provided through a division manager.

In some cases committees are used, especially in larger organizations, to provide staff assistance or to serve in a functional capacity, for example, in research and development. In large firms the finance committee is often an important part of the organizational arrangement.

Working Relationships among People

As we have suggested, people do not always follow the predetermined structure of an organization. Many informal working relation-

FIGURE 9–3

Illustrative Line, Staff, and Functional Organization

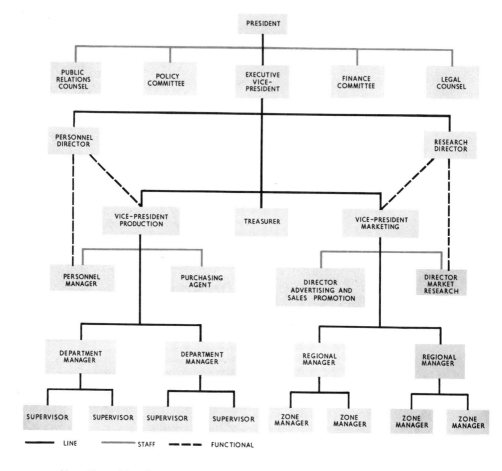

Note: The position of Treasurer will differ in various organizations (this would also be true of the other positions).

ships tend to develop. The marketing research director may play golf with the executive vice-president fairly frequently; business matters may be discussed and the marketing manager to whom the marketing research director would normally report, may be bypassed as a result. Or several production supervisors may lunch together several times a week; they may find that their operations can be co-ordinated more effectively through informal discussions than through formal staff meetings.

People behave much the same way in business firms as they do in other aspects of their lives. They do not follow set patterns. They may take on certain special types of behavior because they are cast in certain roles, but they do this also when taking on the role of chairman of a school board or some other community responsibility.

At some levels of the operations of a business firm people will react against detailed direction; at others they may desire it. Some people welcome the opportunity to make decisions; others prefer not to have such responsibility.

Informal gossip, "the grapevine," may be a more effective means of communicating with various members of the organization than directives, orders, or interoffice memoranda. Effective managers recognize the significance of informal means of communication and often use them to make more formal means effective.

As one writer has pointed out:

> In contrast to organization structure, organization behavior (or performance) represents the patterns of human behavior that take place within the framework of the structure. The performance tells us how things do or do not get done and includes the interpersonal relations, communications, influences, and patterns of co-operation and conflict. Thus organization structure gives us the official or prescribed conduct, and organizational behavior represents the activities as they really are.[4]

In recent years increasing attention has been given to studies of small-group behavior, "group dynamics," and related topics. As a result knowledge about the working relationships among people in organizations has expanded and has been put to effective use by managers. Also, studies of the behavior of people in larger groups have provided increasing knowledge for the guidance of business managers. Considerable attention has been given to the roles that people are called upon to play by their positions in an organization and the effect that this may have on their behavior and their working relationships with others. Increasing attention has also been given to the *motivations* of various members of an organization and the means available to managers to increase total effort through proper motivation.

All of this is not to suggest that the working relations between people in an organization are left to chance. We mean to emphasize the importance of recognizing that special attention must be given to informal arrangements in making a more formally structured organization work in practice. The main purpose is to develop working arrangements among the people in an organization that will be as

---

[4] Carroll L. Shartle, *Executive Performance and Leadership* (Englewood Cliffs, N.J.: Prentice-Hall, Inc., 1956), p. 5.

effective as possible in attaining established goals. Many people in a business firm have personal objectives that are far removed from those of the business organization; often they think of their association with the firm as temporary; in some cases their attitudes may even be hostile. Orientation and training programs, expanding opportunities, a chance to participate directly or indirectly in the activities of the firm, provision for settling disputes before they erupt into difficult problems, and many related activities are often required to make an organization work in practice.

All of this requires a broad understanding of human behavior on the part of managers. People cannot be treated as automatons (except perhaps in military service, and even here this is questionable) if good performance is to be achieved. Somehow the people in the organization must be motivated to carry out the decisions and to perform their functions as effectively as possible.

An organization that is able to survive for very long usually has a substantial number of people whose loyalties and interests are sufficiently identified with the organization to sustain it. In such cases a stability of working relationships has developed through the organization. In the early stages of an organization's life it is vulnerable to the possibility that a sufficient number of key people may quit their jobs in a short space of time to deal it a heavy blow from which it may not recover. Late in an organization's life so many members may take things for granted that it may lose whatever dynamic qualities it once had.

"Inside" and "Outside" Relationships

As we have suggested the people in an organization have various relationships with those outside it. They are members of families, churches, clubs, lodges, unions, political parties, and other organizations. In some cases their outside affiliations may conflict with their loyalties to the firm and its programs.

In setting up or operating an organization the manager recognizes these types of relationships. If he wants an organization that will function and survive for a long time, he needs to provide the incentives, working relationships and arrangements, and opportunities that will cause people to put forth their best efforts rather than give a half-hearted performance or be antagonistic to the organization.

An employee of a firm may have various relations with it other than as an employee. He may be a customer. He may own stock in it. He and his boss may belong to the same church group. His wife may be a good friend of his boss's wife. And so on.

A business organization, thus, cannot be thought of as something distinct and apart from its general environment. It has to be fitted into a number of political and social as well as economic relationships. It must be able to withstand the competition of other business firms in the same line of business. It needs connections with bankers, investors, and suppliers as well as with customers. It needs to be able to work with regulatory agencies, unions, and other types of groups. Above all, it must attract and hold customers.

Organizations in Operation

We have outlined the general nature of organizations and some of the types of arrangements that may be set up for utilizing to advantage human and nonhuman resources in the pursuit of objectives. Many of the more interesting aspects of organizations arise when we view them as "going concerns." When an organization is in operation the activities of the people in it must be directed and co-ordinated. Also operations must be controlled, that is, reviewed and appraised to determine whether established plans are being followed, whether objectives can be attained, or whether decisions need to be revised. We consider these aspects of the manager's work here briefly and also some of the leadership phases of management.

When an organization is in operation there is a constant flow of activity of many types. People are being selected, hired, trained, assigned to duties, and their work relationships established. Their work is evaluated. They are promoted, reassigned, or fired. Old equipment is being replaced by new from time to time, and people are trained to use the new equipment. New markets are being opened up, new products introduced, old products improved. Locations of plants and stores may be changed. Many of these and related topics are considered in Part 4.

The effectiveness of an organization is measured by the degree to which it achieves the objectives that are set up for it. An organization may fail to achieve its objectives either because they are impossible of attainment under the conditions existing or because the organizational structure is faulty in one or another respect. The chief executive may try to do too many things himself and fail to delegate work. Other managers may make the same mistake. The work of the organization may not be properly divided, or if properly divided the organization may not be properly staffed. Sometimes managers are unable to develop loyalty to the firm, or they fail to recognize the problems often generated by people working together. And, of course, there may be other reasons for failure.

As we have said, there is no "best" organizational type. The good manager tries to develop the most effective arrangements possible for co-ordinating to best advantage the efforts of the personnel, material, equipment, and other resources that are available or can be made available to him.

We must recognize that organizations are never static. They are influenced by both external and internal forces as we have suggested, and, consequently, a good manager never considers his organizational arrangements as final.

Organizational arrangements may differ, depending on whether a single short-run effort or a long-term period of activity may be involved. Since most business firms operate over a long period of time, their organizational structure typically makes provision for growth and change.[5] In short, business organizations tend to be dynamic in character. Many business firms make provision not only for training operating personnel but make provision for executive development programs as well. Similarly, organizational structures in more recent years have tended to include research departments so that a portion of the organization's effort will be channeled into the development of new methods and products with a view to increasing the output of the entire organization.

Organizations tend to have a "life cycle." This cycle may be very short; for example, an organization may be set up and fail in a year or two. In some cases this cycle is very long; many of our business firms have celebrated their hundredth birthdays. Quality of management, of course, may make the difference between a short and a long life cycle.

The stages in the lives of organizations has been outlined by one student of the subject as follows:

1. Formation of the organization with high expectations on the part of at least a few of its members.
2. Early difficulties and setbacks, many of which were not anticipated at the beginning.
3. Reorganization and revitalization because of the realities encountered.

---

[5] See for example, Philip Selznick, *Leadership in Administration* (Evanston, Ill.: Row, Peterson & Co., 1957), pp. 102–3.

4. Period of growing achievement.
5. Period of peak achievement.
6. Beginnings of decline because of internal lack of vitality.
7. Serious difficulties and major deterioration.
8. Extinction, absorption by another organization, or major rejuvenation, beginning a new cycle.[6]

Direction and Co-ordination

The chief executive officer provides direction to all phases of an organization's operations. Some of this is done directly, some through subordinates. Direction involves the use of authority or influence of various types. The organization is given a structure in large part to define authority relationships. A hierarchy of decisions is created, as we have suggested. Those in top-management positions have the broadest decision-making powers. They set limits on the next stages of decisions through their authority over the organization. Those at middle-management positions in turn exercise authority over those under their direction. The concept of authority is well stated in the following quotation: "A subordinate is said to accept authority whenever he permits his behavior to be guided by the decision of a superior, without independently examining the merits of that decision." The same author also says, "Of all the modes of influence, authority is the one that chiefly distinguishes the behavior of individuals as participants of organizations from their behavior outside such organizations."[7]

The manager directs through orders (commands), which are communicated to subordinates in the organization. The subordinates accept these orders and govern their own decisions accordingly.

The manager also directs in other ways. He may persuade, advise, suggest, or consult with subordinates. He may use a variety of ways to influence their behavior. He may prefer to direct by the use of authority only as a last resort and try to secure compliance with his decisions by more indirect ways. Sometimes these methods of direction are referred to as "consultative" in contrast to "authoritarian" or "dictatorial," which involve direct commands and direct compliance with them. In a final analysis, of course, the manager can always rely on the authority he possesses.

The following statement is of interest in this connection:

Groups under an authoritarian type of leadership which dictates in detail what shall be done, how it shall be done, and when it shall be done,

---

[6] Shartle, *op. cit.*, pp. 37–38.

[7] Herbert A. Simon, *Administrative Behavior* (2nd ed.; New York: Macmillan Co., 1957), p. 11 and p. 124.

provide a minimum of individual and group freedom of action. The members respond by a reduction of initiative and by a heightened dependence upon the leader for the initiation of activities. The situation is not improved by another extreme: a *laissez faire* type of leadership which provides no goal or task structure. . . . Freedom of action is maximized by a democratic form of leadership which provides some structure and helpful task facilitation but which places a high degree of responsibility upon the group members for task decision and action.[8]

There are limits, of course, to the extent to which people will accept authority in organized activities. Experts and professional people usually are directed by means of suggestion and consultation rather than by direct orders. Routine workers are more likely to accept more specific direction. The manager will make use of different types of influence depending on the people involved and the circumstances under which they work.

Communication

The direction and co-ordination of the operations of an organization depend to a considerable degree on communication. Decisions are transmitted, orders given, and results reported by means of communication. Communication is a two-way process, since orders and information go forward, and reports flow back. There may also be "sidewise" lines of communication as well.

Communications may be oral or written. Memoranda, letters, reports, operating procedures, manuals, and other forms of communication are used by business firms. As we have suggested informal communications such as the "grapevine" often are important as well. In some cases business firms publish "house organs" to provide a steady flow of information that is not in direct channels between the manager and subordinates. A list of the many types of communication in addition to those used in "established channels" includes the following: (1) meetings and conferences, (2) company newspapers, magazines, and similar "house organs," (3) handbooks, and information booklets as well as displays; (4) payroll inserts; (5) bulletin boards and posters; (6) annual reports; (7) films; (8) special-purpose publications such as major announcements, and others.[9]

Effective communication is not always easy to achieve. As one writer has said,

---

[8] Ralph M. Stogdill, *Individual Behavior and Group Achievement* (New York: Oxford University Press, 1959), p. 241.

[9] George R. Terry, *Principles of Management* (Homewood, Ill.: Richard D. Irwin, Inc., 1956), p. 415.

There can be no deep faith without understanding. The effectiveness of an employee is greatly affected by his understanding and acceptance of the action the manager wants taken. And the manager makes his wants known by means of communication. The sender must get through to the receiver if the communication is to be complete and satisfactory. It is an error for a manager to assume that his job is to hand it out and the other fellow is supposed to do all the listening and reading.[10]

Habits and Standard Operating Procedures

Just as an individual may develop habits that govern his decisions and actions, the people associated with a business firm may also develop sets of habits or traditions or accepted ways of doing things that have a wide influence on decisions.

As Professor Simon points out, "Habit is the most general, the most pervasive, of all techniques for making programmed decisions. The collective memories of organization members are vast encyclopedias of factual knowledge, habitual skills and operating procedures. The large costs associated with bringing new members into organizations are principally costs of providing the new members, through formal training and experience, with the repertoire of skills and other habits they need in their jobs."[11]

In many business firms accepted ways of doing things develop and guide a number of minor, and sometimes, major decisions. Orientation and training programs help new employees to learn about such informal guides to decisions and actions. Managers make use of such programs to help co-ordinate decisions and efforts.

Standard operating procedures are often designed to guide the decisions and efforts of the people in a business firm. This is another method of co-ordinating activities in the organization. For example, new orders are placed for certain items when the inventory reaches a given level; interoffice communications are routed in a standard manner; inspections of various machines follow a standard "check list," or new employees are "processed" in a standardized manner. In some cases *manuals* are prepared which summarize operating procedures in order to avoid confusion or conflict in the interpretation of the procedures. From time to time, of course, such manuals may be revised to adapt them to changed conditions.

---

10 *Ibid.*, pp. 406–7.
11 Herbert A. Simon, *The New Science of Management Decision* (New York: Harper & Bros., 1960), pp. 9–10.

Motivation

As was suggested, management has the responsibility for motivating the members of an organization to put forth their best efforts. In smaller organizations the setting of a good example by the manager may provide one means of motivating others. More frequently managers motivate by promising rewards. These may range from promises of higher incomes and promotion to recognitions of various types. In some cases the opportunity for monetary rewards provides adequate incentive; in others, position or status in the organization may be of even greater importance. Thus, appeals may be made to economic motives, the desire for prestige and recognition, or to social standing within a particular group.

A manager may also motivate by the use of fear. This may be called coercive in contrast to inducive motivation. Sometimes the use of fear is called negative in contrast to positive motivation. Members of the organization may be threatened by loss of jobs, reduction in status, or reduction of income.

The type of motivation used will vary widely according to situations and people. Some people respond better to threats than to promises of reward. Others do not respond to motivation based on fear and indeed may become so concerned with protecting themselves that they will accomplish little. Frequently in larger organizations, particularly those that develop bureaucratic arrangements, there is a tendency to take no risks, to follow orders and prescribed procedures exactly, and to put forth no special effort because the chance of gain is not considered worth the risk involved. This is illustrated by the traditional advice of the older army man to the young recruit, "Never volunteer for anything and keep three copies of everything you write."

The setting of goals is often a means of motivating the members of an organization. Sometimes competition proves to be effective, particularly in this country where people are traditionally competitive. Challenges—such as beating the opposition or the quota or setting a new record—have widespread appeal. To a growing extent managers are concerned with increasing the pleasurability of work; thus, the work itself may be an important motivating factor in the years ahead.

Management and Leadership

As we have suggested, organizations need to be directed and co-ordinated. Sometimes these phases of management activities are referred to as "leadership functions." For our purposes, however, we consider all phases of the manager's role as related to leadership. The principal decision makers and those who provide the major direction and co-ordination for the organization may be classified as leaders. They may be leaders in thought, or action, or both.

There are varying degrees of leadership, however. To a degree the captain of a football team is a leader. He is a leader to a lesser dgeree, however, than the president of the university that the team represents. In military organizations distinctions are made between commissioned and noncommissioned officers, thus indicating differing degrees of leadership; also, there are distinctions between general officers and field and company grade officers.

Professor Selznick suggests that the leaders in large business firms are those who make the *critical* decisions, in contrast to routine decisions.[12] Critical decisions are those that define objectives or the mission of the enterprise and those that assure the survival of the institution. Professor Selznick distinguishes between institutional and "interpersonal" leaders. He says,

> ... the role of the institutional leader should be clearly distinguished from that of the "interpersonal" leader. The latter's task is to smooth the path of human interaction, ease communication, evoke personal devotion, and allay anxiety. His expertness has relatively little to do with content; he is more concerned with persons than with policies. His main contribution is to the efficiency of the enterprise. The institutional leader, on the other hand, is *primarily an expert in the promotion and protection of values.*[13]

This distinction helps us to put the difference between the football captain and the university president, the head of a department, and the corporation president, that is, the interpersonal and institutional leader, in proper perspective. They represent leadership in varying degrees, and the distinction between interpersonal and institutional leaders and between routine and critical decision makers may be helpful.

Leaders perform a variety of functions. Figure 9–4 outlines various types of activities in which leaders typically engage. The importance of communication is emphasized in this diagram. The functions of representing the business firm, initiating changes, and interpreting the need for changes are emphasized especially. These types of functions are differentiated from the activities more frequently associated

---

12 Selznick, *op. cit.*, chap. 2.
13 *Ibid.*, pp. 27–28.

FIGURE 9–4. The Functions of Leadership

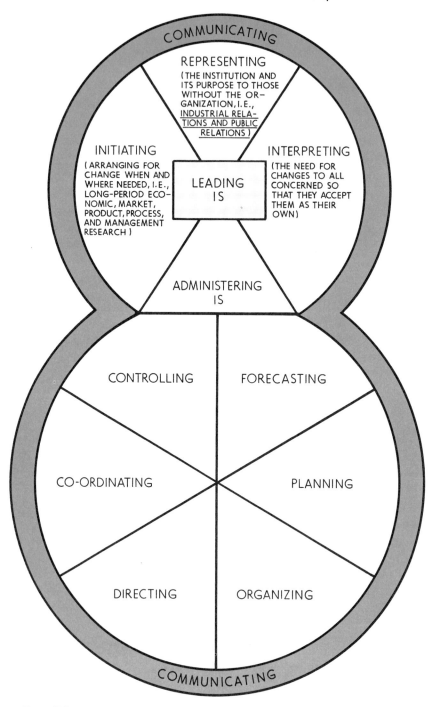

COMMUNICATING

REPRESENTING
(THE INSTITUTION AND ITS PURPOSE TO THOSE WITHOUT THE OR-GANIZATION, I.E., INDUSTRIAL RELA-TIONS AND PUBLIC RELATIONS)

INITIATING
(ARRANGING FOR CHANGE WHEN AND WHERE NEEDED, I.E., LONG-PERIOD ECO-NOMIC, MARKET, PRODUCT, PROCESS, AND MANAGEMENT RESEARCH)

LEADING IS

INTERPRETING
(THE NEED FOR CHANGES TO ALL CONCERNED SO THAT THEY ACCEPT THEM AS THEIR OWN)

ADMINISTERING IS

CONTROLLING

FORECASTING

CO-ORDINATING

PLANNING

DIRECTING

ORGANIZING

COMMUNICATING

Ernest Dale and Lyndall F. Urwick, *Staff in Organization* (New York: McGraw-Hill Book Co., Inc., 1960), p. 29.

with administration or management. As the chart suggests, however, these types of activities are closely related in the practice of management.

Are Leaders Born or Developed?

The question of whether leaders are born or developed has been argued for a long time. Some contend that the inherited abilities of individuals is basic to their achievement of leadership positions. Others argue that the capacities required for leadership are rather widely distributed among the people in our society and that the development of leadership abilities depends upon environmental and educational factors. Those who hold to this view frequently point to such outstanding leaders in our history as Benjamin Franklin and Abraham Lincoln who came from backgrounds that would not suggest the inheritance of opportunities for developing strong leadership characteristics.

Schell in his book, *Techniques of Executive Control,* says,

There seems to be a widespread belief that executive skill is a God-given attribute. It is something you have or you haven't. Your success as a leader of men is a matter of unchangeable destiny. In some measure, this is true. . . .

But between those individuals who have these few qualities in great measure and those who do not have them at all there lies the much greater number of individuals who are gifted in moderate degree.[14]

It appears that at least some of those who have achieved leadership positions *wanted very much to be leaders.* They were strongly motivated to excel. It probably made relatively little difference to them just what type of organization they led so long as they had a chance to lead. This urge or drive toward leadership may arise either from inherited characteristics or from the environment within which the individual developed. The drive toward leadership may be something like the urge toward painting or acting or toward some other of the creative arts.[15]

The work of the management leader resembles in some degree the work of the artist. Indeed the ability to develop new insights, to think creatively, and to bring to his work fresh viewpoints requires artistry of a high order.

---

14 Erwin H. Schell, *Technique of Executive Control* (8th ed.; New York: McGraw-Hill Book Co., Inc., 1957), p. 8.

15 Bernard M. Bass, *Leadership, Psychology and Organizational Behavior* (New York: Harper & Bros., 1960), p. 153.

Attempts to Explain Leadership

If you will think about some of the people you know who are considered to be leaders and try to identify their outstanding characteristics and abilities, you will soon find some wide variations. Leaders range all the way from "the strong silent type," to those with "magnetic personalities," or "quick minds," or "dedicated hearts," to those with other qualities. Leaders in a specialized field of work may be recognized for their professional abilities; political and business leaders for their abilities to make sound decisions and to get things done. Our primary concern is with the latter type of leadership, that is, leadership of organizations.

The subject of leadership is both a fascinating and frustrating area of study. Many attempts have been made to evolve theories or explanations of leadership and of leader-follower relationships, among them being studies which stress the following: (1) leadership traits or characteristics; (2) the leadership requirements of various situations; (3) factors that influence followers; (4) human relations, including "bottom up" or consultative leadership; (5) goal-oriented leadership, for example, "management by objectives;" and (6) others, including attempts to synthesize earlier studies, efforts to study power and influence relationships, and studies of the needs and conflicts of followers and organization requirements. Even this listing is far from inclusive but it will suggest the variety of efforts made to study this interesting subject.

One writer has pointed out, for example: "As we survey the path leadership theory has taken, we spot the wreckage of 'trait theory,' the 'great man' theory, the 'situation critique,' leadership styles, functional leadership and finally leaderless leadership. . . ."[16]

Some of the early students of leadership tended to emphasize leadership traits and have been referred to as the "traitists." They stressed such qualities as physical and nervous energy, enthusiasm, friendliness, integrity, decisiveness, imagination, knowledge, appearance, and the like.[17] This approach has limitations because the traits required for leadership often will vary in importance with circumstances and situations.

Thus, some students of the subject emphasize that leadership is a

[16] Warren G. Bennis, "Leadership Theory and Administrative Behavior: The Problem of Authority," *Administrative Science Quarterly*, Dec., 1959, p. 260.

[17] Roger Bellows, *Creative Leadership* (Englewood Cliffs, N.J.: Prentice-Hall, Inc., 1959), p. 293.

kind of work done to meet the needs of a special situation.[18] These are sometimes called the "situationists." While recognizing that there are some types of persons often with distinctive traits who are more likely to be leaders than others, emphasis is placed on the social situations that they are called upon to handle or lead. Thus, persons who are leaders in one situation may not be leaders in another.

In some cases the factors which influence followers are stressed in studies of leadership. Important leadership characteristics are considered to be the ones that have the greatest impact on followers. General Sir Archibald Wavell, for example, stressed the ability of the leader to motivate and to inspire his followers. He said, for example, "A man does not flee because he is fighting in an unrighteous cause, he does not attack because his cause is just; he flees because he is the weaker, he conquers because he is the stronger, *or because his leader has made him feel the stronger.*"[19]

Some studies of leadership stress "human relations," or the harmonious management of groups as social organizations. Leadership is related to the co-ordination of individual needs and goals with those of small groups and of larger organizations. Emphasis is given to the resolution or minimizing of conflicts and on the development of mutual confidence between leaders and followers. This approach is closely related to "bottom up" or "consultative management" which stresses co-ordination in contrast to the direction of the efforts of those in an organization.

In contrast are explanations of leadership that stress the attainment of desired goals ("management by objectives") and the use of power and influence to obtain the required collaboration between leaders and followers to reach objectives.

There are other theories and attempts to develop general explanations of leadership as well, but those outlined above will suffice for our purposes. Studies in this field are continuing and our knowledge of this subject undoubtedly will expand.

Among the elements that tend to be stressed in leadership studies are *power* and *influence*. The leader-follower relationship appears to be a power relationship in some degree. Power provides the basis for influencing subordinates. Some purpose or goal usually is involved. As has been suggested: ". . . leadership can be defined as the process by which an agent induces a subordinate to behave in a desired manner."

18 Selznick, *op. cit.*, pp. 22–23.

19 General Sir Archibald Wavell, *Generals and Generalship* (New York: Macmillan Co., 1941), p. 18. (Italics added.)

This writer goes on to suggest that three major components are involved: "(a) an agent who is typically called a *leader;* (b) a process of induction or the ability to manipulate rewards that here will be termed *power;* and (c) the induced behavior, which will be referred to here as *influence.*"[20] In this definition, power is related to the control of rewards or punishments; influence to the exercise of control over the subordinate's need satisfaction. The power residing in the leadership agent provides the basis for the influence.

Although this summary provides some basic concepts relative to leadership, we should recognize the variety of leadership situations, forms of power, and degrees of influence that prevail in the diversity of organizations represented in our type of society. Our system is pluralistic. There is widespread opportunity for the exercise of leadership; it may be exercised in many kinds of organizations, in a variety of activities at many levels, and in numerous ways.

Adaptation to Change

Probably the biggest factor in successful leadership in the modern business world is adaptability to change. This is in large part a factor in *institutional* as opposed to interpersonal leadership. As one writer has aptly pointed out, "Most of us could be good businessmen if conditions never changed. But since they do, an executive must make decisions on the basis of indefinite data, and make them with energy, responsibility, intuition, judgment and courage, and reasonably correctly. . . . We cannot supply the intuition, but we can teach the need for it and for the organization permitting it."[21]

The ability to anticipate changes and to adapt to them is probably one of the basic leadership talents. It requires imagination and creativity of a high order. Such leadership keeps the firm from sailing along smoothly on a course that can only lead to disaster. Because this course did not lead to disaster before, does not mean that disaster will be avoided now.

There is always the danger that "good management" will develop too "nice" (really rigid and inflexible) an organization with working relationships that are so smooth that there is no room for flexibility and adaptability. Change often creates conflicts and upsets people. Yet without change the organization may sail smoothly to disaster. In a final analysis, the test of leadership is to introduce change at least

---

20 Bennis, *op. cit.,* pp. 295–96.
21 David McCord Wright, "The Administrative Fallacy," *Harvard Business Review,* July-August, 1960, p. 113–14.

rapidly enough to meet the needs of a changing world, and if possible, to move in advance of general changes. Management leaders dare not forget the warning suggested in this verse:

> Some laud a life of mild content:
> Content may fall, as well as Pride.
> The frog who hugged his lowly ditch
> Was much disgruntled when it dried.[22]

SUMMARY

The manager undertakes the organization of the resources of the firm in order to achieve its objectives through maximizing the results of the efforts of the people in the firm and the use of other resources. Of the various resources available to managers, money is the least specialized, since it can be used to gain command over the abilities of people, land, space, equipment, machines, materials, and other things.

Organization may be illustrated by a team, such as a football team. Usually organization makes provision for (1) division of work; (2) structuring of authority and decision making; and (3) development of sound working relationships among the people in the firm. Equipment, space, machines, and other physical resources, as well as the types of work involved, may influence organizational arrangements. Usually, however, organization problems tend to center around people.

Division of work provides for specialization, economy of effort, and efficient input-output relationships. Work may be organized around basic functions of the firm such as marketing or production, products, locations, markets, processes, or various combinations of these. In some cases, usually smaller organizations, work may be organized around the interests and abilities of key personnel.

Organization structure usually is based on authority relationships and the formal or official relationships often are set forth in organization charts. The more generally used models for such charts include line, line and staff, and line, staff, and functional arrangements.

The informal organization, in contrast to the formal organization is often revealed through studies of organization behavior. Knowledge of organization behavior has been expanded through studies of the behavior of small and large groups, "group dynamics," role assignments, motivations, conflicts of interests, and others including various relationships inside and outside the firm. Organizations in operation are seldom static. They may go through a more or less regular life cycle of shorter or longer duration.

---

22 *Ibid.*, quoted from *Short Stories of Saki.*

The manager provides direction and co-ordination of the members of the organization through orders or commands, persuasion, advice, consultation, effective communication, the use of standard operating procedures, manuals, and in other ways. Motivation may be accomplished by promising rewards. Appeals may be to economic motives, desire for recognition or prestige, or to social standing within a particular group. It may be possible to motivate through the use of fear. Managers may motivate by setting a good example, by developing dedication to established goals, through competition, and by creating greater interest in work assignments.

Leadership relates to all phases of the manager's role. There may be variation in type and degree of leadership as between the making of critical or routine decisions, or between the exercise of institutional or interpersonal leadership. Theories or general explanations of leadership cover a wide range and include those related to leadership traits, the demands of various situations, leader-follower relationships, human relations, management by objectives, and others. Leadership typically involves power-influence relationships. One of the major leadership talents is the ability to anticipate changes and to adapt to them.

QUESTIONS AND PROBLEMS

1. List three organizations of which you are or have been a member. Are there significant contrasts between them?
2. Why is a football team more effective than would be the case if each of the team members followed his own decisions and inclinations?
3. What are the major purposes of organization? Is organization as important for leisure time as for work activities?
4. Organization usually provides for division of work. Why is this? Can you think of an organizational arrangement that does not provide for division of work?
5. On what bases may the work of a business firm be divided?
6. What is meant by the "unity of command" principle? Illustrate.
7. Outline the major differences between a line and a line and staff organizational pattern.
8. Differentiate between the formal and the informal organization in a business firm.
9. Explain this statement by Professor Shartle:
   "In contrast to organization structure, organization behavior (or performance) represents the patterns of human behavior that take place within the framework of the structure. The performance tells us how things do or do not get done and includes the interpersonal relations, communications, influences, and patterns of cooperation and conflict."
10. Do organizations have a more or less regular "life cycle?" Explain.

11. Suppose you are elected president of a student organization. By what means might you motivate the members? Which means do you think would be most effective? Why?

12. Of the various theories or explanations of leadership outlined in the above discussions select two that seem to you to be most plausible and indicate the basis for your selection.

13. Explain the statement by Selznick: "The institutional leader . . . is primarily an expert in the promotion and protection of values."

14. Do you think leaders are born or developed? Explain your position.

15. Why are power and influence important in explaining leadership?

16. What is meant by this statement: "In a final analysis, the test of leadership is to introduce change at least rapidly enough to meet the needs of a changing world, and if possible, to move in advance of general changes."

SUGGESTED READINGS

KAPPEL, FREDERICK R. *Vitality in a Business Enterprise.* New York: Mc-Graw-Hill Book Co., Inc., 1960. Read the first chapter entitled "A Concept of Vitality," which will give you some insights into the organization and leadership problems of a business firm; as will the second, "Goals That Build The Future," beginning on page 35.

LONG, JOHN D. *Workbook to Accompany Weimer: Business Administration: An Introductory Management Approach,* chap. 9. Rev. ed. Homewood, Ill.: Richard D. Irwin, Inc., 1962.

SELZNICK, PHILIP. *Leadership in Administration.* Evanston, Ill.: Row, Peterson & Co., 1957. Read chap. one, "Introduction." You may wish to read more of this interesting volume.

SIMON, HERBERT A. *Administrative Behavior.* 2nd ed. New York: Macmillan Co., 1957. This is a book of major importance in this field. You should become acquainted with it. Read chap. ii, "Some problems of Administrative Theory."

part **3** Decision
Processes
and Guides

6

SUMMARY OUTLINE

BUSINESS ADMINISTRATION—now one of the more exciting areas of study—may be *approached* in an *introductory* manner from the point of view of the *manager*.

He is the central figure in the business firm—the key social and economic institution of our time. It is managed and operated in a highly dynamic environment.

Business Firms are established as individual *proprietorships, partnerships, corporations,* and other forms.

Firms vary in *size* and engage in many *types* of *work*—manufacturing, trade, finance, service, and others.

The *Decision Makers* in business firms are owners, managers, and business specialists.

The *Management Process* involves establishment of objectives, plans, and controls; organization of resources; and leadership.

Decision Making—a central management responsibility—includes problem and *goal identification* and clarification, development and analysis of *alternatives*, appraisal of most likely alternatives, and *choice*.

Decisions may be guided by financial, accounting, statistical, economic, mathematical, and other considerations.

Business Resources and Operations involve effective utilization of the abilities of people—requiring knowledge of personnel and organization behavior—

as well as other resources including

capital, equipment, knowledge, time, and related aids to productivity, plus the place of business—land, buildings, and location—

in the *production* and *marketing* of goods and services to secure *income*.

The *Business Environment* influences management decisions and in turn is influenced by them, particularly in the areas of

business conditions,
governmental and political conditions,
the legal system,
the enterprise system and competing systems,
and international business administration.

Emerging Problems and Opportunities hold promise for the business community, and for you in managing your future.

OUTLINE FOR CHAPTER 10

DECISION MAKING is a major management responsibility
  covering a wide range of problems from
    establishment of objectives to
    utilization of resources in their achievement.

Decision problems are more complicated than information problems, since choices relative to future developments and uncertainties are involved.

Management decisions are complicated by
    competitive conditions,
    strategies, value judgments,
    cost-risk-return relationships,
    time, timing, future uncertainties, and
    ways of implementation.

Major steps in rational decision making include
(1) making an estimate of the situation, covering
      problem identification and understanding,
      definition and clarification of goals;
(2) developing and analyzing alternatives;
(3) appraising most likely alternatives and choosing most
      desirable.

Business decisions are being constantly reappraised and
    reviewed, modified and changed.

Decision making differs from the scientific method, stressing action rather than truth seeking, and striving for reasonable results under uncertain conditions.

Financial, accounting, statistical, and economic decision guides are of major importance; increasing reliance also is being placed on decision guides based on mathematics and the behavioral sciences.

DECISION MAKING

A decision is only a moment in a process.

—Mary Parker Follett

Range of Decisions

You have undoubtedly seen movies which portray the Hollywood concept of the business executive. Typically he is seated at a large desk with two or more telephones ringing almost constantly. Secretaries are running in and out bringing cables, telegrams, and urgent messages. The executive barks out orders, such as: "Cut prices 10 per cent." "Buy all you can get." "Tell the union to go ahead and strike." "Cancel all orders with that company." This sort of scene suggests that the business executive makes major decisions almost without hesitation and that the future of his company rests on the rapidity and accuracy of his snap judgments.

While this Hollywood version of the work of the business executive may provide good entertainment, it does not give a very accurate picture of the manager's activities. As we pointed out in Chapter 3, some managers make their decisions almost entirely on the basis of intuition, haphazard information, or a general "feel of the situation." In some cases they may succeed on this basis. More often, managers try to make use of as many guides to decisions as can reasonably be made available to them. They try to follow a process of rational decision making rather than reaching decisions on the basis of intuition or snap judgments.

Actually most of the business decisions that are made on the basis of snap judgments are of minor importance. The major decisions, those which have an important impact on the programs of a business firm, are seldom reached without careful study and consideration. When decisions are reached quickly, substantial work typically has been done in anticipation of the problem that has developed. The executive often will have available staff personnel who help him in developing information as background for his decisions. These may

231

include all types of specialists such as research workers, business economists, accountants, statisticians, lawyers, engineers, mathematicians, psychologists, and others. In addition the managers of the principal divisions of the business will aid the chief executive in making major decisions. The managers of such major divisions as production or marketing may themselves have staff personnel available to help in the collection and analysis of the information necessary to build adequate backgrounds for the decisions affecting their particular departments.

If the manager is operating a smaller establishment, he may have very little in the way of specialized assistance available to him. In such cases he must develop the information that is required himself, securing whatever assistance he can from current reports that are published in newspapers, magazines, trade journals, and the like; from the records of the company's operations that are maintained; from correspondence with other businessmen; from consultants retained on a part-time basis; or from other sources. In either situation the manager usually is familiar with many types of information and either uses it directly or with the aid of staff specialists in reaching decisions. He tends to acquire either through his experience or his educational development a familiarity with a wide range of subjects.

We might outline some of the types of subjects with which the manager has to deal since this will indicate the pattern of our discussions in the chapters that follow. He is concerned with the processes of decision making almost constantly. We consider this subject in an introductory manner in this, the first chapter in Part 3; followed by Chapters 11 through 14 in which we consider various financial, accounting, statistical, and economic guides to decisions as well as the growing assistance coming from linear programing, game theory, and related areas.

The manager makes use of various human and nonhuman resources in the production and marketing operations of the firm. These subjects are considered in Part 4, Chapter 15 through 19 inclusive. Decisions are made and implemented in a dynamic environment which influences and to a degree is influenced by the business firm; these topics are considered in Part 5. And, since the business firm and its environment tend to change rapidly, we consider some of the potential trends of future development in Part 6.

Types of Problems

In order to understand the manager's role in decision making we may find it helpful to consider the types of problems that he has to solve. We could classify them in a number of ways. We might classify business problems in order of complexity, ranging from problems that can be solved by getting information to those requiring choices or decisions. For example, suppose you have the problem of determining what time the next airplane leaves for Chicago. You call the airline office and get the information. The problem is solved. We may call this an "information problem" to set it off from other types.

Now suppose a friend calls to tell you he is driving to Chicago and invites you to join him. You now are faced with a "decision problem." This involves choices among alternatives. It includes the information problem plus something more—a choice—and typically this will involve a judgment. In the situation outlined above, for example, you have to choose between the airplane trip and the auto trip. Time may be important in your plans, and this may cause you to decide to take the airplane. Or you may know that your friend has a reputation for reckless driving, and this may lead you to decide in favor of the airplane. Or you may enjoy traveling with your friend, even though he is a speed demon, to such an extent that you are willing to sacrifice the time that would be saved by the airplane and run the risks that are involved in your friend's driving with the result that you decide to travel by car.

We should note that in the business world information problems may be very complicated. For example, a business manager may want to know what should be done to improve a product, how much it would cost to do this, and what it might mean in terms of meeting future competition. The development of this information might take a staff of experts several months or longer.

By their very nature, however, decision problems are more complex; they require choices among alternatives which usually necessitate a consideration of strategic factors and the making of value judgments. Decision problems in turn may be divided into those that are of major or controlling significance and those related to minor or supporting activities.

Factors in Business Decisions

How do managers make decisions? Is there a decision-making process that they can follow to aid them in arriving at choices or judgments and conclusions?

Much has been said and written about these subjects, but our knowledge of them is still limited. We tend to think of an orderly process of collecting and analyzing facts prior to making decisions, and of making careful estimates and predictions on the basis of such studies; but we must recognize that managerial decisions involve a great deal more than the collection and interpretation of pertinent information.

As Robert D. Calkins has aptly pointed out, "For many years, the prevailing view in management was that if we got the facts, the solution would be indicated. It was supposed that if the facts were obtained and analyzed, the cause of a problem would become evident; and by treating the cause, we would solve the problem. But few problems are resolved so simply."[1]

Business decisions are complicated by such considerations as competitive conditions and management strategies, by time, and by value judgments that may be involved in selecting a course of action. The situation surrounding the decision and the purposes for which it is made also have an important bearing on the result.

For example, the information available to a manager may suggest that an expanded advertising campaign for one of the firm's products should be undertaken. Such a campaign may require the shifting of funds from other advertising purposes, and this may not be considered advisable. Or a major advertising campaign may be expected to call forth an even greater campaign from competitors. If this happens the end result may be unfavorable to the company and its product. These are questions of *strategy* which we will consider at greater length later in our discussions.

Value judgments may also complicate the result. In the above illustration, the manager may decide to adopt the expanded advertising program because of his desire to expand his market at the expense of his competitors. The manager's personal philosophy and point of view may play a part in his decisions but these are usually subordinated to the objectives of the firm, which provide a value system on the basis of which decisions are made and results judged.

In the business world value systems can be quantified in terms of dollars and cents and thus provide a fairly definite basis for making value judgments. If our objective is to maximize profits in the long run or the short run, we have available a reasonably rational basis for making value judgments. We can compare *costs, risks,* and *returns* and *output* and *input* in dollar terms, and measure results. If our objectives run in terms of prestige or the development of a favorable public

---

[1] Robert D. Calkins, "The Art of Administration and the Art of Science," *Indiana Business Report No. 29* (Indiana University, Bureau of Business Research, 1959), p. 15, by permission. See also, his article in *Business Horizons,* Fall, 1959.

opinion, then our basis for making value judgments is less precise.

Timing is another factor of importance in reaching decisions. Regardless of the scarcity of information available, uncertainty about strategic factors or other considerations, a manager may be forced to make a decision, simply because the business world and his competitors will not wait for him to make up his mind. Conversely, all of the available information may point to a decision, but the manager may not believe that the time is right for it in terms of market uncertainties or possible changes in the programs of competitors.

Decisions are always forward looking; they deal with future, rather than with past lines of action. They may be based on past experience, but they relate to the future. This is why football coaches and captains take such a dim view of "Monday-morning quarterbacks." Almost anyone can determine what a correct decision would have been in retrospect; the decisions that count, however, are made against an uncertain future.

Decisions are influenced both by factors within the business firm and in the business environment—by general economic, political, or social conditions and by potential changes in such conditions. In addition we should always remember that business decisions are action oriented. They are not made as an academic exercise but in order to accomplish a desired result.

We should recognize also that in many situations more than one good decision is possible. Several alternative decisions may be possible and any one of them may lead to approximately the same result. Success often depends on the *implementation* of the decision, on how well it is carried out. We should remember that a "good" decision poorly implemented may be less desirable than a questionable decision that is well implemented.

The foregoing discussion suggests that managerial decision making is a complicated process. Even so we should recognize that some decisions are made on an intuitive basis or after "mulling over" the problem and taking action as indicated by the "feel" of the situation.

Some decisions involve a wide latitude of choices; others are rather sharply limited as to the choices open. For example, when the allies decided that only through the invasion of Europe would it be possible to attain the objective of winning World War II, numerous choices were open. The British favored invasion through the Mediterranean; the Americans favored landing on the coast of France. Once invasion through France was decided by the highest levels of command, plans were developed that would provide the basis for carrying out this basic decision. These plans were made by headquarters groups but at lower levels than the basic decision. Note that these planning decisions did not deal with plans as to any other program of action than invasion through France; the other choices had been eliminated. Once plans were decided upon each had to be implemented through the organization of men, arms, and equipment. Decisions had to be made as to the best types of fighting teams or groups, armies, or divisions. Assignments were broken down for armies, divisions, and smaller units, each integrated with the other. Note that as we move down the scale the decisions become more and more circumscribed. Some are finally governed by standard operating procedures, some by specific orders as to what action to take in a given situation. In these final situations there is little latitude for choice at all.

The important point of this illustration is the *varying degrees of choice* that are open for decision makers at various levels of an organization. The top managers usually have the most difficult decisions since they involve the widest choices, the unit managers and foremen make their decisions under rather definite restrictions and many of them will be indicated by standard procedures and rules. As we suggested in the introduction to Chapter 7, many decisions, other than those made by owners and managers, may be highly important and may set limits on the decisions of a firm's executives. For example, there are decisions of competitors, bankers, government officials, labor leaders, customers, and others.

Classification of Decision Situations

An interesting and stimulating (and somewhat different) method of classifying decision problems has been developed by James D. Thompson and his associates.[2] In this method, decision situations are classified according to (1) outcome preferences and (2) degree of knowledge of cause and effect relationships. Thus, decision problems may be classified as to degree of agreement or lack of agreement, both with respect to outcome preferences and to knowledge of cause and effect relationships. The following diagram summarizes this classification system.

When there is agreement both as to outcome preferences and knowledge of cause and effect relationships, decisions may be made by *computation*. In effect, this means that decisions can be referred to experts and decided on the basis of facts and analysis. A bureaucratic

---

[2] James D. Thompson and Associates, *Comparative Studies in Administration* (Pittsburgh: University of Pittsburgh Press, 1959), chap. xii.

Outcome Preferences

	Agreement	Lack of Agreement
Knowledge of Cause and Effect Relationships — Agreement	Computation	Compromise
Knowledge of Cause and Effect Relationships — Lack of Agreement	Judgment	Inspiration

type of organization usually is involved in this type of situation. Problems tend to be referred to experts who know the cause and effect relationship and who are loyal to the goals sought.

When there is agreement as to outcome preferences but lack of agreement in regard to cause and effect relationships, decisions tend to be made on a *judgment* basis. The organization attempts to refer decisions to people with wisdom and experience who are not necessarily experts in such cases. The persons involved all have about the same types of information and have an equal voice in decisions, with final choices being made on the basis of a majority opinion. Decisions made through political elections are, to a degree, of this type. A jury is another illustration, although where capital crimes are involved unanimous agreement is required. The boards of directors and executive committees of our corporations may be considered as another illustration.

In cases where there is lack of agreement or differences of agreement as to outcome preferences, but where there is general agreement in regard to cause and effect relationships, decisions tend to be made on the basis of compromises or bargaining.

Decisions that result from compromise situations usually are made by a limited number of people who represent the various factions involved. Each of these representatives may carry a veto power. There must, however, be a genuine desire to reach a solution in order to arrive at a decision in this type of situation.

When there is lack of agreement both with respect to outcome preferences and cause and effect relationships, decisions are likely to result from inspiration or intuition or insights. This category relates, at least to a degree, to our discussions of some of the functions of leadership in the preceding chapter.

Few organizations are built around the inspiration or intuition category, although almost all organizations will rely on this manner of decision making to some degree. A disorganized army may respond to inspiration. A new president may, through inspiration, breathe new life into a corporation. Often new scientific developments originate with decisions of the inspiration variety.

To a degree, the computation types of decisions may be related to what Professor Simon refers to as "programmed decisions." These may be the easiest types of decisions to reach. They may be followed by judgment decisions and compromise decisions in that order, with the most difficult being of the inspiration type.

We outline this classification to suggest that decision situations are of many types and that the approaches required to solve decision problems may be of a number of different types as well. An effective organization probably will provide for some means of reaching solutions to decision problems in all of these areas.

We should note that the personnel making up a given organization may be, in effect, reorganized for the solution of different types of decision problems. A case in point might be that of a football team with the same eleven men adopting one organizational pattern for offensive play and another for defensive play.

Stages in Rational Decisions

Often business executives do not realize how they reach decisions. They may be compared to golfers who do not know how they make a good drive. Decision making is in part an art and hence is difficult to study and analyze. To an increasing extent, however, it is becoming a science, at least in the area of rational as opposed to intuitive decision making.[3]

Dr. Robert D. Calkins has outlined five general steps or stages in rational decision making. He says,

---

[3] Professor Simon refers to "programmed" and "nonprogrammed" decisions. He says, "Decisions are programmed to the extent that they are repetitive or routine, to the extent that a definite procedure has been worked out for handling them so that they don't have to be treated *de novo* each time they occur. . . . Decisions are nonprogrammed to the extent that they are novel, unstructured, and consequential." Herbert A. Simon, *The New Science of Management Decision* (New York: Harper & Bros., 1960), pp. 5–6, by permission.

However much they may be obscured or circumvented in practice, there are five general steps inherent in the process of rational decision making. They are: (1) to identify the problem and understand it, (2) to define or clarify the goals sought, (3) to pose alternatives for the attainment of those goals, (4) to analyze the anticipated consequences of each major alternative, and (5) to appraise the alternatives and choose.[4]

Professor Herbert A. Simon treats decision making as synonymous with managing and identifies three principal phases in the process,

. . . finding occasions for making a decision; finding possible courses of action; and choosing among courses of action. . . . The first phase of the decision making process—searching the environment for conditions calling for decisions—I shall call *intelligence* activity (borrowing the military meaning of intelligence). The second phase—inventing, developing and analyzing possible courses of action—I shall call *design* activity. The third phase —selecting a particular course of action from those available—I shall call *choice* activity.[5]

Other writers divide the process in still other ways. It is apparent that there are similarities between the two types of divisions outlined by Calkins and Simon. Using them as a general basis, we may find it helpful for our purposes to use the following steps or stages: (1) making an estimate of the situation, identifying the problem and determining the objectives sought as well as the main obstacles to reaching them; (2) developing and analyzing alternatives for attaining the goal or objective; and (3) appraising alternatives and choosing the most desirable. These three steps may be thought of as the core of the decision process.

In business firms and in most other organizations, decisions are made for the purpose of taking action. In short, the decisions must be *implemented. Plans* need to be developed for carrying out the desired action and this may involve further choices among alternatives. The plan selected often must be worked out in some detail. Resources of men, materials, equipment, and money must be *organized.* The organization is put into action to carry the decision into effect. This is the function of leadership. The action taken is then evaluated; corrections are made as required. Objectives and plans are then modified if necessary.

These stages of planning, organizing, taking action, and evaluating or reviewing the results of the action taken are often thought of as the process of *implementing* decisions, as distinct from decision making,

---

[4] Calkins, *op. cit.,* p. 14.
[5] Simon, *op. cit.,* pp. 1–2.

particularly in terms of the three-stage process we have outlined. This distinction may be a useful way of thinking about the work of managers but we should note also that decision making goes on at each stage of the planning process, the organizing process, the taking of action, and review. Varying degrees of difficulty are involved in these decisions. Further, all of these processes are interrelated. A business firm does not shut down while its managers decide what to do next. Decisions and actions get mixed up together and one modifies the other.

Typically, the identification of problems and objectives is the more difficult part of the process since choices here are wide. At the planning and organizing stages the decisions are narrowed somewhat. At the action stage some decisions will become routine. In the remainder of this chapter we consider the three-part decision process we have outlined.

Estimate of the Situation—Problem and Goal Identification

Most business problems can be thought of in relation to goals or objectives and the obstacles that stand in the way of reaching them. They may range from major problems affecting the very survival of the firm to specific problems relating to the sale of a particular product. Top management is primarily concerned with major decisions; middle managers with decisions of somewhat lesser consequence, although all must tie together ultimately.

Business firms operate in a highly dynamic environment. Managers are concerned constantly with potential changes and their possible impact on the programs of the firm. Thus, they try constantly to identify problems, to see what developments may be creating obstacles for them and to anticipate courses of action that may be taken. The manager typically must search out significant problems. For example, a transportation strike may be threatened. If adequate supplies can be accumulated it may be unnecessary to suspend operations during the strike. A competitor may be ready to move into a new market. A decision to move ahead of him may provide a competitive advantage.

Many business managers make use of elaborate communication systems to detect and analyze developments that may create problems for them. They may employ specialists to help them; hold committee meetings and conferences. We should note that in all too many cases, however, a conference is, as Bernard Baruch once pointed out, ". . . a meeting at which conversation is substituted for the dreariness of labor and the loneliness of thought."

Calkins points out,

. . . when we ask for the meaning of some event the scholar is disposed to explain it, by showing how it arose, what caused it, and why. But for the practical man this is the smaller share of what he needs to know. He must know the future potentialities of the event—what the event is likely to lead to—and since that usually cannot be forecast reliably, he wants to know the event's capabilities, what it *could* lead to, and *how,* and under *what* circumstances. Thus, he wants past experience distilled to yield not just broad universal generalizations, but also a great many special conclusions about how and why things behave in different specified conditions. This will be of practical use to him.[6]

The managers of business firms often outline general objectives for achievement; frequently these are stated as desired rate of return on investment, maximizing profit in the long run, achieving a certain rate of growth, or others. The attainment of such broad objectives may require the establishment of numerous supporting objectives and the making of numerous decisions as to their accomplishment.

Although many business firms have fairly well-defined goals in so far as broad objectives are concerned, there may be shifts in emphasis from time to time. The objectives that are set determine the relative importance of supporting programs. They also help to determine the priorities that may be assigned to one program or process as against another.

As we have suggested, there are various levels of objectives ranging from broad, general goals for the entire organization to specific ones for particular operations. All business decisions, however, tend to have financial implications. They relate to anticipated profits, relations between income or revenues, costs of producing income, and the risks that may be involved in the process.

Often the manager must determine the specific goal that will serve best the broader objectives of the firm. He may find it necessary to clarify relationships between immediate, intermediate, and long-term objectives. Often he selects specific goals within the framework of a rather definite set of cost, risk, and return relationships. These specific or instrumental goals are not final; they serve the broader objectives of the firm. Their careful selection, however, often is a key factor in the success or failure of a firm.

Developing and Analyzing Alternatives

The alternatives among which choices may be made in a given decision situation frequently are far from clear. Often they must be sought out. Only in a limited number of situations is there a choice

---

[6] Calkins, *op. cit.,* p. 15.

between one alternative and another. Sometimes, of course, such choices are extremely difficult to make and the risks of loss may be high. In most situations there are many alternatives. Usually it is not feasible to seek out all of them. Those that appear to be most pertinent are identified and considered.[7]

Often the alternatives are of the "more or less" variety. For example, a business firm may wish to purchase land for expansion. The final decision seldom will be made solely on the basis of whether to buy or not to buy at an asking price. Alternatives will be sought out. The price may be less if a purchase is made in 30 days, the seller may be willing to trade wholly or in part for another property, a long-term lease may be possible, or other alternatives may be open. We should recognize that in many business decisions the alternatives are rather wide. Success may depend on finding the most desirable alternative.

Past experience is often a guide in the posing of alternatives in various situations. The experience of others may also be helpful. For example, practices in a related field may suggest alternatives.

Once the alternatives that are considered pertinent by managers have been identified, some will be eliminated more or less automatically. An alternative may conflict with another aspect of the firm's operations; it may be considered too costly or too risky in terms of the returns anticipated; it may run counter to company policy; or it may involve strategic factors that cause it to be eliminated. Sometimes alternatives are dropped because they are considered unethical or unacceptable to customers, regulatory agencies, or the public at large. Some alternative may seem possible but would involve other changes that are believed undesirable.

After preliminary analysis of the alternatives, some will be considered worthy of further consideration, analysis, and appraisal. In some cases new alternatives will be discovered that supplant the ones originally considered.

Once the principal alternatives have been selected it is necessary to consider the probable consequences of each. This involves prediction or perhaps more properly the establishment of *postulates*. Calkins points out for example:

As I have observed administrators they do not *predict* the future, they postulate it, and ask how a given course of action will work and what results it will have under these postulated conditions. They postulate, for

---

[7] Herbert A. Simon, *Administrative Behavior* (rev. ed.; New York: Macmillan Co., 1957), p. 67, 81. Richard M. Cyert, Herbert A. Simon, and Donald B. Trow, "Observation of a Business Decision," *Journal of Business*, Oct., 1956.

example, by projection or extrapolation, a continuation of business about as it has been, using this or last year as a model for the future; or they assume a rate of growth or recession in line with recent experience. But prudent administrators seldom risk a major decision on the basis of results expected under only one set of postulates. They also ask: "How will this course of action work if we have war, or a depression, or a boom?" They postulate a number of contingencies and consider the consequences under each. They may, and sometimes do, fail to postulate the most likely future, or the one that is later realized, but their several efforts are intended to come fairly close to any set of conditions that may emerge.[8]

Appraisal and Choice

After the decision maker has selected the alternatives that he considers most likely to gain the results desired, he must appraise them and make his choice. At this stage he has weeded out those possible lines of action that may be contrary to established policy, may interfere with other programs, may be unacceptable to members of the firm or financial institutions, regulatory agencies, or the public, or be unacceptable for some other reason. Typically, in business situations, the manager's final choice is made on the basis of attaining his objective in terms of the most favorable set of cost-risk-return relationships.

The decision maker allows for some margin of error in selecting among alternatives. He usually allows a margin of safety by keeping a cash reserve, or providing a reserve of personnel, space, or raw materials. He usually adopts courses of action that permit adjustment to change as new information "feeds back" to him. He may even set up alternative objectives for a course of action, some more difficult of achievement than others. He reviews constantly pertinent developments and potential developments so that he can make adjustments in his commitments and operations.

In these and other ways the business executive makes commitments against an uncertain future. His postulates, projections, or predictions are often based on inadequate information. He may have limited bases on which to make judgments. Ultimately, however, he has no alternative but to proceed.

Professor Simon takes the position that the executive oversimplifies in order to be able to do his job. He says,

Administrative man recognizes that the world he perceives is a drastically simplified model of the buzzing, blooming confusion that constitutes the real world. He is content with this gross simplification because he believes that the real world is mostly empty—that most of the facts of the real world

---

8 Calkins, *op. cit.*, pp. 18–19.

have no great relevance to any particular situation he is facing, and that most significant chains of causes and consequences are short and simple. Hence, he is content to leave out of account those aspects of reality—and that means *most* aspects— that are substantially irrelevant at a given time. He makes his choices using a simple picture of the situation that takes into account just a few of the factors that he regards as most relevant and crucial.[9]

The final choice is an act of judgment and it may be based on objective analysis or on personal value systems. Some executives are disposed to take greater risks than others; some prefer short-term gains, others long-term; some emphasize strategic considerations and competitive position, others return on investment.

Often the decision maker's choice is not final but must be approved by others such as higher officials in the company, an executive committee, or a board of directors. Here the process is much the same as that followed by the executive who originally recommended a decision and action but it will vary with the extent to which reliance is placed on the judgment of the original decision maker. Usually a higher official or a board of directors tries to make sure that all the feasible courses of action have been considered and that each has been analyzed and appraised carefully enough to provide a sound basis for the final decision.

Continuity of Decisions

We have a tendency to think of a decision as final. This is true in a literal sense, but we should recognize that we reappraise and review most decisions and frequently modify them, change them entirely, or supplant them by new decisions. For example, your decision to get a college education may have seemed to you at the time to be irrevocable —and it may turn out that way. Or it may be that after a semester or a year you decide (or the college authorities decide) that you should not continue. Or you may decide that the decision to go to college was a good one, but that the decision to go to the particular school you chose was not. So you may transfer to another school.

Most of our decisions may have the appearance of finality at the time they are made. Many of our decisions, major and minor, are reviewed and reappraised, even if we do not recognize that we are consciously doing this. Often modifications, alterations, or changes are made.

The same thing is true of business decisions. For example, a man-

---

9 Simon, *Administrative Behavior*, op. cit., pp. 25–26, by permission.

ager may decide to lease space for his store. Even before he occupies the location, however, he may have found another one that offers many additional advantages. He may then sublease the first location and occupy the new one. Business managers are constantly reviewing and reappraising the results of past decisions. Often decisions are modified or changed or canceled out. In some cases, of course, it may be impossible to change a previous decision even if the manager wished to do so. In the illustration above, for example, the manager might have found it impossible to take the new location if he had been unable to sublease the first one. Even in this case, however, he may occupy the first location for a time and later be able to make a shift.

As we have suggested, most business decisions have monetary or financial implications. They have a bearing on potential profits. It is through money that many decisions are carried out. Most transactions are accomplished through the use of money or credit. If a businessman sells a plant, for example, this may be a final decision as to that particular property, but he then has the problem of deciding what to do with the money he received from the sale. He has changed the form of a portion of his assets, hence the nature of the problem of what to do with them, but he has not eliminated a portion of his assets by the decision to sell the plant.

This general concept of the continuity of many business decisions— the lack of finality in very many decision situations—is illustrated in the chart presented in Figure 10–1. We begin at about "one o'clock" on the left hand "circle" on the chart with the estimate of the situation, including problem identification, and the definition and clarifi-

FIGURE 10–1

Decisions and Operations

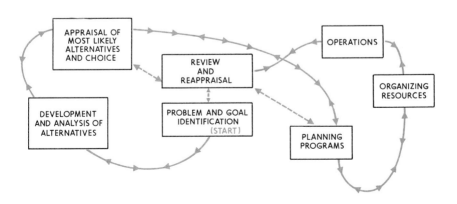

cation of goals (marked "start" on Figure 10–1). We proceed to alternatives, the developing of alternatives, and the analysis of probable consequences of selected alternatives. Finally we move to appraisal and choice. But this does not end the process. We may put the decision into effect, planning programs, organizing resources, and carrying forward operations. Even before doing this there may be reappraisal. Review and reappraisal almost always will follow operations; problems are reidentified or new ones generated as the result of past decisions or new situations; redefinition and clarification is undertaken; new alternatives are discovered and posed; the consequences of the new alternatives are analyzed; and finally appraisal and choice occurs again. And this may not be the end of the process—it may be repeated many times.

At the same time that one decision is being made, hundreds of others may be under consideration. Some of them will be interrelated, particularly since some of them may be supporting decisions, or related closely to major decisions. Often general policies can be worked out to guide the making of supporting decisions. At times, however, it may be necessary to review such policies and to modify or change them.

The business manager is engaged constantly in the making of current decisions, reviewing and reappraising past decisions, postponing some decisions, and undertaking new decisions. The decision-making process is not done in isolation; one decision seldom can be separated from others. In a few cases this is true, for example, a decision to start a new business or to sell an established firm may rule out other alternatives, but even in such cases related decisions may be involved.

Decision Making and the Scientific Method

It is often assumed that the manager in making decisions and the scientist in discovering knowledge follow essentially the same methods and that the more "scientific" the manager may become, the more effective he will be in his work. It is true that managers employ research or scientific methods in collecting and analyzing information. The searching out of alternatives prior to reaching a decision by the manager resembles the establishment of hypotheses by the scientist. The testing of alternative actions and hypotheses may have similar elements. There may be other similarities between the work of the manager and that of the scientist. But there are also marked differences. The scientist is usually not required to make decisions or to assume the responsibility for them; this is the essential element in the manager's work. The scientist typically is not concerned with action.

He is interested primarily in discovering knowledge. While his ultimate objective is prediction in the broad sense, he is usually not concerned with the solution of immediate problems. (In a general sense the ultimate objective of all study and research is prediction.)

As we have suggested in our previous discussions, a knowledge of the scientific method is helpful to the manager or administrator and acquiring such knowledge should be an essential part of his education. It does not follow, however, that the methods of the scientist and the manager are the same. The differences have been outlined by Calkins as follows:

The scientist seeks truth; the administrator effective action. The scientist strives for reasonable certainty; the administrator strives in great uncertainty for reasonable results. The scientist shuns the selection of goals; the administrator chooses and organizes goals to serve an institutional purpose. The scientist aims to discover what is; the administrator strives to realize the possible. The scientist designs a strategy for discovery; the administrator designs a strategy for action.[10]

As is true of the social sciences generally, analytical studies in the field of business administration are complicated by the fact that it is impossible to repeat experiments. In the laboratory sciences, for example, it may be possible to repeat the same experiment many times, to vary one factor in each experiment under controlled conditions, and thus to determine its significance. In the business world even discussing a particular problem may tend to change it.

It is difficult also to maintain objectivity in the process of interpreting information and estimating its significance for future developments in the business world. Each of us has developed a system of personal values that is bound to affect his point of view even in the interpretation of impersonal data. Some allowances for bias in one or another direction may be introduced if one can determine as carefully as possible what his preconceptions or basic attitudes may be. Thus, it may be possible to guard against a tendency toward optimism or pessimism, preferences for stability of operations or rapid expansion, or similar attitudes.

Despite the difficulties, the methods of science are proving to be of increasing value to the manager or administrator. This is especially true in the collection and analysis of information. The high-speed computer is proving to be of special value in this connection. Recent experiments suggest that computers may be able to handle the making

---

[10] Calkins, *op. cit.*, pp. 22–23.

of many types of decisions, perhaps even the major ones.[11] Additional work by mathematicians, statisticians, social scientists, and economists undoubtedly will continue to contribute to the improvement of the work of the administrator.

Decision Tools and Guides

Business managers and their assistants make use of a number of tools or techniques and analytical methods to assist them in various stages of the decision process. For example, much business information is collected and analyzed by means of *accounting* and *statistical* methods; in addition, these methods provide valuable guides to the appraisal of alternatives and to the development of projections or postulates regarding future developments. Widespread use is made of basic *economic* and *financial* concepts in the analysis of information, in the appraisal of alternatives, and the development of projections. Economics proves to be especially helpful in making value judgments related to cost, risk, and return relationships. Often managers and their assistants use various *prediction* methods and *strategic* concepts in the making of decisions. *Mathematical techniques*, notably linear programing, game theory, and related areas, are proving to be of growing value in the solution of many management problems.

In some cases legal methods, historical studies, and case studies prove to be helpful. Frequently, the behavioral sciences are drawn upon to aid in the processes of analyzing information, determining various priorities between goals, either major or supporting, and estimating the potential effects of decisions on the behavior of people within the firm or in markets or in various sections of society as a whole. The physical sciences and engineering often provide basic concepts and data that help to guide decisions. In short, the business manager will draw on the techniques of almost any field that he finds useful for his purposes. Decision making encompasses all aspects of a business firm's life, and relates to all manner of relationships between the firm and its environment.

Diary of a Decision

Suppose you find it necessary to get a job for the summer. Without some added money, you believe it will be difficult for you to carry on your studies in the next academic year. Prior to spring vacation you

---

11 Professor Simon, for example, believes that even unique decision problems may be programed so as to be resolvable by computers. See Simon, *The New Science of Management Decision, op. cit.*

note that a business recession appears to be developing and this may mean a scarcity of summer jobs. You had planned to visit at the home of a friend during spring vacation, but you now decide that you'd better go home to see if a summer job can be arranged.

You have identified your problem and defined your goal in a general way. You now try to see what jobs, if any, may be open. After a few days at home you find that you can work at the bank under a junior training arrangement. The rate of pay is not high, but you will be given good experience and it is understood that this arrangement may lead to a permanent job offer after you finish your university degree.

There is also a job open with a construction company that is erecting prefabricated homes. This part of the construction industry is not unionized in your town so there are no problems on this score. The rate of pay is good, the work is hard, but an outdoor job seems attractive for the summer.

A few days later you find that a neighbor, an elderly woman, will need someone to drive her to the coast for a visit. She will pay all expenses, provide reasonable spending money, and the trip will take about six weeks. You have never been to the coast, indeed have not traveled much, and this possibility has some attractions.

Analyzing Alternatives

So what to do? You try to *project or postulate* the possible consequences of each alternative. You consider that your primary aim is to earn money to return to school next year; this, however, is subordinate to your longer-range objective of finishing your education and developing a career. Also, since you have not traveled much, you recognize that the opportunity to drive to the coast also offers some long-run advantages. You never can tell what may result from a trip of this sort, you tell yourself; you might meet people who will prove to be quite helpful in the future. Still, it will not serve very well your immediate objective of getting enough money to finish the next school year, which is of primary importance for your long-term goals.

You wonder about other alternatives. Could you borrow the added money you will need for next year and thus have the benefit of the travel? You look into this and find the possibilities limited. Also, you reason, you ought to hold your borrowing capacity, even if limited, in reserve in case you should get sick, suffer an accident, or face some other emergency. So you are somewhat reluctantly forced to rule out the vacation travel, much as it attracts you.

About this time you get a call from the bank. You are told that they would like to have your answer within the next day or two because they have another young man in mind for the summer position. You hate to hurry your decision, but recognize that there is no alternative.

Appraisal and Choice

You consider the relative advantages of the bank job and the construction job. On the construction job you will earn about 50 per cent more money and in terms of your immediate goals, this is a highly important consideration. On the other hand, will a letter of recommendation from the head of the construction firm be as helpful later on as a letter of recommendation from the bank? Also, the bank might like your work and offer you a chance at a permanent job later.

You find some other factors entering your problem. A girl friend happens to remark about the exciting aspects of construction work; her brother had a great experience on a construction job last summer. You find that you'd like to impress her, perhaps more than you had realized. At about the same time, you talk to a friend who does business with the bank regularly and he remarks about the large number of good-looking young ladies who work there.

You finally force yourself to think about your problem in more realistic terms; after all, you tell yourself, it's primarily an economic matter, not social. On economic grounds the problem becomes a question of whether you should put greatest emphasis on short-term or longer-term objectives. You make some further calculations about your financial requirements for the next school year and decide that by careful management of your funds you can get along on what you would be able to save from the income from the bank job. Recognizing this, however, raises the question in your mind about whether you are seriously interested in the possibility of a banking career. You consider this further, decide that as a result of the summer's experience you will be a good deal more certain than you can be now, and that you really shouldn't miss the opportunity of trying out this type of work.

It looks as though you are getting close to a final decision, but you still are reluctant to give up the added income from the construction job. You decide to talk to the man in charge of this work again. He tells you that if he gets rushed during the summer there may be a possibility of your doing some "moonlighting," that is working after office hours and on week ends. He can't guarantee this, but indicates that there is a good possibility.

With this added information, you decide to accept the job at the bank, hoping that some extra income may be possible by part-time construction work as well.

Review and Reappraisal

After you return to school you have a chance to reflect further on your decision. You feel reasonably well satisfied with it. On occasion you regret that you will be unable to take advantage of the travel opportunity, but assure yourself that once your education has been completed you will take some time out for travel before you settle into a regular work routine. You conclude that all in all you have made a reasonably good decision. You recognize that unless you had sought out all of the possible alternatives, including the possibility of "moonlighting," however, your decision would have been less satisfactory. You have finally been able to work out an arrangement that serves both your shorter-term and longer-term objectives. You weighed the alternatives carefully, trying to anticipate the consequences of each. You discarded the travel arrangement as impractical fairly early in your attempts to arrive at a sound decision. And your final choice, like many decisions in business, proved to be a compromise.

You recognize that you did not proceed directly from your problem to a solution. You moved back and forth somewhat, re-evaluating your objectives, considering alternatives, seeking out new alternatives, even when you seemed close to a final decision. In short, the decision-making process seldom follows a straight line, it is more appropriately described as a circle or, as we indicate in Figure 10–1, two interlocking circles with decisions and actions closely interrelated in a sort of "lazy 8" arrangement, to borrow a descriptive term from Western cattle brands.

SUMMARY

Management decisions cover a wide range of subjects and are complicated by future uncertainties, since all decisions are future oriented. Decision problems are more difficult than information problems since choices among alternatives must be made.

Business decisions are complicated by competitive conditions, management strategies, value judgments, factors of time and timing, cost-risk-return relationships, the uncertainties of the future, and the effectiveness with which decisions are likely to be carried out or implemented. The results of a "good" decision poorly implemented are likely to be less desirable than the results of a questionable decision that is well implemented.

Top-management decisions typically require selection between a wide variety of major alternatives; the range of decisions tends to narrow after the major ones are made and as policies and procedures are established to guide supporting decisions.

The steps in rational decision making may be outlined in various ways. We suggested a three-step or stage process: (1) making an estimate of the situation, including identifying and understanding the problem, and defining and clarifying the goals sought, along with identifying the major obstacles in the way of attaining these goals; (2) developing and analyzing alternatives for reaching the goals or objectives desired, recognizing that often the most likely alternatives must be sought out; and (3) appraising the most likely alternatives, predicting or postulating the probable results of each, and finally choosing the one that appears to be most promising.

Decisions are constantly being reviewed, evaluated, reappraised and modified, and changed as required. Decisions typically lead to action and actions lead, after review, back to subsequent decisions. There is a continuity to business decisions and operations (as suggested in Figure 10–1).

Various guides to decisions are available to managers including financial, accounting, statistical, and economic, as well as some of the mathematical techniques such as linear programing, game theory, and related areas. The social and behavioral sciences and the physical sciences and engineering are also providing valuable decision guides.

Decision making differs in a number of respects from the scientific method, although a knowledge of the scientific method is helpful to the decision maker. The scientist seeks truth. He is not much concerned with action. The administrator is action oriented; he tries for reasonable results in highly uncertain situations.

QUESTIONS AND PROBLEMS

1. Contrast decision problems with information problems.
2. Why do we say that decisions are future oriented? Why does this make them particularly difficult?
3. Do you believe that if the facts are obtained and analyzed the cause of a problem will become evident, and that by treating the cause, we can solve the problem? Explain.
4. Does the objective of maximizing profits provide a rational basis for reaching business decisions? Why or why not?
5. Why is the manner in which decisions are carried out or implemented of importance?
6. Why does the president of a company face more difficult decisions than the supervisor of the repair shop?

7. Outline the major steps in the process of rational decision making. Can you suggest alternative steps in the process?
8. Why do we say that the manager typically must search out significant problems? Shouldn't these be apparent?
9. Why is it often difficult to identify the alternatives that are available in a decision problem?
10. Is there a difference between predicting and postulating?
11. Can we be sure that we are choosing the most likely alternative in arriving at a decision? Suppose we choose one of the less likely alternatives, what happens then?
12. Why are decisions reviewed and reappraised? Would you be inclined to think of the decisions process as continuous or final?
13. How does the decision process differ from the scientific method?
14. After reading the "Diary of a Decision" do you agree with the choice made by the student? Would you have made a different decision? Why or why not?

SUGGESTED READINGS

CALKINS, ROBERT D. "The Art of Administration and the Art of Science," *Indiana Business Report No. 29*. Bloomington, Ind.: Indiana University Bureau of Business Research, 1959. This report presents an excellent discussion of the decision-making process and its relationship to administration.

EDWARDS, WARD. "The Theory of Decision Making," *Psychological Bulletin,* Vol. 51, No. 4 (July, 1954), pp. 380–417.

LONG, JOHN D. *Workbook to Accompany Weimer: Business Administration: An Introductory Management Approach,* chap. 10. Rev. ed. Homewood, Ill.: Richard D. Irwin, Inc., 1962.

SIMON, HERBERT A. *Administrative Behavior,* Rev. ed.; New York: Macmillan Co., 1957. Read chap. 1, "Decision-Making and Administrative Organization," of this very important book.

————. *The New Science of Management Decision,* New York: Harper & Bros., 1960. Read the first of the lectures published in this short book, "The Executive as Decision Maker."

OUTLINE FOR CHAPTER 11

FINANCIAL GUIDES TO MANAGEMENT DECISIONS are of major
significance because
many objectives are financial in nature such as maximizing
profits, or gaining a desired return on investment which
affect survival, growth or other goals;
financial resources are the least specialized type of business
resource;
cost-risk-return relationships are financial in nature;
business firms compete by means of money as well as in other
ways;
business failure is essentially a financial concept.

Basic financial questions related to business decisions include:
What will be effect on profits?
Do we have the money or can we get it and at what risks and
costs?
Will we get our money back, over what period of time, at
what rate of return?

Financial requirements of a new firm include funds for
studies of market potential, competitive position, and
profit potential; securing a location, required manpower, equipment, and materials.

Financing of operations and expansion requires determination of probable sources of funds, including
sale of goods or services, or other assets.
borrowing, or securing additional equity capital,
in relation to needs for funds for operations or
expansion.

Financial budgets assist in management planning
and control as well as in organization; management is aided by financial standards and
analysis of flow of funds.

Leadership factors in finance include
financial incentives and motivations,
competitive relations,
strategic and risk considerations.

Business failure may lead to liquidation,
directly or through bankruptcy, or to
reorganization and ultimate revival.

FINANCIAL GUIDES TO MANAGEMENT DECISIONS

The great affair, we always find, is to get money.

—ADAM SMITH

Financial Aspects of Decisions

In the preceding chapter we outlined some of the primary characteristics of management decisions and the principal stages of the decision process. In this and the following four chapters we outline various guides to management decisions, including financial guides, accounting guides, some statistical and economic guides to decisions, and the type of help provided by linear programing, game theory, and related areas.

Financial factors are of primary importance in nearly all business decisions. Objectives such as maximizing profits and earning a desired rate of return on investment are financial in nature. Indeed, almost any objective established by a business firm relates to its ability to make profits. This is true of survival, growth, the attainment of a prestige position, or other types of objectives.

Financial resources are the least specialized of any resources available to a business firm. Through financial resources managers are able to gain command over the capabilities of people, land, buildings, materials, machines, equipment, and other things that are needed to produce and market goods and services in order to get income.

Costs are stated in financial terms. Risks are typically reduced to financial relationships. Returns are computed in financial terms. Cost-risk-return relationships are financial in nature.

Business firms compete by the use of money, just as they compete through personnel, production programs, or sales campaigns. The effectiveness with which money is used often in a major factor in a firm's success.

Business failure is essentially a financial concept. While the causes of failure may arise from nonfinancial sources, the insolvency or bankruptcy of a firm is determined on financial bases.

In short, financial factors set limits on and influence nearly all major management decisions and many minor ones. Financial factors impose a discipline on managers and on others throughout the firm because of their potential effect on profits. Financial standards provide an objective basis for evaluating programs, personnel and managers, from supervisors to company presidents.

Some financial decisions are made by managers of the business firm, some are made outside the firm by banks and other financial institutions, which impose limits on the decisions of the managers. Some financial decisions are made by suppliers and customers, which in turn may influence the decisions of managers. Competitors may offer financial plans to customers, for example, that the managers of a firm may find it necessary to match or to better.

The managers of a firm may try to influence these "outside" decisions in various ways. Their ability to make profits is of major importance in this connection. This may be affected by increased revenues, reduced costs, or the handling of risks.

Because of the widespread impact of financial factors on decisions throughout a business firm, the responsibility for financial matters tends to be both centralized and decentralized or "splintered." Major responsibility for finance may be retained by the owner or owners of a business or by the board of directors in the case of a corporation. In other cases responsibility for financial decisions may rest with the chief executive officer, who may delegate some of this responsibility to a vice-president for finance, but it will also be decentralized among the various divisions of the firm.

This is true also of decisions related to personnel. People are a part of all phases of a firm's operations, and decisions often turn on the human factors involved in a particular situation.

The following questions illustrate some of the basic financial considerations that are pertinent to management decisions:

1. What will be the probable effect of the program under consideration on profits? How will this affect survival, growth, or other goals of the firm? Would other programs offer more desirable alternatives?
2. Do we have the money we will need for the program under consideration? If not, can we get it? From what sources? At what costs?
3. Will we get our money back? Over what period of time? At what rate of return?
4. Will the risks undertaken be justified in terms of probable costs and returns? To what extent will management be "locked in," that is lose its ability to maneuver financially? What will be the effect on liquidity? On reserves?

Financial Factors in Business Objectives

It should be apparent from the above discussion that financial factors will have a major bearing on the objectives of a business firm. As we pointed out in our discussions in Chapter 8, objectives are often stated in terms of maximizing profits in the long run. Profits are a financial concept.

Survival is usually a basic objective of most business firms. The objective of survival requires that the finances of a firm be managed in a way that does not leave it exposed to developments that may bring sudden failure. For example, borrowing money on terms that will be difficult to meet may threaten the survival of the firm. Or paying high rates for money may make it impossible to market products at prices that exceed costs. Inability to meet sudden or unforeseen needs for funds may threaten a firm's ability to survive. Loss of credit standing, inability to take cash discounts, or loss of the support of a bank or other financial institutions may bring failure. Probably the best assurance of survival is a good profit position.

Growth is a major objective of many business firms. Financial decisions often are the key to solid growth and expansion. Programs for expansion cannot be undertaken if the necessary funds cannot be provided, and provided on sufficiently favorable terms to allow the projects to "pay out." Solid growth depends not only on the selection of desirable projects but on the efficient financing of such projects in terms of costs, timing, the period for which funds are secured, and the advantages that may be gained over competitors through financing programs.

Many firms pursue *prestige* objectives. They try to be good business citizens, to make the time of executives available for community projects, to establish reputations for fair dealings, to gain recognition for product development, and the like. As we have suggested, all of these relate to the broad purpose of maximizing profits in the long run.

Managers frequently try to attain a *reputation for good financial management* for their firms. People respect "sound financing," even if they may not always be too certain of what they mean by this. The reputation of a business firm may turn to a large extent on its promptness in paying bills, meeting payrolls, providing fringe benefits for employees, and maintaining fairly stable dividend payments. Stable dividends may be more important to the investing public than widely fluctuating dividends, even if total earnings are higher over a period of years in the latter case. In short, financial decisions are as important in the pursuit of prestige objectives as they are in the pursuit of objectives of survival and growth.

In addition to considering financial factors in establishing general firm objectives, management may establish fairly specific financial objectives as well. For example, many firms try to earn a predetermined return on owners' investment such as 8 per cent, 10 per cent, or some other rate. Or they may establish financial objectives in terms of earnings as a percentage of volume of business transacted. For example, the board of directors of a corporation may set as objectives the doubling of sales in a five-year period and increasing earnings from 5 per cent of sales volume to 15 per cent of total sales. In some cases owners will decide to sell a business or to discontinue operations unless financial returns can be increased by a stated percentage.

Typically financial objectives are related to the *risks* that are assumed by business operations. Lower rates of return on investment are acceptable in case risks are reduced, or higher rates are required if it is necessary to undertake operations with higher degrees of risk. Also, financial objectives often are related to general business conditions, a lower rate of return being acceptable if business is depressed than when prosperous conditions prevail.

An interesting illustration of the importance of the degree of willingness to accept financial risks in determining the objectives that may be pursued is provided in the following statement:

The choice between financial alternatives in many, if not all, of the cases depends in part upon the principal's disposition for risk taking. An apocryphal anecdote concerning the late Baron Rothschild will illustrate the need for full recognition of personal factors. It is said that the Baron, while in his prime as a leader of finance in London, received a visit from a young man who had recently inherited a large estate. "Sir," the young man said, "my father told me to seek your advice about how to invest the funds which have come to me." The Baron looked at him for a moment and then said, "Young man, do you wish to eat well or sleep well?"[1]

Financial Decisions and Business Plans

You have probably done some financial planning, although you may not have thought of it in these terms. If you ever have planned a vacation or a trip, you undoubtedly found it necessary to estimate your needs for money to determine whether you would have enough from your own resources or whether you would have to borrow. When you started your college and university studies, you probably did some

---

[1] Pearson Hunt, Charles M. Williams, James T. S. Porterfield, Leonard C. R. Langer, and Robert F. Vandell, *Case Problems in Finance* (3rd ed.; Homewood, Ill.: Richard D. Irwin, Inc., 1959), p. 5, by permission.

financial planning. You may have set up a *budget* to help you manage your program.

Financial planning for business firms is a similar process to that of making your own financial plans. We cannot hope to cover all aspects of this subject here, but we will indicate some of its more important considerations. First, financial planning is related closely to the *general and supporting objectives* that have been set up by the owners and top managers of a business firm as we have seen in the above discussion.

Also, financial planning cannot be carried on in a vacuum; it must be related closely to other areas of a firm's operations and to general business or industry conditions. For example, an expansion in production seldom can be undertaken without the investment of additional money. Whether the investment should be made or not will depend largely on its potential effect on profits. Similarly, increased sales programs almost always require additional financing, which may or may not be warranted on the basis of profit potential. Financial plans will vary depending on how good business conditions are and on whether the industry of which a firm is a part is expanding, remaining stationary, or declining. Similarly, the general conditions of money markets —whether money is readily available on favorable terms or whether "tight" money market conditions prevail—will affect many of the planning activities in a business firm.

Second, all business planning requires that needs for funds be estimated as well as the probable *sources, availability*, and *cost* of funds. Needs may vary according to whether the firm is being started or is in full-scale operations, whether current or longer-term financial requirements are being considered, and whether stable or expanding operations are contemplated.

Decisions often must be made as to whether needed funds can be secured from within the firm or outside the firm. The former include the owners' investment plus income from operations, and the latter include borrowed money, either for short or long terms, or expanded ownership which may result from the sale of additional stock or taking in a partner or an additional partner.

Third, *profit possibilities and risk factors* play a major part in the influence that financial factors have on management planning. Projects of every type are always considered in relation to potential net return or profits, that is, income in excess of costs. The cost of money is an important factor in many business operations and thus plays an important part in management planning. The efficiency with which funds are used, of course, has an important bearing on their cost. The degree of risk involved also is given special weight when financial factors are involved in planning decisions. Anticipated profits must be higher if risky ventures are involved than if less risk is probable. (This does not mean that actual profits will be higher, however.)

Fourth, *competitive considerations* play an important part in financial planning. For example, it may be necessary to match the programs of competitors or to move in advance of them. Potential market changes may argue for a speed-up of operations or for delaying projects under consideration. Business firms compete by means of money as well as in other ways. Thus, the selection of the projects to be financed often is a determining factor in beating competition.

Financial Factors in Establishing a New Firm

At the time a firm is started, funds are usually needed to make studies and estimates of market potential, competitive strength of products, costs of operation, and profit possibilities. Usually the original investment of the founder or founders of the firm will be available for these purposes. Such funds typically will cover the cost of organizing the firm and starting operations. For example, a location for the business firm must be secured, either through purchase or lease. Certain machinery and equipment may be required. People usually have to be hired and paid at least until the firm makes some sales and begins to develop its own income. If the founder does not have sufficient funds for these purposes, he may be forced to borrow from banks or friends or take in a partner. In some cases, if he has a strong credit rating, he may buy raw materials or merchandise "on time," that is, finance by means of what is called "trade credit." Usually trade credit is not extended, however, until a firm has been in business long enough to establish its credit standing.

The financial circumstances surrounding a firm's establishment may dictate the type of ownership that is set up. For example, if it is necessary to raise large amounts of money, the corporate form will usually be preferred since this permits widespread sale of stock and makes possible large-scale borrowing. On the other hand, the amount of money needed may not be great, and this, plus tax considerations, may favor a proprietorship or partnership form of organization.

Financing Operations and Expansion

How can a business firm get money to finance its day-to-day activities or to provide the funds needed for expansion? One method, of course, is by the sale of goods or services. Such services may be personal or may also be property services, that is, the rental of space, equipment, and the like.

This process may be thought of in part as a conversion of assets, for example, the sale of inventories. The firm might also sell its fixed assets, that is, its land, buildings, or equipment and thus get money. The firm may retain earnings rather than pay them out in dividends Some funds will accrue from depreciation changes, as we shall see. The firm might borrow money for short or long periods. It might "join" money, for example, through a partnership or joint venture arrangement.

Thus, the choices on how to get money to finance operations or expansion are wide. Decisions are often difficult. Usually the decisions are made by managers in terms of answers to some of the questions we posed above and especially these:

1. Will we get our money back?
2. Over what period of time?
3. At what rate of return?

Under some conditions it is better to hold money; for example, if loans are falling due and it is essential that cash be available to pay them. In some cases money may be invested in other ventures because chances for gain seem to be greater than by using funds in the operations of the firm.

As we have suggested, after a firm gets into full-scale operations it should be able to produce income. If it is, money will be flowing in from the sales of products or services or both. Such money will be available to meet payrolls, current bills, taxes, and the like.

Most business firms expect to meet their current expenses from current operations, but there are often times when bills "bunch up" due to seasonal or other reasons and then funds typically are *borrowed*, usually from banks. Hence, good financial management requires the establishment and maintenance of effective working relationships with one or more banks. In some cases, banks issue a "line of credit," that is an agreement that the firm can borrow up to a certain amount on stated terms.

Sometimes business firms, especially the larger and better-known ones sell short-term obligations or "commercial paper" in the financial markets in order to raise funds. The selection among alternative sources of funds such as issuing commercial paper, borrowing from banks, using trade credit, or using other sources of funds is an important aspect of financial planning.

For longer-term projects most business firms plan to obtain a substantial share of required funds from *retained earnings,* that is, money left over after all bills due, taxes, and dividends to stockholders are paid. In the postwar years a large proportion of all business expansion has been financed in this way. Typically at least a part of earnings must be paid out to stockholders, although some firms are able to convince stockholders that no dividends should be paid, because of the importance of retaining earnings to finance expansion or other projects that may be in the long-term interest of the company and hence of its owners, the stockholders. Also, many stockholders prefer to have their earnings retained and reinvested since they believe they may secure greater returns in this way than by investing such funds elsewhere.

Another important internal source of funds is *depreciation charges.* These involve charging a certain amount to the cost of goods sold for the use of machines, equipment, or buildings each year so as eventually to recapture the amount invested in them. Such funds ordinarily are not held in a separate account to help finance replacements of the assets but are used for any needed expenditure. It should be pointed out, however, that continued successful operation over a long period of time requires that a firm replace its equipment. If it fails to do so it is said to be "using up its capital."

A business firm may *borrow for long-term* as well as short-term purposes. Usually commercial banks provide funds chiefly for short-term purposes, and insurance companies, investment banking firms, private investors, and others provide longer-term financing. For example, an individual investor might loan funds on the security of a mortgage on the plant of a small firm. In the case of a larger firm, mortgage bonds might be issued and then sold through an investment house to private and institutional investors.

The sale of bonds is usually accomplished by an investment banker who underwrites or guarantees a sale at a certain price and then in turn sells the bonds to others. Somewhat the same procedure is followed in marketing other obligations of a business firm.

Of course, a company may bring in additional owners, that is, provide *additional "equity" or ownership capital* rather than debt capital. For example, a partnership of two persons may take in a third if he agrees to provide certain required funds. Or a corporation may issue additional stock for sale to investors. We should note again that unlike a bond, which is an obligation or debt, a share of stock represents a partial ownership of the business.

Many business managers prefer not to raise money by expanding equity or ownership capital. Added owners may jeopardize the position of present owners. By borrowing money from others there may be a chance to gain additional earnings for present owners since funds usually are not borrowed unless the chances for increased earnings are greater than the costs of the borrowed money. This is called "trading on the equity," that is, using present resources to command additional funds through borrowing and paying a lower rate on borrowed money than can be earned by using it, thus raising the rate of return earned on owner's or equity investment. In case the stock of a company is widely held, however, higher dividends may have to be paid to stockholders to keep their interest in the firm and this, from the standpoint of management, may offset the advantages of "trading on the equity."

Even though borrowing may help to increase earnings on the owner's investment, many managers and owners prefer not to borrow or to borrow as little as possible. This is because of the risks involved in borrowing. Failure to repay loans on the conditions on which they are made may lead to loss of control of the company. Thus many business managers prefer to finance both current operations and capital expansion from income and retained earnings if possible.

Financial Budgets

In order to assist managers in determining the needs for funds and the means by which such needs may be met, financial budgets are often established as we suggested in Chapter 8. Such budgets estimate cash inflow, cash requirements both for current operations and for long-term needs, the outside funds that may be needed, their possible sources, and costs.

You may have had some experience with budgets of your own. In all probability you started with a predetermined amount of income and then allocated your expenditures among essential items such as bills that had to be paid and optional items, such as possible purchases, savings, and the like. The budget might indicate that certain borrowing had to be undertaken as well.

Unlike many personal budget situations, business firms typically have *no definite assurance as to income.* Consequently, incomes have to be estimated for future periods. Requirements for funds in short-term periods for business firms more nearly resemble the items in a personal budget since they are reasonably definite. But optional items are greater in number and variety. Also, long-term requirements often have to be determined well in advance so that plans can be made to meet them. Thus back of financial budgets lie a great many estimates, including those regarding the probable success of both current operations and future expansion programs.

Budgets provide a sort of blueprint for the financial operations of a firm for a future period, usually a year, sometimes for longer terms. Estimates of incomes and expenses are built up from past experience and from the estimates and projections of various departments in the firm. Once adopted, a budget becomes a *general plan* and also a valuable *control device* for management. Operations are reviewed in many firms on a monthly or quarterly basis, comparisons made with the budget, revisions worked out as required, or action taken to correct deviations from the budget as planned.

Financial Factors in Organization

As we have pointed out, financial considerations enter into almost every phase of a business firm's operations. Because of the importance of finance, the boards of directors or owners of some firms do not delegate this function at all but handle it directly or through a finance committee of the board. In individually owned firms the proprietor usually handles major financial matters himself. In some corporations the chief executive officers such as the president or executive vice-president will have the responsibility for financial management; in others a financial vice-president will be charged with this responsibility. In a larger firm there may be a treasurer or controller (sometimes called comptroller) or a chief accountant reporting to the financial vice-president. In some cases combinations of these types of offices will exist. Usually a single division or unit of a firm will disburse funds, typically the treasurer's or accountant's office.

Regardless of the general form of organization of the firm or the organizational arrangements made for financial management, all divisions of a firm will have some financial responsibility. In some cases this is accomplished by means of a budget. Each division will be asked to prepare a proposed budget. It will be reviewed by the financial manager and ultimately by the owner or board of directors. Once adopted, this budget becomes a part of the plan of the firm and a division's budget serves it as an operating guide. The head of the division is in effect a financial officer since he administers a part of the firm's budget. In some cases there will be a specially designated budget officer in each division of the firm. Thus, the financial responsibility tends somewhat to be "splintered" among all divisions of the organization, but with strong central controls being maintained.

The finances of a firm may provide a method for decentralizing authority as well as for centralizing it. In addition, financial standards may be set which establish limits on authority to spend money or to approve expenditures. For example, the manager of a department may have authority to approve expenditures so long as they fall within his budget; or he may be allowed to spend a certain amount for one item, perhaps up to $1,000. If additional funds are needed, he must secure higher approval for the expenditure.

The tendency to maintain central controls over finance in business organizations has been strengthened by the introduction and increasing use of large-scale data processing machines. Such machines usually perform the major accounting and statistical work for the organization and may be the responsibility of the chief accountant, controller (or comptroller) or treasurer, who in turn will be under the direction of the principal finance officer.

As we have suggested, financial considerations may dictate the form that a business firm will take when it is started, that is, whether it will be set up as an individual proprietorship, partnership, or corporation. After a business firm has been in operation for a time, *financial considerations may dictate a change* in the general form or organization. Rapid expansion may cause a shift from proprietorship or partnership forms to the corporate form; the importance of providing special incentives for top managers may dictate the use of stock options or bonuses which can be accomplished best by means of the corporate form or organization.

Many business firms will make use of people outside the firm to assist with their financial operations. Contracts may be let to investment houses or banks to provide for the sale of securities; financial advisers may be employed to advise the officers of the company in regard to special financial problems; accountants, tax experts, and specialized legal counsel may also be included.

Financial Standards and Controls

We have seen how budgets may be used to aid in the financial planning programs of a business firm. Budgets are also an important *control device* to assure that operations proceed in accordance with the plans represented in the budget. The use of budgets for control purposes emphasizes the importance of financial management in the control phase of general managerial operations.

As in the case of other types of controls, the use of the budget for these purposes is a forward-looking process. While it is necessary to relate incomes and expenditures in the past to the budget as established, the purpose of this process is always to determine the most desirable way to proceed *in the future*. Thus, if expenditures for advertising, for example, are running ahead of the budgeted amount, management may decide that advertising should be cut back, or that conditions have changed in such a manner as to justify an expansion in advertising expenditures. In this case some other items in the budget may be reduced to provide the added funds needed for advertising. Consequently, while financial controls must be backward looking to some extent, their purpose is to improve operations in the future.

Financial controls may include other things than those covered by budgets. Certain *standard items* of expenditure may be established either with a top limit or in a range. For example, maintenance costs while a member of a firm is traveling may be set at a top limit per day; mileage allowance on the use of automobiles may be set at a fixed amount per mile; certain officers only may make financial commitments, and the amounts for which they may commit the firm may have a top limit.

Financial controls are an important managerial method for analyzing costs and for improving efficiency of operations. Processing costs are always studied carefully as are sales costs, the cost of holding goods in inventory, costs of borrowed funds, and the like.

One of the important aspects of financial controls is analyses which indicate the *rate at which money is "turned over,"* that is, the number of times per year that it may be used. Money invested in goods in process or in inventory may be turned over several times a year; that invested in machines or buildings may only be turned over once in ten or fifteen years or longer. The rate of turn over of "working capital" or money used to meet day-to-day operations is usually higher than that of "fixed capital" which is invested in the more permanent assets of the company. Rate of turnover is one indication of the efficiency with which funds are being used and hence is an important control factor.

The financial experience of a company permits the establishment of various *financial standards* which may be helpful in controlling operations in accordance with plans. The desired rate of turnover of working capital, for example, may be one of such standards. Relationships between certain major expenditures may serve as standards or guides; for example, the percentage of total sales spent for advertising, the percentage of processing costs involved in payroll, and the like. Desired rates of earnings on owners' investment or rate of return on total investment in the business may be set up as a general standard, although this is such a broad and all-inclusive item that it may be thought of as a general firm objective.

The ultimate purpose of standards and controls—financial or others —is to aid in achieving the general and supporting objectives of the firm. By means of careful evaluation it is possible to determine whether operations are proceeding according to plan, meeting established standards, and moving in the direction of desired results.

The control process, as well as the planning process, in financial management may be understood more easily if you will study Figure 11–1 with some care. This illustration shows how funds may flow through a business firm—where they come from, how they may be used, and the relationship between all phases of the firm's operations. Good financial planning requires that provisions be made for the necessary funds at each stage of operation, and good financial controls help to assure that the funds will be available as required.

Leadership and Financial Management

While we may tend to think of financial management as being a hardheaded, objective type of activity relative, perhaps, to marketing or personnel management, financial affairs have their human side as well as their impersonal aspects. Indeed, the relationships between all officers and employees of a firm may be influenced greatly by the leadership exercised through financial management.

Often the more important incentives that may be provided for the members of a firm are financial. Financial leadership may be responsible for high rates of pay for employees, many fringe benefits, provision for stock purchases or for stock bonus plans, savings programs, insurance programs, and many other things. If a firm is successful financially, it can afford to do many things for its employees; this in turn often contributes to its future financial success.

Some companies attract top managers by offering stock options, that is, allowing a manager to purchase the stock of the company at an established price. Thus, if he helps to make the firm successful, and thus increases the value of its shares of stock, he has an opportunity to profit from his work by exercising his options to buy stock. In some cases stock bonuses are offered; that is, if certain levels of performance are attained, an added payment over and above salary is made as a stock bonus.

Some companies use "profit-sharing" plans. These typically provide bonuses to all employees who have worked for at least a minimum

FIGURE 11–1

Circular Flow of Cash through a Business Firm*

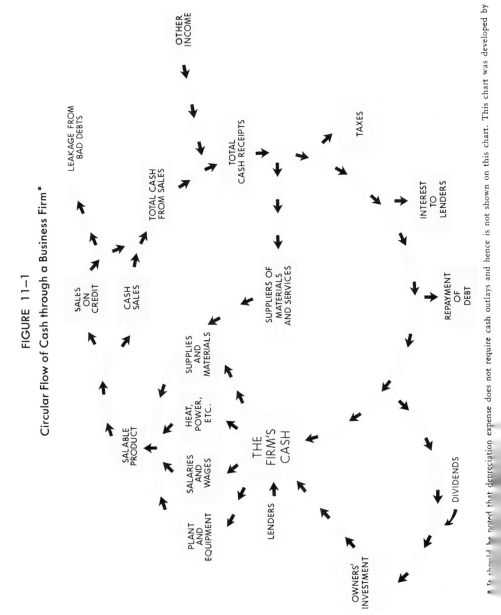

* It should be noted that depreciation expense does not require cash outlays and hence is not shown on this chart. This chart was developed by

period. Such bonuses are paid out of the earnings of the company over and above a stated rate of return on the investment of owners.

Many companies provide special financial incentives for long periods of service in order to reduce personnel turnover. These may be in the form of pensions, added pension payments for longer periods of employment, and other special incentives.

FIGURE 11–2

Corporate Profits, 1929–61

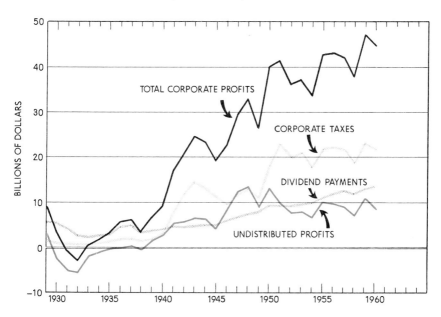

Thus, financial factors may play a significant part in the development of the *motivations* that may be provided to stimulate all of those associated with a business firm to do their best work. Financial factors may have a bearing not only on the financial affairs of a company but may influence other aspects of its operations as well. For example, we have already seen how budgets may be used as a planning and control device throughout a company.

Finance is especially important in the development of *research programs* and in *creating innovations* that will add to efficiency of operations. The creative aspects of management are not found only in the stimulation of research to develop new products or to find better ways of covering a market or of selecting better locations but also in the financial field. The development of a plan that will reduce the cost of borrowed money by a fraction of 1 per cent may mean a big addition to the profits of a firm; anticipation of changes in the financial markets may provide plant and equipment at financial costs that will give the firm a competitive advantage for many years.

Many of the plans for the mergers of firms that have been developed in recent years have resulted from the imagination and careful studies of financial relationships. Tax factors, of course, bulk large in many financial programs, and studies are conducted by many financial managers to avoid unnecessary tax charges or to provide advantages.

Financial Competition

As we have pointed out, business firms compete through their financial programs as well as in other ways. If a firm can borrow money more cheaply than its competitors, it will gain a competitive advantage. Similarly, it may be able to use money more effectively than its competitors, for example, turning its capital over more frequently, or financing projects that yield greater returns, or setting up financial incentives that bring forth greater efforts from the people in the firm, or in other ways.

In their competition with other firms financial managers are always concerned with costs in relation to returns; probable returns in relation to risks assumed; and with strategic factors such as beating competitors to markets, matching the programs of competitors, and anticipating changes in general business conditions or in the financial markets which may give a competitive advantage.

The *cost and availability of money* is always a factor in financial competition. Decisions have to be made as to whether money will be borrowed or whether the firm's activities will be limited to those that can be financed from internal sources. Sometimes there are real advantages in borrowing. Money may be available on favorable terms. The amount earned on it may far exceed its cost, and as a result the return on the owners' or equity investment will be increased. As we have seen, this is often referred to as "trading on the equity."

Borrowing in order to finance either current operations or expansion, of course, involves *risks*. Inability to repay the borrowed money on time may even result in the failure of the firm. Consequently, financial managers try to use borrowed funds to enable them to compete effectively with other firms, but they also try to avoid assuming risks that are unduly great. Thus, a new machine might be bought if funds were available from retained earnings; it might not be bought if it were necessary to borrow in order to buy it.

Business firms try to "work" their money, that is, to avoid large idle bank balances and to turn over capital as rapidly as possible. At the same time some bank balances will be needed to meet sudden or unexpected demands for funds. Sometimes such demands cannot be anticipated very exactly. Hence, some idle money in bank balances may be necessary simply to be sure that funds will be available when needed. Otherwise, important opportunities that might give real competitive advantages may be missed.

To some degree a firm competes by means of its good relationships with banks or other financial institutions. Hence, financial managers make every effort to maintain favorable working relationships with banks, at times borrowing even if funds are not immediately needed to keep up an established program. At other times managers will arrange for loans well in advance of anticipated needs in order to be sure that the money will be available as needed and in order to enable financial institutions to adjust to the needs of the firm.

Careful analyses of general business and industry conditions help a firm in its financial competition. If money is hard to borrow, it may be stockpiled or hoarded just as might be done with other scarce materials. Special efforts will be made to keep lines of credit with banks open at such times. If money is cheap and easy to borrow, expansion programs may be undertaken. Sometimes financial managers try to have expansion projects ready so that they can take advantage of favorable financing terms. On the other hand, periods when money is cheap and plentiful may also be periods of business uncertainty, and despite the availability of funds on favorable terms, money may not be borrowed because of the risks that are believed to exist.

Strategic and Risk Factors[2]

The development of financial programs for a business firm often depends on a number of factors related to the risks involved and the strategic considerations that may affect decisions. For example, how shall selection be made among several desirable projects or programs? Should machinery be replaced by newer machinery? Should a new product be added to the firm's line? Should sales territories be expanded? Should a branch plant be built?

Questions like these often require consideration of broad sets of factors. Usually a business firm will undertake a project calling for the major expenditure of funds for the purpose of improving its profit position either by (1) expanding output and sales or (2) reducing costs.

---

2 See Joel Dean, *Managerial Economics* (New York: Prentice-Hall, Inc., 1951), chap. x.

Management typically is very conscious of cost and return relationships, particularly costs and returns in relation to risks assumed, and the effect of the company's programs on those of competitors or of competitors' programs on those of the company.

For example, a new machine may be purchased to replace an old one in order to reduce costs. Or a machine may be added to expand output. In either case, however, unless the anticipated returns from adding the new machine will exceed costs and exceed them sufficiently to compensate for the risk involved, the project will not be undertaken. In addition, the project may not be undertaken if other considerations are not favorable; for example, timing, rate of payout of the investment, time period involved, or effect on other company programs.

FIGURE 11–3

Corporate Taxes, Dividend Payments, and Undistributed Profits
as Percentages of Total Corporate Profits
1929 Compared with 1960

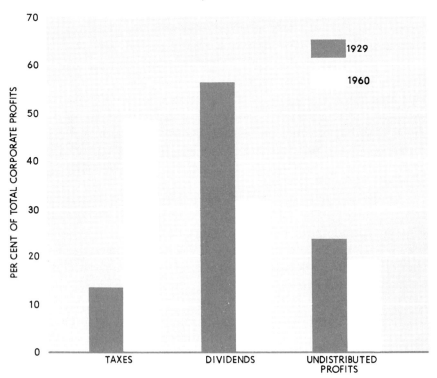

Timing may play an important part in the selection of projects to be financed. The time at which a project is undertaken may be important from a strategic standpoint such as beating a competitor to a market or from the standpoint of waiting to see if a better project comes along. In selecing projects to be financed a business firm, thus, is in much the same position that you are when you buy a new suit. Once you have made your purchase you are ordinarily unable (unless you have a lot of money available) to buy another one very soon even if you find a better value.

The *rate at which an investment will pay out* is often an important consideration in selecting projects to be financed. For example, if a machine will return its investment in a relatively short period of time, less risk is involved than if a fairly long period is required. Of course, anticipated rates of return must always be considered in this connection.

The *risk* element is always a big factor in decisions of this type, as we have pointed out. Ordinarily the shorter the time period involved, the less the risk. Uncertainties increase rapidly as the time period is lengthened. For this reason a dollar that is likely to be earned five years hence is worth substantially less than one that may be earned two years hence. The discounting process is always important in financial decisions since it forces management to think in terms of the *present value* of anticipated income rather than the income itself. In this connection you may find it helpful to refer to Appendix II.

Sometimes the desirability of a project is considered in terms of whether it is *postponable*. This may have some advantages from the standpoint of finding a better opportunity, but postponability by itself as a basis for making decisions may result in complete lack of expansion.

Financial managers sometimes rank various projects that might be selected in order of desirability. Such factors as the over-all objectives of the firm, costs in relation to anticipated returns, the risks involved, strategic considerations, and effect on current operations will be used to determine desirability.

Different projects may be selected, depending on whether a manager wishes to maximize profits in the short or long run, whether the new project may have a bearing on present costs, and whether risks of total operations may be reduced. Many alternatives are possible, of course, and each decision has to be related to a particular firm, its objectives, competitive position, and type of operations.

Risk and Insurance

We have stressed the importance of risk factors in financial management and indicated that some risks may be covered by insurance. Such financial risks as the possibility of loss or destruction of property by fire, windstorm, or theft can be covered by insurance, and most firms do this. In some cases, a firm may have such widespread holdings of property that it will carry its own fire insurance, that is, not pay out insurance premiums but assume the risk of such losses. This may be desirable if the firm has many properties in scattered locations so that a single fire would be unlikely to destroy all of the property that it owned.

Typically business firms transfer all or part of such risks to insurance companies by paying an annual premium for a certain amount of coverage, that is, an agreement on the part of an insurance company to compensate for losses that are insured or for a percentage of loss or for an amount agreed upon as representative of the risk.

In addition to risks of the type outlined above, a firm may insure for public liability, that is, the risk of customers or others being injured or having their property damaged through acts of the firm's employees. Also, workmen's compensation insurance may be provided to cover risk of a worker's loss of life or the risk of his physical incapacity. In addition, health insurance may be established, group life insurance for members of the firm, the lives of key executives may be insured, and many other risks may be covered by insurance of one type or another.

Matters of this type are usually the responsibility of the financial manager or vice-president for finance or treasurer of a company. Some companies have such a breadth of insurance problems that a special insurance department with a manager is set up to deal with them.

In recent years the appointment of "risk managers" has increased because of the growing complexity of insurance problems. Costs have risen and increased risks; progress in automation has created new hazards; insurance premium expenses have been advancing; and many juries have awarded large amounts in accident cases.[3]

Smaller companies rely on independent insurance agencies to handle their insurance for them. The amounts of money and the risks involved have made the insurance area one of growing importance for the financial managers of firms of all sizes.

---

[3] See Russell B. Gallagher, "A Practical Approach to Risk Management," *Business Horizons*, Vol. III (Summer, 1960), pp. 78–86.

Recently there has been some discussion of the possibility of expanding insurance coverage to provide for the stabilization of company income. This would make some risks insurable that now cannot be covered by insurance. For example, long-run averaging of the incomes of a number of firms might create the possibility of insuring the earning of an average income—an area that has never been considered insurable prior to this time. A development of this type would have important implications for financial management.[4]

Business Firm Failures

Each year a large number of business firms fail, go into bankruptcy, or discontinue operations. Business failure is essentially a financial concept. A business firm fails when it no longer can meet its financial obligations or is unable to convince lenders that they should extend further credit or suppliers to supply materials on trade credit or workers to work without any assurance of being paid. When a firm fails, thus, it no longer is able to command a stream of income sufficient to support its operations and the investments made in it. Evidences of weakness will appear in the financial reports of a company, and indications of possible failure when detected in time often can be corrected by prompt and aggressive action on the part of management.

The reasons for failure may be of many types. For example, a firm may lose a major portion of its market to a competitor through the more aggressive advertising and selling activities of the competitor, or a firm may find that its products have been outmoded by new products developed by another firm. In some cases it will fail because of the loss of key managers. Sometimes a firm will fail because of general business or industry conditions. In some cases failure is due to financial mismanagement. For example, a firm may have been put into a vulnerable position because of unwise borrowing, over extension of credit, loss of liquidity, or related reasons. If failure is probable, and if management is unable to take action which will avert it, attempts are often made to discontinue operations in time to meet outstanding obligations and without losing the entire investment of the owners.

In some cases when a firm shows an operating loss, it may be possible to sell the firm because it has a tax loss that can be carried forward, or it may possess certain equipment that can be utilized effectively by another firm, or its particular line of products may fit into the opera-

---

4 See John D. Long, "Stabilizing Income through Insurance," *Business Horizons*, Winter, 1958, p. 93.

tion results. Sometimes this can be accomplished without court action.
tions of another firm. In other cases failure is inevitable and liquida-
In other cases the firm goes into bankruptcy, which is a legal method
of handling failure. By going into bankruptcy, procedures are followed which have been established by law to arrange for the orderly
liquidation of the firm's assets or for its reorganization and ultimate
revival.

SUMMARY

Financial guides to management decisions are of major importance
because of the widespread impact of financial considerations on all
aspects of a business firm's operations. Many business objectives are
stated in financial terms such as maximizing profits in the long run or
gaining a desired rate of return on investment. All types of business
objectives including survival, growth, attainment of a prestige position, or others, depend for their achievement on financial success.

Financial resources are the least specialized of all types of business
resources and may be used to secure command over the capabilities of
people, land, buildings, equipment, machines, materials, and other
elements necessary to production and sales in order to secure income.

Cost-risk-and-return relationships are stated in financial terms,
ratios between them depend to a considerable extent on financial decisions. Basic financial questions include the following: What will be
the effect of a decision on potential profits? Do we have the money?
Can we get it? At what risks and costs? Will we get our money back?
Over what period of time? At what rate of return?

The financial requirements of a new firm often differ to a degree
from those of a going concern. Careful determination of potential
sources of funds from sales of goods and services, sales of other assets,
borrowing or securing additional equity capital is important in relation to needs for funds for operations and expansion.

Financial budgets assist in management planning and control as
well as in the solution of various organization problems. Management
is aided by financial standards, analyses of flow of funds, and related
financial techniques.

Management leadership may be aided by financial factors such as
use of financial incentives and motivations, innovations, improved
capacity to compete financially, and careful handling of strategic and
risk considerations.

Business failure, essentially a financial concept, may lead to direct
liquidation with sale of assets to satisfy claims, or to bankruptcy proceedings with liquidation, or reorganization and ultimate revival.

QUESTIONS AND PROBLEMS

1. Explain why financial guides are highly important to management decisions.
2. Explain what is meant by the statement: profit is a financial concept.
3. What do we mean by the idea that financial resources are the "least specialized" of the resources available to management?
4. Give illustrations of ways in which the general reputation of a firm may be enhanced or damaged by financial factors.
5. In which respects may the financial requirements of a new firm differ from those of a firm that is already in operation?
6. Why do some business managers prefer to raise money for expansion by retaining earnings rather than by borrowing? Set forth a situation in which a banker might control the major decisions of a business firm.
7. Why do we say that financial responsibility tends to be both centralized and "splintered?"
8. How may financial budgets be used for planning purposes? As control devices? May a budget be used to assist management in the solution of organization problems?
9. In which respects may financial factors influence the organization of a business firm?
10. Give illustrations of some ways in which financial factors may be used in exercising management leadership.
11. How may business firms compete through their financial programs?
12. Give illustrations of (a) risks that cannot be insured and (b) risks that can be insured.
13. Why do we describe business failure as essentially a financial concept?
14. What lines of action may be open in the event of business failure?
15. Firm A has made a profit of $50,000 from the past year's operations. Indicate the types of factors that would help to determine whether to (a) pay out the profits to owners as dividends; (b) reinvest the profits in the business; or (c) do part of both.
16. Do you think the stockholders of a business firm should have a right to decide whether the earnings on their shares should be reinvested or paid out to them? Or should management have the right to make the decision?

SUGGESTED READINGS

DEAN, JOEL. *Managerial Economics*. New York: Prentice-Hall, Inc., 1951. Read chap. x, "Capital Budgeting," which is relevant to the discussions here.

HEDGES, J. EDWARD, and WILLIAMS, WALTER. *Practical Fire and Casualty Insurance*. 7th ed. Cincinnati: National Underwriter, 1961. See chap. ii, "The Organization of the Insurance Business."

HOWARD, BION S., and UPTON, MILLER. *Introduction to Business Finance.* New York: McGraw-Hill Book Co., Inc., 1953. This book presents a general review of the subject of business finance; refer to chap. i, "The Meaning and Scope of Business Finance."

HUNT, PEARSON, WILLIAMS, CHARLES M., and DONALDSON, GORDON. *Basic Business Finance: Text and Cases.* Rev. ed. Homewood, Ill.: Richard D. Irwin, Inc., 1961. Read chap. 1, "Introduction," of this well-known text.

JOHNSON, ROBERT W. *Financial Management.* Boston: Allyn & Bacon, Inc., 1959. See particularly chap. 1, "The Role of the Financial Manager."

LONG, JOHN D. *Workbook to Accompany Weimer: Business Administration: An Introductory Management Approach,* chap. 11. Rev. ed. Homewood, Ill.: Richard D. Irwin, Inc., 1962.

SAUVAIN, H. C. *Investment Management.* Englewood Cliffs, N.J.: Prentice-Hall, Inc. See chap. 1, "The Problem of Investment."

OUTLINE FOR CHAPTER 12

ACCOUNTING provides many valuable
GUIDES TO MANAGEMENT DECISIONS

Income is the fundamental fact of economic life.
A firm must produce profits—revenue in excess of costs—to
survive, grow, or pursue any other objective.
Profits may be considered a reward for risk bearing, hence
are *residual* as opposed to contractual income.

Management decisions require adequate methods of accounting for revenues and costs over various periods.

The business firm uses *assets*, things of value that are owned,
and incurs *liabilities* or obligations in the production of
revenue. Excess of asset value over liabilities is owners'
equity or proprietorship interest.

Measurement of revenue, costs, and profits requires a
starting point, for which a *balance sheet* is made; an
ending point or another balance sheet; and a record
of what happened in the interim or an *income
and expense* statement.

The *balance sheet* may be considered a snapshot of conditions at a moment in time; of special importance is
the balance sheet equation — assets = liabilities
+ proprietorship.

The *income statement* may be compared to a moving
picture of operations over time and shows
the flow of revenue into the firm;
the cost of producing this revenue; and
the profits (or losses) resulting.

Management decisions are facilitated by various
accounting relationships such as
current assets to current liabilities;
debt to net worth;
turnover of inventories;
the "Dupont formula"; and others.

Accounting procedures such as auditing, budgeting,
and cost accounting
aid in the management of income
and resources.

ACCOUNTING GUIDES TO DECISIONS

Decisions and Income

Throughout our discussions we have suggested that business firms may pursue varying objectives but all of them depend on securing income, or to use the term preferred by accountants, "revenue." You may think of revenue as a flow of funds from sales into the firm. Of even greater importance, however, is *net* revenue or profit, that is, a flow of funds that is greater than the cost of creating it. Without net revenue or profit a business firm cannot survive, grow, or attain a prestige position. We have emphasized the fact that ours is a profit *and* loss system, that business operations entail risks, and that losses are an ever present possibility.

Income has been referred to as the fundamental fact of economic life. Each of us pursues income in one form or another. Every business firm pursues income, or more technically, net revenue. But revenue cannot be pursued blindly. As we have suggested in our previous discussions, management plans are made in advance of operations to assure in so far as possible that revenues will be maximized. Often financial budgets are used for this purpose, as we have seen. Control measures, including budgets, are used (1) to determine whether plans are being met, or (2) as a basis for adjusting previous decisions or operations.

The business manager needs some way of *accounting* for revenue and the cost of its production as a guide to his decisions. Of course, he will make use of other types of information than those provided through accounting, but accounting and financial data along with analytical studies based on them play a vital role in guiding management decisions. In this chapter we pay special attention to various accounting guides to management decisions. These discussions center first on income or *revenue,* that is, the flow of receipts into the business firm.

Since revenue can only be produced by incurring *costs,* we will consider how costs are determined and controlled. We will also consider what happens to the assets and liabilities of the firm during a period of operations. We will try to find out what the results of operations for a period reveal both in terms of past performance and in terms of future possibilities.

A business manager must have some way of measuring revenue and determining the sources from which it arose and the costs of obtaining it. But it is very important to note that revenue, related costs, and net income must be expressed in terms of some time period. Thus the statement, "The revenue of my business was $100,000," is meaningless because we cannot tell whether the $100,000 was obtained during a year, a quarter, or a month. Similarly, statements about costs and net income, to be meaningful, must relate to a specified time period. In measuring revenue, costs, and net income different time periods are used depending upon the *purposes* for which measurements are made. Management may need reports showing revenue and costs which cover as short a period as a month, week, or even a day. On the other hand, such reports would be of little value to stockholders or other owners not connected with the management. Generally, for their purposes, reports issued quarterly, or even annually, are adequate.

We have pointed out that a business firm produces values to exchange for other values through sales. The values thus received constitute the firm's revenue. The production of the values used in obtaining revenue involves costs. Wages and salaries must be paid to employees; materials purchased; rent paid on leased premises and equipment; interest paid on borrowed money; taxes, insurance, and other obligations met. The net difference between the values received (revenues) and the values given up in exchange (costs) is called *net income* or *profit.*

But business management must do more than account for revenue, costs, and net income. In the process of carrying out its operations, a business firm uses many kinds of things—called *assets.* Thus equipment, machines, land, buildings, and other things of value owned by the business are designated as assets. Furthermore, a business almost always owes some obligations to creditors; for example, amounts owed to the suppliers of materials, to the government for taxes, to banks for money borrowed. These business obligations are called *liabilities.* A solvent, going business always has assets of greater value than the liabilities it owes. The excess of asset value over liabilities is, in effect, an obligation of the business to its owners. This excess value, or obligation to the owners, is called the *proprietorship interest* in the business or the owners' equity. If the business is a corporation, it is frequently referred to as the "stockholders' equity." The firm's assets, liabilities, and proprietorship interest are shown in a report, called a *balance sheet*. This term indicates that the accounts "balance"—that assets are equal to liabilities plus net worth.

We should note that the value of the persons working in a firm or managing it cannot be shown in the balance sheet, although their abilities and efforts may be of greater value to the firm than any of its assets. These abilities, however, will be reflected in the net income earned by the business.

To facilitate their thinking about the financial implications of their decisions, managers often make use of the "entity of the firm" concept. They view the firm as a fictional being—an artificial entity—separate from its owners, managers, or other people associated with it. This is a broader concept than the legal concept of the corporation as an artificial legal being. The "entity of the firm" concept applies to all firms, regardless of how organized.[1] The idea that assets equal liabilities plus net worth or the proprietorship interest is based on the entity of the firm concept.

Profits as a Reward for Risk Taking

We have referred frequently to "profits" or "net income." These are terms which, like many others, everyone knows the meaning of but few are really able to define. Profits are a form of income. Yet they differ from wages, interest, or rent, which are also forms of income. The principal difference between profits and these other forms of income arises primarily from the manner in which they are secured.

Wages, interest, and rent are *contractual* forms of income. A business firm contracts with a bank to pay interest on a loan. If the firm fails to pay interest as agreed, the bank can sue for it; and, through the courts, force performance under the terms of the contract. The same thing is true of wages or of rent. But profits are different. No one can guarantee that you will make a profit if you go into business. If nothing is left after obligations are met or if losses result, there is no one to sue to get profits. Profits are *residuals*, that is, what is left after contractual obligations in the form of wages, rent, interest, and the like are paid.

As one writer has pointed out,

---

[1] See Robert R. Milroy and Robert E. Walden, *Accounting Theory and Practice: Intermediate* (Cambridge, Mass.: Riverside Press, 1960), pp. 19–22.

A firm can make agreements beforehand to pay as costs these incomes to the factors of production. But in the real world, incomes do not turn out as expected. Someone gets a bonus and someone else finds himself short. The resulting unexpected residuals could be shared equally by all factors of production through a profit-sharing plan, but they usually are not. Most people would rather be able to count on a limited income than depend on the uncertain chance of striking a bonanza. In practice, almost everyone gets a commitment from his employer to pay a definite income, and one or a few people (those who own the equity) agree to take what is left as a profit.[2]

Thus, profits are a reward for taking the risks of entering into contractual obligations with workers, landlords, moneylenders, and the like and bearing the uncertainty as to whether the business will produce enough revenue to cover these commitments. Profits are more likely to appear if a firm is well managed than if it is poorly managed. Even so, some poorly managed firms may make profits, either because of luck, highly favorable business conditions, or for other reasons. Profits often result if the management of a firm is creative and alert to the introduction of new ideas and innovations. This is why many firms spend huge amounts on research and development programs. Such expenditures, however, entail great risks and may bring failure as well as outstanding success.

Our interest here is in determining the relative financial success of a business firm's operations; in short, whether it has made a profit, and if so, how much. Regardless of the objectives which its managers set up for a business firm, profits may be thought of as the acid test of the individual firm's performance.

There are differences of opinion in regard to the way in which profits should be measured. We will not undertake to discuss them here. For our purposes standard accounting procedures will be used as a guide, in part because they are widely used by business and in part because you should become familiar with them first, before attempting refinements.[3]

So far we have covered these points: (1) A firm must produce a stream of revenue through its sales (or in related ways). (2) Revenue must exceed costs in order to have profits or net income. (3) Profits are

---

[2] By permission from Joel Dean, *Managerial Economics* (New York: Prentice-Hall, Inc., 1951), p. 4.

[3] If you are interested in some of these problems, you should note that in accounting interest on owners' investment is not computed separately but is lumped with profits, hence "pure" profits tend to be overstated in standard accounting methods. Salaries of managers of corporations, even if they are stockholders, however, are counted as costs and not as profits.

a residual, what is left after contractual obligations have been met. (4) The pursuit of profits involves the assumption of risks. (5) Profits are the acid test of an individual firm's performance.

Measuring Revenue, Costs, and Profits

In order to determine whether a firm has made profits or net income in a period of operations, it is necessary to find out how much, if any, revenue it has produced, what its costs have been, and how much is left over. This sounds simple enough. Unfortunately, it is not. The determination of what is to be counted as revenue and what is to be counted as cost can be a complicated process.

Of even greater importance is the fact that a determination of past success or failure has significance primarily as it *bears on the future.* As we have pointed out repeatedly, business decisions always deal with the future. Management is future oriented. The *measurement* of revenue, costs, and net income pertain to past operations; the *management decisions* in regard to these factors pertain to the future. The use of careful analyses of past operations, however, may provide valuable guides to decisions as to future programs. Furthermore, as management looks toward the future, its decisions tend to be made within a discipline imposed by anticipated revenue, cost, and net income. Anticipations may not be realized, or may be exceeded; to determine what has happened data are collected and analyzed relative to revenue, costs, and profits. These data are generally accumulated through the accounting process.

We must remember that in the measurement, of revenue, costs, and net income (or profits) we are measuring flows—the flow of revenue into the business through sales; the flow of costs incurred for wages, rent, and the like; and the flow of the net difference, that is, profits. We must also remember that while these flows are continuous from the beginning to the end of the firm's life, for purposes of measurement, the firm's life must be broken up into short periods like a month or a year.

We can see how this is done by considering a newly launched firm and how it progresses.

The Balance Sheet

Our firm is Your Company, Inc., which is to engage in the manufacture of student notebooks for sale to college and other bookstores. The owners of Your Company, Inc. (the stockholders), pay in $50,000 in exchange for common stock. Remembering that a balance sheet shows the assets and obligations of the firm to both creditors and owners, we may now prepare the balance sheet shown in Figure 12–1.

FIGURE 12–1

Your Company, Inc.
Balance Sheet
December 31, 19—

ASSETS	STOCKHOLDERS' EQUITY
Cash $50,000	Common Stock $50,000

Your company now has an opportunity to purchase the assets of a similar firm which has decided to discontinue business. Your Company will make payment of $45,000 in cash and agree to pay certain obligations to creditors owed by the old firm. Your Company's balance sheet now looks like Figure 12–2.

FIGURE 12–2

Your Company, Inc.
Balance Sheet
December 31, 19—

ASSETS		LIABILITIES	
Current Assets:		*Current Liabilities:*	
Cash	$ 5,000	Accounts payable	$ 5,000
Inventory	20,000	Notes payable	7,500
Fixed Assets:		*Long-Term Liabilities:*	
Land	12,500	Real estate mortgage...	25,000
Building	30,000	Long-term notes payable	12,500
Equipment	32,500		
		Stockholders' Equity:	
		Common stock	50,000
	$100,000		$100,000

The first thing to note is that the Company owns assets which cost $100,000 but that it has liabilities to creditors of $50,000 and it has an *obligation to its owners for the $50,000 contributed to it for the common stock.* It is easy to see why this is called a balance sheet. On the left-hand side are listed the assets—the things of value owned by the business. On the right-hand side are the obligations to creditors and owners. These must be equal since the amount of the assets which are not required to pay creditors belongs to the owners. As we have suggested, this relationship is sometimes expressed as a balance sheet or accounting equation, thus:

$$\text{Assets} = \text{Liabilities} + \text{Proprietorship}.$$

And to show more clearly the owners' equity:

$$\text{Assets} - \text{Liabilities} = \text{Proprietorship}.$$

It is important to emphasize by means of an illustration the relationship between assets, liabilities, and owners' equity described above. You may find it helpful to construct a new balance sheet for Your Company, Inc., as the illustration progresses.

Suppose that someone steals all of the cash, that is, $5,000, and half of the goods in inventory (total $20,000, one half = $10,000) even before any sales are made. This would reduce assets by $15,000, that is $5,000 from loss of cash and $10,000 from loss of half of the inventory. This would represent a loss to the owners of the business, and in this case the value of common stock would have to be written down from $50,000 to $35,000, reflecting the loss of $15,000. Thus the two sides of the balance sheet would total $85,000 each, that is, assets $85,000, and liabilities $50,000 plus stockholders' equity $35,000. This contrasts with the original situation where assets were $100,000, liabilities $50,000, and the common stock $50,000. The risk of loss is assumed by the owners and whenever losses occur, they are reflected in a reduction in owners' equity.

While the two sides of the balance sheet must be equal in total, there is no necessary relationship between the particular items on either side. In the illustration presented in Figure 12–2, the real estate mortgage has some indirect relationship to the value of the land and buildings but even this merely indicates that if the business should fail the amount received from the sale of the real estate would go first to pay this obligation. In the absence of financial insolvency creditors look primarily to the amount of assets in relation to the amount of liabilities for their protection plus the ability of the firm to maintain profitable operations. Thus, the balance sheet shows that creditors have a claim of a definite value against the business as a whole.

Balance Sheet Items

We should note that both the asset and liability sections of the balance sheet have been subdivided. The assets are classified as current and fixed and the liabilities as current and long-term. The significance of the asset breakdown will be more readily apparent if we consider fixed assets first. These are assets that are not held for sale but rather are for *use* by the business on a more or less permanent basis. Note that land, buildings, and equipment are included here. Current assets are sometimes referred to as the *circulating* assets of the business. This is because specific current assets are continually changing from one form into another. Goods in the inventory today will be sold tomorrow and thus converted into accounts receivable due from customers. As these accounts are collected they are thus converted into cash. But the goods in the inventory may have originally been purchased on credit—either on account or for notes—thus creating current liabilities. But as cash flows into the business, some of it flows out again to pay these obligations. There is a continual circulation from the acquisition of goods through the incurrence of current liabilities to the sale of goods on account, the collection of cash, and the payment of current liabilities. Thus it is generally agreed that current liabilities are those which will be discharged with existing current assets.

Long-term liabilities will not be due for a considerable time—at least one year. When they are about to become due they will be reclassified as current liabilities if they are to be paid by the use of current assets.

The circulating nature of current assets and current liabilities is very important in managerial decision making. Business decisions dealing with fixed assets and long-term liabilities, for example buying a building on mortgage credit, are made only infrequently. But decisions affecting circulating assets and corresponding liabilities must be made daily—what goods to buy, what debts to pay, how much to borrow on short-term credit—are but a few of the decisions that are involved in day-to-day operations.

The names of the specific items listed on the balance sheet should be fairly clear. "Cash" will include money on hand or on deposit in banks. "Inventories" will consist of raw materials or merchandise ready for sale. In the case of a retail firm this item would include typically only goods ready for sale. A manufacturing business, on the other hand, would include in inventories not only finished goods but also raw materials and partly finished goods, generally referred to as "goods-in-process." The valuation of inventories is always a problem. Should original cost, that is, the actual amount paid for the goods, be used or should adjustment be made to reflect current price changes, particularly declines in price? Whatever method is used in valuing inventories, it should be adhered to consistently.

Since the equipment of Your Company, Inc., was recently purchased, it will be shown at its purchase price. It has not been used long enough to suffer any depreciation through wear and tear or to have become obsolete as the result of new developments. We will see how such adjustments are made in Figures 12–3 and 12–4. Similarly the value of land and buildings will be shown at cost.

As already noted, on the liability side the accounts payable are the amounts owed for current bills, typically payments due for goods and services. Notes payable may result from purchases of goods but more typically, they reflect borrowed money which has been secured on the basis of a promissory note. In this case since the notes will probably be paid with current funds, they are shown as a current liability. The real estate mortgage is, of course, a long-term obligation and is secured by the land and buildings. The long-term note is an obligation which is not due until after at least a year.

The stockholders' equity in the business or the proprietorship, or "net worth," as it may be called, is equal to the amount for which the common stock was originally sold, that is, 500 shares at $100 per share, or $50,000.

The Income Statement

In this illustration the firm is just starting operations. Thus far it has neither made nor lost money. Now, suppose that Your Company, Inc., conducts operations for a year. It makes sales. It incurs costs in making these sales. These processes are reflected in the income statement (sometimes called "income and expense statement" or "profit and loss statement") which summarizes operations in our illustration for the period of a year. This information is presented in Figure 12–3.

As we have pointed out, the income statement resembles a moving picture—a summary of events between two points in time. These two points are shown in balance sheets at the beginning and end of the period of time covered by the income statement, in this case one year. Balance sheets are sometimes called "still" pictures or snapshots of financial condition because they reflect the situation at an instant of time. The income statement is a "movie" showing operations during an intervening period. Balance sheets are illustrated in Figures 12–2 and 12–4 while the income statement is illustrated in Figure 12–3.

The income statement shows the flow of revenue into the firm, the costs of producing this flow of revenue, and the net income (or net loss) resulting from operations. The figures in Figure 12–3 summarize what has happened to Your Company, Inc., during its first year of operations. Sales totaled $100,000, after allowing for discounts. The cost of the goods sold totaled $67,500, indicating a gross margin or gross profit of $32,500.

Other costs, in addition to the cost of the goods, were incurred in

FIGURE 12–3

Your Company, Inc.
Income Statement
For the Year Ended December 31, 19—

Gross revenue—sales (less discounts)			$100,000
Less: Cost of goods sold:			
Opening inventory		$20,000	
Manufacturing costs:			
Materials	$17,500		
Direct labor	30,000		
Overhead:			
Depreciation	$ 5,000		
Other mfg. costs	16,250	21,250	
Total manufacturing costs		$68,750	
		$88,750	
Less: Closing inventory		21,250	
Cost of goods sold			67,500
Gross margin (or gross profit)			$ 32,500
Less: Selling and administrative expenses (including depreciation of $250)			18,500
Net operating margin (or profit)			$ 14,000
Less: Interest expense			1,500
Net income before federal income taxes			$ 12,500
Less: Federal income taxes			3,750
Net income			$ 8,750

order to make these sales. There were selling expenses and general administrative or management expenses. These totaled $18,500 in our illustration, thus indicating a net *operating* margin or operating profit of $14,000. But there are still other costs; in this case interest charges of $1,500 which must be deducted, leaving net income before federal taxes of $12,500. Finally, there is the federal income tax bill to be paid. This amounts to $3,750, or 30 per cent of net income, leaving net income after taxes of $8,750.[4] We have thus far ignored the section in the income statement pertaining to the cost of goods sold, including manufacturing costs. As indicated in the illustration in Figure 12–3 the cost of materials totaled $17,500, direct labor costs of $30,000 were incurred, and, in addition, overhead costs were also incurred. These included depreciation charges, which will be discussed below, of $5,000 plus other operating expenses of $16,250, or a total of $21,250.

Note that the value of the opening inventory, $20,000, was added to manufacturing costs of $68,750, making a total of $88,750. Not all of

---

[4] The federal income tax rate varies with the amount of net income, but we will not go into a discussion of this intricate problem here.

these costs were for goods actually sold during the period. Some goods, both finished and unfinished, remained to be sold in the months ahead. These costs are reflected in the closing inventory of $21,250, which is properly deducted leaving $67,250 as the indicated cost of the goods that were actually sold.

If this adjustment had not been made and the inventory position at the beginning and the closing of this period had been ignored, the profits of the firm would have been *understated* by the difference between manufacturing costs of the period and the cost of the goods actually sold, that is, $68,750 in contrast to $67,500, or $1,250, the amount by which inventory was increased during this period. If this procedure were followed then the profits in the *succeeding* period could be *overstated*.

Depreciation Charges

One item of cost shown in the income statement, *depreciation,* is frequently not clearly understood. It may be explained in this way. Assume that included in the equipment purchased by Your Company, Inc., is a delivery truck to which a cost of $2,400 has been assigned. The truck will be used for four years and then junked. Obviously, it would be improper to say that the *entire* $2,400 is a cost of operations during the company's first year. Nevertheless, the entire amount paid for the truck is a cost of doing business since it will eventually be worn out and worthless. The most logical way to handle this is to allocate a portion of the cost of the truck to each year it is used. This allocation is frequently done on what is called a straight line basis, that is, charges made equally to each year that it is estimated the equipment will be used. More refined methods are sometimes used. They generally attempt to allocate the cost among the years on the basis of the estimated ability of the equipment to aid in the production of the firm's revenue. Under the "unit of production method," for example, the cost of a truck would be allocated to the various years on the basis of the relative miles run. The cost of a machine may be allocated on the basis of the number of items turned out. Sometimes a greater proportion of the cost is allocated to the early years of the equipment's life on the ground that it will be more efficient then and hence contribute relatively more to the production of revenue than during its later years.

We should recognize that depreciation charges are estimates only. If depreciation is overstated, it will tend to reduce the profits in the early years of an asset's life, but later the cost of some asset may be fully written off and hence depreciation charges will be lower and profits higher. Problems of this type are involved in the "accelerated depreciation" plans that you may have heard about.

Another aspect of the problem bears consideration. Profits are taxable as we have already seen above. If depreciation is taken rapidly, the computed profits will be lower, hence taxes will be lower. Later on profits will be higher than they otherwise would have been but by then business volume may be down or taxes may be lower and in the meantime the company has had the use of the funds saved on taxes. This explains to some extent why business firms have welcomed "accelerated depreciation" clauses in their defense contracts and the general availability of "fast" methods in more recent years.

Changes in the Balance Sheet

Having surveyed the income statement for the first year of operations of Your Company, Inc., we need to consider the effects that have been produced in the balance sheet at the end of the period. The balance sheet at the end of a year of operations is presented in Figure 12–4. We saw from the income statement that the company made $8,750, after taxes. Since profits made by the business belong to the owners (the stockholders in this case) the obligation of the business to them is hereby increased.

Here the managing officers and directors must make an important decision. Part, or all, of the increased obligation to the owners on account of profits earned may be discharged by paying them a dividend. On the other hand, this obligation may be continued and the money which would otherwise be used to pay a dividend may be retained for expansion and development of the company or to pay off claims of creditors. In the case of Your Company, Inc., the balance sheet shows in the stockholders' equity section that $3,750 of the net income has been retained in the business and $5,000 has been distributed in dividends. Instead of showing the net increase in the obligation of the business to its owners by adding the amount of earnings retained in the business to the value of the common stock, this is indicated separately. The initial investment of the firm is a sort of "trust fund" or basic resource of the business and is not available for dividends. The part of the obligation to the owners arising from earnings which can serve as a basis for dividend distributions should, therefore, be shown separately.

It is important to note that the retained earnings do not correspond to any single asset item any more than the capital interest or creditor

interest do. Rather, retained earnings simply reflect a part of the residual ownership equity. Sometimes a firm will have an increased
obligation to its owners due to profitable operations but most of its
assets will be tied up in inventories, equipment, and other noncash
items which are necessary to expanded operations. It may thus not be
able conveniently to pay a cash dividend to its stockholders despite
large profits.

FIGURE 12–4

Your Company, Inc.

Balance Sheet

December 31, 19—

ASSETS			LIABILITIES		
Current Assets:			*Current Liabilities:*		
Cash	$ 6,500		Accounts payable	$ 4,800	
Accounts receivable	9,800		Notes payable	10,000	
Inventory	21,250	$ 37,550	Taxes payable	3,750	$ 18,550
Fixed Assets:			*Long-Term Liabilities:*		
Land		12,500	Real estate mortgage	$25,000	
Building	$30,000		Long-term notes payable .	10,000	35,000
Less: Accumulated			Total Liabilities		$ 53,550
depreciation ..	2,000	28,000			
Equipment	$32,500		*Stockholders' Equity:*		
Less: Accumulated			Capital stock	$50,000	
depreciation ..	3,250	29,250	Net income $8,750		
			Less: Dividends		
			paid 5,000	3,750	53,750
			Total Liabilities and		
Total Assets ...		$107,300	Stockholders' Equity		$107,300

There are several new items in the balance sheet reflecting the
financial condition of the business as of the close of its first year of
operations. There is a "taxes payable" item which did not appear
before. The income statement indicated the amount of income taxes
assessed because of the amount of the net income earned. Since these
taxes would not usually be paid by the end of the year they must be
set up as an obligation to the government as a creditor. Other unpaid
costs, such as wages, rent, and the like (generally called "accrued expenses") may have to be set up in a similar manner. If this were not
done, the proprietorship interest would be overstated and the creditor
interest understated.

We should note that "accounts payable" dropped from $5,000 in the first balance sheet, Figure 12–2 to $4,800 in the second one, Figure 12–4. "Notes payable" increased by $2,500; however, "long-term notes payable" dropped by a like amount. This probably indicates that a portion of the long-term notes comes due each year and hence is moved from the long-term liability section to the current liability section. The real estate mortgages item remained unchanged.

On the asset side, several changes have also occurred. Cash has been built up from $5,000 to $6,500. A new item, "accounts receivable," appears indicating that customers have current bills due Your Company, Inc., in the amount of $9,800. We have already commented on the change in inventories from $20,000 to $21,250.

We can also see the manner in which depreciation is handled. Remember that a part of the cost of the building and equipment was charged as an expense on the income statement. Instead of writing down the cost figure for buildings and equipment, the cumulative amount charged as expense is subtracted from the cost figure. This procedure has the advantage of showing the balance sheet reader both the original cost of the fixed asset and the amount of the cost which has been charged against revenue as an expense of operations. This charged-off amount may be indicated as *accumulated depreciation.* The term "reserve for depreciation" is sometimes used but this terminology is somewhat misleading as it tends to imply that there is a reserve of funds with which to replace the asset. Actually, as we have just seen, the accumulated depreciation figure merely indicates the portion of the cost of the asset that has been "expensed."

In the case of Your Company's equipment, it will be noted that one tenth of the cost has been allocated to expense in the first year of operations. If the straight-line method of computing depreciation is used, an estimate that this equipment will be worn out or obsolete in 10 years is implied. From the information on the balance sheet, you can determine that the estimated useful life of the building is 15 years, that is, $2,000 per year for 15 years will equal $30,000, the value placed on the building.

The assets of the firm have increased $7,300 and so have the liabilities and proprietorship interest; the liabilities by $3,550 and the proprietorship interest by $3,750.

Significance for Management Decisions

We stressed the point early in our discussion in this chapter that while it was important for management to know what happened in terms of revenue, costs or expenses, and net income and what changes occurred in assets, liabilities, and proprietorship as a result of operations, it was even more important to use this information as a guide to decisions relative to *future* operations. What can management learn from the materials presented in Figures 12–2, 12–3, and 12–4 that will be helpful in making decisions affecting the future?

Several things would be apparent to a trained accountant at once. We cannot hope to go into great detail at this stage of our discussion, but several examples of the types of information that will help in management decisions regarding the production of income in the future will be indicated.

If we compare the two balance sheets, Figures 12–2 and 12–4, and look at the current assets and current liabilities of each, we see that in Figure 12–2 the ratio between these two items is two to one. That is, cash in the amount of $5,000 and inventories of $20,000 total $25,000 in comparison to current liabilities of accounts payable of $5,000 and notes payable of $7,500, or $12,500. After a year of operation this ratio has remained just about the same, with current assets totaling $37,550 and current liabilities $18,550. This "current ratio" is always watched closely. It indicates the ability of the firm to operate without being dependent on short-term creditors and to meet sudden and possibly unexpected demands for funds.

The firm has increased its debt in this period of operations, long-term and short-term debt totaling $53,550, but the debt is approximately equal to the stockholders' equity which for this type of business probably indicates a greater dependence on credit than would be desirable. The relative position of debt to stockholders' equity has changed little from that at the start of operations.

The "accounts receivable" item indicates that customers or others owe the firm amounts equal to nearly 10 per cent of sales. Whether these amounts are excessive will depend on the terms of sale. If thirty-day credit is extended, this amount is not excessive; if ten-day credit is used, it is higher than desirable.

In view of the rising debt and the volume of business, questions may be raised as to the advisability of paying a dividend of $5,000 to the owners of the business. If this money could have been put to work for the business it would have permitted the reduction of debt by this amount if desired, or the expansion of operations. From the standpoint of the firm and its management, retaining all of the earnings and "plowing them back" into the business at this stage of its development would appear desirable; the owners, however, may have preferred a cash dividend.

Considerable information can be provided for the guidance of management in the future from the income statement, Figure 12–3. For example, with cost of sales of $67,500 and with opening inventory of $20,000 and closing inventory of $21,250, we see that inventories have been "turned over" approximately three times in the year. Management may find it possible to raise this to perhaps five, six, or even ten times, and if so, the company can reduce its short-term debt, and thus save interest charges. The amount invested in inventories is thus "worked" more effectively.

By comparing this income statement with those of other firms in this business—we assumed that Your Company, Inc., was manufacturing student notebooks—we could decide whether certain costs appeared reasonable or out of line. Since we do not have such information available, we may note that while the figures on the cost of materials and direct labor seem reasonable the "other operating costs" may bear investigation. Comparisons with the experience of other firms will be helpful.

Managers and accountants will study statements of this type with considerable care in order to find clues to improve operations in the future. They will use various ratios such as applied in the case of current assets to current liabilities, total liabilities to stockholders' equity, inventories to cost of sales, plus others. They will also use comparative information secured from the reports of other companies—and, of course, will have much more detailed information available from other records than we have presented here. We have tried, however, to indicate some of the ways in which information on balance sheets and income statements may be used, not only to see what has happened as a result of past operations but also as guides to management in the future.

Operating management will have available much more detailed knowledge than can be provided by these statements. Detailed cost analyses, special operating reports, and the like are very important in day-to-day management decisions.

Also, many managers work out special formulas to show relationships between various phases of their operations. One such formula that has been used rather widely is referred to as the "Dupont formula."[5] It places primary emphasis on return on investment as a goal, and then shows the factors and the relationships between them that affect the final result. Return on investment responds to movements

---

[5] T. C. Davis, "How the Dupont Organization Appraises Its Performance," *Financial Management Series No. 94* (New York: American Management Association, 1950), p. 6.

in two factors: (1) earnings as a per cent of sales, that is, the net operating profit on sales and (2) turnover. For example, if there is no change in selling price, an improvement in turnover indicates that the firm is getting increased sales from the same plant and working capital; or with no change in selling price an improvement in profit margin shows that costs are being reduced in proportion to the sales dollar. The formula is outlined in the chart in Figure 12–5.

FIGURE 12–5

Chart Based on the "Dupont Formula"

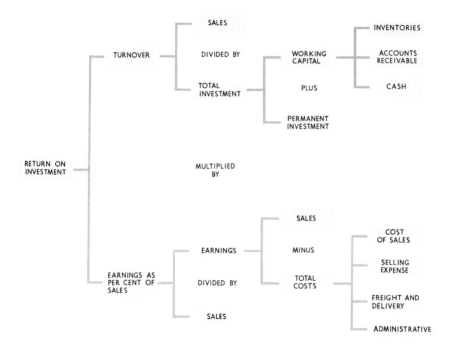

Auditing

Whenever a business firm reaches the end of a period of operations, such as a year, and prepares statements—balance sheets and income statements—it is often desirable to have them audited by an independent Certified Public Accountant. The CPA will determine the accuracy of the records and thus provide the management of the firm with certified information that may be used in arranging bank loans or in other transactions that require an impartial report of the firm's financial condition. Many firms publish their audited statements and often include in such published reports important explanatory material about the firm's operations.

Larger business firms may employ auditors on a full-time basis in addition to independent accounting firms. Full-time or internal auditors make certain that recording systems are being used as intended and that records are being kept accurately. Such auditors also serve a control function to assure that expenditures are being made in accordance with company policies. They help to guard against errors or fraud.

Budgeting

The types of information presented in Figures 12–2, 12–3 and 12–4 will be of substantial value in preparing a budget to plan the company's operations in the year or years ahead. It would have been possible, of course, to set up a budget for planning purposes at the time the firm was started. Now, after a year of operations and with the records available of those operations, a much more realistic budget can be prepared for use as part of management plans.

For example, the firm can set up an estimate of sales in the year ahead, probable costs of materials, direct labor costs, other operating costs, selling and administrative expense, interest charges, and the like. Profits can be estimated. Indications of cash needs will be provided.

The effect of budgeted operations on the balance sheet a year hence can also be forecasted, and the relationships between various balance sheet items anticipated. Thus, if it appears that debt may be rising too rapidly, short-term liabilities increasing faster than short-term assets, and the like, adjustments in the budget can be made to try to avoid unfavorable developments.

Ae we pointed out in our discussions in Chapter 11, budgeting is a valuable aid to financial planning and control. It is facilitated by good accounting reports and analyses.

Cost Accounting

One of the more valuable guides to management decisions is cost accounting. We can see something of the uses of cost accounting from the information in the income statement in Figure 12–3. If we assume that we are selling the student notebooks for one dollar each, we know that we sold 100,000 of them during the year and can determine the cost of producing each unit. Since the cost of goods sold totaled $67,500 and we sold 100,000 units, we know that it cost on the average

$0.675 to produce each item. But cost accounting would show us which part of the process was most expensive. Also, if we were producing three or more models of notebooks, cost accounting would tell us the relative costs of each.

Over a period of time we could compare several income statements and use other data to give us trends of costs and of various items in costs. We could compare direct labor costs, materials costs, other operating costs, and the like to see whether ratios between them were changing or whether one or another cost was moving up rapidly. Such information helps management to spot problem areas.

Over a period of time it is possible also to compare costs with volume of output and with sales at different levels. This would help management to know whether expanded operations reduced costs per unit or raised them.

In addition cost accounting helps management to determine the point at which a firm's operations will "break even," that is, where costs and revenue will just balance.

After a period of operations it may be possible to establish "standard costs" for various operations. These can be used for control purposes—for forecasting costs at various levels of operations— and hence may be helpful in budgeting.

Management of Income

Our discussion in this chapter should help you to gain some idea of the importance of income and the proper management of income in the success of business firms. As we pointed out in the introductory paragraphs of the chapter, the acid test of the success of a business firm is its ability to make profits. This requires that a stream of revenue be channeled into the firm and that the costs of securing this revenue stream be controlled and kept at levels that will assure the earning of net income or profits.

In order for income to be managed effectively, it is necessary that objectives be established. These may be stated in a number of ways; for example, earnings equal to a desired rate of return on owner's investment, or total investment, earnings as a percentage of total sales, an increase in profits over the preceding year's performance, plus many others. Some firms try to maximize profits in the short run; others in the long run.

Many firms do not try to maximize profits in the short run. They prefer a "reasonable" short-run profit, and what is reasonable may be defined in a number of ways. Thus, a firm may prefer to keep profits lower than would be possible in the short run because this makes for a more pleasant working situation rather than one where everyone is constantly under pressure. As a result long-run profits may be maximized. Similarly, the management of a firm may hope to keep the demands of organized labor down by limited short-run profits. In some cases this is done to discourage new firms from entering the field, to prevent adverse public relations, to discourage politicians looking for reform issues, and the like.

In short, not all business firms pursue maximum profits as a goal, although most firms do in the long run. Hence, the management of a firm's income requires a clear understanding of the objectives that are to be achieved.

Once established, such objectives provide a sound basis for the planning, organizing, and controlling of operations from an income standpoint. In connection with such planning, budgets provide an important tool. The records of operations and the accounting statements which result are of great help in the budgeting process.

The management of income relates to every division of the firm's organization. Weaknesses in any part of the organization can, of course, have an adverse effect on its income-producing ability.

Management of income requires careful controls. The control process is facilitated by cost accounting, auditing, and budgeting. The budget becomes both an instrument of planning and of control.

Finally the management of income requires careful direction of the financial affairs of the firm. All of the people in the firm must operate efficiently in order to maintain a proper balance between costs and returns.

SUMMARY

Income has been referred to as the fundamental fact of economic life. Every business firm must secure revenue, and revenue in excess of costs, that is, *profit* if it is to survive or grow. Revenue cannot be pursued blindly. The business manager has to know how effectively his business is pursuing revenue, which revenue sources are best, and how revenue can be increased. Thus the business manager must have some way of accounting for revenue, of knowing the sources from which it arose, and how much it cost to obtain the revenue that was secured.

The net income of the business firm is usually referred to as "profit." This is a *residual* income in contrast to contractual forms of income such as wages, interest, or rent.

Net income is usually measured by accounting processes. In order to measure income, the accountant sets up "balance sheets" for the beginning and ending of the time interval covered and an "income statement" for the period between. Thus, the balance sheet is a snapshot or still picture of a business firm on a specific date; while the income statement is a motion picture covering the interval of time involved.

While it is important for management to know what has happened in the past in terms of revenue and cost, it is even more important that information of this type be used as a guide to decisions on future plans and operations. Auditing, budgeting, and cost accounting provide a variety of guides to management decisions.

QUESTIONS AND PROBLEMS

1. Why are profits referred to as "residual income" in contrast to contractual forms of income?
2. Explain the significance of the following statement which is quoted in this chapter: "A firm can make agreements beforehand to pay as costs those incomes to factors of production. But in the real world, incomes do not turn out as expected. Someone gets a bonus and someone else finds himself short. The resulting unexpected residuals could be shared equally by all factors of production through a profit-sharing plan, but they usually are not. Most people would rather be able to count on a limited income than depend on the uncertain chance of striking a bonanza. In practice, almost everyone gets a commitment from his employer to pay a definite income, and one or a few people (those who own the equity) agree to take what is left as a profit."
3. What is meant by a "balance sheet"?
4. Explain the meaning of "assets." Distinguish between current assets and fixed assets.
5. What is meant by "liabilities"? Distinguish between current and long-term liabilities.
6. What is the balance sheet equation?
7. The assets of a business firm total $200,000, current liabilities are $25,000, and long-term liabilities are $75,000. What is the proprietorship interest of this firm?
8. What is an income statement? How does it differ from a balance sheet?
9. Why is accumulated depreciation set up for various types of assets?
10. What is an acceptable ratio between current assets and current liabilities?
11. A business firm shows an opening inventory of $50,000, a closing inventory of $52,000, and its cost of sales totaled $150,000. How many times have inventories been "turned over" in the period covered?
12. What is meant by "auditing"?
13. How is budgeting used to aid management?
14. What is meant by "cost accounting"?

SUGGESTED READINGS

KELLER, J. WAYNE. *Management Accounting for Profit Control.* New York: McGraw-Hill Book Co., Inc., 1957. If you have a special interest in the field of accounting and especially its managerial aspects you may wish to refer to this book and in particular to read chap. i, "Organization for Management Accounting"; chap, xix, "Income Accounting"; and chap. xx, "Budgets and Forecasts."

LONG, JOHN D. *Workbook to Accompany Weimer: Business Administration: An Introductory Management Approach,* chap. 12. Rev. ed. Homewood, Ill.: Richard D. Irwin, Inc., 1962.

MILROY, ROBERT R., and WALDEN, ROBERT E. *Accounting Theory and Practice—Introductory.* Cambridge, Mass.: Riverside Press, Houghton Mifflin Co., 1960. Read chap. i, "Introduction to Accounting," of this excellent accounting textbook.

SAMUELSON, PAUL E. *Economics: An Introductory Analysis.* 5th ed. New York: McGraw-Hill Book Co., Inc., 1961. This widely used economics textbook has a good summary discussion of the accounting process which is presented as an appendix to chap. v covering pages 99–109. Read also chap. v, "Business Organization and Income."

OUTLINE FOR CHAPTER 13

This discussion of SOME STATISTICAL AND ECONOMIC GUIDES TO DECISIONS covers various types and uses of information which are important in management decisions.

Statistics, a body of methods of obtaining and analyzing data for decision purposes, is a branch of the scientific method. Included is the collection of data; evaluation and analysis of data by determination of points of similarity and difference.

Uses of statistics are many, such as
estimates of business volume,
determination of consumer preferences,
analysis of past performance, and
projections rearding future developments.

Erroneous uses include
shifting of definitions,
incorrect classifications,
assumption of causal relationships, and
inappropriate use of charts and scales.

Methods of prediction include
persistence prediction, trends,
cycles, associative prediction, and analogy.

Economics is generally concerned with attainment of ends with least expenditure of resources; it includes "micro" and "macro" branches.

Relationships between forces of *demand*, *supply*, and *price* are of basic importance in understanding markets and competition.

Degrees of competition range from "pure" to monopoly; manager's decision limits vary, typically being restricted in highly competitive conditions; wider under monopoly conditions.

The *theory of the firm* aids in explaining cost-volume-return relationships, optimum operating levels, types of costs, and break-even points.

SOME STATISTICAL AND ECONOMIC GUIDES TO DECISIONS

Any line of action is commonly termed economic when it attains its end with the least possible expenditure of money, time and effort.
—KEYNES

Types of Decision Guides Considered

We have reviewed various financial and accounting guides to decisions in the preceding two chapters. Important as they are to the management of business firms, many other types of decision guides are used. For example, the manager makes use of information arising from many sources and he uses a variety of methods for analyzing it. Some of this information will come from within the firm; some from outside sources. The manager tries to get as much assistance as he can from the information at his disposal, making use of economic analysis, statistical analysis, and mathematical techniques of various types. He may draw also on the behavioral sciences or other areas of knowledge as well.

We have been paying attention to general decision guides. They may be used in connection with all types of decisions, those relating to broad problems of the firm as well as to specific resources or areas of operation. We continue our discussions along these lines in this chapter and the next. In the following sections of the book we direct our attention more specifically to managerial problems related to business resources and operations and to environmental factors.

The manager makes use of the best thinking he can give to a problem, drawing on his experience, judgment, imagination, and even intuition. He tries to avoid errors in making assumption, in using logic, in making use of statistical or other data, or in reasoning from the known to the unknown. As we have suggested he makes use of the scientific method since it forces logical and hard thinking, but he makes use of it for action purposes. He uses a variety of information and techniques of analysis. In this chapter we review several types of decision guides drawn from economic and statistical analysis. In the next we consider some of the help for decision making that comes from such quantitative techniques as linear programming, game theory, and related areas.

Variety of Information

In the preceding chapter we considered various types of accounting information. A single business firm may have millions of transactions; much of the recording work often is done by machines. The result is a large body of data, which, as we have seen, must be analyzed to make it useful. The operations of a business firm will produce information of many other types as well. There may be reports of salesmen in regard to competitors' products; reports of personnel directors on union-management relations and workers morale; reports from purchasing agents about price changes for materials; and many others.

In addition to the information resulting from the operations of the firm, business managers may use a variety of information made available by government agencies, trade associations, chambers of commerce, private reporting and consulting services, and other sources. Managers are always "hungry" for information since it may help to throw light on their problems.

Some information is quantitative in nature; other information is not. The former includes statistical data of many types; the latter may include the personal impressions reported by a company official after an inspection tour of the firm's plants, a legal decision in regard to the firm's liability to a customer who was hurt in one of its stores, the ruling of a government agency affecting the firm's products, and many other types.

In some cases it is difficult to get the information needed; for example, it may not be possible to find out a competitor's costs of producing a given model of a product, or the amount of goods he has in inventory. Information sometimes is available on an industry-wide basis, but not for specific firms. Often estimates are made to give approximate information.

Sometimes voluminous information is available and the problem is one of selecting what will be pertinent. Also, the degree of detail required will vary; the president of the company may need summary reports; the purchasing agent may need much more detail.

When electronic data processing equipment began to be used by business firms, there was a tendency to assume that most data collection and analysis problems were well on the way to solution. The potential of such equipment, however, is so great that its sheer capacity has made it necessary to think in terms of complete *systems* of data collection and processing that fit the over-all requirements of the firm, rather than providing separate means to supply the needs of each division of the firm.[1]

Much business information can be reduced to quantitative terms, since financial and accounting relationships are so prevalent in business activities: Often, however, it is possible to quantify information only by making such broad assumptions that the data may suggest much greater precision of measurement than in fact exists.

Use of Information

If we have information, what it means to us, or to a manager, depends a good deal on how we think about it. How we think about it will depend in part on our purpose or objective, in part on what the information can be made to reveal, and in part on what we may be able to imagine, project, or sense on the basis of it.

What the information can be made to reveal depends to a considerable extent on our ability to "think straight." It depends also on our techniques and capacity for analyzing the information. Beyond this much depends on the means available and our capacity for making the information lead us on to think creatively. We can make information more meaningful for our purposes if we break it down, classify it, find points of similarity and difference, determine relationships within it, or do other things. We can secure considerable help in these processes from statistical analysis.

We can make information help us by applying previous knowledge, for example, principles or theories that provide general explanations of relationships. Or we may develop hypotheses or hunches—tentative explanations of the information available and its meaning for our purposes. These can then be tested, adopted, modified, or abandoned as the case may be. We can also construct *models,* ranging from skeleton outlines such as the diagram of a football play to complicated mathematical formulas to help us use the information in moving from the known to the unknown.

Economic analysis often is helpful to managers in this connection, since economics provides a body of theories, principles, and hypotheses that often helps to bring out the significance of information. Economic

---

[1] E. W. Martin, Jr., *Electronic Data Processing: An Introduction* (Homewood, Ill.: Richard D. Irwin, Inc., 1961), p. 23.

analysis also makes use of a number of models, some mathematical and others not, which often prove to be useful to managers and others.

In recent years we have found increasing help from operations research and various mathematical techniques in constructing models and in giving us tools to analyze complicated information. The computer has helped greatly in this process.

Valuable as these and other aids to decisions are proving to be, it is well to remember a statement made by the famous Justice Holmes: "To rest on a formula is a slumber that, prolonged, means death." Theories, principles, models, formulas, and related aids to thinking are only as good as our ability to make use of them, not only in current solutions to problems, but also in moving on to better solutions.

Examples of Information Uses

How information, hypotheses, and methods of thinking about information and problems may be used in practice may be illustrated by a problem faced by a baseball manager. He is trying to select his line-up for the day's game. He looks at the batting averages (statistical information) and is able to select six men without difficulty, but the next four players are about at the same level. A general principle in baseball is that right-handed hitters do better against left-handed pitchers and vice versa. The manager knows that the opposing team will use a left-handed pitcher. This enables him to select his seventh man. The final choice (except for the pitcher and he is not going to be selected on the basis of his hitting ability) is still in doubt. The man whom the manager would ordinarily select is in a batting slump. The manager would like to "shake him up" a bit, and at the same time provide some experience for a new member of the club. This new member has a good record, but has been nervous when playing. Sometimes he has hit fairly well, other times poorly, but his long-term average is good. The manager develops an idea (hypothesis) that by playing the new man, the regular man who is now in a batting slump may be motivated to improve; at the same time the new man, who has never been started in the line-up may have his confidence bolstered as a result. The manager decides to proceed this way.

Here we see the use of data, principles, and hypotheses in the solution of a problem; most business problems are more complicated but the methods are similar.

For example, Wallis and Roberts provide a number of interesting illustrations of the use of statistics by business firms.

In order to place orders with manufacturers, a mail order company wanted to predict how total sales of a certain garment would be divided among individual styles. To a randomly selected sample of catalog receivers, the company mailed, in advance, a special booklet made up of the catalog pages describing the various styles of the garment. Actual orders from recipients of the special booklet were then tabulated, and predictions were made on the basis of these orders. These predictions were found, at the end of the sales season, to have been substantially more accurate than the predictions of experienced buyers.

A flour manufacturer wanted to bring out a new pie crust mix. The proposed mix was put in plain packages with only an identifying letter, and the same was done with the pie crust mix of the leading competitor. Each of 75 families was given a package of each of the two mixes and asked to fill out a questionnaire comparing the two brands for taste, texture and other qualities. The competitor's product was preferred by most of the 75 families. The flour company therefore revised the formula of its mix. The revised formula was tested on another group of 75 families and found still to be less preferred than the competitor's mix. The same thing was repeated several more times. Meanwhile, another competitor introduced a new mix which gained preference over all others. The company made similar tests of its proposed formulas against this new competitor. Finally, a mix was developed that seemed to be preferred to all competitive products. When it was marketed it proved highly successful.

A personnel manager wanted to find out the times during the year when the largest number of accidents occurred in his plant. With this information he hoped to be able to give safety instruction when the need for it was greatest. A statistical study of the accident records for this plant showed that while there were variations among the months in the number of accidents these variations were no greater than might reasonably be expected by chance alone. Thus, there was no best season for safety indoctrination, and the decision could be based on other grounds.[2]

Many firms make use of statistical studies as a basis for quality control, that is, assuring that products meet standards without testing each one. In fact, in order to test some products it would be necessary to destroy them, as in the case of determining whether a fuse would meet quality standards. By means of sampling quality controls can be worked out, saving time, and cost without sacrificing quality.

Interest in Statistics

Statistics has been defined as "a body of methods for making wise decisions in the face of uncertainty."[3] Ordinarily we think of numbers or numerical data when we use the term "statistics" and it is quite proper to use this term in this way. But statistics also refers to a body of knowledge; in this sense it is similar to accounting or finance.

---

[2] W. Allen Wallis and Harry V. Roberts, *Statistics: A New Approach* (Glencoe, Ill.: Free Press, 1956), pp. 20–23, by permission.

[3] *Ibid.*, p. 3.

Hence, the following statement is helpful: "The subject, in this sense of statistics, is a body of methods of obtaining and analyzing data in order to base decisions on them. It is a branch of the scientific method, used in dealing with phenomena that can be described numerically either by counts or measurements."[4]

Our interest in statistics arises primarily from its practical uses in business decision making. It helps in determining management objectives, in planning, in control, and in making organization decisions.

You will recall from our earlier discussions that the scientific method usually includes several stages. For our purposes here we may think in terms of the following: (1) observation, the collection and study of facts that are relevant to the problems; (2) hypothesis, the development of hunches or preliminary ideas that explain the facts; (3) prediction, estimating what may result from more facts (for the business manager this may be a forecast or a postulate based on known facts and on what the facts suggest); and (4) verification, or the collection of new facts to test predictions or hypotheses—and the cycle may be started over again with the first step or observation. (Sometimes steps two and three are combined.)

As Wallis and Roberts have pointed out,

Statistics is pertinent chiefly at the first and fourth stages, observation and verification, and to some extent at the second stage, formulating a hypothesis. The methods most important at the second stage, however, are primarily those of intuition, insight, imagination and ingenuity. Very little can be said about them formally; perhaps they can be learned, but they cannot be taught. As someone has said, referring to an apocryphal story, many men noticed falling apples before Sir Isaac Newton, yet no interpretations of comparable interest were recorded by these earlier observers.[5]

In the collection of observations or facts, statistics performs one of its most useful functions. Here are encountered many problems such as what to count, how to do it, how to record results and report them. Statisticians usually refer to the "population" or the "universe" in determining the totality of observations that might be made. For example, a census or actual counting of each member of the population is one way to proceed; it may be too expensive, however, and samples may be taken. The determination of what is a reliable sample that is representative of the entire population (or universe) is far from an easy task. Yet, unless we know the validity of data, we may soon be led to erroneous conclusions.

---

4 *Ibid.*, p. 4. See also pages 4–16.
5 *Ibid.*, p. 6.

Analysis of Data

After the collection of observations, data usually must be analyzed to be useful. This generally involves determining points of similarity and difference. For example, if you count the students in a classroom you are making observations or collecting facts. If you not only count the number of students but also secure information about such things as age, height, sex, and weight, you would be able to classify the students according to these characteristics. You could analyze information of this type, for example, determining the percentage of men and women or the percentage in various age groups. You might determine the *average* age or height, either on the basis of an arithmetic average or determine the most frequent age or *mode* or the middle or *median* age when the data were arranged in order from lowest to highest in an *array*. You might study the *range* of ages and heights. You could study the extent to which there were variations from averages.

FIGURE 13–1

Grade Distribution

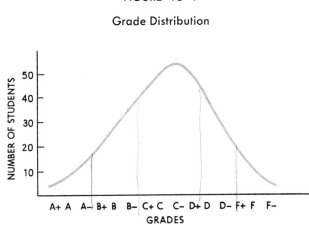

If you were in a hurry and did not have time to secure complete information about each student, you might use a sample of the group. Many public opinion polls, of course, are based on samples of the total population. If you were able to study the student group over a period of time, you might determine *trends* or directions of change in height or other characteristics.

In using business data the manager is concerned with many of the same types of information. Determining the types of information needed and the purposes it will serve is of primary importance. For example, in the case of Your Company, Inc., discussed in the preceding chapter, we computed the average cost of notebooks. We might also have wanted averages by type and style and a manager would be interested in sales reports from various types of bookstores—and of course many related items of information.

Various types of averages and deviations from averages may be illustrated by a diagram showing a "bell-shaped curve." You may have heard about instructors marking according to "the curve." The meaning of this expression is indicated in the diagram in Figure 13–1. It means that in a given class the largest number of grades would be "average" or according to some marking systems, "C" grades; next in frequency would "B" grades and "D" grades in the same proportion on each side of the C's; beyond these would fall the "A's" and "F's" in still smaller quantities. The plus and minus grades would fall between the others as indicated on the chart.

FIGURE 13–2

Average Book Cost Distribution

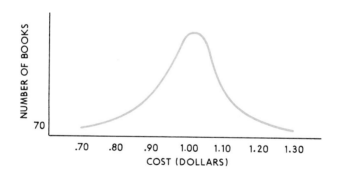

Or to use a business illustration from Your Company, Inc., as outlined in the past chapter, we found that the average cost of notebooks was $1.00; but had we charted the actual costs we might have found some notebooks costing slightly more, perhaps produced during an overtime period; others costing slightly less, perhaps during a period when everything went just right (see Figure 13–2). If deviations from the average became too wide at any time, of course, corrective measures would be taken. One of the important uses of statistics in business is for control purposes.

Additional Examples and Dangers

One author presents a number of interesting illustrations of the uses of statistical methods in business.[6] For example, some business firms have been able to estimate the probable volume of business by weighing the mail. Railroads, airlines, and bus lines can estimate from records their service requirements in various localities at different seasons of the year. Advertising agencies and departments of business firms are able to determine the effectiveness of various advertising methods and media by the use of statistical data. One of the oldest uses of statistics is found in the life insurance field. Life insurance premiums are based on statistical tables of life expectancy.

Some companies use statistical methods to estimate the preferences of consumers for one or another type of product. Clothing companies use statistics in regard to the distribution of the height and weight of men and women to set their production quotas for various sizes of clothing. Among the more important types of numerical data used by business firms are indexes of prices. Some labor contracts, for example, contain "escalator clauses" which tie wage rates to consumer price indexes.

Suppose we return to our baseball manager. Obviously, he is concerned with batting averages since they show the relative success of various players in getting hits and also compare the performance of the same player from day to day and even from season to season. Similarly, the number of singles, doubles, triples, home runs, walks, and sacrifices may be analyzed, player by player or team by team. Such information assists the manager in selecting his players and in changing his line-up as required.

Similarly, a business manager may use records in regard to his operations in order to guide his decisions. For example, a baseball player may have a batting average of 0.300 but also have a record of failing to hit when "the chips are down"—when the tieing or winning run is on third base, with two out in the last of the ninth inning. Despite the over-all batting average of this player, his poor performance under pressure would probably cause the manager to decide on a pinch hitter when a situation of this type occurred.

Similarly, a salesman might have a good sales record but also show a consistent failure to sell "the big ones," that is, the key accounts that

---

[6] B. J. Mandell, *Statistics for Management* (Baltimore: Dungary Publishing Co., 1956).

might mean a lot of future business. If a sales manager has information of this type, he may assign such key accounts to another salesman.

Often business firms will employ specialists in statistical and other research methods to aid managers in developing useful information to guide their decisions. Such specialists also help managers to avoid erroneous uses of statistical and related data. But because statistics may be twisted either through design or error, it is imperative that managers have a basic knowledge of statistical and other research methods in order that they may evaluate analyses of data carefully before basing important decisions on them.[7]

Some illustrations of the erroneous uses of statistics include the following: Definitions may be shifted; for example, reports of the banking business as a whole are used for part of an analysis, reports for a specific bank or the banks in one region of the country are used for the remainder. Incorrect classifications of data may be used, as in the often-mentioned fallacy of comparing apples and pears. In some cases the persons compiling the original information may classify items incorrectly, for example, a salesman may report a customer as a poor credit risk rather than report he is using a competitive product. Causal relationships may be assumed where none exist, as for example, a retailer assuming that an increase in sales is due to his advertising campaign when in fact it may be due to an expansion of employment in a nearby plant. Frequently, statistics are made to lie by the inappropriate use of charts. The scales used are improper or misleading. One may show the curve depicting sales of a product as going up when in fact the chart may be labeled to indicate declining sales at an increasing rate.

These illustrations indicate some of the hazards of using statistical data and the ease with which erroneous conclusions may be drawn unless one is on his guard. Too many people assume that because information is quantified and presented in chart form, it is accurate. Good managers make every effort to avoid being misled by erroneous data or inaccurate interpretations of data.

Predictions and Postulates

As we indicated in our discussion of the steps or stages in decision making in Chapter 10, managers are faced constantly with the making of estimates regarding the future. They postulate, that is, make assumptions regarding the probable course of events. In greater or

---

[7] See, for example, Darrell Huff, *How to Lie with Statistics* (New York: W. W. Norton & Co., Inc., 1954).

lesser degree they make predictions. One of the main reasons for collecting and analyzing information of many types is to provide guides to such estimates, postulates, or predictions. Having reviewed some of the ways in which statistics may be helpful in this process, we turn now to a consideration of various ways of making predictions. An interesting discussion of methods of prediction has been presented by Irwin D. J. Bross in his *Design for Decision*.[8] One of the basic methods of prediction is to assume the persistence of the situation as it exists now. This is referred to as *persistence prediction*. For example, in predicting the weather it may be assumed that tomorrow will be like today. Or in predicting stock-market changes persistence prediction may be used; that is, unless there are important reasons for believing otherwise, the current situation in the market will be expected to continue. This method of predicting works best in relatively stable situations or under slowly changing conditions. It is often very useful for short-term business decisions. The life insurance industry, for example, bases its insurance premium rates on the assumption that death rates will change very slowly. Similarly, worker output usually changes slowly. The morale of the personnel of a business firm usually changes slowly and market preferences typically do not change very rapidly.

A second method of predicting is based on trends of development or persistent change in a given direction. For example, if the price of wheat has been moving upward gradually for a period of time, it may be assumed that this *trend* will continue. Predictions of this type are used in the business world in connection with estimating population growth, changes in productivity, changes in interest rates, and the like. Typically a trend must be in operation for some period of time before it can be useful for decision purposes.

A third method of prediction is the *cycle* type. Essentially this method assumes that history will repeat itself. It assumes that whatever goes up must come down and that there will be a tendency for market activity or activity of other types to move in wave-like patterns or cycles. You have often heard of the business cycle or the movement from prosperity to depression and back to prosperity. While business activity has tended to follow cyclical patterns, the extent and duration of the cycles have varied so greatly that it is difficult to make use of this approach, especially for short-range business decisions. It may be useful in various situations, however. For example, there are fairly

---

[8] Irwin D. J. Bross, *Design for Decision* (New York: Macmillan Co., 1957), chap. iii.

regular seasonal variations which tend to fall into a wave-like pattern. There may be cycles of price changes for a product or of worker output and others. A much disputed but interesting theory of history is based on the cycle principle. This theory was developed by Oswald Spengler and published in his book, *The Decline of the West*. His general thesis suggests that history tends to follow cyclical patterns with one civilization developing, reaching maturity, and then declining, with another taking its place.

Another method of prediction is that of *associative prediction*. In this method one event or type of activity is used as the basis for predicting a related event or activity. War scares in the past have usually been associated with sudden advances in prices. The price of one commodity may move in association with the price of another. For example, the price of sheep may advance and bring about an increase in sheep production. This may increase the supply of wool to the point where it will move in the opposite direction from the price of sheep.

Still another approach is by means of *analogy*. In this type of prediction a relationship is assumed to exist between two situations or sets of events. For example, all of the people in a market may be assumed to react like a panel of consumers. That is, an analogy may be drawn between the panel and the entire market. The strategy being followed by the management of a business firm may be compared to the strategy of a military commander. For example, too rapid expansion may be considered as analogous to a general pursuing his enemy too rapidly and overextending his line of supplies. Mathematical models are sometimes worked out to predict the possible interaction of various sets of events, and then analogies are drawn between the model and the actual business situation to which it is believed to apply. The use of electronic data processing machines has increased greatly the possibility of using mathematical models for business purposes.

Help from Economics

Economics provides us with a body of principles, theories, and hypotheses which often is helpful to managers in thinking about their problems and in guiding their decisions. We saw earlier in the chapter how the baseball manager made use of the general principle that right-handed hitters do better against left-handed pitchers and vice versa. There are a number of principles of economics that are similarly useful to business managers. We review only a few of these in our discussions here to indicate the general nature of this field of knowledge and some of the ways that it may be applied to the solution of management problems. As you move on to more advanced studies you will have opportunities to explore this area more intensively.

J. M. Keynes, the noted British economist of a generation or so ago, pointed out:

Any line of action is commonly termed *economic* when it attains its end with the least possible expenditure of money, time, and effort; and by *economy* is meant the employment of our resources with prudence and discretion, so that we may derive from them the maximum net return of utility.[9]

For business purposes we usually think in terms of maximum net return on investment, or maximum profit, rather than utility, which is a broad concept relating to the general satisfactions enjoyed by society as a whole. But the concept of economy and of principles explaining economic relationships are similar (though not necessarily identical) whether an entire society or a single business firm is under consideration.

Economics is of assistance to managers both in terms of analyzing "outside," that is environmental factors, or those primarily related to the firm itself. The former type is referred to as "macroeconomics," and deals with the economic system as a whole or broad sectors of it; the latter is referred to as "microeconomics." Environmental factors affect the decisions of managers with respect to the people they hire or want to hire, the machines and materials they buy, the impact of government regulations, and the conditions under which they undertake to sell their goods or services—and, of course, many other things also. Internal factors pertain to costs, level of operations, relationships between costs and potential returns, and other relationships.

Many of the principles of economics relate to markets and to various market relationships. Markets vary in the degree to which competition prevails, ranging from such highly competitive markets as the commodity exchanges and the stock exchanges to the market for water in a community supplied by one public utility. Under highly competitive conditions several general principles of market behavior tend to prevail. (Economists set up a model of "pure" competition assuming complete knowledge of buyers and sellers, none of whom act under compulsion and all of whom have free access to markets in which there is complete substitutability of products, but we will not consider these refinements here.)

---

[9] John Maynard Keynes, *The Scope and Method of Political Economy* (4th ed.; New York: Kelley & Milliman, 1955), p. 1.

Market Relationships

Some well-established market relationships are these:

1. The forces of demand, supply, and price tend to move toward equilibrium. If one factor is changed, the others will change so as to restore equilibrium. On the basis of this tendency the other relationships outlined below follow logically.
2. Increasing the price of a commodity, other things being equal (which is assumed in each of these propositions), will result in a smaller quantity being demanded by purchasers and a greater quantity being made available by suppliers.
3. Lowering the price will tend to increase the quantity demanded and reduce the quantity supplied.
4. An increase in supply will tend to cause a reduction in price if demand conditions do not change.
5. A decrease in supply will lead to an increase in price if demand conditions are constant.
6. An increase in demand will bring a rise in price if supply remains the same.
7. A decrease in demand will result in a lower price if supply does not change.

These sets of relationships help to explain what is likely to happen in markets as a result of changes in any of the principal factors involved: price, demand, or supply. Even if highly competitive conditions do not prevail (as is often the case) these basic tendencies help to explain and to anticipate changes that may be occurring in underlying market forces.

For example, firm A introduces a new machine that reduces the cost of producing power lawn mowers. It can reduce the selling prices of lawn mowers, drawing business from its competitors. They may soon introduce such machines. The result is likely to be that the power lawn mower industry will sell more products but at a lower price. The manual mower field may be hurt as a result, but it in turn may find a way to cut costs and win back some of the market.

Or suppose that the taxes on theater tickets are increased. We could expect (if there were no income changes and the like) that fewer theater tickets would be sold. Or if a tax on tickets were reduced or removed, we might expect more sales. This explains why lower taxes on some items produce more total revenue than higher levels of taxes —the quantity sold rises more than in proportion to the lowering of the tax. In such cases demand is said to be *elastic*, that is, having great responsiveness to price change; little responsiveness to price change is called a "condition of inelastic demand."

From the standpoint of the society as a whole, competition is one method of regulating business in the public interest. Market competition forces a businessman to keep prices in line. Without competition it would be necessary to fix prices by law and provide for some means of rationing the goods available (as was true of some things in World War II). Markets also ration goods—at higher prices we demand less and make the existing supply "go around." Often we forget the regulative role of market competition, and think only of what it means to a manager in making business decisions or to a consumer in deciding whether or not to buy, or buy more or less.

Impact of Competition

In making his decisions the manager is always conscious of the limits that are imposed on him by his competitors. He may wish to increase revenues by expanding sales but finds that this is not possible under the current competitive situation. He may consider reducing prices in order to capture a larger portion of the market, but finds upon investigation that his competitors might be able to reduce prices even more. He may decide that he needs two additional assistants to help improve budgeting procedures. He may locate the men he wants and offer them starting salaries that are in line with what he can pay. He may find, however, that competing firms are willing to offer more.

These illustrations suggest in a preliminary way the *discipline* that is imposed on managers by competition. The degree of competition varies from time to time and between markets and industries. In some situations managers have substantially more latitude in making their decisions, at least from the standpoint of competition, than in others.

We may outline the varying degrees of competition ranging from "pure" or perfect competition, as explained above, to pure monopoly. Neither of these two models ever exist in reality, but it is useful to think in these terms to identify the major characteristics of varying competitive situations. Between these two extremes are conditions usually referred to as "monopolistic competition," or "imperfect competition." The term "monopoly" means one seller (or producer); the reverse situation with one buyer is called "monopsony." If there are two sellers the situation is described as "duopoly"; a few or limited number of sellers is referred to as "oligopoly."

Under conditions of pure competition the manager's decision-making latitude is limited. He can only buy or not buy or buy more or less; sell or not sell or sell more or less. He cannot fix prices. He may put a price on a product but it may not sell until he lowers the price. Thus the market rather than the individual businessman sets prices under these conditions. Products are standardized; all firms are relatively small with no single one dominating the market.

Theoretically, the manager would have wide decision-making powers in a monopoly situation since there would be only one seller and he would dominate the market. He would be able to establish his prices at the point where he could realize maximum profits on the quantity that could be sold. In fact, of course, monopolies are usually regulated directly by government rather than through competition; hence, the manager's decision-making latitude may be rather sharply curtailed.

It is in the situations between pure competition and pure monopoly that we find most business firms operating. Under these conditions managers have fairly widespread latitude in making decisions. They have some control over prices. They can advertise and differentiate their products from those of competitors. They may produce a variety of products for many markets, at home and abroad. They may undertake public relations programs and related activities to create a favorable "image" which in turn may give them special competitive advantages. Often managers will engage in a certain amount of political activity, either directly or indirectly, in order to improve their positions or to restrict the operations of their competitors. Thus, the manager is always struggling for more "elbow room" than he can enjoy under a highly competitive situation.

Theory of the Firm

Economists have undertaken to develop a body of principles related to the operations of business firms and these principles are often referred to as the "theory of the firm." In its simplest form the theory of the firm assumes a model or projected set of conditions that include pure competition, standardized products and numerous small firms. (Other models also may be constructed representing varying degrees of competition.) In its simplest form efforts will be made by a manager who is trying to maximize profits to operate at a level where the spread between revenues and costs will be largest, that is, at an optimum level.[10] Since conditions will change in terms of consumer demands,

---

[10] See George Leland Bach, *Economics: An Introduction to Analysis and Policy* (3rd ed.; Englewood Cliffs, N.J.: Prentice-Hall, Inc., 1960), chap. 21 for a more complete discussion.

a firm may not achieve this optimum level or, if it does, may not operate at this level for very long. But the manager's aim, when the firm is not at this optimum level will be constantly to move toward it.

If we assume that the price of the product is fixed by the market, the manager cannot raise prices without losing his market. Hence, his decisions will aim at the "best" or optimum level of operations, the point at which his costs are lowest in relation to output. Such a situation is illustrated in Figure 13–3. The total revenue, cost, and profit are shown on the scale at the left side of the diagram; the output per period of operations, say a month, is shown on the base line of the diagram. In this case total costs exceed total revenues until an output of 200 units is reached; thereafter revenues exceed costs by varying degrees until an output of 1,000 units is reached, after which costs advance beyond the revenue. Under these conditions the manager would aim at an output of about 600 units, since this is the point at which profits would be maximized.

FIGURE 13–3

Revenue, Cost, and Profit Relationships at Various Output Levels

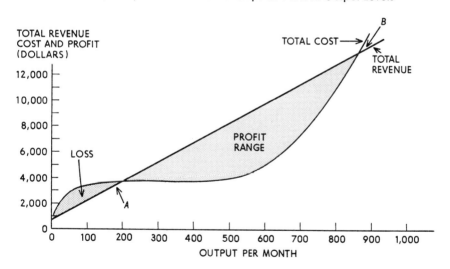

In this type of situation the manager would make his decisions on what is called "marginal" analysis. If he wished to maximize profit, he would expand output to the point where marginal revenue (the income from one added unit or block of units) equals marginal cost (the cost of producing the added unit or block of units). It is at this level of operations where the difference between average revenue and average cost is the greatest. If he expands beyond this point his income from each added unit would be less than his cost (see Figure 13–3).

Points A and B are "break-even" points. Usually managers refer to the situation indicated by Point A as a break-even point, since thereafter revenues exceed costs during the specified range of operations. Many businessmen use break-even analysis to a greater extent than marginal analysis.

It may be helpful to describe costs to a greater extent, since in a highly competitive situation the manager would have little opportunity to influence price. Oversimplifying, in most business firms some costs are rather definitely fixed and must be borne whether a few or many units are produced; these are called *fixed* costs. For example, the rent paid for a place of business will be the same whether it is used intensively or not. When output is expanded, however, some costs will move upward somewhat in proportion to the expansion in output; these are called *variable* costs. For example, the number of workers employed is likely to increase if a manager increases output and under these conditions labor costs would be variable.

Fixed costs and variable costs added together represent *total costs*. This concept may be stated as a formula: $TC = FC + VC$ (total costs equal fixed costs plus variable costs). If we divide total costs by the number of units produced, we have *average costs*; or in formula terms $AC = TC/Q$ (Q stands for quantity produced). *Marginal* costs represent the increased cost for producing one added or incremental unit. We show these relationships in the following table (Figure 13–4).

This figure outlines a number of relationships. In terms of quantities produced and sold we move from 200 to 1,800 as over-all possibilities (we are assuming that quantities can be changed only in units or "batches" of 200). Total revenue possibilities range from $1,800 to $9,000. But note what happens to marginal revenues, that is, the increased return for each "batch" or unit of 200 items. It moves from $1,800 to a low of $200. Total costs range from $3,000 to $15,300. Fixed costs stay at $1,400. Variable costs range from $1,600 to $13,900. Note that marginal costs move from $1,100 down to $300, and then rise gradually to $4,100. Average costs drop from $15 to $5.42 then move up to $8.50.

Where will the manager stop production? Certainly he will not produce beyond 1,400 units because at a level of 1,600 units he would actually be losing money. If he wished to operate at the optimum level, he would stop production at 1,000 units, since his revenue relative to costs is greatest at this point.

FIGURE 13–4

Cost and Revenue Relationships

	Expenditures						Revenues			
Quantity	Total Fixed Cost	Total Variable Cost	Total Cost	Average Cost	Total Marginal Cost†	Marginal Cost per Unit	Total Revenue	Average Revenue	Total Marginal Revenue‡	Marginal Revenue per Unit
200	1,400	1,600	3,000	15.00	.....	.....	1,800	9.00	1,800	9.00
400	1,400	2,700	4,100	10.25	1,100	5.50	3,400	8.50	1,600	8.00
600	1,400	3,300	4,700	7.83*	600	3.00	4,800	8.00	1,400	7.00
800	1,400	3,600	5,000	6.25	300	1.50	6,000	7.50	1,200	6.00
1,000	1,400	4,100	5,500	5.50	500	2.50	7,000	7.00	1,000	5.00
1,200	1,400	5,100	6,500	5.42*	1,000	5.00	7,800	6.50	800	4.00
1,400	1,400	6,900	8,300	5.93*	1,800	9.00	8,400	6.00	600	3.00
1,600	1,400	9,800	11,200	7.00	2,900	14.50	8,800	5.50	400	2.00
1,800	1,400	13,900	15,300	8.50	4,100	20.50	9,000	5.00	200	1.00

* Rounded to the nearest cent.
† Additional cost incurred in producing each additional 200 units.
‡ Additional revenue received for each additional 200 units sold.

SUMMARY

Management's use of various statistical and economic—as well as other—guides to decisions depends on effective use of information, some of which is quantitative, some of other types. A wide variety of information usually is available to a manager. Complete systems of data collection and processing have evolved from the use of the computer.

Our uses of information are facilitated by straight thinking, techniques for collecting and analyzing data, application of previous knowledge in the form of theories or principles, development of hypotheses or hunches, use of models, and related techniques.

Statistics is a body of methods of obtaining and analyzing data for decision-making purposes; a branch of the scientific method, it deals with phenomena that can be described numerically. It involves the collection of facts and the analysis of facts by determination of points of similarity and difference. Widespread uses are made for decisions, predictions, and various control purposes. Errors often are made in the uses of statistics by shifting definitions, using incorrect classifications, using improper charts and in other ways.

After data are collected and analyzed they may form the basis for predictions or postulates, using such methods as persistence prediction, establishment of trends, use of cycles, associative prediction, and the use of analogy.

Economics provides a body of principles, theories, and hypotheses that often is helpful to management decisions. In general, economic thinking or action attempts to attain its end with least expenditure of resources. It is helpful in the analysis of environmental factors "outside" the firm ("macroeconomics") as well as factors related to the firm itself ("microeconomics"). Many economic principles relate to markets and well-established market relationships between the forces of demand, supply, and price are especially helpful as guides to management decisions.

There are varying degrees of competition and these determine in part the latitude of management decisions. In a highly competitive situation the manager's decision-making latitude is limited; as we move in the direction of monopoly his decision-making latitude tends to widen. Of course, it may be circumscribed directly by regulation in many monopoly situations.

The theory of the firm helps to explain various cost-volume-return relationships, optimum levels of operation, relationships between various types of costs, marginal analysis, and related factors. It is especially helpful in indicating what may happen under highly competitive situations. Many managers make use of "break-even" analysis in determining desirable operating levels.

QUESTIONS AND PROBLEMS

1. Why do managers make use of such a wide variety of information? Indicate how a manager may utilize information to help him reach decisions.
2. Give an illustration from your experience of the use of "facts" that were not true or only partially true.
3. Mr. A. M. Edwards is manager of a department store. His wife and three daughters are enthusiastic about some dresses they bought while on vacation. They urge Mr. Edwards to purchase dresses of this type for sale in his store. Should he do so? Why or why not?
4. How would you define "statistics" as a body of knowledge?
5. Identify the types of averages in the following statement: Sales ranged from 100 to 250 units per week; average sales were 175 units per week; the most frequent number of sales per week was 177.
6. Draw a "bell-shaped" curve. Assume this represents the volume of sales of a restaurant which opens at 9:30 A.M. and closes at 4 P.M. The manager wants to reduce costs. How might this be done?
7. Give an illustration of persistence prediction. Of prediction based on cycles.
8. Mr. E. E. Long who is already independently wealthy inherits a large estate. He wants to give this money away to support various educational activities. Is this an economic problem?
9. Because of an increase in printing costs, the price of textbooks has been advanced. If other things are equal, how is this likely to affect the demand for textbooks? If you were in the textbook publishing business, are there any decisions you might make under these conditions to try to gain a larger part of the market?
10. The price of cigarettes is advanced from 30 cents to 35 cents per package. Sales drop by a little over 1 per cent. Would you say that the demand for cigarettes was elastic or inelastic? Why?
11. Differentiate between duopoly and oligopoly.
12. What is meant by "fixed costs"? By "variable costs"? By "marginal costs"? Illustrate each.
13. Indicate what is meant by a "break-even" point.

SUGGESTED READINGS

BACH, G. LELAND. *Economics: An introduction to Analysis and Policy.* 3rd. ed. Englewood Cliffs, N.J.: Prentice-Hall, Inc., 1960. This is an interesting introductory textbook in economics. Read especially chap.

20, "The Business Firm and Its Costs." You may also wish to read chaps. 21 and 22.

BROSS, IRWIN D. J. *Design for Decision*. New York: Macmillan Co., 1957. chap. iii, "Prediction."

LONG, JOHN D. *Workbook to Accompany Weimer: Business Administration: An Introductory Management Approach,* chap. 13. Rev. ed. Homewood, Ill.: Richard D. Irwin, Inc., 1962.

SAMUELSON, PAUL A. *Economics: An Introductory Analysis*. 5th ed. New York: McGraw-Hill Book Co., Inc., 1961. This is a widely used and well-known textbook in economics. Read chap. 24, "Equilibrium of the Firm: Cost and Revenue."

WALLIS, W. ALLEN, and ROBERTS, HARRY V. *Statistics: A New Approach*. Glencoe, Ill.: Free Press, 1956. Read chap. 1, "The Field of Statistics," of this highly regarded book on statistics.

OUTLINE FOR CHAPTER 14

DECISION HELP has come increasingly
FROM LINEAR PROGRAMMING, GAME THEORY,
AND RELATED AEAS.

Such help is often of special importance to managers of firms
operating on a *multinational, multiproduct basis,*
under conditions of imperfect competition or oligopoly.

Operations research refers to the use of the scientific method,
and advanced mathematical and statistical techniques in the
solution of decision problems.

Linear programming is helpful in solving problems involving
several sets of linear relationships; a linear relationship
exists if one value varies directly with another.

The "graphic method" illustrates use and is applicable
with a limited number of variables; more complex
methods are used with aid of computer.

Managers may adopt solutions indicated, or
others that change the problem situation.

Game theory is helpful in decision problems where results
depend in part on actions of competitors ("conflict of
interest" situations).

Where losses of one firm are gains of another "zero-
sum" game theory is used; in other situations
"nonzero-sum" concepts are applied.

Decision problems under uncertainty require arbitrary adoption of some criterion to guide decisions, if there is
no knowledge of probabilities of possible outcomes; or
if there is knowledge or possible assumption as to
outcome,
adoption of strategy that will maximize expected
return in the risk situation.

Simulation involves developing a sort of "advance history" of potential developments, by means of
mathematics and the computer.

Limitations of mathematical guides to decisions arise
from difficulty of defining objectives for all parts of
systems; and complexity of people's behavior; hence
decision making remains an art, even though it
increasingly uses the methods of *science.*

14

DECISION HELP FRO LINEAR PROGRAMM GAME THEORY, AND RELATED AREAS[1]

It was an historical accident with large consequences that the same war which spawned operations research saw also the birth of the modern digital computer as a practical device.

—HERBERT A. SIMON

Complex Decision Situations

Many business firms now operate on a multiproduct and multinational basis. Often they operate under conditions of imperfect competition or oligopoly. Their range of decisions is wider under these conditions than if they operate on a one-product, one-country basis in highly competitive markets. Not only is the range of their decisions wider, but also the problems with which they contend are much more complicated.

It is more difficult to determine costs if several products are being made and marketed. The cost of producing one may be related to that of producing another, or may be unrelated. Large firms producing a number of products for many markets, at home and abroad, face very complicated revenue-cost relationships. Furthermore their managers are likely to be especially conscious of public reactions to their programs and to the roles they are expected to play. It may be difficult to detect changes in customer attitudes and preferences if markets are not highly competitive. The relatively slow introduction of compact cars by American automobile companies is a case in point. Objectives may be less clear-cut than in a one-product firm operating in a highly competitive situation; there may be conflicting objectives as between different parts of a large company.

To help managers cope with problems of this type a number of techniques have been used to an increasing extent in recent years. We consider some of them here in an introductory manner. One group arises out of the combination of modern mathematics, statistics, and eco-

[1] I am indebted to Professors John D. Long and E. Wainright Martin, Jr., for valuable assistance in the preparation of this chapter.

nomics to form a discipline that is called "operations research," and we consider some aspects of this subject in this chapter. Another group is based on behavioral and organization studies to which we will refer in the next chapter.

Increasing Help from Operations Research

Operations research (or "O.R." as it is often referred to) had its beginning in World War II when teams of scientists representing different fields of knowledge undertook to bring their combined knowledge to bear on particular problems. Thus, we usually think of teams of various specialists when we refer to operations research. Business firms, especially the larger ones, have used such teams increasingly in recent years.

As one author has pointed out:

The words "operations research" refer to the use of the scientific method and advanced mathematical and statistical techniques in the solution of management decision problems. Frequently referred to as "management science," "operations analysis," or "quantitative analysis," operations research and the concepts and techniques associated with it are becoming of increasing importance to management. It is possible to trace the history of the use of the scientific method to solve management decision problems back through Frederick W. Taylor and Thomas A. Edison to ancient Greece and the contributions of Archimedes to the defense of Syracuse. However, not until World War II, when teams of scientists were formed into operations research groups to study the problems associated with the use of new weapons systems, did the idea that the scientific method could be applied to the complex problems associated with the management of organizations begin to achieve widespread acceptance. Thus, the development of the use of operations research parallels that of the electronic computer, and the two are closely interrelated.[2]

One of the basic concepts of operations research is the use of a mathematical model, which is a system of equations representing an abstract concept of the situation or problem under consideration. The "bell-shaped curve" which we outlined in the preceding chapter is a simple form of such a model. Or a formula may be set up as a model; the familiar law of falling bodies is stated as a formula: $S = 16t^2$, that is, the space an object will fall will be equal to 16 feet (the drop in the first second) times the number of seconds (t) squared. A diagram of a football play is a simple form of model, as we have suggested.

For business purposes a mathematical model may be set up to ex-

---

[2] E. W. Martin, Jr., *Electronic Data Processing: An Introduction* (Homewood, Ill.: Richard D. Irwin, Inc., 1961), p. 382.

press in numeric form the relationships between alternatives and objectives and thus provide help in reaching decisions. The solution may be useful if the abstraction represented by the model resembles fairly closely the real problem; that is, if it has been possible to set up a model that reflects the actual situation. Often new lines of action may be suggested through the use of such a model. We should remember that the manager is not necessarily looking for a specific, single solution. It may be just as important to change the problem situation as to solve the problem under consideration. As we have suggested, the manager can in varying degrees influence his environment and the conditions under which he is working.

Operations research views the business firm as a *system*, or as a series of systems. Its purpose is to maximize the performance of a system. A system in turn is viewed as a "complex" or organic unit of functionally related elements. A system could be a political party, a military organization, or a church. From the standpoint of the manager, a business firm is a system. It is made up, especially if it is of larger size, of a series of subsystems. Each of these subsystems may have its own objectives but somehow they must be tied into the over-all objectives of the firm and brought into proper balance. It may be necessary that some of the subsystems be given objectives that are less than the optimum they might achieve but which will be best for furthering the over-all objective of the firm. This is referred to as "suboptimizing," that is, determining what is optimum for the subsystem within the entire system or firm itself. Operations research has been frequently concerned with solving problems of this type.

As Professor Martin points out, "Among the new mathematical areas that have been important in quantitative analysis have been linear programming, dynamic programming, the theory of games, queueing theory, statistical decision theory, information theory and servomechanism theory. Also, such older areas of mathematics as calculus, calculus of variations, set theory, matrix theory, differential equations, difference equations, and the theory of probability have been of great importance."[3]

We attempt little more here than to illustrate several of these areas and some of their uses. You will be making further use of these approaches to decision problems as you undertake more advanced work. (A good foundation of mathematics will be especially helpful as you move to more advanced studies.)

---

[3] *Ibid.*, p. 385.

It should be emphasized that operations research, employing the tools of the scientist, is not magic. Mathematics is indeed a powerful language for examining relationships in a way that allows rigorous manipulation and the application of formal logic to the derivation of solutions. On the other hand, in order to express a complex problem in mathematical form it is necessary to have an even more thorough understanding of the problem than we usually have, for each factor that can influence the outcome must be specified and expressed in measurable form. The relationships between these factors and the outcomes must be determined in so far as possible in advance. The process of meaningfully abstracting a real-life problem into mathematical form requires understanding and discrimination as much as it requires a knowledge of mathematics. Thus, the manager typically participates actively in this process. He cannot simply turn the problems over to specialists. He must be able to communicate with the specialists that have a thorough knowledge of the tools that may be employed.

Linear Programming

There are several techniques employed in finding solutions to linear programming problems but we will content ourselves here with one of the less complex types, the graphical method. A linear relationship exists if one value always varies directly with another; for example, if for all possible values of one item (X) and another (Y), a given change in the value of X produces a constant change in the value of Y.[4] An increase or decrease in sales, for example, might affect the amount of profit in direct proportion to the increase or decrease in sales. If for every added sale profit is increased by $5, the relationship between units of sales and dollars of profits would be linear; but if for each added sale profits would rise somewhat more or less than for the previous sale, the relationship would not be linear. If we plotted sales (S) and profits (P) as on the graph (Figure 14–1), the relationship between them would be a straight line—that is linear. In equation form, $P = 5S$.

Linear programming is helpful in solving problems involving several sets of linear relationships. For example, suppose we are turning out two models of power lawn mowers, the R model and the T model. We have three main production activities: metal working, motor assembly, and final assembly. Because of the machinery required, each of these activities is limited in capacity. In metal working there are 600

---

[4] R. Stansbury Stockton, *Introduction to Linear Programming* (Boston: Allyn & Bacon, 1960), p. 13.

FIGURE 14–1

Linear Relationship

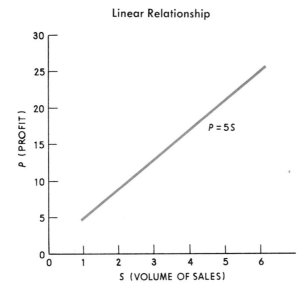

machine hours available in the time period under consideration. Each unit of model R requires one hour in metal working, while each unit of model T requires 2 hours. Thus if we build one unit (R) of model R and T units of model T, we require $R + 2T$ hours in metal working, so $R + 2T$ must not exceed 600. Each point on the graph of Figure 14–2 represents a combination of production of model R and model T. For example, the point M represents 300 of model R and 150 of model T, while the point N represents 200 of model R and 400 of model T. The metal working restriction specifies that the combined production must stay on or below the line shown, which represents the equation $R + 2T = 600$. Thus the point M represents a production that is feasible for the metal working activity, while the production represented by point N is not feasible (because $200 + 2 \times 400$ equals 1,000, which exceeds 600 hours). See Figure 14–2.

In motor assembly 7 hours are required for each unit of model R and 8 hours are required for each unit of model T, while a maximum of 2,800 hours are available. Thus $7R + 8T$ cannot exceed 2,800, and this restriction means that feasible production must stay on or below the line shown in Figure 14–3.

In final assembly two hours are required for each unit of model R and one hour for each unit of model T; 600 hours are available. This restriction forces production to stay in the area on or below the line

FIGURE 14–2

Metal Working

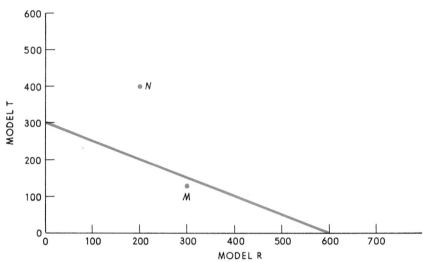

FIGURE 14–3

Motor Assembly

FIGURE 14–4

Final Assembly

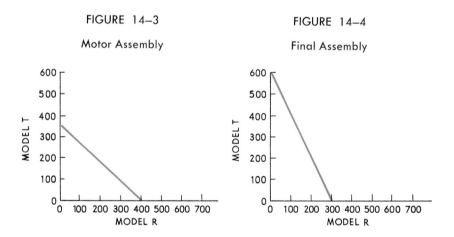

shown in Figure 14–4. The combination of these three restrictions limits production to the shaded area of Figure 14–5.

How much of each model should be produced? This question is not very meaningful unless we have further information. If we wish to maximize profit, and if we know the profit contribution of each model, and if these profits may be combined in a linear relationship, then linear programming can be used to determine the production schedule

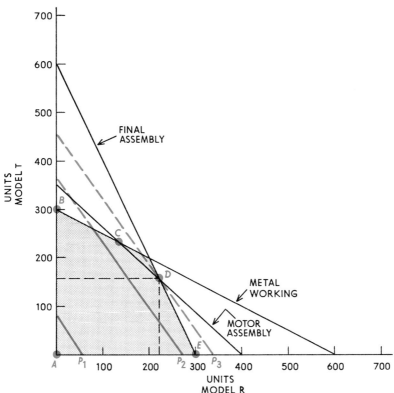

FIGURE 14–5

Production Limits

that will maximize profits under the specified restrictions. Suppose that the profit on each unit of model R is \$40 and the profit on each unit of model T is \$30. Then the profit is $P = 40R + 30T$.

The best possible or optimal solution is that set of values for R and T which: (1) is feasible, i.e. lies within the shaded area, and (2) also maximizes profit. It can be shown that this set of R and T values will be represented by one of the corners or points (B, C, D, or E) in Figure 14–5. For example, line P_1 indicates those combinations which will result in a profit of \$240. These are feasible but not very profitable combinations. The various combinations of line P_2 are more profitable (\$10,800) although not all of them are feasible as shown by the dotted portion of the line. Only one point (D) on line P_3 which represents \$13,530 is feasible within the limits stated. The production of approximately 222 R units and 155 T units indicated by point D is not only feasible but is also the most profitable mix.

Lines P_1, P_2, and P_3 are parallel because their slope of 4/3 is determined by the relative profitability of the two products. Four units of model T are required to produce the same profit which is yielded by three units of model R. Hence, the slope of these lines is 4/3. A major change in the profitability ratio will usually change the solution point. For example, if the profit contributions for the models were reversed, the slope of the profit lines would be 3/4 and point C would become the optimal solution. On the other hand, if the profits were $65 on R and $30 on T, the slope would become quite steep (65/30) and the solution would be point E. In this case we would produce 300 units of R and none of T. The profit would be $19,500.

The graphic method of solution is directly applicable in such problems only when the number of products does not exceed 2. If we had 30 or 40 variables and 12 restrictions, we would use the simplex method and an electronic computer to calculate the solution. Our main purpose here is to indicate the types of problems that may be solved or in which considerable help can be secured by the use of tools of analysis of this type.

Often the manager's decision may differ from that specified by the use of these techniques. In the above illustration, for example, the manager may decide to increase capacity in order to obtain more profit. In this case a glance at Figure 14–5 will tell him that he can increase profit by enlarging the capacity of final assembly or of motor assembly —the metal working restriction is not involved as Figure 14–5 shows. In more complex problems the simplex method would indicate the increase in profit that would be obtained by any increase in capacity, and thus contribute to this "higher order" management decision. Likewise, if the solution indicated that only model R should be produced, the manager might decide to produce some of model T for public relations or other reasons. In this case the simplex method would indicate the cost of deviating from the indicated solution.

Game Theory

Many of the problems of a business manager require decisions where results depend in part on the action of competitors, union officials, or others. The best course of action for the firm may depend on the course of action chosen by another person (or persons) who is a "protagonist." The business manager's job is to try to choose the best offsetting strategy, taking into account the possible actions and counteractions of those with opposing interests. On the basis of our discussions in earlier chapters, you can understand that many problems in business fall under this heading.

Growing assistance in problems of opposing interests has been coming in recent years from developments in "game theory." The central idea in game theory is that an individual or a business firm (1) has certain preferences or goals, which are in conflict with those of one or more other persons, (2) faces two or more alternative courses of action, (3) does not have full control over the outcome of any course of action, and (4) is subject to some extent to the control of the other person or persons whose interests are in conflict with his own. Thus, game theory is said to involve "conflict of interest" situations.

John McDonald in his book *Strategy in Poker, Business and War* elaborates on this conflict aspect by pointing out:

> The strategical situation in game theory lies in the interaction between two or more persons, each of whose actions is based on an expectation concerning the actions of others over whom he has no control. The outcome is dependent upon the personal moves of the participants. The policy followed in making these moves is strategy. Both the military strategist and the businessman act continuously in this state of suspended animation. And regardless of the amount of information given them—short of the ideal of perfect information—they generally act in the final analysis on hunch; that is, they gamble without being able to calculate the risk.[5]

While initial use of game theory was preponderantly in military problems, it has had a growing influence on the approach of business decision makers faced with conflict situations.

The "Minimax" Concept

Among the useful ideas developed in game theory have been the "minimax" and the "maximin" concepts. The former involves a minimizing of the maximum loss, while the latter involves the maximizing of minimum gains. Both of these concepts—often for convenience referred to simply as the "minimax" concept—have useful applications to business and have found their way into the thinking and vocabulary of many business executives and also into business literature.

A simplified illustration may help you to appreciate some of the fundamental ideas involved. Suppose that Firm 1 and Firm 2 are competitors in the manufacture and sale of a certain product, that Firm 1 is larger and more powerful than Firm 2, and that these two firms

---

5 John McDonald, *Strategy in Poker, Business and War* (New York: W. W. Norton & Co., Inc., 1950), pp. 16–17.

control about all of the market for this product. Suppose further that Firm 1 is considering three alternatives it can use in an attempt to wrest sales away from Firm 2 and that Firm 2, in turn, has three alternative courses of action it might take in its effort to capture more of the market from Firm 1. Suppose further that neither the management of Firm 1 or Firm 2 wants to cut price directly and that both firms must choose a course of action at the same time which cannot be changed on the basis of the competitor's choice. While this situation is grossly simplified, it can be used to illustrate some aspects of game theory.

For the sake of brevity let us use symbols to denote the possible alternative courses of action in the following way:

For Firm 1:

    A—Launching of extensive advertising campaign.
    B—Hiring of more salesmen.
    C—Extension of easier credit terms.

For Firm 2:

    X—Improvement of quality of product.
    Y—Speeding up of delivery service.
    Z—Absorption of more transportation costs.

Suppose that the management of Firm 1 has prepared estimates of the effect on its sales of various combinations of actions by Firm 1 and Firm 2. Game theorists characteristically summarize such estimates in what they call "pay-off matrixes."

"Pay-off Matrixes"

You have undoubtedly encountered a "matrix" before, particularly if you have made use of mileage charts set up so as to show the distances between cities in a manner that reads both "across" and "up and down." For example, the illustration of a mileage chart (Figure 14–6), showing the distances between cities A, B, C, D, and E, is

FIGURE 14–6

Mileage Chart Matrix

City	A	B	C	D	E
A		300	500	700	1,000
B	300		400	600	1,200
C	500	400		250	100
D	700	600	250		1,350
E	1,000	1,200	100	1,350	

set up in the form of a matrix. A "matrix," in the sense in which the word is being used here, is simply a form or frame which embraces something else—in this case the pay-offs.

"Pay-off matrixes" present pertinent information in a form in which it may be easier to analyze the various "strategies" involved in order to pick the best one for the occasion. The pay-off matrix shown below presents the outcome to Firm 1 (in units of sales) of each pair of courses of action that the two firms can take. Positive numbers represent increases in sales of Firm 1 and negative numbers represent decrease in the sales of Firm 1.

| | | Firm 2 | | |
		X	Y	Z
Courses of Action	A	4,000	7,000	5,000
	B	1,000	3,000	6,000
Firm 1	C	−2,000	8,000	−3,000

"Zero-Sum" Games

A similar pay-off matrix might be constructed by Firm 2, showing its anticipated outcome for each pair of courses of action. If the gains to Firm 1 represent losses to Firm 2, and vice versa, the game is said to be "zero-sum" and the outcomes to both are expressed by the pay-off matrix shown above. It should be noted that in most situations the gains of one participant will not correspond to losses for his competitor. For example, Firm 1 by advertising might be able to increase its sales by an amount larger than the decrease in the sales of Firm 2. As we will see later, if this is the case and the game is not zero-sum, strange things can happen. In particular, *the techniques of analysis that are successful in the zero-sum case do not provide satisfactory solutions to nonzero-sum situations.*

With these remarks, let us continue our analysis of the illustration in which one firm's gain is the other firm's loss. All estimates such as these are crude at best. Assume for the sake of the illustration that they are reasonably accurate. A look at the matrix shows that for most of the combinations of opposing actions Firm 1 would be successful in capturing some of the market from Firm 2 and that some outcomes would be much more favorable than others. For example, if Firm 1 chooses course of action *A* and Firm 2 choses *Y*, Firm 1 will gain 7,000 units of sales in the period under consideration. In only two combinations would Firm 1 lose sales to Firm 2 according to the estimates reflected in the matrix. For example, if Firm 1 chooses C and Firm 2 chooses X, Firm 1 will lose to Firm 2 an estimated 2,000 units of sales. The big question, of course, is: which alternative should Firm 1 follow? (We could just as well look at the problem from the standpoint of Firm 2, but suppose we stay with Firm 1.)

A basic assumption of the theory is that your competitor is at least as smart as you and that he knows as much as you about the pay-off matrix. This leads one to the rather negative approach of focusing attention on the size of the gain that can be guaranteed at the worst. Likewise, Firm 2 management will be interested in determining how small the loss can be kept at the worst. Looking at the matrix again, we can identify the minimum figure in each row in order to learn the least that could be expected by Firm 1 in following that alternative. These are the row minima. At the same time, we can look for the largest figure in each column to learn what each course of action would cost Firm 2 at the worst. These are the column maxima.

Firm 2

		X	Y	Z	*Row Minima*
	A	4,000	7,000	5,000	4,000
Firm 1	B	1,000	3,000	6,000	1,000
	C	−2,000	8,000	−3,000	−3,000
Column Maxima		4,000	8,000	6,000	

Examination of the row minima and column maxima shows that Firm 1 can guarantee itself the largest minimum gain by choosing alternative *A* where the minimum of the row is 4,000. This is the maximum of the minima (4,000, 1,000, and −3,000); hence it is called the "maximin." Notice that alternative *C* might yield a larger gain to Firm 1, assuming Firm 2 chooses alternative *Y*, than would alternative *A* at the best. (A pay-off of 8,000 is better than 4,000, 7,000, or 5,000, the pay-off in alternative *A*.) On the other hand, it does not *guarantee* as much gain; in fact, it might involve a loss. (For example, if Firm 1 chooses alternative *C*, Firm 2 might choose alternative *X* and this would result in a loss of 2,000 units or worse yet, alternative *Z* where the loss would be 3,000.) Looking at the Firm 2 situation, we can see that alternative *X* is the one which holds the possible loss to the lowest level, namely, 4,000. Other column maxima are 8,000 and 6,000. Hence, the minimum column maximum is called the "minimax." On the basis of this analysis Firm 1 would choose *A* and Firm 2 would choose X, and the "value" of the game to Firm 1 would be 4,000 units.

This matrix was designed deliberately to present an example of what game theorists call a "saddle point," which exists when the maximum of the row minima and the minimum of the column maxima are the same. While saddle points are infrequently encountered, games with saddle points are the easiest of all to analyze and to explain. This solution is stable, for even if Firm 2 knows that Firm 1 is adopting choice A, Firm 2 must still select choice X, and vice versa.

Since saddle points are uncommon in pure game theory and even more uncommon in business situations, let us change the matrix slightly by assuming that the 1,000 and the 4,000 in the estimates are reversed. (A and B in the X column.) The adjusted matrix would be as follows:

| | | Firm 2 | | | |
		X	Y	Z	Row Minima
	A	1,000	7,000	5,000	1,000
Firm 1	B	4,000	3,000	6,000	3,000
	C	−2,000	8,000	−3,000	−3,000
Column Maxima		4,000	8,000	6,000	

Now there is no saddle point because the minimum of the column maxima is still 4,000 but the maximum of the row minima has become 3,000. Thus Firm 1 can guarantee itself a return of 3,000 by choosing alternative B. Firm 2 can assure that it will lose at most 4,000 by choosing alternative X. However, the actual result that will be arrived at cannot easily be predicted for if Firm 1 knew that Firm 2 would choose X, Firm 2 would choose B. On the other hand, if Firm 2 knew that Firm 1 would choose B, it would choose Y, because this loss is lower than any other possibility in this row. If Firm 1 knew that Firm 2 would choose Y, Firm 1 would choose C. The process of trying to "second guess" could go on and on. Hence, there is no longer equilibrium in the open choice of a given alternative by each firm.

In situations like the above, there is no one alternative (such as A, B, or C) which each firm can follow consistently in order to maximize its expected returns. Game theory indicates that the largest expected return comes rather from following a "mixed strategy" where various alternatives are used in a certain relative frequency.

For example, game theory can show that in the above situation Firm

1 should choose alternative *A* and alternative *B* in the ratio 1:6 and should not use alternative *C* at all. (The method of computing this "mixed strategy" ratio will not be explained here.)[6] In this way, Firm 1 can expect to obtain a larger return (3,571 units) than would result in any other method of selection. How we arrive at 3,571 units is explained below. In the language of game theory, Firm 1, by doing this, is "maximizing its minimum guaranteed security level." The important point to observe is that in no other way could Firm 1 achieve an expected return of this much. Notice that alternative *A* guarantees Firm 1 only 1,000 units, alternative *B* guarantees Firm 1 only 1,000 units, and alternative *C* guarantees Firm 1 only a *loss* not to exceed 3,000 units.

A difficulty, however, comes in that Firm 1 must not let Firm 2 know in this case what alternative within this "mixed strategy" Firm 1 will take at any time. If Firm 2, for example, knows that Firm 1 will choose *A*, Firm 2 will choose *X*. If on the other hand Firm 2 knows that Firm 1 will choose *B*, Firm 2 will choose *Y*. Hence, secrecy is needed. Even if Firm 2 deduces the "mixed strategy" which Firm 1 will follow to maximize security (as it can be assumed to do), Firm 1 should try to prevent Firm 2 from knowing which choice is to be made at any particular point.

One way for Firm 1 to do this is to "mix" its choices between *A* and *B* on some sort of "random" basis. Following this procedure and having already decided on its "mixed strategy" of *A* and *B* in the ratio 1:6, Firm 1 could use a randomizing device which would result in the choice of *B* six times for every one choice of *A* over the long run. One such device which game theorists have talked about is a "fair wheel" whose circumference is divided into equal segments. In this case there would be seven equal segments. Six of the segments would be labeled *B* and one of them *A*. A spin of the wheel would indicate the course of action. This type of decision making may strike you as unrealistic. The idea that a business manager or military commander would make an important decision on the turn of a wheel of chance or toss of a coin may seem strange. And perhaps it is. All game theorists are saying, however, is that such a randomizing device can be used to prevent the opponent from being able to figure out what alternative you are going to choose. Remember, the general "strategy" at this point has already been developed.

---

[6] To learn more about such "games" and how they might be solved, you may wish to read one or more books on game theory. A good one to start on is J. D. Williams, *The Complete Strategyst* (New York: McGraw-Hill Book Co., Inc., 1954).

Notice further that even though the choice is to be made only *once* (and most real-life problems *are* solved only once), game theory suggests that the "mixed strategy" still be followed. In the above example, if Firm 2 knew that Firm 1 would choose B for the one-time play of the game, Firm 2 would choose 3. Firm 1's expectation would then be only 3,000 units instead of 3,571.

Using the same idea of "mixed strategy," Firm 2 could develop a pattern of action to guarantee its own minimum level of security (in this case, of course, a loss, but a *smaller* loss than might otherwise be the case). This "mixed strategy" for Firm 2 in this case would be the use of X and Y in the ratio of 4:3 (with Z not being used at all). In following this strategy, Firm 2 could hold its expected losses to 3,571 units. The point to observe here is that in no other way could Firm 2 keep this expectation so low. In order to prevent Firm 1 from knowing which alternative Firm 2 will choose (even though Firm 1 might have figured out the "mixed strategy" being followed by Firm 2), Firm 1 could make its choice on some random basis.[7]

Before you leave this section, try to make sure that you understand that the expected return of Firm 1 in this situation is 3,571 units and that the expected loss (negative return) of Firm 2 is the same quantity (3,571). For example, if Firm 1 uses its "mixed strategy" of A and B in the ratio of 1:6, it will average against the X choice by Firm 2 following: $(1 \times 1,000 + 6 \times 4,000)/7 = (1,000 + 24,000)/7 = 25,000/7 = 3,571$ units. Against the Y choice by Firm 2, the expected return by Firm 1 will be the same amount as shown by the following: $(1 \times 7,000 + 6 \times 3,000)/7 = (7,000 + 18,000)/7 = 25,000/7 = 3,571$ units. Computation of the expected loss by Firm 2 is illustrated as follows against choice A of Firm 1: $(4 \times 1,000 + 3 \times 7,000)/7 = 25,000/7 = 3,571$ units. You might double check your understanding of this idea by trying to compute the expected loss by Firm 2 against choice B by Firm 1. You should wind up with the same figure, namely, 3,571 units.

"Nonzero-Sum Games"

As was mentioned before, when a conflict situation is not "zero-sum" the analysis becomes quite difficult. This is also true when the number of participating interests exceeds two. For example, the farm problem may be succinctly expressed in game theory terms as follows: Assume for simplicity that each farmer has but two alternatives, full production and restricted production, and that the action of an in-

---

[7] If Firm 2 used a "fair wheel" such as described above, the equal segments should again be seven in number, four of them being marked X and three of them being marked Y.

dividual farmer has no appreciable effect. Looking at the situation from the standpoint of an individual farmer, we can construct a pay-off matrix showing his profit for each of these choices under various possible alternatives determined by the per cent of all farmers that restrict production.

Per Cent of All Farmers Restricting Production

	0%	25%	50%	75%	100%
Full	$300	$750	$1,500	$2,250	$3,000
Restricted	$200	$500	$1,000	$1,500	$2,000

Note in this pay-off matrix that full production is better for the *individual* farmer than restricted production, *no matter what the other farmers do*. Thus it appears that the rational course of action for each farmer is full production, in which case each makes $300. On the other hand, if they all adopted the irrational strategy of restricting production, each would make $2,000.

In the above and similar situations there is no solution that all game theorists can agree upon. Indeed, one lesson that may be drawn from these illustrations is the fact that, contrary to what everyone would wish, there exist decision-making situations in which *complete knowledge* of the possible outcomes plus rationality and logical reasoning on the part of the decision makers do not lead to a satisfactory solution. Some believe that a major function of government is to change the rules and pay-offs in such situations so that rational men can arrive at socially desirable solutions. Certainly one may conclude that the most practical alternative of a manager faced by such a situation is to attempt to change the environment to produce a problem that he can solve, rather than passively choosing a course of action.

Decision Making under Uncertainty

In still other types of business problems managers do not face "conscious adversaries" but still are forced to choose in the face of the unknown. In many cases they know that more than one outcome is possible in any course of action but they may not have the faintest idea of the likelihood of any particular outcome.

Problems of this type are known technically as "decision problems under uncertainty." This means that the probabilities of the outcomes of alternative courses of action cannot be known. In recent years much attention has been given to problems of this type. As a result, several guides have been worked out to aid business managers who have to take action without knowing many things that they would like to know concerning the possible consequences.

Decision problems under uncertainty may be thought of as requiring a choice between two or more alternatives where any one of two or more "states of nature" may exist. (A "state of nature" may be the condition of the weather as of a particular time, for example, or the health condition of a person or a group at a given time.) The difficulty arises from the fact that the decision maker does not know and cannot meaningfully predict which state of nature will exist as of the time of this choice.

In situations of this type some business managers prefer to use the minimax concept and settle for the alternative that *guarantees* the largest minimum gain (or smallest maximum loss), regardless of which state of nature prevails. Others will prefer to shoot for the largest possible gains even at the danger of suffering a calamitous loss. Still others will prefer to choose so as to minimize the maximum possible regret from having made the wrong choice. And some others will prefer to act on the "principle of insufficient reason" as though all of the states of nature were equally likely.

These behavior patterns, and others that may exist, may appear somewhat confusing to you, for none of them is completely satisfactory. Some people prefer one pattern and others different patterns. The point is that each one of these patterns (and others) has its champions, each claiming that a decision maker who acts "rationally" should follow his patterns. When faced with this type of problem, the decision maker is forced to select some basis on which to proceed. What is "best" depends on which of these decision criteria (or others) he adopts to guide his choices.

Example of Decision Problem under Uncertainty

Perhaps another example—also highly simplified—will suggest to you some of the ramifications of decision making under uncertainty. Assume you have a chance to buy a concession to sell ice cream bars at the homecoming football game. You can get the concession for a certain area of the stadium for $5 plus rental of a container for $3. Cost of the ice cream bars is five cents each; the sales price at the game is 25 cents. Suppose that you can also get a concession to sell hat covers that have a bill and hence may be bought as protection against either rain or sun. This concession costs $5, but there is no container rental. Moreover, it covers a larger area of the stadium. The hat covers cost five cents each and sell for 25 cents each. Assume further for the sake of simplicity that you can return any unsold items in either concession but that you must pay the full rental on the container no matter how many or how few ice cream bars you might sell. As another assumption, suppose that you could have *either but not both* of the concessions and that you had already decided that you wanted one or the other of them. The problem is: which one should you take?

The difficulty, of course, is that the sales of each concession item is highly dependent on the weather and that you do not know what the weather will be. In this situation the alternative courses of action are taking the ice cream bar concession or taking the concession for hat covers. The alternative states of nature are the various weather conditions which might prevail during the game. Let us suppose for the sake of this illustration that you must decide a week before the game which concession to take and thus you are unable to obtain enough information about weather conditions to be of any significant use to you in trying to predict the weather at the time and place of the game. Hence, let us assume that you consider yourself completely ignorant about the way the weather will develop.

You might attempt to classify weather conditions and then make some estimates of your sales and profits under each alternative concession for each weather condition. Suppose that you did this and came up with the following estimates of net profit under several possibilities. This breakdown of the weather, of course, does not exhaust the possibilities. They are being used to keep the problem reasonably simple.

Weather Conditions	*Dry Warm*	*Dry Cold*	*Wet Warm*	*Wet Cold*
Ice Cream Bar Concession	$22.00	$7.00	$17.00	$ 4.00
Hat Covers Concession	5.00	3.00	23.00	29.00

From earlier discussions in the text you can recognize that estimates such as these which involve speculation as to revenue and costs are often subject to large error. Ignoring for the moment, however, possible errors in the estimate and assuming that the weather will fall into one of these four categories, let us consider what you should do.

According to the minimax decision criterion, you should choose the concession for ice cream bars. The reason is that even with the "worst" weather you would make an estimated $4.00 profit, whereas the least profit under the hat covers concession would be an estimated $3.00.

On the other hand, if you wanted to choose in such a way as to minimize the most regret you could have as the result of having made a poor choice in the first place, you would take the hat covers concession. The idea here is that regret is measured by the profit "lost" by making the wrong choice, given the state of the weather. For example, if the weather turns out to be dry and warm, you would make only $5.00 with hat covers but $22.00 with ice cream bars. Hence, if you had chosen the hat covers, your "regret" at making the wrong choice would be $17.00. If you had chosen the ice cream concession, you would have had no "regret" since the weather turned out to be dry and hot. If you analyze the other three states of nature in a similar way, you can see that your "regret" would be as follows: if the weather is dry and cold, $4.00 in case you chose hat covers; if the weather is wet and warm, $6.00 in case you chose ice cream bars; and if the weather is wet and cold, $25.00 in case you chose ice cream bars. The following matrix summarizes the various "regrets." After studying the matrix you would choose the hat covers concession, assuming you wanted to minimize the maximum possible "regret." It would be $17.00 as opposed to $25.00 if you picked the ice cream concession and the weather at game time was wet and cold.

Regret Matrix

Weather Conditions	Dry Warm	Dry Cold	Wet Warm	Wet Cold
Ice Cream Bar Concession	0	0	$6.00	$25.00
Hat Covers Concession	$17.00	$4.00	0	0

This concessions example could be used to illustrate several other criteria for decision making under uncertainty. Only one more will be cited. Suppose that, because you did not know the likelihood of any weather condition, you decided to regard each of the four conditions as equally likely. The decision criterion based on the "principle of insufficient reason" would lead you to choose the hat covers concession. The estimated value of this concession, assuming the four weather conditions are equally likely, is $15 ($5 + $3 + $23 + $29 all divided by 4). For the other concession the estimated value is $12.50 ($22 + $7 + $17 + $4 all divided by 4).

Maximizing Expected Return

Although this example is much simpler than most real life situations, it does provide you with some insight into the nature of decision making under uncertainty. The crucial factor is the selection of the particular decision criterion which is to be used.

If in the above example historical data and long-range weather forecasting techniques can be used to estimate the probabilities associated with the various weather conditions at the time and place of the game, a simple yet powerful analysis can be used.[8] In this case the decision maker would probably choose to maximize expected return (or more specifically, the expected utility of the returns). Suppose that the weather *probabilities* turned out to be: .4 for dry warm (that is 4 out of 10); .3 for dry cold; .2 for wet warm; and .1 for wet cold. In such a situation you should choose the ice cream bar concession with an expected return of .4 ($22.00) + .3 ($7.00) + .2 ($17.00) + .1 ($4.00) = $14.70. The expected return from the hat covers concession would be .4 ($5.00) + .3 ($3.00) + .2 ($23.00) + .1 ($29.00) = $10.40.

This helpful knowledge of probabilities, in turn, often results from research. This is another illustration of why research often is helpful to business decision making.

Simulation

We have been able to simulate various types of conditions in a number of ways. One of the more interesting, of course, is simulated space flights for the training of astronauts. Simulated flights were used widely in training aviators during World War II. Role playing is a form of simulation that is often highly effective. The "executive game" is a method of simulating executive decision making, and is used increasingly by students and by practicing executives. (You may have an opportunity to engage in one of these exercises in connection with this course.)

Such exercises can be made to approximate complicated business problems by the use of advanced mathematics and the computer. The performance of an organization or part of an organization can be represented over a period of time, thus providing a sort of "advance history" of potential developments. Various factors can be changed keep-

---

[8] Some authors suggest that, with these probabilities known or reasonably assumable, the decision problem solving takes place under conditions of "risk" rather than "uncertainty." For detailed treatment of this distinction as well as a comprehensive summary of utility theory, game theory, and decision problems under uncertainty, see R. Duncan Luce and Howard Raiffa, *Games and Decisions* (New York: John Wiley & Sons, Inc., 1958).

ing others the same, and thus it is possible to compare performance to determine which course of action may be most desirable. In particular, such techniques have proved to be valuable in connection with job-shop operations on problems of scheduling and of assigning machines.[9]

Limitations of Decision Guides

In this chapter we have considered a number of guides that are helpful to the manager in making decisions. Of special importance is the determination of objectives, since these set general value standards for a firm. In the large multiproduct, multinational firms, the determination of over-all objectives may not be difficult, if stated in terms of profit maximization, but the establishment of objectives for parts of the firm or subsystems may be exceedingly difficult. Carefully defined policies may be subject to misinterpretation and frequently may need to be re-evaluated. Financial and accounting guides to decision have the appearance of being rather definite, as do economic concepts in their simpler forms. But even these leave much to be desired and we move on to mathematical methods to try to get further assistance. While many of the mathematical techniques may appear to provide rather definite guides, it is usually necessary for the manager to exercise a good deal of judgment in determining what is to be quantified in order to apply such techniques.

We must remember, too, that the business world is made up of people, as well as things, numbers, ratios, and mathematical or economic relationships. People are highly complex beings or "systems." Their complexity adds to the difficulty of management decisions but at the same time assures that decision making will always be a most challenging area of activity, which will continue as an art, even if it uses increasingly the methods of science.

SUMMARY

In highly complicated managerial situations increasing reliance is being placed on linear programming, game theory, and related areas for help in the solution of decision problems. This is particularly the case when firms operate on a multiproduct and multinational basis under conditions of imperfect competition or oligopoly.

Operations research (or "O.R." as it is often referred to) had its

---

9 See, E. W. Martin, Jr., "Simulation in Organizational Research," *Business Horizons*, Vol. II (Fall, 1959), pp. 68–77.

beginning in World War II when teams of scientists from different fields undertook the solution of complicated problems such as those associated with weapons systems. Also referred to as operations analysis, management science, operations analysis, and quantitative analysis, operations research has been used increasingly by management in recent years; it involves the use of the scientific method in combination with advanced mathematical and statistical techniques, facilitated by the use of the computer. Widespread use is made of mathematical models to represent abstract concepts of the problems under consideration.

Linear programming is helpful in solving problems involving several sets of linear relationships. A linear relationship exists if one value always varies directly with another so that a given change in one produces a constant change in the other. For example, an increase in sales adds $5 to profit for each unit of increase. The relationship is linear. The "graphic method" illustrates the use of linear programming and is applicable when the number of linear relationships is limited; for more complex situations more complicated methods are used with the aid of the computer.

Game theory is helpful in the solution of decision problems where the results depend in part on the actions of competitors; these are called "conflict of interest" situations. In cases where the losses of one firm are the gains of another, "zero-sum" concepts are used; in other situations "nonzero-sum" concepts may be applied.

The concepts of the "minimax," that is minimizing of maximum losses, and the "maximin," that is maximizing of minimum gains, are used increasingly to aid in the solution of decision problems. Pay-off matrixes often are constructed to summarize the possible outcomes of various alternatives and facilitate the development of strategies.

Decision problems under uncertainty present a particularly difficult set of conditions. The solution of such problems requires the arbitrary adoption of some criterion to guide decisions, since there is no knowledge of the probabilities of possible outcomes.

When there is knowledge or assumed knowledge of possible outcomes, the strategy is indicated that will maximize expected return in the particular risk situation.

Simulation involves the development of a sort of "advance history" of potential developments by means of mathematics and the computer. Other examples of simulation include the "executive game," role playing, and simulated training situations.

Decision guides of the type discussed here have their limitations since it is often difficult to define objectives with sufficient precision for all parts of complicated systems to permit the application of mathematical techniques; in additions the complexity of the behavior of people assures that management decision making will continue as an art, even though it uses the methods of science to a growing extent.

QUESTIONS AND PROBLEMS

1. Which developments have caused managers to make increasing use of advanced mathematical and statistical techniques in the solution of some of their decision problems?

2. How did World War II contribute to the development of operations research? What other terms are used frequently in referring to this general area?

3. Give an example of suboptimizing. Could this concept be applied to sports as well as to business?

4. Explain why the manager must participate actively in the solution of problems by the use of operations research and related methods?

5. What is meant by "a linear relationship"? If each constant addition to or decline in sales means an addition or loss of one dollar in profits, is this a linear relationship? If profits increase $5 per unit for the first 100 units of output and $8 thereafter, is this a linear relationship throughout the range indicated?

6. In the example of linear programming (using the graphic method) presented in this chapter, why might the manager decide to increase capacity in final assembly or motor assembly, rather than to accept the solution indicated? What is the value of methods of this type, if managers do not accept the indicated solutions?

7. Why is game theory said to involve "conflict of interest" situations?

8. What is meant by the "minimax" concept? The "maximin" concept?

9. What would the matrix on page 000 look like if it were set up to reflect outcome to Firm 2?

10. Give an illustration of decision making under uncertainty.

11. In the illustration of the ice cream bar and hat covers concessions presented in this chapter, would you prefer the solution that would minimize maximum losses or minimize maximum regrets?

12. What is meant by the statement that simulation provides "a sort of 'advanced history' of potential developments"?

13. Do you agree that decision making will continue as an art, even though it is using increasingly the methods of science?

SUGGESTED READINGS

Long, John D. *Workbook to Accompany Weimer: Business Administration: An Introductory Management Approach,* chap. 14. Rev. ed. Homewood, Ill.: Richard D. Irwin, Inc., 1962.

Martin, E. Wainright, Jr. *Electronic Data Processing: An Introduction.* Homewood, Ill.: Richard D. Irwin, Inc., 1961. Read the introductory chapter.

McDONALD, JOHN. *Strategy in Poker, Business and War.* New York: W. W. Norton & Co., Inc., 1950. Read what you can of this interesting discussion.

STOCKTON, R. STANSBURY. *Introduction to Linear Programming.* Boston: Allyn & Bacon, 1960. Read the first three chapters of this introductory discussion of this subject.

WILLIAMS, J. D. *The Compleat Strategyst,* chaps. 1 and 2. New York: McGraw-Hill Book Co., Inc., 1954.

part

Business
Resources
and
Operations

SUMMARY OUTLINE

BUSINESS ADMINISTRATION—now one of the more exciting areas of study—may be *approached* in an *introductory* manner from the point of view of the *manager*.

He is the central figure in the business firm—the key social and economic institution of our time. It is managed and operated in a highly dynamic environment.

Business Firms are established as individual *proprietorships, partnerships, corporations,* and other forms.

Firms vary in *size* and engage in many *types of work*—manufacturing, trade, finance, service, and others.

The *Decision Makers* in business firms are owners, managers, and business specialists.

The *Management Process* involves establishment of objectives, plans, and controls; organization of resources; and leadership.

Decision Making—a central management responsibility—includes problem and *goal identification* and clarification, development and analysis of *alternatives,* appraisal of most likely alternatives, and *choice.*

Decisions may be guided by financial, accounting, statistical, economic, mathematical, and other considerations.

Business Resources and Operations involve effective utilization of the abilities of people—requiring knowledge of personnel and organization behavior—

as well as other resources including

capital, equipment, knowledge, time, and related aids to productivity, plus the place of business—land, buildings, and location—

in the *production* and *marketing* of goods and services to secure *income.*

The *Business Environment* influences management decisions and in turn is influenced by them, particularly in the areas of

business conditions,

governmental and political conditions,

the legal system,

the enterprise system and competing systems,

and international business administration.

Emerging Problems and Opportunities hold promise for the business community, and for you in managing your future.

OUTLINE FOR CHAPTER 15

PERSONNEL represent a major resource of the business firm, AND ORGANIZATION BEHAVIOR is important in the firm's performance.

Individual behavior may be explained on the basis of the individual's "internal state"—his history and what is stored in memory—and his environment.

Changes in memory content are learning; content of memory is brought out by "evoking" process; stimuli may bring out habitual or other responses.

Manager attempts to anticipate behavior of individuals and groups. Understanding interactions between individuals and groups is important in building effective organizations.

Responsibility for personnel is both
  centralized and
  "splintered."
Personnel specialists usually work in staff capacity.

Achievement of the firm's objectives usually depends on a basic work team of strongly committed members;
  on efficiency in terms of costs and returns;
  on balancing of interests and conflicts of the individual and the firm.
    Incentives are important—economic, social, or others.

Personnel plans relate to other plans of the firm, include job analysis, job description and specification, job classification; use of personnel budgets which also serve control purposes. Standards are used to measure individual and group performance.

Organizations are built by attracting people to them; proper selection; orientation and training programs; direction; motivation; good communication; job assignment; recognition; adjusting conflicts; protections against hazards; fair standards; development of loyalty; anticipating changes.

Union-management relations continue as major problems both for the firm and the economy as a whole.

PERSONNEL AND
ORGANIZATION BEHAVIOR

The property which every man has in his own labour, as it is the original foundation of all other property, so it is the most sacred and inviolable.

—ADAM SMITH

Resources and Operations

We have been considering a number of topics related to the overall management of business firms, including some of the approaches and guides to broad decision problems. We turn now to a discussion of the management of business resources and operations. We may classify resources in a number of ways. For our purposes, however, attention is centered in this and the following two chapters on (1) the people in the firm; (2) the machines, equipment, tools, and other things used by these people to help them in their work; and (3) the plant or other installation in which the work is done as well as its location. Following these discussions we turn our attention to the management of production and marketing operations.

We have suggested that money may be considered as a general resource of the business firm because it is typically used as a means of commanding other resources. Hence, we considered the general subject of finance in relation to central decision problems. Once money has been used to hire people, or to buy or rent machinery, equipment, materials, or real property, the resources of the firm become more specialized and the management problems related to them take on somewhat different aspects.

Although we break down our discussions by various types of resources, we should recognize that all of them are interrelated. A single resource is seldom productive by itself. People need tools and machines, a place to work, materials to work on, other people to work with. It is difficult to discuss personnel, for example, without regard to other resources of the firm. For study purposes, however, it is almost essential that we make some divisions. In a final analysis, of course, we are concerned with the ways by which managers put together a totality of resources of various kinds to produce and market the goods and services necessary to secure income.

Human Resources

We turn our attention first to personnel (manpower or human resources), to the people in the firm, and to various problems related to the behavior of people within business organizations. Looking at people as a resource is not always easy. As we have pointed out their abilities are not "owned" by the firm, as are equipment and machines. This would be contrary to the Thirteenth Amendment to our Constitution which abolished slavery. The abilities of people do not appear on the balance sheet of the firm, yet such abilities are a resource; they cost money; and with proper management, they bring returns.

After our discussions in the last five chapters you may have begun to think about management problems in an abstract manner, and it is often helpful to do so. But you must never forget that business firms are made up of people, that such firms are social and political as well as economic institutions, and that few business decisions are likely to "make sense" unless consideration has been given to the people who will be affected by them.

As one executive has aptly said: "Whether management problems are problems of production, sales, engineering, or finance, they have human dimensions. Pushed back to basic fundamentals all the management problems of running an enterprise are rooted in human judgments, actions, interests, and attitudes. Only people have problems; only people solve problems. This constitutes a continuing challenge to the personnel administrator."[1]

The business manager is concerned with people outside the firm as well as within it—with customers, suppliers, investors, bankers, stockholders, government officials, labor union representatives, trade association officials, and the public at large. In this chapter, however, we center our attention primarily on the people within the firm. They cannot be separated entirely from those outside, since they interact on each other. Also, new people are being drawn into the firm, those in the firm are retiring, or moving on to other jobs, or being separated from the firm. Yet a "going concern" continues.

---

[1] E. H. Van Delden, "The Task of the Personnel Administrator in the 1960's," *Personnel Administrator*, American Society for Personnel Adm., June-July, 1960, p. 20.

Illustration of a Personnel Program

If you have participated in the activities of a student group, a fraternity, a sorority, or similar club, you have probably had some experience with personnel and human relations problems even though you may not have recognized them as such. For example, you probably tried to attract new members to help achieve the organization's objectives. This is comparable in some ways to the function of hiring people. You listed or had in mind the general qualifications of new members, and you developed plans for attracting the people you wanted into your organization. You tried to set up inducements that would get them to join the group. After you added new members, you usually provided programs for their development. Even though of an informal type these programs acquainted the new members with the club, its rules, traditions, objectives, and programs. You were concerned with maintaining the general quality of your members and providing opportunities for them. You probably arranged to give younger members the experience that would qualify them to become club officers at the proper time. In some cases you may have expelled a member or put him on probation or taken some other disciplinary action.

The organization probably had an over-all program for making effective use of the talents and abilities of the members in furthering the purposes of the club. There may have been times when it was necessary to resolve differences of opinion, to make certain that good work on the part of various members was recognized, and to do a number of other things that were necessary to keep the organization operating effectively.

In a brief and somewhat oversimplified view this illustration indicates what is involved in the development of an effective work team for a business firm and some of the personnel and human relations problems that may be encountered in the process. To make sound decisions a manager needs to understand the behavior of people as individuals and in groups of varying size.

People are a primary resource of business firms and hence, a knowledge of human behavior is important for the solution of all types of management problems. It would be a mistake to think that a manager made one set of decisions on the basis of financial factors, another in terms of materials and equipment, and another in terms of human behavior. All types of factors are interrelated in business decisions, and the behavior and anticipated behavior of people affects them all.

Just as in the types of problems outlined above in the illustration of a club's personnel problems, the business manager has the problems of (1) attracting people to the organization, (2) training and developing them, (3) directing their decisions and activities through the proper exercise of authority and by means of effective communications, (4) motivating them to put forth productive effort, (5) compensating them fairly, (6) recognizing good performance, (7) maintaining required discipline, and (8) providing for personal satisfaction in work and association with the organization.

We consider these topics in a preliminary way here. It may be possible to understand them more readily, however, if we review briefly some of the factors that help to explain the behavior of people as individuals and as participants in organizations. In larger organizations these are the areas for personnel specialists who assist line executives in carrying forward their responsibilities.

Behavior of Individuals

The study of individual behavior is generally the area of the psychologist, and group behavior that of the sociologist and cultural anthropologist, although these distinctions overlap. Hence we often use the term "behavioral sciences" to cover these areas of study.

March and Simon explain individual behavior on the basis of (1) the "internal state" of the individual—his past history and what has been stored in the individual's memory, and (2) the environment.[2] The individual may call out of his memory certain things that have a bearing on his behavior at the time, called an "evoked set" of things stored up in memory. In turn other content of the memory may be brought out by an "evoking" process. The changes in the content of the memory takes place slowly through education and experience; many things are accumulated over time. This process is referred to as *learning*. Thus, behavior can be influenced by learning, or adding to the total of things in memory, or by changing the things that may be called out to bring to bear on a particular situation or problem, that is, by evocation.

Similarly, environment may influence behavior but some aspects of the environment will have a particular bearing at a given time; these are called *stimuli* by the psychologists. Other aspects of the environment may have little or no influence at a given time. The stimuli are closely related to the evoked set of factors that are called out of memory; the stimuli that are present will determine what is evoked;

---

[2] This discussion based on James G. March and Herbert A. Simon, *Organizations* (New York: John Wiley & Sons, Inc., 1958), pp. 9–11.

and the evoked set at any given time will determine what parts of the environment will be effective as stimuli. There is interaction among these processes; it is a dynamic rather than a fixed or stable set of relationships. There will be variation as between intervals of time—the longer, the larger the part of the memory that will be evoked and the larger the number of environmental factors that may be effective as stimuli.

As March and Simon point out:

The memory content, thus divided into "active" and "passive" elements can also be classified in a different way. It includes: (*a*) values or goals; criteria that are applied to determine which courses of action are preferred among those considered; (*b*) relations between actions and their outcomes: i.e., beliefs, perceptions, and expectations as to the consequences that will follow from one course of action or another, and (*c*) alternatives: possible courses of action.[3]

There may be various associations between these factors; for example, through the learning process a particular goal may have become associated with a particular action and *habitual* responses may occur. There may be no conscious reaction in such cases.

In short, the human organism is viewed as "a choosing, decision-making, problem-solving organism that can do only one or a few things at a time, and that can attend to only a small part of the information recorded in its memory and presented by the environment."[4]

The manager's problem is to try to predict or to anticipate the behavior of individuals. We must recognize, however, that human beings are very complex and that predicting their behavior is far from easy. For example a stimulus may have unanticipated consequences because it evokes a larger set than expected, or a different set than expected, or a given stimulus may be mistaken for another, or the stimulus may include unintended elements.

Basically, the manager is interested in getting people to become participants in the organization and to participate productively so that their contributions will exceed the cost to the firm of their participation. The individual normally is willing to participate in the organization and to participate productively if he feels that according to his values the returns exceed his contributions. He agrees to accept a given authority relation to the organization, and to adjust his decisions, within some limits, to those of the organization as reflected in its objectives, policies, work rules, and the like. If the individual feels

---

3 *Ibid.*, p. 12, by permission.
4 *Ibid.*, p. 12.

that his contributions exceed his rewards, he is likely to leave the organization, or to reduce his contributions; similarly if his goals conflict sharply with those of the firm, he may leave or reduce his contribution. He is likely to remain identified with the organization if he feels rewards are adequate, the work is compatible with the other roles he plays in life, if the characteristics of the job conform to his characterization of himself, if there is consistency of supervision practice and if related factors are favorable.

People and Organizations

The manager of a business firm is interested in developing an organization that will enable him to achieve the objectives of the firm. This means that as a minimum the organization must have sufficient stability to survive, and beyond this, if possible, to grow.

While economic objectives typically are paramount, to achieve such objectives the manager must create not only an economic organization but a social and political one as well. Increasingly managers have studied individual and group behavior in order to increase their ability to establish and develop organizations of the type needed to accomplish their goals.

A manager may make various assumptions about the behavior of people in relation to his organization. For example, he may view people as (1) "passive instruments," capable of performing work under direction but having little impact on others or on the organization as a whole. In this situation the manager would probably develop a highly centralized organization with little latitude for participation by members. (2) Or a manager may assume that members of the organization bring to it *attitudes, values, and goals,* that it is necessary to motivate or induce them to participate in the activities of the organization, recognizing that there may be conflicts between individual and organization goals and that factors of morale and attitude are important in influencing the behavior of people in the organization. Under this assumption emphasis would probably be given to human relations programs. Further, (3) a manager may view the members of the organization as decision makers and problem solvers, which implies that perception and thought processes are of basic importance in explaining the behavior of people in organizations.[5] In this assumption the organization may tend to stress decentralized decisions and individual participation by members of the organization.

---

[5] *Ibid.,* p. 6.

All of these propositions have some validity. They provide a useful starting point for thinking about the behavior of people in organizations as well as about management problems related to their behavior. The way in which managers view the people in their organizations will have much to do with the kind of people hired and the way in which they are organized. Managers will be influenced by the objectives they seek to attain, the size and type of organizations they consider it necessary to establish and operate; the kind of work that will be required; the kinds of people and the abilities they must have to do the work; the situations and conditions in which the organization will operate; and related considerations.

An organization may be made up of various types of participants. Those who control entry into the group help to determine its general character; but once people are made a part of it they in turn have an important effect. It is the job of management to create a hierarchy of decision-making arrangements, and to provide decision guides through policies, orders, instructions, training programs, standard operating procedures, and the like. But it is necessary to understand how the people involved react to the organization as a whole, to the authority imposed on them, to the conflicts of their personal goals with those of the organization, to the incentives and motivations provided, and in other ways.

Interactions

The effective management of personnel requires an understanding of the interactions between individuals as members of subgroups or divisions of the organization and the organization as a whole. As we have suggested, an individual interacts with other individuals and they in turn on him. Beyond this, he interacts with subgroups or with the organization as a whole, and these in turn on him. These relationships expressed in this way sound relatively simple, but they often become exceedingly complex.

Professor Bass points out:

Definitions of "group" can be clustered into six categories. We can define a group as a collection of persons in definite interaction, or as a collection with common goals, or as a collection with interlocking roles, or as a collection with shared norms, or as a collection with shared perception of their unity . . . if we conceive of groups as collections of persons, which collections are reinforcing to the membership, it is possible to proceed to deduce many theorems concerning leadership and group behavior. . . .[6]

---

[6] Bernard M. Bass, *Leadership, Psychology and Organizational Behavior* (New York: Harper & Bros., 1960), pp. 22–23, by permission.

He goes on to suggest:

Groups vary in the extent to which they are rewarding to their members. The extent they reward is their *effectiveness*. Groups also vary in the extent they are expected to reward. The anticipated goal attainment is the *attractiveness* of the group. A potentially rewarding group is attractive; a group which actually rewards is effective.[7]

The relative effectiveness and attractiveness of groups vary widely. Each of us is a member of many economic, social, political, and other groups. An individual may work for a firm but still feel that his major identification is with one or more outside groups—the union, church, social club, or others. Or he may feel a primary identification with the firm, in contrast to identification with outside groups. He may feel a close identification with his job or with his work activities; this is often true if he is a specialist in one or another field. He may identify with subgroups in the organization itself; for example, he may identify himself with people in his particular department or his territory or those associated in producing a particular product.

One way of thinking about the manager's work with respect to his organization is in relation to his attempt to create what has been called "organizational equilibrium,"[8] that is, the basic set of conditions that allows for the survival of the organization itself. This point of view involves several relationships: (1) the organization is viewed as a system of interrelated social behavior of the participants; (2) each participant receives inducements (wages, salary, opportunity for training or advancement, or others) for which he makes contributions; (3) each participant continues with the organization so long as inducements offered (measured by his values and in terms of the alternatives open) are greater than contributions made (again his values); (4) all contributions taken together are the source of the inducements that can be given to participants; and (5) the organization is "solvent" from an organizational viewpoint so long as the contributions are great enough to provide the required inducements to keep the organization going.

Management of Personnel

We turn now to a consideration of some of the personnel and human relations problems usually encountered by the managers of business firms. Since people play such an important part in determin-

---

[7] *Ibid.*, p. 42.
[8] March and Simon, *op. cit.*, p. 84.

ing the success or failure of a business firm, the responsibility for personnel rests primarily on the chief executive officer, but it rests also on everyone who has any supervisory responsibility within the organization. Thus, the responsibility for the management of personnel is both centralized and "splintered" among all of the divisions of a firm. In a small firm the owner-manager or top administrative officer will usually do the work related to personnel programs himself. In somewhat larger organizations these functions may be delegated to a subordinate who may combine them with others. In still larger firms a specialized personnel manager usually is employed. In some cases an entire personnel department may be set up to perform these functions. A personnel manager or personnel department typically occupies a "staff" relationship with the other divisions of a business firm and assists supervisors at all levels of management in carrying out their responsibilities relative to personnel and human relations.

Some personnel responsibilities, however, are never delegated by the chief executive. These will include the hiring and training of key management personnel, fixing the compensation of such people, and firing people with major executive responsibilities whose performance has not been satisfactory. Some personnel and industrial relations matters are nearly always retained by owners or boards of directors, including the hiring, compensation, and firing of the chief executive officer, approval of major contract negotiations with unions, adoption of major policy changes affecting rates of compensation of major executives, fringe-benefit programs, and the like. The top-management group thus has the power to determine who will be participants in the organization and the basis of such participation.

Also because of the special types of problems involved, the hiring, training, compensating, and firing of the sales personnel may be the responsibility of the sales manager. The same thing may be true of other department heads and their specialized personnel.

We pointed out in our discussion of objectives (see Chapter 8) that the general targets or objectives of a business firm are usually broken down into more specific goals for various divisions of the firm. This means that effective personnel and human relations programs begin with a determination of objectives and the establishment of a working relationship between these objectives and those of the firm as a whole. Both the broad and supporting objectives of the firm are important factors in motivating the personnel of the organization.

The functions of personnel management have been outlined as follows:

Personnel management involves the entire management process as it is applied to the essential personnel relations functions of recruiting and selecting, developing, utilizing and maintaining an adequate and satisfactory work force. The personnel or industrial relations program is a course of planned action designed to embrace these essential functions, so that when they are performed in line with company policies they will contribute directly to the organization's success.[9]

Human Relations

As we all recognize, people are complex beings. They vary widely in their abilities, hopes and fears, likes and dislikes, value scales, interests, and attitudes toward life in general. Despite these differences managers must find ways to get people to join their organizations, to develop, to work together as a team, to motivate them to put forth their best efforts in order to achieve the objectives of the firm. This involves "human relations," a subject of growing importance which has been defined by Professor Keith Davis as, ". . . the integration of people into a work situation in a way that motivates them to work together productively, cooperatively and with economic, psychological and social satisfaction."[10] It involves also the establishment and maintenance of good working relationships between the people *within* the firm and those *outside* the firm.

Those working in the firm typically are directly dependent on it for a living for themselves and their families. The relationship of others to the firm may not be so direct. Some may have financial interests in the firm such as investors and owners but may or may not be primarily dependent upon it. Some may have relations with the firm as suppliers of goods and services, for example, or as customers.

In addition, there are public officials who may have regulatory or protective relationships with the firm, including inspectors, policemen, firemen, tax collectors, and the like. Some quasi-public officials, such as the representatives of trade associations, or chambers of commerce, or labor unions, will have important relationships with the business firm. And finally the members of the public at large will determine the general reputation of the firm and its products.

Obviously, the business manager cannot influence all of these people to the same degree. The greater their ties with the firm, the greater

---

9 John F. Mee and Edgar G. Williams, "Managing a Successful Personnel Relations Program," *Indiana Business Information Bulletin Number 33* (Bloomington, Ind.: Indiana University, Bureau of Business Research, 1958), p. 8.

10 Keith Davis, *Human Relations in Business* (New York: McGraw-Hill Book Co., Inc., 1957), p. 9, by permission.

is his opportunity to influence them and to enlist their aid in achieving successful operations. The manager may have relatively little influence on government officials, or on union representatives, or on the public at large, and usually he can influence to only a limited degree the general environment within which his firm operates.

With respect to people outside the firm the manager has the responsibility for relationships with government, the community or public at large, customers, investors, suppliers, and others. The extent to which he can "manage" these elements may vary considerably from the extent to which he can manage operations within the organization. His responsibility, however, includes all of these things.

General Firm and Personnel Objectives

As we indicated in our earlier discussions, the major objectives of the firm are supported by various subobjectives or supporting objectives. Typically the personnel obectives of a firm will fall in the latter category, unless, of course, the major firm's objectives are stated in terms of personnel goals. Typically, this is not the case.

Frequently, the personnel objectives of the firm are stated in terms of securing and maintaining a well-knit and highly productive team, the members of which derive reasonable satisfaction from their work and the returns that it provides. Personnel policies and plans are usually developed to assure such a result.

The manager of the firm is concerned with efficiency, that is, favorable returns in relation to the personnel costs of operating the organization. This includes consideration of the rate of worker turnover, which is often expensive, especially if lengthy training programs are involved; losses due to accidents or absenteeism arising from sickness or other causes; and other factors. The attitudes of employees may have an important bearing on public and customer relations and thus present difficult problems of computing cost and return relationships.

Many firms find it advisable to develop a reputation as a good place to work in order to attract competent personnel and because such a reputation may have public and customer relations values. Policies such as promotion from within, paying salaries and wages that are above the average for the industry, protection of employees against hazards and similar ones often help to attain over-all firm objectives.

The survival of a business firm often depends on the stability of its basic work team. Usually a firm will have a "hard core" of members who are strongly committed to it. Growth, however, often awaits the development of a larger and well-integrated team.

The objectives of the owners, managers, and employees of a business firm do not necessarily coincide. Usually the owners and managers identify themselves with the firm and its objectives more definitely than do employees. Managers try to develop mutuality of interests on the part of all participants in so far as this is possible.

The people in a business firm may be influenced by a wide variety of factors ranging all the way from the job situation and income to the attitudes of members of their families. There may be problems of conflicting loyalties between the firm and the union, or between the firm and the local community, or others, as we have seen.

Employer interests tend to run in terms of low personnel costs relative to returns, high productivity, good worker morale, a stable work force, and employee loyalty. The interests of employees tend to center around fair wages and salaries (relative to similar work), economic security and opportunity, recognition, interesting work, safe and healthy working conditions, desirable hours, opportunity for expression and development, and fair and efficient leadership.[11]

Incentives

Many of the differences in interests listed above can be blended, but some divergence of interests frequently persists. Increasingly personnel managers have studied the goals, wants, and needs of employees in efforts to provide the incentives that will produce effective team effort.

A British industrialist approached this problem by raising the question, "Why do men work?"

He answered:

The short, blunt answer is "because they have to." But that is only the beginning of the matter. It is like saying that men swim because if they do not they sink. That is true enough, but it does not explain the difference between swimming enough to keep one's head above water and the whole range of speed strokes which gives a man mastery over water and makes swimming a thing of delight.

It is that difference which is covered by the word "incentives." It reflects the fact that, though men work because they have to, they also work because they want to. And it is that last increment—the increment that comes of willing work—which really generates power, and produces pretty well all that is worth having in the world.[12]

This statement suggests that people may be motivated to put forth their best efforts in most types of business situations. It is manage-

---

11 Mee and Williams, *op. cit.*, p. 12.

12 Sir Frederick Hooper, *Management Survey* (2nd ed.; New York: Pitman Publishing Corp., 1961), p. 95.

ment's job, of course, to find the right motives and to provide the corresponding incentives.

One way of looking at this problem is in terms of the *wants and needs* of people. While generalizations about matters of this type are hazardous, we may consider the suggestion of Professor Keith Davis that needs may be arranged in the ascending order according to the diagram in Figure 15–1.[13]

We should note that monetary income means more to some people than to others and that recognition may be a stronger incentive than income in a number of cases. There is always the question of whether people will respond more to incentives that appeal to their self-interest, their group interest, their unselfish or philanthropic interests, or their urge to create.

Creativity, of course, may be as much a selfish matter as desire for a higher income. Indeed, the desire for a higher income may be largely an unselfish matter since a worker may want more money to benefit the other members of his family or for some other similar purpose. Group interest may be selfish in the sense that one wants acceptance from a group for his own reasons rather than because of his interest in the group. Even doing things for the love of humanity in general may arise basically from selfish motives.

Approaches to the problems of incentives include provision of: attractive pay scales, rates of pay set according to the importance of jobs, development through training and related programs, opportunities for promotion and advancement, recognition for outstanding work, guarantees against risks and insecurity, and others.

Compensation Problems

Just as a dynamic and progressive society may contain elements of instability, so a business firm that is developing rapidly may run the risk of unstable operations. Most of the employees of a business firm are interested in opportunities for advancement, but they also are concerned about the certainty of their incomes both currently and in the future. Because of family and other obligations many of them may not feel they can run major risks.

Consequently, some workers will prefer jobs that may offer lower salaries than others but that provide reasonably certain employment with little risk of layoffs or loss of jobs. Similarly, some workers will accept jobs at lower rates of pay than offered by other firms if provi-

---

13 Davis, *op. cit.*, p. 41, fig. 3–1.

FIGURE 15–1

Priority of Human Needs

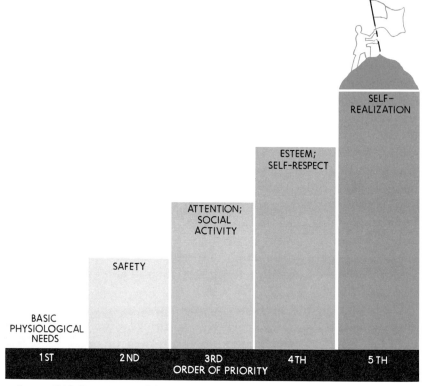

Source: Keith Davis, *Human Relations in Business* (New York: McGraw-Hill Book Co., Inc., 1957), p. 41.

sion is made for retirement income, hospitalization programs, protections against sickness, accidents, and the like.

The manager of a business firm must decide on the total program of compensation he can offer, relating it to the type of business in which he is engaged, the competition for workers from other firms, and the demands of unions or the requirement that may be established by legislation. Obviously, the manager of a firm with wide seasonal fluctuations cannot offer great stability of employment. Some firms, of course, have been able to iron out seasonal factors at least to a degree. The automobile industry is a case in point. Model changes in fall rather than in spring have helped to regularize employment.

Competition often will determine not only rates of pay offered but "fringe benefits" of various types. Thirty years ago fringe benefits accounted for only about a cent per hour on the average; today they exceed 25 cents per hour.

In some cases collective bargaining agreements with unions call for the guarantee of a minimum number of weeks of work per year. Minimum wage laws set floors below which wages may not be paid. Increasingly unions attempt to secure guaranteed work plans or guaranteed annual wage árrangements.

FIGURE 15–2

Labor Force

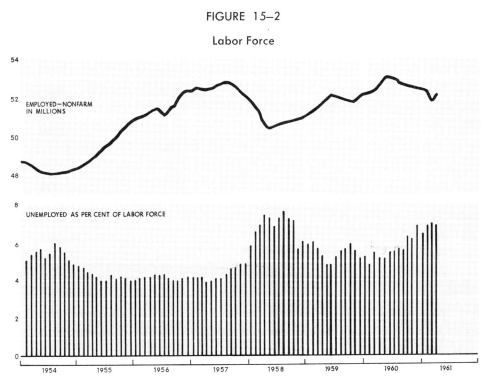

All of these factors affect decisions regarding a compensation program. Fundamentally, however, the manager of a firm is interested in establishing the type of program that will provide the greatest incentive for those in his organization to put forth their best efforts. In some cases this may mean that greater stress will be given to protections against insecurity than in others. The total compensation program is one of the important points at which the mutuality of interest of the firm and of its employees tends to center.

Sometimes employees through their union organizations will resist the introduction of new methods and processes since they believe they will be "working themselves out of a job." This is understandable from the worker's point of view. People fear most the things they do not understand. It is the job of management to make certain that members of the organization understand how changes may lead to greater productivity and more successful operations and hence greater opportunities for those associated with it.

Thus, while progress involves uncertainty and instability, the only real security for a business firm and for the economic system as a whole is the advance that comes from the introduction of new methods, products, and processes which result in greater productivity per man-hour. In the case of the economy as a whole we undertake to provide protections against major instabilities such as would result from "boom and bust" types of development. We must recognize, however, that if we put a strait jacket on the economy or on a businesss firm in the interest of stability, we tend to destroy the conditions that make progress and greater productivity possible. While our labor force is larger (see Figure 15–2, page 371), the number of people who will need jobs is growing rapidly.

Personnel Planning

The manager of a business firm develops personnel plans that will help him to achieve his objectives, just as he develops financial plans, production plans, marketing plans, and plans of other types. Personnel plans relate to the type of organization he believes to be essential for his purposes. He needs to determine the number of jobs, the kinds of jobs, the degree of training and skill for each job or block of jobs, when various jobs must be filled, the extent to which tney can be filled by hiring people or the extent to which people will have to be trained, the probable rate of turnover, and many related factors.

Usually the top manager of a business firm with his assistants will undertake to estimate the goods or services that can be marketed in the year ahead, the volume of production that will be required to meet such market demands, the timing of the production, whether a highly seasonal pattern of work or a more level pattern of operations will be followed, the number and types of employees needed plus the production equipment and facilities that will be required. Thus, personnel needs are closely related to all other aspects of a business firm's operations; hence, personnel planning seldom can proceed very far except in relation to other planning processes.

In addition, however, personnel managers may undertake special plans for testing, orientation, and training programs, for attracting workers with special abilities, or for experimenting with new programs of various types. Often the plans of a firm to open a branch or to start operations overseas or to shift to new products require highly elaborate types of personnel planning. Experienced workers may need to be shifted to new plants or stores and in turn replaced by new employees, who may need special training. Often personnel plans attempt to anticipate developments by a year or two or more in order that adequate lead time can be available to develop plans to the point where they may become operational.

The personnel departments of business firms typically study the various jobs; this is usually called "job analysis." Out of such studies comes a series of "job descriptions," and "job specifications," indicating the requirements of each job. The jobs are then classified in appropriate relationships to each other and a "job classification" system is developed. Often *personnel budgets* are used to facilitate planning. Plans also may be developed for attracting new employees, for improving programs of promotion and compensation, for studying new fringe-benefit proposals, and for undertaking the perennial problem of improving union-management relations.

Standards and Controls

Personnel plans often establish the basis for controls since they indicate the avenues by which objectives are to be reached. Such controls depend, of course, on the establishment of *standards of performance* against which to measure. Standards are established for group activity and for individual performance. Merit rating methods are often used for appraising individual performance; the performance of a production line, plant, store, or other unit may be measured in terms of units of output or sales, costs, contribution to profit or in other ways.

The performance of individual employees may be evaluated in many ways ranging from check lists and rating scales to fairly complicated methods. Standards may be relative, that is, comparisons with performance of other employees, or absolute comparisons being made against a predetermined standard. Those who do the evaluating often are supervisors and use the ratings as a basis for trying to improve performance.

In some cases performance can easily be measured on an individual basis, as in the case of sales personnel where it is readily apparent whether the volume of sales is meeting quotas or whether a particular salesman's performance compares favorably with others. In many cases, however, it is difficult to measure individual performance because one job is essential to the next. In such cases group performance can be measured against established standards and the members of the group evaluated on a comparative basis. A particular worker may be holding back the production of an entire group, hence must be weeded out and dismissed or shifted to other work. Sometimes lack of good communication results in poor performance. Standards may be set at too high a level and discourage rather than encourage workers.

In short, personnel controls are forward looking. Their purpose is to identify problem areas so that corrective action can be taken promptly in order to improve future performance. Ultimately the performance of the firm is evaluated by its ability to compete with other firms. Anticipating the factors that will have a bearing on effective performance, however, is usually essential.

Building the Organization[14]

Building a good work force includes the selection and hiring of people, assigning them to appropriate jobs, training them as required, and providing the necessary motivations to bring out their best efforts. The latter includes proper incentives in terms of income, recognition, and opportunities for advancement. A good "work climate" often yields dividends in terms of worker performance. Protections against various types of hazards usually are set up, in part to make certain that the firm is not running unnecessary risks and in part to help the work climate.

People may be attracted to a firm, held against competitive offers, and motivated to give their best performance in a variety of ways, as we shall see. We should note that it is the responsibility of management and not of workers or of unions to build effective work teams. For example, if a manager cannot find the "right" people for his team, he must use less well-qualified people and develop them to the point where they will perform like superior people. If management cannot afford to pay high wages or salaries, some other incentives must be developed to attract people to the organization and to hold them against the competition of others.

---

[14] You may wish to review the discussions on direction, co-ordination, and motivation in Chapter 9.

Personnel may be located through employment agencies, public or private, through management consulting firms, university placement bureaus, advertising efforts (the familiar "help wanted" ads that you have often seen), labor unions, and in other ways. Often present employees are helpful in locating new people. By means of promotions from within some job requirements are met without going outside the organization. Such policies are often helpful in developing employee morale.

Selection of employees may be an informal or highly formalized process. Many companies now use interviews, elaborate tests, analysis of employment history, recommendations, and related data. Managers try to use such information to predict the future performance and behavior of a prospective member of the organization. Physical examinations are now required by many firms. Once selections are made employees may be placed directly in jobs or orientation and training programs may be involved.

Orientation and Training

Once a new employee is hired, it is necessary to acquaint him with the job, in some cases assigning him for a time to a special orientation program, but as a minimum familiarizing him with rules and regulations, company policies and problems, methods of compensation, payroll deductions, special programs, and the like. Proper introduction of a new employee often plays an important role in determining his success, and his future attitude toward the company and his work.

Many firms have programs for the training and development of their employees. These may be formal or informal types. For example, apprenticeship training has been used for a long time to develop the skills and abilities of employees. Much training is done on the job. In some cases special courses may be set up ranging from the teaching of operative skills to management development or executive programs. Internship training, that is, joint programs of schools and business firms, is sometimes used to advantage. Courses outside the company may be available with the firm paying all or a part of the costs. Some programs may provide for general education as well as specialized training related to the job. Others may be vocational in nature. Some companies send "middle" management and top-management personnel to universities for special programs designed to develop executive abilities. Training and development programs are often important factors in the morale of an organization, and they frequently play an important part in the public relations programs of the firm as well.

Continuing Operations

The development of an organization is a continuing process. It involves efforts to improve the performance of individual members of the organization, various divisions, and the entire organization as well. Hiring the best possible people, of course, is one approach to the problem. But a team of stars sometimes is not as effective as a well-knit team of somewhat less competent individuals.

Well-designed orientation and training programs often are a means of developing the members of the organization and the organization itself. But the management of a successful going concern involves more than this. Careful assignment of people to jobs and movement to new jobs as opportunities arise are important.

Recognition through better pay, increased responsibility, and greater status in the organization is essential to the development of individuals and the total organization as well. For every person who can be recognized, in one way or another, however, there may be several who cannot be recognized, or who are not yet ready for recognition. Difficult human relations problems often are involved. Conflicts often arise from factors of this type or from other causes. There may be conflict between individuals due to competition between them. Conflict may arise between subgroups or divisions of the total organization. Differences in goals, in points of view, or in value scales often bring about conflict. Misunderstanding or lack of communication may be sources of conflict.

Some conflicts can be solved by removing the cause, that is, by specifically solving the problem. Some conflicts can be resolved by persuasion, getting one person or group to accept the point of view or the goals or value scales or attitudes of another. In some cases, however, conflicts must be adjudicated, either by management decisions and efforts to "sell" the decision or through bargaining or what are essentially "political" processes.

Protections against hazards both while working and while away from work are important aspects of most personnel programs. Health and safety programs, regularization of employment, medical protections, insurance plans of various types, provision for retirement, and related programs are widely used in this connection. Fair standards of performance and fair treatment in evaluations often are essential elements in the development of an organization. Provision for airing grievances and for correcting the situations that cause them; good communication systems that provide for two-way flows of information and opinion; effective and fair supervision; satisfaction and pride in work; and many related areas play a part.

Through these and related methods, managers try to develop loyalty to the organization, build good morale, and provide for effective leader-follower relationships. Recent studies by behavioral scientists have helped to throw light on various problems of this type.

As is true of other aspects of business operations, the effective management of personnel requires imagination to foresee probable changes in lines of development and their potential impact on the organization. For example, anticipated changes in markets may bring a change in product line and hence require workers with greater skills. Market changes may result in a new sales area being opened up and this may require the staffing of a branch operation. Competition may force the merger of one firm with another and require the development of an entirely new organization structure.

A firm's relationships with unions may be undergoing changes. Rates of pay may be rising rapidly and force management to introduce new and better machinery or to develop other ways to increase worker output to the point where the higher wages can be paid without jeopardizing the success of the firm.

Managers may anticipate changes in government regulations or in tax patterns and as a result may find it necessary to change personnel policies. Withholding taxes, for example, created numerous problems for business firms. The business world is a dynamic place; organizations and their leaders must be dynamic to compete, survive, and grow.

Union-Management Relations

Just as there are many types of business firms, there are also many kinds and varieties of unions. While we typically think of the large national unions, such as the AFL-CIO combination, the United Auto Workers, the Steel Workers and others, it is important also to think in terms of the local union organizations, city labor organizations, state organizations, and many others.

Some unions are very conservative in their social philosophy; others are far to the "left." A few of our unions have been dominated by communist leaders. Others have leaders who are more conservative than most business executives.

Some unions are organized on *craft* lines like the carpenters; others on *industrial* lines like the automobile workers. In some situations the national organizations are dominant and bargain on a national basis with large employers; in others the local union is of major importance.

It is well for us to recognize these and many other points of difference between unions so that we do not reach prejudiced opinions when we discuss the subject of union-management relations. In some cases business firms find unions to be a distinct asset in building an effective work team; in others the unions are a stumbling block, not only in building an effective work team but in other areas. Union membership today includes more than a quarter of the total labor force in this country (see Figure 15–3). In many industries the union plays a major role, sometimes helpful and sometimes not.

There are many theories which attempt to explain the rise of

FIGURE 15–3

Membership of the Seven Largest Labor Unions
1946 and 1958

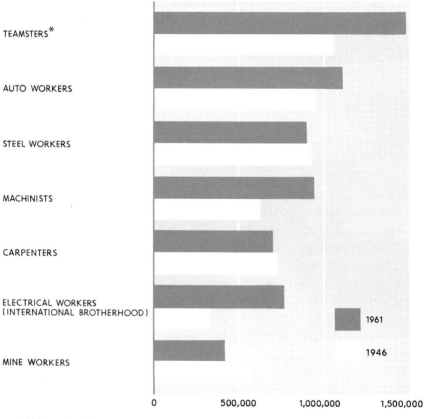

° 1960 membership.

unions. They may have resulted from the rise of larger business firms and the inequality of the bargaining positions of business firms and workers. For many years workers were at a great disadvantage in bargaining. Unions worked to provide balance, and then in some cases gained advantages over business firms. Unions may have arisen because of the lack of opportunity for the participation of individual employees in the affairs of the business firm. They probably arose at least in part from the desire for fraternal association on the part of those engaged in the same line of work as well as from political factors and the desire to present a united front on various public issues. They have influenced public sentiment considerably over the years.

Of major importance is the union's role in collective bargaining, that is, in determining the wages that will be paid, the "fringe benefits" that will be provided, the hours of work, conditions of work, and related factors. In some situations today a worker virtually must join the union in order to secure employment. This is particularly true where "closed-shop" conditions prevail. (The closed shop as an institution is illegal but the condition still prevails in some industries.) In such situations the union typically assumes a considerable responsibility for providing properly trained workers for the company, of taking disciplinary action against workers who fail to live up to the rules which have been agreed upon, for assisting in the negotiation of grievances, and other activities.

In order to understand the operation of unions it is well to recognize that their internal organization is essentially *political* in nature. Their officers are elected, and this puts them in somewhat the same position as the elected officers of any other organization or political party. Consequently, the officers of unions must win and hold support. Their motives are essentially related to the attainment and holding of power within the union organization.

There is little doubt that unions will continue to play an important role in the American economy and that sound programs of union-management relations will be essential to our future prosperity. Such programs must be more than a testing and balancing of power between business firms and unions. They must always give appropriate consideration to "the party of the third part" in labor contracts—that is, the public at large.

Dean G. L. Bach has made the following summary comment about unions which is well worth considering:

To describe unions as merely a mechanism through which workers can bargain collectively for higher wages and shorter hours is to miss much of the flavor of unionism in the American scene. Individual dignity and the feeling of belonging may be even more important to millions of workers than higher wages and better working conditions. Unionism today is a far-reaching social and psychological institution, as well as a powerful economic and political mechanism. Over the past quarter-century the rise in the status and security of the American working man has been greater than is easy to understand without having personally lived through the pre-New Deal days and the New Deal struggles of the 1930's. Much of this improvement has been due to unions. But much has also been due to the changing sympathies of the American public, and to management's own initiative in doing a better, more broadly conceived job than was true in most firms a generation ago.

Unionism versus no unions is no longer the central issue in America. Workers who want unions have them. The issue today is how well unions, as democratic organizations, can serve their members, and how the growing power of great labor organizations and their leaders can be channeled effectively toward the public welfare.[15]

SUMMARY

Understanding the behavior of individuals and groups is important to managers in building effective organizations. Individual behavior may be explained in terms of (1) the "internal state" of the individual —his past history and what has been stored in his memory—and (2) the environment; he may call out of memory things having a bearing on his behavior—an "evoked set." Content of memory may be brought out through evoking, that is, reaction to environmental and other stimuli. Changing content of memory is referred to as "learning." Responses to stimuli may be habitual or of other types.

The manager attempts to anticipate individual and group behavior; his assumptions regarding people may influence the type of organization he builds, whether he stresses highly centralized organization, human relations, decentralized arrangements, or various combinations. Management typically controls entry into the organization; establishes hierarchy of decision arrangements and decision guides; adjusts conflicts of individual and group goals; provides required inducements; and strives for efficiency in operations.

Responsibility for personnel management is both centralized and splintered in most firms. Typically, personnel specialists operate in a staff capacity.

Achievement of the firm's objectives is usually dependent on the development of a basic work team of strongly committed members, on efficiency in terms of cost-return relationships, on balancing interests

---

[15] George Leland Bach, *Economics: An Introduction to Analysis and Policy* (Englewood Cliffs, N.J.: Prentice-Hall, Inc., 1960), p. 580, by permission.

and conflicts of individuals, various subgroups and the firm. Incentives of all types are important in balancing interests and conflicts and in working toward the firm's objectives.

Personnel plans are closely related to other plans of management. Included are such techniques as job analysis, job description and specification, and job classification. Personnel budgets are used both for planning and control purposes. Standards are important for measuring performance and in achieving proper controls. Difficulties arise in measuring performance in complicated work situations.

Organizations are built by managers through the attraction of desirable members; proper selection of members; use of orientation and training programs; provision of good leadership; fair standards; proper job assignments; offering of fair compensation and other forms of recognition; establishing protections against hazards; development of loyalty to the firm and its objectives; increasing attractiveness of work; anticipating changes; and in related ways.

Union-management relations continue to pose both problems and opportunities for management. Problems in this area are important for the firm and for the economy as a whole.

QUESTIONS AND PROBLEMS

1. Why is it difficult to consider personnel as a resource of the business firm separately from other resources? What is distinctive about personnel or manpower resources?

2. Which fields of study typically are included in the behavioral sciences? How may managers make use of knowledge in these fields to predict or forecast individual and group behavior?

3. What is meant by the "internal state" of the individual? By his "environment"? How do they interact?

4. What is meant by "learning"? By "stimuli"? By "habitual responses"?

5. Why do we say that in order to achieve the economic objectives of a firm the manager may find it necessary to build a political and social as well as an economic organization?

6. How may the assumptions made by a manager about the behavior of people affect the way in which he sets up his organization? The kind of people he hires? The decision-making hierarchy he establishes?

7. Why do we say that the responsibility for personnel management may be both centralized and "splintered"? List some of the types of responsibilities that are never delegated by the chief executive.

8. Give illustrations of the importance of human relations in organization performance.

9. Show how personnel objectives are related to the general objectives of a business firm. How are costs affected by labor turnover? By absenteeism? By employee attitudes toward the firm?

10. Why do managers try to develop a mutuality of interests on the part of all participants in the organization? Contrast employer and employee interests.

11. Comment on the question, "Why do men work?"

12. How may conflicts between a firm and its members be adjusted? How are compensation and recognition related to such problems?

13. What is meant by "job analysis"? Job description and specification? "Job classification"? How may these be used in personnel planning?

14. How may personnel budgets be used in planning and control processes?

15. What is meant by "performance standards"? Give illustrations of how individual and group performance may be measured.

16. Of the various ways in which a manager may build an organization, indicate which you believe to be most important and indicate why.

17. A manager finds that he is losing employees to a competitor. What kinds of action might he undertake to cope with this problem?

18. Reports from the marketing department indicate that sales of a major product are slipping. How may this affect the personnel program of the firm?

19. How can you explain the rise of unions in this country?

20. What are the primary problems in labor-management relations at the present time?

21. Why is the "party of the third part" (the public) important in labor-management relations?

SUGGESTED READINGS

BACH, G. L. *Economics: An Introduction to Analysis and Policy.* 3rd ed. Englewood Cliffs, N.J.: Prentice-Hall, Inc., 1960. Read chap. 30, "Labor Unionism and Collective Bargaining."

LONG, JOHN D. *Workbook to Accompany Weimer: Business Administration: An Introductory Management Approach,* chap. 15. Rev. ed. Homewood, Ill.: Richard D. Irwin, Inc., 1962.

MARCH, JAMES G., and SIMON, HERBERT A. *Organizations.* New York: John Wiley & Sons, Inc., 1958. This is a significant book, though probably somewhat advanced for you at this stage. Read chap. 1, "Organizational Behavior."

MEE, JOHN F., and WILLIAMS, EDGAR G. "Managing a Successful Personnel Relations Program," *Indiana Business Information Bulletin No. 33.* Bloomington, Ind.: Indiana University, Bureau of Business Research, 1958. You can read this report in its entirety and obtain an interesting survey of work of the personnel manager.

OUTLINE FOR CHAPTER 16

CAPITAL EQUIPMENT AND OTHER AIDS TO PRODUCTIVITY present difficult management decision problems, and have certain special characteristics, including:

ownership and leasing possibilities;

long life, hence, difficult cost-risk-return determinations;

investments may be "locked in"; may have a potential impact on personnel.

The *Industrial Revolution*, a late phase of the Renaissance, laid the basis for modern production methods and requirements for improved business management and organizations.

Automation—the use of machines to run machines—often is referred to as the "second industrial revolution."

Knowledge and time are highly productive forces;

they form the basis of capital (unspecialized productive power) and capital goods;

income from capital and capital goods may be *capitalized*, reflected in present value;

depreciation and obsolescence represent risks to investment.

Natural resources, while gifts of nature, probably worth no more than capitalized value of time, effort, and other resources required to make them productive; *technology* is tending to replace geography in importance.

Manager's range of choices on capital and capital equipment decisions typically are wide; objectives need sharp definition; risks are high; and long-range plans are required.

Choices often include:

capital equipment versus direct labor;

ownership versus leasing;

one versus another type of equipment;

financial versus other considerations;

quick versus long-term return (based on present value estimates)

Research and Development programs involve great risk, little certainty of return, but may be essential to survival.

Management research and improvement of the management of research programs are increasing in importance.

16 CAPITAL EQUIPMENT AND OTHER AIDS TO PRODUCTIVITY

. . . everybody must be sensible how much labour is facilitated by the application of proper machinery.

—ADAM SMITH

Human versus Nonhuman Resources

In the preceding chapter we considered some of the factors that have a special bearing on management decisions related to personnel and to the behavior of people as members of organizations. We turn our attention now to the nonhuman resources of the business firm; in this chapter to capital equipment, tools, and related things that help people do their work more effectively; in the next chapter to the land, buildings, and other improvements on land that serve as a place of business as well as to the location of such facilities.

People are almost always involved in some way in making use of nonhuman resources. Even so, we could conceive of a situation in which you, as the manager of Your Company, Inc., were the only person in the firm. As you sit at your desk you might be getting reports by telephone on market conditions for your products, which are being turned out by automatic machines under contracts that you have let. You may have other contracts for supplying the necessary materials for these operations. You may have arranged for independent retailers or a chain-store organization to market your products. By means of telephone or other communication facilities you could keep in touch with bankers and investment houses in regard to required funds. Thus, in a situation without assistants or other employees it would be possible to operate a firm, provided you had the necessary equipment as well as contractual and other legal arrangements to assure that necessary operations were carried out.

In ordinary situations, of course, you would employ a number of people and organize them into an effective work force to carry out the activities of your firm, as we indicated in the preceding chapter. Also, you would provide each of these people in so far as possible with mechanical aids and with electrical or other types of energy or power to help them do their work. Such aids may be thought of as combining knowledge, time, and capital or savings. The types of resources we are discussing in this chapter serve to *extend the abilities of people*. For example, accounting machines extend the abilities of clerks and tellers in a bank. They enable a few people to do the work that formerly required many people when it was performed by hand. The electric typewriter saves the physical energy of the stenographer and enables her to turn out more work per day than would be possible with a mechanical model. The telephone extends our range of communications and cuts down on the time required to transmit and receive messages. And, of course, in factories electric motors operating a wide variety of machines extend the abilities of workers in the plant many fold.

In physical terms human energy is the most expensive of all types of energy. As pointed out in the study of the Twentieth Century Fund, *America's Needs and Resources—A New Survey,*

Electric energy is delivered at a cost of a penny or two per horsepower hour; a draft horse—if one can be found—can be hired for $10 a day; while the present rate of $1.25 an hour for common labor means that the least expensive human energy (on the basis of one horsepower equivalent to 20 manpower) costs $25 per horsepower hour. On the whole, animal power probably costs from fifty to a hundred times as much as "mechanical" power, and manpower more than a thousand times as much. Only the most backward nations can afford to use even slave labor on a bare subsistence basis for tasks that machines can perform.[1] [See Figure 16–1.]

As we move up in the scale of things, we find the energy of people to be more productive. Skills increase the efficiency of people; knowledge and know-how do so even more; judgment and the capacity to make decisions along with the ability to create ideas represent the highest achievements of people. But they often need machines and equipment to use their abilities to greatest advantage.

The work of business firms that can be reduced to routines usually can be accomplished better and more cheaply by machines than by human effort. Even operations that require a considerable amount of skill and dexterity often can be accomplished more effectively by the use of machines than by people. This is why American business firms

---

[1] J. F. Dewhurst and Associates, *America's Needs and Resources—A New Survey* (New York: Twentieth Century Fund, 1955), p. 910, by permission.

FIGURE 16–1

Machine Power Costs Less than Muscle

COST PER HORSEPOWER=HOUR

MECHANICAL $0.02   ANIMAL $1.25   MAN $25.00

currently invest on the average between $15,000 and $20,000 per worker in plant, machines, and equipment.

We are beginning to make programed decisions by means of the computer; even some nonprogramed decisions may be made at least in part by the use of computers in the future. Research in heuristic problem solving is attacking problems of this type.[2]

The term "heuristic" refers to discovery. It is based on the Greek word "heuriskein"—to discover. It pertains to methods of argument or demonstration that are persuasive rather than logically compelling, or on methods that lead one to find out for himself. In current usage the term "heuristic," thus, is often used to indicate nonstructured or nonlogical approaches to the solution of problems. (Incidentally, in the "Buck Rogers" comic strip, one of the characters was referred to as "Dr. Heuer.")

Characteristics of Nonhuman Resources

As has been pointed out, people are almost always involved in some way in making use of nonhuman resources. There are several factors, however, that characterize nonhuman resources. First, many of them can be owned, whereas the abilities of people cannot be commanded in this way. Slavery was outlawed by the Thirteenth amendment to our Constitution. Nonhuman resources may also be leased, and management often has to make difficult choices between owning and leasing major items of equipment.

---

[2] See Herbert A. Simon, *The New Science of Management Decision* (New York: Harper & Bros., 1960), p. 35.

Second, some types of nonhuman resources have a long life, both physically and economically. Hence, it is difficult to determine cost, risk, and return relationships. At the time machines are purchased, for example, specific costs are incurred, but whether such costs are warranted will not be determined for some time—usually several years or longer. Some costs are not apparent; for example, the money invested in resources with a long useful life could earn returns if put into alternative uses, and such returns might be higher. Further, resources of this type depreciate over time and are subject to obsolescence, as we have seen. The risks are high and very difficult to estimate. Also, returns are difficult to estimate since they are earned over a period of time. Hence, decisions related to resources of this type are usually made on a "present-value" basis, as we shall see.

Third, because cost, risk, and return relationships are difficult to estimate, the objectives that nonhuman resources are designed to serve often must be established with great care. This is due to the fact that once commitments are made to buy or to lease for long periods major items of equipment or land and buildings, managers tend to be "locked in" by such decisions. Such resources often cannot be sold, leased, or subleased to advantage. Often machines are designed for special purposes and may have little value to other potential users. Land and buildings often cannot be sold or leased without loss. Decisions related to resources with a long life require careful long-term planning. Once plans are made, it is often difficult to modify them. Further, organizational arrangements frequently are dictated by long-term commitments regarding the place of business or major items of capital equipment.

Fourth, human and nonhuman resources interact on each other. Decisions related to nonhuman resources may have important personnel implications. Most machines must be operated by people. A machine that runs at a certain speed requires that the people operating it adapt themselves to such speeds; a machine that must run continuously for efficient performance requires rigid scheduling of the people who operate it; a machine that produces dust, dirt, and undesirable odors makes for unpleasant working conditions.

Beyond this, various machines and other nonhuman resources compete with people. They add to the productivity of people, but they also replace people in specific jobs and thus often create special problems for managers. The replaced people may have to be fired, or absorbed in other operations, or restrained for new duties. Each of these alternatives may present special sets of management problems. Many of the problems related to automation are cases in point.

Classification of Resources

The classical economists (Adam Smith, Ricardo, Mill, and others who lived and worked about the time of the Industrial Revolution) classified the factors of production as "land, labor, and capital." In some cases a fourth factor, entrepreneurship or managerial ability was added. There have been varying classifications of productive resources or factors of production. Professor Frank H. Knight suggested that an "ultimate" classification might be made in terms of "nature, man, and time." This would suggest the general type of division we follow here since we separate the abilities of people (at all levels) from natural resources and man-made resources such as machines and power equipment.

The business manager tends to separate people and their abilities from nonhuman resources. The latter he tends to divide into cash or resources that can rather quickly be turned into cash, that is, current assets; and fixed assets, those that require a period of a year or longer in which to be "turned over" or converted into cash. We outlined this distinction in our accounting discussions in Chapter 12.

Some current assets are significant as aids to people. For example, protective clothing may be essential to some factory operations. It may wear out in a few months and be treated as a current expense for accounting purposes. Similarly, some tools may wear out in a short time. The significant factor from our standpoint is that management decisions regarding such items that aid people in their work usually are not very difficult to make. Their short life enables managers to estimate their usefulness relative to costs without undue difficulty. It is the long-term commitments for major items of capital equipment or for research and development programs that pose extremely difficult decision problems for business managers.

Another method of classifying various resources that aid people in raising their productivity is in terms of (1) natural resources, (2) products of past accumulation of capital and knowledge, or (3) things that will be forthcoming in the future. The third type would involve investments in research and development programs that might produce significant results in the future. Current capital equipment is the product of past accumulations of capital and knowledge. To a degree natural resources may be classified in the same way, since they represent in addition to original gifts of nature, substantial investments in effort, time and thought.

While natural resources are to a degree more closely related to our discussions of location, land, and buildings in the next chapter, we should note that most managers make little, if any, distinction between land or other natural resources and man-made machines and related types of resources. From a manager's standpoint both are fixed assets.

We might divide nonhuman resources into *tangible* and *intangible* categories. For example, a business firm may own a delivery truck. It will also have a piece of legal paper called a "title," which is evidence of ownership of the truck. This is an intangible resource, but it may be as important for business purposes as the tangible resource of the truck itself. Similarly there are intangible resources such as the "good will" of a business. This refers to the value of its general reputation and the public following and established customers it enjoys. Large expenditures may be required for advertising and public relations programs to build good will. Once established good will helps to accomplish the work of the firm. Of a similar type is "going concern value," that is, the worth of the momentum of a firm that is in operation in contrast to a new firm that has not yet started operations or one that has been forced to close down.

Another division may be made between resources that are privately owned and those that are publicly owned. Resources that are provided through federal, state, or local governments may have great significance for the success or failure of a business firm. For example, a major highway may form the very basis for the success of a filling station or a shopping center. If the highway is moved or rerouted, major losses or even business failure may result. Similarly, the provision of electrical power at favorable rates may give a firm a competitive advantage. Sewage disposal systems, schools for the children of a firm's employees, and community facilities of many types often are important for the success of business firms, even though such things are not paid for in the usual market sense. In some cases, of course, business firms balance local tax rates in one city against the public services provided and make comparisons with similar analyses of other cities in order to select locations. We have more to say about this in the next chapter.

All of the above ways of classifying nonhuman resources have certain advantages. For the purposes of our discussions here, however, after a brief review of several background topics, we center attention

in this chapter on management decisions related to ('
ment—machines, tools, engines, and the like, and
development programs. The former represents know
know-how plus time and savings arising out of past effort
represents efforts to add to knowledge, which in turn may crea
capital equipment or new final products.

The Industrial Revolution

You have undoubtedly read about the Industrial Revolution and
know something of its importance in the evolution of modern business. It is difficult to define the Industrial Revolution very exactly
since it included a wide number of developments that took place over
a considerable period of time, principally in the second half of the
eighteenth century. We should note, however, that many of the revolutionary developments of this period continued to influence events
for many years and continue to do so today. Indeed, the events associated with the recent development of automation are often referred to
as the "second industrial revolution."

Basically the Industrial Revolution refers to the introduction of
many laborsaving devices and machine methods to production processes. Many of these changes came so rapidly and influenced other
aspects of life and work—distribution as well as production, political
as well as economic attitudes, population movements, and financing
methods—that the term "revolution" may properly be applied to
them. A series of inventions such as Arkwright's cotton spinning
machinery and James Watt's steam engine set off significant changes
and laid the basis for the factory system of large-scale production.

The Industrial Revolution was in large measure a late phase of the
Renaissance, the period of exploration and discovery, the emergence
of modern states, the establishment of large areas over which trade
could be carried on safely, and related developments. Business organizations evolved which made possible the pooling of large supplies of
capital that were essential to finance large-scale production operations.

The impacts of the Industrial Revolution affected all phases of life.
Handicraft and home production methods in many lines were supplanted by factory operations; specialization resulted from larger-
scale production processes and reduced the importance of craftsman-
ship; factories attracted large groups of workers and laid the foundations of modern cities with some of their earlier problems; transportation systems developed to make it possible to assemble the necessary

˰en, materials, and equipment to carry on large-scale operations. Interchangeable parts made mass production of machines possible and provided ready means for their repair.

For our purposes the Industrial Revolution is especially significant since it marks the period in history when capital equipment and other major aids to people were introduced and hence when modern management problems began to emerge. Prior to the Industrial Revolution most of the work of the world was done by sheer physical man power and animal power; thereafter, new forms of energy and machines were used to increase the efficiency with which people could work. The average number of hours worked per week declined substantially (see Figure 16–2).

FIGURE 16–2

Average Weekly Working Hours

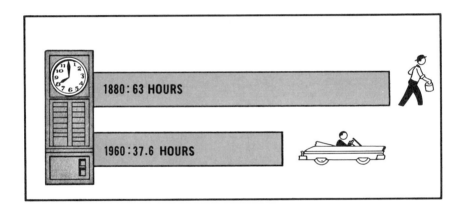

The events growing out of the Industrial Revolution made modern business management necessary. Prior to that time most business units were relatively small and their operations were far from complex. After the Industrial Revolution, business firms grew in size and resources, management decisions increased in complexity, and managerial abilities became increasingly important.

Automation

As we have suggested the events associated with automation often are referred to as the "second industrial revolution." Automation is essentially a process of production in which machines are used to operate other machines, and which in turn may operate additional machines. It may be a one, two, three, or more stage process. One of the simplest illustrations of automation is that of the thermostat. You can set a thermostat at a given temperature and it will run your furnace, turning it on and off automatically to provide the desired temperature. Prior to the invention of thermostats it was necessary for us to regulate our furnaces directly. This required a good deal of attention, and even so, we were seldom able to insure a reasonably even flow of heat. By contrast we now set a thermostat and virtually forget the temperature problem. It regulates the temperature more efficiently and effectively than is possible by manual means.

To an increasing extent we have been able to apply automation to various business operations. Of major importance has been the development of machines to operate machines in our factories, but we have also been able to adapt automation to other types of business activities.

The large-scale computer has contributed greatly to the expansion of automation. Machines of this type made it possible to "store" a vast amount of information and to call it out as required for various purposes. That is, these machines have a "memory" and thus can be made to operate highly complicated machines and processes. Still another stimulus to automation is likely to come from the peacetime uses of atomic energy.

Automation may be thought of as another step in the process of providing aids to people in increasing their productivity. We have had *automatic* factory processes of various types for a long time. There is the case of Oliver Evan's automatic grist mill in Philadelphia in the 1780's. This mill, which was later copied widely, operated automatically from the time the grain was unloaded until the flour dropped out of a chute.[3]

But automatic operations are not the same as automation—the difference can probably be illustrated best by contrasting an adding machine or hand calculator, which are automatic devices, with an electronic computer, which is an illustration of automation, of machines which may be used to operate machines, as we have seen.

There has been much discussion of the possible effect of automation on *employment*. Many trade-union leaders have contended that such processes will result in displacing numerous workers by machines.

It is true that some workers may be displaced directly by the introduction of automated processes. In terms of total employment, how-

---

[3] Keith Davis, *Human Relations in Business* (New York: McGraw-Hill Book Co., Inc., 1957), p. 379.

ever, automation is likely to produce expanding rather than fewer opportunities for our people. This has been true of laborsaving machinery throughout history. By reducing costs and enabling business firms to sell products for less, many more people can afford to buy, and thus by expanding markets, total employment is increased.

Knowledge and Time

As we have suggested human knowledge has been accumulating over the course of recorded history. Much knowledge is available on our public library shelves for the taking. The Library of Congress is thus a great national resource that is generally available to all. Knowledge in books, of course, means little when it is gathering dust on library shelves. Someone must make use of it. The fact of its availability, however, is important.

Many business managers develop knowledge through studies of their operations as well as through their research and development programs. Such knowledge is acquired at a cost, often a substantial cost, and in some cases it may be copyrighted or patented. Thus protection is secured for its exclusive use. In this way a property right may be created in such knowledge which may be bought or sold directly or assigned through leasing or royalty arrangements.

Time is a resource that has many general as well as business implications. Knowledge accumulates over time. Saving requires time. Because of time we are willing to pay more for a shipment of goods by air than by rail or truck; we are willing to pay more for a long-distance telephone call than for a stamp to mail a letter; and we find it desirable to pay more for a ditch-digging machine than for several hundred shovels. The ditch-digging machine represents an embodiment of time as well as ideas and knowledge. It took time to save the money to create it. The machine represents a way of getting work done that is spread over time—a roundabout or capitalistic method of production. Like most other resources, of course, time has little significance except in relation to people. We may wonder whether time would exist in any meaningful sense if there were no people on the earth.

Because of time we *discount* the future. We pay more for funds now than a year from now or five years from now. If you borrow $100 at 5 per cent interest, you have reached the conclusion that $100 now is worth $105 a year from now. Five years from now you would pay back substantially more—$100 today is worth approximately $127.63 five years from now at 5 per cent compound interest (see tables in Appendix II). Or stated another way the present value of $100 five years hence is $78.35 (discounted on the basis of 5 per cent per annum). Similarly we would pay less for a property that we could occupy five years from now than if we could have immediate occupancy. This concept of discounting the future is an essential element in understanding long-term management decisions.

Capital and Capital Goods

As we have seen, knowledge, ideas, and time are essential ingredients in the development of capital. We usually think of capital as money or as funds available for investment. Capital in this sense means an accumulation of savings over time. It is unspecialized productive power that may be used to gain command over machines, materials, and the like. This concept is helpful in the sense that liquid capital or uncommitted funds or unspecialized productive power may be put to a variety of uses. Decisions as to what these uses will be are among the more difficult that managers have to face. Investments may be made in machines or equipment. These are referred to as *capital goods* or "capital equipment," or in accounting terms, "fixed assets." This investment can earn a return in the form of interest (if borrowed funds are involved) or dividends (if owners' funds are involved) only over a period of time and the investment can be recaptured only through earnings of the machine or equipment over a period of time, unless of course, there is a sale. In this case liquid funds or liquid capital become available again and may be reinvested.

At the time a business firm is set up it usually must have some capital, an investment of funds of owners or of people who are willing to loan money to the business. These funds are then used to secure the necessary real properties, machines, tools and equipment, goods, or materials for processing and to hire the people required to carry operations forward. Ultimately the sale of products provides a stream of income from which payments can be made in the form of wages and salaries, reimbursement for materials, and goods in process, and as interest to compensate those who loaned funds to the business, plus dividends or compensation to owners for the funds they advanced.

It may be helpful to think in terms of capital as economic power either available for a variety of purposes or as invested in certain machinery or other capital goods. The earnings from such investments may be viewed as a *flow* of income. The value of the investment then is related to the size, nature, and length of the income stream that it creates. The character of the income stream, of course, must be estimated, since one cannot be sure of the future course of events. Such estimated earnings can be *capitalized,* that is, reflected in present value. Anticipated earnings can be projected over the expected life of the machine or other piece of capital equipment and this income stream is then translated into a present lump sum to indicate its current value. Thus, the value of a delivery truck to a business firm is in reality the present value of the estimated amount of earnings it can produce over its economic life.

For example, if a machine or other property produces a net income of $1,000 per year, if it appears that such an income can continue to be earned indefinitely, and if a rate of return of, say 10 per cent is necessary to attract funds of investors in order to secure the capital necessary to buy the machine, then its value will be approximately $10,000. This is secured by dividing $1,000, the estimated annual average or stabilized return, by 10 per cent ($1,000 ÷ .10) which equals $10,000. Thus future earning power is reflected in present value. In effect, this relationship means that $10,000 now is equal to $1,000 per year forever at an annual rate of return of 10 per cent. "Forever" of course in business and economic term means relatively little since values decline rapidly if the time at which they may be enjoyed is postponed for a number of years.

The relatively simple relationship outlined above indicates the basic relationships between capital goods or equipment and the income they may produce. The problems arising from these relationships, however, may become quite complicated for managers, as we shall see.

We should note here that the use of capital is not limited to the so-called "capitalistic" countries. A socialist or communist state will also use capital in the form of machines, tools, and equipment. The difference, however, arises from the type of ownership. In our society we permit productive agents such as capital goods to be owned privately by individuals, business firms, or other organizations while in other types of systems such things are typically the property of the central government or of a smaller unit of government.

Depreciation and Obsolescence

It is important to recognize that machines and equipment wear out. This does not usually happen suddenly but gradually over a period of time. We usually refer to this process as *depreciation,* that is, the gradual wear and tear that finally causes a machine to wear out. The term "depletion" is used to indicate the using up of a natural asset such as an oil well.

FIGURE 16–3

Business Investment

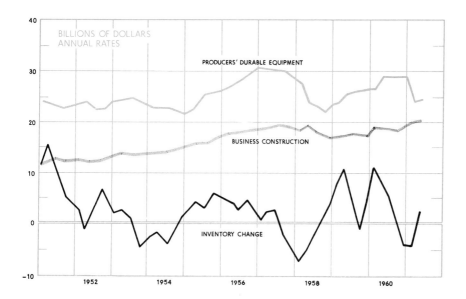

Of major importance for managers is the process of *obsolescence,* that is, the elimination of a machine or piece of equipment by a newer and more efficient one. For example, the diesel replaced the steam engine; the electric typewriter is an improvement over the manual kind. Many other illustrations might be mentioned.

Obsolescence does not always result from changes of this magnitude. A slight improvement in a machine may give it an advantage over its predecessor and cause obsolescence. Machines are not the only capital goods subject to obsolescence. For example, improved designs of buildings may make older ones obsolete, even though they may still be physically in good condition. Even a new method of testing applicants for jobs may be thought of as making previously used methods obsolete. It is important to recognize that a business firm must recapture through earnings investments in capital equipment rapidly enough to stay ahead of rates of depreciation or obsolescence.

One of the important characteristics of American business firms and their managers has been their *willingness to scrap obsolete equipment* and methods and to introduce newer and better equipment and methods as soon as they become available. This is not typical of managements in many parts of the world. Often it is considered wasteful to scrap equipment before it is physically worn out or fully depreciated. Managers in this country, however, generally recognize that the real waste results from attempting to use machines and equipment after better models have made their appearance, since to do so denies workers and the buyers of goods and services the benefits that may be derived from the improved models.

Higher rates of change increase the risk of obsolescence. This is one of the difficult aspects of decisions related to the purchase, sale, or leasing of capital equipment.

Natural Resources

Whether natural resources such as the fertility of the soil, minerals, virgin forests, and the like should be considered as gifts of nature or whether they are a type of capital goods has been a subject of much discussion. At the time this country was settled originally, people were able to make a living largely because of the abundance of natural resources available. It must be recognized, however, that considerable time, effort, and machinery were required to make such resources productive. There is a real question whether such resources are worth more than the capitalized value of the time and effort of people and other resources that have to be expended in order to bring them into productive use. Nevertheless, the availability of certain natural resources will be of vital importance to business processes at least until we are able to create in the laboratory on an economic basis synthetic materials that will take the place of agricultural, forest, mineral, and other natural products.

The ready availability of an abundance of natural resources has been a big factor in the economic growth and development of this country. This point was emphasized during World War II when access to some raw materials was cut off. For example, it was necessary to develop a synthetic rubber industry to provide a substitute for the rubber which had previously been imported. As technology advances, of course, we will become less dependent on natural resources.

Walton Hamilton has said: "It may be too much to say that technology has replaced geography in determining what commodities any nation may economically produce. But it is quite safe to say that technology has come to share this throne, that its dominion is increasing, and that geography is rapidly becoming the lesser of the two partners."[4]

---

[4] By permission from Walton Hamilton, *The Politics of Industry*, lectures on the William W. Cook Foundation (New York: Alfred D. Knopf, Inc., 1957), p. 115.

Range of Choices

You are undoubtedly familiar with the story of Robinson Crusoe. The tools, canoe, and other things he fashioned in a primitive way may be thought of as capital equipment. He took time from leisure and saved on what he would eat in order to create such equipment; thus his savings flowed directly into such equipment rather than through money and financial institutions as is the case in modern society. He brought previous knowledge plus what he learned on his island to bear in the solution of his problems. Even so, he continued to do much of his work "by hand" or with the aid of his man Friday.

The business manager of today has somewhat the same set of problems. He is almost constantly faced with such questions as these: How much work is to be done by unskilled workers? How much by workers trained to various levels of proficiency? How much by machines, mechanical power, and other aids to the efforts of people?

The decisions that are reached will vary from firm to firm depending on its objectives, on the scale of its operations, on the type of work in which it is engaged, on the resources that are available or can be made available, and on related things. The decisions of modern managers grow increasingly complicated as the ranges of choice expand. It is not only a question of manpower versus machine power but also questions of which types of machines are preferred to others, and of whether research and development programs should be supported to find ways of doing work even more effectively than by means that are already available.

Over the course of the history of the Industrial Revolution and its aftermath we have been provided with a growing body of knowledge and increased savings which have given us many means of supplementing human effort and making it more productive. The modern business manager, however, is not content to make use of existing knowledge and equipment; he tries to push forward to innovations that will give his personnel definite advantages over those in other firms.

In order to guide his decisions the manager determines the objectives he is trying to achieve as carefully as possible. If his objective is to produce a quick return and to sell the business as rapidly as possible he is unlikely to invest very much in capital equipment or in research and development programs. If his objective is to develop a rapidly growing firm, he is likely to put more resources in capital equipment and to put special emphasis on research and development.

What kind and how much capital equipment relative to personnel will be provided depends in part on the type of business, the extent to which processes can be mechanized and routinized, and the relative costs of man power and capital equipment. Even today some industries can use to advantage only limited amounts of capital relative to man power.

Decisions that commit funds for long periods of time require careful long-range planning. The risks are high. Changes may come rapidly that will reduce the value of the investment. Such planning usually begins by a determination of long-range market potential for the product involved and the development of estimates as to the income that may be earned. If these relationships appear to be favorable, more specific plans are worked out regarding the particular type of capital equipment that may prove to be most desirable. Capital budgets are often developed to provide both a means for developing plans for making capital investments and as a device for evaluating and controlling the results.

As we have suggested, capital commitments may "lock in" a business firm for some period of time after investments have been made. They may also commit the firm to a specific type of organizational arrangement and to the specified geographic and market coverages. Decisions related to capital or other long-term expenditures are seldom made without consideration of their implications for the people who make up the organization.

Decision Factors

We have already suggested the controlling influence of objectives in regard to decisions as to making long-term capital investments in equipment. Other factors that are often considered by managers in this connection are the following:

1. Capital equipment versus direct labor. How much will the equipment save in labor costs? Will the saving compensate for the cost? Or will there be added earnings in addition to the saving in labor?

One of the important considerations here is the direct control a manager exercises over capital equipment. It is owned. It does not belong to a union. It does not resign from the firm and take valuable knowledge and know-how to a competitor. It does not create conflicts within groups in the organization (although it may be the basis of worker irritations at times). It does not have divided loyalties. Still, it costs a lot of money; it is subject to depreciation; and tomorrow a new machine may come along that will produce twice as much at half the cost.

2. Ownership versus leasing. In some cases it is possible to lease equipment on a year-by-year or longer basis. Such arrangements reduce the capital investment required. Costs can be borne as they are incurred rather than being spread over time. From a tax standpoint the entire leasing charge is a business expense. It is unnecessary to worry about depreciation or obsolescence (unless a long-term lease that is noncancellable is involved). So leasing often has advantages. But there are advantages in ownership. A lease may expire and the owner of the equipment may be unwilling to renew on favorable terms. Operations may be interrupted. Thus, the degree of control under leases may be somewhat less than under ownership. Depreciation allowances for tax purposes may be attractive in many situations and favor ownership. Also, ownership may lead to modifications and improvements that would be unlikely in the case of leased equipment.

3. If decisions to invest in capital equipment rather than leasing are made, the determination of whether to invest in this type or another type of equipment is often difficult. In some cases, of course, there is only one particular piece of equipment that will meet requirements. Usually, however, there will be several types that will serve equally well, each with certain advantages and disadvantages. Choices typically turn on the specific requirements of the particular firm and the situation in which it operates.

4. Decisions often depend on the financial condition of the company. It may be forced to meet bank loans and be more interested in the sale of capital equipment and plants than in their purchase, even if, for long term purposes, such a sale would not appear to be advisable. Or working capital may be short and leasing arrangement only may be possible. In some cases a company will have high earnings, fear they may not continue, hence invest heavily in capital equipment in the hope of reducing costs in the future.

5. The situation in which a manager is working will tend to indicate the factors to which he gives greatest weight in arriving at capital investment decisions. For example, he may stress the period of payback. It may be important to recapture the investment at an early period. Or he may stress returns per dollar of outlay, without respect to the timing of the return. He may emphasize average annual proceeds per dollar of outlay (that is giving consideration to the number of years and averaging the return per year). The manager may esti-

mate average income on book value of the investment, that is, after depreciation has been charged against the investment. The method considered highly desirable by many managers is the discounted cash flow method; that is, computing the present value of the earnings that will be secured over a period of time.[5]

We will not consider these methods here since they are more properly a discussion for more advanced courses. We should note, however, that each of these methods may lead to a different conclusion in regard to a problem of investing in capital equipment. There is no necessary "right" answer as we have suggested, since much will depend on the situation in which the manager is working. If other things are equal, however, the approaches which make it possible to consider the present value of anticipated returns have much to commend them.

Investment Illustrations

To illustrate the types of decisions that managers often face in determining whether to undertake the purchase of major items of capital equipment, we may consider several situations. Suppose that you have been operating a neighborhood grocery store. Customers have been coming to the store and carrying out their purchases with them. You have provided some delivery service by hiring a small number of students to make deliveries for you in the afternoons after school hours. You now are considering the purchase of a delivery truck since you are of the opinion that you can add substantially to your business by making deliveries throughout the day. The cost of the truck will be $3,000. A driver will cost $75 per week. Costs of gas, oil, insurance, and maintenance are estimated at $15 per week. You have been paying the students an average of $15 per week, employing from four to six, depending in part on volume of business, in part on whether the students show up for work. You decide that the cost of the driver of the truck and that saved by not using students will just about cancel out.

The main problem, of course, is whether the truck will earn more than its cost. This question will have to be answered by an estimate. You know that you have lost some business to other stores because they have delivery service at any time of the day. You are somewhat

---

[5] For a discussion of these methods see Harold Bierman, Jr., and Seymour Schmidt, *The Capital Budgeting Decision* (New York: Macmillan Co., 1960), chap. 2. The authors mention other related methods, including the "yield of an investment method." See also Donald F. Istvan, "The Economic Evaluation of Capital Expenditures," *Journal of Business*, Vol. XXXIV, No. 1 (Jan., 1961), pp. 45–51.

concerned that your delivery boys may have built up some personal customers, and that they may take such customers to other stores if you eliminate them from your operation and they go to work for others.

You decide to compute some costs. You can borrow the $3,000 at the bank since your credit is good, at 6 per cent interest. This will represent an annual cost of $180 or $15 per month. This, plus estimated outlays of $15 per week for gas, maintenance, insurance, etc., will mean a monthly cost of slightly over $75. You decide that this will not be difficult to earn through increased sales. But then you consider the value of the truck. Clearly it will be worth less a year from now than when you buy it; in two years with an average of 100 miles a week, which you estimate as easily possible, the truck will have covered over 100,000 miles and may be pretty well worn out. If you need another truck at that time you face a write-off of at least $1,500 per year in terms of depreciation. This means an average of $125 per month. If this is added to your earlier cost estimates you see monthly costs of over $200, and it will require a substantial increase in grocery sales to earn this much, to say nothing of gaining a return for you beyond costs.

You look at the problem in reverse. True, the delivery boys are not always reliable, but they are far from expensive. They enable you to serve a limited number of customers, who are "regulars." You could serve them with the truck, but they would probably not buy more. You begin to wonder whether delivery service, except for good steady customers is worth the cost. You consider the savings on the loan at the bank and its repayment. If you repaid at the rate of $125 per month you would have your money back in two years and ready for another truck purchase. But suppose the truck did not earn this amount?

You study your market and make some estimates. You decide that the truck could not extend your market very far since there are other stores in the vicinity already providing grocery delivery by truck. You decide that at best the truck could increase business by $700 per week, and this would not be enough to increase earnings sufficiently to cover the costs involved.

This illustration suggests several things. One is the importance of depreciation in making decisions regarding investments in capital equipment. Another is the alternatives and the relative desirability of alternatives, in this case, the delivery boys versus the truck. Another is the time required to get the investment back. Assume in the above case that the truck would earn exactly its cost of $3,000 in two years. Then at the present time it is worth less than nothing to you, since interest costs will total $180 per year.

If a piece of equipment with a longer life, say a fork-lift truck for stacking groceries in a warehouse, had been involved, there is the added danger of obsolescence, that newer and better equipment would make its appearance at lower costs than the original item. This is a risk that cannot always be foreseen, but that is increased the longer the time before investment is recaptured.

The longer the period of time involved, the more difficult it is to compute cost, risk, and return relationships. The higher the risk, of course, the greater the rate at which a future income stream must be capitalized, and the lower the value of the investment.

Suppose you have an opportunity to buy two store buildings, each priced at $50,000. One is in a stable neighborhood, the other in a rapidly changing neighborhood. You can lease each building for the same amount, $5,000 per year, and the person leasing the building pays taxes, insurance, and upkeep. This indicates approximately a 10 per cent return. Suppose you decide that this rate of return is satisfactory for Property A in the stable neighborhood but because of the rapidly changing character of the neighborhood in which Property B is located the risk is so high that you should have a 15 per cent return. If then we apply a 15 per cent rate for capitalizing purposes, $5,000 (the annual rate of return) divided by 15 per cent (the rate desired), then $5,000 ÷ .15 gives us a valuation of $33,333, rather than $50,000 for the property. In short, you could not afford on this basis to pay $50,000 for Property B.

This relatively simple illustration indicates what happens if the rate of return is changed. Suppose Property B, however, will pay a return of $7,500 per year. Then even though you expect a 15 per cent return, the property would be worth $50,000 ($7,500 ÷ .15) and it would be a matter of indifference to you which building you purchased.

Now suppose that you were more concerned about getting your money back than anything else. In this situation you would select Property B, since you would recapture your investment in 6⅔ years (without making allowance for interest on the recaptured amount), while in the case of Property A ten years would be required for you to recapture your investment (again eliminating interest return). In fact, the higher rate of return of 15 per cent is imposed for just this reason. When anticipated rates of change are high, risks are high. A higher rate of return recaptures the investment more rapidly.

Research and Development

Among the more difficult decisions faced by many managers today are those related to research and development. These may be classified as decisions under uncertainty as outlined in Chapter 14. Should a firm invest in its own research programs? The risks are great, since no return may be forthcoming at all. But the potential returns are also great, since one new discovery may give the firm a competitive advantage for many years. A new product may be developed that gives a firm a long lead on competitors. Or new knowledge may be discovered that will form the basis of an entire new industry.

Decisions related to programs of this type are usually approached in much the same way as decisions related to capital equipment, which we considered above. Many firms, however, do not have sufficient earnings to support research programs of any consequence. To a large extent the research programs carried on by American business firms are conducted by those of larger size. But the number of firms engaged and the amounts expended by them for these purposes per year is growing rapidly.

In 1959 American business firms spent over $9 billion for these types of programs. If the expenditures of government, universities, and other research organizations are added, the annual total is $12.5 billion, two and a half times the amount spent for these purposes in 1953. In a sense there has been growing up a new "industry of discovery," as the late Professor Sumner Slichter characterized it. In 1960 business firms expenditures for these purposes totaled more than $10 billion, and for government, universities, and other research agencies more than $5 billion or a grand total of over $15 billion.

As Dexter Keezer and his associates have pointed out,

Out of the research now reaching a commercial stage will come an increasing flow of new materials—such as plastics, metallic alloys, and ceramics—for use in both consumer goods and capital goods. In consumer goods especially, the new materials will make possible rapid changes in styling and packaging. In capital goods we can expect faster, more compact machines and great improvements in the automatic control of machinery. As a result of these developments, which are already in progress, it seems safe to predict that over half of all capital expenditures in 1965 will go to make new products or install new machines that were not on the market in 1958.

The flow of new products and new processes, from advanced research to commercial testing, is already reaching these proportions.[6]

We should note further that of the hundred largest business firms operating in this country as of 1926, forty-one have since been supplanted by others. Most of the firms eliminated from this list were older companies where rates of growth had slowed down. They were displaced by companies in newer and more rapidly growing industries.

Even in specific companies the rates of change brought on by research and development are often startling. In one case two thirds of the sales in a recent year were from product lines that were not even in existence five years previously. A considerable number of companies report that as much as 80 per cent of sales volume now results from products that were unknown ten years ago.

It may be that managers in the future will be under increasing pressure to engage in research and development programs. Even firms of modest size may be forced to undertake some research. The risks are great; but the risks of not undertaking such programs may be even greater.

Management Research

It is not enough to develop new products or to improve old ones, however. It is necessary to determine their commercial feasibility. Possibilities of patents and licensing relationships need to be explored. It is necessary for management to evaluate the relationships between possible new products and present operations. Marketing factors must be surveyed and, of course, cost-profit relationships estimated. In short, management research is an essential partner of product research.

Management research designed to improve management processes may be conducted by the business firm directly or by other organizations such as schools of business, management consulting firms, research foundations, trade associations, or government agencies. Such research has for its principal purpose the improvement of management decisions and operations. It may lead to important economies in operation and contribute materially to improving the productivity of the people working in a business firm.

Important examples of developments along this line in recent years include improvements of inventory controls, production quality con-

---

[6] Dexter M. Keezer and Associates, *New Forces in American Business* (New York: McGraw-Hill Book Co., Inc., 1959), pp. 50–51, by permission.

trols, management development programs, improved organizational structures, better communications systems, and the adaptation of electronic data processing to many types of business operations.

Some business firms and other organizations as well have developed "operations research programs." Such programs provide for the combination of a wide variety of research techniques and methods in the solution of business problems, as we pointed out in Chapter 14. For example, mathematicians, psychologists, sociologists, and anthropologists may be brought together into a team to study the organizational problems of a firm. Such a combination of knowledge, research techniques, and specialized abilities often leads to the solution of problems that cannot be solved by the usual research methods.

Also, increasing attention has been given to the management of research programs. This is an area in which opportunities are likely to expand in the years ahead.[7]

SUMMARY

Capital equipment and other aids to productivity may be thought of as extending the abilities of people. They are significant in reducing costs and increasing the productivity of people but present difficult management decision problems because:

1. They may be owned or leased, in contrast to the abilities of people.
2. Most of them have a long useful life, both physically and economically, hence, it is difficult to determine cost, risk, and return relationships.
3. Objectives to be served must be sharply defined because of the danger that investments will be "locked in." Long-term planning is required; organizational arrangements may be dictated by machines and equipment.
4. Human and nonhuman resources interact on each other; in some cases people must be adapted to machines rather than vice versa.

Nonhuman resources may be classified in a variety of ways. The classical economists referred to "land, labor, and capital," and later entrepreneurship was added to this list; an alternative is "nature, man, and time." Other classifications include current and fixed assets; natural resources, past accumulations of capital and knowledge, or things that may be forthcoming in the future; tangible and intangible factors; or privately owned and publicly owned resources.

The industrial revolution laid the foundation for the widespread

---

[7] See, for example, "Consultation: How Should Scientific Research Be Administered?" *Business Horizons*, Vol. I, No. 3 (Summer, 1958), pp. 52–62.

use of capital and equipment and modern management methods. Automation and related developments in more recent years are often referred to as the "second industrial revolution."

Knowledge and time are highly productive forces. Knowledge accumulates over time, and time is required to accumulated saving or capital. Before investment, capital is unspecialized productive power, capital goods are specialized productive power. Income from such factors of production may be capitalized, that is, reflected in present value. Natural resources, although gifts of nature, probably are worth no more than the time, effort, and other resources required to bring them into productive use. Technology is growing in importance relative to natural resources.

The manager's range of choices relative to capital and capital equipment decisions is wide; risks are high and decisions are difficult. Types of choices include capital equipment versus direct labor, whether to own or lease, which among alternative types of equipment to purchase or lease, the balancing of financial requirements such as need for liquidity against the longer-term advantages that may come from investments in capital equipment, and others. In making such decisions managers tend to rely increasingly on the discounted cash flow method or computing the present value of earnings that will be secured over a period of time.

Research and development decisions represent another set of difficult choices. Risks are extremely high but potential returns are great. Decisions are made on bases similar to capital equipment investment decisions; they are good examples of decisions under uncertainty. Increasing emphasis is being given to research in management methods and processes and to the management of programs of research and development.

QUESTIONS AND PROBLEMS

1. Why do American business firms currently invest on the average between $15,000 and $25,000 per worker in plant, machines, and equipment?
2. What is meant by "heuristic" problem solving?
3. Outline some of the major characteristics of nonhuman resources.
4. Why is it difficult to determine cost-risk-return relationships in the case of capital goods?
5. How do we distinguish between tangible and intangible resources?
6. What do we mean by saying that capital equipment is the product of past accumulations of knowledge and capital or savings?
7. What is meant by the industrial revolution? Why do we sometimes refer to automation and related developments as the "second industrial revolution?"

8. What is meant by discounting? Explain why $100 now is worth $105 a year from now at 5 per cent interest. By using the tables in Appendix II, indicate the present value of $1,000 ten years from now at 6 per cent.

9. Distinguish between "capital" and "capital goods".

10. What is meant by "capitalizing earnings"? A machine earns $1,200 per year. A rate of 6 per cent is required to attract investment into this field. What is its value? Explain. Why are computations of this type important for management decisions?

11. Explain this statement: An investment of $10,000 is the equivalent of an income of $1,000 per year forever at 10 per cent.

12. Why do depreciation and obsolescence complicate management decisions in regard to investments in capital equipment?

13. In recent years there has been a number of claims filed by Indian tribes for reimbursement on lands sold to our government many years ago. If you were asked to determine the value of such lands, would you try to justify any value for them? Explain.

14. How will a manager decide whether to buy capital equipment or employ direct labor? How will he decide between ownership and leasing?

15. Why do some managers prefer a rapid pay back of investment?

16. What is meant by the discounted cash flow or present value of earnings method of reaching capital-equipment decisions?

17. Machine A will cost $10,000; it is expected to earn $1,000 per year; Machine B will cost $20,000; it is expected to earn $1,500 per year, but will last twice as long. Which would you buy? Why?

18. Why are business firms engaging to an increasing extent in research and development programs? Why are decisions in this field difficult to make?

19. Why is increasing attention being given to the improvement of management methods and processes?

SUGGESTED READINGS

BIERMAN, HAROLD, JR., and SCHMIDT, SEYMOUR. *The Capital Budgeting Decision,* chap. 2. New York: Macmillan Co., 1960.

KEEZER, DEXTER, and Associates. *New Forces in American Business.* New York: McGraw-Hill Book Co., Inc., 1959. Chap. 3, "Research—Key to Growth and Stability."

LONG, JOHN D. *Workbook to Accompany Weimer: Business Administration: An Introductory Management Approach,* chap. 16. Rev. ed. Homewood, Ill.: Richard D. Irwin, Inc., 1962.

ROBERTSON, ROSS M. *History of the American Economy.* New York: Harcourt, Brace & Co., Inc., 1955. This book surveys the economic history of this country. Chap. viii, "Industry in First Transition" presents an interesting discussion of the emergence of large-scale factory production methods.

OUTLINE FOR CHAPTER 17

THE PLACE OF BUSINESS plays a vital role in a firm's success; decision problems include those related to LAND, BUILD-INGS, AND LOCATION.

A good place of business should enable a firm to pursue its objectives effectively, and should fit the requirements of its organization and operations.

Physical factors—land and buildings—and their location are important, but chiefly as they relate to economic consider-ations.

Special decision problems are involved in the place of business due to

uniqueness of each real property;

localized nature of real estate markets; and

interdependence of private and public property and decisions.

Also, the large amounts of money involved and long life of properties complicate decisions.

Decisions often are made centrally by top management; some-times decentralized, within limits; decisions are made infre-quently in many firms; use of experts is widespread.

Location decisions include

regional and local community factors; and choices be-tween specific sites;

access to raw materials; and to markets, workers, and supporting business.

Transportation and communication facilities often are im-portant in location decisions; future impact of such facilities on location decisions is likely to be great.

Decisions related to installations include problems of

cost-risk-return relationships;

depreciation and obsolescence;

and neighboring influences.

Typical installation decision problems include

buy or lease;

use existing facilities or develop new ones;

operate from one installation or more; and

finance from borrowed or company funds.

THE PLACE OF BUSINESS: LAND, BUILDINGS, LOCATION

Under all is the land. *
—ANON.

Importance of the Place of Business

Unless it is a very simple activity that a man may carry forward from his home or from a post office box, a business firm usually must have a place of business—a plant, office, store, or other installation in which and from which business operations can be carried on. The place of business may be owned or leased; arrangements for occupancy may be short term or long term in character, although the latter are more typical. A business firm may occupy one or many places of business including installations abroad.

The place of business determines the general physical environment and work arrangements for those in the firm with "inside" jobs, for example, clerks in a store in contrast to house-to-house salesmen. The kind of housing provided for the firm including design, space arrangements, and layout have an important bearing on the efficiency of operations. Cost, risk, and return relationships may be affected greatly by the place of business. The location of the place of business determines its accessibility to markets, materials, workers, transportation routes, suppliers, public services and utilities, power sources, community facilities, and many other things. The place of business is an important factor in reflecting the total personality or "public image" of the firm. It is one of the ways by which customers and potential customers, investors and potential investors, and employees and potential employees evaluate the business firm and its probable future.

Thus, decisions related to the place of business often are of critical importance in the success or failure of a business firm. Such decisions depend on the over-all objectives and plans of the firm's owners and

---

* Slogan used by National Association of Real Estate Boards.

managers, but once made they may in turn impose significant limits on the objectives that can be pursued. As Winston Churchill once observed, we control the planning of our buildings but once constructed the buildings control us. This is as true of business firms as of individuals and families. Decisions related to the place of business often involve large monetary commitments that are made for a long period of time. Once made such decisions may impose severe limitations on the ways in which a firm may be organized and operated.

What Makes a Good Place of Business?

The question of what makes a good place of business must have a wide variety of answers. Otherwise all business firms would want essentially the same things in regard to a location or installation. In a general way we may answer the question of what makes a good place of business by saying that (1) the place of business should enable the firm to pursue its objectives and plans effectively, and (2) it should fit the requirements of its organization and operations.

We have pointed out repeatedly that one business firm may pursue objectives that are different from those pursued by another; hence a variety of locations and installations is required. For example, a firm that has rapid expansion as a primary objective may need a different place of business than one concerned primarily with achieving a stable level of operations. Growth needs may have to be anticipated well in advance since it is often difficult to acquire additional space and facilities at a given location. If the owners of a business firm want it to operate on a national scale they may need a number of locations and installations in contrast to a firm that undertakes to serve a local area only.

The organization and operation of a business firm will be influenced by its place of business in terms of the physical facilities available; the economic implications of such facilities; location in terms of access to materials, markets, man power, and supporting activities; volume of business; competitive conditions; and related factors.

A place of business typically involves the ownership or leasing of some real estate—land and buildings plus certain equipment. Thus, such physical factors must be considered as the size and shape of the lot, if one is involved; square feet available for office, plant, or store area; quality, type, and design of the building or the portion of a building that is used; and similar considerations. Similarly the physical *location* of the place of business relative to other places of business, to markets, suppliers, workers, transportation routes, utilities, and community facilities are related to the problem of what makes a good place of business.

These physical factors have their major significance in so far as they affect *economic* considerations. For example, number of square feet of space is considered in relation to cost and potential income; the price or rental of one location is considered in relation to another, judging the advantages and disadvantages of each; or the cost in relation to potential returns of one type of building is considered in relation to others.

A good place of business provides for an efficient and attractive relationship between the people in the firm and the machines, equipment, tools, and other things that make the efforts of people more productive. A crowded space, for example, may make it impossible to arrange work processes efficiently; too much space may lead to scattered operations. The design and layout of work areas, their comfort and convenience, and the general climate or environment created by working arrangements may have an important bearing on the efficiency with which the people in a firm can operate. Similarly a good place of business is attractive to customers and investors.

The *type of business activity carried on* will determine in part what makes a good place of business. A manufacturer of heavy equipment usually requires a single-story factory building covering a substantial amount of land, while a firm engaged in light manufacturing operations may be able to occupy space on an upper floor of a building. A department store requires a different type of business place than a specialty shop; a supermarket needs something quite different in terms of an installation from a corner grocery. Similarly a bank needs a different set of facilities than a small-loan office.

It is apparent also that *volume of business* will have a bearing on what makes a good place of business. A firm with many customers will require a place of operations quite different from that needed by one with few.

Limitations on Decisions

As we suggested in our discussions in the preceding chapter, the general framework within which management decisions are made regarding capital goods and equipment applies also to those involving the acquisition, development, or use of land and buildings. From the manager's standpoint, both types of resources are fixed assets, long term in character and decisions related to them involve difficult problems of translating future potential income streams into present values. Even so, there are some factors relating to land and buildings that, to a degree at least, require special consideration.

Of major importance is the fact that land and buildings are *fixed in location*. The land obviously cannot be moved; buildings can be moved only at what are usually prohibitive costs, hence for practical purposes are also fixed in location. Thus, decisions related to the place of business are basically real estate problems; they are also problems of transportation and communication, as well as of access to public utilities and services. Further, such decisions involve "neighboring" relationships, since a piece of real property is influenced greatly by its physical, social, and economic surroundings; in turn it has some influence on them. Thus, decisions related to the place of business typically require consideration of a whole complex of regional and local community relationships.

Second, every piece of real property is *unique*. No two points on the earth's surface are exactly alike. Each property is a unique point on a changing economic framework. Several buildings, of course, may be constructed to identical specifications but the lots on which they are located will differ, perhaps only slightly, but still will not be identical. Except in the relatively rare cases of reclaiming land from the sea or lakes, we are unable to manufacture land. This suggests that every major decision involving the place of business is unique and usually requires special study and analysis. Because of the unique character of such decisions and the fact that for many firms decisions relative to the place of business are made rather infrequently, the possibility of error tends to be greater than in many other phases of business administration and management.

Third, the market for real estate tends to be localized to a greater extent than the markets for other fixed assets. This has important implications for management decisions. Land and buildings cannot be moved to the market; the market must be induced to come to them. Hence, the risk of being "locked in" by real estate investments may be greater than for various items of capital equipment. This is particularly true of special-purpose properties.

Fourth, privately owned real property almost always must be used in conjunction with publicly owned property. As has been pointed out:

Rarely can a piece of real estate be used except in conjunction with some public land, and the interdependence of private and public land tends to increase as the community becomes more complex in structure and organization. In order to have access to private land, there usually must be either a public road or street or an easement providing a right-of-way over another private property. Since private arrangements of the latter type are usually difficult to make, we normally depend on public streets and roads for access to our properties. . . . In addition to the problems of access to real properties, provision must be made for water, drainage, and disposal of sewage; for electricity, gas, telephones and other utilities and conveniences; and for police and fire protection.[1]

Thus, the private decisions of the business firms inevitably come up against *public* decisions whenever there are problems involving the place of business.

As we point out later in our discussions, a real property has a definite relationship to the "urban plant," that is, the complex of streets, sewers, utilities, conveniences, and services as well as schools, churches, hospitals, and other community facilities that in toto make up the public and quasi-public properties, facilities, and conveniences which make private real properties valuable and productive.

Other characteristics of the place of business vary from those related to capital goods in degree rather than kind. For example, large amounts of money may be involved in the acquisition or development of a place of business but this is also true of capital equipment. Also, the long life of real properties has special significance for management decisions. Various items of capital equipment also have a long life; that of real properties may be somewhat longer, but differences, as we have suggested, are of degree rather than kind. Usually, however, decisions related to the place of business involve long-term commitments. A few business firms rent space for short periods of time, such as a year or two. Most leases, however, run for ten years or longer and many business executives prefer to own rather than to lease the properties in which they conduct their operations.

Who Makes Decisions

Management decisions related to the place of business are usually made by the chief executive officer of the firm or by some other major company official such as the controller or treasurer. Sometimes the owner or a committee of the board of directors will keep the responsibility for final decisions in this area. In some cases real estate transactions are handled by a subsidiary company; for example, the owner or principal owner of a business will have a separate company which owns the real estate and which in turn leases it on a long- or short-term basis to the operating company.

---

[1] A. M. Weimer and Homer Hoyt, *Principles of Real Estate* (4th ed.; New York: Ronald Press Co., 1960), p. 103.

In retail organizations such as chain stores the real estate function may be delegated to the sales manager or marketing manager, since the location of retail outlets may be important factors in the total sales effort of the firm. Sometimes companies arrange for leases to local dealers, as in the case of gasoline filling stations. For example, a large company like Standard Oil or Texaco will purchase sites, construct filling stations, and then lease them to local operators. In such cases the real estate transactions may be handled by a separate division of the firm or by the sales or marketing division.

Often in cases of this type top-management officials will determine the general policies under which real properties will be purchased or leased. The selection of specific properties will then be accomplished by specialists in this particular field of operations. In some cases limitations will be put on transactions in terms of the amount of dollars that can be committed without additional authority.

Top-management officials and those operating more specifically in real estate matters for the firm often make use of specialists such as architects, engineers, land planners, real property lawyers, appraisers, real estate brokers, market and location analysts, financial experts, and others in arriving at their decisions. Some firms will employ specialists of this type on a regular basis, others utilize them as needs arise. Financial institutions often are an important source of information and guidance; indeed, the willingness of a financial institution to support a particular project may make the difference between undertaking it or abandoning it. Similarly, transportation companies often provide useful information and assistance; public utility officials often play a critical part in determining the feasibility of developing a particular property. In addition, government officials on local, state, and national levels often provide considerable assistance in indicating what may be feasible as to special arrangements and the interrelationships between various public and private facilities.

Decisions on Locations and Installations

Decisions related to the place of business may be divided into two broad areas: (1) those pertaining to location; and (2) those pertaining to the installation itself, the store, plant, office, or other facility involved.

From the standpoint of location, managers are typically concerned with regional factors, local community factors, and considerations pertaining to specific sites. Location analyses include such topics as access and cost of access to raw materials, markets, workers, and supporting types of businesses. Thus, transportation and communication factors are considered along with real estate factors in decisions based on these types of analyses.

With respect to the installation itself managers are faced with a variety of problems ranging from the physical facilities involved, as we have seen, to such alternatives as buying or leasing; operating from one installation, several, or many; financing with borrowed funds or the firm's funds; determining when to change locations; and the operation of properties by company personnel or outside specialists. Other types of problems also are involved; but these will illustrate the types of decision problems with which managers typically are concerned in this general area.

Location Decisions[2]

In some cases the owners and managers of a business firm have an opportunity of selecting locations as between regions, towns, and cities, or of selecting between specific sites within a given city. New branches may be involved in such a program. In some cases business firms are moved deliberately from one locality to another. For example, the textile industry migrated to a large extent from New England to the South; many firms in other lines have moved to the southern and southwestern regions of the country in recent years.

Obviously climate may be an important factor in the regional location of business firms. Population movements which usually follow areas of expanding opportunities often will bring the movement of business firms in their wake. The location of raw materials often is an important factor. For example, the steel industry tends to locate at a point that provides an economical meeting place of coal and iron ore. Note the location of the steel industries in Chicago, Pittsburgh, and Cleveland in relation to the availability of coal by rail and water transportation and iron ore by means of the cheap transportation on the Great Lakes. Availability of adequate water supplies often is important for manufacturing activities. Availability of power at reasonable costs may control the location of some firms.

Business firms that supply goods and services for factories tend to locate near the industries that they serve. Thus, there is a heavy concentration of industry on the so-called "New York-Chicago axis." Often nearness to markets is an important factor in determining the location of a firm. The heavy concentration of population and in-

---

2 *Ibid.*, chaps. 17, 18, and 19. For a theoretical analysis of various location factors see Walter Isard, *Location and Space Economy* (New York: John Wiley & Sons, Inc., 1956).

comes in the northeastern part of the United States serves as a magnet to many firms as do the new concentrations in Florida and southern California.

Locations of business firms within a *region* may be dictated by access to routes of transportation, nearness to raw materials, or other factors. If it is necessary to be near the center of the national railroad network, a location near Chicago will be indicated; if there is heavy dependence on ocean shipments, locations near a port like New York, Baltimore, New Orleans, or San Francisco will be attractive.

In some cases concentrations of industries or industrial "complexes" make for special economies of operation. Pools of skilled labor may be available at such places. Supporting business activities may be concentrated there. Financial institutions may be well acquainted with the problems of such industries. Local governments may be sympathetic and avoid restrictive legislation.

Transportation economies or diseconomies often determine how far a firm can be located from sources of materials and markets. The location problems that a manager must solve grow increasingly complex in a multiproduct firm operating from several locations. Analysis of problems of this type has been aided by the use of linear programming techniques and queueing theory[3] (see Chapter 14).

Often a business firm may be located to equal advantage in any one of a dozen or more cities. In such cases the selection of a specific city will turn on such factors as local taxes; attractiveness of the community in terms of schools, hospitals, churches, and other facilities; transportation rates and types of transportation available; other types of business in the area; availability of workers with the required abilities; and sometimes the promotional efforts of local chambers of commerce or similar organizations. In some cases cities provide special inducements to attract business firms. While sometimes of importance, typically other factors of the type listed above will carry greater weight in managerial decisions regarding locations.

Selection of Specific Sites

Location within a city usually depends on the type of business, the availability of space and its cost, and the special requirements of the firm. Large department stores, variety stores, and apparel stores are usually found in the central business district near what is known as the "100 per cent" retail location—that is, the point of heaviest concentration of shoppers and buying power. In the central business dis-

---

[3] See Isard, *op. cit.*, chaps. 4, 5, 6, and 7. See also his *Methods of Regional Analysis* (New York: John Wiley & Sons, Inc., 1960), chaps. 7 and 10.

trict shoppers can compare goods, prices, and qualities easily. The major financial institutions and the office buildings which serve as the headquarters of many business firms and agencies of government are usually located in the central business district of a large city.

Obviously the space for business firms in the central business districts of cities is expensive and often not readily available since much of it is under long-term leases. Many business firms, however, find it advantageous to pay the high prices and rents that are required for such locations.

The automobile has created a major revolution in regard to the location of many types of business firms. The development of outlying retail shopping centers has resulted largely from the construction of throughways and the provision of parking areas. Such locations typically require much less expensive land than is available in downtown areas.

The automobile also has made it possible for factories to move outward from the center of cities since workers with their cars can reach them from almost any point in the city. Provision of parking is also important in this connection. Also the development of truck transportation has freed many industrial plants from the necessity of locating on railroad lines or spurs.

The automobile has brought a substantial spreading out of city areas. Throughways, freeways, and superhighways have made it possible for many business firms to locate at points that are far removed from the centers of cities and yet to operate successfully.

The movement of the locations of some business firms from the center of cities to outlying locations has been brought about also by cheaper taxes in outlying areas, greater availability of land at favorable prices, and by improved land planning and development programs.

As pointed out in another connection:

The extent to which economic activities have been redistributed in metropolitan regions varies greatly. For most of them, however, retailing and manufacturing have tended to move from the city center or core area to outlying locations. . . . Headquarters offices for business firms and government agencies, however, have shown little tendency to decentralize; to a lesser degree this holds true for specialized activities and those requiring a diversified mixture of skills and materials.[4]

---

[4] Arthur M. Weimer, "Investors and Downtown Real Estate—Opinion and Comment," *Technical Bulletin 39* (Washington, D.C.: Urban Land Institute, 1960), p. 12. See also, Raymond Vernon, *The Changing Economic Function of the Central City* (New York: Committee for Economic Development, 1959), and Homer Hoyt, "Changing Patterns of Land Values," *Land Economics*, May, 1960.

Area Changes

We mentioned the importance of "neighboring" factors on decisions related to the place of business, that is, the effects of the immediate environment on the place of business and in turn the effects of the place of business and its operation on the environment. You have undoubtedly read and heard about the numerous problems emerging in our urban communities ranging all the way from those related to traffic congestion and excessive concentration to those related to slum areas, decentralization, "urban sprawl," and urban renewal and development. Many of these problems, of course, have a direct bearing on the decisions of managers in regard to their places of business.

Decisions related to the place of business often necessitate estimates regarding the future changes in an urban area in which a firm is located or in which a location is contemplated. Such estimates often make it necessary to analyze probable changes in the internal growth and structure of an entire urban area, probable changes in the competition for land uses, potential changes in transportation systems, and the likely trends of change in government policies.

For example, the continued decentralization of our cities suggests that many of the outlying business centers will develop more rapidly in the years ahead than will central business districts. Even so, many business firms will continue to find their greatest opportunities in central locations. It may be also, that some reversal of decentralization tendencies will occur, particularly if urban renewal programs help to reclaim some of the present slum areas. Improved transportation facilities, however, have opened up a wide variety of location possibilities for business firms and technological developments may expand even further the areas within which various business firms can operate advantageously.

As we have suggested, it is often helpful to think in terms of "an urban plant" when considering problems related to the place of business. By this term we mean the entire complex of urban facilities—streets, sewers, water systems, utility lines, and related things that enable business firms to operate in urban communities and in effect support such operations. Expansion of the urban plant is a costly process, largely borne at public expense, but this in turn affects the taxes borne by business firms and private individuals. Yet, it may be more desirable in some instances to expand the urban plant than to rebuild it. Business managers have a major interest in the effectiveness with which the urban plant operates in relation to the costs that must be borne by their firms through taxes, special assessments, and other changes.

To an increasing extent managers are recognizing the potential impact of many of their decisions on the urban community. In turn they are increasingly aware of the significance of public policies and potential changes in such policies for their places of business.

Movement of Goods and People

Although a business firm may occupy a single location or a number of locations if it has branches or other divisions, management is faced constantly with problems of moving goods and people into and out of the place of business. Management is concerned with local and regional and often with national and international modes of transportation and the cost and quality of the services that may be available.

Local transportation, of course, includes subways, elevated trains, belt lines, streetcars, bus lines, taxis, and private automobiles. Type and volume of business activity will usually determine the extent to which management is concerned with matters of local transportation. Even a highly specialized business firm such as an accounting firm, however, will need to consider the problems of employees reaching the place of business conveniently and also of accessibility to customers and clients who may come to it for business purposes.

Of major importance in regional, national, and international transportation are railroads, motor trucks, bus lines, water shipping facilities, airplanes, and pipelines. Each of these modes of transportation may have special advantages for a particular business firm, and a number of management decisions will turn on the type, quality, and cost of the transportation available. Each type of transportation may have special advantages for certain kinds of business activity. Some transportation facilities have major advantages for passenger traffic; others for the movement of goods. Some businesses rely heavily on express services such as those provided by the Railway Express Agency, and some on the parcel post system operated by the United States Post Office.

In the postwar years automobiles and motor trucks have increased quite rapidly and have changed the pattern of doing business for a number of firms. Illustrations include the emergence of the large regional shopping centers, the decentralization of many manufacturing operations, and the development of office buildings in suburban locations. The motel industry has emerged largely in recent years in response to such developments. The federal highway program undoubtedly will have increasing impact on the location of business firms as it is carried through to completion.

There has been some tendency in recent years for railroad services to decline relative to other types of transportation, although it should be noted that the role played by railroads especially in connection with heavy industries is of vital importance to American business. The use of airplanes has increased, and this is especially true in the field of air freight. Jet aircraft have added a new dimension to air transportation. Helicopters are coming into use for the solution of some short-range transportation problems.

Traffic Management

When business firms attain some size, problems of the type discussed above are usually assigned to a traffic manager. In some cases an entire traffic department may be established to aid in the solution of problems in this field.

A specialist in traffic management typically needs a thorough knowledge of the kinds of transportation facilities that are available, their rates, schedules, special advantages or disadvantages, and related things. Careful planning and the study of transportation facilities and costs, organization of the movement of goods and people, and the exercise of careful controls often yield major economies in the operations of a business firm. For example, the proper type of transportation arrangements may reduce the size of inventories that may be required. In some cases the use of truck transportation will reduce costs because of the reduction in the number of times that goods must be handled. Sometimes the traffic manager can speed up deliveries of goods and thus improve the competitive position of the firm.

Communication Facilities

Closely allied with transportation in terms of its impact on managerial decisions is communication—the facilities and methods available which enable business managers to receive and to disseminate information rapidly and accurately. *Time* as well as *space* considerations are involved. Today it is possible by transoceanic cable and radio to communicate quickly with all but the most remote regions of the world. Within this country it is possible to dial an increasing number of long-distance numbers directly. The importance of the telephone for local, regional, national, and even international communication services can hardly be overemphasized. The telegraph, ticker-tape services, television, radio, and other facilities make it possible to do business over wide areas and in short periods of time.

The operations of a business firm are often facilitated by special communication equipment and services. For example, business firms with branch operations often use ticker-tape services to speed up the internal activities of the company. Closed-circuit television is used by some firms for internal communications, as in the case of verifying signatures in financial institutions.

Of special importance for business communications is the U.S. Postal Service. The large bulk of business transactions is carried out by means of correspondence, letters, memoranda, reports, and the like, much of which passes through the mails. Not only does the Postal Service provide efficient handling and transmission of the mails, it protects the privacy of communications. Air mail, of course, has increased rapidly in recent years. Many business firms also use special delivery and registered mail services to facilitate their communication problems.

In considering communication facilities we should include newspapers, magazines, journals, and similar publications. These publications serve important advertising purposes along with radio and television. They also bring basic information to the business manager every day. The widespread use of the *Wall Street Journal* by business is a case in point.

These so-called mass media of communication are used by business firms either on local, regional, or national bases. Many periodicals provide national coverage, as do the large radio and television networks. Local markets play a major role in the operations of many business firms, and hence local radio and television stations and local newspapers and other publications serve many valuable business purposes in such cases.

Impact of Transportation and Communication

You can understand the impact of transportation and communication facilities on management decisions if you will think of an office building or a store or a factory located in the middle of a remote desert. Such a location would make it almost impossible for any kind of business firm to carry on successful operations. Regardless of the amount of money spent on such facilities, they would be valueless for practical purposes simply because there would be no ready means of access to them without incurring heavy costs. Hence, there would not be a stream of income accessible to such business firms.

You can also gain some insight into the significance of transportation and communication facilities by thinking of the changes they have brought in business throughout our history. In the early periods of our history there was heavy reliance on water transportation and the location of business places near harbors on the ocean or on inland waterways was a matter of prime importance. The growth of railroads represents one of the dramatic chapters in our economic history. Railroads permitted the development of the interior of the country, made possible the movement of materials and people over wide areas, and brought heavy concentrations of business firms at such points as Chicago, Cleveland, Pittsburgh, and St. Louis.

The rise of the automobile and improved highways added another chapter in the influence of transportation on business firms. Many smaller towns and cities lost their economic reasons for existence; most larger places decentralized with business firms spreading over wide metropolitan areas.

The airplane has had important effects in more recent years, although the full impact of this mode of transportation has not as yet been made on business and the American economy. Of major importance has been the ability of the air lines to move people and the more valuable and less bulky commodities rapidly over wide regions.

The evolution of improved communication facilities has also played a dramatic role in the history of American business. The telegraph which made its appearance in 1832, the telephone in 1876, radios after the turn of the century, and television in the postwar period, all have made it possible for business firms to carry out transactions more and more efficiently over wider and wider areas in shorter periods of time.

Television has created a minor revolution in the advertising field, and its impact on business in the future promises to be great. There is no doubt that telephone services will continue to be extended and made available at lower costs. Offset printing, new reproduction techniques and facilities, better photography and motion picture techniques, transistor radios, communication satellites, and many related developments will have a far-reaching impact on business communications in the years ahead.

Decisions Related to Installations

Management decisions related to the selection and operation of specific installations or properties depend on the over-all objectives and plans of the firm as we have indicated. They depend also on the adaptation of the firm's organization and operations to one or more installations that may be available for purchase or lease. In some cases, it may be necessary to develop new facilities in order to fit the firm's requirements more specifically.

Decisions in this area, as in most others, depend to a large extent on potential cost, risk, and return relationships. Since long-term commitments often are involved, decisions may be extremely difficult. For example, it may be necessary to sign a lease for ten years or longer in

FIGURE 17–1

Value of $100,000 Business Building for Immediate Occupancy
and for Occupancy at Future Times

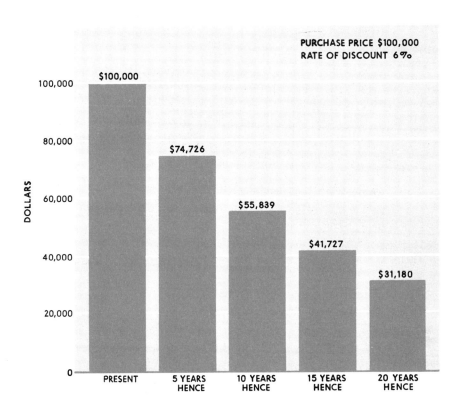

order to secure a particular property or space for a business firm. Hence, it will be necessary to make long-term estimates of incomes and costs and relate them to the probable risks that may be involved in occupying the particular installation. Such long-term estimates are subject to wide margins of error. Present values of potential incomes and costs are difficult to determine but such analyses are usually essential for arriving at rational decisions (see for example Figure 17–1).

Factors of depreciation and obsolescence generally are involved. Most structures used as places of business suffer physical wear and tear or depreciation, as we have seen. The rate of depreciation may vary widely depending on the type of structure, condition of the structure, kind of business operations carried on, intensity of use, and related factors. In addition newer buildings with improved designs and better facilities are being developed constantly and as a result older buildings suffer obsolescence and loss of competitive advantage.

As we have seen, "neighboring" influences may have a vital effect on a specific installation and often these are difficult to anticipate. Population shifts, changes in land uses, rearrangements of transportation facilities and traffic patterns, changes in zoning laws and taxes, and related developments may affect a particular installation favorably or adversely. Often changes of this type are difficult, if not impossible, to anticipate.

To illustrate some of the kinds of decisions often faced by managers with respect to specific business installations we will consider the following: (1) whether to buy or lease; (2) use existing facilities or develop new ones; (3) operate from one installation, several, or many; and (4) finance from borrowed or company funds.

Own or Lease

Whether ownership or leasing will be preferred by the manager of a business firm will depend to a considerable extent on the alternatives open and the effect of alternative arrangements on the firm's operations. Often a firm has special requirements as to location and facilities. In such cases it may be difficult to work out lease arrangements.

A rental payment is a direct business expense; hence, it is deductible for tax purposes. This may argue for leasing arrangements. On the other hand, depreciation charges and interest also are deductible expenses for tax purposes. Often the rate of depreciation that is allowed will be a controlling factor.

Leases expire at stated intervals of time. Options for renewal may or may not be available. A manager may prefer not to run the risk of moving from an established place of business upon the expiration of a lease and hence may prefer to own even though this may be a somewhat more costly arrangement.

It may be possible to turn over the money of the firm more rapidly through current operations than is possible when such money is invested in land and buildings. Hence, leasing may be desirable. This has been the case in most "sale and leaseback" arrangements in which stores, for example, are sold to an investor and then leased back by the selling company.

In some cases decisions in this area are controlled by established company policies. For example, there may be a preference for ownership or for avoiding ownership on the part of top management. Such a preference may be based on considerations that are broader than the relative cost-risk-return relationships involved in a specific choice between the ownership and rental of a property. The owners of a firm may prefer to own the original place of business because it is a part of the general image presented to the public. Some properties have important advertising and public relations advantages as in the case of a building dominating the sky line of a city and thus providing a "billboard" effect.

Conversely some business owners and managers have encountered heavy losses through the ownership of property and hence have adopted general policies requiring that all real property used by the firm be leased.

Existing versus New Facilities

Decisions as to whether existing facilities will be used for a place of business or new buildings will be constructed often depend on the kind of space needed, whether existing properties can be made to meet the firm's requirements, and relative cost-risk-return probabilities. New facilities often provide such added advantages as improvement of the "public image" of the firm, attraction of workers, and incidental advertising values. Often new facilities can be tailored directly to the needs of the business firm. Special advantages such as adequate parking facilities may be provided.

On the other hand, older facilities may be less costly; they may be more centrally located; leasing may be possible rather than ownership; they may provide locations in established centers of operation with nearby supporting activities. In some cases older buildings can be modernized and made to provide many of the advantages of newer structures. In some cases combinations of older and newer facilities may be possible with headquarters activities centered in older and established locations and other activities located in new facilities on less expensive land.

Sometimes managers have only limited choices in regard to older and newer locations. Space of the type required simply may not be available in older facilities. Or it may be that only by means of new developments is it possible to provide the facilities that will meet the firm's operating requirements.

When a firm has been operating at a given location for a long time the potential losses that may be incurred by moving to another site may be so great that managers will not undertake to move, even though from the standpoint of the physical facilities needed a new location would offer many advantages.

In some cases new installations may be essential, regardless of the adequacy of established locations for former purposes. Typically, new locations are sought when expansion at an established location is not possible or when the neighborhood in which an installation is located changes and affects adversely the operations of the firm. Such changes may affect customers, employees, investors, or all of these groups in varying degree.

Sometimes transportation routes are changed; for example, a new highway may bring a rerouting of traffic and make a change of location desirable. Tax burdens may change and dictate relocation. New community facilities may become available such as water supplies or power supplies that will bring decisions to change locations. There may be new developments such as an office building that will offer special attractions or an industrial park or a shopping center that may bring decisions to change the location or locations of a firm.

One or More Installations

Many firms start operations in one place, gradually expand, and then find it impossible to expand further at that site. In such cases they are faced with the alternative of moving completely to another location, or of operating from two or more installations. Much will depend in such cases on the type of business operations. A department store may find it advantageous to open branches in outlying shopping centers rather than to undertake expansion in a central location. A manufacturing firm may have no alternative except to move to another site, since it may be essential to have a number of processes conducted in close proximity to each other. A bank may find it impossible to operate from more than one location because of state laws that prohibit branch banking.

As some firms expand they may find it desirable to separate the office staff from production activities. It may be advantageous to have the executive offices located near the center of the city so as to provide easier access to major customers, suppliers, and investors.

As our cities have tended to spread over wider areas increasing numbers of business firms have tended to operate from more than one location. This is notably true of firms in retailing activities but it is also true in other fields. Downtown locations may be too expensive even for routine office activities which may be moved to outlying locations. Warehouses and other storage spaces often need not be directly accessible to other phases of a firm's operations and hence may be located on less expensive land.

Legal requirements may result in a variety of locations; it may be desirable to manufacture goods in one state but sell them from another. To an increasing extent the managers of larger business firms find it desirable to have a headquarters office in New York or in a major regional center. Financial activities are tending more and more to center in New York. Also, as American business firms increase their operations abroad they find it advantageous to operate from several locations. The European Common Market is stimulating the location of branch manufacturing plants of American firms within the Common Market countries.

Often decisions to operate from one or more locations will turn on the solution of complicated sets of relationships such as the advantages of locating near to markets, possibilities for covering markets more intensely, relative costs of moving raw materials and finished goods, taxes, special charges made by various states such as truck license fees, and many others.

Alternative Financing Arrangements

If a business firm owns its place or places of business, the method of financing often poses difficult problems for management. Usually these problems center around the question of the extent to which financing should be accomplished by company funds or with borrowed funds. If money can be borrowed on favorable terms many managers prefer to free the capital of the firm for other purposes. Other managers, however, fear the risks of borrowing; mortgages may mature at times when it is difficult to pay them off or to arrange for refinancing. In such cases the financial solvency of the entire firm may be threatened.

If managers expect to sell one or more properties, there are arguments for carrying fairly heavy mortgages on them since prospective owners will not need to raise as much cash as would be the case otherwise. Or if managers prefer not to run the risks involved in carrying heavy mortgages they may find it necessary to finance sales to others through the use of company funds, and find themselves short of cash for operating purposes.

Decisions as to whether to finance real properties by means of company or borrowed funds tend to turn on the interest rates and borrowing terms that may be available on the one hand, and the relation of costs of borrowing to the returns that can be expected by the use of company funds in operating activities, on the other.

Special considerations, of course, may be involved. General company policies may frown on heavy borrowing, regardless of the price of money or other conditions. Or company policies may set limits on the proportion of company funds that may be tied up at a given time in real property.

Other Decisions Related to Business Installations

The above types of problems illustrate some of the decisions faced by business managers with respect to the installations which serve them as a place or places of business. Many others might be considered as well but those covered should help you to see some of the types of problems involved and their relationships to various other problems and policies of business firms.

Among the other problems that might be considered, for example, is the extent to which real property should be purchased or leased in advance of current needs to provide for future expansion. Another problem is that of managing the properties themselves. Real properties require continuing attention and it is necessary to determine whether this will be done by the business firm directly or by a real estate management firm retained for this purpose. Insurance must be arranged, taxes paid as required, programs for servicing and repairing the facilities carried forward on a continuing basis, plans developed for alterations and improvement, and the like. Some managers find it desirable to "farm out" these duties, others prefer to handle them within the firm. Difficult problems often arise in deciding whether to demolish existing buildings and construct new facilities on established sites.

There are continuing problems of determining the impact of management decisions on local community affairs, for example, staggering hours of work may help to relieve traffic congestion; providing special fire fighting facilities may reduce the burden imposed on the local fire department; company police may relieve the work of local city police. Illustrations of this type could be multiplied.

SUMMARY

The place of business plays a significant part in determining the degree of success of a business firm. It determines the firm's general physical environment; affects cost-risk-return relationships; and determines accessibility to markets, materials, workers, transportation routes, suppliers, public services and utilities, power sources, and community facilities. It reflects the personality or public image of the firm.

What makes a good place of business depends on how well it enables the firm to pursue its objectives and plans and how well it fits the requirements of its organization and operations. Physical factors, including the land, buildings, and special equipment are important, but chiefly as they have economic implications, including effect on worker morale and efficiency, attractiveness to customers and investors, and adaptability to the type and volume of business carried on.

Decisions in this area often are complicated because land and buildings are fixed in location; every piece of real property has certain unique characteristics; and the market for real estate tends to be localized, hence, risks of being "locked in" are great. In addition, privately owned property must almost always be used in conjunction with publicly owned property. Thus there is often considerable interaction between private and public decisions. Also, large amounts of money typically are involved. The long life of real properties often complicates decision problems.

Decisions related to the place of business tend to be centralized, although in some firms such as chain operations, there is a degree of decentralization. Experts such as architects, engineers, real property lawyers, real estate appraisers, property managers, market analysts, and others are used widely.

Location decisions include those related to regional and local community factors, and choices between specific sites; as well as problems of access to and costs of access to raw materials, markets, workers, and supporting businesses. Transportation and communication facilities play a significant part in many location decisions and may be even more important in the future.

Decisions related to installations include a variety of problems such as those involved in cost-risk-return relationships; depreciation and obsolescence, and neighboring influences. Installation decisions cover a variety of problems; typical of those often encountered are these: (1) whether to buy or lease; (2) whether to use existing facilities or develop new ones; (3) whether to operate from one installation, several, or many; and (4) whether to finance from company funds or by means of borrowed funds.

QUESTIONS AND PROBLEMS

1. Indicate some of the important ways in which the place of business may affect the success of a business firm.

2. What makes a good place of business? Who determines what makes a good place of business?

3. The selection of a place of business involves primarily a consideration of real estate problems. Why are these likely to be difficult problems from a managerial standpoint?

4. Why do private decisions relative to the place of business usually come up against public decisions?

5. What is meant by the "urban plant"?

6. Indicate the major factors involved in making choices between regions in regard to a location for a place of business.

7. If a firm can be located to equal advantage in any one of several cities, which factors are likely to be given major consideration by managers in making a final choice?

8. You have been asked to recommend one of three sites for a filling station. Which factors would you consider in deciding on one of them? Would the same factors apply to the selection of a site for a supermarket? For a small manufacturing establishment?

9. Why may it be advisable to analyze city structure and directions of growth when selecting a specific site for a place of business?

10. Indicate several of the ways in which the cost and availability of transportation and communication facilities may affect the location of a place of business in the years ahead.

11. You own and operate a small department store. You have an opportunity to buy a building that fits the needs of your store, or to lease it. The cost of the building is $100,000. The lease runs for ten years at an annual rental of $7,000 (the owner pays property taxes, fire insurance, and is responsible for exterior repair only). Which arrangement would you prefer?

12. On what bases would you decide whether to make use of an existing building for your place of business or to construct a new one?

13. You have decided to buy a building for your business firm that costs $120,000. You have funds available to pay for the building. However, you find that you can borrow $80,000 on a first mortgage at 6 per cent. Funds invested in your business have been earning 10 to 11 per cent. Would you borrow or finance with your own funds?

14. Study the Acme Brass Manufacturing Company Case presented here and answer the following questions:

    a) Do you believe that the location decision was critical to the future of the firm?

    b) Would you have made the same decision? Why or why not?

    c) Does this case suggest that many industries may move to smaller towns? Why or why not?

ACME BRASS MANUFACTURING COMPANY[5]

The fiscal year ended June 30, 1949, had been very disappointing to the stockholders of Acme Brass Manufacturing Company of Detroit, Michigan.

This family-controlled firm was incorporated in 1906 for the manufacture of brass castings, valves, and cocks as original equipment for makers of gas ranges, driers, and heating appliances. The company was successful for several years but met sharp reverses during the 1930's, and was on the verge of bankruptcy in 1938 when Mr. Robert T. Herbert, son of the founder, bought out his two brothers and reorganized the company.

Heavy indebtedness made it impossible immediately to replace inefficient, outmoded equipment with modern machinery. Very little progress had been made on this problem prior to World War II and the very low earnings that had been made during the base period, 1936 to 1939, subjected the firm to heavy excess profits taxes. Again, because of this and other wartime factors, the company was prevented from modernizing its facilities as rapidly as needed to keep abreast of competition.

From 1938 on the management had been practically a one-man operation, but in September, 1947, Herbert told his son-in-law, Grant C. Willman, then production manager, that he intended to have Willman become familiar with the commercial and financial phases of the business. Before these intentions could be carried out Mr. Herbert died suddenly in November, 1947, and Willman was made president and treasurer.

Before joining Acme Brass in 1939 Willman had been employed in the Chevrolet Division of General Motors, where he had received training in warehouse management, supplemented by training in sales and in analysis of dealer costs and earnings. This experience had convinced him of the importance of close control of costs and also of the advantages of efficient organization with clearly defined chain of command and areas of responsibility and authority.

Fortunately a new cost system had been put into operation in October, 1947 and was functioning well when Mr. Willman assumed his new responsibilities. This system provided him with a daily analysis of labor variance from standard in each department and enabled him to keep a close control on manufacturing costs.

A study of the profit and loss statements for the fiscal years ended June 30, 1947 and 1949 reveals the following:

Net sales	$565,860 decrease
Cost of sales	478,460 decrease
Gross profit	87,403 decrease
Selling and advertising	9,325 increase
Administration and general*	5,870 increase
Other income	5,054 increase
Other deductions	7,762 decrease
Net profit before federal income taxes	83,912 decrease

---

* Case writer's note: The "selling and administrative" figures were supplied by the case firm from actual records and given as approximations.

[5] Adapted by permission of the Small Business Administration and the Graduate School of Business, Indiana University.

The high wage rates prevailing in the Detroit area were only partially responsible for Acme's excessive manufacturing costs. The company occupied 96,000 square feet in a three-story building at the corner of West Fort Street and Junction Avenue. The dimensions of the building were approximately 300 feet by 200 feet; a central open courtyard, 106 feet by 192 feet, took out an area of approximately 20,000 square feet in the center of the building. Trucks entered and left the court through an arched driveway in the center of the front section of the building.

The foundry was on the second floor, cleaning operations were on the first floor, and sand for molds was stored in the basement. Purchased parts were also stored in the basement. Machining operations were performed on both the first and second floors. Offices were on the third floor. Some space on the first floor was rented to an outside firm.

Elevators were inadequate for the company's operations and did not meet the requirements of the Detroit building code. A reliable contractor estimated that an expenditure of $50,000 would be necessary to put the elevators in satisfactory condition. The building repair bill in 1947 was $17,160. The cost of coal for heating was as much as $7,302 annually, while real estate taxes were approximately $7,800 a year.

The situation had been discussed at length with the stockholders. In December, 1948 a decision was reached to purchase vacant property in a Detroit suburb on which a modern one-story plant could be erected. Soon afterward an option was taken on some land in Plymouth, Michigan, and architects' plans and elevations for the new building were prepared.

The estimated cost of the new building was $195,500. It was believed that the company could realize $237,500 net from the sale or trade of the plant on West Fort Street and Mr. Willman planned to apply $150,000 of the proceeds on the new building, with a bank loan being used for the balance. No immediate major purchase of new equipment was contemplated.

It was estimated that monthly savings of $4,952 in wages plus $436 in the reduction of fringe benefit costs could be realized in the new location. Annual savings in the cost of heating and in taxes were estimated at $8,067.

Negotiations were undertaken for the simultaneous sale of the existing plant and the erection of the new plant in Plymouth. When the West Fort Street factory was advertised for sale, Mr. Willman called the employees together and showed them the architects' drawing of the proposed new building, so that they would not think the company planned to go out of business.

At this juncture it was learned that Ford Motor Company had purchased a large tract of land adjacent to the site under option to Acme Brass and that Ford planned to begin the erection of a new factory there in the immediate future. Mr. Willman and the other stockholders realized that if they went ahead with their plans they would be forced to match Ford wage scales or lose their skilled workers to better paying jobs at the Ford Plant.

ALTERNATIVES OPEN TO

ACME BRASS MANUFACTURING COMPANY

Needless to say, the directors of Acme Brass were very disappointed by the turn of events in Plymouth, Michigan. They had looked forward to being able to make substantial savings in direct labor as well as in charges for repairs and maintenance and in property taxes. They felt Acme could not afford to pay wages comparable to those which would prevail in the adjoining Ford plant. On the other hand, Acme would not hold its skilled workers if it paid a lower wage than Ford paid for similar jobs.

At the same time, they were convinced that Acme Brass would not earn a satisfactory profit if it continued to operate in the West Fort Street plant because of the inefficient layout, the high wage and property tax rates, costly repairs and maintenance, and excessive fuel costs. In addition, the necessity of making expensive changes in the plant elevators to comply with municipal ordinances would seriously affect the company's working capital position.

There were several alternate courses open to the Acme management. Among those considered were:

1. Continue with plans for the new plant.
2. Continue to operate in the present location as long as possible, hoping for relief from the cost/profit squeeze.
3. Go out of business and liquidate the company.
4. Explore the possibilities of getting into some more profitable business, in which most of the existing equipment and labor force, and possibly the existing plant, could be used.
5. Move to some location entirely outside the Detroit area and continue in the line of business in which the company was presently engaged.

For reasons already presented, the stockholders felt that the first possibility was not feasible. They thought that the second alternative threatened them with a gradual but almost certain loss of their entire investment. The third option was actually considered but was rejected, basically because the owners had faith in the future of the type of business the company was in and therefore hoped for a better solution. The fourth choice did not appear practical at that time. The last alternative presented several serious problems. The move to another section of the country would involve considerable expense, would seriously interrupt production, would expose the company to a loss of goodwill, and would necessitate training virtually an entirely new crew of operators. Willman estimated that six months would be required in the new location before efficiencies could be expected to equal those attained in the Detroit plant.

In spite of these considerations the last alternative was selected as the most promising, and the stockholders directed Mr. Willman to investigate possible sites outside the Detroit area. Willman spent a large part of the next year and a half checking into possible locations in Michigan, Ohio, and Indiana, and even in certain midsouthern states.

Willman looked for a small town in which no large company was already located, thus hoping to avoid the dominance of a large company in labor rate and personnel problems. He also hoped to find a location which would not involve too radical an adjustment for the families of key personnel moved from the Detroit plant. Good transportation facilities and a spot reasonably centered with respect to the principal customers of Acme Brass were requisites. A favorable climate of labor relations and friendly co-operation and assistance from members of the new community were also desirable.

FINAL DECISION

Willman eliminated several locations which qualified in other respects because prevailing labor rates in these areas were higher than Acme Brass could afford to pay. He finally decided in favor of Baker, Indiana (1956 population estimated as 3,425), for the following reasons:

1. Labor rates were not high. A small clothing factory was operating successfully there.
2. The nearest large metal working plant was several miles away at Bedford, Indiana. General Motors had a foundry in Bedford but was not performing any parts machining at the Bedford plant, and Smith did not plan to operate a foundry immediately. (He subsequently added a foundry at Baker.)
3. The local tax structure was satisfactory.
4. Land for the plant would be donated by the town.
5. The secretary of the local chamber of commerce was capable and did a good job of presenting the advantages of moving to Baker.

The Detroit plant was sold for $250,000 and a new plant was built in Baker for $180,000. To provide enough cash for moving expenses and working capital, bank loans were obtained in the amount of $90,000. Later this short-term paper was converted into long-term notes with an insurance company.

Including warehouse and foundry (4,000 square feet each), the Baker plant covers 45,000 square feet. A greater volume of business is done in this space than was handled in the 96,000 square feet of the Detroit plant. By late 1959 the Baker plant was operating at consistently higher efficiency than had ever been achieved in Detroit.

The estimated savings have been more than realized. In addition to savings in labor, about $2,700 has been saved annually in fuel. Property taxes in Baker for 1959 were $12,800 less than paid in Detroit in 1948.

SUGGESTED READINGS

LONG, JOHN D. *Workbook to Accompany Weimer: Business Administration: An Introductory Management Approach*, chap. 17. Rev. ed. Homewood, Ill.: Richard D. Irwin, Inc., 1962.

VERNON, RAYMOND. *The Changing Economic Function of the Central City*. New York: Committee for Economic Development, 1959. This is a very interesting brief statement that outlines some of the important changes affecting our cities.

WEIMER, ARTHUR M., and HOYT, HOMER. *Principles of Real Estate*. 4th ed. New York: Ronald Press Co., 1960. Read chap. 6, "Economic Characteristics of Real Estate," and chap. 24, "Commercial and Industrial Real Estate."

OUTLINE FOR CHAPTER 18

PRODUCTION of goods and services is a basic function of all firms; the DECISIONS AND OPERATIONS included are among major management problems.

Production involves the creation of values:
changing form of things; changing place or location;
provision at desired times and amounts; plus
adding values or serving convenience needs.

Production decisions and operations are related directly to the firm's objectives and other programs, notably marketing.

Major production decisions include those related to
what is to be produced,
whether to buy or make, and
type of processing.

Product line planning requires choices between
single and multiple products;
one or another "product mix"; and others.
Decisions usually are based on cost-risk-return
expectations, and strategic factors.

Design of product usually is based on market preferences and includes
mechanics of design, and
aesthetics of design.

Procurement requires decisions on
buy or make, or
combinations of alternatives;
effect on profit usually is controlling.

Processing includes manufacturing operations or those corresponding operations in nonmanufacturing firm. Alternatives include continuous processing, processing to order, or combinations.
Production standards, controls, and costs are important.

Disposition of products is accomplished
through sales, or
adding to inventory, or
supplying next stage of processing.
Inventory controls are improving.

PRODUCTION: DECISIONS AND OPERATIONS

The sailor or the railway-man who carries coal above ground produces it, just as much as the miner who carries it underground; . . .
—ALFRED MARSHALL

Importance of Production

Like each of us a business firm cannot exist unless it has income. We get our incomes by marketing our services or our property. Our income may be in the form of wages or salaries as payment for our work for others or as rent for property that we own, interest on money lent to others, or dividends on stock owned. There may also be income from others, as when parents help to pay for the education of sons or daughters. Income may be derived from the sale of property, from inheritances, and in other ways.

A business firm gets its income by marketing goods or services. It may on occasion sell plant or equipment or other things, but its principal source of income is from the sale of products. In order to have something to sell *it must produce goods or services* or both. Our discussions in this chapter center around decisions related to the production operations of business firms.

As we have seen, production must be related closely to marketing since few business managers are interested in producing something for which there is no market, or such a weak market that sales cannot be made at prices which exceed production costs. Production is also related closely to finance. Production cannot be undertaken unless adequate funds are available to finance the operation. As we pointed out in Chapters 8 and 9 production factors enter into many of the decisions of top managers in establishing objectives and plans as well as in the organization of the firm's resources.

We consider production here primarily from the point of view of the chief executive officer of the firm but consider also the work of the production manager or other executive responsible for this function.

Consequently, our interest centers in the types of decisions that are involved in (1) relationships between production and other management problems; and (2) the production phases of a firm's operations, including what is to be produced, how much, for whom, at what rate, by what methods, and at what costs.

Creating Values

Production is the process of *creating values or adding values.* We may think of values as things that people want and are willing to pay for. They may be in the form of goods like a pair of shoes or a bar of candy or in the form of services such as a haircut, a movie, or a taxi ride.

Anything that is useful but not available in sufficient quantity to meet all demands for it has *economic value.* As we know, air has no economic value. It is highly useful, but there is plenty of it to meet the needs of all on this planet. In outer space air would have very high value.

As we have pointed out, the objective of production in the case of most business firms is to *secure income.* Values are created in the hope that they will bring income to the firm, and preferably income in excess of the cost of producing it.

Most of us think of production as involving some manufacturing process. Actually, production in an economic sense involves *any value creation*—ranging all the way from manufacturing, mining, and farming, on the one hand, to retail stores or the provision of such services as transportation, entertainment, or the delivery of goods to a customer, on the other.

Every business firm must produce something of value in order to exist. This may be done by changing the *form* of things, as in the case of manufacturing; by changing their *location*, as in the case of transportation; or providing them at a certain *time* and in *convenient amounts*, as in the case of wholesaling and retailing, or in related ways. Similarly, a service may be provided either by *adding value* to goods such as repairing a piece of machinery or serving the convenience needs of customers and clients or by providing personal services of one type or another.

A grocery store, while primarily a marketing or selling firm, engages in *production* in that it provides groceries in convenient amounts and at a given place. A *bank produces financial services* assembling savings and making them available to those who wish to borrow money. *Every business firm, thus, is engaged in production.* It is involved also, of course, in marketing or selling the goods or services (values) that it produces.[1]

Production Management Functions

Production and marketing are the principal operating functions of business firms. In smaller firms the chief executive officer may discharge the responsibility for production himself; in larger firms he will delegate this responsibility to a production manager or superintendent. Production and marketing functions may be divided but there must be close co-ordination between them. Indeed, many business managers now organize their activities by product, with a single manager responsible for both production and marketing, rather than by dividing activities between the production and marketing of a variety of products.

The management of production requires the performance of the basic functions of planning, organizing, and controlling, just as the general management of the firm involves these functions. Objectives are established, plans developed to achieve these objectives, an organizational structure and team is set up, controls are exercised, and the entire process is activated through leadership.

Obviously, production objectives must be related to the over-all objectives of the firm and integrated with the objectives established for the marketing division. It is the job of the general manager or chief executive officer to establish proper relationships between general objectives and those related specifically to the areas of production or marketing. For example, the production manager may set quality standards too high for the market his firm is serving; or he may set a goal for total output that is beyond the capacity of the firm to finance or sell.

Production planning and organization must also be related to the general plans and organizational framework of the firm. Of special importance in the integration of production and general planning is the *budget*. Volume of output, of course, is basic to estimates of the gross income that may be produced by the firm, and production costs frequently bulk large in total projected expenditures.

In connection with production planning it is necessary to decide what is to be produced, how much, and for whom. Production planning includes the procurement of the necessary materials and man

---

1 See, for example, Howard L. Timms, "Production," in Frank C. Pierson and Others, *The Education of American Businessmen* (New York: McGraw-Hill Book Co., Inc., 1959), pp. 475–81.

power, the flow of work, routing and scheduling of work, determining production rates, relationships between stages in the production process, and the cost and quality standards that will be observed.

Organization for production involves the division of the total work load into manageable parts and the establishment of proper relationships between production and other phases of the firm's activities, especially marketing.

Production controls range all the way from the control of product lines to inspection of the quality of output. Typically the effectiveness of production controls depends largely on the establishment of standards that can be made sufficiently definite to measure against. This includes deciding how many units are to be produced or handled, of what quality, at what cost, and in how much time.

As we have suggested, when we think of production management, we tend to think in terms of factory processes, and more often than not of large-scale factory operations. While production management is important in such operations, it is equally important in a financial institution, a store, and even in an office type of activity.

Marketing and Production

The managers of a business firm, as we pointed out above, usually will not undertake the production of goods or services unless they have good reason to believe that these things can be sold and sold for amounts that will exceed the costs of producing them. Thus, *sales begin even before production starts*. Decisions have to be made before production starts as to the kind of product that will be appealing and acceptable to buyers, will meet the competition of other business firms, and can be produced at costs which will be below sales prices. Note that the producer of a good or service may try to set a price above costs, but he can do this only if the market is strong enough to sustain such prices. Only under monopolistic or partially monopolistic conditions can managers really control prices.

Before a new automobile model is produced for example, designers develop plans, the engineering and manufacturing departments of the firm compute costs, and markets are studied often with sample surveys being made of various segments of the market. Finally, the models selected represent a balancing of all of the factors involved ranging from estimated costs to probable consumer preferences. Materials are then selected and ordered; production machines developed, purchased or leased, and installed; advertising and promotional campaigns planned; and financing programs arranged. In deciding what will be produced, how much and for whom, business managers are involved constantly with balancing costs and returns, trying to make their resources go as far as possible.

Production and Financing

It is impossible for business managers to undertake the production of anything unless they are able to finance the process. At the time a firm is established, financing may require the assembly of sufficient funds through the resources of owners or through the borrowing of money to purchase or lease a place of business, provide the necessary equipment, and pay the employees until products can be sold and create a stream of income which, in turn, will finance a continuing production process. Thus, production requires financing of several types.

As we have seen, long-term financing will be required. This money will be needed to provide the place of business and the necessary machinery and equipment.

Also, short-term financing or operating capital will be required, that is, sufficient money to purchase the necessary materials that will go into the production process, to carry raw materials or partially finished products in inventory until the time of sale, and to meet payrolls.

Production Alternatives

Some indication of the types of decisions that are involved in the production field may be provided by outlining several of the alternatives that frequently are open to managers. Of major importance, of course, are decisions regarding *what is to be produced*. Shall effort be concentrated on one product, or several, or many? If more than one product is to be produced shall the products be complementary or represent a diversity of lines?

Closely related is the question of whether the firm will *buy or make* its products, or the degree to which it will buy or make them. Relatively few firms process products from original raw materials to final consumers. Some products are bought, altered slightly, and then sold; some are processed from raw materials to partially finished products.

Often managers must select the *type of processing*—that is, will they produce to order or undertake continuous production for the mass market. They also have alternatives of trying to *regularize* levels of output or to allow operations to follow seasonal or cyclical patterns. In some cases choices, especially as to cyclical patterns of operations, may not be open to managers.

Managers may face many other alternatives as well. For example, shall production be carried on in one place of business, or several, or many? On what scale shall production be carried forward? When should new products be added? Old ones discarded? What quality standards should be imposed?

We consider here a few of the types of alternatives outlined above in order to illustrate managerial decisions related to the production of goods and services in order to secure income for the business firm.

Production Steps or Stages

One method of organizing our thinking in regard to production decisions is to consider the various steps or stages or the major functions that may be involved in the production process. These have been variously identified.[2] For our purposes, however, the following outline may be helpful:

1. Product line planning, including the determination of the product or products that will be produced in order to achieve the objectives of the firm. Such planning typically includes a careful consideration of the results of market studies and analysis, financial factors, costs, competitive situation, and related matters.
2. Design, including the design of the product or products as well as the production processes that are to be utilized.
3. Procurement—this stage involves the purchase of raw materials, partially finished goods, or even completed products.
4. Processing, that is, the manufacturing activities of the firm or those corresponding to them in nonmanufacturing firms, along with such functions as production control, quality control, cost control, and maintenance. As we shall see, various types of processing may be undertaken by business firms; some use highly automated processes, others use less advanced methods; in some cases continuous operations are carried on, in others the firm processes to order.
5. Disposition, that is, final sale of products or holding goods in inventory pending final sale or further processing; problems of inventory control are particularly important at this stage. We should note, however, that they are important at all stages of processing, including the raw-materials and work-in-process stages.

We consider each of these stages and various decision problems related to them in the remaining discussions in this chapter.

Product Line Planning

The multitude of goods and services produced by business firms almost defies one's imagination. Furthermore, the rapidity with which

---

[2] Edward H. Bowman and Robert B. Fetter, *Analysis for Production Management* (rev. ed.; Homewood, Ill.: Richard D. Irwin, Inc., 1961), pp. 7–10.

new products are added and old ones are outmoded is one of the principal characteristics of our business system. Each product, of course, involves a special set of problems. Some of these are highly complex; others are relatively simple.

The question of what to produce is of continuing importance to the success of a business firm. Shall it specialize in one line or attempt to provide a series of products, either related or unrelated? In some cases by-products offer special opportunities. Often complementary products can be put on the market to advantage. Two or more seasonal products may enable a firm to achieve reasonable regularity of operations. Some firms attempt to produce and market a wide diversity of product lines in order to guard against sudden changes in their competitive position or to insure against quick changes in consumer preferences.

There are instances of a single firm making cowboy boots and underwear; a dairy producing chemicals; a weaver of woolen and worsted fabrics producing sheet metal products; and similar widely diversified product lines.[3] Difficult decisions often are involved in developing a desirable "product mix" for a firm. By this is meant the kind and relative amount of products that will maximize net income. As we have suggested, sometimes this means a mixture of complementary products, sometimes diversified products.

In some cases firms carry production through a series of integrated steps from original procurement of raw materials from mine, forest, or farm through various stages of processing to the final sale of completed products to consumers. In other cases they specialize in the production of a single item. Usually the decisions reached by the managers of a firm in regard to product lines turn on (1) profit factors, short and long run; and (2) strategic considerations such as offsetting competition, expanding market coverage, or improving cost patterns.

Joel Dean has quite aptly pointed out that "There are two questions to answer in considering any product addition: (1) Does it have adequate economic promise (even if technically feasible)? and (2) Can the company appropriately exploit this economic opportunity?"[4]

Thus, a firm will not ordinarily undertake to add a product to its line unless the chances for making profits are favorable. This will depend, on the one hand, on the potential market for the added product and the competitive situation in which it will be placed. On the other hand, profit potentials will depend on costs not only for the

---

3 See, for example, Russel B. Robins, "New Products by Proxy," *Proceedings* of the 1957 Stanford Business Conference, p. 51.

4 See Joel Dean, *Managerial Economics* (New York: Prentice-Hall, Inc., 1951), pp. 115–20.

added product but on the total cost picture, that of the added product as well as the older products.

For example, the cost situation would tend to be favorable to the addition of a new product if there were excess capacity. This might be excess capacity in terms of machinery and equipment; man power, either engaged in production or sales; executive talent; or other resources. Sometimes a firm name has been developed through advertising and can be made to carry an additional product.

As we suggested above, some firms add products in order to provide a hedge against cyclical or other variations in general business activity or changes in a particular industry. It may be that no amount of diversification can guard against a widespread deterioration of general business conditions. Different products, however, may experience varying degrees of decline in sales during a general business recession, and sales for some may actually expand, even when general business activity falls off fairly sharply. In some cases, operations on a multinational basis are helpful in this regard.

From the standpoint of profitability it has been found that unless potential additional products are considered with great care, the results are likely to be disappointing. Business firms, of course, may establish different standards by which they measure profitability, and their objectives may be sufficiently broad to justify adding a product even if profit expectations from it are not great. For example, a firm may add a product and expand employment in a specific community in anticipation of future needs because of a surplus of labor there. It may do this in part to be assured of a future labor supply and in part in the interests of community relations. A firm in a different situation might not consider the addition of a product under similar conditions.

Product Strategy

We should note also that *strategic considerations* often play an important role in determining the product line or lines that a firm will undertake to produce. For example, it may be strategically advisable to keep on producing a particular item even if its profitability has declined because it has been identified with the firm over a long period of time and has attained a prestige position. This position may help to carry other products that the firm may undertake to market.

In some cases a company wishes to have its products cover a complete range of markets, or to reach all geographic regions in the country, or to obtain other coverages. Sometimes a product is added for defensive purposes, that is, to prevent a competitor from moving into a specific field, or if he does move in to offer as much competition as possible.

This subject of the strategic factors involved in developing product lines is a broad and fascinating one. We have tried to indicate some of the factors that will be involved in arriving at managerial decisions relative to the selection and addition of products. The problems of each firm are peculiar to it. For example, the management of one firm will decide to specialize in a single product because of its know-how in the field. The management of another firm will decide to diversify product lines for the same reason in the belief that this type of know-how is transferable to another or to several more products.

New products may be developed by a company through its own efforts, or products may be purchased from other firms. Sometimes products are secured by buying the firms that make them; in other cases licensing or other arrangements are set up to give a firm control of a particular product. When new products are developed by a firm, they may result from its research and development programs, or from ideas of managers or employees or others; they may grow out of methods for using by-products, or result from other programs.

Sometimes it becomes desirable to discontinue a product either because it can be bought more cheaply than made, or because of market changes, or because other products can be produced more profitably. Thus, decisions about product lines are being made almost constantly by the managers of business firms. Indeed, some businessmen believe that if a firm does not change its product or product lines in the space of around ten years, it is very likely to fail.

Design

As we have suggested, design problems relate both to product and the production process. Bowman and Fetter point out, for example:

Product design is concerned with the planning involved in determining the attributes of the finished product. The stimulus to new design or redesign usually originates in marketing which reflects consumer preferences and desires. But the actual function is primarily one of engineering and consists of two phases as follows: the mechanics of design—determining primary function or performance of the product; and aesthetics of design—determining appearance, color, etc.[5]

Once the product has been designed, it is necessary to design the methods by which it can be made economically. In some cases it may be possible to purchase it from another business firm that agrees to make it according to design specifications. Often, the product will be

---

[5] Bowman and Fetter, *op. cit.*, p. 8, by permission.

produced in whole or in part by the firm that designed it. The aim generally is to create the conditions and methods that will make it possible to provide the product in accordance with the standards that have been specified under cost conditions that will meet competition. Such factors as efficient plant layout and the design or selection of the required tools typically are involved in accomplishing this purpose. Decisions related to plant layout include choices between such alternatives as whether all of the equipment required to make a product can be made available at a single location, thus permitting an easy flow of materials; the type and amount of equipment that will best meet requirements; and the type of structure that will best serve the equipment and the flow of work.

Buy or Make?

As we have suggested, management often must decide whether to make products or buy them or follow various combinations of these alternatives. *Potential effect on profit* is the basis on which questions of this type usually are decided.

FIGURE 18–1
Production Stages

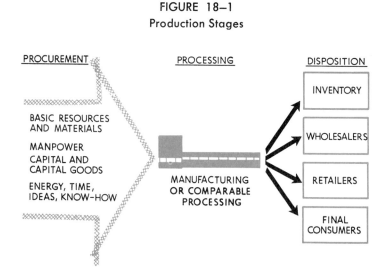

In some cases it is advisable to discontinue making a product and to buy it from another firm. A particular firm, for example, may prefer not to make the investment in new equipment that would be required to produce an item as economically as it can be produced elsewhere.

There are situations in which a firm may wish to buy rather than to make a product because its production facilities are already used to capacity. Its sales force, however, may be more productive if another line is added. In some cases manufacturing firms may make a part of a product but buy other parts from other firms.

Some business firms use the *subcontracting* system to a great extent. This is particularly true in the construction industry. The parent firm or general contractor, for example, may do very little construction itself but subcontract to other firms various subdivisions of a project.

In the case of a service business something like subcontracting may be used in the form of letting out concessions. For example, a barber shop may let out the shoeshining concession for a percentage of income taken in or for a rental of the space used. A hotel may prefer not to operate a restaurant and let out a concession for this purpose. Or an automobile repair shop may lease space to a filling station.

In short, the various stages and levels of production may be broken down in many ways. Each firm tries to find the best combination of products and the most efficient methods for making them available to its customers. What is "best" will vary widely from one firm to another but will usually be decided in terms of anticipated effect on profits.

Procurement Problems

In the purchasing of materials needed to support production activities, numerous decisions are required, many of which must be made from day to day. For example, there is the problem of the rate of purchasing and the arrangements for the dates on which goods will be delivered. Decisions along these lines usually are related to the level of inventory that is desirable and to the rate at which production is carried forward. The timing of purchases is very important. Sometimes because of seasonal factors, for example, substantial savings can be accomplished by buying goods for future delivery.

The problem of timing also raises the question of whether a firm will engage in speculative buying or whether it will time its purchases to fit its immediate requirements. There is a tendency for many firms to build up inventories, for example, when prices are advancing, and to liquidate inventories rapidly when prices are moving downward. This reflects speculative buying.

Like so many other problems in business, purchasing problems cannot be solved by themselves. They must be related closely to the total production processes, and they may in some cases have a bearing on other aspects of the firm's operations as well. Frequently, the problem of reciprocity has to be faced; that is, whether to buy from companies which are customers of the firm or whether it may be advisable to place orders with companies who may become customers in the future.

Numerous losses can result from errors in the buying process, including delays of delivery resulting from faulty order placement or the necessity of making use of rush orders because needs have not been anticipated adequately in advance.

It is important to recognize that *goods well bought are half sold*. In most business firms, purchasing, thus, becomes an important key to successful operations. It has been given increasing attention by the managers of business firms of all types and is a field of expanding opportunity.

In larger companies a purchasing agent or similar official will be given the responsibility for buying the materials needed for operations. His position in the organization will vary with the type of work in which it is engaged. Often he reports to the president, in some cases to the chief financial officer or chief production officer. In retail operations buying is of such importance that purchasing may be centered in the merchandising manager or in a vice-president. Closely related to procurement problems are those of the transportation and storage of the required materials. Also the reclamation of scrap and waste materials represents a closely related set of problems.

Processing

The processing stage of production includes manufacturing operations or those which correspond to this stage in nonmanufacturing firms. For example, in a warehousing firm processing is largely a matter of materials handling; in a bank it includes the handling of money and documents; in a legal firm the preparation of briefs; and in a grocery store the movement of goods from delivery to the store to the hands of the customer.

Thus, the processing stage of production may be a relatively simple activity, or it may involve the most complicated types of machine operations. From a management standpoint the most important decisions tend to center around (1) the type of processing, (2) the rate of output, and (3) the maintenance of standards.

In earlier stages of our history handicraft methods of manufacturing were used to a predominant extent. In some firms these are still adequate. Processing is accomplished largely by direct labor using simple hand tools. In most fields, however, it is advantageous for business firms to break down processing activities into small units and to use machines to do the work, that is, to apply the principles of mass production.

In order to make such processing economically possible, large-scale operations usually are required. Also, machines must operate as nearly automatically as possible, have interchangeable parts, and be relatively easy to repair. Even in small-scale operations, the substitution of machines for hand operations is often practical. Office type operations, for example, are making increasing use of accounting and statistical machines.

In most firms a choice must be made between *continuous processing* or *processing to order*. Continuous processing usually involves production for an impersonal and often a mass market. Processing to order involves job lots with production being undertaken for specific customers. In this case sales usually precede production; in continuous operations sales typically are made after production is completed. In some cases processing is carried on intermittently to replenish the firm's inventory.

Various combinations of these alternatives also may be followed. For example, automobile manufacturers typically produce for a general mass market. Some cars of completely standardized design may be produced on a continuous basis, others of less standardized design may be produced in intermittent lots to replenish finished inventory as they are sold. Still others with unique design features will be made to order, being sold in advance of manufacture; for example, a completely bullet-proof "bubbletop" car for the President or other head of state. When all three types of processing are performed in one plant, the scheduling and controlling of operations often represents a highly complex set of problems.

The National Homes Corporation, a large manufacturer of prefabricated houses, engages in continuous processing, but all houses are sold in advance of being made; thus, production processes are operated continuously but materials are scheduled on a job-order basis. In this case the local builder-dealer, whose work corresponds roughly to that of an automobile dealer, sells houses from samples, that is, from "show houses" or demonstration houses, and orders from one of the plants of the parent company the number of houses he needs and arranges the time of delivery to coincide with his local processing operations.

This is an interesting case of the use of both handicraft and large-scale manufacturing operations in the processing of a final product. The local builder-dealer uses machines to an increasing extent but still relies on handicraft methods to a degree in assembling the panels and other house components that have been processed in a factory by mass-production methods.

Rate of Output and Break-Even Points

One of the major management problems in the processing stage of production is that of establishing a desirable rate of output. Continuous operations may provide such economies that production may be carried forward, with finished goods held in inventory well in advance of sales. Unless sales materialize, however, the economies of continuous operations will be lost.

Managers typically are highly conscious of "break-even points" in their scale of operations. (Preliminary comments about the break-even point concept were made in the discussion in Chapters 6 and 13.) By this we mean the output required in order to cover costs, that is, to break even in terms of costs and returns. If markets are strong, all output beyond the break-even point may be sold at a profit. As we observed in our discussions in Chapter 13 a business firm typically incurs both fixed and variable costs. In combination these represent total costs. Such total costs will rise as output rises up to a point but not as rapidly as total revenue. Thereafter, added output will add to profits, since total revenues are increasing more rapidly than total costs. The break-even point, as you will recall, occurs where total costs and total revenues are in balance.

Problems of break-even analysis are more complicated if a firm makes several products and each has a different break-even point. Modern mathematical techniques have been helpful in solving problems of this type. Also, we should remember that the market will not always absorb all that a firm can produce without some downward adjustment in price. This would tend to shift the break-even point, since such a downward adjustment in price would affect all units and not only the final ones produced. An exception, of course is that of a "clearance sale" to dispose of an inventory erroneously purchased or produced in excess of market demand at normal price, for example, style goods.

In some cases firms find it advantageous to use existing plant and facilities more intensively by operating on a two- or three-shift basis. This tends to wear out the equipment more rapidly, and thus, sets up still another variable to complicate management decisions.

A firm may find it desirable in special situations to operate with some employees working overtime. This raises production costs, of course. But it may be desirable to meet the requirements of special customers, to adjust to overloads of some machines so as to avoid making additions to others, to test out a market before making larger commitments for equipment, or for other reasons.

Thus, it should be apparent that the determination of a desirable rate of output involves a number of difficult decisions. Such decisions tend to increase in complexity as a firm adds more product lines and markets.

Flow of Work

Efficient operations usually require careful co-ordination of the flow of work, especially in the processing stage of production, although this is true of other aspects of the firm's activities as well. One step in production typically depends on a preceding one and in turn sets the stage for the next.

Materials must be procured at a rate that will support the various steps in processing. The rate of processing must be co-ordinated with sales or requirements for further steps in production.

The importance of the flow of work has been stressed by Sir Frederic Hooper who has said in this connection:

The scientific approach to production commences with a complete analysis of the job, down to its smallest single component part. The production of each is preplanned in terms of the optimum material and taking account of the resources in labour and plant available. The whole is then fitted into a closely-integrated programme of production, the ideal of which is that each component shall be ready on time, in the correct balance of quantities, at the right place; that the flow of work shall be logical and in a single direction; that the distances travelled and the amount of lifting and handling during this flow shall be the minimum possible; that machines and men shall be employed to capacity, without breaks or delays due to shortages or errors in the programme; that supervision of the programme at each point is adequate and exercises complete control in timing, quality, and quantity. The result is a pattern of very great complexity, always in motion, yet never, in the ideal, allowed to fall out of rhythm or balance.[6]

Analysis of Work Processing

A number of techniques ranging from relatively simple flow charts to exceedingly complex mathematical models are used by managers to aid them in reaching rational decisions in regard to production processes. Flow charts and diagrams are used to show the order of occur-

---

[6] Sir Frederic Hooper, *Management Survey* (2nd ed.; New York: Pitman Publishing Corp., 1961), pp. 39–40, by permission.

rence of events. Standard symbols are used by many firms to show such sequences of events. For example, note the following:

Operation: This includes any work done. When blacked in this symbol indicates "do" operations in contrast to "make-ready" or "put-away" activities; make-ready activities referring to preparations necessary to do the work, and put-away referring to returning tools to proper places, cleaning up, and the like.

Inspection: This symbol refers to any comparison of work activities with predetermined plans or standards.

Transportation: This symbol refers to the movement of materials and the like between work centers or stations and storage.

Storage: This symbol indicates any delay or storage of material, workers, or paper work—which may involve delays in regular work flows.[7]

Symbols of this type are used in developing flow-process charts indicating how a particular set of operations should be carried out. It becomes in effect a highly "programed" decision at this stage.

In addition to flow charts, *multiple activity* charts often are used to record the times required to do work which involves both men and machines of various types. Again standard symbols are generally used.

		Man	*Machine*
	Independent Activity:	Work that is independent of a machine or other worker.	Work done by a machine without help of an operator or worker.
	Combined Activity:	Work done in co-operation with a machine or other worker.	Operating time when an operator is needed for the machine.
	Idle:	Time in waiting for machine.	Time in waiting for operator.[8]

Also in use are operator charts which show the essential activities or motions of a worker in performing a particular job. Routine sequence diagrams indicate the flow of information to points where work is done and then the flow of work. Assembly diagrams indicate the requirements as to working time for subassembly and final assembly of products.

---

[7] See Bowman and Fetter, *op. cit.,* p. 39.
[8] *Ibid.,* p. 44.

Widely used aids to the management of production processes are the Gantt Charts. As Bowman and Fetter point out:

The concept of the Gantt chart is simple. Vertically are listed the kinds of capacities to which various requirements must be allocated or orders to which capacities are to be apportioned. The horizontal axis represents the available time for this work. Allocation is accomplished by assigning the times necessary for performance of the given tasks to the available capacities or requirements by trial and error until some feasible fit is discovered. This, then, becomes the program for the time covered by the chart, and the chart may be used as a control device on performance. As the passage of time reveals under- or over-performance, the various allocations can be shifted to conform with new information.[9]

We reproduce in Figure 18–2 an illustration of a Gantt chart. Such charts are used for scheduling work loads and determining progress.

In addition managers make use of block diagrams, organization

FIGURE 18–2

Gantt Layout Chart

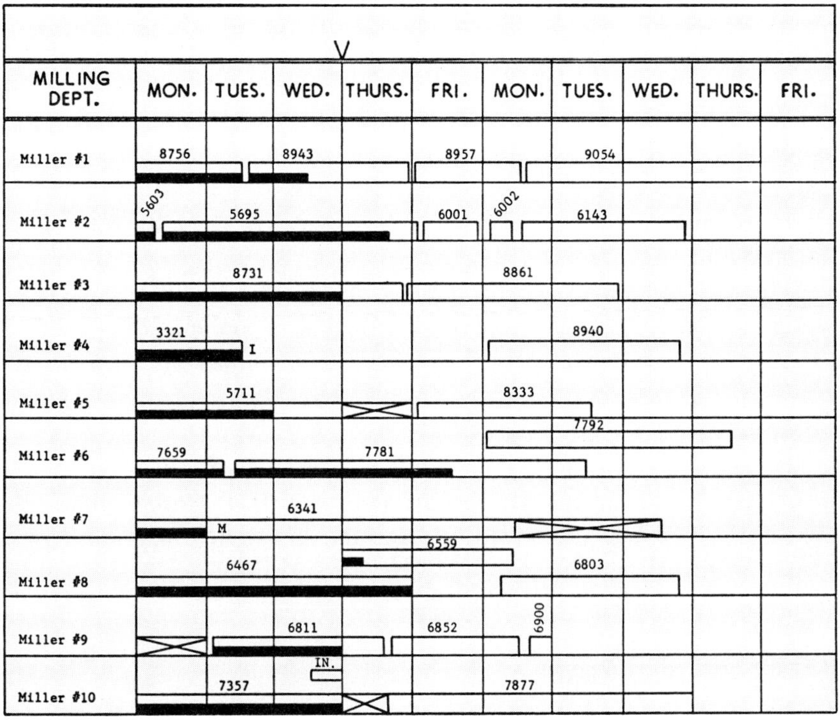

MILLING DEPT.	MON.	TUES.	WED.	THURS.	FRI.	MON.	TUES.	WED.	THURS.	FRI.
Miller #1	8756		8943		8957		9054			
Miller #2	5603	5695			6001	6002	6143			
Miller #3		8731				8861				
Miller #4	3321		I				8940			
Miller #5		5711				8333				
Miller #6	7659			7781			7792			
Miller #7		M	6341							
Miller #8		6467			6559		6803			
Miller #9			6811		6852	6900				
Miller #10		7357	IN.		7877					

From Bowman and Fetter, *Analysis for Production Management* (rev. ed.; Homewood, Ill.: Richard D. Irwin, Inc., 1961), p. 57.

_____

[9] *Ibid.*, p. 55, by permission.

charts, and similar methods to assist them in managing production processes. Major advances in recent years, however, have come in the use of mathematical, statistical, and economic analyses, most of which are beyond the scope of our discussions here. Introductory outlines of some of these types of analyses were presented in Chapter 14. We should note here that linear programing has been of vital help to the solution of many production management problems. You may wish to review our earlier discussion of this topic or refer to Bowman and Fetter, *Analysis for Production Management*, rev. ed., to which we have made several references.

Production Standards

Another important aspect of production is the maintenance of standards. Most goods and also services must meet certain standards if they are to be marketable. Standards may be qualitative or quantitative in character; the former have greatest bearing on acceptability to buyers, the latter on production costs and operating rates. *Inspection* of finished products, either item by item or on a sample basis is a typical method of assuring the maintenance of standards. *Reactions of customers,* of course, provide the final test. Such reactions will be conditioned at least in part by the competition of other products.

The maintenance of standards is a complicated matter when processing includes many stages of manufacturing. In such cases the quality of the results of one stage have an important bearing on the succeeding stage, and to a degree the reverse is true as well. In the case of the prefabricated house manufacturer and his local builder-dealer to which we referred, the success of the local builder-dealer's operations will depend to a large extent on the quality of the components delivered to him from the factory. In turn, the success of the manufacturer depends at least to a degree on the standards of construction maintained by the builder-dealer.

This subject could be discussed at considerable length. It has many interesting ramifications. In recent years statistical control methods have helped greatly in developing standards and in measuring performance against such standards. The use of sampling in inspection has increased greatly.

Maintenance and Repair

Almost all types of production activities require maintenance, repair, janitorial, and related services. An office must be kept clean, its typewriters and calculating machines in repair, and its furniture in good condition. A store requires continuous attention to the condition of displays, equipment, windows, and its general appearance. In large factories maintenance is a major operation, including everything from keeping the premises and the plant clean and orderly to testing, servicing, and repairing major pieces of equipment. Waste products must be disposed of, and sometimes this is a very costly process. In other instances waste and scrap products have a ready market or may be used in a secondary production operation.

Even if all other phases of production are well managed and handled, lack of adequate maintenance and repair programs may lead to ultimate failure. Sound programs, on the other hand, help to prolong the life of machines, and thus reduce costs; they may prevent breakdowns of machines and costly work stoppages, and they often have a bearing on the attitudes of workers and customers.

A poorly maintained place of business repels rather than attracts customers and often sets the stage for slipshod rather than neat and orderly work. Poor maintenance often suggests inefficient management, and thus may affect the point of view of prospective investors, bankers, or others.

Production Costs

Nearly all production problems finally center in costs. If costs cannot be kept below selling prices, except perhaps for brief periods, failure will inevitably result. There are many concepts of costs, as we have pointed out; see Chapter 13, for example.

For management decisions *anticipated costs* or future costs are more important than past or historical or original costs. While past decisions that have committed a firm to a line of action may affect costs in the future, it is impossible to make the decisions over again. All that can be done is to take action that may result in a more favorable future cost situation.

Costs will vary with the *mixture* of labor, equipment, materials, or other resources used in the production process. Thus, it is often helpful to state problems of cost in terms of units of "input" relative to units of "output." This is another way of saying costs relative to returns, but by stressing the idea of units of input we recognize more readily that costs are not usually fixed; that by varying the proportion of "input items," for example, labor and machines, costs may vary significantly. For example, high wages may be compensated for in part by the use of more machinery or by stepping up research and development programs which will lead to improved production methods.

If a manager believes that wage rates will continue to advance over a period of years, he will probably try to bring in laborsaving machinery as rapidly as possible. If he thinks that wages will stabilize, he may introduce such machinery more slowly.

Cost will typically vary with the *level and rate of output,* with *size of plant, efficiency of management,* and related things as well as with the mixture of input factors.[10] For every production activity there is an optimum or most favorable size of plant. In some operations this means that costs tend to decline as plant is increased in size until finally a point is reached where costs either stabilize or move upward. Most mass-production manufacturing operations are of this type. In other cases the best size for production activities is a relatively small one, since costs begin to move upward at an early stage as output is expanded. Firms in the personal service fields typically have this type of cost experience. Increased mechanization and automation will tend to favor larger-scale operations.

Efficiency of management, of course, affects all aspects of a business firm's operations and has a definite bearing on costs. In some firms managers are not sufficiently aware of their cost problems or fail to give adequate study to them. In others, costs are analyzed with care, and efforts are made to keep them at their most desirable levels relative to potential returns. Also through research and development programs, attempts are made to introduce more efficient and less costly methods. In a final analysis, efficiency of management is a basic factor in determining the kind of cost pattern that a firm is likely to experience.

Disposition of Products

After processing takes place, products must be disposed of. Usually production is undertaken for the purpose of having something to sell. Thus, *sales* represent the final disposition of products. As we have suggested, however, production may at times be carried on for the purpose of making *additions to inventory.* It may be desirable to maintain a given level of inventory, and whenever supplies drop below this level, production may be increased in order to re-establish it. Sometimes certain ratios must be maintained between the availability of two or more products, and this may require some production for inventory.

The purpose of one stage of processing may be the provision of ma-

---

10 See Dean, *op. cit.,* p. 253.

terials for the next. In this case disposition is not through final sales but through the *supplying of the next stage of processing.* If these stages are separated by companies, of course, disposition is made through sales.

The processing of some products follows a seasonal pattern because supplies become available at certain times during the year. This is true, for example, in the canning industry. In such cases peak levels of production are attained at certain times and products must be stored for future sales. Costs of storage including not only rental of space but supervision, maintenance, insurance, and all related costs may be very great. In other cases they can be absorbed and, thus, allow a firm to more nearly regularize processing between seasons.

Inventory Control

In recent years business managers have paid increasing attention to the control of inventories with a view to increasing efficiency of operations. Ideally, inventories of goods, whether they are for sale or for use in processing activities, should be maintained at optimum levels with no overflows, on the one hand, and no gaps in the availability of materials, on the other. This requires careful determination of the rates at which purchases or other methods of procurement must be arranged to maintain the desired levels of inventory.

Proper inventory control is an important key to the flow of materials through the production process. This depends on careful order planning, receipt and storage of materials, inspection of materials as received, identification and labeling of materials, routing them directly to production or to stock rooms or to sales floors as required.

Effective inventory control rests on an adequate *record system.* The use of accounting and statistical machines has greatly facilitated this work for business firms.

At least once a year most business firms take a complete inventory in order to determine the amount of goods on hand and to classify them by type. Such periodic counting is necessary to determine losses of materials or goods through damage, misplacement, or theft, or the deterioration of materials that may result from the passage of time. This periodic counting is also desirable to establish an accurate value of inventory which is needed to determine operating cost for the period covered. Determining the item "cost of goods sold" in the profit and loss statement requires an accurate figure for the value of ending inventory. (See the discussion in Chapter 12.)

Analytical Methods

In recent years substantial progress has been made in adapting statistical, mathematical, and economic analyses to the solution of various problems related to production management decisions. We referred to some of these in Chapters 13 and 14, and to several of them in our discussions in this chapter. Many of them are beyond the scope of our discussions here. We should note, however, that several types have come into widespread use, and you will undoubtedly be encountering them in your more advanced studies. For example, "total value analysis" offers a number of mathematical models that have managerial uses. The problem of economic lot size is one of these uses, that is, deciding the size of the lots of goods that will be put into stock at various intervals. Determination of scale of operations is a similar use—deciding how large a particular operation should be such as a plant, a warehouse, or other production unit. Inventory problems of various types are also adaptable to these types of analytical methods, as are servicing problems, waiting time problems, and many others.

We should remember, however, that a manager often has an opportunity to change the conditions in which he is operating. Often analytical methods of the type referred to above indicate when, in what directions, and to what extent the manager should try to change the conditions surrounding a problem. Such action may be more desirable than simply relying on the solutions to which analytical methods point.

SUMMARY

In order for a business firm to have something to sell it must produce goods or services or both. Production is the process of creating values or adding values. It includes changing the *form* of things, for example, manufacturing; changing location or *place* available, for example, transportation; provision at desired *times* and in convenient amounts, as in the case of wholesaling or retailing; or providing for repairs or serving the convenience needs of customers or clients.

Production programs are of basic importance in achieving the firm's objectives and are closely co-ordinated with other programs, especially marketing. The financial and other resources of the firm must be adequate to carry the production programs desired.

Major production decisions include those related to such problems as what to produce, whether to buy or make, and the type of processing that will be utilized. Product line planning requires choices between single and multiple products, related or not related, in various possible "product mix" alternatives. Decisions usually turn on anticipated effect on profits, that is, on expected cost-risk-return relationships. Strategic considerations often are involved as well.

Design of products usually is based on market studies but centers around the mechanics of design and the aesthetics of design. Once a product has been designed the necessary production processes and methods are designed to meet desired standards at competitive costs.

Among procurement problems are those related to the general choice of making or buying products or using various possible combinations of these alternatives. Expected effect on profit usually is the controlling factor in such decisions.

Processing includes manufacturing operations or comparable operations that correspond to manufacturing in a nonmanufacturing business, for example, the processing of checks in a bank. Major alternatives are continuous processing or processing to order. Various combinations also may be possible. The rate of output often is dependent on various types of costs and their combination in relation to market opportunities and competitive conditions. Problems related to rate of output often are extremely difficult in multiproduct firms.

Analysis of work processing is important in achieving efficiency of production. Various techniques such as flow charts and diagrams, multiple activity charts, Gantt charts, and others are used. Production standards and controls play an important part in successful operations. Production costs or potential changes in costs often are controlling factors.

Products may be disposed of through sales, by adding to inventory, or by supplying the next stage of processing. Inventory controls have improved with the introduction of new techniques.

Analytical methods are being used increasingly in the solution of production problems, particularly as statistical, mathematical, and economic analyses have been adapted to these purposes. Such methods may indicate to managers how the conditions surrounding a problem may be changed to advantage, as well as pointing to specific solutions to the problem.

QUESTIONS AND PROBLEMS

1. What is meant by "production"? Does a grocery store engage in production? Why or why not?
2. What types of value are created or added by an airline? A manufacturing plant? A bank? A retail store?
3. What is meant by the statement, "sales begin even before production starts"?

4. You are engaged in the production of outdoor sporting goods. On what bases would you decide whether to add a line of indoor sporting goods?
5. What is meant by a desirable "product mix" for a firm?
6. Give an illustration of a situation in which it might be desirable to continue producing an item though its profitability has declined.
7. What is meant by "product design"? Indicate some of the major factors involved in the design of production processes and methods.
8. You are engaged in the production and sale of office supplies. Your plant is operating at capacity. Your sales force, however, seems able to handle more business. What might you do under these circumstances, reduce your sales force, add another product line, or take other action?
9. Differentiate between continuous processing and processing to order. Give illustrations of each type.
10. How may "break-even" analysis affect decisions relative to rate of output?
11. What does this symbol $\bigtriangledown$ indicate in flow charts or diagrams? This symbol?
12. Why are maintenance and repair programs important in production operations?
13. What are production standards? Why are they important? How does a manager make sure that production standards are being met?
14. Do high wages necessarily mean high production costs? Why or why not?
15. Why is inventory control important to managers?

SUGGESTED READINGS

BOWMAN, EDWARD H., and FETTER, ROBERT B. *Analysis for Production Management*. Rev. ed. Homewood, Ill.: Richard D. Irwin, Inc., 1961. This is a relatively advanced book, but the first chapter, "Introduction," is of a general type and may stimulate your interest in this subject.

DEAN, JOEL. *Managerial Economics*. New York: Prentice-Hall, Inc., 1951. Read chap. 3, "Multiple Products."

LONG, JOHN D. *Workbook to Accompany Weimer: Business Administration: An Introductory Management Approach,* chap. 18. Rev. ed. Homewood, Ill.: Richard D. Irwin, Inc., 1962.

OUTLINE FOR CHAPTER 19

MARKETING is a basic function of every business firm; effective DECISIONS AND OPERATIONS in this field are vital to its success.

Markets arise from the mutually beneficial nature of exchange; They perform major functions for the economy by indicating what should be produced, how much, and for whom.

Understanding the *market environment* is essential to developing and carrying out successful marketing programs.

Demand analysis helps management to understand the conditions under which products will be sold. Major factors likely to influence demand for a product include:

price of the product,
prices of substitute or complementary products,
incomes of consumers and their borrowing capacity, and
preferences of consumers.

Sales forecasts may be based on demand analyses and help to determine product lines, rate of output, price policies, market strategies, and financial requirements.

Cost and profit analyses are at least as important in marketing as production.

Product selection is basic to successful marketing programs; marketing really begins even before production starts.

Promotion policies and programs include advertising, sales, and related programs.

Selection of *marketing channels* often depends on firm's position in market.

Prices and price policies are related to the competitive situation, estimated sales levels, and costs; plus alternatives to price competition.

19 MARKETING: DECISIONS AND OPERATIONS

But without the disposition to truck, barter and exchange, every man must have procured to himself every necessary and conveniency of life which he wanted.

—ADAM SMITH

Marketing and Top-Management Decisions

In our preceding discussions we have stressed repeatedly the concept that business managers make use of a variety of resources in order to produce goods and services that can be marketed in order to provide revenue. In this chapter we pay particular attention to the marketing aspects of the manager's work.

We indicated at various points in our discussions that many marketing decisions are so closely related to production decisions and to decisions as to the financial and other resources required to secure net revenue that they are made by the chief executive officer. Many of the major planning decisions are based on marketing considerations; for example, probable changes in markets often are the major causes of changes in basic company policies and programs. In addition to the role of marketing factors in top-management decisions, many management problems are related more specifically to the marketing of products. For example, a decision as to the size and general nature of the advertising program usually will be made by top management; a decision as to the allocation of the program between different types of advertising media is more likely to be made by the marketing manager.

In business firms of smaller size the chief executive officer typically makes many of the marketing decisions himself. As firms increase in size the marketing function tends to become more highly differentiated. Many firms have marketing managers or vice-presidents for marketing. Reporting to the marketing manager may be a sales manager, advertising manager, a market research manager, and other officials.

Also, in some cases the work related to marketing will be divided according to products or on some other basis.

Regardless of how organized, the work of the marketing manager (or similar executive, regardless of specific title) is concerned with sales to produce revenue for the firm. The marketing manager often participates in central or general firm decisions, particularly as marketing factors are involved; in addition he directs activities related to the making of sales including required analyses of markets and the market environment, and the development of effective programs for meeting the competition of other firms with respect to products, promotional efforts, and prices. He is concerned also with the marketing of his products (goods or services) on bases that will exceed costs and thus enable the firm to survive, grow, and pursue prestige or other objectives.[1]

Range of Marketing Decisions

As we have suggested, market decisions range all the way from those that affect the profit objectives and the very survival of the firm to those related to specific marketing programs such as the selection and training of sales personnel. Our discussions of the general subject of marketing and marketing management will be divided into two broad parts: first, the determination of the market situation and environment within which a firm's products may be sold; and second, selecting and developing programs to meet market conditions.

With respect to the determination of the market situation we consider types of markets, demand analysis, sales forecasting, and related topics. In the selection and development of marketing programs the following subjects are considered:

1. Selection of effective products.
2. Choice of potentially successful promotional policies and programs.
   a) Advertising programs.
   b) Sales organization and effort.
3. Selection of marketing channels.
4. Determination of appropriate prices, price structures, and policies.

Before turning to a consideration of each of the topics outlined above, we discuss briefly the significance of markets in our society, the

---

[1] Our discussion in this chapter centers around marketing management in relation to other management functions. Marketing has been stressed increasingly in recent years. Indeed, Peter Drucker maintains that the two primary functions of business firms are marketing and innovation. See his *The Practice of Management* (New York: Harper & Bros., 1954), p. 37. See also Richard H. Buskirk, *Principles of Marketing* (New York: Holt, Rinehart & Winston, Inc., 1961), pp. 10–12.

relationship of the firm to its market environment, and the interrelations between marketing and production.

Role of Markets

If you have ever sold or traded anything, you have had some experience with marketing. You know from such experience that sales result from an agreement to exchange certain things—books for money, history books for mathematics books, fountain pens for notebooks, and the like. As a practical matter money enters into nearly all of the transactions that take place.

As we have pointed out, *exchange is a mutually beneficial proposition*. If you buy a fountain pen for five dollars, you must want the pen more than the five dollars and the merchant who sold the pen to you must want the five dollars more than the pen. Otherwise no exchange would occur (unless some element of compulsion were involved). Thus, in a free society there would be no buying or selling if exchange were not a mutually beneficial proposition.

Through exchange it is possible for each of us to *specialize* in the type of work he likes best and to exchange the income from such work for goods and services. Through exchange it is possible for a business firm to specialize in one or a few products and through their sale to obtain income for workers, owners, and creditors as well as for further production.

Exchange takes place in markets. Some markets are highly organized like the great commodity and security exchanges such as the Chicago Board of Trade and the New York Stock Exchange. Other markets are very informal affairs with no very direct ways of bringing buyers and sellers together. Some markets are world-wide in scope, like the market for wheat; others are limited to a single community, like the market for single-family homes. Regardless of degree of organization or scope, markets reflect the relative strength of buyers and sellers through the prices that are set by competition. Markets may be specific places like the stock exchange or may be less formally organized. It is often helpful to think of a market as an area over which buyers and sellers are in sufficiently close communication so that the same product will sell for substantially the same price. Thus, under highly competitive conditions, with allowance for transportation costs, a market would be the area in which a product would be sold for only one price at a given time. This is what we mean by saying that the market for wheat is world-wide in scope; wheat sells for substantially the same price in London as Chicago (allowing for shipping charges). Single-family houses, however, might sell for a great deal more in Chicago than London or New York or Detroit. The market for single-family houses is limited to a local area because the supply available cannot be moved from one place to another.

We use markets to make many of our general economic decisions regarding what is to be produced, how much, and for whom. If buyers bid up the price of fountain pens, for example, business firms will undertake to produce more of them. Some of us, however, as a result of the higher prices, will prefer not to buy fountain pens or to buy fewer of them, and thus the higher prices *ration* or allocate the pens among those who want them most. Through prices markets indicate what people want and are willing to pay for, how productive resources will be allocated among a variety of uses, and the rate at which economic growth and progress will take place.

We use competitive markets in this country, thus, to perform a number of significant economic functions for us. If these functions were not performed through markets, it would be necessary to have them performed by direct government action or in some other way. Because of our reliance on markets, we undertake through various government programs to make them as competitive as possible. If monopolies develop, we either regulate them directly, recognizing that competition may not work effectively in the field involved, or break up concentrations of economic power so as to restore competition. Some markets are more competitive than others. The market for some luxury goods such as fur coats, for example, is generally not as competitive as the market for wheat. But there is enough competition to allow for reasonably effective allocations of resources and products.

The degree of competition that exists in markets is a factor of major concern for business managers. In highly competitive markets their range of choice and action is much more limited than in markets where varying degrees of imperfect competition or oligopoly prevail, as we pointed out in Chapter 13.

As we suggested in the preceding chapter, production may be thought of as the process of *creating values*. This concept includes more than changing the form of things as in manufacturing. It includes also changing their location and availability as well as the provision of related services. In the same vein, marketing may be thought of as a later stage in the process of making values available to users. Thus, the values created by the firm must be *transferred* to others in exchange for revenue.

Such transfers are usually made through sales. In some cases outright sales are not involved, since goods may be leased for a period of time, that is, rented rather than being sold. In such cases there is a transfer of the use of things even though ownership is not transferred, hence, marketing has still taken place.

Similarly, the performance of services may be thought of as resulting from a transfer or sale. For example, you exchange money for a haircut. This is a sale and differs little from your purchase of a package of cigarettes or a bar of candy.

Marketing processes may be thought of as *adding values* for the users of goods and services. Many costs are incurred in arranging for the transfer of goods and services from business firms to users. Such costs add values to the final utilities (or satisfactions) of the users of goods and services. Advertising may add to the attractiveness of one product over another in the mind of the ultimate buyer. Sales effort may influence a buyer to prefer one set of goods and services to another and add to the final satisfaction of the user.

Specialized Marketing Firms

As we have pointed out, every business firm engages in marketing. This is one of its primary functions. Some business firms, however, specialize in the marketing of goods or services for others. These include wholesalers, manufacturer's agent, brokers, retailers, and others. Each of these types may be broken down further into numerous divisions. Thus, the "service wholesaler" buys merchandise in large lots, resells it in smaller units, provides storage facilities as required, extends credit, maintains a sales force, and makes deliveries. By contrast there are "limited service" wholesalers who may not extend credit, or may not maintain a sales force but rely on mail orders, or may not provide storage as in the case of a "drop shipper," and the like. Similarly, there are many types of retailers, including department stores, specialty shops, mail-order houses, chain stores, independent retailers, and others.[2] And, of course, various combinations may exist such as a chain of department stores or a combination of mail-order and chain-store operations. Some firms may specialize in the marketing of industrial or "producers" goods; others in "consumer" goods. Specialized marketing firms may also include advertising agencies, market research organizations, and others.

Specialized marketing firms, like manufacturing firms, engage in production activities, as we have pointed out. Typically, however, they do not make things, or more specifically change the form of things. They procure by buying; they process by making goods or

---

[2] See Kenneth R. Davis, *Marketing Management* (New York: Ronald Press Co., 1961), p. 138.

services available in convenient amounts, places, and times; and they dispose of things by sale or lease either to final consumers or to another stage in the production process. Specialized marketing firms, of course, stress marketing activities, and that is why we make particular mention of them here.

Our discussions in the remainder of this chapter, however, center around the management of marketing operations regardless of whether a manufacturing firm, a financial institution, a specialized marketing business, or some other type of business firm is under consideration. We do this because the basic function of marketing is much the same for all types of business firms.

The Market Environment

As we have suggested, the management of the marketing activities of a business firm requires, first, an understanding of the market situation in which the products of the firm must be sold; and, second, the development and execution of programs which will result in the successful sale of products within this situation.[3] In other words, the marketing or sales manager must understand the environment in which he is working before he can develop effective marketing programs.

In some cases the manager has limited opportunity to affect the environment or set of conditions in which his products are sold. This is typically the case in highly competitive situations. In other situations, usually where competition is less intense, the manager may, through promotional programs, be able to influence in varying degrees the market environment.

As one author aptly points out: "For our purposes, we shall recognize those factors that are beyond the control of the firm as demand conditions to which the firm must adapt. Those factors that are *within* its control are demand conditions that the firm can manipulate.[4]

In either case the manager needs an understanding of the forces at work. For example, general business conditions, the situation in the industry or line of business, the extent and intensity of competition, income levels, regional factors, and government policies are all among the forces likely to affect the market for a product.

General business conditions, that is, the degree of prosperity or recession, will be an important consideration. Similarly, conditions within a given line or type of business are generally considered. For

---

[3] See John H. Howard, *Marketing Management* (Homewood, Ill.: Richard D. Irwin, Inc., 1957), p. 3.

[4] By permission, Davis, *op. cit.*, p. 207.

example, the market for TV sets or for some other product may be weak even if general business conditions are favorable.

The markets for producer's goods (machines, trucks, and the like) typically present different conditions from those for consumer's goods (food, clothing, pleasure cars, etc.). Also, the markets for perishable and durable goods vary widely, as do the markets for goods in contrast to those for services.

As we have suggested, competition is carried on very broadly in the modern economy. To a degree *every product is in competition with every other one* for a slice of the consumer's dollar. There is competition between saving and spending for current things, and between spending for one good or service as against another. Also the markets for goods and services in one field will have a bearing on those of another; for example, new and used cars; automobiles and tires; synthetic fibers and cotton and wool.

General levels of income have an important effect on markets. Markets are not simply people, but rather, *people with money in their pockets or the ability to command credit.* The demand for many products will vary with income levels. Typically the demand for durable goods like automobiles, refrigerators, television sets, radios, and the like will vary considerably as incomes change. If incomes fall, the demand for such goods tends to drop even more sharply probably because purchases of this type are postponable. The demands for some services are quite responsive to income changes including taxi rides, domestic services, and others.

There are some important regional differences in markets. For example, in some regions incomes tend to advance faster than the national average during a period of prosperity; in others they rise more slowly. As we point out in Chapter 24 there are significant differences between international markets.

Markets are influenced by governmental policies, not only with respect to the regulation of markets or prices as in the case of the antitrust laws or "fair-trade" regulations but also tax laws and changes in such laws, monetary and credit policies, defense spending programs, highway construction, and many other government activities.

Degree of Competition

One of the important factors for management to consider in the development of marketing programs is the degree of competition for the sales of a product. If a product is generally standardized and there are many buyers and sellers with general freedom of entry into the market, competitive conditions tend to exist. By contrast, if there are only a few sellers, they may be able to regulate the supplies put on the market and thus control prices to their advantage.

As we have seen, there may be varying degrees of competition in markets, depending on the number of firms, the number of customers or suppliers, and the extent to which there may be co-operative agreements between firms in the market. Conditions may range from highly competitive situations to those with varying degrees of imperfect competition, oligopoly, or monopoly. In some markets a particular firm may enjoy a *leadership* position; that is, it is sufficiently strong that other firms typically follow its lead, especially in making price changes. United States Steel is a case in point.

To some extent products may be "differentiated" by giving them brand names. This introduces an element of monopoly into what would otherwise be a competitive market situation. For example, "Palmolive Soap" is differentiated from soap in general; "Ford cars" from other cars; and "Pendleton" shirts from shirts in general. While a degree of competition prevails in markets for products of this type, buyers usually do not move as easily from one product to another when prices are changed as they would in the markets for more highly standardized goods.

Sometimes competition becomes chaotic. For example, "cutthroat" competition may develop if demand deteriorates and firms find it necessary to sell below costs because of the heavy investments and fixed charges they are carrying. Sometimes "predatory" competition develops, as in the case of one company deliberately pricing below cost in order to drive its competitors out of business.

Managers usually study the market situation in which they operate with great care. The degree of competition that exists has an important bearing on the extent to which the demand for a product may be manipulated.

Demand Analysis

To an increasing extent managers are undertaking analyses of demand in order to develop a more complete understanding of the conditions under which their products are sold. The analysis of demand rests in part on economic principles and theory and in part on concepts developed by behavioral scientists, including sociologists, psychologists, and cultural anthropologists.

The factors that are most likely to influence the demand for a product are (1) the price of the product; (2) prices of substitute products or complementary products; (3) incomes of consumers plus their ability to borrow; and (4) the preferences of consumers. The first three of these represent largely economic considerations. The fourth, however, represents a variety of factors and we rely increasingly on the behavioral sciences for explanations of consumer preferences.

The price of a product is a major factor in determining the demand for it. If the other three factors listed above are constant, then the higher the price of a product, the less will be the demand for it. (By "demand" we mean desire for the product plus the ability and willingness to pay for it.) Usually, however, the other factors listed above will also vary. Of major importance are the prices of substitute products. For example, if the price of beef goes down, the price of pork may be forced down, since people may substitute one for the other. The opposite effect may result in the case of complementary products; for example, if the price of razors goes down this may increase the sale of razor blades, even with no change in their price. We often refer to this situation as one of *joint demand.*

If the incomes of consumers decline, the demand for a product is likely to go down, even if its price is the same or somewhat lower. Demand may not go down if the price is dropped more than the decline in incomes, although the reactions of consumers under these conditions may vary widely as between products. Typically consumers will continue to buy necessities or what are often referred to as "conventional necessities," that is things considered necessary to a certain scale or standard of living, even when their incomes decline but they will reduce substantially their purchases of products considered less essential. We should note that a tightening of credit, for example, increasing interest rates or the terms on which money can be borrowed or credit extended by sellers, may have an effect generally comparable to a decline in incomes. When incomes rise, of course, demands tend to be stimulated. The demand for luxuries may be stimulated more than the demand for necessities. Easier borrowing terms and credit extensions may have much the same effect as a rise in incomes.

Consumer preferences arise from a wide variety of factors, many of which we find difficult to explain or understand. Some are due to custom and tradition or accepted standards of behavior. Some arise from reactions to style changes or fads. It may be considered fashionable to prefer one product to another. The preferences of social and community leaders may be followed by others. Professor Davis points out, for example:

. . . consumer behavior theory encompasses (1) the analysis of certain biological drives, an area examined largely by the psychologist in his laboratory; (2) the analysis of psychological drives, an area studied largely by the clinical psychologist who examines the balancing of biological drives with socially acceptable behavior; and (3) a final group that places greater emphasis on environment as against the individual, claiming that his motives can only be understood as we understand the environment in which he lives. This last group encompasses the area of social psychology. These avenues of analysis in studying consumer behavior are becoming increasingly important to marketing management.[5]

Motivation research has been developed to help explain consumer behavior, and if possible to establish cause and effect relationships. Often depth interviews are used in studies of this type.[6] There is considerable uncertainty as to how far in practice research of this type may prove to be useful. There is also uncertainty as to the applicability of various concepts of the behavioral scientists to the problems of the marketing manager. Progress in the use of such methods and concepts, however, is being made.

We should recognize that research in the general field of consumer preferences and behavior is difficult because in some cases consumers are themselves unaware of the reasons for their behavior or are unable to explain it. For some products consumers understand and are able to explain their likes and dislikes very well; for example, one ball-point pen writes better than another selling for the same price. Consumers often prefer one product over another, can explain their preferences, but are unwilling to tell others about their preferences. For example, you may buy a car in the higher-price field because of a feeling that it gives you a higher status in the eyes of your neighbors, and you might be unwilling or reluctant to admit or to discuss this reason for your decision. There may be subconscious reasons for consumer preferences that are susceptible to various interpretations, and the risks of drawing the wrong conclusions are very great.

Studies of consumer buying habits often are helpful in the analysis of demand. Finding out where a product typically is bought, whether for cash or credit, at what season of the year, and by which member of the family often throws light on consumer preferences as well as on buying habits. For example, if the sale of golf clubs goes up prior to the Christmas holidays, gift purchases probably are indicated.

---

[5] By permission from Davis, *op. cit.*, p. 222; see also, R. Ferber and H. Wales, *Motivation and Market Behavior* (Homewood, Ill.: Richard D. Irwin, Inc., 1958), especially pp. 4–14 by Charles Cannell and pp. 21–31 by Ernest Dichter.

[6] See for example, James F. Engel, "Motivation Research—Magic or Menace," *Michigan Business Review*, March, 1961, pp. 28–32.

Also studies of the behavior or potential behavior of competitors often throws light on the marketing manager's problems. The manner in which consumers react to the programs of competitors may help to guide management decisions. Also the range of choice of one firm relative to another may help in selecting marketing programs. For example, nonprice competition may offer greater possibilities than price competition for gaining a bigger part of the market, since competitors may be able to match price changes.

Sales Forecasts

Analysis of demand and related studies are usually undertaken in order to make sales forecasts. Of course, some firms may not undertake to study their markets or the demand for their products, or may study them only in a casual manner. Sometimes they are able to operate successfully simply because general market conditions are sufficiently favorable to allow them to do so. In other cases, however, failure to analyze market conditions may lead to disastrous results.

Sales forecasts may help to determine product lines, rate of output, price policies, market strategies, and financial requirements. Thus, the development of accurate sales forecasts often is of major importance in the successful operation of business firms. Such forecasts may form the basis for estimates of personnel, production, and financial requirements. Forecasts of sales potentials also guide the development of future marketing programs, for example, determining the extent and intensity of advertising campaigns, selection of price policies, allocation of sales personnel to various territories, and in other ways.

In developing sales forecasts various information based on analysis of demand typically is used. In some cases the market for an industry as a whole will be forecasted and then the company's share of this entire market will be estimated. Sometimes sample surveys are made. Reports of salesmen, since they are close to the market, often are helpful. Studies of past market performance may be useful, particularly if patterns or trends are revealed.

An interesting diagram of the elements in sales forecasting is presented in Figure 19–1.[7] This diagram shows how national and industry data, the firm's own records, reports based on consumer studies, and related data may be assembled and processed to provide forecasts that can be used as the basis for management decisions.

---

[7] See James B. Boulden, "Fitting the Sales Forecast to Your Firm," *Business Horizons,* Winter, 1958, p. 66.

FIGURE 19-1
Elements of Sales Forecasting

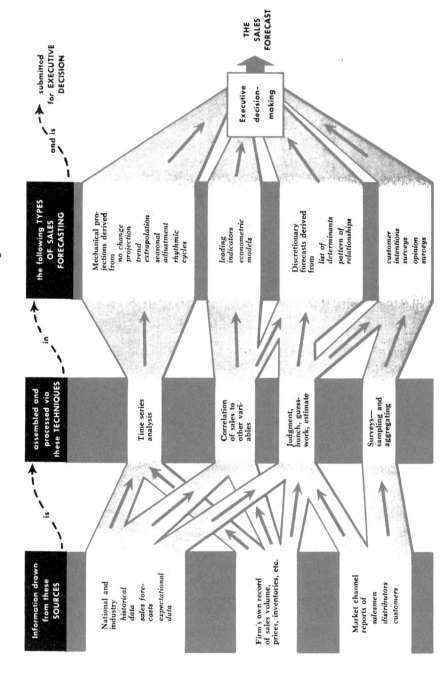

Cost and Profit Analysis

In the preceding chapter we discussed costs related to production. In Chapter 13 we referred to various types of costs incurred by the business firm. We should note here that a variety of costs is involved in marketing. "Selling expense" is one of the items that almost always appears in income and expense or profit and loss statements. For business firms as a whole marketing costs probably represent about half of the ultimate price of products. There are wide variations, however, between products, between goods and services, and between types of markets involved.

Advertising costs, and the salaries and commissions of salesmen, of course, are easily recognized as marketing costs. Often, however, it is difficult to allocate costs as between marketing and production or other functions of the business firm. The costs of a market analysis may be directly related to marketing, but may also be highly valuable in the design of products. Packaging a product in an attractive manner may be largely a marketing cost but production costs also are involved. Similarly, making a product available in a variety of styles and sizes will increase production costs, may require larger inventories, hence greater financial costs because inventory turnover is reduced.

Cost analysis typically is undertaken to allocate as realistically as possible the costs incurred so that the manager may be able to see more clearly than would otherwise be possible relationships between costs and revenues. He is concerned primarily with net revenues or profits. For example, advertising costs may be prohibitive unless they can be spread over a large enough number of units; salaries of salesmen may be out of line unless larger territories can be covered or unless each salesman can handle several products.

Most marketing costs have long-run effects, hence are hard to measure. An advertising campaign may have an effect on the sale of a product long after the campaign is over, hence, costs per unit of sales are most difficult to measure. Even so, it is often helpful to analyze costs, even if their measurement is difficult. Costs may be allocated between various marketing functions; for example, advertising, selling, warehousing, and the like. Costs may be allocated to individual products or groups of products, to territories, to various marketing channels, types of customers, sizes of orders, and to other bases.

Often cost allocations are arbitrary, hence, may lead to erroneous conclusions. It is possible in some cases to relate costs to contribution to profit. One territory may have a better record than another, one product may sell better and produce more revenue than another and through comparisons of this type, managers may be able to determine cost-profit relationships that are helpful in reaching decisions.

Profits as a percentage of sales may provide the manager with a useful measure. This is a widely used type of relationship. A more precise measure is profit as a percentage of investment. Both are used, often for different purposes.

Profits as a percentage of sales often provides an easy method for comparing the performance of firms in the same line of business, since it is often difficult to secure a realistic valuation of the investments of the firms. Similarly, profits as a percentage of sales may provide a useful comparison between the products or divisions of a firm. Managers usually look to sales volume, share of the market, and margins or markups in studying cost-profit relationships.

Marketing Programs and Product Selection

Studies and analyses of markets, as well as of the general economic, governmental, and social factors related to them, will indicate to managers the general conditions within which they may develop their marketing programs. (Some of these topics are considered at greater length in Part 5 of our discussions.) Such programs are the ways by which the managers develop revenue and pursue the firm's over-all objectives. For example, a firm may vary its products, its promotional programs, and its price structure and policies.

As we suggested in the preceding chapter, *marketing really begins even before production starts.* In a manufacturing firm, for example, the marketing manager may provide the factory manager and the chief executive with information that will be helpful in deciding whether to continue making present products; to change them to a greater or lesser extent, for example, improving their packaging or completely redesigning them; or to substitute new products for old ones. In a retailing firm problems of this type center in selecting goods for sale— the proper "mix" of goods and services and related decisions. A bank may develop new services or combine new services with established programs.

As we indicated in the preceding chapter the selection of product lines and the variation of products (including both goods and services) are among the important decisions for the management of a business firm to make, not only at the time the firm is started but at various times throughout its history.

When a new product idea is under consideration attempts are made to estimate the potential size of the market and the extent to which existing products are serving that market. Consideration is given also to the probable effect of the new product on present products sold by the company; for example, it may substitute for existing products and reduce their sales or stimulate sales by complementing them. Costs and profit potentials are usually weighed carefully. A new product may help to make use of surplus capacity, gain advantages in the purchase of required materials, or improve inventory turnover; or, of course, it may have adverse effects.

Often new products are sold on an experimental basis in test markets in order to determine their acceptability to the entire market. For example, a new product may be introduced in a particular city or to a predetermined but widely scattered group of consumers. Follow-up studies are then made through questionnaires, interviews, reports of consumers, and in related ways.

Once product selection and modification have been determined (a process that goes on almost constantly) sales efforts and programs are developed. Our attention will center on the following topics in these discussions: (1) promotion policies and programs including (*a*) advertising, (*b*) sales organization and effort, and related programs; (2) selection of marketing channels; and (3) prices and pricing policies, as well as alternatives to price changes including services made available, credit extensions, guarantees provided, and related programs. We also consider briefly the integration of marketing programs with those of the firm as a whole.

Advertising

Advertising is an important tool of competition. Typically advertising costs are incurred in the hope of increasing the demand for a firm's products, and hence its sales.

Firms of substantial size usually will have their own advertising departments. In addition they may make use of independent advertising agencies. When a firm has its own advertising department, it is usually a part of the marketing division with the advertising manager responsible to the sales manager or marketing manager or the vice-president for marketing. Because of the importance of advertising in the general policies and programs of a business firm, major advertising decisions are often matters for decision by the chief executive officer, or even by the board of directors of the company.

The primary purposes of advertising are to make potential buyers *aware* of a company's goods or services and to influence their *attitudes* toward them. The extent to which this can be done will vary with the advertising effort put forth, and this in turn will vary with the size of the advertising appropriation, the copy and media used, and the frequency, continuity, and size of the advertising effort. Advertising efforts are undertaken to get new customers, hold old ones or increase the size of their accounts, provide leads and support for the sales force, and for other purposes. The ultimate objective, of course, is to create net revenue or profit for the business firm. General relationships between these factors are set forth in the accompanying diagram (Figure 19–2), adapted from a similar one prepared by Professor Kenneth R. Davis.[8]

Managers may undertake advertising programs to defend themselves against the actions of competitors; or they may go on the offensive and attempt to move ahead of competitors, trying to gain a bigger share of the market.

FIGURE 19–2

Advertising Program Relationships

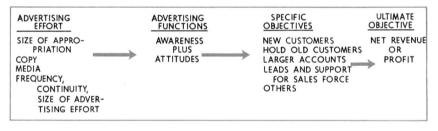

Adapted from Kenneth R. Davis, *Marketing Management* (New York: Ronald Press, Co., 1961), p. 571, by permission.

In some cases advertising is of an "institutional" type, stressing the company rather than its products. In other cases the products are given primary emphasis. Some advertising stresses "hard" selling, that is, products or prices are stressed; others are of the "soft" selling variety—indirect rather than direct in their appeals. Sometimes advertising is carried out co-operatively for an entire industry to help firms in it to compete more effectively with those in other industries.

The decisions in regard to advertising programs involve the size of the effort; the types of advertising and media, such as newspaper, magazine, TV, radio, direct mail, and the like that will be used; the relationship of advertising to other promotional and sales efforts; and costs.

---

[8] Davis, *op. cit.*, p. 571.

Decisions as to the *size and scope of the advertising effort* often turn on the type of product, since buyers are more responsive to advertising in some fields than in others. For example, advertising is not used to any marked extent in the sale of heavy machinery but is used widely in the sale of luxuries and conventional necessities, such as cigarettes, perfume, vacation travel, and the like.

The size of the advertising effort often depends on the alternative methods of reaching buyers. Usually the principal alternatives are either advertising or selling by salesmen, and managers try to develop the best balance between programs in these two closely related fields. Advertising, of course, supports the efforts of salesmen and may also attract buyers who cannot be reached by the sales force directly.

People get information about products in many ways, of course. Some have previous experience with a product. There is often informal discussion among people about products and companies. Feature stories in magazines, use of products in movies or TV shows, and many other things provide ideas and information about them. Efforts are made by certain consumer organizations to give information about products. For example, there are product-evaluating services such as Consumers Union and Consumers' Research. These organizations give comparative ratings to various products.

Advertising Costs

A major factor in determining the kinds of advertising programs that will be carried on is that of *costs*. How much to spend depends on the total marketing program, the programs of competitors, and the results that may be achieved. As a general guide, some managers spend a certain percentage of sales volume on advertising. Others use what is called the "objective and task" method. In this method estimates are made of the amount of sales that could be made without advertising and the amount that may be made by means of advertising. The difference is the "objective," and the "task" is the volume of advertising necessary to achieve it.[9]

In some cases past programs are studied and decisions are based on the effectiveness of past performance. Some managers believe they should spend all the funds that may be available—that is, all they can afford—on advertising; others relate efforts closely to those of competitors.

---

[9] See Howard, *op. cit.*, p. 335.

Once the total amount to be spent on advertising has been determined, decisions are made as to the allocation of this total to various media, the rate of spending over time, and the amount to be spent for specific products or advertising messages. Decisions of this type will vary widely from industry to industry and from company to company. The area covered, whether national or local, the media available and within the economic reach of a company (ranging from local newspapers to national magazines and TV programs), the types of customers, and past experience will have a bearing on final decisions.

Personal Selling

Many firms make use of salesmen in order to market their products. The requirements of business firms, of course, vary widely ranging from the seller of complicated industrial machinery to the door-to-door selling of consumer goods. In some cases the sales personnel work "inside," for example, the clerks in a department store; in others they work "outside," calling on prospective customers at their places of business or their homes.

The marketing manager of a business firm in co-operation with other company officials decides on the general size of the personal selling effort, the kind of sales organization that is required, and the allocation of sales effort between products and territories. Personal selling is an area of very direct competition between business firms. Hence, the size, quality, and aggressiveness of the sales force often are determining factors in the success of a firm.

The size of the sales appropriation will be related to other phases of a company's marketing programs. For all companies as a whole more is spent in personal selling than in any other promotional effort. As we have suggested, there is typically a close relationship between advertising and personal selling programs. It is recognized that sales may be increased by a larger sales force in most situations, but the real question from a management standpoint is the optimum sales force; that is, the one that will produce greatest return in relation to cost, effort, and alternative selling methods.

Organization for Sales

Selling organizations are sometimes built around products; in other cases, around territories or geographic areas; and in still others, around customers. For example, division may be made between industrial, wholesale, or retail customers. Combinations of these methods may also be used.

"Under this new incentive plan every salesman that meets his quota will get to keep his job."

Source: *Wall Street Journal* (by permission of Cartoon Features Syndicate).

If the organization centers around products, there may be sales managers for various product lines with sales personnel responsible to them; in the case of geographic organization there may be regional, state, district, and local managers. In some cases local communities will be subdivided into sales territories. There may be sales managers for various regions and districts and sales supervisors for smaller areas.

The decision as to how to organize the sales force often turns on the character of the firm's products or the markets for its products. Such a decision will depend somewhat on the way competitors' sales forces are organized and on the strength of the market.

How big a salesman's territory should be depends in part on estimates of its potential and forecasts of how much sales effort will be required to achieve this potential. A "sales quota" is often set up to give the salesman a specific objective to reach. His performance may be judged in terms of the degree to which he approximates the quota established. In some cases performance is measured by average sales volume over a period of time; in others, by number of sales or in terms of *added sales*. The number of new customers is often considered important, especially in terms of longer-run sales expansion.

Of major importance is the salesman's *contribution to profit*, and this requires a measurement of performance not only in terms of total sales but of sales relative to costs incurred.

The compensation of salesmen is usually related to some extent to volume such as the payment of commissions on sales. In some cases, however, salesmen are compensated on a regular salary basis, or combinations of salaries and commissions may be used. Sometimes products are classified with higher commissions being paid for some than for others.

Sales Personnel

The selection, training, and organization of a sales force is a matter of major importance in successful marketing management. Because of the unique qualities often required of salespeople, their selection may be made by the sales manager rather than by the personnel department. Some types of sales jobs require a great deal of technical knowledge, as in the case of selling industrial machinery, for example. Such salespeople sometimes are called "sales engineers." Other types require adaptability to different situations, determination, ability to "wear the customer's shoes," social skills, and related abilities. Skill in verbal expression is important to most salespeople, as is ambition, energy, drive, and an understanding of people and their wants.

The manager's job is to select those people who are most likely to fit the requirements of his program, his products, and his markets. Selection is only part of the process of building an effective selling team, however. Training may also play a major part in this process. In addition most companies hold periodic "sales meetings" which give the members of the sales force an opportunity to exchange experiences. The sales manager typically uses these meetings for generating enthusiasm about the company, its products, and its sales force.

Motivation is a big factor in the success of sales personnel. In most cases well-motivated salesmen will be more successful than others. Thus, management leadership has a special role to play in this area of operations.

The importance of selling for business firms and for the American economy in general can hardly be overestimated. To a large extent *products are not bought—they are sold.* Sales efforts create demands and produce revenue for the firm. Assuming markets, that is, people with money in their pockets or access to credit, whether Product A or Product B is successful often depends on the extent and quality of the sales effort.

Related Programs

Closely related to selling efforts and advertising programs are sales promotion, publicity, product display, and location.

Sales promotion is largely a reinforcing or supplementary activity designed to make direct selling or advertising programs more effective. Typically sales promotion involves a variety of activities designed to stimulate interest and motivate the people involved in all of the stages of selling. Sales promotion efforts are directed toward a firm's own sales force, its distributors and dealers, and customers.

Publicity is a form of promotional program that is intended to develop favorable public attitudes toward a business firm, its personnel, or its products. News releases are used widely along with speeches and public appearances and services of company officials. Industrywide publicity efforts are sometimes used. This is the general area of "public relations" or "community relations" activities of many business firms.

Product display takes many forms; it may be a part of advertising programs. In some cases it involves participation in business conventions and trade fairs. Some product displays are highly elaborate and costly arrangements and represent a significant part of a company's promotional efforts.

In their selling efforts business firms compete through their locations as well as in other ways. We discussed a number of location factors in Chapter 17, and you may wish to refer back to some of the points that were considered in that chapter. As we pointed out there, the location of a place of business may have an important bearing on its success. A manufacturing firm, for example, will try to locate at a point which will give it a competitive advantage in terms of bringing materials and workers to the plant, on the one hand, and in transferring products to customers, on the other.

The importance of location for a retail store is fairly obvious. The large department stores like Marshall Field's or Macy's typically locate in the heart of the business districts of large metropolitan areas where the volume of pedestrian traffic is heavy and where the store is accessible to a large number of buyers. By contrast a neighborhood grocery store or drugstore will locate at a point that will enable it to serve conveniently people living in a particular area.

Thus, the type of operations carried on by a firm and the objectives that have been established for it, including the kind of company that the owners want it to be, will all have an important bearing on location decisions. From a marketing standpoint such considerations as ease of access for customers, competitive advantage of one location over another, and the coverage of the market are especially important.

Costs are an important element in location. Business firms located in the downtown sections of metropolitan areas have high location costs; those located less centrally typically have lower costs. On the basis of costs per unit of sales, however, there may be little difference. Suburban location costs are usually lower than for downtown locations relative to the amount of space provided. In each case it is necessary for management to decide whether high costs will be justified in terms of the volume of sales generated, the competitive advantage secured, or the coverage of the market that will result. For example, management may decide on a less expensive location but compensate for this by heavier advertising programs, sales promotion, or adding to the sales force.

Marketing Channels

A company may have a number of alternatives from which to choose in channeling its products to its customers. A manufacturing firm, for example, may sell directly to customers. It may make "bulk sales" with the disposition of all or a major part of output to a single buyer. It may sell to ultimate users through company representatives, as in the case of the Fuller Brush Company. A company may own its retail outlets. It may sell by mail, sending out catalogues or other literature. It may advertise products through newspapers and magazines and invite direct orders.

On the other hand, a manufacturing company may sell to a retailer who then sells to ultimate buyers. Or the company may sell to a wholesaler who in turn sells to a retailer who makes final disposition of the products. In some cases various sales agents and brokers may be involved at different stages of the marketing channels that are followed.

In some cases firms make use of dealers who are authorized or "franchised." In such cases the manufacturer does the national advertising and sales promotion work, and this assists the local dealer in making sales. The local dealer is expected to conform to certain policies as laid down in the franchise agreement, although these vary widely.[10] Franchise arrangements are found in the automobile, petroleum, appliance, electric product, prefabricated housing, and other fields.

The marketing channel problem must be considered from the point of view of the firm's position in the market. A retailer, for example, will consider whether to buy from a wholesaler, broker, or agent; whether to enter into arrangements with other retailers to buy in quantity and eliminate a wholesaler from the "normal" chain of distribution; and whether to enter into franchise agreements. Also he may select among various other alternatives.

The rise of the *chain store* has reduced the importance of the wholesaler in many lines since wholesaling and retailing are centered in one management. It has brought various combinations of buying and selling efforts on the part of "independent" retailers, that is, separately owned stores in contrast to chains. The rise of supermarkets, shopping centers, and discount houses has changed the structure of distribution, especially in the postwar years. The supermarket and the discount house both emphasize price and self-service or limited service.

The rise of *shopping centers* has reflected the shift of people from downtown to outlying suburban centers and has caused many firms to reconsider their outlets, including financial institutions and department stores as well as specialty shops.

Department stores handle a wide variety of lines usually of apparel, home furnishings, and the like; *specialty shops* usually offer items that customers are willing to make special efforts to buy, which often include "high-fashion" merchandise.

In choosing among the alternatives that may be open to him in regard to marketing channels, a marketing manager typically considers the coverage of the market that he will secure, the assistance he will receive in promotion, and the cost involved. The importance of these factors will vary with the type of product and the position of the firm in the distribution system.

Pricing

Many firms compete for sales by means of price. Consequently, marketing managers attempt to develop price policies that will fit their markets. A firm can set prices so high that it will price itself out of the market, or it can offer prices so low that losses are inevitable.

---

[10] Charles M. Hewitt, "The Furor over Dealer Franchises," *Business Horizons*, Winter, 1958, pp. 80–87.

Usually price policies are related to the *competitive situation* within which a firm is operating and to general economic and market factors. If general business or industry conditions are depressed, price policies usually will be different than if such conditions are more favorable. If prosperous conditions bring a "seller's market," that is, one in which most of the advantages are on the side of the seller, a manager may eliminate all but the most profitable outlets and price accordingly. Such a line of action may cause problems when conditions shift to a "buyer's market." In a buyer's market prices usually must be competitive, and in some cases may drop below cost.

The price of a product is usually related to the prices of competing products, potential competition, services offered, credit terms, and the general level of consumer acceptance of the product. Price decisions are usually made by managers within a range of possible alternatives. Existing or anticipated competition usually will have a bearing on such decisions. The degree of competition in the market often is a factor. Managers may have more latitude in pricing policies under oligopoly than under highly competitive conditions. The estimated *level of sales* at various prices will also play an important part. Sometimes a product may be priced high in order to allow for concessions, for quantity purchases, or to provide strategic advantages, or for other reasons. Most prices, other than those at retail, are set at levels that will permit discounts for cash or payment in a short period of time.

Prices may be related to costs, as in the case of "cost-plus" pricing, that is, setting prices at a certain percentage above costs. Sometimes prices are set with a view to earning a desired return on the investment in the firm or to achieve a certain profit level as a percentage of sales.

While cost-plus pricing is used widely, such a policy may fail to give adequate consideration to the competitive situation. Also there is always the question of how costs shall be measured; and, since costs typically vary with output, some level of output has to be assumed when pricing is handled on a cost-plus basis as we noted in the preceding chapter. Flexible markups may be used. These are adaptations of the cost-plus method and are used when conditions are undergoing changes as when new products are being introduced.

We should note also that products may be tailored to fit a market situation. In other words, managers may work back to product from prices and markets rather than the other way around.

The degree of *responsiveness of quantity sold to price changes* is an important factor in the determination of prices for an entire industry. It may also affect the pricing of the products of a particular firm, especially if that firm is in a price leadership position in its industry. Some firms because of their leadership position may establish prices for a substantial segment of a market.

Sometimes managers must price in such a way as to *limit losses* rather than to attempt to *maximize gains*. For example, they may find it necessary to sell products below cost in order to keep idle capacity at a minimum.

Experimentation is often undertaken in determining price policies. For example, a price change for a nationally distributed product may be tried out in a few localities. Sometimes tests are made by comparing sales in limited markets at different prices. In some cases when a new product is brought out it is introduced into several localities at different prices and the results are compared before general pricing arrangements are made.

A number of pricing problems demand almost continuing attention. For example, some firms use price differentials, that is, they undertake to sell the same product at different prices. A useful example is the prices of theater tickets, differential pricing being used for matinee and evening performances, or for children and adults. Electricity is often priced differently for large-volume users than for normal users. Products may be introduced into a territory at special prices, lower than in established markets. Often differentials exist between foreign and domestic markets. There may be "off-season" pricing as in the case of summer rates at winter resort hotels. Cash discounts may be included as an example of differential pricing.

Special problems are often encountered in establishing prices for a product line, particularly if the products in the line complement each other or if costs of producing them are interrelated. For example, a high-quality product such as a suit may be priced high but will be used as a means of selling other suits in the line that are offered at lower prices.

Establishing prices at the time a product is introduced often poses special problems. The price may be set low in order to penetrate the market, or set high to compensate for heavy costs of introducing it. Much will depend on its position relative to competitors and whether it enjoys a protected position. A high price may skim off areas of strong demand; the price can then be lowered to expand the quantity sold. Over time, of course, prices are adjusted to changing demand and cost conditions as well as to changes in the competitive situation.

We should recognize, of course, that companies vary in the extent to which they may set prices. Often the market rather than the company is the determining element. This is notably true if competition is intense, less so if oligopoly conditions prevail. Also, governmental regulations such as the Sherman Act and the Clayton Act impose limits on the pricing policies of business firms.

Alternatives to Price Competition

We should remember that products compete in other ways than through price. Rather than cut prices, for example, some firms may offer *easier credit terms*. This is one of the ways that neighborhood stores may compete with discount houses, even though the prices of the former may be higher.

In some cases *more extensive services* may be offered in lieu of price advantages. Delivery services, repair programs, and the like are often highly important in the sale of various products. Repair facilities are especially important in the case of automobiles, TV sets, electric appliances, and other durable consumer goods. Such services often play a big part in the sale of machinery and equipment, since the availability of repair services may mean more to a buyer than a price concession without assurance of prompt repairs in the event of a breakdown.

Guarantees of quality may also be used in lieu of price concessions. A buyer may be attracted to a greater extent by assurances of "satisfaction guaranteed or your money back" than by low prices. Usually "brand names" develop reputations for quality, and the seller of such products may find it somewhat less necessary to compete through price than is the case with more standardized commodities.

SUMMARY

Marketing decisions and operations are of major importance in a business firm's success; they center around the determination of the market situation and environment within which a firm's products may be sold, and selecting and developing programs to meet these conditions.

Markets arise from the fact that exchange is a mutually beneficial proposition. Markets perform useful functions for the entire economy, helping to determine what is to be produced, how much, and for whom.

Understanding the market environment is essential to the development and execution of successful marketing programs. In some situations the manager may influence the market environment to a greater or lesser degree; in others he must adapt to it. The degree of competition that prevails usually indicates the extent to which the manager may influence the market environment.

Demand analysis helps to develop an understanding of the conditions under which products will be sold. The factors most likely to influence the demand for a product include: (1) its price, (2) prices of substitute or complementary products, (3) incomes of consumers and their ability to borrow, and (4) the preferences of consumers. Motivation research and studies of consumer buying habits and the behavior of competitors have been helpful in various types of demand analysis.

Sales forecasts may be based on demand analyses and help to determine product lines and "mix," rate of output, price policies, market strategies, and financial requirements. Cost studies may be even more important in marketing than in production operations; difficult measurement and allocation problems often are involved. Profit studies tend to center around profits as a percentage of sales for marketing management purposes.

Product selection is of continuing importance for marketing programs, as well as for production operations. Marketing really begins even before production starts.

Promotion policies and programs cover a wide range of activities, including advertising, sales organization, and effort, as well as such related programs as sales promotion, publicity, product display, and location.

Selection of marketing channels is among the major marketing management decision problems. Selection often is determined by a firm's position in the market and anticipated effect on costs, returns, and profits.

Decisions as to prices and price policies are often based on a firm's competitive situation, estimated sales levels, and probable costs. Various alternatives to price competition may be used such as easier credit terms, provision of more extensive services, and guarantees of quality.

QUESTIONS AND PROBLEMS

1. Do you think markets would exist if exchange were not a mutually beneficial proposition? Explain.
2. What are the principal functions which markets perform for our economy? One day you cannot find a parking space for your car. The next day there are spaces available. Parking meters have been installed. How has the market helped to ration parking space?
3. Differentiate between a service wholesaler and a limited service wholesaler.
4. Explain the statement: Markets are not simply people, but rather, people with money in their pockets or the ability to command credit.

5. How are some products differentiated? How does this affect their markets?

6. Indicate the factors most likely to influence the demand for a product. If the price of golf balls is reduced, is this likely to affect the demand for golf clubs? Explain.

7. How are sales of conventional necessities likely to be affected by a drop of incomes? How may a drop in incomes affect the pricing policies of a firm in the perfume business?

8. You are engaged in the business of manufacturing and marketing a product. Sales in the industry as a whole have been going down gradually. Is this likely to have any significance for your sales in the future? Explain the conditions under which it may, and those under which it may not.

9. Why is it frequently difficult to allocate marketing costs? How important is it for a marketing manager to be able to relate costs to contribution to profit?

10. Explain the statement: "marketing really begins before production starts."

11. Your firm sells automobiles, one of the "Big Three" cars, as well as used cars. You have an opportunity to add a line of foreign sport cars. What factors would you consider in deciding whether or not to add this line?

12. What is meant by "defensive advertising"? By "institutional advertising"? On what bases may a manager decide how much to spend on advertising?

13. Under what type of situation would you prefer to build a selling organization around products? Around territories?

14. Do you agree with this statement: "To a large extent products are not bought—they are sold?" Explain your position.

15. Explain what is meant by "marketing channels." List some of the factors that will guide a manager's decisions in regard to the selection of marketing channels.

16. Give an example of price differentials for a product. Give an example of "off-season" pricing.

17. (This is an illustration of the "in-basket" technique of instruction.) Steve Miller has just been appointed Director of Marketing for California Industrial Corporation. He has just arrived in Palo Alto, California, the company's Business Equipment Division headquarters. The promotion has brought him from the Air Conditioning Division in Chicago, Illinois, where he was Director of Sales. The reason for the sudden promotion was the unexpected resignation of Bruce Young, former Director of Marketing. (See organization charts, page 495.)

Today is Saturday, July 4. It is 9:30 A.M. and Steve has just arrived at the office. He must, however, leave at 11:45 A.M. to catch a plane for New York for a week-long advertising conference where the advertising program for the entire firm for the next year will be developed. He will return to work on Monday, July 13. His secretary, Mrs. Holt, is on vacation and will return on Monday, July 6. The following memos were in the in-basket on Steve's desk.

Instructions: Assume that you are Steve Miller. You are to go through all of the memos and take whatever action you think necessary. However, every action should be written down, including memos to your secretary, to others, and to yourself. Make a note for every telephone call. Draft or write whatever letters are necessary. Write out plans or agendas for any meetings. Remember, you must take some action on all memos. The decisions are yours.

MEMO

To: BRUCE YOUNG
From: B. CARR
Date: MAY 29
Subject: CONSUMER PRODUCTS, INC.

As you know, our electronic data processing office in Atlanta has been quite active in developing a complete installation plan for electronic data processing equipment for Consumer Products' new home office. In the future all record keeping will be centered there. Their target date for occupancy of the new building is December 1.

On May 27, GBK Machines, Inc., made a bid that was approximately 14 per cent below our maximum sales discount.

In view of the importance of this customer, will you agree to our matching GBK's bid?

B. CARR
Manager, Sales Section

MEMO

To: BRUCE YOUNG
From: E. MACK
Date: MAY 24
Subject: ADVERTISING PROGRAM

The advertising agency called me this morning with a very fine proposal. The third page (from the front) of *Business Week* will be available September 1.

We could have it on a three-year contract. This could replace our biweekly ad in the same publication and possibly some others.

This is the kind of thing you and I have hoped for over the years.

The agency must have a confirmation by July 20.

E. MACK
Advertising Manager

MEMO

To: MR. YOUNG
From: DOTTIE HOLT
Date: MAY 29
Subject:

Just to remind you, Sunday, July 5, is Mr. Tuttle's twenty-fifth wedding anniversary.

DOTTIE

MEMO

To: BRUCE YOUNG
From: J. P. TUTTLE
Date: MAY 29
Subject: PROGRESS REPORTS

July 15 is the deadline for Employee and Supervisory Annual Progress Reports to be in my office. They will be discussed at our monthly meeting on July 22.

Thank you.

J. P. TUTTLE
Vice-President, Equipment Division

MEMO

To: BRUCE YOUNG
From: J. GORDON
Date: MAY 19
Subject: EXPENSE ACCOUNTS

The expense vouchers sent in from the New York City Sales Office have been 20 per cent to 30 per cent above the limit for the past six months.

May I please discuss this with you at your earliest convenience.

Thank you.

J. GORDON
Director, Finance Department

SUGGESTED READINGS

DAVIS, KENNETH R. *Marketing Management.* New York: Ronald Press Co., 1961. Read especially chap. i, "Nature and Scope of Marketing Management," and chap. ii, "Marketing Management Decisions."

HOWARD, JOHN H. *Marketing Management.* Homewood, Ill.: Richard D. Irwin, Inc., 1957. Read chap. i, "Introduction," of this widely used text.

LONG, JOHN D. *Workbook to Accompany Weimer: Business Administration: An Introductory Management Approach,* chap. 19. Rev. ed. Homewood, Ill.: Richard D. Irwin, Inc., 1962.

California Industrial Corporation
Organization Chart

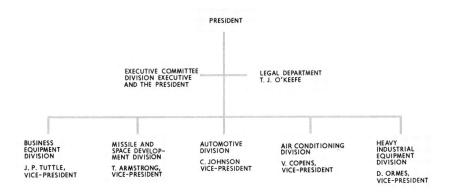

Business Equipment Division
Organization Chart

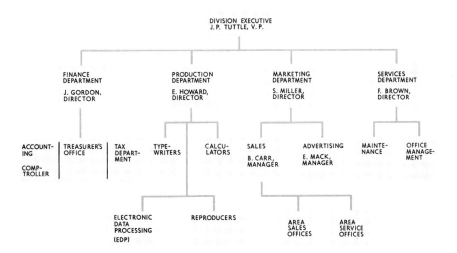

part 5 The Business Environment

SUMMARY OUTLINE

BUSINESS ADMINISTRATION—now one of the more exciting areas of study—may be *approached* in an *introductory* manner from the point of view of the *manager*.

He is the central figure in the business firm—the key social and economic institution of our time. It is managed and operated in a highly dynamic environment.

Business Firms are established as individual *proprietorships, partnerships, corporations,* and other forms.

Firms vary in *size* and engage in many *types of work*—manufacturing, trade, finance, service, and others.

The *Decision Makers* in business firms are owners, managers, and business specialists.

The *Management Process* involves establishment of objectives, plans, and controls; organization of resources; and leadership.

Decision Making—a central management responsibility—includes problem and *goal identification* and clarification, development and analysis of *alternatives*, appraisal of most likely alternatives, and *choice*.

Decisions may be guided by financial, accounting, statistical, economic, mathematical, and other considerations.

Business Resources and Operations involve effective utilization of the abilities of people—requiring knowledge of personnel and organization behavior—

as well as other resources including

capital, equipment, knowledge, time, and related aids to productivity, plus the place of business—land, buildings, and location—

in the *production* and *marketing* of goods and services to secure *income*.

The *Business Environment* influences management decisions and in turn is influenced by them, particularly in the areas of
business conditions,
governmental and political conditions,
the legal system,
the enterprise system and competing systems,
and international business administration.

Emerging Problems and Opportunities hold promise for the business community, and for you in managing your future.

OUTLINE FOR CHAPTER 20

BUSINESS CONDITIONS, of major importance in the business environment, have important implications for management decisions and programs, and influence general public and business attitudes.

Managers may follow varying policies relative to expected environmental changes:

they may adapt to them,
move contrary to them, or
attempt to change them.

Changes in business conditions are reflected in measures of gross national product, price levels,

industrial production,
income levels, employment and unemployment,
spending programs and plans, and others.

Types of variations in business activity include

seasonal changes,
cycles, and secular trends.

Predictions of changes in business conditions may be based on plans of major spending divisions of the economy, including

consumers, business firms,
and government agencies.

Gross national product and income analysis covers expenditures for product items—

personal consumption,
gross private domestic investment,
net sales abroad, and
sales to government units; and

income items, including

compensation of employees,
returns to nonfarm unincorporated enterprises,
income of farm proprietors,
rental income of persons,
corporate profits (before taxes), and
net income, plus adjustments.

Industry forcasts usually are based on special studies. Economic and managerial "audits" may be used by managers.

20 BUSINESS CONDITIONS

There is a tide in the affairs of men
Which taken at the flood leads on to fortune.

—SHAKESPEARE

Impact of Environment

In the preceding section we considered a number of topics pertaining to business resources and operations. In that section as well as in our earlier discussions we recognized that management decisions were influenced both by factors within the firm and outside the firm, that is, by the firm's environment. We emphasized the point that *business firms do not operate in a vacuum.* Their managers are influenced greatly by what is going on around them, in the industries of which their firms are a part, markets of many types both domestic and foreign, economic and business conditions, international relations, and the general economic, social, and political climate.

We have seen, for example, that when the manager hires people he is concerned with the labor market and often may find it necessary to deal with labor unions. Government officials may be involved in various types of labor relations. When the manager buys machinery, equipment, and materials he is brought into close contact with the markets for these things. When he buys or leases a place of business, he enters the real estate market of his community or of several communities, if his company operates from several locations. Decisions as to borrowing money are influenced by conditions in the money markets and by general monetary and credit policies. Markets for the goods and services sold by a firm are affected greatly by domestic and foreign business conditions and by conditions in specific areas and localities.

Thus, we have recognized the importance of the business environment and its impact and potential impact on management decisions and operations throughout our discussions. You may wish to review

501

Chapter 4 at this point since we considered there the importance of the business environment as a part of our introductory discussions.

You may recall that we outlined three general alternatives as typically being available to managers: (1) they may adapt to anticipated environmental changes; (2) move contrary to anticipated trends; or (3) attempt to change the environment.

We turn here in Part 5 of the book to a consideration of a variety of important factors in the business environment, including business conditions, governmental and political conditions, the legal system, the enterprise system and competing systems, and various regional and international factors in the business environment.

Significance of Business Conditions

In his day-to-day operations, few matters concern the manager more than the general state or condition of business. While most people are likely to open conversations with discussions of the weather, businessmen typically ask, "How's business?"

This is no idle question like most of those pertaining to the weather. The manager is genuinely concerned with levels of business activity. He knows that conditions in one line of business are likely to affect another; that when business generally is good, his own operations are likely to benefit; and when business activity is declining, his problems are likely to grow more difficult.

As we have seen, the plans of business managers are influenced greatly by what is going on around them and the general trend of business activity is an important element in the business environment. Of course, business is not always either "good" or "bad." In an economy as diversified as ours some areas may be expanding while others are declining or remaining stationary. Or one business firm may be undergoing expansion while the programs of others in the same industry or area are being curtailed.

When the over-all levels of business activity are good, however, the general psychology of the public at large—customers, investors, suppliers, employees, and others—is likely to be optimistic. And, of course, the opposite is true when business activity is declining.

In making his decisions the manager tends to be affected by the general psychology in which he works. He may deliberately try to guard against this, attempting to think in pessimistic terms when others are optimistic, or vice versa. In so far as possible the business manager tries to maintain an objective point of view, to base his decisions on information rather than general public attitudes or the impressions of those around him. He tries also to avoid "getting into a rut" in his operations—to alter them as general conditions may indicate.

The importance of this was recognized by Machiavelli, who pointed out:

On this depends also the changes in prosperity, for if it happens that time and circumstances are favorable to one who acts with caution and prudence, he will be successful, but if time and circumstances change, he will be ruined because he does not change his mode of procedure. No man is found so prudent as to be able to adapt himself to this, either because he cannot deviate from that to which his nature disposes him, or else because having always prospered by walking in one path, he cannot persuade himself that it is well to leave it; and therefore, not know how to do so and is consequently ruined: for if one could change one's nature with time and circumstance, fortune would never change.[1]

In making his estimates of probable changes in business conditions and in planning his programs with respect to such changes, the manager must decide: (1) whether present conditions will persist into the future or change. If change is anticipated, whether it will be in the direction of expansion or decline. (2) Whether conditions in his own line of business will follow more general trends or deviate from them. (3) Whether he should move with general trends of business activity or those in his own line of business, move against them, or try to change them.

Sources of Information

The question "How's business?" can be answered in more specific terms than "good," "bad," or "fair." Various measures of business activity are available to us, and many of them are followed closely by business managers. These measures enable us to look at all or part of the economic system, to compare current and past performance, and to form a basis for predictions in regard to the probable trend of business activity in the future.

Indicators of business conditions are numerous. The President's Council of Economic Advisers, a three-man board of experts with a considerable staff, was established to provide information and advice on economic trends for the head of our government. The Council watches a large number of indicators of business activity.

Most business executives will not undertake to study current business developments as extensively as the Council of Economic Advisers. Many of the larger corporations, however, have established depart-

---

[1] Machiavelli, *The Prince* (New York: Oxford University Press, World Classics, published by the New American Library, 1952), pp. 132–33.

ments of business economics to engage in rather extensive studies of this type and to advise management. A number of such departments carry on studies almost as extensive as those of the Council of Economic Advisers. Some business firms hire economists on a consulting basis to help them with this work. In other cases the managers of business firms rely on their own analyses of business conditions.

Many business managers watch the *stock market* rather closely since they consider this to be a "sensitive" or a "lead" indicator. They keep an eye on levels of employment and unemployment. Some businessmen consider the automobile industry to be a "bellwether" of general conditions. Many subscribe to services such as the "Kiplinger Washington Letter" or rely on publications provided by financial institutions. A number of government publications are used widely, including the *Survey of Current Business* published by the Department of Commerce, the *Federal Reserve Bulletin* published by the Board of Governors of the Federal Reserve System, and *Economic Indicators* published by the Council of Economic Advisers. Indeed, the provision of information about business conditions is one of the more important services provided by government for the business community. Such private publications as *The Wall Street Journal* and *Business Week* are read widely by business managers as well as more general magazines such as *Newsweek, U.S. News and World Report, Time,* and *Fortune.*

There is available also a wide variety of publications dealing with specific lines of business. Many of the publications of the Bureau of the Census provide information of this type, including the *Census of Manufacturing, Census of Housing,* and others. In addition the trade associations in many fields provide detailed reports on current conditions in their respective industries.

Types of Information

In the foregoing discussion we suggested a few of the more generally used sources of information about business conditions. It is apparent from this discussion that we may distinguish (1) general and (2) special or industry measures of business conditions. In addition there are regional measures and state and local measures.

The business manager uses those that most nearly fit his purposes. If he is operating on a national or international basis, he will be especially interested in general measures of business conditions at home and abroad; he may also be interested in some special line of business such as the automotive field, pharmaceuticals, clothing, or others. If operations are of a local nature, special attention will be paid to local indicators of business conditions.

General measures of business conditions include information about *gross national product,* that is, the total value of goods and services produced in a given period, usually a year; *price levels* including wholesale and consumer prices; *industrial production* reflecting the output of mines and factories; *population changes; personal incomes* —wages, salaries, and other incomes; *spending* by business firms, by governments, and by individuals; *savings trends; employment;* and a host of others.

Several types of information that arise out of special areas of business may also have general significance for business managers. For example, widespread use is made of banking information; car loadings; retail sales on national, regional, or local levels; housing starts; agricultural production and marketing; and many others.

Indeed, it is not possible to present in any brief discussion more than a general indication of the variety and range of information about business conditions that may be used by business managers. Businessmen attempt to determine what is going on in the business community generally as well as in their own lines of business. They use this information as a background for their day-to-day as well as longer-range decisions.

Types of Variations

Before undertaking a brief discussion of some of the methods used to predict or anticipate changes in business conditions, we should recognize that there are several types of variations in business activity. Three major types may be distinguished. One of these is long-term changes, upward or downward, usually referred to as *"secular trend."* The others are *seasonal fluctuations* and *cycles.*

Secular trends may be useful in predicting activity in a single line of business or in the economic system generally. A secular trend reflects fundamental forces that continue in operation for decades at a time. For example, the increase in the birth rate during and after World War II will bring about long-term population growth and changes in the age distribution of the population. Another example is the gradual trend toward a larger output of goods and services in this country. Total output has tended to expand for more than half a century at an average rate of about 3 per cent per year.

Long-term trends or secular changes are especially important to business managers in making long-range plans. Favorable long-term growth prospects in a particular industry, for example, may form the basis for decisions to undertake long-range programs of expansion for a business firm in that industry. Publishers of college textbooks expect an expanding market in the decade of the 1960's because the number of people of college age will be increasing rapidly, reflecting the higher birth rates of the middle 1940's. House builders expect a rapidly expanding market by the late 1960's and early 1970's for the same reasons. Long-term trends of this type may be expected to persist into the future, barring some major interruption such as a global war.

We should note that long-term trends or secular changes are not always easy to identify. In the thirties, for example, many people believed we were heading toward a "mature" economy with limited growth potential. Actually, long-term growth trends had been interrupted but not changed by the great depression of those years. We should note also that secular trends are not always upward; they may move downward as well. For example, the production of horse-drawn vehicles tended downward after the advent of the automobile, new synthetic fibers may bring a downward trend for the more traditional materials, and oil and gas furnaces have brought a downward trend in the production of those using coal.

Seasonal Fluctuations

In contrast to secular changes or very long-run trends stand *seasonal fluctuations,* that is, changes in business conditions that take place from one season to another. Some of these changes are due to the weather. For example, fewer houses are built in the winter than in the summer; hence, comparisons of July and January housing starts can only be made if this seasonal factor is taken into account. Many retail establishments make a third or more of their sales in the Christmas shopping season; others have a big volume of business around Easter. Vacation periods affect many lines of business, some favorably, some adversely. Many business managers make effective use of seasonal variations in their planning. In some cases off-season programs such as the introduction of a complementary product or production for inventory may help to regularize operations; in others seasonal patterns influence advertising and sales programs. Some business firms have been able to modify or even to eliminate the seasonal pattern.

Sometimes seasonal patterns change or can be changed. By introducing automobile models in the fall rather than the spring the companies in this industry were able to reduce previous seasonal fluctuations. The increasing popularity of winter vacations may modify somewhat the depressing effects on many businesses of the traditional summer vacations.

Business Cycles

A third major type of business fluctuation is the *cycle.* Perhaps more has been written and said about business cycles than any other kind of change in business activity. You undoubtedly have had some personal experience with cyclical variations in business activity. At times nearly all business firms enjoy a high volume of activity, earnings are good, and few people are unemployed. At other times many firms experience a decline in business volume, earnings are reduced, and substantial numbers of people are unemployed. Cyclical variations in business activity generally include the stages of prosperity, recession, depression (if the downward movement is severe), recovery, and prosperity again (see Figure 20–1).

FIGURE 20–1

The Business Cycle

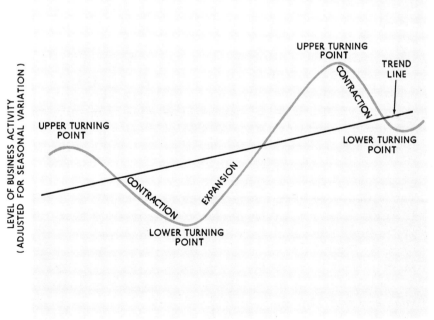

TIME

There are cyclical variations in general business activity and in specific lines of business. Even a particular business firm may experience cyclical fluctuations which may or may not coincide with those of its industry or with business conditions generally.

If business managers could find a definite cycle with a given length for business activity generally or for their own industries, it would, of course, greatly simplify their problems. Many try to find such a "key" or pattern. Unfortunately, we have never been able to find a "rhythm" or set pattern for business cycles generally or even for a given line of business. Studies indicate that cycles of general business activity vary in length from two years or less to around twelve years. The deep depression of the early 1930's, for example, may be contrasted with the relatively minor recessions of 1948–49, 1953–54, 1957–58, or 1960–61. Each business cycle appears to have its own individual characteristics. The forces in operation differ somewhat from previous cycles.

It is important for the manager to recognize the implications of cyclical variations. He may not be able to anticipate them very definitely, but even so, he knows that he must be prepared for variations in his business volume, in earnings, and in many other phases of his operations. Thus, he usually tries to choose the periods when new products may be introduced to advantage, when costs may be cut, when competition will grow more intense, when plant and facilities may be expanded, when personnel may be hired to advantage, when money can be borrowed on favorable terms, and the like.

Many activities can be carried out successfully only if their timing is "right." Unfortunately, the choice of the most favorable times to undertake one or another program is far from easy. No one can foretell the future, regardless of the volume of information at his disposal. This is because so many decisions made by so many people—literally billions of decisions made by millions of people—business executives, government officials, farmers, trade-union leaders, consumers, investors, and others—all affect the level of business activity. It is extremely difficult to make estimates of the direction of such a multitude of decisions, or of sudden changes in the patterns of decisions.

In addition the American economy is now highly diversified—and is growing increasingly so. In the 1920's agriculture, for example, accounted for about a quarter of total output each year; currently it accounts for less than 10 per cent. Thus, declines in one line of economic activity are less likely to affect the whole economic system than was formerly the case.

Further, the people in this country enjoy a high standard of living relative to many parts of the world. Hence, many of the demands of consumers as well as business firms in this country are *postponable*. The demand for new plant and equipment is postponable. The same thing is true of many consumer demands notably for automobiles, consumer durables, and houses. Even the demand for clothing is postponable when many people have two and three suits rather than one.

Factors of this type are of varying importance in many foreign countries. A firm operating on a multinational basis often finds it necessary to evaluate similar types of data for several countries quite differently.

Predicting Business Conditions

In view of the wide variety of information available and the difficulties encountered in making predictions based on it, how is the business manager to proceed? Is there any method or procedure that he may follow to help him in making estimates of changes in business activity?

Some managers and analysts study various of the indicators of business activity we have outlined above or others and then attempt to determine whether changes will occur and their probable extent and direction. Unfortunately, some indicators of business trends may suggest expansion, while others indicate that declines are likely to occur. It is necessary to relate one type of information to another and to determine the relative importance of the forces in operation. How can this be done?

In more recent years many managers, business economists, and analysts have tried to do this by paying special attention to the principal spending divisions of our economic system—consumers, business firms, and government agencies, plus exports to foreign countries. Ours is an exchange economy; hence, the level of business activity tends to reflect the volume of spending. Various guides to the intentions of consumers, business firms, and government agencies in regard to spending have been developed and have proved to be highly useful in estimating the probable levels of general business activity at least for short-run periods of time.

For example, studies of consumer buying intentions are available and are published in business magazines, newspapers, and journals. The Survey Research Center of the University of Michigan provides such information. The Bureau of the Census collects information of this type and it is published in the *Federal Reserve Bulletin*. These analyses provide information about current income levels, the general financial condition of consumers, their income expectations, and their plans for spending. Such studies are made on a sampling basis and, consequently, are subject to varying degrees of error. In

addition, consumers may change their minds rather rapidly in response to new developments. Nevertheless, information of this kind
has proved to be quite valuable in making estimates of the probable
trends of consumer spending.

Information is compiled by the Department of Commerce, the Securities and Exchange Commission, and by the McGraw-Hill Publishing Company in regard to business plans for capital spending, that is,
expenditures for plant and equipment. Reports of such studies are
presented in the *Survey of Current Business* and *Business Week*.
While these reports are based on expectations and subject to the same
types of error as the studies of consumer income and spending expectations, information of this kind has proved to be quite helpful in predicting the trend of events.

Of special importance for short-term changes in business conditions
are changes in business inventories. Current information about business inventories is usually made available through reports published
in the *Survey of Current Business,* and also information of this type
typically appears in financial publications such as the *Wall Street
Journal.* For example, if inventories are rising in a period of declining
incomes and prices, difficulties may be encountered in attempting to
liquidate them, and further declines in prices and incomes may result.
Conversely, when incomes are expanding and prices are tending to
rise, business firms may add to inventories more rapidly than normally, and thus provide a further stimulus to expansion.

A third principal area of expenditure is the government, not only
the federal government but state and local governments as well. One
of the best indications of federal expenditure plans is provided by the
President's Budget Message which is submitted to Congress early in
each congressional session. Of course, this is a tentative program and
may be modified by congressional actions relative to appropriations
and taxes. Appropriations are not nearly so important in terms of their
effect on business as actual expenditures which may come about many
months after the budget is approved. The budget, however, provides
an indication of the probable level of future government expenditures. Information about anticipated expenditures on the state and
local governmental level are less generally available, but reports on
past expenditures can be secured from such sources as the *Federal
Reserve Bulletin.*

The three principal areas of spending outlined above are of major
importance in determining the general trend of business activity. In
addition, the difference between our expenditures in foreign coun-

tries and receipts from them may at times be important for their effects on domestic business activities. Our situation, of course, differs from such economic systems as those of Holland and England. Nevertheless, we are subject to the discipline of the balance of payments between countries and our position in international trade and finance often has important implications for domestic business and government policies.

Gross National Product Analysis

You will not proceed very far in your studies of business and economics before you will encounter discussions of the gross national product (GNP) and economic analyses using the gross national product or national income or national income accounting methods which now are in widespread use. Indeed, we have already referred to the gross national product at several points in our preceding discussions.

It is not our purpose here to explain specific methods of economic analysis that are based on studies of the gross national product or income. Rather we will try to explain some of the principal factors that are included in such studies.

Today many business managers, government officials, and economists for government agencies or business firms rely heavily on gross national product and income studies. Basically, such studies group together the major income and product or expenditure accounts for the nation as a whole. Consequently, this method of economic analysis is sometimes referred to as "national income accounting."

Although much greater detail might be presented, Figure 20–2 indicates the principal "accounts" that are involved. If you will look at the right-hand column of this table first, you will note that we have represented here the principal *spending sectors* of the economic system which we discussed briefly above. As we have pointed out, the gross national product is the total value of goods and services produced in a period, usually a year. The sum of the expenditures of these major groups is equal to the total product or output of the economy.

We refer to "gross" product because the production of goods to replace those worn out is included. The total value of product includes every type of goods or services to which a market value can be assigned, such as government services, food produced on farms for home consumption, and the rental value of owner occupied homes. Only *final* products are counted, however, in order to avoid counting items several times as they pass through the various stages of production to final sale. Thus, GNP reported in dollars reflects changes in market values as well as in physical output.

FIGURE 20-2

Gross National Income and Product in the U.S., 1960 and 19—*

(In Billions of Dollars)

INCOME	1960	19—	PRODUCT (OR EXPENDITURE)	1960	19—
Compensation of employees	294.4		Personal consumption expenditures	327.8	
Business and professional income	35.9		Gross private domestic investment	72.8	
Income of farm proprietors	12.0		Net exports of goods and services	3.0	
Rental income of persons	12.5		Government purchases of goods and services	99.7	
Corporate profits and inventory valuation adjustment (before taxes)	44.3				
Net interest income	18.7				
Equal Net National Income	417.8				
Plus: Indirect taxes	45.1				
Plus: Adjustments†	−2.5				
Net National Product	460.4				
Plus: Capital consumption allowances	43.2				
Equal Gross National Income	503.6		Equal Gross National Product	503.3	
	(503.2)‡			(503.2)‡	

---

* You may fill in these blank spaces to show current conditions.

† Includes business transfer payments, statistical discrepancy, and surpluses of government enterprises minus government subsidies.

‡ Figures rounded—hence, items will not necessarily add to the totals indicated.

Product or Expenditure Accounts

On the right-hand side of this account, as outlined in Figure 20–2, are included sales for personal consumption such as food, clothing, books, entertainment, travel, and so on. Some problems are involved in allocating certain items; for example, an automobile purchased for personal use would be included in "sales for personal consumption," but if bought by a business firm, would be considered a capital expenditure. Houses in all cases, however, because of their long life, are counted as capital goods.

The item, gross private domestic investment, includes expenditures by business firms for capital goods such as machinery, equipment, plants, stores, and the like. Included also is a plus or minus factor to show changes in business inventories. As we have noted, new houses are included in gross private domestic investment; sales of old houses are not included since they do not reflect an addition to total output.

The item, "net export of goods and services," or frequently referred to as "net foreign investment," indicates the differences between sales abroad and purchases from other countries plus some other international balance of payment items.

Government purchases of goods and services cover federal, state, and local governmental units, and include compensation for employees (those in the armed forces as well) plus purchases from business firms usually under government contracts of one type or another. Investments by the government in installations such as those of the atomic energy commission are included; that is, both capital and current expenditure items are grouped together in this account.

These items of expenditure by consumers, business, and government plus net sales abroad account for total output—that is, the gross national product, measured in terms of what was actually paid for this output by such expenditures.

Income Accounts

The items on the left-hand side of the above table indicate *who receives* various types and amounts of *income*. The total of these various incomes is gross national income.

There are indicated the earnings of employees, business and professional income, incomes of farm proprietors, rental incomes or corporate profits and inventory valuation adjustment, and income from interest payments. These items constitute net national income, or usually this is called "national income." In order to account for total payments, however, other items must be included such as indirect business taxes, depreciation allowances or capital consumption allowances, and the like, plus adjustments of various types to allow for statistical discrepancies.

These accounts show the principal items of income and those on the right-hand side of Figure 20–2 show product or expenditure accounts for the economy as a whole for a year. By studying changes in these accounts from year to year or more frequently, business economists and analysts are able to formulate estimates of the probable trend of general economic activity.

Detailed analyses of gross national product and income are usually made by experts. Business managers, however, have found it highly useful to become acquainted with the principal items or "accounts" involved and to develop an understanding of the significance of changes in these accounts.

Other Methods of Analysis

Although the national income accounting or gross national product type of analysis is now in widespread use, there are several other methods that should be mentioned. We do not undertake a detailed description of them, but you will undoubtedly be encountering them in your future studies or work experience and a brief outline of them is in order here.

One of these methods is referred to as "flow-of-funds accounts" or sometimes as "moneyflows." This system is more elaborate than GNP analysis, and to some extent complements it, rather than being an alternative approach. It has been used chiefly by economists in the Federal Reserve System with annual reports made available in the *Federal Reserve Bulletin.* As Professor Lewis points out:

Whereas the purpose of national-income accounting is to provide reliable estimates of the scope and structure of the economy's productive achievement and of the income which this generates, the purpose of flow-of-funds accounting is to supply a comprehensive, revealing picture of the economy's uses of money and credit and of the sources from which these funds arise.[2]

For some purposes, the flow-of-funds method provides analysts with valuable guides in estimating directions of economic change.

---

[2] John P. Lewis, *Business Conditions Analysis* (New York: McGraw-Hill Book Co., Inc., 1959), p. 75.

FIGURE 20–3

The Flow of Money Income and Expenditures: The Circular Flow in a Given Time Period

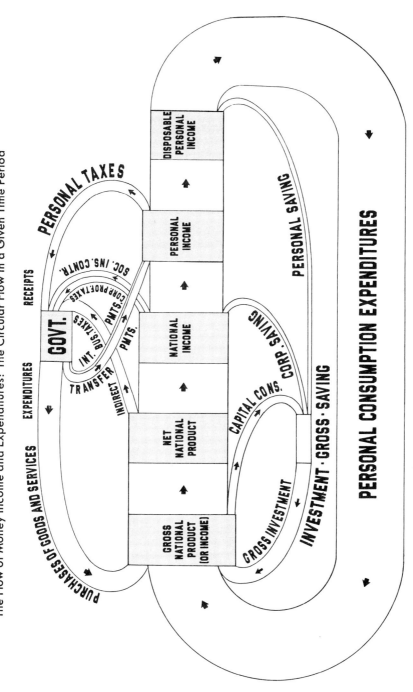

Adapted from *America's Needs & Resources: A New Survey*, Twentieth Century Fund.

Another system that has been developed and which offers promise for the future is referred to as "national wealth statistics."[3] The purpose of this system is to provide measurements of the size and composition of the wealth of the entire economic system and to record changes in them. It resembles for the economic system as a whole an individual firm's balance sheet; GNP accounts more nearly resemble a firm's income statement. It may be that regularly published government figures based on this national balance-sheet concept will soon be forthcoming.

Other methods of analyzing changes in the economy include input-output tables and balance-of-payments accounting but we will do little more than mention them here. The former makes provision for dividing the economy into a large number of industries or final demand sectors and the various inputs of goods and services they get from each other and outputs supplied to each other provide the basis of the tables that are set up. These are arranged in the form of a matrix or cellular table, with the same industries listed at the top and at the sides, thus forming a "matrix"[4] (see Chapter 14). The calculations that are made, however, are more complex than we can consider in these discussions, and indeed, it is the complexity of the calculations that has prevented this method of analysis from achieving more widespread use.

Balance-of-payments accounting is used primarily for measuring the volume and composition of a nation's international transactions. Both current and capital accounts are used. The Department of Commerce has provided data of this type for a number of years. They are especially useful for analyzing relationships between the American economy and those of the rest of the world.

We should recognize that significant work is going on constantly to provide improved methods for analyzing and forecasting potential changes in economic activity and business conditions. Even so, the future will always remain an enigma. A sudden outbreak of war, a major shift in public attitudes, new technological developments and new products, improved institutions for facilitating business transactions, and many other changes can never be anticipated with any high degree of accuracy. Business managers and those who assist them, however, continue to improve the techniques by which they can develop their forecasts.

---

[3] See R. W. Goldsmith, *A Study of Saving in the United States* (Princeton, N.J.: Princeton University Press, 1955); see also Lewis, *op. cit.*, pp. 80–81.

[4] Lewis, *op. cit.*, pp. 81–82.

Industry Forecasts

As we have suggested, businessmen base their forecasts or postulates of the future course of business conditions, not only on general trends, but also on potential changes in the particular industry or line of business within which they carry on operations. All industries, of course, do not move in the same direction as the entire economic system. Our economic system is now so diversified that a number of industries may be expanding at the same time that others are declining. Hence, business managers study industry as well as general business conditions in developing backgrounds for their predictions and decisions.

In many industries trade associations prepare special reports for managers dealing with recent changes and potential developments that are of special significance to a particular line of activity. In a number of instances monthly or quarterly reports are published such as *Banking* and the *U.S. Savings and Loan News* in the field of finance; *House and Home, Architectural Forum,* and *Engineering News Record* plus other related publications in the construction field; *Railway Age* and *Traffic World* in transportation; and the *Department Store Economist* and the *Journal of Retailing* in the retail field.

Various professional associations also make available published materials that carry useful information along these lines; for example, the *Journal of Finance* published by the American Finance Association, *Journal of Marketing* published by the American Marketing Association, and the *Accounting Review* published by the American Accounting Association. In addition numerous government reports are available in specific fields, notably in housing, wholesaling, retailing, manufacturing, and others.

In some instances trade associations in various lines of business activity retain business economists and research workers to prepare industry studies and to explain them to business managers in order to help them develop sound predictions relative to their own fields of work. Frequently, conventions and conferences are sponsored by various industry groups in order to provide useful information along these lines either based on statistical and related information or in some cases to present the views of leaders in the industries.

As in the case of information about general business conditions, the business manager himself or in co-operation with his staff undertakes to prepare forecasts which will guide him in making plans for his future operations. Ultimately, of course, he must make up his own mind as to his expectations regarding the future trend of events in business activity generally as well as in his industry. Then he makes his plans accordingly.

Economic and Managerial Audits

Business managers need to look ahead, to anticipate economic changes, and to adjust their decisions to potential trends; they also need to look back in order to determine how well they have adjusted their plans and programs in the past to anticipated economic changes. To do this it is possible to make use of *economic and managerial audits*. In effect, the manager may review or "audit" the principal decisions of a past period such as a year and determine the extent to which such decisions correctly anticipated changes in economic and business conditions. Analysts such as business economists may assist in making such audits.

By means of an audit of this type, using hindsight with "20-20" vision, the manager of a business firm can determine the extent to which price changes, shifts in competitive patterns, changes in business conditions, and related developments have been correctly anticipated in his decisions. To the extent possible any necessary adjustments can be made in past decisions. Implications for future developments can be determined. As a result of such audits, future projections and decisions may be improved.

For example, if a decision was made six months previously to add to inventories in anticipation of a price advance and if prices have not moved upward since that time, the decision may have added to costs by the expansion of inventories. A study of potential price changes may be undertaken to determine whether inventories should be worked down or partially liquidated, or whether the added stock should be held because upward pressures on prices are expected to bring price increases soon. The earlier decision may have been premature, rather than in error. Many other types of decisions may be audited including such things as the timing of the introduction of new products, letting of contracts for major plant additions or improvements, expanded or reduced advertising programs, personnel recruiting programs, and the like. Audits of managerial decisions in the light of changes in business conditions may be made at the time the budget for the next year's operations is prepared. Or they may be made in connection with the development of other management plans. Audits may be fairly complete covering a large share of a firm's operations, or partial, or they may be directed to only one phase of activities.

Uses of Economic Forecasts

We have outlined in a very introductory manner some of the indicators of changes in business conditions and various methods that may be used in analyzing them. As we have pointed out, business managers are vitally concerned with prospects for the future—whether business will get better, worse, or remain the same.

In making his decisions against the background of one or another estimate of the trend of business conditions, the business manager often uses the types of analysis discussed under the heading of "Game Theory" and "Decision Making under Uncertainty" in Chapter 14. For example, he might ask: what is the worst that could happen and how can I maximize my minimum gain or minimize my maximum loss? In such a case he would attempt to select the "maximum" alternative on the assumption that business would deteriorate sharply. On the other hand, he might choose to act in such a way as to minimize his regrets or to act on the assumption that each one of several possible future conditions of business were equally likely. Or he may feel optimistic and ask himself what is the best that can happen and choose accordingly. Of course, his estimates of the "payoffs" under the various "states of nature" are necessarily very rough.

If he has information about the probabilities of various possible future business conditions, he may try to choose a course of action to maximize his "expected return." Many managers analyze their possibilities less formally. For example, they may raise such questions as these: What is the *worst* than can happen? Assuming that business conditions deteriorate sharply, what will be the probable effect on my situation? Conversely, he may ask, given an estimate of conditions, what is the *best* that can happen? In other words, what is the most optimistic result that may be expected?

Between these two extremes, on the basis of a sort of "worst-best" type of analysis, he arrives at a decision. The assumptions of the worst possible developments indicate the maximum probable loss that may be encountered. The assumption of the best possible situation indicates the maximum gains that may be anticipated. Programs can then be undertaken, dropped, postponed, or undertaken on an expanded or reduced basis in terms of such estimates.

Usually, business conditions do not change with great rapidity. While managers often are caught with long-term commitments which may be difficult to carry in a period of recession, they usually come out all right if they can hold on long enough. Short-term commitments such as excessive buying for inventory may bring short-term losses when conditions deteriorate sharply.

SUMMARY

General business conditions represent a significant part of the business environment. Changes in business conditions may affect the markets for the things that business firms buy and sell, and may have an important bearing on the attitudes of business executives and the public generally. Thus, business conditions, and especially anticipated changes in business conditions, may have substantial significance for many management decisions.

Either directly or with the aid of business economists and other specialists, managers study and analyze various sources of information in order to keep abreast of business conditions generally or in specific industries or sectors of the economy. The indicators of business conditions that are usually watched closely include gross national product; wholesale and consumer prices; industrial production; personal income; anticipated expenditures for plant and equipment; consumer expenditures; spending programs by governments; changes in employment; changes in population; and others. Attention is given to secular trends, cyclical fluctuations, and seasonal variations in business activity.

Gross national product or national income methods of analysis have been especially helpful to managers and analysts in their attempts to forecast changes in business conditions. In addition some use is made of "flow-of-funds" accounts, input-output tables, and balance-of-payments accounting.

Industry forecasts typically are based on special studies of specific industries or lines of business activity. Managers may make use of "economic and managerial audits" in reviewing and evaluating past decisions, which.in turn may form the basis for future decisions. Game theory and decision making under uncertainty may be helpful in developing programs to meet anticipated changes in business conditions; more typically a "best-worst" kind of analysis is used. Regardless of the methods used (or lack of them) decisions based on forecasts of changes in business conditions usually are difficult to make.

QUESTIONS AND PROBLEMS

1. You are asked to describe current business conditions. Indicate several sources of information that might be helpful to you.

2. On the basis of current conditions, do you think that business activity will expand, remain stable, or decline in the months ahead? Justify your estimate.

3. Contrast secular trends, cycles, and seasonal fluctuations. What are the principal stages of a business cycle? Which stage do you think we are in now?

4. Do you think that cylical variations in business activity will be more or less severe in the future? Why?

5. Why do business managers and analysts pay so much attention to the principal spending divisions of our economic system when they undertake to forecast probable changes in business conditions?

6. Do you agree or disagree with the comments made by Machiavelli that were quoted in this chapter?

7. Why are many of the demands of business firms and consumers in this country postponable?

8. Give an example of a sensitive or "lead" indicator of changes in business activity.

9. Under what circumstances might a manager decide to move contrary to general trends of business conditions?

10. What is meant by "gross national product or national income accounting approach" to the analysis of business conditions? List two other methods of analysis.

11. What are the three principal spending sectors of the American economy?

12. Why is it important for a manager to study the industry in which he is operating as well as general business conditions?

13. You are the manager of a college book store. You find on the basis of the evidence available that local student enrollments are expected to rise, that national enrollments are expected to remain stable, and that general levels of business activity are tending slightly downward. Under these circumstances would you expect your sales to expand, remain stable, or decline? Explain.

SUGGESTED READINGS

Lewis, John P. *Business Conditions Analysis.* New York: McGraw-Hill Book Co., Inc., 1959. This is an outsanding book in this field. Read especially chap. 1, "The Subject and the Book," and chap. 2, "The General Architecture of National-Income Accounting." You may also want to read chap. 16, "General Forecasting Techniques."

Long, John D. *Workbook to Accompany Weimer: Business Administration: An Introductory Management Approach,* chap. 20. Rev. ed. Homewood, Ill.: Richard D. Irwin, Inc., 1962.

Maisel, Sherman J. *Fluctuations, Growth and Forecasting.* New York: John Wiley & Sons, Inc., 1957. Chap. iv, "Long Run Growth," and chap. v, "Short Run Fluctuations," are pertinent to the discussions in this chapter.

OUTLINE FOR CHAPTER 21

GOVERNMENT AND POLITICAL CONDITIONS have a major impact on business decisions and operations.

Business firms have many responsibilities to government, such as
conforming to laws and regulations,
collecting and paying taxes,
co-operating in voluntary programs, and others.

Governments have responsibilities to business firms, such as
establishing and enforcing laws and regulations;
maintaining order and protecting persons and property;
providing for defense;
providing systems of money and credit;
protecting against "booms and busts"; and
providing services, information, and facilities.

Relationships between government and business cover wide ranges of programs and controls.

Types of controls include
formal and informal,
inducive and coercive,
direct and indirect, and those
supplementing or supplanting competition.

Types of government and political changes include
long-term trends,
election cycles, and
sudden changes.

Analyses of government and political conditions
are based on
information,
observation, and
expert advice and special studies.

Business managers are tending to emphasize
public and community relations programs,
as well as political activity and business
statesmanship.

GOVERNMENT AND
POLITICAL CONDITIONS

Government is a trust, and the officers of the government are trustees; and both the trust and the trustees are created for the benefit of the people.

—HENRY CLAY

Impact of Government and Politics

As we indicated in our discussions in Chapter 20, the business manager attempts to forecast changes in business conditions and to use such forecasts in making his decisions. Much the same thing may be said in regard to the governmental and political forces operating in the environment of business firms.

By this stage of your studies, you undoubtedly recognize that the activities of all business firms are affected in greater or lesser degree by government programs on federal, state, or local levels. Changes in such programs, especially those of major importance, are usually the result of significant shifts in the political weather—in the attitudes, preferences, and objectives of the voters generally. If the business manager can anticipate changes in government programs or in the political forces back of them, he may be able to operate much more successfully than would otherwise be the case.

Anticipated changes in government programs or in the political climate may call forth the manager's support or opposition; but of even greater importance, they may bring about directly or indirectly major or minor changes in his decisions and operations. He may find it necessary to alter or modify his objectives, his plans, his organization, or his control methods. He may be called upon to exercise unusual qualities of leadership in the process.

In order to gain at least a preliminary understanding of the manager's work in adjusting his decisions and operations to changes or anticipated changes in the governmental and political sector of the environment, we discuss briefly the following topics: (1) responsibilities of business firms to government, (2) responsibilities of government to business firms, (3) ranges of business-government relationships, (4) types of controls, (5) types of government and political changes, (6) analysis of government and political conditions, (7) public and community relations programs, and (8) business politics and statesmanship.

Responsibilities of Business Firms to Government

In order to give you at least a general idea of the responsibilities of business firms to government, we may outline a few of the more important. It is obvious, of course, that business firms must obey the laws of federal, state, and local governments. Such laws and regulations may range all the way from required procedures for starting a business to the inspection of the products of the firm. Licenses may be required to carry on certain types of business; employees must be protected against industrial hazards; minimum-wage laws must be observed; taxes must be paid to local, state, and federal units of government; and many other things.

In many cases business firms serve as tax collection agencies for government. For example, they collect income taxes for the federal government by withholding stated amounts from the salaries and wages of employees. They are required to withhold and pay social security charges. In some cases taxes are collected for state and local governments, such as state income taxes or sales taxes.

Business firms often co-operate with government agencies on a voluntary basis in connection with various programs such as withholding from salaries and wages for the purchase of United States savings bonds or giving special assistance to local governmental units in connection with educational or recreational programs.

Many business firms bid on government contracts, and if they are successful, carry out the resulting projects in accordance with required specifications and standards, submitting to inspections as necessary.

Under certain conditions business firms may institute suits against government agencies in such cases as recovery of taxes believed to be paid in error or disagreement in regard to contracts or rulings. In the case of the federal government, business firms or individuals may not sue except with the consent of the government.

In some cases business firms make executives or other officials available for government service. Such persons may at times be appointed to government posts and be given leaves of absence by their companies. In other cases business firms may contribute the services of various officials on an advisory basis. You have undoubtedly heard the expression, "dollar-a-year men." In such cases business executives serve government, but their salaries are paid by their firms.

Business managers may undertake to influence government programs. They may try to secure changes in laws or regulations affecting the activities of their firms or those of competitors. While rather rigid limitations are now imposed on the contributions which business firms may make to political campaigns, many make such contributions. Through their trade associations or other organizations, they may carry on lobbying activities, attempting to secure the enactment of the kind of legislation they prefer or to prevent the enactment of legislation which they oppose.

Basic Government Responsibilities to Business

While business firms have a wide variety of responsibilities to government, as we have seen, government also carries out a variety of activities in discharging its responsibilities to business. Governments *establish and enforce the laws and regulations* under which business activities are conducted. Provisions for private ownership of property and enforcement of contracts are basic to our system of business. The government has the responsibility for providing the "rules of the game" which make the business system work and which help to maintain competition, or if monopolies develop, to break them up, regulate them, or supplant them by government operations. It is the responsibility of government to enforce the laws and to provide a system of courts for adjudicating differences between business firms, individuals, or government agencies.

Government agencies have the responsibility of *maintaining order* and protecting persons and property. Without the maintenance of order, it would be impossible to carry on peaceful activities. Business firms would have to provide all of their own guards to protect their plants or stores and the movement of goods to customers.

It is the responsibility of government also to provide for the *national defense*. In effect, our national government maintains a monopoly of force and in this manner assures the maintenance of order and the protection of persons and property. To as great an extent as possible our government protects its citizens and their property in other parts of the world.

The federal government provides a *system of money and credit* by means of which business transactions can be carried on. It is the responsibility of government also to regulate money and credit, and in so far as possible to protect the integrity of the dollar, that is, to guard against rapid changes in its value. In the postwar years and particularly with the enactment of the Employment Act of 1946, the federal government has assumed important responsibilities for the maintenance of reasonably full employment, of protecting the economic system against "booms and busts," and of pursuing the objectives of orderly economic growth.

Governments on nearly all levels undertake important responsibilities in the field of *education*. The availability of well-trained and educated personnel is, of course, of vital importance to business firms of all types. Furthermore, the system of public education from lowest to highest levels is one of the greatest assurances we have of the maintenance of reasonable equality of economic opportunity in this country.

Government agencies also provide a large volume of *information* which is used extensively by business firms. At various points in our earlier discussions, we have referred to the publications of the Departments of Commerce, Labor, Agriculture, and the Treasury, the Bureau of the Census, the Council of Economic Advisors, the Board of Governors of the Federal Reserve System, and other agencies which carry on important activities in providing business firms and private citizens with objective and impartial information about business activity in general, about specific lines of business, and about many other things of interest to business managers. Many state and local governments also provide a variety of information that is valuable to business firms in the conduct of their activities. In addition to the provision of information, many government agencies provide advisory services of certain types. Various activities of the Small Business Administration and the Departments of Commerce and Agriculture are cases in point.

Our federal government has assumed major responsibilities for a system of *federal highways* for the movement of goods and persons. State governments make provision for state highway systems, and local governments provide for streets, sewers, and many other local community facilities without which business could hardly be transacted. The Post Office Department, of course, provides for carrying the mail and, thus, makes available a highly important communication system for business.

Special Government Programs

Many governments conduct important *inspection* activities, assuring consumers of the quality of products. In some cases they license various types of activities. For example, many state governments license real estate brokers, insurance agents, barbers, and many other people who provide services which it is believed require special competence. Assurance of such competence is provided the buying public through licensing systems.

Governments may in some cases *compete* with business firms either for the purpose of regulating competition, often referred to as "yardstick competition," or in some cases supplanting private activities by government programs. This is often the case if "natural" monopolies exist. In other cases government agencies regulate the rates that may be charged, as in the case of railroads, telephone companies, local utilities, airlines, and many others.

You are quite familiar, of course, with the responsibilities of local governments for regulating traffic, establishing zoning regulations to determine how various types of land will be used, requiring building permits for the improvement of properties, and others.

The above discussion is not in any way intended to be complete. Rather, it is designed to suggest the multiplicity of responsibilities of government to business and the many types of programs which may affect business firms in the modern community. It is obvious that business has a major stake in good government. Thus, many business managers are deeply concerned with the relationships of government agencies to them, and their relationships to government agencies in turn. Like business, government is far from being a static type of activity. Governmental programs must be adapted to changing conditions and must cope with new problems as they arise.

The administration of government agencies, of course, involves many of the same types of activities that are carried on by the managers of business firms in the conduct of their day-to-day operations. This is why business managers often can be especially helpful in the administration of government programs.

Ranges of Business-Government Relationships

In order to understand the wide range of relationships that may exist between business and government, we may distinguish two extremes: (1) complete government ownership and operation of all economic activities, and (2) minimal government activity in the economic field. Between these two extremes a multitude of arrangements is, of course, possible, with a preponderance of government activity in some situations, and in others a preponderance of private business activity.

Of course, neither of the two extreme positions outlined above is ever likely to be found in reality. Rather these extremes represent concepts or idealized "models." Even in the most complete dictatorship in the history of the world, it is difficult to think of a situation in which there would not be some economic activity carried on by private persons or interests. The absolute monarchies of the pharaohs of ancient Egypt came close to this concept, since they owned all the people as well as all other resources. Conversely, it is difficult to think of a set of conditions in which there would be a complete absence of government activities, if only to provide roads or maintain order. The pioneer community of an earlier period of our history illustrates this type of situation.

The extent to which private activities or those of government dominate an economic system will vary with conditions, for example, the pioneer community versus modern urban communities; and with the objectives, attitudes, and mores of the people. Even in the pioneer period experiments were carried on of completely socialized communities. Jamestown, when first settled in 1607, started as a socialized community, and New Harmony provides a later example. Sometimes religious motives inspired the establishment of communal types of social organizations in pioneer settlements.

In our country there has been a historic preference for a wide range of private economic activity. Even so, government has played a big role throughout our history, even in the pioneer period. As our society has grown more complex and interdependent, the role of government has tended to expand. Still, we have tried to keep government always in the role of servant rather than master; to provide widespread opportunities for the establishment and operation of private business firms; and to rely on competition as a regulator of economic activities to as great an extent as possible, rather than on direct government ownership and operation of numerous economic activities.

While we must in some situations—such as total war or major depression—rely heavily on government, we try, when emergencies have passed, to restore to as great an extent as possible economic freedoms for individuals and private firms. In all probability, the true test of whether one is a socialist turns not on whether he may favor government programs to meet emergencies but on whether he favors returning the activities covered by such programs back to private individuals and companies once the emergency has passed.

In fact the minimal amount of government action that is required for the operation of our economic system today is substantially greater than most people realize. Businessmen, of course, often complain about governmental interference in their affairs. They recognize, however, that substantial programs of government are unavoidable in order to make our system function. They are concerned, as are many persons in other lines of activity, with the *types* of governmental programs and actions that are undertaken. They recognize perhaps more clearly than most of us the importance of avoiding the types of programs that will change the essential character of our system. They favor programs that will keep our system competitive, productive, and progressive—programs that will enable each individual to go as far as his ambition, energy, and luck will carry him in the "pursuit of nobler things in a nobler way."

Types of Controls

We should recognize that business is not something apart from controls. As J. M. Clark has said, ". . . when we speak of the 'social control of business,' we must take pains to avoid the implication that business exists first and is then controlled. Control is rather an integral part of business, without which it could not be business at all. The one implies the other and the two have grown together."[1]

In order to understand some of the interrelationships between business and controls, it may be helpful to consider various types and levels of controls of business activity. Thus, we may distinguish between formal and informal controls, between constitutions, legislation, and common law; between inducive and coercive controls; between direct and indirect controls; and among various levels of control relative to competition.

By *informal* controls we mean the types of regulations that various groups develop themselves out of their own needs and customs. Business firms in various lines of activity develop customs, informal agreements, and accepted ways of doing things that have important regulative implications. These change very slowly over time, and usually create no special problems for management in terms of forecasting probable future changes.

The common law is to some extent an informal type of control since it grows by precedent and court interpretation rather than formal action. We will consider this general type of control to a greater extent in the following chapter. We should note here, however, that the common law does not usually change rapidly. It adapts to changing conditions, it is true, but tends to follow rather than to lead developments

---

[1] By permission from John M. Clark, *Social Control of Business* (2nd ed.; New York: McGraw-Hill Book Co., Inc., 1939), p. 12.

in the business world. Hence, the manager is seldom faced with possibilities of rapid change in this area.

Formal controls are usually those resulting from legislation. The most formal of our controls is the Constitution of the United States and the constitutions of state governments. They may be changed at times, but the process is a slow one requiring formal procedures that are not easy to meet. Legislation, of course, comes out of every session of Congress, every state legislative session, and on a somewhat less formal level out of many meetings of local governmental organizations such as boards of aldermen or councilmen. Often when we think of government control of business we are referring essentially to legislation. Important as this is, we should remember that it is but one of many types of control. It is, however, one of the most volatile areas, and the area which is often of major concern to business managers in planning and carrying out their operations.

Related to legislation are the regulations of administrative tribunals such as public-utility commissions, the Interstate Commerce Commission, the Federal Communications Commission, and many others. While not so formal as legislative enactments, these regulations have important implications for business managers and often are subject to fairly rapid change.

As we have suggested, we may distinguish also between *inducive* and *coercive* programs. Basically, coercive regulations or programs require performance of certain actions or restraint from actions in order to avoid penalties. For example, either you pay your taxes or suffer fines or possibly imprisonment. By contrast, inducive regulations or programs hold out promise of reward for compliance with desired lines of action. For example, subsidies may be granted to stimulate certain programs. A good example is the insurance of mortgages by the Federal Housing Administration if they conform to established standards. Another example is the offering of accelerated depreciation charges if business firms build plants that are required for certain war or defense programs.

In this country both inducive and coercive types of programs are used extensively. Business firms typically prefer the former, although it is recognized that they will not be effective in all cases.

We may also distinguish between *direct* and *indirect* regulations. For example, if government wishes to halt price rises, prices may be fixed, that is, controlled directly, or monetary and credit controls may be used to reduce the availability of funds and thus halt price advances indirectly. In this country we tend to favor indirect controls of economic activity, particularly if the alternative is direct interference with business processes such as would result from price controls.

We may also classify regulations and programs in terms of their *relationship to competition:* for example, (1) government regulations designed to make competition work such as enforcing antitrust laws, (2) government regulation of rates, charges, or earnings as in the case of privately owned monopolies such as utilities (3) government competition with business firms as a means of setting standards of com petition, or (4) direct government ownership and operation, thus supplanting competition.

We have listed some of the types of controls of business activity, not with a view to presenting an exhaustive list but rather to give you some insight into the variety of relationships that exist as between business firms, on the one hand, and government, law, custom, and other regulative methods, on the other. As we pointed out, business cannot exist without some system of regulation. In part this system is largely nongovernmental, being based on customs, accepted ways of doing things, and the common law; in part it is legislative, or related directly or indirectly to legislation.

The importance of these relationships from the standpoint of the business manager arises from the possibility that they will change, that change will bring risks, and that such risks will have implications for the manager's decisions relative to plans, organization, or control processes. In order to anticipate such changes as may occur, the manager needs to study and analyze current conditions and trends. We will consider this topic, now, beginning with the types of changes that may occur and proceeding with a discussion of some of the methods that are used in analyzing them. The manager attempts to estimate the degree of risk—the relationship between possible gains and losses—that may arise from changes in governmental or political conditions. He does this in a manner similar to estimating the risk arising from changes in business conditions.

Types of Governmental and Political Changes

In our discussions of business conditions in Chapter 20 we pointed out that at least three types of changes in business activity could be identified: secular trends, cyclical variations, and seasonal changes. Similarly several types of changes in the governmental and political field may be distinguished. For example, there are *long-term* political changes that to some degree resemble secular trends in business conditions. Usually long-term political and governmental changes reflect basic shifts in the attitudes and viewpoints of the public generally. Thus, there have been continuing trends toward programs that will help to prevent depressions; to protect people against the hazards of illness, old age, or economic insecurity; and to establish minimum standards such as wages per hour. All of these trends reflect a quickening social conscience, on the one hand, and sufficient economic strength to support programs of this type, on the other.

The business manager who is able to identify long-term trends in political and governmental affairs may be able to use them as guides to his decisions and operations. They may be as important, or in some cases even more important, for his purposes than secular changes and trends in the economic field.

Unfortunately, basic long-term political changes are not always easy to distinguish, and in some cases may lead to unanticipated results. For example, unsettled international relations and tensions—a major factor in shaping government programs in the recent years—resulted in man-made earth satellites and other space vehicles. From this came increased emphasis on scientific education, and to some degree a re-evaluation of many of our educational programs. This illustration points up the difficulty of estimating the effect which long-term political forces may have or in determining their significance for the managerial programs of specific business firms.

In contrast to long-term forces making for political change, *sudden shifts* in political and governmental conditions may occur. For example, a sudden "scare"—fear of an economic depression, outbreak of war, or other national emergency—may bring quick political reactions that are almost impossible to anticipate.

Something like *cyclical* changes may also be distinguished in political and governmental affairs. The elections every two years set up a sort of cycle of political activity which is accentuated in the years of presidential elections. In election years, government tends to be somewhat more responsive to popular opinion than in the "off" years. Business managers often are able to make use of this political cycle of changes in developing their plans and programs. For example, years of presidential elections are often years of major uncertainty for the business community, and a number of business managers may be reluctant to start new programs at such times. On the other hand, some managers may try to anticipate the results of elections and develop programs in advance of them, in the hope of gaining advantages over competitors.

In addition to the above types of changes—long-term political changes, election cycles, and sudden shifts or "scares"—regional fac-

FIGURE 21–1

"I'd hate to have to go out and make a living under those laws we just passed."

Source: *Wall Street Journal* (by permission of Cartoon Features Syndicate).

tors often require special attention. For example, agricultural considerations may dominate the political scene in some states. In many states the conflicts between city and rural areas are of great importance politically; most state governments are dominated by rural interests, even though they may represent a minority of voters. Illustrations could be multiplied, but the above examples should help you to see some of the factors that a manager must consider in attempting to predict political and governmental changes on national, regional, or local levels.

Analyzing Political and Governmental Conditions

From our above discussions it should be apparent that governmental and political factors play a major role in shaping the environment in which business firms operate. Thus, many business managers try to study and analyze this sector of their environment with a view to predicting probable developments, estimating the risks involved, and adjusting their decisions and operations to anticipated changes.

This is far from an easy task. While information about government and political affairs is presented in every daily newspaper, it is difficult to select the key information or to determine its implications. Furthermore, business managers do not usually have expert assistance available to them in this field. A number of trade associations and other organizations maintain offices and personnel in Washington and in various state capitals for the purpose of bringing together information about governmental and political activities that may be of value to their members. On the local level, chambers of commerce are often helpful in this connection. In some cases lawyers undertake to analyze proposed pieces of legislation and to estimate chances of enactment. The business manager often can secure useful information from congressmen or senators in Washington, his legislative representatives in state government, or city councilmen or aldermen on the local level.

In more recent years various "public opinion polls" have attempted to give advance indications of the attitudes and preferences of voters. You have undoubtedly read various reports of polls of this type prepared by Gallup, Roper, or others. Essentially these reports are based on sample surveys and employ much the same types of techniques used in sample surveys of consumer spending plans, product preferences, and the like. Their reliability varies with the adequacy of the sample taken and the accuracy of the interpretation of results.

Like the politician, the businessman may "put his ear to the ground," that is, try to determine trends of opinion. In the normal course of their work businessmen talk to people of many types. They read widely. They may set up public relations departments or employ public relations firms to help them in this and related activities. Business managers need to know how to evaluate newspaper and magazine reports, to try to see behind the headlines, news stories, and editorials. Often government officials or politicians issue statements that are designed to "smoke out the opposition" or to "send up a trial balloon" to test public reaction or to lay out a claim to an area in which there is likely to be new legislation. The business manager soon develops a healthy skepticism in regard to current news reports. He tries to understand what is back of them, what the motives of government officials or politicians may be, and what kind of results may be anticipated. He attempts to think in terms of who exercises the real power in political and legislative campaigns. Often the actions of elected representatives or public officials are taken with one eye on those who control important blocks of votes or who provide substantial financial support for political campaigns.

In short, *things are not always as they seem* to be in this interesting sector of our business environment. It is not easy to figure out the strategy of a politician or government official, to determine whether he is acting in his own interests or the interests of others, or to estimate the relative strength of one or another program. As we have suggested there are few "experts" to whom the manager can turn for advice in trying to estimate the probable trend of political and governmental events. In some cases political scientists may provide valuable assistance.

Predicting Political Changes

Regardless of the difficulties involved, the manager has no alternative but to make predictions, projections, or postulates as to what will happen in government and political conditions and how such changes may affect his operations. If he ignores developments in this area, he is making the assumption that his operations are unlikely to be affected or may be affected to such a limited degree that he need not be concerned with political or governmental trends. In most cases, he is vitally interested and makes every effort to develop the best estimates that are possible.

For example, there may be the possibility of tax increases or reductions. Either of these developments might affect a manager's decisions and plans significantly. Various expenditures might be expanded in anticipation of a tax increase on the theory that government would bear an increasing share of costs, or the timing of programs might be changed in order to shift income between tax periods in anticipation of a tax cut. Changes in defense or defense-related programs may expand or reduce opportunities for business firms in various lines of work. Government programs in the international field have special implications for business firms carrying on foreign operations as we shall see in Chapter 24.

We might expand this discussion to great length. It should be clear, however, that the analysis of governmental and political conditions and the forecasting of changes are an important aspect of the business manager's work, that it is an area of considerable uncertainty and difficulty, and that much remains to be learned about it.

Public and Community Relations

Prior to the great depression of the 1930's the public relations programs of business firms consisted largely of "puff" stories in newspapers designed to call favorable attention to a business firm, its products, or its officials. Sometimes such stories dealt with public issues and presented the business side of such issues.

The great depression of the early thirties resulted in considerable loss of prestige for business firms and their leaders. Their contributions to the tremendous production programs required in World War II and the Korean War helped to restore the prestige of business. Some of the antitrust actions in more recent years were damaging to business prestige. As a result of these developments, the public relations programs of business firms have taken on quite a different character from those of a generation ago.

While there are still "puff" stories and propaganda of various types, the better public relations programs now attempt to develop a broad range of understanding between business firms and the public at large. Recognition is given to the importance of local community relations, to the relationships between a firm and the people who work for it and their families, to participation in public-service programs and activities, and to the development of two-way communication between the firm and its customers, employees, suppliers, investors, and the public at large.

Many firms give emphasis to the development of a desirable "image" in the minds of the members of the various publics that are served. As one corporation executive has said: "The corporate image —or corporate personality—is nothing essentially new. It is, in its essentials merely the picture which your organization has created in the minds of your various publics. . . ."[2]

In an earlier period the public relations programs of business firms were concerned primarily with "explaining away" problems and disagreements. Today, such programs undertake to find out what people really think about a business firm, or an entire industry, or to investigate other related topics. Efforts are made to get objective information about the reactions and attitudes of customers, investors, suppliers, employees, other companies, and the public at large to a business firm, its products, or its officers. On the basis of such information corrective action can be taken.

Thus, it is not enough to assume that a business firm or its management is "misunderstood" and that a few good propaganda efforts will change things. It is important to find out what public attitudes really are and if possible what lies behind them, regardless of whether they are favorable or critical.

---

[2] Statement by Lee H. Bristol, Jr., of Bristol-Myers Company. See, *Directors Digest*, Vol. XX, No. 5 (May, 1961), p. 16.

To some extent the public and community relations programs of business firms are used to influence political or government action. As we have suggested, such programs may aid the business manager in "putting his ear to the ground" in order to determine basic attitudes or possible changes in attitudes.

If a firm engages in a public controversy, care is usually taken to present factual information and to avoid the appearance of "propaganda." For example, a local government program may be proposed that would be detrimental to the operations of a firm. Presentation of the significance of the program in regard to the potential growth of the firm or its competitive position will go much farther toward assuring careful consideration of the proposal than denouncements and threats on the part of the firm's management.

Similarly, many business firms have found that their published "house organs," magazines, or reports become far more effective when they present straightforward information or discuss frankly problems of relationships between workers or customers and management than if one-sided points of view are reflected. As another illustration, the annual reports of many firms now provide helpful analyses of the result of operations rather than merely a technical accounting and statistical summary.

Business owners and managers generally recognize that they have important joint interests with the public they serve and the public at large. They understand that the public today is much better informed than was formerly the case and that it is not easy to win its approval. Yet, that approval is important to the long-term future of the business community at large as well as to specific firms. To win it, of course, requires sound operations, the provision of goods and services produced efficiently and made available at prices that give good value per dollar. Public relations programs that are well planned and carried out can also help in this process of gaining public acceptance and approval.

Business Politics and Statesmanship

Despite some of the statements in the popular press, which suggest that business is losing its influence in shaping public policies and government programs, the fact remains that business executives play a major role in this field. In part this is due to the many relationships between business firms and federal, state, and local government agencies, and in part it is due to the increasing responsibility which many business leaders have shouldered relative to matters of public policy.

Some businessmen are active in the political field in their own right, running for public office and discharging the duties of public office. Their number, however, is not great. To a larger extent businessmen work through organizations like their trade associations or chambers of commerce in attempts to influence legislation and government programs. Thus, there is a sort of "politics of business," not with respect to the internal affairs of business firms as in the case of "office politics" but in the area of public policy issues and programs.

There is a considerable controversy between business managers as to the extent that they should engage directly in political activities. One group believes that business executives should participate actively in political affairs, working with political parties, serving as precinct captains, and party committeemen, running for elective office, and serving in such offices. Another group contends that partisan political activity is not desirable either for the executives of a particular firm or for business generally. This group takes the position that partisan politics tend to alienate those in the opposition party, hence will lose customers and potential investors. Also, they think that too many business executives would tend to work with one party rather than another and thus make the entire business system a matter of party politics.

Regardless of the merits of these positions, and there is merit on each side, business executives to an increasing extent are taking an active part in political and governmental activities. Prominent business executives serve as cabinet officers and top administrators in both Republican and Democratic administrations in Washington, as well as in state and local government capacities.[3]

Business executives today often sponsor directly, through trade associations or through political parties various types of legislation. Some of this activity has for its purpose the improvement of business practices, protection against unethical methods, or the elimination of regulations that lead to increased costs without improving quality of products. In some cases, of course, there are ulterior motives back of such proposals. Sometimes legislation is proposed by established firms to reduce the possibility of competition by new firms or to give a competitive advantage to one kind of business over another. For the most part, however, the legislative proposals of business executives and their organizations serve many useful public purposes.

For example, local chambers of commerce perform many useful

---

[3] See, for example, Theodore Leavitt, "Business Should Stay Out of Politics," and Willard V. Merrihue, "The Business Leader's Role in Politics," *Business Horizons*, Vol. III, No. 2 (Summer, 1960). See also, Morrie S. Helitzer, "How Do Business Men Do in Washington?" *New York Times Magazine*, May 7, 1961, p. 37.

services in studying traffic problems, sanitary codes, building permit regulations, zoning laws, fire protection systems, and countless other difficult, practical, day-to-day issues, and make recommendations for improvements. Often chambers of commerce concern themselves both on state and local levels with good government rather than with issues related directly to business operations. Trade associations often recommend legislation that will protect the public against sharp practices. Frequently, legislative representatives cannot know the details of business operations or what may be required to improve or regulate them adequately. In such cases they must rely on the recommendations of business executives or trade associations and similar organizations.

Businessmen directly or through trade associations engage in a broad range of lobbying activities. While such activities are often criticized, we should note that they may serve highly useful purposes in bringing problems and issues to the attention of lawmakers and providing information that is valuable in the consideration of proposed legislation. Lobbying activities, of course, are not carried on solely by business firms or trade associations representing them but also by labor unions, various consumer groups, reform groups, farm organizations, and other sectors of our society.

Business firms have a vital interest in good government. The very life of many firms depends on honest and efficient government. If rules and regulations are applied unfairly as between business firms, competition soon breaks down. If firms following high standards are not protected against illegal practices, the public at large is not protected. If the "rules of the game" under which business firms operate are changed drastically with every session of Congress, the cost of doing business becomes prohibitive and the public suffers as a result.

Thus, the interests of business firms and the public at large tend to coincide to a substantial extent. Obviously, there are broad areas in which the public at large must be protected against questionable business practices. But usually these are carried on by a small minority of the members of the business community. Indeed, the principal reason for such a wide variety and diversity of laws and regulations relative to business firms is this small minority who operate on the basis of the letter rather than the spirit of the law.

Today many of the heads of our larger corporations occupy an almost *quasi-public position.* They cannot discharge their responsibilities to their companies without giving careful consideration to the implications of their actions and decisions for the economic system as a whole. Many other business executives are recognizing to an increasing extent the implications of their programs for the public generally as well as for their own industries and firms. Such "business statesmen" are exerting a growing influence in business and in public affairs.

SUMMARY

The decisions of business managers are affected more or less continuously by government programs on federal, state, or local levels. Business managers attempt to anticipate changes in such programs, and this necessitates the prediction of shifts in the political weather, that is, in the attitudes, preferences, and objectives of the voters generally.

Business firms have a number of responsibilities to government. They must observe the laws and conform with various regulations. In addition, they may serve as tax collection agencies, they may bid on government contracts, and they may participate in various voluntary programs. Under certain conditions they may institute suits against government agencies. Also, business firms may undertake to influence government programs.

In turn, government has a number of responsibilities to business including the establishment and enforcement of the laws and regulations under which business activities are conducted. Government agencies maintain order, protect persons and property, provide for the national defense, make provisions for a system of money and credit, protect against "booms and busts," collect and publish significant information, provide roads and numerous services such as the post office, support educational programs, and various other things.

The possible range of the relationships that may exist between business and government are wide, with complete government ownership and operation at one extreme and minimum government activities in the economic field on the other. While we have maintained a wide area for private economic activity in this country, government has played a significant role throughout our history. Indeed, control is an integral part of our business system. Controls may be informal or formal in nature. They may be inducive or coercive, direct or indirect.

Government and political changes may be of several types: (1) general long-term trends, (2) sudden shifts in political conditions due to unusual occurrences, and (3) cyclical changes centering around election periods. Business managers, either directly or through trade associations, various professional services, or in other ways, attempt to analyze political conditions in order to anticipate changes that may take place in government programs.

Business managers have paid increasing attention to their relationships with local communities and to the public generally in recent years. They have attempted to develop a *two-way* communication process in their public relations programs rather than simply to present the points of view of the business firm.

Business executives play important roles in the political and governmental fields, not only in terms of lobbying and related activities but also in participating in direct political activity, serving in important government posts, or as leaders of business and public opinion, that is, as business statesmen.

QUESTIONS AND PROBLEMS

1. How may possible changes in political conditions or in government programs affect the decisions of business managers?
2. If there appears to be sentiment favoring a reduction in federal income taxes for business firms and individuals for the year ahead, how may this affect the plans and operations of a business firm?
3. List and illustrate several of the major responsibilities of business firms to government; the major responsibilities of government to business firms.
4. Do you think the federal government should continue to assume responsibility for maintaining reasonably full employment and protecting the economic system against "booms and busts?" Why or why not?
5. Comment on this statement, which was quoted in this chapter: ". . . when we speak of the 'social control of business,' we must take pains to avoid the implication that business exists first and is then controlled."
6. Contrast formal and informal types of government regulation; inducive and coercive controls.
7. The Board of Governors of the Federal Reserve System announces a reduction in the discount rate which usually brings about a reduction in the interest rates charged business firms. Do you consider this a direct or an indirect method of regulating business activity? Explain.
8. Is it possible to identify changes in political activity that resemble such changes in business activity as secular trends, cylical variations, and seasonal changes? Explain.
9. Why is the business manager often skeptical about current political news reports?
10. A business manager reads in his newspaper that a bill is being introduced in Congress that will impose special regulations on his particular type of business. How could he go about determining whether this bill has a reasonable chance of being enacted into law?
11. Contrast the public relations programs of business firms currently with those of the 1920's. How do you account for the change?

12. Do you think business executives should or should not participate directly in political activities? Give reasons for your position.
13. Do you think it is appropriate for business firms to engage in lobbying activities? Why or why not?
14. Do you think business executives will play a larger or a smaller role in public affairs in future years? Explain your position.

SUGGESTED READINGS

CLARK, JOHN M. *Social Control of Business.* 2nd ed. New York: McGraw-Hill Book Co., Inc., 1939. This is virtually a classic in the field of social control of business. Read especially chap. i, "Introduction and Fundamental Conceptions," and chap. iv, "Purposes of Social Control."

———. *Economic Institutions and Human Welfare.* New York: Alfred A. Knopf, 1957. Read chap. 10, "The Interdependence of Politics and Economics."

LONG, JOHN D. *Workbook to Accompany Weimer: Business Administration: An Introductory Management Approach,* chap. 21. Rev. ed. Homewood, Ill.: Richard D. Irwin, Inc., 1962.

WILCOX, CLAIR. *Public Policies toward Business.* Rev. ed. Homewood, Ill.: Richard D. Irwin, Inc., 1960. Read chap. 1, "Public Control of Business," and chap. 2, "Methods and Instruments of Control."

OUTLINE FOR CHAPTER 22

BUSINESS AND THE LEGAL SYSTEM have many interrelationships. *Owners and managers* of business firms operate in a framework of law, and legal factors affect specific business decisions and transactions in terms of

    legality of actions, relations between benefits and obli-
    gations, and legal risks.

The *legal system* is an outgrowth of
    custom and tradition,
    the common law,
    legislation,
    constitutions, and
    agency and administrative decisions.

The *legal framework* is based on principles of
    freedom to act,
    rule of law versus rule of men,
    necessity for settling disputes,
    rights and obligations, and
    enforceability of law through
        civil action or
        criminal action.

Basic legal relationships encompass
    property such as
        real and personal, and
        tangible and intangible types;
    contract, which involves
        offer and acceptance,
        consideration, and
        enforceability;
    agency; and
    remedies.

Various instruments and security devices are used; *negotiable instruments* being of special importance.

Managers are concerned especially with
    legal risks and
    protection against risks.

BUSINESS AND THE LEGAL SYSTEM

Reason is the life of the law ... the common law itself is nothing else but reason....

—Sir Edward Coke

Law and the Business Environment

You have had enough experience with law to recognize that it forms an important part of our economic, social, and political climate or environment. You rely on the protections of law and conform to its requirements. There are a number of things we may not do, and others that we must do in order to observe "the law." The same thing is true of business firms.

The owners and managers of business firms make their decisions within a general framework of law. It would be impossible to do business without it. There must be provision for protecting persons and property, for enforcing contracts, for balancing the rights and obligations of persons or business firms, for providing remedies in case of wrongs, and for many other things that are necessary to an orderly society and an effective system of business.

"The law" in this country is a composite of customs, constitutions, legislation, court decisions, rulings of administrative boards, and institutional factors. We grow up with a feeling of respect for law. The general weight of public opinion is back of our legal system.

The business manager, of course, must operate within this broad framework of law and opinion. More specifically, legal factors will enter into nearly all business transactions and influence many important managerial decisions. The manager's situation relative to the law may be compared in a general way to your position in regard to traffic regulations. You know that there are general regulations that apply to all drivers. In addition, such regulations apply to you specifically, and will influence your decisions in regard to the speed at which you will drive or the precautions you will take in operating an automobile.

Legal Aspects of Management Decisions

Our interest in this chapter centers in the legal system and in the implications of legal factors for management decisions. An illustration may help you to see the relationships between our discussions in the preceding chapter and this one. Because of a new government project such as the federal highway program, for example, a business manager may decide to expand the operations of his firm. To do this may require the purchase of additional real estate. Numerous legal problems may be involved including zoning regulations, taxes, and others. Whether one property or another is purchased may turn on legal factors, on whether the title to one property is clear and the other "cloudy," or whether there are legal restrictions on the use of one property and not on the other.

In short, our attention here is centered on such questions as these: (1) Is a contemplated course of action legal? (2) Must a transaction be carried out in a certain way in order to conform to law? (3) What benefits may be gained, and what types of obligations are assumed in a given transaction? (4) Are there risks that may be shifted or minimized by appropriate legal arrangements? (5) If agreements are not carried out, what sorts of remedies are available?

It is obvious that the business manager cannot be a lawyer any more than he can be an economist or an expert in political science. As in the case of these other fields, however, he needs to know enough about law and especially the business aspects of law to avoid taking action that will expose him to unnecessary risks. Often he will need to rely on legal advice in arriving at specific decisions. It has been suggested that he who is his own lawyer has a fool for a client.

As one writer has said, "In law as in chemistry and elsewhere, a little knowledge can be a dangerous thing. Businessmen acting without proper legal counsel frequently find themselves expensively, sometimes disastrously, involved in legal entanglements when their intentions were of the very best and they thought they were proceeding lawfully to accomplish entirely justifiable ends. More often than not, such entanglements could have been avoided by timely reference to competent legal counsel."[1]

In many business firms legal departments form an integral part of the organization. The head of the legal department may serve as a vice-president or general counsel of the company in such cases. Com-

---

[1] C. B. Dutton, "Business Law," in *Chemical Business Handbook* (New York: McGraw-Hill Publishing Co., Inc., 1954), Sec. 15, p. 15-1.

panies of smaller size usually employ independent law firms to advise them relative to legal problems, either retaining them on a continuing basis or for assistance on specific problems as they arise.

Legal Predictions

Obviously, a lawyer cannot make a manager's decisions for him. Legal advice may help a manager to decide on one course of action as against another, to weigh the risks in the alternatives open to him, and to estimate the relative chances for success or failure that may arise from legal factors. In short, the lawyer like any other expert, such as an economist, engineer, or accountant, helps the manager to make predictions and through them to arrive at decisions.

For example, a lawyer may help the manager by predicting that a contract drawn in a certain manner has a better chance of being sustained in court in case of suit than another drawn in a different manner. Or he may predict that the enforcement of a given contract will be extremely costly, or that a particular document is faulty, or in many other ways aid the manager to reach decisions. The decisions, however, are always the manager's, and he must assume the responsibility for them.

The legal aspects of business frequently pose difficult problems because "the law" is not a set of definite and specific rules that may be applied with certainty in reaching decisions. In some situations, the legal points will be clear; in others, clouded and uncertain. Also, the law changes over time, either as a result of court decisions, or legislative enactments, or judicial interpretation of legislative enactments. Our legal system must adapt itself to the changing requirements of the business community and of society as a whole. It is not the function of law to protect the status quo—to keep things as they are. Law has reflected the dynamic nature of our social and economic system. While legal changes create problems and risks for management, such changes are essential to the improvement of our economic, social, and political system.

Background of Legal System

As Professor Harold F. Lusk points out: "A legal system is one of the essential institutions of a civilized society. The cultural level, the religious beliefs, and the economic status of the people, as well as the form of government which has been established, all make their contributions to the development of the legal system, and in turn are influenced by that system."[2]

There has been a gradual growth of our law over a long period of time. In part it is the result of custom and usage which reflect the habits and mores of society and the business community. These, of course, change gradually over time. In part our law arises from the common law, that is, judge-made law, resulting from court decisions. In this country, the federal Constitution and the constitutions of the various states form a basic source of our law. Another source is legislation, acts passed by Congress, or state legislatures, or local governments. Also government commissions and agencies through administrative decisions develop regulations that affect business.

In the medieval period of history merchants held their own courts to settle disputes. As decisions gained acceptance, they became a part of established ways of doing business.

In England the common law arose out of the settlement of private disputes and controversies. As decisions were recorded they gradually evolved into a body of principles to which lawyers and judges could refer in working out solutions to new problems. The basic principle of judge-made law is "stare decisis," that is, to stand by decided cases and adhere to precedent.

Common law tends to center around the *settlement of individual controversies*, between persons or business firms, in contrast to legislative law, which usually involves group or general regulations. Often the effects of a common law decision thus are retroactive, while in legislation we follow the principle that there shall be no "ex post facto" regulation, that is, that such laws shall not be retroactive. Through legislation, thus, we are more likely to change law to meet changing requirements.

In this country we adopted many of the methods and principles of the English common law. In contrast to the English system, however, we drew up a formal written constitution, and the same practice was followed in each of the states. These constitutions may be amended, and sometimes this happens. The process is relatively difficult, however, and changes in constitutions are likely to come largely from interpretations of the courts. The Supreme Court, for example, may determine whether a piece of legislation is constitutional and thus exercise restraints on legislative bodies and assure that constitutional rights and liberties are not infringed on through legislation. Some-

---

2 By permission from Harold F. Lusk, *Business Law: Principles and Cases* (6th ed.; Homewood, Ill.: Richard D. Irwin, Inc., 1959), p. 1.

times, of course, such decisions have far-reaching effects on business and personal relationships.

Certain basic rights, obligations, and freedoms are spelled out in constitutions. In the federal Constitution, for example, the Bill of Rights, the first ten amendments, spells out a number of such basic concepts.

Basic to our system of enterprise and democracy are the rights of private property and the principles of contract. The authority of business firms to organize and to carry on operations rests chiefly on the private property concept. Relationships between business firms, or such firms and persons, are largely matters of contract.

The Legal Framework

Our legal system is based on the *principle of freedom to act*. This may sound strange in view of the wide variety of regulations and controls of business activity. Nevertheless, the basic concept of freedom to act will help you to understand our legal system.

To a large degree our law is a process of spelling out what people may *not* do, and to a lesser extent what they must do. We may do what pleases us or suits our purposes, but the law comes into operation to restrict our freedom to act when our activity will interfere with the freedom of others, who enjoy equal rights with ours. The law thus is a process of making adjustments between individual freedoms.

Our system of law is based on the concept of *rule of law* as against rule of men, the law being considered as something superior to the highest government official. Since traditionally we have been suspicious of authority, we have emphasized the separation of powers, between federal, state, and local governments and between legislative, executive, and judicial branches of government.

Basically laws grow out of the *necessity for settling disputes*. The interests and obligations of individuals or business firms must be determined and adjusted. In this connection one writer has said, "Law arises out of the need of settling disputes; hence its very nature is the defeating of certain interests that others may prevail. Ultimately it becomes an instrument for furthering the purposes and ideals prevailing in the community, but always it faces the necessity of defeating certain interests."[3]

The rights and obligations that are involved in a legal relationship must be enforceable if they are to mean anything. For example, my

---

[3] By permission from John M. Clark, *Social Control of Business* (2nd ed.; New York: McGraw-Hill Book Co., Inc., 1939), p. 71.

right under a contract to receive a book from you is based on your obligation to deliver the book. Your right to receive money from me for the book is based on my obligation to pay you for the book. If either of us fails to fulfill his obligation, it can be enforced in the courts.

FIGURE 22–1

A Balance of Rights and Obligations

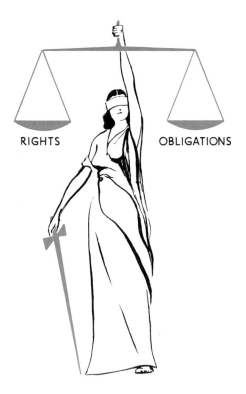

RIGHTS   OBLIGATIONS

To be enforceable laws must be backed up by power to compel persons to conform to regulations and to honor obligations. The courts ranging from Justices of the Peace to the Supreme Court of the United States settle disputes and may invoke the power of the executive branch of government to enforce their decisions. If you violate a general rule of society, for example, stealing property, *criminal* action may be taken against you; that is, the state takes steps to enforce the law. If you break a contract, *civil* action may result if the other party sues you for damages or the enforcement of the terms of the contract.

A *crime* may be thought of as a breach of one's duty to society as a whole and is punishable by society acting through government agencies.[4] If there is a breach of one's duty to an individual resulting in injury or loss to him, this is referred to as a *tort*. A tort is independent of contract. It is a wrongful act against an individual rather than society as a whole, and legal action can be taken to secure redress or as the lawyers say "remedy."

We should note that business firms may be involved in criminal action as well as individuals. Failure to pay taxes, for example, or to conform to sanitary or other regulations may result in criminal action against business firms or their officials. Antitrust prosecutions have involved some of the larger business firms of the country. Similarly business firms may be involved in legal actions because of torts.

In terms of the legal aspects of business our attention centers largely on property, contracts, agency, various legal instruments and security devices, and remedies. Our discussion of these basic legal factors involved in business transactions is brief. You need a familiarity with them to understand what may be involved in various business operations. In addition you can hardly appreciate the problems of management in regard to the legal aspects of business and the impact of the legal system on business decisions without at least an elementary understanding of some of these factors.

Basically the manager faces a number of *risks* in every transaction. Some of these are legal. We will discuss various legal risks and various adjustments that may be made to them after a brief review of several fundamental legal concepts and relationships.

Property

Property may be defined in a nontechnical way as the exclusive right to exercise control over economic goods.[5] In effect private property is a "bundle" of rights and liberties. The rights center largely around the exclusion of others from the use of the property, and the liberties in the use of property in any way that does not infringe on the rights of others or is specifically prohibited by law.

The essential requirements for private property are the following: (1) an owner; (2) a property object, which must be a thing of economic value; and (3) an organized government to protect and enforce property rights.

There are three major sets of reservations on private property rights: taxation, eminent domain, and the police power. Taxes on

---

[4] Harold F. Lusk, *Legal Aspects of Business* (Homewood, Ill.: Richard D. Irwin, Inc., 1949), pp. 122–23.

[5] For a more technical discussion, see Lusk, *Business Law: Principles and Cases, op. cit.*, chaps. xxix and xxx, and especially pp. 590–95.

private property must be paid or the property may be sold to satisfy the claim for taxes. Eminent domain means the right of government to take private property for public use. It is a right to compel sale by the owner, since compensation is always paid. The police power is a broad set of regulations considered necessary to safeguard the public health, morals, and safety, and to promote the general welfare. The establishment of zoning laws to restrict land uses, for example, is an illustration of the police power. Until a few generations ago one was free to use a tract of land for industrial, commercial, or residential purposes. We found, however, that the establishment of a factory in a residential area or a residence in an industrial area tended to diminish the value of adjacent properties. Hence, zoning laws were set up to regulate land use. The "bundle of rights" that makes up private property was thus redefined.

Property may be tangible or intangible. Tangible property is made up of rights in physical things. Intangible property is made up of rights in things that have no physical existence, for example, patents. Whether tangible or intangible, however, they are usually referred to as "things." The two major legal classes of things are "things real" and "things personal," or in ordinary language real property and personal property. The land and all things permanently attached to it are considered to be real property, and other things are classed as personal property. Goods, wares, merchandise, stocks, bonds, and money are all personal property. Most business tools and equipment, as well as patents and copyrights, are classified as personal property. In some cases personal property can become real property, as in the case of heating equipment being permanently installed in a building. This is usually called a "fixture."

Obviously, business firms use all types of properties. They may buy, sell, use, lease, or mortgage property. They may pledge it or take options to purchase it or give options to sell it. They may change its use; consolidate ownerships or subdivide them; improve real property by putting buildings on it; and many other things.

Contract

Contracts are essentially enforceable promises.[6] We should distinguish between social promises and unenforceable agreements, such as an engagement to meet for lunch or a promise to meet for a business conference, and contracts which may be enforced as a matter of public policy.

---

[6] *Ibid* , chap. iv.

In order for a contract to exist there must be an *offer and acceptance*. The subject of the contract must have economic value. The contract must be for a legal purpose, enforceable, and entered into by "legally competent" people; that is, they must be of age and of sound mind.

In some cases, depending on state statute, contracts must be in writing to be enforceable. Usually such agreements run for more than a year and involve $500 or more. For example, most real estate contracts must be in writing.

Enforceability is basic. Many types of contracts cannot be enforced, such as those in restraint of trade, those made under duress, that is, threats or pressure, those made by company officials if they exceed their authority to act, those made by incompetent persons, or for illegal purposes. As J. M. Clark has said, "The power to enforce carries with it the power to interpret, and the legal conception of a contract includes not merely the agreement itself but the entire body of law governing its interpretation and enforcement so that social control becomes an integral part of the contract itself."[7]

It is obvious that many business transactions involve contracts. Indeed without a workable system of contracts it would be impossible to carry on business activity. The basic principles of contract have changed relatively little for some time. There have been changes resulting from the establishment of minimum standards such as the minimum wage, standards governing conditions of work, and the like. The development of labor contracts—broad agreements covering wide ranges of problems entered into by unions and business firms—has been an important development of the uses of contracts in recent years.

We should make brief mention of "sales acts" in connection with this discussion. Such acts have been passed in all but a few states and provide for a reasonably uniform set of principles and definitions for the guidance of those involved in buying and selling goods and for the settling of disputes between merchants. These acts are complemented by judicial decisions, thus providing a fairly well-integrated law of sales which has been very helpful in the commercial development of this country.

Agency

The owner or principal executive officer of a business firm cannot personally enter into all of the negotiations involved in the many transactions that are carried on. Consequently, representatives or "agents" conduct much of the business in the name of the firm. A body

---

[7] By permission from Clark, *op. cit.*, p. 100.

of law has developed to govern the relationships that arise when a person performs work for or enters into contracts through or for someone else. The term "agent" is used to designate anyone who acts for another, who is his "principal."

Closely related are the relationships between employer and employee and "master and servant." In common usage an agent is considered to be a representative, such as a salesman or a purchasing officer, an employee as a clerical or factory worker, and a servant as one engaged in domestic work. Legal usage varies somewhat from the more common meaning of these terms, but they will be adequate for our purposes.

The chief problems in the agency relationship arise from the ability of the agent to make contracts for his principal with "third parties," that is, persons who may not necessarily be familiar with the agency relationship that exists in a specific case. The situation is complicated by the inability of third parties to know the direct or implied authority which the agent may have. Typically an agent may not sign checks or other negotiable instruments for his principal. Officers in companies may be granted authority to obligate the company within the limits of a certain amount of money or within a stated range of activity.

The responsibility of an employer for employees, arising out of the common-law doctrines of principal and agent and related relationships, for injury or losses has been greatly expanded and spelled out in the "workmen's compensation" statutes. Also many aspects of labor relations are based on the legal doctrines developed to govern relationships between principal and agent, employer and employee, and master and servant. Numerous statutes on federal and state levels have been enacted to clarify various aspects of labor relations, especially in dealings between companies and unions. Three important areas of development may be noted: (1) provision of safety standards, (2) minimum wages and maximum hours, and (3) standards of conduct for collective bargaining units. After contracts have been entered into by companies and unions, of course, their provisions govern the specific relationships between the parties during the period that the contracts are in force.

Remedies

As we suggested earlier in our discussions in this chapter, certain "remedies" or relief are available, principally through the courts, when the rights of a person or a business firm have been infringed by another. The most common form of remedy or relief is that of *mone-*

tary damages. There are two principal types of damages: compensatory and punitive. Consequently damages are awarded to repay a person (or firm) for losses that have been incurred, as in the case of failing to honor obligations under contract; punitive damages are somewhat like criminal penalties, but are recoverable by persons rather than the state under legal policies that impose payments for conduct that is considered unlawful or improper as in the case of torts.

In addition to damages of various types, relief or remedies may be sought through *injunctions.* An injunction is an order by a court to stop a certain designated type of activity. Thus, it is not a remedy for a past wrong as in the case of damages but a means of preventing a wrong from being continued or occurring in the future. An injunction may involve a restraining order by a court, a temporary injunction as an emergency measure and in some cases a permanent injunction. Sometimes mandatory injunctions are issued not to stop an action but to require that action be taken. Failure to comply with an injunction of any type renders a person subject to penalty for contempt of court.

Another type of remedy is called "specific performance," that is, the court orders a party to an agreement to carry out its terms specifically and not simply to award damages for failure to comply. For example, most agreements involving real estate are specifically enforceable. Property that is wrongfully taken may be returned to its owner. Most contracts involving services, however, are not specifically enforceable, since this would involve involuntary servitude. There are some limits, however, on persons who break contracts for services in making their services available to others.

There are various other legal remedies, but we do not undertake much more than a mention of them here. For example, suits to quiet title, to clarify ownership, often serve as a remedy; similarly the division of interests in property or "partition" may be used for this purpose; contracts may be rescinded as a means of securing relief in some circumstances; a declaratory judgment may provide a remedy. This involves the court ruling on a point of law without being called upon to decide the rights of one party as against another; and also writs of mandamus and prohibition may be used to compel a public officer to perform duties or to prohibit him from taking a contemplated action.

A basic familiarity with remedies will help you to understand how a manager may estimate the legal risks involved in specific transactions and the protections that may be available through remedies if other parties do not honor their obligations or commit wrongful acts. Usually various security devices may be employed to reduce risk, but if these are not effective or adequate, recourse may be had to legal remedies.

Instruments and Security Devices

Documents and papers are involved in many business transactions. Some of these are formal; others informal. If of a formal type, the documents may be referred to in some cases as "instruments." Of special importance for business purposes are "negotiable instruments," that is, documents which may be used to facilitate exchange and in effect take the place of money. Checks, notes, and drafts, for example, fall in this category. A check may be endorsed and passed on to a third, fourth, or later party in a series of transactions and thus be used as a medium of exchange.

In an exchange economy it is essential that the process of exchange be facilitated. The law has responded to this need of business by giving to negotiable instruments certain special characteristics that distinguish them from other property. Thus, if your hat is stolen you have a right to try to recover that specific hat even from someone who may have bought it from the thief in good faith. If money or a check is stolen and a third party takes it in good faith and without knowledge that it is stolen, he does not have to return it. You can see how important this arrangement is in facilitating exchange; without it no one would be certain whether to accept a check or even money in settlement for a payment due.

You may think of negotiability then as transferability with certain protections for one who is a "holder in due course," that is, who accepts a negotiable instrument in good faith and without knowledge of any problems that may have developed relative to earlier parties to the instrument. The instrument itself must be in writing, signed by the maker or drawer; contain an unconditional promise to pay a stated amount in money; payment is indicated as on demand or at a fixed date, and made "to order" or "to bearer."

The details of the relationships that may cause problems in connection with negotiable instruments need not concern us here, but we should note that various liabilities exist which have been carefully spelled out; that rules govern such things as orders to stop payment on checks, forged instruments, or endorsements, unauthorized signatures, and others. Many legal documents are not negotiable: for example, shares of stock, which are usually reissued by a transfer agent; deeds to real property, which involve the transfer of ownership; and others.

A number of *security devices* have been developed to facilitate business transactions. Typically these provide for the pledge of real or personal property to assure payment of a debt or the performance of an act. The real estate mortgage, for example, is a widely used security device. It provides for the pledging of a stated interest in real property. Chattel mortgages may also be used, that is, the pledging of personal property to facilitate a transaction. In some cases property is pledged by placing it in the personal possession of a lender or other party. Collateral loans are of this type, and to some extent assignment of accounts receivable fits this general classification. Warehouse receipts are often used as a security device; various liens such as mechanics liens also may be involved.

Many business transactions are facilitated by the use of security devices. They provide a direct protection for the performance of agreements rather than making it necessary to look to general remedies such as may be obtained through suit in courts or in other ways.

Legal Risks

As we suggested in the introductory sections of this chapter, managers need to develop a basic understanding of the legal aspects of business in order to determine the legal risks that may be involved in business transactions and to establish protections against such risks in so far as this is possible. Suppose we consider some of the types of legal risks that may face business managers.

For example, there is the risk of not knowing the law in a particular situation. Ignorance of the law, of course, is no excuse for violations. In such cases, the manager may consult a lawyer, and as a result reduce risk or calculate it more exactly than would be possible without legal counsel. In short, the business manager needs to know when to consult a lawyer in order to avoid or reduce legal risks.

Again, there is the risk that the law is indefinite. A new piece of legislation often is a source of legal uncertainty until it is tested in the courts. Even a skilled lawyer may not be able to predict very exactly what the results may be.

Risks may arise, of course, from changes in laws or regulations. Usually specific agreements already entered into will not be affected by new legislation directly since there are safeguards against "ex post facto" legislation; however, legislation may change the circumstances surrounding an agreement in such a way as seriously to affect it. Court decisions may change conditions and thus have retroactive effects. For example, the Supreme Court decided some years ago that restrictions in the deeds to real property which prohibited sale to persons other than members of the Caucasian race would not be enforceable in the courts. This in effect set aside assurances which many holders of real estate believed were available to them at the time they bought their properties.

Risks arise from the possibility that securities pledged may be inadequate or that enforcement of the pledges will be costly. Similarly there are risks that the remedies available in case of default on obligations or wrongs incurred will be inadequate in specific transactions or that the costs involved in enforcing agreements and obtaining remedies will be so high that the remedy is worthless for practical purposes. Indeed, most business managers prefer to avoid court actions, if possible, and to arrange settlements out of court. Legal actions are costly; often innumerable delays are involved, and additional and unforeseen risks may arise from a court action itself.

Some legal risks arise from differences in laws between states, that is, from lack of uniformity. For example, laws affecting mortgages vary widely as between states. In some, the borrower enjoys a long period of time in which to redeem the pledged property; in others this time period is brief.

Numerous other legal risks may be mentioned. Risks may arise from improperly drawn instruments, from errors in the judgment of lawyers or managers, from legal incapacity of parties, from fraud or misrepresentation on the part of various parties to agreements, from inability of parties to carry out agreements, and from many other sources. We have tried to point out a number of sources of legal risks without undertaking anything like a detailed or adequate coverage of the subject in order to illustrate some of the problems that managers face in this area.

Protections against Legal Risks

Business managers may undertake to protect their firms against various types of legal risks, to reduce such risks, or to shift them. Good legal counsel, of course, is one way of trying to avoid risky commitments. For example, properly drawn documents may aid greatly in reducing legal risks, or the careful interpretation and evaluation of agreements in advance of making commitments may prevent the assumption of hazardous transactions.

In some cases "performance bonds" may be set up as a method of reducing risks. In such cases the funds posted under a performance bond are forfeited in case of failure to complete an agreement.

Penalties sometimes are established. For example, if payments under an installment contract are not met, the entire debt may fall due at once. Financial institutions sometimes insert a penalty clause for the early repayment of a mortgage since costs are involved in putting the loan on the books. Sometimes bonds may not be callable prior to a certain date or before maturity without the payment of a penalty.

Insurance may be used to shift various legal risks, either entirely or in part. An example is title insurance which may be purchased to gain protections against unknown defects in the title to real property. Or a firm operating a store may buy public liability insurance to provide protection against injuries to customers and the suits that might result. Similarly, workmen's compensation liability may be covered by insurance.

Security may be required in connection with an agreement in order to reduce risk. For example, real property may be mortgaged, personal property pledged under a chattel mortgage, or goods may be sold under a conditional sales contract. Collateral loans are a case in point, that is, a manager may pledge stocks, bonds, or other securities in order to borrow money, or to borrow it on more favorable terms. In some cases recording in public records helps to reduce legal risks. Recording is required in the case of documents pertaining to real estate transactions and in various other cases. This involves filing the required documents with a "Recorder" or other appropriate official so that they become a matter of public record. In this way, all who wish to do so may consult the records and thus avoid making erroneous commitments.

Various other methods may be used to reduce or shift legal risks. The above illustrations, however, will help you to see some of the ways that are open for the use of managers.

Management and Legal Risks

Even though the types of protection against legal risks are numerous, many risks cannot be anticipated or cannot be estimated with any degree of even reasonable accuracy. Such risks are assumed by the business firm in the ordinary course of its operations. The assumption of risk by business firms, of course, is an essential ingredient of the enterprise system. Risks are assumed in the hope of gaining profits. Thus, in a final analysis the chance of making a profit must be present in order that business firms will undertake the many legal and other risks of doing business.

It is the job of management to gauge the risks of doing business. In the legal field the hazards are often great, as we have seen. Legal factors of varying degrees of complexity are involved in nearly every business transaction. To a degree skilled lawyers can help managers to avoid risks or indicate how they may be minimized. There may be danger, however, that legal complexities will discourage managers from undertaking new programs. This situation plus the increasing costs of litigation have in some cases tended to restrict business expansion.

Lawyers often are unduly conservative and may be inclined to recommend against action, since this usually cannot lead to much legal difficulty. To an increasing extent the manager needs legal counsel that will help him find ways of undertaking new programs rather than indicate why they should not be undertaken.

Increased uniformity of laws as between states, clarification of obscure legal points through legislation, improvement and streamlining of court procedures, development of simplified legal forms, elimination of cumbersome procedures as in the case of real property law, and related developments would aid greatly in reducing the legal risks involved in doing business. The best efforts of businessmen, lawyers, government officials, and students of law and business administration will be required to effect improvement in the broad area of legal aspects of business.

SUMMARY

Law forms an important part of the economic, social, and political climate of business. It would be impossible to do business without it. In this country "the law" is a composite of customs, constitutions, legislation, court decisions, rulings of administrative boards, and institutional factors.

Whenever a business manager faces an important decision, it is necessary for him to understand its legal implications. He must determine whether the action contemplated is legal, and if so, whether the transaction will be carried out in a manner that will conform to legal requirements. He will be concerned with the possibility of minimizing or shifting risks through legal arrangements. The types of remedies that may be available are also important in reaching decisions. To aid managers in regard to legal problems, business firms typically have legal departments or retain the services of lawyers.

To be effective, laws must be enforceable. Such enforcement may take the form of criminal action if a general rule of society such as stealing property has been broken, or civil action may be involved as in the case of suits to enforce agreements.

Our legal system centers, to a considerable extent, around property and contract. Important legal factors in business include agency, remedies, various instruments such as negotiable instruments and security devices, and others.

Business managers, with the aid of legal counsel, attempt to anticipate legal risks and to set up protections against them. Such protections may include performance bonds, penalties, insurance, requirement of security, recording, and other procedures.

Increased uniformity of laws as between the states, the clarification of obscure legal points, development of simplified legal forms, and streamlining of court procedures would all be helpful in improving the operation of the legal system.

QUESTIONS AND PROBLEMS

1. Why does business need a general system of law?
2. Since a business manager seldom is a lawyer, how can he make certain that he understands the legal implications of his actions?
3. If you were serving as the manager of a business firm and were confronted with a decision that had a variety of legal implications, what basic questions would you try to consider?
4. Is "the law" a set of definite and specific rules that can be applied with certainty in reaching decisions? Explain.
5. Outline the principal sources of the law under which modern business operates.
6. Explain this statement: "Our legal system is based on the principle of freedom to act."
7. Explain the essential difference between a criminal action and a civil action.
8. What is meant by "tort"?
9. Which basic conditions must be met in order for private property to exist?
10. What are the primary differences between real property and personal property? Give illustrations.
11. What is meant by "contract"?
12. Comment on this statement by J. M. Clark that was quoted in this chapter: "The power to enforce carries with it the power to interpret, and the legal conception of a contract includes not merely the agreement itself but the entire body of law governing its interpretation and enforcement so that social control becomes an integral part of the contract itself."

13. If you enter into a contract with me by which I agree to pay you $5 for every red traffic light you are able to pass, is this an enforceable contract? Explain.

14. If you are acting as the agent for a business manager could you typically sign checks for him?

15. What is meant by "a negotiable instrument"? Give illustrations. Is a check a negotiable instrument?

16. Is a mortgage a security device? Explain?

17. Why are legal remedies important to a business manager?

18. Give illustrations of several types of conditions that may create legal risks.

19. Give several illustrations of ways by which a business manager might protect himself against legal risks.

SUGGESTED READINGS

EELLS, RICHARD, and WALTON, CLARENCE. *Conceptual Foundations of Business.* Homewood, Ill.: Richard D. Irwin, Inc., 1961. Read pages 175–82; chap. 7, "Private Property"; and chap. 8, "Contract."

LONG, JOHN D. *Workbook to Accompany Weimer: Business Administration: An Introductory Management Approach,* chap. 22. Rev. ed. Homewood, Ill.: Richard D. Irwin, Inc., 1962.

LUSK, HAROLD F. *Business Law: Principles and Cases.* 6th ed. Homewood, Ill.: Richard D. Irwin, Inc., 1959. Read chap. 1, "Nature and Source of Law."

OUTLINE FOR CHAPTER 23

Understanding THE ENTERPRISE SYSTEM AND COMPETING SYS-
TEMS is essential to effective management.

The Enterprise System provides the general framework of our
economy and reflects
competition and political democracy;
common law, property, and contract;
dispersion of power; and
individualism.

This system, representing a special type of social control, is
distinguished by equality of economic opportunity,
broad participation in decision making, and
interrelationship of means and ends.

Social systems may be classified by the extent of choice
available.

Socialism may be characterized by state ownership and
operation of the chief means of production.

Communism, in terms of doctrine, stands for
revolutionary socialism,
the "withering away" of the state, and
theoretical anarchy,
but in *practice* results in
forced acceptance of doctrines, and
all-powerful dictatorship.

Dangers to the enterprise system include
cyclical fluctuations,
monopolistic tendencies, and
equality problems.

Strengths of the enterprise system center in
capacity for growth and increasing
productivity;
freedom of inquiry, choice, and
enterprise;
creativity and innovation;
adaptability to change; and
equality of economic opportunity.

THE ENTERPRISE SYSTEM
AND COMPETING SYSTEMS

A free society relates freedom and responsibility; a society which is not free tries to separate them and destroys both.
—ROBERT J. BLAKELEY
Vice-President
Fund for Adult Education

Management and the Social Organization

Our discussions shift now from various sectors of the business environment to a consideration of the significance of our general system of social organization for business firms and their management. The term "the enterprise system" is often used to designate our general economic organization. Sometimes the term "capitalism" is used to distinguish our type of organization from others. For our purposes we may use these two terms interchangably.

Our system is one in which economic activities are regulated largely through competition, but government has important responsibilities for making it work. The enerprise system can hardly be thought of as separate from political democracy or the common law, both of which are essential aspects of the system.

In addition to competition, political democracy, and the common law, other basic ingredients of the system include private property, contract, dispersion of power, and the concept of the importance of the individual relative to the state. We will have more to say about the characteristics of the system later in this chapter.

It is essential that business managers understand the basic characteristics of the system in which they carry on their operations. And since many business firms conduct operations throughout the world their managers need a knowledge of many types of systems. The competition between Western and Communist Bloc countries has added to the need for understanding the essential nature of our system and the way in which it differs from communism.

565

The system of enterprise and democracy has important implications for the day-to-day activities of business firms as well as for long-term programs of business development. The nature of the enterprise system affects the types of objectives that business firms may pursue, the manner in which they may pursue them, and the relationships between business firms and other divisions of our society.

What we call the "enterprise system" today differs significantly from the economic order to which we also applied the same term a hundred years ago. Yet this is not inconsistent. The essential nature of the system has been preserved, but it has been adapted to meet new requirements and conditions in part through changes in customs and mores, in part by legislative enactments, in part by legal and judicial adaptations, and in part by redefining competition and other basic processes as required.

What we call the enterprise system today will be quite different from this system a hundred years from now. Changes are going on constantly, and business managers need to be aware of them in order to guide the operations of their firms successfully. Indeed, we would soon supplant the enterprise system by something else if it did not adapt itself to the changing requirements of business and society.

Meaning of the Enterprise System

In the first place the enterprise system is a *system of social control.* This may strike you as a highly questionable statement, since most proponents of the enterprise system argue that it is a system of no social control or of limited social control. You probably recognize in view of our discussions in the preceding two chapters that business and social control go hand in hand, that only in a system of anarchy could there be an absence of social control, and that the effectiveness of business firms and of business management turns in considerable measure on the nature of the control system in which they work. It is true that the enterprise system represents a particular kind of social control; this is control to a substantial extent through competition and through the maintenance of conditions that make competition possible. The fact remains, however, that it is a system of control—of the social control of business and of various other sectors of our organized society.

In the second place, the enterprise system is an *incentive system.* People are induced to work for the good of the whole rather than coerced or forced to do so. Possibilities of reward are held out to those who try to achieve desirable goals, and people with ability respond.

In order to get responses to incentives, the rewards or the possibilities of reward must be handsome. The rewards must be of various types so as to have a widespread appeal: economic as in the chance to gain profits, or own property; prestige, for example, the opportunity to gain recognition, position, or power; and service with the appeal to altruistic motives.

Third, the enterprise system may be called an *opportunity* system. This may be thought of as a corollary to the concept that it is an incentive system. To make incentives real they must be fairly generally available to all; to make them available there must be reasonable equality of economic opportunity. A basic premise of the enterprise system is that there will be freedom of entry into business, into various lines of work, and into competition for leadership positions. There is also widespread freedom to produce ideas and to reap the benefits that arise from new ideas. Ideas can come from any sector or level of society. Ideas do not create power over others. An idea, even if protected under patent or copyright laws, does not result in "your more being my less." Our system or enterprise and democracy appears to provide a good climate for idea production; this may constitute one of its main strengths in the competition with communism.

Fourth, the enterprise system is one of *widespread leadership.* By means of the private ownership of property and enterprises many opportunities for leadership are opened up. This stands in sharp contrast to a dictatorial system in which leadership is highly centralized, and while there are provisions for many subsidiary leaders, their positions carry limited authority.

In many respects the enterprise system stresses leadership above everything else. It is through the provision of leadership that the rewards of society may be gained. The enterprise system is not a system in which rewards go to those who gain dominance over others, but to those who can contribute through leadership to the common good. The right to lead has to be demonstrated by deeds. Leadership positions must be won, and once won must be held against the competition and challenge of others.

Fifth, the enterprise system is one of widespread freedom of choice and of *broad participation in decision making.* Each of us and each business firm may choose objectives, and within legal limits the ways by which they may be pursued. The system does not make basic decisions for us. Rather it establishes the general framework within which decisions may be made. Of course, we cannot pursue courses of action that would interfere with the rights of others, and our system of law and regulation is designed to establish appropriate limits on the actions of individuals or business firms. People are inclined to work harder and be more productive if they can pursue programs that to a large extent they establish themselves, including freedom of choice of expenditures as well as type of work activity.

Sixth, and as a corollary to the concept of widespread freedom of choice, the enterprise system is one in which the *means become the ends*. No attempt is made in the enterprise system to get agreement on the ends or objectives that will be pursued. Rather this is left to the individual choice of people or business firms (or other organizations). Freedom of choice applies to many areas of life—to leisure time as well as work activities, to spending for current things as well as to investing, and to social life, religion, political activity, and other areas.

Of basic importance is the maintenance of a set of conditions that makes possible widespread freedom of choice as to ends and widespread opportunity as to their achievement. Thus, the principal objective of the system may be thought of as the development of appropriate means to make and keep it workable.

Compromise is often necessary to make the system workable. Indeed, the capacity for compromise within the system may be one of its significant characteristics. It is not a system of "blacks and whites" or of extremes; there are many "gray" elements.

A system of this types is likely to be prized and appreciated only in rather advanced, even sophisticated societies. This has been one of our problems in appealing to some of the less developed countries in our competition with international communism for their support.

What the Enterprise System Is Not

In part a definition turns on what a thing is *not*. The enterprise system is not a system of exploitation. We have undertaken to protect people and business firms against exploitation by government or by each other. To accomplish this has required redefinition of various rights, liberties, and obligations from time to time.

The enterprise system does not put a premium on the enjoyment of wealth. It puts a premium on the use of wealth constructively. Thus, this system stands in sharp contrast to some of the societies of the Middle and Far East in which much of the productive capacity of the people and their resources are used to support the luxurious living of their rulers rather than to produce more wealth. Funds are more likely to go in such situations into diamonds and jewels rather than into machines and factories.

The enterprise system is not static. Class lines are hard to find. It makes for a dynamic and fluid type of society. There are few protections for those who have won success since they must continue to meet competition. Old concepts and ideas must compete with new ones; old methods and processes with the most recent developments. It is not a stable system but changeable, and change creates problems. One of the main arguments against the system arises from its instabilities, even though the conditions that create them are one of its sources of strength.

The enterprise system is not a system of big business. While big business may flourish under it, small and medium-sized business firms may prosper as well. The mere fact of size is seldom a protection against competition, and if it is, government action is taken to bring competition into play or to regulate the enterprise.

Alternative Social Organizations

We may distinguish two principal types of social organizations: (1) pluralistic systems with separate areas of action for individuals, or business firms, or voluntary associations, and the state; and (2) totalitarian systems with the state supreme over individuals, business firms, or other organizations.[1]

Our system of enterprise and democracy falls clearly into the first of these two categories. A democratic system must permit freedom of thought and expression, hence widespread decision making, and this affects education, research, expression, publishing, the arts, and many other areas of life as well as economic activity. Totalitarian systems are characterized by limited freedom of choice, centralized authority, and a lack of or substantially limited individual freedom of thought and expression.

Another way of classifying social organizations is by means of the extent to which choice is permitted. Thus we may distinguish among (1) a status or caste system in which no choices or decisions are made by anyone, everything being decided on the basis of tradition or station in life; (2) a dictatorship (or absolute monarchy) in which there is in effect only one decision maker—who makes all basic choices; (3) an autocracy (closely related to dictatorship) in which a few people, members of a select group, make decisions; (4) democracy in which decisions are made basically by the majority, although there are important protections for minorities; (5) the enterprise system in which

---

[1] See John M. Clark, *Social Control of Business* (2nd ed.; New York: McGraw-Hill Book Co., Inc., 1939), p. 500.

decisions are made on a widespread basis but in terms of economic rather than political factors, through competitive markets; and (6) theoretical anarchy in which all may make decisions and choices and all would agree.[2]

This latter possibility can exist only in the abstract, at least in terms of the evolution of mankind to date. It does represent a theoretically possible system and hence should be noted. Similarly the other types outlined above seldom exists in any "pure" form in reality. We may think of them rather as "ideal types" or models.

Our system today contains some elements of nearly all of these possible arrangements. Some families, business firms, and other organizations may be dominated by tradition and certain elements of the caste system; some are operated largely on dictatorship principles. Some of our organizations may be run by small groups. But the society as a whole is organized essentially around the principles of democracy and enterprise. Decision making is widespread, and individuals, families, business firms, and voluntary associations enjoy wide latitudes of action with the state serving them rather than vice versa.

Socialism

Where do socialism and communism fit into the patterns outlined above? Experience with them to date puts them largely in the dictatorial or autocratic groups even though they profess to follow essentially democratic principles. Basically, socialism involves the ownership and operation of the principal means of production by the state. Varying degrees of socialism may be distinguished, ranging from the extent to which some private types of business activity may be allowed to the evolutionary or revolutionary character of the processes by which socialism would be established.

In theory most socialists believe in democracy and believe that democratic processes may be applied in reaching the decisions as to what should be produced, how much, and for whom. In an enterprise system most of these decisions, of course, are made through markets and through the choices of people as to how they prefer to spend their money. Complete socialism would abolish private enterprise in all its forms and would do away with profits, rent, and probably interest.

In our society we allow the socialization of some types of economic activity, typically those which cannot be controlled through competition and which may be classified as "natural" monopolies. In some

---

[2] See Frank H. Knight, *The Economic Organization* (Chicago: University of Chicago Press, 1933), pp. 22–30.

cases we leave even such activities in private ownership but regulate them closely. But some "mixture" has almost always been necessary. The important factor is not that some activities may be socialized in our society but that this is not the normal course of things; if this happens it would represent a shift from a system of enterprise and democracy to one of socialism.

Communism

The major challenge to our type of system today comes from communism, and more specifically communism as exemplified by Russia. In theory communism started as "revolutionary socialism," the overthrow of established orders by force in order to socialize or collectivize the principal means of production. Included in the theory of communism, however, is a considerable amount of anarchy, the concept that eventually all men will choose among the many alternatives of life and all will agree. When this condition has been reached the state will "wither away." According to communist doctrine the principal conflicts arise between those who own property ("the bourgeois") and those who do not "the proletarians"). This is what communists mean by the "class struggle." Hence, they contend that eliminating private property, at least of the type that produces monetary income, would eliminate major conflicts. All would then become unselfish and would serve the good of all.

As one student of the essential differences between capitalism and communism has said: "The myth which Marx taught and Lenin elaborated, the myth which has fired the minds of thousands of intellectuals, has been one of an eventual literal anarchy, obtained through a present strict control...."[3]

While there are obvious defects in the theory of communism, the appeal of a final theoretical withering away of the state has been widespread. The application of communist doctrine in Russia, however, has deviated far from the classical concept. Instead of tending to "wither away" the state has become all powerful; agreement among people has been achieved through liquidations and "brain washing"; freedoms of many types in addition to the right to own property have disappeared; and doctrine has been changed to serve the purposes of a ruling dictator or ruling clique.

Proponents of the system point to industrial and scientific progress in Russia, the lack of recessions and depressions, and the gains in inter-

---

[3] By permission from David McCord Wright, *Capitalism* (New York: McGraw-Hill Book Co., Inc., 1951), p. 9.

national position and strength in the world. Industrial progress has been made but has been purchased by forced saving, by severe limitations on consumer goods, and in some instances by starvation. Scientific advance has been made in limited "approved" areas, typically those which have military or industrial potential, for example, the space programs; absence of recessions or depressions overlooks slave labor, some famine, and relatively low living standards (it takes a prosperous country to have a recession); and gains in world position have been accomplished largely by military might or the threat of it and by infiltration of established governments.

To quote from Professor Wright again:

But the Marxian promise, at least in its modern communist version, is one not only of industrialism but of *developing* industrialism—an outlook idealizing scientific discovery—yet insisting it conform to the "party line" —the current interpretation of an ambiguous social oracle. To glorify change and yet restrict it; to stimulate the restless inquiry of the West and then expect it to conform spontaneously to the vague rules of a complex and evasive gospel concerning whose meaning there may, in utmost good faith, be scores of different interpretations; to feel an utter, fierce conviction that the salvation of mankind depends upon the survival only of the correct (your) interpretation, surely there could not be a social outlook, less likely ever to dispense with coercion or eliminate conflict.[4]

Threats to the Enterprise System

The enterprise system has been under attack, especially by "left-wing" groups, but also by those of the "right-wing." Among the criticisms usually included in such attacks are these: (1) The enterprise system is subject to cycles of activity going from periods of full capacity to substantial unemployment of people and machines. (2) The system does not provide for "planning," hence has no specific goals and no defined means for attaining them. (3) Labor is exploited by capital. (4) Monopolies tend to develop thus furthering exploitation. (5) "Pressure groups" tend to develop and have somewhat the same effect as monopolies. (6) The system does not lead to equality of persons.

There are also dangers from "gangster" elements that infiltrate and dominate some unions and business firms. Whether this will prove to be a growing danger depends on the effectiveness of law enforcement and the capacity of union leaders and members and of business owners and managers to resist them.

There is the danger also that unions and business firms will combine to carry on programs that in effect "hold up" the public. Closely re-

---

4 *Ibid.,* p. 27.

FIGURE 23–1

Electric Power Production and Population

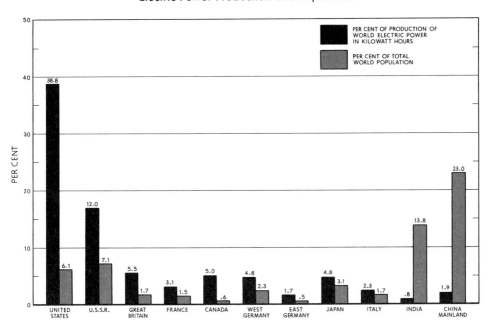

Source: Developed from United Nations data.

lated is the danger of political party and business or labor combinations.

Other arguments against the system are often advanced as well, but the above are encountered frequently and illustrate some of the dangers to the enterprise system that exist, either real or imagined. We must recognize, of course, that the enterprise sysem, like others, has various weaknesses. If we defend it, this does not mean to suggest that we consider it "ideal" or "perfect" in any way. Rather our contention is that it has advantages over other systems, that these advantages are worth preserving, and that, hence, dangers must be recognized and corrected if at all possible. Indeed, a major danger to the enterprise system is that it will not change or will not change rapidly enough to meet the requirements of a dynamic society.

We have already pointed out that the enterprise system is something quite different from the system of a century ago. The fact that it can change and has changed suggests that it will continue to do so in the future. Its strength lies in part in its adaptability, and it is important that this quality be preserved.

But suppose we consider some of the dangers to the system that we have listed and undertake to evaluate them.

Cycles and Instability

It is true that the enterprise system does not run on an even keel, that typically periods of expansion alternate with periods of decline or at least readjustment. We discussed this subject briefly in Chapter 20. When cycles dip very low and carry us into a deep depression, as was the case in the early thirties, great suffering results.

We have tried to learn from the experience of the early thirties and of that with cycles before and since that time. Various safeguards have been developed. In the Employment Act of 1946 the federal government undertook a major responsibility for attempting to protect us against the extremes of cyclical fluctuations. Certainly progress has been made. But there will undoubtedly be cycles of business activity in the future. Within limits, they are probably desirable. There are few persons, business firms, or other organizations that develop at a constant rate or that maintain stability in their activities or operations. All of these are part of the economic system and hence affect its functioning. Reduction of business fluctuations to a bare minimum would probably require such a volume of controls as to render the system unworkable. Such controls undoubtedly would include licensing of investment, determining when new inventions or ideas could be introduced, limiting replacement of old machines by new ones, and other similar measures. As a result the dynamic qualities of the system would probably be destroyed.

Our objective is not to eliminate cycles but rather to limit their extremes; and at the same time to maintain a set of conditions that will encourage economic growth and progress. Cycles of limited magnitude are a relatively small price to pay for the dynamic qualities of the system.

We should note also that it is probably impossible to find an economic system that is not subject to cycles of a sort unless we are content with a simple agrarian type of society. The Russians do not report cycles of economic activity and insist that they never have unemployment, but we know that they encounter periods of grave economic shortages from time to time.

Social Planning

The argument that the enterprise system does not provide for planning depends for its validity a great deal on what we mean by this term. It is true that the enterprise system does not provide for central planning of the type that allows a national authority to decide how many shoes or cars or suits of clothes will be produced next year. Such decisions are left to the business firms in these industries. Sometimes this leads to surplus amounts of goods, with the result that production is cut back until balance is restored. But the assumption that central economic planning of this type is preferable assumes that it would be possible to gauge more exactly by central authority what requirements are likely to be than to have this done by numerous independent business firms. Central planning can lead to surpluses or shortages, too.

In addition, we attempt to "plan" by various indirect means. The Board of Governors of the Federal Reserve System, for example, attempts to restrain a too-rapid expansion of the economy and to retard declines by means of monetary and credit policies. Our tax policies can also be adapted to avoid extremes of economic activity. Special provisions are made for particular industries as well. As a result the enterprise system is planless in terms of the establishment of quotas for specific industries or products but allows for direction through the establishment of conditions that will tend to influence the planning of business firms, local government units, individuals, and families.

Exploitation

The idea that the enterprise system is based on the exploitation of "labor" by "capital" is a part of the Marxian ideology. Undoubtedly there has been exploitation of workers by businessmen at various stages of history; there may be instances of it today. But the greatest protection against exploitation is competition. If you work for Mr. A and believe he is exploiting you, it is possible in a competitive situation for you to go to work for Mr. B or Mr. C. Of course, if Mr. B or Mr. C do not have jobs to offer, Mr. A may be able to take advantage of your situation for a time. But usually such time periods are brief. And they are likely to be brief in the future. Greatest exploitation is possible if there is only one employer of labor, and it would make little difference whether such a single employer were a governmental or private agency—either would be in a monopoly position.

What does the record have to say about exploitation?

Over the past half century, a period for which we have fairly good comparative statistics, the relative position of labor has steadily improved, and it has improved much more rapidly than the position of owners or managers or investors. Indeed, both the extremes of great poverty or great wealth have been reduced. We have gone a long way toward the elimination of distress arising from low incomes. Improvement in the future depends on the dynamic qualities of the economy and its capacity for growth and expansion. "Redistribution" of such wealth as we have would solve few problems. There are not enough millionaires to improve very much the lot of the rest of us even if we deprived them of all of their money.

Monopolies

We have mentioned monopolies and their dangers at various points in our discussions. The greatest danger to the enterprise system is monopoly in all its forms, whether monopolies of the "left" or the "right."

Unrestrained competition might eventually lead to a system of monopolies. But the enterprise system that we know is not a system of unrestrained competition; it is a system which uses competition as a major means of social control. Hence, if monopolies develop we undertake to deal with them in various ways. The Sherman and Clayton acts, which you will encounter often in your studies, are "antitrust" laws, that provide for the breaking up of blocks of economic power or the prosecution of those who engage in collusion in order to reduce competition. Not only does the Department of Justice prosecute business firms and business executives from time to time but the threat of prosecution undoubtedly operates as a significant restraint on tendencies for monopolies to develop in specific industries.

Where monopolies are "natural" or inevitable or essential for the national defense, provision is made for the socialization of the activities involved or for their regulation.

The monopoly problem has always been a threat to the enterprise system. It will undoubtedly be a major problem in the future. But as we have noted, there are governmental as well as private monopolies. Socializing an area of "natural" monopoly does not make it less of a monopoly; it shifts control to government as against private interests. So long as government is responsive to the wishes of the electorate and prevents exploitation from developing from socialized monopolies, reasonable conditions prevail. But, if all economic activity were socialized, a system of giant monopolies would be created, which would provide those in power with the means to exploit all of the members of our society as they wished.

"Pressure Groups"

It is often argued that our system is being divided into pressure groups or blocks—sometimes these are spelled out as business, agriculture, and labor. To a degree this is true. But at every period of our economic history there have been pressure groups, and at times this has led to great national difficulty, as in the case of the Civil War or the War between the States, whichever you prefer to call it. This was essentially a conflict between "pressure groups" that could not be resolved by peaceful processes.

The fact of the existence of pressure groups is not a peculiarity of the enterprise system. They may exist in any kind of system. The important factor for the success of a system is the extent to which such groups will pursue their own interests as against the common interest. If extreme positions are taken and if the short-run advantage of a pressure group is given precedence over the long-term advantage of the system as a whole, real difficulties will result.

At the present time many business leaders are recognizing the necessity of supporting the interests of our society as a whole as well as their own interests. At least to a degree the same thing is true of "labor" and "agriculture" to the extent that such specific interests can be identified. Fortunately, our society is not split very decidedly into these three divisions but into dozens or hundreds of types of interests. On some issues a businessman will agree with a farmer; on others with an intellectual; on others with a consumer group; and on others with labor.

One of the discouraging factors in the current situation is the concern of a few labor leaders over their particular and immediate interests and their relative lack of interest in the general welfare. This is illustrated by the following statements by Professor Sumner Slichter, who often expressed views that were favorable to the position of organized labor: "Powerful unions have existed in the building trades for well over a generation, but no important thinking on the difficult problems of housing has originated with unions in the building industry. Few officers of these unions have taken the lead in bringing about modernization of building codes, in fostering city planning, or in sponsoring better municipal government—all needed to encourage the construction industry."[5]

One may, of course, say much the same thing about some farmers, some professional men, and some businessmen. It is important for the community as a whole and for the business community, as well as other sectors of our society, that somehow the various pressure groups maintain a reasonable balance between their special interests and the interests of the whole. Our system provides a fair chance that this can be

---

[5] By permission from Sumner H. Slichter, *The American Economy* (New York: Alfred A. Knopf, Inc., 1948), p. 61.

done, in part because of the dispersion of power that continues to prevail and in part because leaders of many "pressure groups" are recognizing the increasing interdependence of all sectors of our society.

The Problem of Equality

One of the charges often made against the enterprise system is its failure to provide for equality of persons. Sometimes this charge is made in terms of equality of incomes or wealth; sometimes in terms of equality of opportunity; and in some cases in terms of a sort of "literal" equality. The latter, of course, is impossible so long as human beings differ in wants, capacities, and aspirations.

From the standpoint of equality of income and wealth, there are serious questions as to whether such a condition would be desirable. The concept of taking from each according to his ability and giving to each according to his needs fails to consider that ability may respond to different incentives, that recognition in some form calls forth greater effort (whether the recognition is in economic or in less tangible forms), and that as a result there is no longer any equality. Or looking at it from the other side, the capacity to consume—to develop greater needs—is in itself a reflection of lack of equality. Thus, inequality persists even if measured in no other way than by some standard of "need."

All of us are attracted to a greater or lesser degree to some sort of ideal of equality. When we are asked to define what we mean by this term, however, we have difficulty in giving any very satisfactory answer. Probably the closest we can come to such an answer is in terms of equality of opportunity. And in this regard the enterprise system holds a rather good record. Probably no system in history has gone so far in making provision for a "chance to rise on independent terms," of recognizing ability in many forms, and of providing means for its development. The great guarantor of equality of opportunity is our public school system, and it is supplemented by the programs of numerous foundations and special funds created by individuals and business firms.

The danger to the enterprise system from the standpoint of the question of equality arises largely from the chance that we shall be unable to provide as much equality of opportunity in the future as in the past. If monopolies develop, if trade-unions become more exclusive and greatly restrict membership, if it becomes more difficult to start new business firms, if educational opportunities are denied to important segments of the population, if political considerations or seniority rather than ability become the main tests of selection for advancement, then all who are interested in the maintenance of reasonable equality of economic opportunity have something serious to worry about. Fortunately, current trends do *not* suggest that there will be less rather than more equality of economic opportunity in the future. On the contrary, the record of recent years points to continuing advance in this area.

Other Criticisms

Various other criticisms of the enterprise system are made from time to time. For example, in recent years comparisons have been made between the rate of economic growth in Russia and in this country. Some politicians, economists and others contend that the American economy is not growing as rapidly as it could or should; that Russia's rate of growth is higher than ours; and that she will soon overtake us. By implication at least it is suggested that our type of system has limited capacity for economic growth or less capacity for growth than Russia's system. On the other hand, it is argued that rates of growth are not a good basis of comparison, since Russia represents an earlier stage of industrial development and starts with a smaller base; a gain from ten to twenty is a hundred per cent gain; a gain from one hundred to one hundred and fifty is a fifty per cent gain, but in terms of absolute amounts is more significant. It is also contended that rate of growth by itself has little significance, that the important element is the type of growth, the extent to which growth is balanced, and the degree to which all sectors of society participate in economic growth. This controversy over "growthmanship" is likely to continue.

Sometimes the enterprise system is criticized because it is cumbersome, that it does not respond rapidly enough to changing conditions. At times this may appear to be the case; but the record of history suggests that the system is highly adaptable, even though some changes may come fairly slowly.

The criticism is sometimes made that the enterprise system cannot adequately serve the needs of a highly complex and interdependent society. To a degree this criticism is similar to the charge that the system is cumbersome. Although we cannot forecast the shape of things to come, the record of the adaptability of the system in recent years suggests that it has substantial capacity for responding to the needs of an increasingly complex society. We should note, also, that the implied assumption that other systems may be more effective in dealing with the needs of a complex society is not necessarily correct. There is little evidence to support such an assumption.

Strengths of the Enterprise System

Having reviewed some of the dangers to the enterprise system, we should consider some of its strengths. Does it have the strength to meet the challenge of communist Russia? Are its strengths likely to increase? Or is the system living on borrowed time, on the strengths of the past?

It is often contended that the enterprise system is more productive than any other. This contention was seriously challenged by the rise of Russian military might and was pointed up by the success of the Russians in space exploration.

There is no doubt that any dictatorial system may in the short run expand production in a given direction very rapidly, and probably more rapidly than the enterprise system. This was demonstrated by Hitler, Mussolini, Stalin, and more recently by Khrushchev. A dictatorial state, whether of the fascist or communist variety, can center efforts on a predetermined objective and register great gains.

In the longer run, however, the enterpise system has an enviable record of expanding production and of increasing output per man-hour worked. This record is in large part the result of freedoms—of scientific inquiry which leads to technological advance; of enterprise which leads to more effective co-ordination of men, materials, machines, and ideas; and of free people who willingly give of their best when called upon rather than being forced to do so. The freedom to think, develop new ideas, choose, adventure, work, and if necessary sacrifice is a major strength of the enterprise system and makes it highly productive and probably more productive than any other over a period of time.

The main strengths of the enterprise system probably rest in these freedoms and in its adaptability to change. More than any other system it requires democratic institutions for its success and in turn supports them. Labor leaders who are often critical of the system support it because they feel that it serves their interests better than could a system of collectivism while at the same time protecting personal freedoms.

The enterprise system has a demonstrated capacity for adaptability to the changing requirements of society, and this is a source of major strength. As Professor John M. Clark has said, ". . . private enterprise as it now exists is an evolving thing and affords a basis for further evolutionary change of the most flexible sort available, with the most nearly voluntary methods of adjustment of conflicting interests and changing rights. This seems the most cogent reason for wanting it to continue."[6]

Is Freedom of Enterprise Important?

You have undoubtedly heard or participated in discussions and arguments on the relative desirability of the enterprise system. Some argue that socialism or communism are preferable, giving various reasons for their positions. Some contend that property and most business enterprises could be socialized, perhaps exempting family stores, service establishments, and farms, and that this could be done without losing political or other liberties.

While we can never be sure of answers in regard to arguments of this type, the weight of evidence from what we observe happening in other countries and notably in communist Russia suggests that our basic freedoms are so interrelated that the loss of one threatens the loss of all.

Professor John M. Clark says in this connection: "Is there any reason why personal liberty, as distinct from business liberty, should not be as unrestricted under socialism as under the present system, or more so? I believe there is; and the reason centers upon the coercive potentialities of a central administrative authority that has ultimate power over the livelihood of every citizen. This is a power of whose full impact we in this country have no direct knowledge, though we have recently had some hints, and elsewhere people have learned its fulll meaning by experience."[7]

A highly centralized authority, that is, a dictatorship, undertakes to protect itself from attack and criticism so censorship is established and the freedom of the press and expression are curtailed. This soon leads to the curtailment of political activity and political parties. Then education is censored, followed by control of research, religious activities, and enterprise; and the restriction of other rights and liberties soon follows.

Private enterprise helps to disperse power, to prevent concentration of both political and economic power in the hands of a few and essentially the same men, and thus helps to protect and preserve many personal liberties. Through competition, entrenched positions are subject to attack and displacement by new ideas, products, and methods.

---

[6] John M. Clark, *Economic Institutions and Human Welfare* (New York: Alfred A. Knopf, Inc., 1957), p. 259, by permission.
[7] *Ibid.*, p. 98.

Thus, whatever its shortcomings, the enterprise system helps to assure many of our personal liberties.

Business Firms and the Enterprise System

Business firms are dependent on the enterprise system for their existence. They do not exist in communist Russia. The "business firms" (if they may be called that) that exist in dictatorial states are quite different from those in an enterprise system. Usually cartels or state sponsored or approved monopolies are all that may exist.

Thus, competitive business-firms are peculiarly a creation of the enterprise system. By contrast, families, clubs, churches, and various other social institutions may be found in almost every type of system, although their character may be somewhat different. Business firms, thus, have a special interest in the preservation and improvement of the enterprise system. If it should cease to exist, business firms would also cease to exist, at least in anything like their present form. Similarly labor unions in anything like their present form would cease to exist.

The recognition of their dependence on the system has brought an increased feeling of responsibility on the part of many business leaders for it, especially in recent years. They recognize that its continuation depends on its performance, which in turn depends on the performance of individual business firms. To continue its existence the system must be acceptable to all sectors of our society and to the people at large, the final source of authority in this country.

Business owners and managers have a variety of attitudes toward the enterprise system. While nearly all support it, some support it blindly while others support it more rationally.

A growing number of businessmen as exemplified by the Committee for Economic Development recognize that the enterprise system involves social control in large part through competition with reasonable freedom of business firms to pursue their opportunities. They recognize the importance of positive programs on the part of business firms, trade associations, and government agencies to maintain a set of conditions that will enable the system to work effectively. In short, the system cannot be expected somehow to work by itself, to correct its own mistakes, and to develop without direction.

Like other systems it is made up of people, and it can function no more effectively than the people who have major responsibility for it. Such responsibility rests not only on the business manager but also on leaders in other sectors of our society. If labor leaders follow narrow and special interests to the detriment of the whole, they can do great damage to the system's effectiveness. The same thing is true of farm, professional, educational, or governmental leaders. The desire and the will to make the system work is an important part of its strength.

Businessmen have an important responsibility to support and promote the will to make the system work. This can be done through the development of greater understanding of the system and its methods of operation, through promoting good government on all levels, by managing the operations of individual firms in a way that will provide more and better goods and services at lower costs, and above all by helping to maintain and expand equality of opportunity for all to "pursue nobler things in a nobler way."

SUMMARY

Our general system of social and economic organization is often referred to as the enterprise system or "capitalism." It contrasts in various respects with other systems. Managers need to understand the essential characteristics of the enterprise system and competing systems.

The enterprise system provides for the regulation of economic activities largely through competition, but government has important responsibilities for making this system work. Basic ingredients of the system include private property, contract, the dispersion of power, and emphasis on the importance of the individual as against the state. This system is dynamic, hence sometimes unstable, but has demonstrated its abilities to adapt to changing conditions and needs.

Despite widespread freedoms the enterprise system is a system of social control. It is an incentive system and an opportunity system which allows general participation in leadership and decision making. It is a system in which, to a large extent, the means are the ends, that is, the maintenance and development of a set of conditions that allows widespread freedom of choice becomes the general objective, with each individual and business firm relatively free to establish specific ends or objectives.

In comparison with totalitarian systems, the enterprise system exhibits a number of important advantages. It provides for greater dispersion of decision making and idea generation than is possible under other systems, it provides protection against monopolies which are not available either under socialistic or communistic systems, and it protects the individual against central authority more effectively than does communism even though the general theory of communism envisages the ultimate "withering away" of central authority.

Dangers to the enterprise system arise from extreme cyclical fluctuations in business activities, the faith of many people in centralized planning, the belief that labor is exploited by capital, the special problems created by monopolies and pressure groups, and the confusion of many people relative to the meaning of equality. Such people fail to recognize that equality of economic opportunity rather than some concept of literal equality is of major importance in our system.

Principal strengths of the enterprise system center in its expanding output and productivity over the long run; in the widespread freedom of people to think, choose, adventure, and innovate; and in its demonstrated capacity to adapt to change. Business firms are dependent on the enterprise system for their existence since they could not flourish in a communistic or socialistic state. Consequently, an increasing number of business managers are recognizing their responsibilties for making the system work.

QUESTIONS AND PROBLEMS

1. What are the principal distinguishing characteristics of the enterprise system?
2. Contrast the major features of social control in the enterprise system with those characteristic of socialism and communism.
3. Explain the extent to which widespread leadership characterizes the enterprise system.
4. Explain this statement: "An idea, even if protected under patent or copyright laws, does not mean that 'your more is my less.' "
5. Explain the concept that in a system of enterprise and democracy the *means* become the *ends*.
6. Do you agree or disagree with this statement: "The enterprise system does not put a premium on the enjoyment of wealth. It puts a premium on the use of wealth constructively."
7. What are the principal points of difference between the enterprise system and communism?
8. What do you consider to be the major dangers to the enterprise system? Which of these dangers do you believe will become increasingly important in the future?
9. Do you think we need more centralized planning in our system? Why or why not?
10. Mr. Khrushchev has declared on a number of occasions that Russia will "bury us" economically. Does this suggest fundamental strengths in his system in comparison to ours? Explain.
11. How may various pressure groups damage the enterprise system? Can you give illustrations?
12. Do you think labor tends to be exploited under the enterprise system? Under communism?

13. Mr. John W. Gardner has suggested that the critical lines of tension in our society grow out of emphasis on individual performance and restraints on individual performance. (See John W. Gardner, *Excellence* [New York: Harper & Bros., 1961], p. 28.) Do you think these lines of tension may diminish? Why or why not?

14. Do you think equality of economic opportunity is the most important form of equality? Why or why not?

15. What do you consider to be the three major strengths of the enterprise system? Explain. Is the enterprise system likely to gain new strengths in the years ahead?

16. Do you agree with the following statement that was quoted in this chapter: ". . . private enterprise as it now exists is an evolving thing and affords a basis for further evolutionary change of the most flexible sort available, with the most nearly voluntary methods of adjustment of conflicting interests and changing rights."

17. Do you think business executives have a special responsibility for making the enterprise system work? Why or why not?

SUGGESTED READINGS

CLARK, JOHN M. *Economic Institutions and Human Welfare.* New York: Alfred A. Knopf, Inc., 1957. This book is a series of essays dealing with a number of topics of current interest. Refer especially to chap. xi, "Free Enterprise and a Planned Economy," and chap. xii, "The Relation of Western Economic Thought to the World Struggle."

LONG, JOHN D. *Workbook to Accompany Weimer: Business Administration: An Introductory Management Approach,* chap. 23. Rev. ed. Homewood, Ill.: Richard D. Irwin, Inc., 1962.

WALLICH, HENRY C. *The Cost of Freedom.* New York: Harper & Bros., 1960. This is a stimulating book that may be of interest to you.

WRIGHT, DAVID McCORD. *Capitalism.* New York: McGraw-Hill Book Co., Inc., 1951. This book presents a discussion of some of the principal characteristics and problems of capitalism. Of special interest for our discussions here are chap. i, "Government and the Social Problem," and chap. iv, "Democracy, Capitalism and Growth."

OUTLINE FOR CHAPTER 24

INTERNATIONAL BUSINESS ADMINISTRATION is an area of growing importance for American business firms and their managers and specialists.

Regional environments may be divided as to
    local or "little" economies,
    sections of the country,
    national, and international areas.

Significant developments in the international environment
    include
        the population explosion,
        the ideological conflict,
        rising aspirations, and
        new institutions.

Major types of international business operations cover
    exporting,
    licensing arrangements, and
    establishing manufacturing and distributing facilities abroad.

Management problems for multinational firms include
    those arising from multiplicity of government regulations and compliance with them;
    taxes, incentives, and guarantees;
    personnel and labor relations, notably
        training programs,
        bargaining agreements, and
        wage scales;
    ownership arrangements;
    remote control difficulties;
    language barriers, and
    foreign currencies.

Managers develop a variety of policies for guidance
    in international business operations;
    National Cash Register Company provides examples.

International Business Administration represents a
    challenging field of study and
    an area of expanding opportunity.

INTERNATIONAL BUSINESS
ADMINISTRATION

Imagination rules the world.

—NAPOLEON

Regional Environments

In our discussions in the preceding chapters in this section of the book we considered various topics relating to the business environment including economic and business conditions, government and political conditions, the legal system, and the enterprise system and competing systems. We now change our viewpoint somewhat with respect to the business environment and consider it in terms of *regions,* with major emphasis on the international environment of management decisions. We may view the business environment in terms of regions, first, from the standpoint of local communities or areas, or as the Committee for Economic Development has suggested the "Little Economies."[1] The various sections of the country represent another group of environmental factors; for example, the Southwest, the Far West, the South, the Midwest, and the Northeast. The various countries and major regions of the world form still another dimension of the business environment. It is with this latter aspect of the business environment that we are primarily concerned in this chapter.

Business owners and managers often encounter quite a different set of environmental factors in one local community than another. Adapting to the environment of a locality or undertaking to change it may be quite a different set of problems in City A than in City B or City C. Attitudes of local government leaders may vary widely, as may tax levels in relation to public services, desire for economic growth on the part of local residents, availability of skilled workers, or other potential resources, and many other things.

Most of us are aware of some of the major differences between the various sections of this country. While sectional differences are tend-

---

[1] See for example, *The "Little Economies"* (New York: Committee for Economic Development, 1958).

ing to become less pronounced, there are still significant contrasts in terms of resources, attitudes, rates of economic growth, customs, and other environmental factors.

Differences in the business environment, of course, become much more pronounced when we move into the international field. Various countries or blocks of countries represent substantial differences in resources, types of government, legal systems, economic and social systems, currencies, trade practices, customs, traditions, languages, and cultural standards. In the international field business managers encounter some of their most difficult problems. The impact of the environment on their decisions and operations tends to be very heavy. Despite the problems, the number of multinational business firms is growing rapidly and the field of international business administration is one of expanding opportunity. By "multinational" firms we mean those that have their homes or headquarters in one country but operate under the laws of other countries as well.

Businessmen in the United States have always played a significant role in international business activity. In the colonial period of our history international trade and commerce were of major importance. As our internal economy developed we relied to a relatively lesser extent on international business activity.

As has been pointed out:

American businessmen have had the capital and enterprise to venture into foreign lands since the days the Salem Clipper sailed to China and have been a major factor in foreign markets since Commodore Matthew Perry forcibly opened the Japanese market with two steamships and six sailing vessels. Early in the twentieth century, as the United States slowed down its rate of capital imports for its own development and started exporting capital on a big scale, some of the largest American companies, especially those in mining and food production, began to make direct investments abroad under the tacit protection of the U.S. government.[2]

In terms of proportion of gross national product involved, the international area still represents only about 5 per cent. This may not be an adequate measure of its importance, however, since it does not reflect the output of the plants and branches of American firms operating in other countries. The volume of international operations is growing; more and more business firms are operating on a multinational basis and are investing substantial amounts of capital in other countries. Even many smaller and medium-sized firms are moving into the international field. Thus a knowledge of the international en-

---

[2] Harlan Cleveland, Gerald J. Mangone, and John Clarke Adams, *The Overseas Americans* (New York: McGraw-Hill Book Co., Inc., 1960), p. 99.

vironment of business is becoming increasingly important for business managers and for students of business administration.

Population Explosion

One of the significant elements in the international environment is the rapid rise in population. In the years since 1920, roughly at the end of the first World War, the population of the world has increased by some 800 million. Estimates indicate a further rise of a billion in the next generation.[3] This rapid rise of population presents some real problems because of the difficulty of increasing economic output fast enough to provide for rising living standards, or even to prevent living standards from falling.

Annual production of goods and services in this country averages about $2,500 per capita. In many of the other industrialized countries it is under $1,000; and for the less industrialized areas, which include about a billion people, output per capita is only about $120 per year. The Communist Bloc countries have been producing at the rate of about $300 per year. (Figures are not regularly available.) While low by our standards, the output of the Communist Bloc countries is sufficiently above that of the less industrialized areas of the world to hold promise for them. The Communists claim that they can make output rise faster than population; we have demonstrated that we can do so. The methods used, of course, often are quite different.

The Ideological Conflict

If population growth poses one of the significant facts of the international environment, a second certainly is the ideological conflict. The Western nations and the Communist Bloc countries are engaged in a major struggle for the minds of men throughout the world. This struggle is waged in part through military and defense programs, in part by propaganda and psychological warfare, and in part through economic competition. We are concerned primarily with the latter in these discussions, although we should recognize that all of these types of conflict are interrelated.

The ideological conflict is in part a conflict of economic and social doctrines including basic attitudes and philosophies regarding "ultimate" values of life. The conflict is also a matter of power politics, including the use of military might, diplomatic efforts, and political strategy to gain increasing control over the minds of men in all parts

---

3 Dexter Keezer and Associates, *New Forces in American Business* (New York: McGraw-Hill Book Co., Inc., 1959), p. 218.

of the world. The conflict has centered in recent years particularly in the less industrialized parts of the world. It continues, however, in other areas as well. Despite the tensions created by the ideological conflict and the varying degrees of cold war that it generates, the world has been sufficiently peaceful to permit an expansion of international business activity.

The competition between East and West has tended to become more intense in the economic field in the last few years. Russian threats that "we will bury you," by economic competition represent an extreme position in this competition. Despite Russian efforts to expand economic activities abroad, American progress in this field continues to be great. It is supplemented by substantial expansion of foreign economic activity by countries in western Europe and by Japan.

Economic rivalry between Communist and Western countries has created various opportunities for American business managers, since our government has developed inducements as well as new and improved institutions to assist in stimulating the volume of international business carried on by firms headquartered in this country.

Rising Aspirations

Another fact of significance in the international field is the rising aspirations of people around the world.[4] Not only those in the more highly developed countries, but also those in countries just emerging from a relatively primitive life, are aspiring to improved economic and social conditions. Throughout the world there appears to be a rising tide of aspirations for a fuller and better life. There is a growing interest in education, in greater economic opportunities, in higher living standards, and in greater cultural attainments.

All of this represents a climate of expanding opportunity in the broad field of international business administration. Expanded opportunity for all of the people in the world can be provided through greater exchange of goods and services, taking advantage of the possibilities for increased regional and international specialization and division of labor. Many countries and areas have an abundance of natural resources that can provide the basis for trade with nations that have an advantage in the production of finished products. Forces

---

[4] The Rockefeller brothers report refers to "the revolution of raising expectations," see, *Foreign Economic Policy for the Twentieth Century*, Report of the Rockefeller Brothers Fund, Special Studies Project III (New York: Doubleday & Co., Inc., 1958), p. 6. See also Cleveland, Mangone, and Adams, *op. cit.*, p. 5, with their reference to the "triple revolution" of rising economic expectations, rising resentment against inequality, and rising determination to be free.

of nationalism, however, often lead to the establishment of barriers to international trade. Unstable currencies and economic policies add to the problems involved.

There is great need for the investment of capital, both in private and public programs, in the countries that are at an early stage in their economic development. Some of this capital is invested via government channels and largely in the public sector of the economies of lesser developed countries. A substantial amount of capital is being invested by private firms, and the potential for such investment appears to be rising.

New Institutions

Prior to the two World Wars international business activities tended to follow the "natural" division of labor between various areas of the world. Bananas are easier to grow in the tropics than in areas with temperate climates. International trade makes it possible to exchange the goods that can be produced economically in one area, such as bananas, with those that can be produced economically in another, such as radios.

The two World Wars, however, resulted in a variety of restrictions on the flow of goods, capital, and persons between countries. New nations established tariffs to protect their infant industries. Fear of war built trade barriers. Many nations tried to achieve some degree of self-sufficiency in order not to be dependent on others. Often such developments exhausted financial resources and inflation resulted. Currencies lost value; it became increasingly difficult to convert one into another. In some cases currencies were "blocked," so that they could not be converted into gold or U.S. dollars.

In order to cope with situations of this type the United States, various western European nations, and the United Nations undertook to develop new institutions that would bring a revival of international business activity. Two major institutions, the International Bank for Reconstruction and Development and the International Monetary Fund, were set up with the United States subscribing a substantial share of the required funds.

Closely related to these institutions is the Export-Import Bank, a U.S. agency that has financed a large volume of trade. Grants under the Marshall Plan, which was a significant invention, and subsequent aid programs all helped to encourage world-wide business activity. The International Cooperation Administration and the Development Loan Fund are examples of other institutions that have been set up to facilitate international business operations. More recently the Agency for International Development has consolidated a number of U.S. programs.

Various agencies of the United Nations have contributed to the improvement of the international business climate as well as the North Atlantic Treaty Organization (NATO) and others. The emergence of the European Common Market, is an important development. This is a six-nation group, France, Germany, Italy, Belgium, the Netherlands and Luxemburg, with Greece as an associate member. Closely related is the European Free Trade Association, or "Outer Seven" countries that ring the Common Market area. (Finland is an associate member.) There are continuing moves to bring these two groups closer together. Both of these groups represent significant developments and essentially new institutions that have considerable importance for international business. Latin American countries have been undertaking to develop a Latin American Free Trade Zone. There is also the Central American Customs Union, the Arab group, plus others.

All of these developments have helped to change greatly the general climate for international business activities. Some trade barriers, at least, have been broken down. Some currencies have been stabilized. Capital is again moving between different parts of the world, not always easily, but moving. Some loans and grants are being made in "soft" currencies, that is, on the basis of repayment in local currencies that are not convertible into gold or U.S. dollars.

Important as these developments have been, much remains to be accomplished in this field. Many American business firms have been stimulated to move into the international field but many more would enter it if barriers and risks could be further reduced. Over all hangs the uncertainty of the trade policies of the Communist countries. For political reasons they may operate on a noneconomic basis. For example they may sell below costs, as they have from time to time; hence, they can disrupt trade arrangements, in some cases temporarily, in others for longer periods.

Types of International Business Operations

Business firms engage in three broad types of foreign operations: (1) exporting, (2) licensing arrangements with existing local manufacturers in foreign countries including provision of technical aid and "know-how," and (3) establishing manufacturing and distributing facilities abroad.

Exporting may include the exporting of services as well as goods; for example, a business consulting firm may export its services. The export of a product by an American firm may be accompanied by the export of a certain amount of service for repair, replacement, or training of operators. Exporting may be accomplished in a variety of ways; for example, an American company may sell to foreign wholesalers, enter into arrangements with brokers or agents, or in some cases sell directly to retailers abroad. Conversely, of course, some firms in this country operate as importers from abroad.

Under licensing arrangements an American firm enters into agreements with a foreign company to manufacture and distribute one or more products. Usually the foreign company has an exclusive contract for the product or products for a stated time and covering a designated area such as a country or several countries in a market area.

A firm may establish a branch office abroad to market and service its products. Sometimes this happens after a period of experience as an exporter, after business volume grows to the point that a branch office with company representatives becomes possible.

To an increasing extent American business firms are establishing manufacturing as well as distribution facilities abroad. Often large amounts of capital are involved in such enterprises. In 1961, for example, foreign investments of this type accounted for about 10 per cent of the total capital expenditures of American manufacturing companies.[5] With reference to the establishment of manufacturing and distribution facilities in other countries, Ralph J. Cordiner, president of General Electric, observes:

This should not be thought of as a substitute for exports, or considered as "moving United States jobs overseas." Sales made by overseas operations are for the most part sales that could not be made on an export basis, and hence create wholly new jobs in these markets. In addition, overseas investments help to build up the economies of other countries and make them better customers for export products from the United States as well as the products of local industries.[6]

The emergence of the European Common Market has stimulated a substantial expansion of investment by American companies in the member countries. Similar developments, however, are taking place in many parts of the world.

---

[5] McGraw-Hill Survey of Capital Expenditures, as reported in *Business Week*, April 29, 1961, p. 32.

[6] Ralph J. Cordiner, "Managerial Strategy for International Business" (Schenectady, N. Y.: General Electric Co., 1960), an address to the World Trade Division, National Foreign Trade Council Convention.

Management Problems in International Business Operations

As we have indicated, an increasing number of business firms, both American and those of other countries, have expanded their international operations. In large part, they do this because they see expanded opportunities in foreign markets or access to resources abroad. There may be production advantages, and in some cases, opportunities for spreading risks.

When business firms operate on a multinational basis their managers encounter a number of problems that differ from those involved in domestic operations. They must do business under the laws of one or more governments in addition to the government of the United States. Often regulations conflict or difficult problems of interpretation of laws and regulations are involved.

Taxes usually represent a series of problems and uncertainties. Also, U.S. and foreign guarantees and subsidies may be involved as well as various fees and related charges.

The hiring and training of the nationals of other countries often presents a series of difficult managerial problems. Also, the extent to which and the way in which the citizens of other countries may invest in American firms operating abroad often has a significant bearing on success or failure.

Beyond these problems are those arising from the management of operations at a distance. These may be referred to as problems of remote control.

Language differences pose problems. The customs, traditions, and business practices of other countries often differ widely. Currencies may be unstable or not convertible into American dollars. Movements of funds often present almost insurmountable difficulties.

Government Relations

Managers undertaking international operations need a familiarity with the laws and regulations of the countries in which they do business. International lawyers and lawyers in other countries, of course, can be very helpful. Some laws are enforced outside the territorial limits of the country involved; for example, our social security laws are applicable to Americans working abroad. There are also various neutrality laws and antitrust laws that may cause a variety of difficulties.

Not only is it necessary to understand the laws and regulations of other countries where business is being done, but the problems of complying with these laws often are difficult. Close working relations with the ministries and officials of other countries usually are essential. Sometimes agencies of the United Nations provide valuable assistance. As one writer points out with reference to international business administrators:

They must become as familiar with the specialized UN economic agencies and international banks as with their own governments, and they must learn to walk in the halls of the European and other economic communities as knowledgeably as they walk in the halls of their own state department, department of commerce or board of trade.[7]

Learning to do this is far from easy. Every country has its own set of laws governing alien corporation registration, the ownership of various types of resources, notably land or the stock of local corporations, licensing arrangements, and many others. Often the manager working abroad is involved in extensive negotiations with government officials on many levels. The attitudes of such officials is not always sympathetic to foreign business firms. In some cases, notably in the newer countries, business firms may actually be in partnership with governments. In other cases the major contracts of American firms are those made with foreign governments. Business operations under such arrangements often require diplomacy of a high order.

Taxes, Incentives, and Guarantees

Tax laws usually differentiate between domestic and foreign corporations, with the advantage going to the former. Because of this, many firms establish separate corporations in the countries in which they carry on business activities.

The tax laws of the United States often provide special arrangements for income derived from foreign operations. In some cases there are important tax credits for certain types of international business activity.

Obviously, strict compliance with the tax laws of the countries in which a firm is operating is a necessity of the first order. But compliance often involves a variety of interpretations that complicate business affairs.

In some types of situations our government provides investment guarantees to assist American firms doing business abroad. Various countries have guarantee arrangements with the United States; others

---

[7] David Lilienthal, "The Multinational Corporation," in Melvin Anshen and G. L. Bach, *Management and Corporations, 1985* (New York: McGraw-Hill Book Co., Inc., 1960), p. 126, by permission.

offer special guarantees to the exporters of capital goods sold on long-term credit.

A number of countries offer incentives to business firms in order to stimulate investment and business activity within their borders. Tax concessions such as "tax holidays," and others, often are used. In their application, however, local government officials may resent the special advantages going to foreign business firms and attempt to impose interpretations that take away some of the intended benefits. Often special problems arise at the time that incentives expire, particularly if they are subject to renewal.

Personnel and Labor Relations

The variety of employment practices and regulations relating to employment throughout the world is so great that few general statements can be made. Of major importance for American managers with operations abroad is the recognition of the wide differences that prevail.

In many foreign countries labor law tends to be highly complicated and to regulate employment and related practices much more specifically than in this country. As a result political factors often enter into employment relations. Unions abroad often are more politically oriented than in the United States. There are typically fewer opportunities for local collective bargaining agreements. The provisions of one collective bargaining agreement may be extended to people who were not involved in the original contract as in the case of France, for example.

Training problems often are staggering. In some situations American firms or those from other countries set up operations in newly developing countries and find it necessary to train workers with very limited abilities and skills in the industrial field. Many have had no experience except in village and agricultural life. Labor turnover often is high under such conditions.

Establishment of wage scales often presents major difficulties. In some countries government regulations as to methods of compensation are stated in specific terms; they may include minimum wage scales, a variety of fringe benefits beyond those to which a company may be accustomed in the United States, and many detailed rules. Also, in some parts of the world seniority and family size may be given greater weight in determining rates of pay than ability and skill. Social insurance may represent as much as 40 per cent or more of the payroll in some European countries.

As one observer has said:

Personnel administration in this climate demands a departure from the United States norm, which emphasizes policies rather than persons, insists on uniform standards of behavior and judgment and is pre-occupied with creating an enlightened in-plant atmosphere and high morale. Such a system, if transplanted without modification into other societies, could arouse great resistance and antagonism.[8]

Ownership Problems

American companies often find it advantageous to establish separate corporations for various foreign operations. This is often due to tax factors and government regulations. An American company, for example, may establish an international division to co-ordinate its foreign operations. This may take the form of a separate corporation established in this country. In turn, separate corporations may be set up in several countries abroad. In some cases an American firm may buy a controlling interest in an established firm in another country; in others new firms may be established with part of the stock owned by citizens of the local country. Sometimes joint ventures are arranged.

Whatever the specific arrangement, there are often problems in regard to the extent to which people in other countries participate in ownership. In some cases the laws of the country require that at least half of the stock be held by local citizens. Thus, control by means of ownership may not always be possible. In some cases, however, control is exercised in this way. Difficult problems of public relations may arise from the ownership arrangements that are made. Many people in foreign countries feel that they have a right to some participation in the ownership of companies that are operating there.

Problems of Remote Control

To a considerable extent problems of remote control center in communication, which in turn is complicated by distance, language and cultural barriers, and government regulations. We have already mentioned the latter types of problems.

Even in this country there are often conflicts and problems in the relations between the home office and regional and local offices. Such problems tend to increase in complexity as operations are extended to foreign countries.

Company objectives and policies often must be adapted to the po-

---

8 Dan H. Fenn, Jr. (ed.), *Overseas Operations* (New York: McGraw-Hill Book Co., Inc., 1957), p. 143.

tentialities and requirements of foreign situations. Preparation of budgets, quotas, and goals for specific foreign operations requires special care. Authority for various decisions often needs to be very carefully spelled out. Controls often become a most difficult problem, since the evaluation of operations frequently requires a knowledge of the situation in a specific foreign market.

Many American companies arrange for key executives to travel rather extensively to foreign operations. Nothing takes the place of a personal inspection of a remote installation and the development of a "feel" of the local situation. In addition, managers of foreign operations often are brought to the home office at frequent intervals in order that they may understand views of top management and to become well acquainted with their associates in this country.

Improved communication facilities and jet aircraft have helped to solve some of the management problems that arise from remote control. The time required for key executives to reach many parts of the world has been greatly reduced. Even so, the translation of central management plans into action in specific local manufacturing and marketing operations in many parts of the world continues to be a most difficult process.

Language Problems

Since World War II there has been an increasing interest in the study of foreign languages and a growing number of people in this country have a familiarity with at least one foreign language. Even so, American firms often encounter difficulty in locating people with the desired language ability. Many companies undertake special language training programs to try to cope with this problem. It is possible for many people to gain a working knowledge of a foreign language in a few months. In some cases, this will be adequate. But when business firms enter into complicated contracts with foreign corporations and governments, expert knowledge of both English and the foreign language is required.

As one writer[9] has pointed out, "There is little need to belabor the point that many of our overseas representatives are seriously handicapped by a lack of language facility. The lamentations from the field are overwhelming proof that not enough linguists are available to be sent overseas and that too few Americans learn foreign languages even when they work abroad."

---

[9] Harlan Cleveland, Gerald J. Mangone, and John Clarke Adams, *op. cit.*, p. 242, by permission.

Some indication of the time required for acquiring various degrees of facility in using a foreign language include the following: People with high language aptitude can gain sufficient proficiency to satisfy routine travel requirements in two to four months in most of the western European languages; up to six months may be required for people with average aptitudes. For eastern European and some Asiatic languages about two additional months are required. To gain basic familiarity and to conduct routine business added time is needed, and for fluency in the language and ability to read newspapers up to a year of training is needed for the western European languages for people with average aptitudes. An additional six months is needed for eastern European and some Asiatic languages. For Chinese, Japanese and Korean almost twice as long may be required and for Arabic, Burmese, Thai, and similar languages up to two years more.[10]

Language proficiency by itself, while valuable, needs to be supplemented with a feel for the local culture out of which the language grows. Thus, language study has been combined increasingly with efforts to gain an understanding of the history, culture, and attitudes of the people who use the language.[11]

Valuable as a command of a language and a knowledge of the local culture and environment may be, business activities can be conducted despite these barriers. The number of bilingual and multilingual people abroad is much greater than in this country. Business firms make extensive use of interpreters, local secretaries, local lawyers, and others to bridge the language and culture barriers that exist. As time goes on, however, the increasing emphasis being given to language and area studies will provide business firms with increasing numbers of people who may prove to be very useful in foreign operations.

Foreign Currencies

The transfer of funds between countries is complicated even under highly favorable conditions. When the currency of a country becomes unstable, international business operations are affected adversely. Instability of currency may lead to numerous controls of the movements of funds. A business firm may find it difficult, if not impossible, to move profits out of a country to say nothing of the original investment of capital. In some cases businessmen engage in a series of complicated transactions through which they are able to return at least some of their earnings to this country. The banks in Switzerland have long

---

10 *Ibid.,* pp. 250–51
11 Lilienthal, *op. cit.,* pp. 148–49

FIGURE 24–1

"With the government trying to attract foreign tourists we'd better sharpen our bargaining methods! . . don't forget how the first foreigners swindled us out of this country!"

From the *Chicago Sun Times*, April 13, 1961.

served as intermediaries for foreign transactions. Many firms find it advantageous to have subsidiaries established in Switzerland for this reason and because of various tax problems and relationships.

It requires a good deal of financial sophistication to carry on business operations in the currencies of several countries with varying degrees of stability or instability. Because of this many business firms are reluctant to engage in international activities, but in turn, this increases the opportunities for those who are willing to undertake the problems and risks involved.

Experience of National Cash Register Company

The experience of business firms varies so widely in the field of international business operations that generalizations are difficult to make. Hence, it would be a mistake to assume that the experience of one company could set the pattern for the policies of another. It is interesting, however, to note some of the conclusions reached by Stanley C. Allyn, president of the National Cash Register Company, as a result of his company's experience in the international field. This company has been in world trade almost since its founding in 1884. It carries on operations in more than a hundred countries and sales abroad account for some 40 per cent of total sales volume.

The essentials of the programs followed by this company have been summarized by its president as follows:

> When we go into any foreign country, we go in for keeps.
>
> We believe in a company operation overseas instead of general agencies.
>
> We believe in staffing our overseas operations with nationals of the countries concerned.
>
> We have learned that—for us at least—*service* comes ahead of *sales*. I am using the word "service" to mean rejuvenation of overage machines, new parts for old and skilled repair work.
>
> We consistently invest part of our profits in the countries where those profits are earned.
>
> We do not look on our overseas employees as stepchildren. We treat them exactly as we treat our staff at home.
>
> We try to give the foreign market the product it wants—not the product we think it ought to have.
>
> We believe in firsthand contacts with our foreign markets, so we are constantly traveling.
>
> We are extremely careful to respect the customs, traditions, religions and sensitivities of other peoples.

These nine principles are the fundamentals of our working pattern, but they do not follow any particular order of precedence. One principle might take priority in one nation, and another be considered the most important one in a different land.[12]

Study of International Business Administration

Because of the growing importance of international business operations increasing attention is being given to the study of international business administration. Several universities now pay special attention to this field. Courses in foreign trade and in international economics have been offered for a long time by many universities and colleges. These courses, however, seldom approached international economic relationships or activities from the standpoint of the business firm or in terms of the decisions of the business manager. It is this point of view that tends to be stressed in the study of international business administration.

---

[12] Stanley C. Allyn, "American Business Goes Abroad: A Case History," Dan H. Fenn, Jr. (ed.), *op. cit.,* pp. 61–62, by permission.

Since this is a new and challenging area of study you may want to consider its implications for your own future as well as for the business manager in the process of adapting his operations to a rapidly changing and dynamic environment. The language problems and related problems of understanding the cultures of different parts of the world have a bearing in the development of this field. Also, there are the political, governmental, legal, and regulative problems to which we have referred. Comparative business systems form an important element of study. In addition, the applications of management methods to the vastly different environments of the world requires special competence and education. Management decision making in the international field differs from the domestic scene in degree, rather than kind, but the differences in degree often are great enough to make a sound solution to a decision problem in one country an incorrect one in another.

People from this country who conduct business operations abroad often need to have a greater understanding of our system than do those conducting business activities solely on a domestic basis. People in other countries often hear criticisms of the United States and of our system. They often ask our nationals who are doing business abroad for explanations of our system or for replies to some of the criticisms that have been made. Thus, information of the type covered in the preceding chapter may be particularly helpful in such cases.

The potentialities in the field of international business administration are great. As David Lilienthal points out:

Already there is the beginning of a new class of men and women, who spend a considerable part of their existence living and working in foreign countries. These are the managers and the technicians of multinational corporations, and their families. In a sense, they are two-way ambassadors. Abroad, they represent their native lands; when they return home, they reflect some of the attitudes of the countries in which they have temporarily resided. In time the managers and their families may even have two—or more—nations in which they will be equally at ease; they will form a new class. They will be trained in one of the most sophisticated outlooks in our world, that of the international businessman.[13]

SUMMARY

International business administration is a field of growing importance to many American business firms and their managers. Expansion has been especially rapid in recent years.

---

[13] Lilienthal, *op. cit.*, pp. 144–46, by permission.

The business environment may be viewed from the standpoint of regions, beginning with local or "little" economies, moving on to the major sections of the country, to nations, and finally to the international scene. Within the international environment significant developments in recent years include the population explosion and the difficulty of expanding economic output at a high enough rate to keep pace; the ideological conflict, particularly communism versus democracy; rising aspirations around the world and notably in the lesser developed areas; and the establishment and expansion of new institutions to facilitate international business operations.

International business operations typically include exporting arrangements of various types, licensing arrangements with existing local manufacturers in foreign countries, and establishing manufacturing and distributing facilities abroad. Various combinations of these types of operations may exist.

The problems encountered by business managers in international operations cover a wide range. Of special importance are those arising from the multiplicity of government regulations at home and abroad and the difficulty of complying with many of them. Also, special problems are posed by taxes, incentives, and guarantees. Personnel and labor relations present a special set of challenges including training programs, special bargaining arrangements, and establishment of wage scales.

Special problems may arise from ownership arrangements, the difficulties of managing operations by remote control great distances from home offices, language barriers, and foreign currencies. Highly sophisticated financial operations are often required in order to achieve success in the international field.

Managers develop many types of policies for guiding their international programs; an interesting case in point is provided by the experience of the National Cash Register Company. Because of the diversity of problems, international business administration represents a challenging field of study and an area of expanding opportunity.

QUESTIONS AND PROBLEMS

1. If the business environment is viewed from the standpoint of regions, identify the principal types which we considered in these discussions.
2. What is meant by a "multinational" firm?
3. Why is the population explosion important for the field of international business? The struggle between the Western nations and the Communist Bloc?
4. Of what significance are rising aspirations around the world and notably in the lesser developed countries for international business operations?

5. What is meant by a "blocked" currency? By the European Common Market?

6. Explain why the trade policies of Communist countries may pose special problems for American business managers in their overseas programs.

7. What is meant by exporting? How does this differ from licensing arrangements?

8. Why have many business firms established manufacturing and distributing facilities abroad?

9. Explain how the multiplicity of government regulations may create special problems for managers in their international operations. Give examples.

10. Give examples of the types of incentives offered by various countries to business firms in order to stimulate investment and business activity within their borders.

11. Do managers typically find it easier or more difficult to comply with labor laws and regulations abroad than in this country? Why? Why may training programs abroad pose special sets of problems?

12. Give examples of some of the ownership problems that may be encountered by business firms operating abroad.

13. What is meant by "problems of remote control?" Illustrate.

14. Why do currency problems discourage some business managers from undertaking international operations?

15. Read the accompanying article which appeared in the July, 1961, issue of *Reader's Digest* and answer the following questions:
    a) Is pay for overseas work better than at home? Explain.
    b) How many American companies are now doing business abroad?
    c) What are the primary requisites for overseas employment?
    d) Do you think you would like to work in the international field?

SO YOU WANT TO WORK OVERSEAS?

NEW CAREERS FOR AMERICANS

*There is need for qualified people. The rewards
are considerable, but so are the difficulties.
A survey of international opportunities.*

By ROBERT O'BRIEN

When President Kennedy created the Peace Corps a few months ago, volunteers reacted swiftly. Letters and applications, 6000 a week, descended on Washington. This dramatic response pointed up the fact that young Americans want to work abroad, but it tended to obscure the equally arresting fact that thousands are already doing so.

According to latest State Department figures, Americans working, studying or living as expatriates overseas total about 298,600. With their 367,000 dependents, they form a huge community of nearly 666,000 American men, women and children, *not* including members of the armed forces or their families.

These Yankees are manning embassies in Paris, Rome, Rio, Djakarta, Istanbul. They're clearing jungles in Guatemala, planting apple trees in Iran. They're teaching biology in Zanzibar and English in Ecuador. They're typing government reports in Kuala Lumpur, fighting smallpox in Pakistan and delivering babies in Kabul. Their backgrounds are as varied as their posts. A high-school graduate from Scranton, Pa., is an Air Force typist in Berlin. A young economist from California is a foreign-service officer in Athens. An engineer from Vermont is building dams in Ghana. An accountant from Ohio is checking oil-company payrolls in Arabia.

The pay, for most, is excellent—higher, when you consider housing, cost-of-living and other allowances, than for similar jobs in the United States. Base incomes range from about $4000 a year for Defense Department clerks to $20,000 a year and up for career ambassadors and business executives.

But it's not all plush living. Many get along without plumbing or central heating. Many boil water before drinking it, keenly aware that the nearest American doctor may be 2000 air miles away.

The good pay and allowances help make up for these hardships. But most Americans working abroad are in it for something bigger—the thrill of being in the thick of history. "We overseas Americans are performing the most important task in the world today," a young missionary doctor from the Philippines told me. "We're helping millions to help themselves."

What are the chances of joining the legion of overseas workers?* For qualified people, they've never been better.

Economists, figuring the annual turnover of employes at about ten percent, estimate that replacements alone will open up 10,000 more jobs abroad every year. On top of this, some experts foresee a steady increase in jobs of all kinds overseas.

Some 3300 American companies are now doing business abroad. True, they all employ as many foreign nationals as possible. But they will continue to need sales and plant supervisors, engineers and other key staff personnel from home.

Opportunities for overseas jobs are booming in nearly every branch of government service. The foreign service needs more personnel trained in commerce, science, economics and administration. The United States Information Agency (USIA) wants college graduates with language ability. Nearly all U.N. and government agencies sending Americans abroad, such as the International Coöperation Administration (ICA), are short on technicians. Soil conservationists, rural-credit experts, agronomists, livestock and poultry advisers, veterinarians are urgently needed. Says Rep. Henry R. Reuss of Wisconsin, "Only 6000 Americans are serving overseas on technical projects; the need is for many times that number."

---

* The 298,600 overseas Americans divide roughly as follows: 41,340 government workers, 40,000 American-company employes, 35,000 missionaries. The rest are employes of foreign firms, students, scholars, self-employed and—a large category—expatriate and retired Americans living abroad.

The shortage of qualified health workers is acute. A Protestant-church-council pamphlet calling for missionary nurses says, "More nurses are needed than the church boards can find." Most pressing of all is the need for teachers. Assistant Commissioner O. J. Caldwell, U.S. Office of Education, estimates that some 20,000 Americans are currently teaching abroad. The teaching force should be doubled in the next decade.

What is the primary requisite to get you a job abroad? Proficiency in a foreign language is obviously a vital asset. But the foremost qualification is a skill: the proved ability to do something practical that someone wants done overseas. In technical-assistance jobs in underdeveloped countries, the required skill may be knowing how to build roads, increase egg production, repair high-tension power lines, fight malaria, extract teeth, or teach English to school children. A heavy-machinery man in Ghana, a Negro, had Army-ordnance and trade-school training, and no college background. "Here is what sold us," the personnel man said, and read the first line from the applicant's letter: "I am skilled in diesel and automotive engineering, and I want to work abroad."

The premium on skills has opened up exciting "second careers" for older professional men. A successful city editor I know decided in his early 50's that he wanted to work abroad—for his country. He resigned his job, joined USIA as a press attaché. In the last few years, he's done vital work at American embassies in Tehran, Baghdad and Bonn.

ICA is actively recruiting in 90 occupational fields. Its needs range from horticulturists to housing advisers, from economists to crime experts. Age limit? There is none. Pay ranges from $7500 to $12,500, and may be augmented by cost-of-living allowances and travel expenses. Says ICA's Stephen A. Tripp, "We need men with 10 to 20 years of experience who can pass along what they know to the people of other countries."

But qualities other than skill are important. In a unique survey by Syracuse University's Maxwell Graduate School of Citizenship and Public Affairs, researchers agreed on the five elements that contributed most to the performance of 244 Americans employed in a wide spread of jobs abroad. Ranked next to technical skill was belief in mission—an absorbing enthusiasm for the job, driving faith in oneself and the value of one's work.

Listed third was "cultural emphathy"—a talent for understanding and accepting other people's customs and ways of doing business. Rated fourth was a "sense of politics"—a sensitivity to political realities and trends. The final helpful qualification was a talent for organization—for making people and institutions grow.

What can you do now, if you're a college undergraduate, to improve your chances of getting a job overseas? Three things:

1. While pointing toward a graduate specialty, get a broad liberal-arts education. Increase your knowledge of America and its position in world affairs. At the same time, learn all you can about the history, geography, art, literature, religion and politics of the foreign country where you'd like to work.

2. Plan on a least a year of graduate work, or its equivalent in actual job time, in the skill you will need. "Get your professional base established

here at home first, then go after your overseas job," says Assistant Secretary of State Harlan Cleveland.

3. Seize every opportunity to go abroad while still in college. Try to go to Europe or South America for a summer. Stay in one place. Find out what's it's like to live in a foreign country, preferably under an organized group program such as the American Friends Service Committee international work camps. Better yet, study abroad with an overseas program, such as those offered by Syracuse, Stanford and Georgetown universities. "You learn to live abroad by living abroad," says Secretary Cleveland. "There is no other way."

Without this advance experience, some Americans have had difficulty adjusting to life overseas. "On many posts there are no devices for fun or diversion—no TV or movies, no golf or swimming," says Commissioner Caldwell. "A serious hobby is a great help—hunting, fishing, the study of the art, music or dance of the country." One teacher in Burma hiked as a hobby, and took 200-mile walking trips to outlying native villages. A teacher in Pakistan started classes in canning fruit and vegetables. A French teacher stationed in the West Indies started a local radio program on child care and home improvement.

The most practical advice is to plan far ahead. If you're interested in missionary work, get in touch with your own church board of missions; it will have all the preliminary information you need. For those wanting overseas government work, there is abundant information available in government pamphlets. Looking for American firms doing business overseas? The *College Placement Annual 1961* lists nearly 200. Advertise in and check the "Help Wanted" pages of publications covering international commerce, such as the New York *Times, Export Trade* and *International Trade Review*. Certain employment agencies specialize in jobs abroad. If there's one in your city, have it place your name on file. Many overseas jobs are filled through personal leads from bankers, salesmen, brokers; let men like these know that you're looking for work abroad.

An enterprising young Texan I know decided in his junior year at college that he wanted to work abroad. On the advice of oil-company recruiters, he specialized in Latin American studies. Both he and his pretty financée buckled down to learn Spanish. Because of well-organized preparation, he was able to earn a master's degree in geology in one year of postgraduate work. Two months later he was married, on the oil-company payroll at close to $8000 a year, and en route to join an exploration field crew in Venezuela.

In the years immediately ahead, as more and more young Americans plan for careers abroad, this kind of direct, efficient approach will become commonplace.

"Opportunities overseas are, and will remain, on the increase," says Secretary Cleveland. "Any American youth who is well prepared, and strongly motivated, will be able to find work in foreign lands. For the right kind of American, the rewards will be priceless. He'll be able to say, 'I'm doing my part in the great movement for education, democracy, and a better world.' "

SUGGESTED READINGS

CLEVELAND, HARLAN, MANGONE, GERALD J. and ADAMS, JOHN CLARKE, *The Overseas Americans*. New York: McGraw-Hill Book Co., 1960.

KEEZER, DEXTER, and Associates. *New Forces in American Business*. New York: McGraw-Hill Book Co., Inc., 1959. Read chap. ten, "U.S. Business and the World Overseas."

LILIENTHAL, DAVID. "The Multinational Corporation," in M. L. ANSHEN and G. L. BACH, *Management and Corporations, 1985*. New York: McGraw-Hill Book Co., Inc., 1960.

LONG, JOHN D. *Workbook to Accompany Weimer: Business Administration: An Introductory Management Approach,* chap. 24. Rev. ed. Homewood, Ill.: Richard D. Irwin, Inc., 1962.

ROBOCK, STEPHAN H. "Six Visiting Marxists Meet U.S. Business," *Business Horizons,* Vol. IV, No. 1 (Spring, 1961), pp. 29–38.

part **6** Emerging
Problems
and
Opportunities

SUMMARY OUTLINE

BUSINESS ADMINISTRATION—now one of the more exciting areas of study—
may be *approached* in an *introductory* manner from the point of view of
the *manager*.

He is the central figure in the business firm—the key social and economic
institution of our time. It is managed and operated in a highly dynamic
environment.

Business Firms are established as individual *proprietorships, partnerships,
corporations,* and other forms.

Firms vary in *size* and engage in many *types of work*—manufacturing,
trade, finance, service, and others.

The *Decision Makers* in business firms are owners, managers, and
business specialists.

The *Management Process* involves establishment of objectives,
plans, and controls; organization of resources; and leadership.

Decision Making—a central management responsibility—includes problem
and *goal identification* and clarification, development and analysis of
alternatives, appraisal of most likely alternatives, and choice.

Decisions may be guided by financial, accounting, statistical, economic, mathematical, and other considerations.

Business Resources and Operations involve effective utilization of the
abilities of people—requiring knowledge of personnel and organization behavior—

as well as other resources including

capital, equipment, knowledge, time, and related aids to
productivity, plus the place of business—land, buildings,
and location—

in the *production* and *marketing* of goods and services to secure *income*.

The *Business Environment* influences management decisions and in turn
is influenced by them, particularly in the areas of

business conditions,

governmental and political conditions,

the legal system,

the enterprise system and competing systems,

and international business administration.

Emerging Problems and Opportunities hold promise for the business
community, and for you in managing your future.

OUTLINE FOR CHAPTER 25

The emerging PROBLEMS AND OPPORTUNITIES OF THE BUSINESS COMMUNITY will influence the future management of business firms, and the character of the business environment.

Changes are probable in the following areas:

Number and size of business firms.

Owner-management relations:
  who controls, and
  extent of ownership.

Business objectives,
  possible value changes,
  balancing of interests, and
  degree of public acceptance.

Use of capital equipment,
  automation, and
  new power sources.

Management by machines.

Research development,
  basic and applied programs, and
  research management.

Character of markets,
  size,
  degree of competition, growth of "interurbias,"
  extent of decentralizing.

Nature of industrial relations,
  power and character of union leaders,
  attitudes of owners and managers, and
  interests of the public.

Extent of economic growth and development,
  population and labor force, and
  rising productivity may be affected by fears of
    war,
    inflation, and
    depression.

Changing levels of education may influence
  quality of economic growth,
  values and social attitudes, including
    concepts of the "good life."

On balance emerging problems and opportunities justify an optimistic outlook.

PROBLEMS AND OPPOR-
TUNITIES OF THE
BUSINESS COMMUNITY

On what principle is it that, when we see nothing but improvement
behind us, we are to expect nothing but deterioration before us?
—MACAULAY

Importance of Future Trends

We begin here the last section of our discussions. This section deals primarily with the future; first, in this chapter, with the future of business firms and the environment in which they are managed; and second, in the following chapter, with your own future.

In our discussions we have emphasized the point that management decisions are future oriented. This is also true of other types of decisions including those related to your personal life. Hence, it seems appropriate to consider the possible shape of things to come. As we all know, we must be interested in the future since that is where we will spend the rest of our lives.

At the same time it is well for us to recognize that none of us can foretell the future. We can make some guesses in regard to the probable trend of events and their potential significance. As a minimum we may raise pertinent, or perhaps impertinent, questions about some of the problems and opportunities that may lie ahead.

Problems and opportunities often turn out to be different sides of the same coin. Hence, it would not seem desirable for us to present a discussion of problems or of opportunities separately.

In this chapter we undertake a consideration of some of the problems and opportunities of the business community ranging from those related rather directly to the management of the business firm to broad issues and problems that are likely to shape the business environment. Primarily we are interested in speculating about the future of the firm, its size, management, ownership, objectives, resources, and its role in our society. We are interested also in the emerging trends and forces that will shape the management of business firms in a dynamic society, particularly those arising from the fears, hopes, and aspirations of people at home and abroad.

Larger Firms? And More?

Will big business firms get bigger and small ones smaller as is often contended? Will mergers and combinations lead to a reduction in the number of firms until there are only a few large ones left?

While it is difficult to suggest definite answers to these questions, we may tentatively answer both of them in the negative. Mergers and combinations undoubtedly will go on. Capital requirements for many lines of business will tend to expand. The number of firms operating on a multinational basis undoubtedly will continue to increase. Also, more firms are likely to operate on a multiproduct basis. It does not follow, however, that we will have fewer firms in the future. We may have larger firms but it is doubtful that the number of firms will decrease.

Many types of business firms will never require large amounts of capital to get started or to continue in operation. This is particularly true in service businesses, and these are areas in which substantial expansion may be anticipated. Many people will aspire to own and operate their own firms. New products and new processes will open up opportunities for many new firms, some of which will be small in size. The advantages of flexibility, rapidity of decisions, and adaptability will continue to favor smaller business firms. In addition, they are likely to continue to enjoy certain tax and political advantages. Also, the small firms enjoy some advantages with respect to union contracts. Typically, they are not part of national bargaining agreements.

Many people have been concerned about the large number of new enterprises that are started which have a very short life. Most failures of new firms may be traced to a lack of management ability. Plans are not carefully worked out. Risks are not estimated realistically. Markets are not analyzed. Production processes are not subjected to painstaking study. Financing is often carried out on a "shoestring" basis.

Yet the opportunities for aspiring and ambitious people who have a reasonable grasp of management fundamentals are great. Indeed, there is a good chance that the future will see more rather than fewer developments in the small business field.

A Management Revolution?

In the early 1940's a book entitled *The Managerial Revolution* made its appearance.[1] In it the argument was developed that control

---
[1] See James Burnham, *The Managerial Revolution* (New York: John Day Co., 1941).

of business firms was passing from owners to hired, professional managers.

We may seriously question whether an owner-manager is any less a "professional" manager than a nonowner-manager. The term "professional," however, has come to refer largely to a nonowner or hired manager. To a degree the *operation* rather than *control* of firms has passed to management from owners. For in a final analysis, owners retain control and can "fire" managers if their performance becomes unsatisfactory. What is considered unsatisfactory finally depends on the standards established by owners. Customers and employees may have a part in determining what is unsatisfactory but their opinions ultimately have an impact on return on investment, continuity of operations, rate of growth, or other objectives. We may note that civil servants are often less subject to control than are nonowner professional business managers.

Control by owners over management is significant even when ownership is "splintered" among many persons. While action may not be so direct as in cases of greater concentration of ownership, groups of stockholders may pool their interests to gain control over management; or if the stock slips in price, certain owners may acquire enough shares to give them effective control. Nonowner managers, thus, usually are quite concerned about a downward trend in the price of the company's stock, especially if the decline is faster than that of other stocks or if it occurs when other stocks are rising in price.

Stockholders are taking a more active interest in the affairs of corporations than ever before. One evidence of this is the growing interest in annual corporation meetings.

Increasing attention is being given to protecting the rights of minority stock owners. Cumulative voting for directors is one trend in this direction. It has also been suggested that the individual stockowner should have the right annually to determine whether and to what extent he will invest his share of the firm's profits. Frederick A. Hayek has said, for example:

It seems to me that nothing would produce as active an interest of the individual stockholder in the conduct of a corporation and at the same time give him so much effective power as to permit him annually and individually to decide what part of his share of the net profits he was willing to reinvest in the corporation.[2]

---

2 Frederick A. Hayek, "The Corporation in a Democratic Society: In Whose Interest Ought It and Will It Be Run?" in Melvin Anshen and G. L. Bach, *Management and Corporations, 1985* (New York: McGraw-Hill Book Co., Inc., 1960), p. 110 by permission.

Even under present conditions the ownership of the stock of a company carries important control elements. While nonowner managers may avoid such control for a time, they generally are highly responsive to the desires of owners. Managers are likely to continue to try to serve the best interests of owners. This does not mean that they will be unresponsive to the wishes of employees, of customers, and the public at large. But the interests of employees and customers may tend to conflict. The attitudes of the public at large often are difficult to gauge. Such attitudes, however, help to determine the general climate in which business firms are managed. We discuss this topic later in this chapter.

More Ownership?

The ownership of business firms in this country is being extended to more and more people. In part this is the result of a growing number of small business firms but it is due also to the rising number of individual investors in corporate stocks and to the growth of mutual funds and the number of investors in them. More widespread ownership is taking place in other countries as well. Western Europe presents a number of cases in point. In Japan the number of owners of corporate shares increased from a million and a half before World War II to around 10 million in 1960.[3]

Thus, the trend toward more ownership seems almost certain to continue, barring a major depression or other development that would undermine the confidence of people in the earning capacity of business firms.

In many companies there is a trend toward the recombination of management and ownership by the use of stock option and purchase plans for the compensation of top managers or the establishment of trusts which assure control of operations by the board of directors and management. The latter arrangement is being followed by some family-owned corporations.

Many firms are finding it necessary to offer ownership opportunities to good managers in order to hold them against the competition of other firms. The salaries of managers lose their appeal after the higher tax brackets are reached; hence, compensation by stock purchase options or bonuses probably will increase in importance.

Use of hired or professional managers will grow in importance in

---

3 David Lilienthal, "The Multinational Corporation," in Anshen and Bach, *op. cit.,* p. 141.

large firms or smaller firms that are bought by larger ones. As we suggested earlier the number of firms, however, is likely to increase over future years as opportunities expand. Many of the new firms will be managed by owners. A number of people will start their own businesses or buy established ones. Opportunities for smaller business are likely to be found especially in the service fields where small firms are able to compete to advantage.

Thus, the "managerial revolution" in terms of greater *operation* of firms by hired managers will continue, but there is likely to be little change in terms of control. The owner-manager will remain an important factor in business operations. Many hired managers may be offered increased opportunities for acquiring important ownership rights.

Different Objectives?

Will the objectives of business firms or of managers change in the years ahead? For example, will present objectives be replaced by new ones, or are there likely to be changes in the relative importance of objectives?

You will recall that we identified the major objectives of business firms as (1) survival, (2) growth, and (3) prestige or recognition. We pointed out that profits are the "acid test" of the ability of business firms to pursue these or other objectives; that the objectives of individual firms may differ greatly or the objectives of the same firm may change over time; and that there may be differences between the objectives of owners, managers, employees, customers, and others in respect to a particular firm.

In our earlier discussions we pointed out also that business firms must either consciously or unconsciously aid in achieving the objectives of our society as a whole. Otherwise they would not be allowed to continue their existence.

Little change is likely to occur in regard to the points outlined above relative to the objectives of business firms or in their relationships to the objectives of society as a whole. Changes may occur in emphasis, however, rather than in type or direction.

For example, there appears to be a trend toward a greater "community orientation" of business. Owners and managers are increasingly aware of the importance of favorable public opinion in regard to products, methods, or dealings with the public. These trends are likely to continue.

Similarly, business owners and managers are increasingly conscious of the importance of their relationships with government on state, local, or federal levels. This does not mean, however, that business firms or their managers will try to alter the traditional separation of economic and political activities. As A. A. Berle has pointed out:

There is another reason, though perhaps negative, for their [corporations] survival. They have maintained a comparative divorce from the political system. This meant in substance that they were not primarily agents of a political government. . . . A substantial part of the economic system had to be kept free of direct control by the state, for somewhat the same reason that the separation of church and state is accepted as a political necessity. . . . There seems to be no reason for thinking that America will abandon this pluralism.[4]

Also the owners and managers of business firms appear to be increasingly conscious of the impact of the firm on its employees. There is growing interest in increasing the challenge and the pleasurability of work at all levels. This is taking place in part as automation and mechanization continue to reduce the number of routine jobs. It is occurring also because of the growing recognition on the part of managers that worker productivity depends to a considerable degree on the provision of challenging opportunities and interesting work and work relationships.

Some firms are increasingly concerned with the avoidance of great fluctuations of operations. In part this is due to cost considerations and in part to the desire to provide fairly regular employment. As a result, diversification of product lines is pursued by an increasing number of firms, a trend that may continue. For the same general reasons many firms are placing increasing emphasis on research and on new product development. Many firms try to maintain a stable record of earnings and of dividend payments, a factor of some importance in owner-management relationships.

Many firms pursue growth as an objective and will continue to do so; they may become increasingly concerned with growth at regular rates. Reasonable stability of growth helps firms in their relationships with unions and in the development of favorable collective bargaining agreements. This is also a factor of some importance from the standpoint of financial institutions and potential investors. Growth is likely to result from increasing diversification in the future, although expansion of existing lines will continue to be an important part of the growth process.

---

[4] A. A. Berle, Jr. "The Corporation in a Democratic Society," in Anshen and Bach, *op. cit.*, p. 75, by permission.

Greater or Less Public Acceptance?

Business firms will continue to be concerned with survival in the future; indeed, competition is likely to grow more intense and make the survival objective increasingly difficult to achieve by many firms.

Business owners and managers are increasingly aware of their dependence on favorable public opinion, both with respect to their own firms and in terms of public attitudes toward the business community generally. Thus, it is often contended that business owners and managers should undertake to stress their service to the public and to emphasize the public interest, rather than to be primarily concerned with profit maximization, even over the long run. While this question is debated widely, as we have seen in our earlier discussions, most businessmen believe that public acceptance and favorable attitudes depend primarily on the provision of better products—goods and services—at lower cost, greater convenience, and on more favorable terms. Pursuit of long-run profits appears to be the objective that is most likely to bring about this result.

An interesting comment in this connection has been made by A. A. Berle, Jr.:

> . . . the real reason for corporations' right to continued existence lies precisely in the fact that they can organize, apply and use capital to meet increasing and changing economic wants with a speed, an economy, and an efficiency greater than most other forms. They can apply new methods and pioneer new fields . . . corporations can move more swiftly, construct more rapidly, arrange for distribution of products more effectively, than other forms of economic institutions.[5]

Increasing efforts are being made by businessmen to make sure that the public understands what they are trying to do. Hence, we may see continued emphasis on public relations programs, on programs of economic education, and on efforts to increase public understanding of the economic system and the role of the business firm in our society.

Business executives are likely to increase their participation in public and quasi-public activities. Primarily, however, they are likely to extend their efforts to understand the preferences and attitudes of the public, American and world-wide, and to try to provide the public with the products and opportunities that it wants. It now appears that for the forseeable future the American public (and to a large degree the world) wants expanding opportunities for work and income, higher living standards by means of better products at lower costs,

---

5 *Ibid.*, p. 75.

protections against hazards and uncertainties arising from war, inflation, depression, illness, accident, old age or loss of employment, opportunities to save and invest savings to advantage, and freedom to set and pursue their individually selected objectives. To the extent that business owners and managers are able to help people pursue these aims, they will gain in public acceptance for their firms and their work.

More Machines?

In our earlier discussions we mentioned some of the possibilities that may arise from the introduction of energy derived from nuclear fission and fusion and the expansion of automation. It may well be that electricity can be produced so cheaply in a relatively few years that it will not even pay to meter it. If you let your imagination run a bit, you can see what this might mean to the operation of business firms and to the ordinary processes of living.

Developments of this type undoubtedly would mean increased use of machinery, thus requiring more highly skilled and better trained workers who will hence have an opportunity to earn higher incomes. It probably means some dislocation of employment and the emergence of new opportunities as old ones dry up. It means new investment opportunities as new business firms take root from new products and new production methods. It probably means lower prices and greater values per dollar for consumers. Power probably can be made available over wider areas and this may bring still greater decentralization of industry and related business activities than has occurred to date.

It would be a mistake, however, to assume that cheaper power, improved machines, and more automation will affect all types of business firms in the same way or to the same degree. Some firms, notably those in the personal service field, will be affected little. Others, especially those in the heavy industry lines, will be affected greatly.

There is little doubt that production and also marketing will be affected by new improvements in transportation, with jet aircraft and helicopters undoubtedly playing a major role. It is in the movement of people and goods for shorter distances, however, that we probably need greatest improvements. Even today it is easier to travel long distances than short ones. To a considerable extent this is also true of the movement of goods. The helicopter may offer some real possibilities for improvement of travel for shorter distances, or there may be other and even more revolutionary developments that will help to solve these problems.

Improved production methods may be associated in part with new products. There are already in development such products as wall panels that will heat and cool homes, built-in vacuum cleaners that will clean homes at the touch of a button, sewerless toilets, and new building materials including plastic and aluminum panels. Automobiles will change greatly as new fuels become available in commercial form. We have already seen important changes in clothing as nylon, dacron, and other synthetic fibers have been brought into use, and there will be other equally revolutionary changes in the future.

It may be that new production methods will make it possible for some production activities to be carried on in the home in contrast to factory production, which provides such a large proportion of our goods at the present time.

There will undoubtedly be important developments in the medical and pharmaceutical fields equivalent to the discovery of penicillin and other antibiotics and the Salk vaccine only a short time ago. Some foods will be synthetic in nature, not relying on animals or vegetables for their origin.

Many of us may find it difficult to adjust to the rapidity of change that may lie ahead. We will need to develop adaptability, resilience, and ability to withstand tensions at least as great as possessed by our immigrant and pioneer forefathers. New products and new production methods also present problems for our educational and social systems. When we see how well people have adapted to change in the post World War II years, we may be encouraged in regard to the future.

Nevertheless, the problems of abundance, even recognizing that they may create frustrations, are nicer problems than those of scarcity. The problems of change are more challenging than those of stability.

Potential changes in products and in business operations undoubtedly will make management more difficult, will increase risks, and will intensify competition. At the same time they will create new and greater opportunities for many owners and managers of business firms and for all of us.

Management by Machines?

The increasing use of the electronic computer in the solution of many types of management problems almost inevitably raises questions about the role of such machines in the future. Will there be more management by machines? Will some nonprogramed as well as various programed decisions be made by machines? How great will be the impact of such machines on management thinking and methods in the years ahead? How will the organization of business firms be affected?

At least a few of these questions can be considered briefly here. To follow through many of their implications, however, would soon carry us beyond the scope of these discussions.

Professor Simon has predicted a tremendous expansion in the potential use of computers and automated processes. He says:

Closely allied to the development of complex information-processing techniques for general-purpose computers is the rapid advance in the technique of automating all sorts of production and clerical tasks. Putting these two lines of development together, I am led to the following general predictions: Within the very near future—much less than twenty-five years—we shall have the *technical* capability of substituting machines for any and all human functions in organizations. Within the same period, we shall have acquired an extensive and empirically tested theory of human cognitive processes and their interaction with human emotions, attitudes, and values.[6]

He goes on to point out, however, that while we may have these technical capacities, we are most likely to use them in areas where they provide greatest advantages, rather than in all of the areas where it may technically be possible to make use of them. The genuinely automatic factory, without workers, is likely to be technically feasible in the not too distant future. In all probability, however, practical developments of such installations will come slowly. As time goes on, however, more and more factories are likely to resemble present-day oil refineries, generating stations, and similar operations that employ relatively few workers in relation to the machines and equipment that are used.

Large-scale clerical operations are likely to be automated to an increasing extent. Both the office and the factory will include more equipment and machines than at present. Investment per employee will rise. But output will also rise.

There are likely to be significant shifts in occupations as a result of these developments. For example, there will be fewer routine workmen, more maintenance personnel, and more people at the professional and general management level.

With respect to the substitution of machines for managers, it is likely that the area of programed decisions will expand, perhaps well into middle-management levels. Even so, as Professor Simon con-

---

6 Herbert A. Simon, "The Corporation: Will It Be Managed by Machines?" in Anshen and Bach, *op. cit.*, p. 22, by permission.

cludes, "My first guess is that man will retain a greater comparative advantage in handling ill-structured problems than in handling well-structured problems."[7] He suggests that management and other professional activities may constitute about the same proportion of all occupations in a generation as at present.

Whether or not we agree with Professor Simon's conclusions, we must recognize the magnitude of some of the revolutionary forces that are at work. They are bound to affect future investment and employment opportunities as well as the work of business managers. They should help to make work in business firms at all levels more challenging and rewarding.

More Research?

Perhaps the future development about which we can be most certain is the expansion of research. In 1960 expenditures for research and development totaled around $13 billion, in contrast to $3.8 billion in 1952 and only a third of a billion in 1940. By 1970 programs of this type may account for $25 billion annually or more.

Dexter Keezer and his associates point out:

Spending on this massive scale is enough to create a major industry overnight. In one sense, research and development *is* an industry—the "industry of discovery," as Professor Sumner Slichter of Harvard University has aptly called the current efforts in industrial research. And it is an industry whose achievements will determine the outlook for new capital investment —in fact, the outlook for much of the U.S.'s growth and prosperity—in the years ahead.[8]

It is difficult to indicate the directions toward which research will lead us. Much will depend on scientific "breakthroughs" as well as on the extent to which new knowledge can be applied. We may have a system or set of devices that provides complete protection against missiles, cures for cancer, even civilian space travel. There may be widespread use of solar energy, nuclear energy, or energy provided by harnessing the ocean tides. The new home of the future may be essentially a "factory for living," with many added types of equipment, and the possibility of changing its shape at will. The car of the future may differ greatly from today's model.[9]

The trend of research and development programs will depend to a considerable extent on business executives, on their attitudes toward

---

[7] *Ibid.*, p. 49.

[8] Dexter M. Keezer and Associates, *New Forces in American Business* (New York: McGraw-Hill Book Co., Inc., 1959), p. 48, by permission.

[9] *Ibid.*, pp. 52–54.

research, their willingness to undertake the risks and problems involved, and their ability to administer programs of research. Mr. J. Irwin Miller, Chairman of the Board of Cummins Engine Company points out:

> The inventive capacity and mechanical inspiration of man has never been higher than it is today, and, therefore, in the years ahead the businessman should anticipate and assume the rapid obsolence of all his products and should endeavor through research to be, himself, the one who obsoletes them, realizing that whatever he is doing, whatever he is making, there is a better way of doing it and a better way of making it.
>
> Today's businessman should also realize that research can be the most purely wasteful of all his business activities. If the head of a business indulges in research, as many do, just to solace his own fears of the future, and plays no personal part in this agonizing function, then he will only come to the end of his cycle all the sooner. If research is to be fruitful, it must be a major daily concern of top management; and, if it is to succeed, those who conduct the research must have a solid understanding of the true needs of their company, of its industry, and of its customers. Unless the top management of a company and its research staff are in the most constant and intimate kind of communication, research will amount to little and can be a great drain on any company.
>
> Research, therefore, is a genuine "business risk," but it is one which must be undertaken. Despite all its perils, the truth remains that in this wildly imaginative technical world in which we find ourselves, a business manager should not sleep too easily at night unless he accepts the fact that there is a better way to do everything that he does and a better way to make everything that he makes, and unless he is determined, himself, to engage in disciplined effective research to obsolete his own ways and his own products.[10]

Management has a great deal to learn about the administration of research activities. For example, the processes of planning research and organizing research activities appear to be somewhat different from those which fit other types of business operations. Research projects tend to be planned from the "bottom up" rather than from the top down. Much depends on the individual research worker and on the support that is provided for him to carry forward his investigations. Probably applied research such as product research can be managed more nearly like other business operations than is the case with respect to basic research. The entire area of activity related to the management and administration of research programs is one that undoubtedly will expand greatly in the years ahead.

---

10 J. Irwin Miller, "The Real Challenge of Research," *Business Horizons,* Vol. I, No. 1 (Winter, 1958), p. 10. See also "How Should Scientific Research be Administered?" Vol. I, No. 2 (Summer, 1958).

Bigger Markets?

There is little doubt that markets will be bigger in the years ahead. Population growth plus rising incomes will form the basis for such expansion. Markets also will be different as new products make their appearance, as the wants and tastes of consumers change, as expenditure patterns shift, as demands for capital equipment expand, and as competition at home and abroad grows more intense.

Professor Robert C. Turner has estimated that our economic growth potential is very great. He says:

If a 4½ per cent rate of increase should continue for another 15 years, until 1975, total output should rise to nearly $900 billion in today's prices. Real standards of living would rise by over 50 per cent. Per capita after-tax income, now about $1,900 should rise to about $2,900 in today's dollars. The mean [arithmetic mean] income per family before taxes, now about $6,500, should rise to about $10,000.[11]

The increasing use of machines of all types in production will generate large demands for capital equipment and will require continued high levels of saving and investment. Both business and consumer spending patterns are likely to change. Demands for services are likely to rise relative to goods. Public expenditures are likely to rise relative to private expenditures. Defense programs undoubtedly will continue to be a major market for many business firms, but many other government programs on state, local, national, and international levels will represent important markets for business firms.

It is probable that markets will grow more competitive in future years. Competition will become more intense between firms in the same line of business, and the trend toward increasing competition between industries and widely divergent products will also continue. As the economy grows more diversified, this trend will be accentuated. Under the impact of new products and increased diversification, competition will accelerate the supplanting of old products by new ones, and there will be increased emphasis on the improvement of present products. In addition, there is likely to be more international economic competition.

The automobile, which has greatly affected consumer markets in the postwar years, undoubtedly will continue to exert a major influence. The federal road-building program will play an important part in these developments.

---

11 Robert C. Turner, *Lectures on Economic Growth* (New Orleans: Tulane University, 1960) p. 30, by permission.

Competition between outlying and downtown retail areas will probably grow more intense. It will be necessary to solve some of the important problems of congestion in the downtown areas, including the movement of traffic and parking. Urban renewal programs may prove to be an important market.

Managers are likely to emphasize market research as competition grows more intense. Market measurement, demand analysis, and motivation research are all likely to expand. It may be that more intense competition will result in more one-man or Caesar type of management in contrast to the group type of management that has been popular in recent years.

Mass marketing is likely to grow in importance, but as we grow more prosperous, greater opportunities are likely to open up also for highly individualized products and services. Thus, we may see widely divergent movements in this area with expansion of supermarkets, shopping centers, sales by vending machines, automatic self-help stores, and the like, and at the same time greater development of highly personalized marketing activities.

In all probability international markets will expand in the years ahead. While many problems exist including trade barriers of various types and various other regulations, many American firms have already expanded operations in foreign markets, as we pointed out in the preceding chapter, and this trend undoubtedly will continue.

One of the interesting possibilities regarding market changes arises from the increasing urbanization and suburbanization of the country. It has been suggested, for example, that by 1980 the nation will be dominated by some fourteen already forming "interurbias," that is, metropolitan strips connecting a number of cities. For example, the east coast metropolitan areas now represent virtually one 600-mile city stretching from Maine to Virginia. This area, which covers less than 2 per cent of the nation's land area, includes a fifth of its population and about a fourth of its retail sales (see Figure 25-1).

There is a possibility that an "interurbia" may develop around Pittsburgh, Youngstown, Canton, Akron, and Cleveland. Still another possibility includes Lansing, Pontiac, Flint, Detroit, and Toledo. The lake shore communities north of Chicago, including Milwaukee, Racine, Kenosha, and Waukegan, and those to the south—Hammond, Gary, and South Bend—already form an "interurbia." One is developing around Puget Sound including Seattle, Tacoma, and Salem. Then Los Angeles, of course, with extensions to the south toward San Diego and also to the north includes an important interurbia development

FIGURE 25–1

Interurbia by 1980—Connected by the Projected System of Interstate Highways

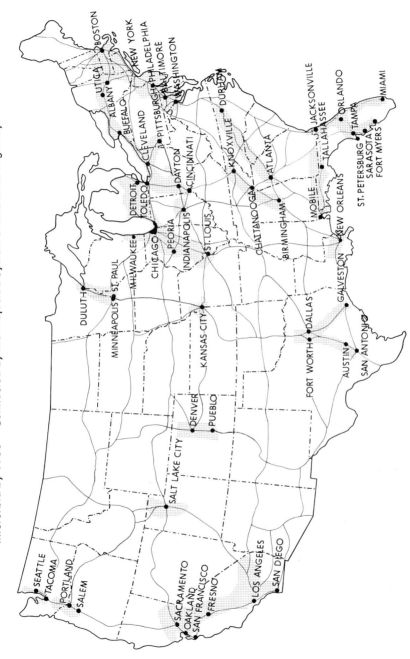

Source: John M. Willem, "Interurbia Is Here to Stay," *Business Horizons*, Vol. I, No. 2 (Spring, 1958), p. 28. By permission of the Foundation for Economic and Business Studies, Indiana University.

and one that will undoubtedly expand in the future. There are several in the South—Dallas and Fort Worth; Atlanta, Birmingham, Chattanooga, and Knoxville; plus others.[12]

Improved Industrial Relations?

The field of industrial relations holds for the future such questions as these: Will business owners and managers be able to solve the problems posed by their relationships with unions? If the power of union leaders continues to increase, will they impose demands that will interfere seriously with the operation of business firms?

The answers to these questions turn in part on the character of union leadership that emerges in the years ahead. If leaders emerge who understand the relationship between wages and labor productivity and the common interests of employees, managers, owners, and the public in successful operations, then we may be optimistic about the development of satisfactory relationships between unions and business firms in the years ahead. Thus, if the demands of labor are kept within the capacity of business firms to meet, the problems of industrial relations are susceptible of solution. But if demands of unions run strongly ahead of the productivity of workers, managers, and machines, then some difficult problems may lie ahead in this field.

Prolonged strikes and work stoppages, for example, will be costly and will arouse the displeasure of the public. As a result both unions and business firms may lose. Both must merit public confidence. If unions are directed by shortsighted or unethical leaders, by gangster elements or by incompetent persons, the problems in the field of industrial relations could become very grave indeed.

The point of view of certain trade-union leaders may have to undergo somewhat the same evolution as took place in the point of view of management in more recent years, that is, giving greater consideration to the public interest.

Developing a greater unity of interest between those involved in industrial disputes is a task that is likely to fall largely on the shoulders of management. There will be some difficult questions to solve, such as: Do workers have a right to share in profits? Do workers have a right to a job? Should managers consider worker welfare when inaugurating technical changes? Does management stand in a trustee relationship relative to employees?

---

[12] See John M. Willem, "Interurbia Is Here to Stay," *Business Horizons,* Vol. I, No. 2 (Spring, 1958), pp. 25–32.

More Economic Growth and Development?

There is every reason to believe that the dynamic qualities of our system will continue to stimulate economic growth and progress in the years ahead. While it is impossible to estimate very exactly the rates of growth that will be achieved and while we must recognize that growth is not likely to be continuous but rather that it will proceed in wave-like movements of varying duration, still the prospects for growth appear to be good. In part this growth may be expected to represent a continuation of forces already in existence. In part it will result from new developments.

FIGURE 25–2

Population Growth by 1975

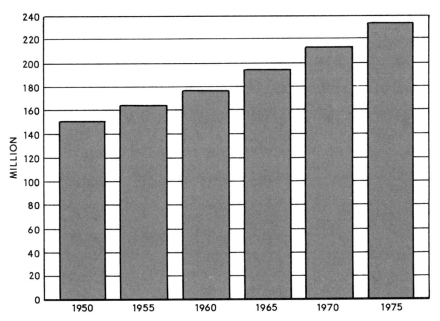

Source: Robert C. Turner, *Lectures on Economic Growth* (New Orleans: Tulane University, 1960), p. 25.

There is some question as to whether a rapid increase in the population will create more problems than it solves, but in any event the population will be larger and there will be more people in the productive age groups during the years ahead than at the present time. If they can be provided opportunities for employment and employment that enables them to work with increasing productivity, there is a good probability that our total output, output per worker, total income, and income on a per capita basis will expand in the years ahead.

The total population of this country is expected to reach about 210 million people by 1970 and to 235 million by 1975 (see Figure 25–2). All people, of course, do not work; some are too young, some too old, and some are not physically or mentally able to work. A number are housewives and not classified as "gainfully employed." Thus, by 1970 it is expected that there will be around 86 million people in the labor force. Something in excess of two million are likely to be in the armed forces, and if between three and four million are unemployed, civilian employment may total something like 80 to 82 million.

We probably will have about a 37-hour week in 1970. If productivity continues to rise at established rates ranging from $2\frac{1}{4}$ to $3\frac{1}{4}$ per cent a year compounded annually, output per man-hour in 1970 would range between $4.29 and $4.96 (in constant dollars). This does not mean hourly earnings, but total output and includes the work of machines, contributions of management, and the like. This would mean a total output for the American economy of between $660 and $815 billion, or an annual rate of growth of about 4 per cent a year[13] (see Figure 25–3).

Encouraging as these prospects are, they will not be achieved automatically. They will require better trained workers; more competent managers; more and better tools, machines, and equipment; new ideas and technological developments; and a favorable economic climate. Better trained workers will mean more and better education for all of our people. This will be provided through our school system and also by improved training programs developed by business firms. As we suggested, there is a good probability that managers will become more proficient, in part as the result of increased knowledge and experience and in part because of more effective use of machines.

More machines and equipment will require increased savings, not only by business firms but also by individuals and families. The level of savings may be affected by our tax structure and by fears of inflation. Probaly the greatest unknown in our potential economic growth is the extent to which we may be able to add to our knowledge, ideas, and technology. We are placing great reliance on research as a key to future economic growth and expansion.

Our growth potential may be influenced by three types of fears: war, inflation, and depression.

---

13 Turner, *op. cit.,* pp. 27–29.

FIGURE 25–3

Projection of Gross National Product through 1975

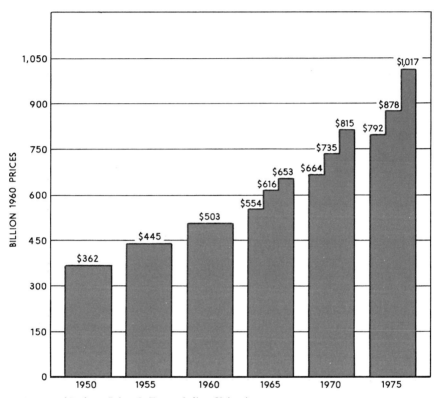

Courtesy of Professor Robert C. Turner, Indiana University.

Fear of War

Most of us realize that the capacity of the human race for destruction is now so great that another war could mean the end of the world itself or at least the end of civilization. It has been said that at the end of the next war there will not be enough living to bury the dead.

We live in great fear of another war. Yet we may take hope that such a disaster will be avoided by the knowledge of the destructive forces that we possess and that other nations, notably the Russians, possess.

So far at least fear of war has not retarded economic growth. To a degree it has stimulated it by making available larger research support in many fields and by emphasizing the importance of economic strength. The shift from military to economic rivalry between the Communist Bloc and the Western Alliance probably has tended to stimulate economic growth in this country, and to some degree at least in others.

But the fear of war has had its impact. Some of our people are inclined to take a "what's the use?" attitude toward life and work. Some are certain that human folly, stupidity, or simply miscalculation will bring on another war and possibly self-destruction. Thus, if we could somehow assure ourselves that war would not again break out the net effect probably would be a stimulation of economic growth and well-being.

Improvements in transportation and communication have greatly reduced the size of the world and forced a closer set of interrelationships among the people of all lands. Problems have been created as a result, but opportunities for better relationships among people in all parts of the world also have been created. The United Nations may have made limited progress but it undoubtedly will play a role of growing importance in world affairs. It may provide the basis for synthesizing some of the divergent viewpoints and objectives that tend to divide the world today and thus to generate fear of war.

Fear of Inflation

Economists tell us that over the historical long run we have had inflation in this country, that is, the value of the monetary unit, the dollar, has tended gradually to decline. This decline has not occurred at a regular rate. There have been periods of rapid decline in the value of the dollar, notably those coming in war periods or in periods immediately following wars, but there have also been periods of considerable stability in the value of the dollar and some in which it has gained in value. In the postwar years inflation has created a considerable amount of concern. Dean Neil H. Jacoby has said in this connection:

> The most important economic problem to be faced by the United States during the next twenty years is how to prevent price inflation, while maintaining full employment and full production, in a free economy. Preventing inflation—rather than reducing unemployment—has become the primary U.S. problem, because powerful and enduring new forces of economic expansion were set in motion by World War II.[14]

Inflation creates a number of problems, particularly for people who live on fixed incomes such as retired persons. Thus, group pressures may be generated because all groups are not affected in the same way

---

14 Neil H. Jacoby in *Problems of United States Economic Development* (New York: Committee for Economic Development, 1958), Vol. I, p. 153, by permission.

by inflationary tendencies. Inflation also creates problems for business firms because of the difficulty of measuring accurately the results of their efforts. Thus inflation may give the appearance of prosperity to business activity and conceal certain types of costs. New firms may be attracted into business as a result, thus intensifying competition.

One of the major problems created by inflationary tendencies is that of saving. In order to achieve continuing economic growth, we will need more and better machinery and equipment. This can only be provided out of capital which can only be created by saving. A considerable amount of saving, of course, is done by business firms through retained earnings, but much of it is done by individuals and families. If we should begin to lose confidence in the value of the monetary unit over the long-run future, the desire to save might be greatly undermined and as a result serious problems created in providing the necessary capital for expansion. Or savings might be put into jewels or gold or some other unproductive form of wealth.

Inflation creates some important problems for business firms in making long-term commitments such as are involved in mortgages, bond issues, or long-term leases, and it creates other uncertainties. For example, business firms may assume that they are prosperous because their monetary incomes are increasing, even though in fact they may be using up capital. If they fear inflation, investors tend to channel funds into equities, that is, common stocks as against bonds or debts. This may create financing problems for some business firms.

There are, however, good possibilities that inflation in the foreseeable future will not attain proportions of a type that will do great damage to our economic system. Indeed, there are reasonably good prospects for price stability. The Board of Governors of the Federal Reserve System has made significant efforts toward restraining inflation. The very fact that our system does not expand continuously but in wave-like movements provides periods in which the pressures toward inflation are restrained. Increasing competition and the growing diversity of the economy may help to restrain inflationary tendencies.

We should note also that the measures of inflation, the price indexes, fail to reflect many changes. For example, it is almost impossible to compare the goods that a dollar will buy today with the goods that a dollar bought fifty years ago. There are many more goods on the market today. To a lesser degree the same thing may be said of periods as short as ten years ago. For example, how can we compare the cost of living before and after television became available? Or before and after penicillin? Or before and after jet aircraft? Thus, while comparisons with such uniform commodities as bushels of wheat may be made by price indexes, it is impossible to reflect other changes, and even bushels of wheat may not be used for the same purposes in the future as at present.

Fear of Depressions

As we suggested in our earlier discussions, a dynamic economic system is also an unstable system. While it would be possible to work out a system which was largely stable in character, this type of situation probably would be purchased at the expense of significant economic growth. We must recognize the possibility, however, that the wave-like movements of economic activity, even if the long-term trend is upward, may at times create so many difficulties that people will prefer to purchase stability even at the price of economic growth and progress.

Such a development would be highly damaging to the type of business environment that is favorable to business firms, and we might find it difficult to maintain our type of economic system under such conditions. It is imperative, therefore, that we find ways and means of limiting the extremes of economic fluctuation without at the same time eliminating the dynamic qualities of the system.

While substantial progress has been made in the years since the end of World War II, much remains to be done, both in learning how to restrain periods of too rapid advance and to limit the extent of economic declines. While the record of the past is encouraging, it would be a mistake to assume that further improvement will be achieved more or less automatically.

This problem has been stated in a very interesting fashion by David McCord Wright as follows:

If we cannot overcome the blind urge for security, and if we cannot at the same time find some method of easing pressures toward restriction by keeping disturbance within bounds, future historians may well write the epitaph of our civilization as follows:

From freedom and science came rapid growth and change.
From rapid growth and change came insecurity.
From insecurity came demands which ended growth and change.
Ending growth and change ended science and freedom.[15]

---

[15] David McCord Wright, *Democracy and Progress* (New York: Macmillan Co., 1948), chap. vi, p. 81, by permission.

Higher Levels of Education?

While our physical environment will change greatly in the years ahead—more and better roads, new buildings with improved architectural treatment, elimination of at least some of our slum areas, better planned communities, and the like—our general environment will be shaped largely by the competence and attitudes of our people.

We have suggested that educational programs, including those provided by school systems, by business firms, and by other means, will tend to expand in the years ahead. Such expansion will be important for our future progress not only in terms of economic advance but in all aspects of life.

Currently the typical young adult around thirty years of age has completed four years of high school, his father completed around a year of high school, and his grandfather as a rule did not go beyond grade school.[16] The period between World Wars I and II saw very rapid advances in general levels of education. Provision for the education of veterans under the "G.I. Bill" after World War II and the Korean War had an important impact on educational development. The continuing competition with Russia has stimulated greater interest in education.

In view of the rapid growth of the population, a significant expansion of our educational facilities and teaching personnel will be needed even if no provision is made for increased education opportunities. If more people, and especially those with real capacity, are to have the benefits of more education, marked expansion in this field will be required.

Improvement of our educational system will be essential for meeting the requirements of life in the years ahead, qualifying for the kinds of work that will have to be done, and making our system of enterprise and democracy work successfully. President James Madison recognized the importance of education for good government when he said, "Popular government without popular education is a prologue to a farce or a tragedy."

Much the same thing may be said about the enterprise system. A system of widespread decision making cannot work unless the people in the system have the competence to make wise decisions. An economic system which is rapidly eliminating routine jobs, requires people of competence to do the work that is necessary.

---

16 See J. F. Dewhurst and Associates, *America's Needs and Resources—A New Survey* (New York: Twentieth Century Fund, 1955), p. 380.

Professor Turner has stressed the *quality* of growth and suggests that this will depend to a considerable extent on education. He says:

We need further economic growth in the years ahead. Even more, we need to improve the quality of economic growth. The only ultimate way to improve the quality of economic growth, I am convinced, is to improve the quality of the human mind. We will get the kind of growth that we ask for —the kind of growth that corresponds to our value systems as manifested in our spending and taxpaying decisions. If we want further economic growth to emphasize the finer, more enduring things of life, we must first want these things and have enough understanding and ability to reason to know what we want.[17]

New Concepts of "The Good Life"?

Our system of education has an important impact on the value scales, general attitudes, and points of view of the public generally. Are there likely to be important changes in what people consider "the good life" in the years ahead? In the ways by which the good life is to be achieved? In attitudes toward business firms? Labor unions? Government agencies? Welfare problems? Minority groups? International relations?

It would be impossible for us even to guess some of the changes in value scales and attitudes that may occur. We should recognize, however, that such changes will have a profound impact on shaping the business environment, and indeed our general environment in the years ahead.

What will be considered "the good life" will continue to be variously defined by different people. Fortunately, we are likely to see the continuation of a set of conditions that will allow each of us generally to set our own goals in work; leisure time activities; the place we will live; community, church, or cultural activities; and others.

How will the majority of people define the good life? Obviously we cannot provide very definite answers to this question. Physical security in terms of health, reduction of hazards, and defense against attack by other nations will continue to be important. People probably will approve the expenditure of substantial parts of our annual income to provide for defense. Similarly, we will continue to support programs that will protect and promote health. Development of medical education and research will undoubtedly be considered of major importance in the years ahead.

Protection against hazards of various types will come in for continuing attention—illness, accident, unemployment, and old age are all

---

[17] Turner, *op. cit.*, p. 63, by permission.

parts of this set of problems. Efforts undoubtedly will be made to reduce highway and other travel accidents as well as accidents in plants, stores, offices, and homes.

As levels of competence for employment are raised, it may be necessary to approach some of the problems of unemployment from a social rather than solely an economic standpoint. There will be more older people, and they will require proper support. At the same time they will gain in relative importance in our voting population.

Economic opportunity and increasing equality of economic opportunity will play an important part in the thinking of people in the years ahead. Indeed, work may become a more significant part of our lives with greater satisfactions coming from work than from leisure time or other activities.

Maintenance of the basic freedoms—political, economic, religious, and academic; freedom of inquiry, expression, and other freedoms—undoubtedly will be placed high on the list of requirements for achieving the good life.

Changing Value Scales and Attitudes?

How people will prefer to achieve the various objectives they set up is also difficult to predict. We have tended to place considerable reliance on government in recent years as a means of solving our problems. Too great a reliance on government may create problems for business and for other sectors of our society in the years ahead.

Attitudes toward business firms are likely to reflect the success of such firms in meeting the needs of the people generally. Wide fluctuations in economic activity may, as we have suggested, call forth demands for greater regulation of business, and this in turn may inhibit economic expansion. The loss of prestige of business in the major depression of the 1930's has at least to a degree been regained. But various antitrust prosecutions have recently had an adverse effect on public attitudes. Some sections of the public continue to have an attitude of suspicion toward business that may create real problems in the years ahead. Programs that will lead to greater economic understanding, more effective public relations on the part of business firms, and above all the continued provision of good values per dollar of consumer expenditure are all important for business firms in this connection.

In all probability labor unions will come in for a greater amount of government regulation in the years ahead. The actions of a number of labor leaders have brought disappointment and some loss of confidence on the part of the public generally.

While people are tending to take an increasing interest in international affairs, there are and probably will continue to be important isolationist elements in our population. In general, however, there appears to be a trend toward increased interest in the United Nations, in the problems of underdeveloped countries, and in the position of the United States in world affairs. Gradually we are assuming the responsibilities that go with a position of world leadership, even though somewhat reluctantly.

The author of a recent book has pointed out:

Whether the problem be that of a burgeoning population and of space in which to live with peace and grace, or whether it be the depletion of the materials which nature has stocked in the earth's crust and which have been drawn upon more heavily in this century than in all previous time together, or whether it be that of occupying minds no longer committed to the stockpiling of consumer goods, the basic demand on America will be on its resources of ability, intelligence, and education. The test will be less the effectiveness of our material investment than the effectiveness of our investment in men. We live in a day of grandiose generalization. This one may be made with confidence.[18]

The gauging of general public opinion and changes in value scales is an important factor in estimating the shape of things to come. It is important that each of us try to do this in order to plan our lives. It is especially important for the business manager in his attempts to plan the future operations of his firm.

An Optimistic Outlook

Despite the many uncertainties and problems that lie ahead, our record to date suggests that we may with good reason take an optimistic view of the future. Progress is never achieved automatically. It takes thought, effort, and in all probability, some luck. Progress is made by people, not things, although the availability of things may be helpful in the process. Similarly, a workable social organization for channeling our efforts toward the achievement of our objectives is an important element in progress. As we have suggested, the means may be more important than the ends in terms of general social objectives and social organization. But there are other factors in economic progress as well. One economist has stated it this way:

It begs the question to say that the American people are more enterprising, more disposed to take risks and to make mistakes and quicker to learn and recover from them that other peoples (although all this is true). But

---

18 John K. Galbraith, *The Affluent Society* (Cambridge, Mass.: Riverside Press, 1958), p. 355, by permission.

why are they so? Not, I am convinced, because they are born so. I can offer no better suggestion than that, whether by good chance or by design, the United States has created within itself a set of institutions which implants in its citizens the habits and arts of adjusting themselves to the everchanging facts of life and of recovering in resilient fashion from the blows of fortune.[19]

SUMMARY

The problems and opportunities of the business community that are likely to emerge in the next few years will undoubtedly influence the management of business firms and the general character of the business environment. The potential changes that may have significance in these terms are many and varied. Of these several were selected for discussion including the following: the number and size of business firms—whether large firms will grow larger or small ones smaller and the possible impact of such developments; changes that may occur in owner-management relations including problems of control; shifts that may take place in business objectives because of the problems of balancing the interests of various groups and the need of business firms to gain greater public acceptance.

In addition, the problems and opportunities related to automation and the potential uses of new energy sources were considered, along with potential developments in research, in the character and size of markets, and in the broad field of industrial relations. All of these potential changes relate in some degree to the growth prospects of the American economy. Fears of war, inflation, and depression may have a restraining influence on economic growth and development.

Improved levels of education and related developments may affect the quality of economic growth, social values and attitudes, and general concepts of what constitutes "the good life." On balance, this review of the emerging problems and opportunities of the business community justifies an optimistic outlook for the future.

QUESTIONS AND PROBLEMS

1. Do you think it may be possible to foretell the future to a greater extent in the years ahead than has been true in the past? Why or why not?
2. On the basis of present trends do you think large business firms will become larger in the future? Explain your position.
3. Do you think relationships between owners and managers will change to any marked extent in the years ahead? Explain.

[19] John Jewkes in *Problems of United States Economic Development* (New York: Committee for Economic Development, 1958), Vol. I, p. 262, by permission.

4. Comment on this statement, which was previously quoted: "It seems to me that nothing would produce as active an interest of the individual stockholder in the conduct of a corporation and at the same time give him so much effective power as to permit him annually and individually to decide what part of his share of the net profits he was willing to reinvest in the corporation."

5. Are there likely to be significant changes in business objectives in future years? Why or why not?

6. Are managers likely to pay greater attention to increasing the pleasurability of work at all levels? Explain.

7. What are the major problems likely to arise from increased automation? From the standpoint of the business firm? The worker? The investor?

8. Comment on this statement, ". . . the problems of abundance, even recognizing that they may create frustrations, are nicer problems than those of scarcity. The problems of change are more challenging than those of stability."

9. To what extent are we likely to see management by machines in the years ahead?

10. Why are we likely to see substantial expansion in expenditures for research in the future?

11. Indicate some of the probable changes that may take place in our markets. Which of these appear to be most important?

12. Do you think that problems of industrial relations will become more or less complex? What will be the main factors influencing directions of development in this field?

13. There is a possibility that the gross national product of the American economy will reach around $750 billion by 1970. What conditions will be necessary to reach such levels of output? Why?

14. How are fears of war, inflation, or recession likely to affect future growth?

15. Do you think there will be changes in what people consider to be "the good life?" Explain.

SUGGESTED READINGS

ANSHEN, MELVIN, and BACH, G. LEE. *Management and Corporations, 1985.* New York: McGraw-Hill Book Co., Inc., 1960. Read especially the summary article pp. 199–238: "Management and Change," by MELVIN ANSHEN, and if you are interested, the following articles in this highly stimulating book: pp. 17–61: "The Corporation: Will It Be Managed by Machines?" by HERBERT A. SIMON; pp. 63–98: "The Corporation in A Democratic Society," by A. A. BERLE, JR.; and pp. 99–117: "The Corporation in A Democratic Society: In Whose Interest Ought It and Will It Be Run?" by FREDRICH A. HAYEK.

KEEZER, DEXTER M., and Associates. *New Forces in American Business.* New York: McGraw-Hill Book Co., Inc., 1959. Read especially chap. eleven: "The Last Round-up."

LONG, JOHN D. *Workbook to Accompany Weimer: Business Administration: An Introductory Management Approach,* chap. 25. Rev. ed. Homewood, Ill.: Richard D. Irwin, Inc., 1962.

TURNER, ROBERT C. *Lectures on Economic Growth.* New Orleans: Tulane University, 1960. Read this thought-provoking series of lectures in its entirety, or, as a minimum, the concluding lecture.

OUTLINE FOR CHAPTER 26

MANAGING YOUR FUTURE requires
   selection of objectives; careful planning; organization of resources; and evaluation of performance, plus self-direction,
   motivation, and development.

Personal objectives may be defined in many ways, such as the
   attainment of
      outstanding goals; modest goals; or multiple goals.

Areas of opportunity may be found in
   expanding industries and problem areas, or
   in established fields.

Special opportunities may arise through
   owning your own business or
   acquiring other ownership interests.

Personal planning requires determination of
   what will be required to achieve your objectives;
   when and where programs will be undertaken;
   how objectives will be pursued; and
   who will be involved in addition to yourself.

Organizing your resources involves
   evaluation and analysis; multiplication and supplementing of your personal resources; and
   careful management of personal finances.

Evaluation of personal programs involves:
   self-discipline; analysis of past performance
   periodically; and analyzing your strengths
   and weaknesses.

High standards of personal conduct and values
   will aid in the pursuit of success and yield
   great satisfaction in achievements.

MANAGING YOUR FUTURE

I had rather have to lament my fortune than be ashamed of my victory.

—ALEXANDER THE GREAT

Management of Personal Programs

In the introductory chapter of this book we suggested that you might study business administration for a variety of reasons—as preparation for a career in business, the government service, law, or a related profession; as a citizen and consumer; as an investor now or in the future; as a student of economics or one of the other social sciences; or from the standpoint of general intellectual interest. We suggested that you had an important management job to do in order to succeed as a student. You should recognize also that the job of managing your life and your career will be a big one. To help you in the early stages of this process, we consider in this chapter some of the possibilities and opportunities that may lie ahead for you.

You recognize by this time that every managerial task, whether in business, personal life, or in some other area, requires (1) selection of objectives, (2) careful planning and policy formulation, (3) appropriate organization of resources, and (4) controls to make certain that objectives will be attained. The same processes are involved in managing your future.

Whether your career objective lies in the general field of business administration or in other areas, this discussion may help you to identify your goals more specifically and to develop at least preliminary plans for achieving them. We try to indicate some of the important areas of opportunity that may unfold during the years ahead which will be important for a business career and also for other fields of activity. We try also to indicate, at least in a general way, how you may help yourself to reach the goals that you set.

We have suggested that education is a continuous process, that it goes on throughout life. We have indicated also that fundamentally education is something you achieve yourself. You must be responsible for your own development now and in the future. The discussions in this chapter should help you to establish a program for continued growth and development, not only during the period you are going to school but also after you enter actively into the field of work that you plan to pursue.

Personal Objectives

Each of us defines success in a different way. For some of us success means the attainment of outstanding goals such as becoming the president of an important business firm; developing into the best market analyst, the best accountant, or the best sales manager in the country; making a million dollars or some other significant amount of money; or reaching the top in a profession, in politics, or in other public service. Others will establish more modest definitions of success. Some will prefer to achieve success in several aspects of life, centering a part of their attention and energies on a business or professional goal but developing other interests including a successful family life, participation in community projects, the pursuit of interesting hobbies, and the like. As we have seen from our preceding discussions, one of the important freedoms we enjoy is the freedom to define success as we wish.

The first step in managing your future is that of defining your objectives. At this stage you may not be able to do this very exactly, but even a general definition will be helpful. For example, you may be able to determine whether your interests center primarily in (1) working with people or things, (2) becoming an expert or directing the activities of others, (3) pursuing big goals or more modest goals, and (4) getting your major satisfactions from work or from leisure-time activities.

There is much to be said for trying to achieve outstanding success in some field. The pursuit of big goals is likely to be more rewarding than the pursuit of more modest ones. As we have suggested in our preceding discussions, some of the greater satisfactions in life are likely to be derived from work rather than from leisure-time activities. Most leaders in business or in other fields devote a major part of their energies and attention to their work, almost to the point of being dedicated to it. The achievement of outstanding success usually requires this. Satisfactions of this type have been described in various ways, of which the following statement is a good example: "The philosophy of life which the writer believes to be most fundamentally democratic, and the one hitherto most congenial to the modern man, is the philosophy of the artist—the searcher. The nineteenth century 'utility calculus' slurred over most of the important things of life. Man is not merely a consuming machine. Nor for that matter is he merely a contemplating one."[1]

Areas of Opportunity

Whether you set your sights high or on more modest targets, your goals will be easier to achieve if you select the areas of greatest opportunity for your operations. In our discussions in the preceding chapter we indicated some of the expanding opportunity which the future may provide. The service industries, business operations related to leisure-time activities, and new areas of development such as plastics and electronics may be particularly important. Certain regions of the country are developing more rapidly than others, notably the South, Southwest, and Far West. The emergence of interurbias and their probable significance for future markets may suggest opportunities, as may the growing importance of research—a field that has been called a "new industry of discovery."[2]

One way of identifying areas of opportunity is to determine where the principal problems of the future may develop. People will pay for goods and services that help them solve their problems. For example, they would like to get their work done more easily, to eliminate or reduce onerous chores, to reduce the hazards of illness and accident. Business firms will welcome help in the solution of major problems such as collective bargaining, cost reductions and controls, improving business community relationships, making work more challenging at all levels of business activity, and reducing areas of conflict between owners, managers, employees, customers, and the public generally.

Since problem areas typically present opportunities, the bigger the problems, the bigger the opportunities that may emerge. For example, anyone who can solve the problems of traffic congestion in our central cities obviously will be highly successful. Anyone who can find solutions to some of the difficult problems of union-management relationships should find a broad avenue of opportunity open to him. Anyone who can provide good housing at half its present cost or make available

---

[1] David McCord Wright, *Democracy and Progress* (New York: Macmillan Co., 1948), p. 197, by permission.

[2] Statement by Sumner Slichter.

any other important product that is in wide demand at a lower cost will certainly succeed. The whole field of international business administration gives promise of rapid expansion.

Another way of identifying areas of opportunity is to determine how new ways can be devised for doing old jobs. Ideas that are developed through your own creative thinking may well be the most important key available to you in attempting to achieve success in future years. This is not to suggest that all of the opportunities are in new fields; many established areas also hold great promise. In fact, opportunities in established fields may be overlooked because of the glamour often associated with new developments.

You may find it helpful to consider from time to time such questions as these: What is the best possible idea for a new business? What is the best way for improving an existing business or a prevailing business practice? Which combinations of present businesses may be valuable? What don't people like about one or another product, and how might it be improved? Where are the greatest wastes in business? What are the problems that are most in need of solution?

We might add many questions to this list, but these suggest the types that may stimulate your thinking and your imagination. The development of an inquiring attitude of mind, the constant searching for improvements and solutions to problems, and the development of an inventive point of view will be important assets in your quest for success.

Your Own Business?

Among the objectives that you may select is the possibility that you may go into business for yourself. You may have an opportunity to enter a family business or to acquire an interest in an existing firm or to start a new one. There are many satisfactions in the pursuit of such an objective. Opportunities for making a good income are open. Indeed, many people fail to recognize that a successful independent business may yield far greater returns than can be earned by working for a salary, even if one attains a position of considerable responsibility. Of course, such returns are possible only through the assumption of greater risks and responsibilities than are borne by those who work for a salary.

You may find it advisable to gain some experience for a few years by working for an established firm, and then as opportunities become available, to start a new firm or buy all or part of an existing business. In some cases family businesses need to bring in outside people, either because there are no heirs or the sons and daughters of the family prefer not to go into that line of work.

Acquiring Ownership

Incidentally, you may find it advisable to get *ownership* whenever this is possible under favorable conditions. Thus, if you have a chance to acquire stock options or a share in a business with a modest salary, on the one hand, or a higher salary, on the other, you may find it advantageous to move in the direction of ownership. Of course, not all ownership is desirable. There is no advantage in becoming the owner of a "white elephant." If the future of a business firm is in serious doubt, you would obviously prefer the higher salary to a lower salary plus a chance at an ownership interest. But if future prospects are reasonably good, ownership has many advantages, not the least being the tax situation. If you acquire the stock of a business firm or a share in its ownership and sell it, the gain, if any, may be taxable at the capital gains rate. Most salaries, at least after the lower brackets are passed, are taxed at significantly higher rates.

But there are other reasons for acquiring ownership when this can be done under favorable conditions. For example, we discussed the general problem of long-term inflation. Ownership, of course, provides a hedge against inflation since the money value of things goes up during a period of inflation, while the value of the dollar goes down.

The ownership of an interest in a business firm, or a piece of productive property, or other investments, gives you a source of income in addition to what you may receive by marketing your personal services. If your health breaks down or some catastrophe befalls you which reduces your working ability, income from such sources, of course, can be very helpful.

Ownership may take a variety of forms. You may become the owner of securities of many types which may represent ownership shares or debts of business firms; debts of local, state, or federal governments; real estate of various types; insurance, savings accounts, annuities, and other things. To do this requires saving, and this should be a part of your personal program.

Personal Planning

Having considered some of the many objectives that may be open to you in the years ahead, suppose we turn our attention briefly to the topic of planning as a means for attaining the objectives you establish.

As we have suggested in previous discussions, plans may be of many types, general and specific, short- or long-range, simple or complex. Plans may serve as guide lines to personal policies.

Good plans are programs of future action. Good plans are based on good predictions and projections—careful estimates of probable lines of future development. Consequently, you need to consider *what* will be required to achieve your objectives: The education and training that you will need; the financial or other resources that will be required; the assistance of others that may be essential; the costs that will be incurred; the risks that you are assuming; and related things.

Your plans should include decisions as to *where* you will carry out your program of action. For example, will it be essential that you be located at some specific place? Will travel be involved? If so, how much? Some people prefer to select a place to live first and try to find career opportunities there. Others are willing to locate almost anywhere, giving priority to the places that offer greatest opportunities. Some people do not like to travel and will prefer work that keeps them in one place; others enjoy travel and try to find work that will enable them to cover a lot of places.

A time schedule is of basic importance to most plans. *When* will you try to take various steps in your career? For example, how long will you plan to go to school? When will you perform required military or other services? How long will you plan to stay with your first job? When will you move from one job to another? If you wish to go into business for yourself, how soon will you plan to undertake such a program?

Questions of this type cannot always be answered exactly. A time schedule, however, often is helpful in your planning even if you can only establish it in terms of general ranges. For example, you may plan to stay in school only long enough to finish your bachelor's degree, but you may also consider the possibility of taking a master's degree, thus giving you a range of time rather than an exact time schedule for planning purposes.

How you will plan to achieve your objectives will require the consideration of numerous alternatives. In part the "how" aspects of your planning will be conditioned greatly by the type of objectives you set up. Beyond this, you will find it advisable to consider such questions as whether you will try to achieve your objectives largely through personal efforts, whether you will need the assistance of others, for example, financial aid or assistance in getting a starting job; how you will organize your resources in order to use them most effectively; how costs will be met; how risks will be borne or shifted and numerous other related questions.

Who will be involved in your plans also requires consideration. Primarily, of course, you will be the one to carry them into effect. But you may also have to consider other people and the implications of your plans for them—parents, friends, your own family when you establish one, advisers, sponsors, those who have provided or will provide financial support, and others.

These are some of the basic questions you will need to consider in developing plans for your future. Many others, of course, may also be involved. Those outlined above, however, should give you a start in the direction of establishing some fairly well-considered plans. And, of course, like the manager of a business firm, you will find it necessary to revise and refine your plans from time to time. This can be done effectively by setting up a specific time such as the start of a new calendar year or a new school year or on your birthday when you will reconsider your plans in the light of the knowledge and experience you have acquired since you set up your plans or reviewed them previously.

Organizing Your Resources

How can you best organize your resources to accomplish the objectives that you want to achieve? Your first step will probably be that of defining your principal resources. Do these consist largely of your personal abilities and energy? Or do you have financial resources or the support of family or friends to count on as well?

Ordinarily when we think of organizing as a managerial function we are concerned with the development of a team effort, putting together the abilities of several or a great many people. In your own case, however, you are concerned largely with organizing your own energies, time, and whatever other resources may be available to you. You will find it helpful to evaluate your resources as realistically as possible. Is your health good? Do you have an abundance of energy or only a limited amount? How good is your mental ability? What are your principal deficiencies? Can they be corrected?

An objective analysis of your resources may help you to avoid undertaking types of work for which you are not adapted. It should help you to "put your best foot forward."

Another important factor for consideration in organizing your abilities grows out of your likes and dislikes. What types of things do you really like to do? What kind do you try to avoid? Each of us tends to do better the things he likes. While we cannot always have our preferences, the extents to which we can channel our efforts into things we like often determines whether we do a job well or only in a routine manner. At the same time most of us have more capacity than we realize for developing interest in new or unfamiliar activities.

In a final analysis each of us faces the competition of others with about the same level of abilities as our own. There are some outstanding exceptions, of course, such as people who have phenomenal ability of one or another type, but for most of us the differences in native ability are not unusually great. The difference between success and failure often turns on the effectiveness with which abilities are used and managed rather than the level of ability we happen to possess. It turns also on our desire to succeed and to make the sacrifices that may be required—or as it is sometimes put, on our willingness to be inconvenienced.

Multiply Your Resources

If you wish ultimately to achieve outstanding success, you will need something more than the opportunity to market your personal services. Even if one becomes a highly skilled specialist and can command a very good rate of pay per hour or per day, there simply are not enough hours available to achieve a significantly high level of income. For example, if you could command a hundred dollars per day for your efforts, this would mean an income of around $25,000 per year since there are about 250 working days per year. If you worked every day including Sundays' your annual income would reach $36,500 per year. Either of these income levels may be satisfactory. But if you have your goals set higher, it is necessary to recognize that in some way you must be able to multiply or supplement your own personal abilties.

Popular singers could not begin to attain the income levels they enjoy without the ability to multiply their personal efforts by means of records and motion pictures. Similarly, a lecturer may make a good income by delivering lectures; he may make a great deal more by turning his lectures into a book, which in effect enables him to multiply his abilities. You can often multiply your efforts through the work of others. Learning how to use assistants is a part of this process. Learning how to organize them into an effective work team will carry you even farther.

Thus, in considering the resources that may be available to you in the future, you may find it advisable to devise ways and means for multiplying them. Or we might state this idea in another way: You can't achieve outstanding financial success by relying entirely on the marketing of your personal services.

Savings Program

Most of us believe in saving. Few of us do it. Yet a sound program of saving often represents the difference between a happy and a difficult personal situation. You can save on almost any level of income if you want to do so. Even a few dollars a week can in a period of time amount to a considerable sum. If you save five dollars per week, the total at the end of the year will be $260, plus interest since most savings institutions will pay interest or dividends every six months. In some cases this is done quarterly or even daily. If you put $1,000 to work for you each year for ten years at 5 per cent interest and allow the interest to accumulate, that is, to compound, you would have at the end of the period $12,578. If you save only five dollars a month, put it into a savings account drawing 3 per cent interest and allow the interest to compound, it will amount in five years to $323.45, in ten years to $698, and in fifteen years to $1,133.15. You may be interested in reviewing the Tables in Appendix II in this connection.

If you are able to accumulate even a small amount of savings, this may enable you to make a down payment on a well-located piece of property and give you an opportunity to command the income from it while you are paying the balance due.

You may find it advantageous in planning your personal program to think in terms of at least three levels of saving: (1) for emergencies —"rainy-day" savings such as sudden illness or accident or other need for an unforeseen expenditure; (2) for specific purposes such as accumulating a down payment on a home, financing a vacation, purchase of presents, for example, joining a "Christmas Club" for savings purposes, or for some other specific reason; and (3) for investment such as the purchase of securities or property in order to gain additional income from this source.

A good savings program, of course, will include regular payments for required insurance of various types, retirement programs, social security, medical and hospital insurance, and the like. These are usually considered as "contractual savings" in that a stated and agreed-upon amount is paid at regular intervals. Optional savings may be treated in the same way. Funds that are free for whatever use you may wish to make of them may be accumulated best by saving a stated amount each week or month, taking this amount from your current income first. In other words, you "pay yourself" before paying bills or other obligations. This is probably the most effective method of carrying on a savings program.

You will not find it easy to save. Marketers will do their best to get you to spend all you can earn plus all you can borrow. There will be pressure to "keep up with the Joneses." Buying on installment arrangements often means paying high carrying charges. Borrowing requires interest payments, and in some cases the charges are high.

This is not to suggest that you should never borrow; in some cases, it might be highly advantageous to do so. For example, few of us could become homeowners if we had to pay the purchase price in cash. It is essential, however, to borrow on terms that are as favorable as possible. Savings programs help us to avoid "panic borrowing," that is getting money for emergencies or special purposes almost regardless of cost.

Managing Personal Finances

As we suggested in the introductory chapters of this book, you must learn to manage yourself before you can manage others. Similarly, you must learn to manage your personal financial affairs, not only because this is advantageous in itself but also because it enhances your reputation among your associates and in the community generally. Some people are able to make money "go farther" than others. This is because they manage it better. There are numerous cases of people with limited incomes who are able to accomplish more through careful management, savings programs, and shrewd investments than others who earn high incomes but fail to manage them effectively.

Without realizing it many of us are judged by the care with which we manage our personal affairs, and especially our personal finances. People who fail to pay their bills as due are often "talked about," and this information filters back to employers and others who may have an important influence on the opportunities that may unfold for us.

Building a reputation for financial responsibility may play an important part in shaping your future. No one has much regard for persons who "throw their money away" or fail to exercise ordinary common sense in managing their financial affairs or meeting their obligations.

Controls

For the management of your personal affairs the most important control available is that of self-discipline. You establish the standards by which to judge your performance. You analyze your progress to see whether things are moving according to plan. You take such corrective action as appears to be indicated.

As we suggested above, "taking inventory" or reviewing your performance periodically is a good control procedure in connection with personal as well as other programs. In addition, studying your weaknesses is as important as analyzing your strengths. Just as in the case of business management, control in connection with your personal program is forward looking. Past mistakes cannot be corrected, but similar mistakes may be avoided in the future.

By studying and analyzing past performance you may find it advisable to alter or modify your plans and in some cases your objectives. You may find that you have set your goals too high or too low; or your plans may not be realistic in one or another respect. Thus, the control aspect of the management process can be adapted to your personal programs to good advantage.

Trends of Development and Your Future

Many of us tend to assume that we will be swept along by the general forces of expansion that are at work in our country. If the future generally is bright, as we have suggested it may be, we may consider our prospects to be favorable as well. This type of assumption can lead you into difficulty. Your chances of moving with the forces of expansion are good only if you are able to take advantage of them.

At the height of the postwar boom many people, some of them with good educational and experience backgrounds, were far from prosperous. The same thing may be said of some business firms. By contrast, at the bottom of the major depression of the early 1930's some people and some business firms were prosperous. They had been able to move contrary to general trends.

Thus, it is a mistake for you to assume that success will be easy to achieve in the years ahead simply because we painted in the preceding chapter a fairly bright picture of the future of business and the American economy. It should be somewhat easier to succeed in an expanding system, of course, than in one that is static or declining. Ultimately, however, your success will turn on your own efforts, abilities, and luck.

We should note also that your own future may be better in a stable line of business than in an expanding area simply because your talents may fit best into that situation, and, of course, the opposite may be true as well. Identification of your abilities, selection of the areas into which they may fit best, projection of probable lines of development, and above all managing your abilities and resources carefully are essential ingredients of your future success.

Who Will Succeed?

Which types of people are most likely to succeed in the years ahead? While our answers to this question will pertain especially to the field of business, they are applicable to other areas as well.

Probably the quality that will be needed most is *adaptability*. In a rapidly changing world the ability to adapt, to fit into changing circumstances, and to adjust to new conditions and requirements is a highly valuable quality.

Adaptability is at least in part a matter of attitude, of willingness to make adjustments. Most of us are highly adaptable, but often we resent change and resist the adjustments that must be made to it. Military training often helps to develop adaptability. One recognizes that he has little control over his situation and can accept and adjust to it and be reasonably happy or resist and resent it and be miserable. Few of us can do much in the way of altering the general trends or directions of change. If we learn how to adapt ourselves to new conditions and developments, our chances for success tend to increase. This depends in part on our ability to predict, to anticipate the types of changes that are likely to occur, and also on the way we manage our own abilities and resources in attempting to adapt to anticipated changes.

Willingness to compete is a second quality that may be important in your future success. While the future may see expanding opportunities in many fields, there will also be an increasing number of people pursuing these opportunities. Those who are able to compete most effectively are likely to win them.

The desire to compete is often developed through college athletics or through student activities of various types. It is not an easy quality to define, being a combination of pride, a desire to excel, high standards, plus other things, but it is likely to be a very valuable quality in the years ahead.

Closely related is *determination*—unwillingness to accept defeat, dedication to the goals set. These combinations of qualities may be considered a third important factor in determining the degree of success you are likely to enjoy in the future.

Thus, we may say that the *desire to succeed* is in itself a basic requirement for success. To put it in plainer language, you've got to want to. Unless this basic desire exists, no other qualities are likely to be sufficiently strong to bring success. The will to succeed is basic.

Often the champion in a sport does not have greater skill than his rivals. He simply refuses to be beaten. Somehow he calls forth the added ounce of effort that makes the difference. Much the same thing can be said about careers in business or in other fields as well.

Willingness to work—to be *industrious*—may be considered a fourth quality of importance in the development of a successful career. While this has almost always been true in the past, it is likely to be especially significant in the future. As one company president has pointed out, "Lack of talent may often be overcome by sheer hard work."[3]

You have undoubtedly heard the statement that genius is 10 per cent inspiration and 90 per cent perspiration. In large measure this is true. The ability to apply yourself to the task at hand—to work hard and for extended periods of time—is a factor of real importance in any successful career.

A fifth important quality is *creativity*—imagination, ingenuity, inventiveness, and a searching and inquiring mind that can spark new ideas and make use of them. Not all of us have this ability, and if we do not, there is some question of whether it can be developed. It takes many forms. Some of us can be creative in one area and not in others. There are various degrees of creativity as well, ranging from the level of the original thinker or artist to that of the routine worker who may be able to find better ways of doing his work.

Sixth, *objectivity*—the ability to think in realistic terms, to be "hard-headed—often spells the difference between wrong decisions and sound ones. For every line of action you will pursue, there are numerous alternatives. The ability to select among them on the basis of carefully developed information and realistic value standards is an ability that is likely to increase in importance in the more complex world that lies ahead.

We might mention other qualities of importance for the development of a successful career. Certainly mention should be made of the ability to get along with people, since most careers, especially those which exceed the average to any marked degree, involve work with people, and to do this effectively requires that you understand them and be able to adapt to them. Of course, we should recognize that any-

---

[3] James R. Price, President, National Homes Corporation. See also Theodore O. Yntema's statements in Chapter 2.

one with leadership ability, however this may be defined, has a greater chance of achieving outstanding success than one who does not have leadership capacities.

Value Standards

Each of us develops consciously or unconsciously a set of personal standards. By these we judge what is right or wrong, important or unimportant, ethical or unethical. Our value standards will tell us when success is being purchased at too high a price, as, for example, rigging contracts or competing unfairly or engaging in other practices that are not acceptable to most of us or to the community at large. Most of us are able to avoid obvious errors of this type. We recognize that if success is purchased by conduct or quality of work that does not meet our personal standards, the results can hardly be satisfactory. Often, however, there are less obvious choices. For example, choices between loyalty to friends and to an employer or between company interest and public interest or between family preferences and career preferences often may be difficult. Questions of this type will turn largely on your own standards and your evaluation of the alternatives that are present.

Sometimes we may think that high value standards interfere with rather than aid in the pursuit of success. Over the long run, this is not likely to be the case. Temporary gains, of course, may be achieved by pursuing lines of action that can only be justified by questionable value standards. The big jobs, however, and the major responsibilities seldom go to those with mediocre personal value standards.

Some people contend that only the unethical can attain major financial or other success. You may have heard it said, "Show me a millionaire and I will show you a crook." There is no doubt that some people have achieved success and wealth by questionable means, but for the vast majority this simply is not true. Indeed, it is harder to succeed in the long run by following unethical standards than by living up to high standards of personal performance.

One of the big satisfactions in life is the sense of achievement that comes from the attainment of difficult objectives. Such satisfactions are likely to be denied when objectives are achieved through questionable practices and conduct.

We have suggested in our earlier discussions that for our type of society the *means* become the *ends*. By this we are trying to say that in a system of widespread freedom of choice of objectives, the real goal becomes the preservation of a set of conditions that makes such freedom of choice possible. We might suggest also that for most of us success may be measured not so much in terms of the attainment of our objectives but rather in their pursuit. If this is true, the manner by which we pursue our objectives and the value standards by which we judge our performance will play a major part in measuring our ultimate success.

Confidence in the Future

Despite the many problems that may lie ahead for our economic and social system, for business or for each of us personally, the progress that has been achieved in the past justifies confidence in the future. Our problems will not solve themselves, it is true, but if we approach them with a willingness to experiment and to adventure, in short, to be enterprising, we should have little to fear.

Many great careers will be carved out of the years that lie ahead. Yours can be one of them. The risks are great, but so are the opportunities.

A future without challenge is no future at all. A future that is bright with promise but also beset with struggle unfolds before you. Its rewards both in contributions to society and in personal satisfaction can be as great as in any age of history.

If we accept this challenge with confidence in ourselves and in the future, we can say with Justice Holmes: "Through our great good fortune in our youth our hearts were touched with fire. It was given to us to learn at the outset that life is a profound and passionate thing . . . above all we have learned that whether a man accepts from Fortune her spade . . . or from Aspiration her . . . cord . . . the one and only success which it is his to command is to bring to his work a mighty heart."

SUMMARY

Each of us defines success in a different way. One of the important freedoms we enjoy is the opportunity to define success as we wish. Definition of your personal objectives is necessary if you are to manage your future effectively. While some will prefer to aim for modest goals, there is much to be said for trying to achieve outstanding success in some field.

Regardless of the type of objective established, it will be easier to achieve if areas of greatest opportunity are selected. Some of these may include the service industries, business operations related to leisure-time activities, new and emerging industries, or rapidly growing regions. One way of identifying areas of opportunity is to determine where the principal problems are likely to develop. Among the opportunities available, that of owning your own business or of acquiring ownership rights in other businesses should not be overlooked.

As is true of business management, good planning will help to achieve your personal objectives. Similarly, it will be advantageous to organize your resources effectively and to extend and multiply them. Good control processes also may prove useful, particularly the practice of reviewing past performance periodically in order to avoid making the same mistakes over and over again.

Those are most likely to achieve success in the years ahead who are adaptable, willing to compete, determined, industrious, and who have the qualities of creativity and objectivity. The degree of success that you may achieve will be measured finally by your personal value standards.

QUESTIONS AND PROBLEMS

1. Indicate the line of business in which you think the greatest opportunities are likely to be found. Do you think this may also provide the best opportunities for you? Why or why not?

2. Would you prefer to look for opportunities in problem fields, new fields, or established fields? Give reasons for your choice.

3. Would you give first priority to the place you want to live and try to find work in that locality, or would you reverse these in priorities. Explain.

4. What are the main advantages in acquiring ownership in business firms or in other economic resources? If you had $10,000 to invest would you prefer to put it in a savings account, insurance, stocks, bonds, other investments, or combinations of these? Give reasons for your choice.

5. Which factors do you give highest priority in developing your plans for the future? Why?

6. What do you consider to be the principal resources available to you in trying to achieve your objectives? Are these likely to change over time? In what ways? How may you be able to multiply your resources?

7. Do you think it is important to manage personal finances carefully? Why or why not?

8. Do you believe that high standards interfere with or aid the pursuit of success? Explain.

9. Comment on the following excerpts from the *Monthly Letter* of the Royal Bank of Canada, Vol. XLII, No. 3, entitled, "In Search of a Happy Life."
"Long, long ago, men and women moved from birth to death as it were on a stream, obeying unquestionable laws, taboos and totems. Today,

we are more subject to the burden of choice. No warm-blooded youths want to go to sleep in the bottom of the boat, letting the elements carry them wherever chance leads. Instead, they wish to sit up and learn to sail into the wind and against the thrust of the tide, with stars to steer by. They wish to be, if not masters of their fate, at least pilots of their craft. . . .

"Life is an endless succession of choices. When you go to a ball game you reject an infinite number of other things you might have done with your time. . . .

"Life is also a set of skills. Your education and your preparations need to be suitable to your hopes and the greatness of the enterprise upon which you are embarking. . . .

"What is the happy life?

"This was the greatest question of antiquity, as it is of the modern world. . . . But the good life should lead us steadily toward happiness, and happiness is a satisfied self, not merely a succession of gratified impulses and desires. . . .

"Let us say, tentatively, that there are five components of the happy life: health, work, interests, friendships, and the pursuit of an ideal. . . .

"Happiness should not be looked upon as a reward for a good life, but as the natural effect of it. . . .

"To be chattered about in the newspapers, to be feted and dined, to be sought after because of wealth: these are not vital ingredients of the good life. A disillusioned comment was given us by Collingwood, who succeeded to command of the fleet upon Nelson's death at Trafalgar: 'Fame's trumpet makes a great noise, but the notes do not dwell long on the ear'. . . .

"The truly important man is one who is conscious of his powers and is bent upon developing them, and thus becomes great by design. You cannot be great in anything unless you have a vision of the greatness possible in it. *Your success is the ratio of your accomplishment to your capacities.*"

SUGGESTED READINGS

GATES, JAMES E., and MILLER, HAROLD. *Personal Adjustment to Business.* Englewood Cliffs, N.J.: Prentice-Hall, Inc., 1958. This book can be helpful in your career planning. Refer especially to chap. i, "The Importance of Career Planning."

LONG, JOHN D. *Workbook to Accompany Weimer: Business Administration: An Introductory Management Approach,* chap. 26. Rev. ed. Homewood, Ill.: Richard D. Irwin, Inc., 1962.

Appendixes

GLOSSARY

Accounting. The recording, classifying, summarizing, and reporting of financial data pertaining to business transactions; it includes the interpretation of such information in a manner which aids management in making and implementing decisions.

Accounts receivable. Amounts owed to an individual, business firm, or other organization for purchases made on credit.

Adaptability. The ability to accept and adjust to a new situation.

Administration. See *Business administration and management.*

Administrative expenses. Those expenses chargeable to the general management of the business which are not attributable to either producing or selling operations.

Advertising. Public announcements and messages sponsored and paid for by sellers presented in various media—newspaper, magazine, TV, radio, or other forms—the purpose of which is to aid directly or indirectly in the sale of goods or services.

Agency. A relationship between two or more persons, by which one party, usually called the agent or attorney, is authorized to do certain acts for, or in relation to, the rights or property of the other, who is usually referred to as the principal (or employer).

Analysis. Systematic study by means of classification, determination of points of similarity or difference, and evaluation.

Annuities. Literally, a series of equal payments at annual intervals; used in a popular sense to refer to equal payments at monthly intervals, particularly as represented by a contract sold by insurance companies in which benefits are payable to the recipient for a specified time or for life.

Antitrust laws. Regulations as provided by the Sherman Act, Clayton Act, and others to restrict combinations by business firms in undue restraint of competition.

Appraisal. An estimate of the nature or worth of something.

Arbitration. Submitting a dispute or controversy to a disinterested party or board for decision.

Array. In statistics, an arrangement of observations or numbers in order, frequently from highest to lowest.

Asset. Any property or right to property having a money value owned by an individual, partnership, or corporation, or other form of organization.

Assignment of accounts receivable. A process of pledging accounts owed to a firm as security for a loan.

Audit. The review and examination of financial records to determine that they are accurate and that they were properly prepared.

Authority. Right and power to command or to act officially.

Automation. A process of production in which machines are used to operate and control other machines; may involve one stage as in the case of a

Automation—*cont.*
thermostat or a series as in the case of electronic computers.

Balance sheet. A statement of the financial condition of a business firm as of a given date.

Balance sheet equation. Assets equal liabilities plus net worth.

Bankrupt. One by or against whom a petition in bankruptcy has been filed; a person generally insolvent, whose financial condition makes him liable to action by his creditors for the seizure and distribution among them of his property.

Basic freedoms. Political, economic, religious, academic, and related freedoms of inquiry, expression, investigation, publication, competition, and enterprise.

Blocked and controlled currencies. Monies upon which limitations have been placed as to movement between countries.

Board of Directors. The principal governing body of a corporation, representing the shareholders; minimum number of members usually three.

Bond. An evidence of a debt; an obligation which usually represents a promise to repay a sum certain at a specified time and to pay interest at a specified rate on the indebtedness; the duration from borrowing to repayment is usually many years and thus qualifies the indebtedness as a long-term or fixed liability of the business firm.

Break-even point. The volume of output (and sales) for a stipulated time period at which total costs for the period equal total revenues for the period.

Budget. A plan for the systematic receipt and expenditure of funds for a specified period such as a year; a budget may be set up also in terms of personnel or other resources.

Bureaucracy. Formalization in an organization which results from classification of positions, establishment of hierarchies of authority, and de-

Bureaucracy—*cont.*
velopment of specialized procedures for acquiring information, making decisions, communicating information, hiring, firing, initiating changes, or taking other action.

Business. The complex field of commerce and industry in which goods and services are created and distributed by private enterprises in the hope of profit within a framework of laws and regulations which makes this possible. The term is also used more generally as in personal business, public business, or even church business. In its most general sense a state of being busy.

Business activity. Volume of production and distribution of goods and services as indicated by volume of transactions, employment, or other measures. See also *Business conditions.*

Business administration. The direction of business affairs including the formulation of goals, the choice of ways and means, the direction of people, and the co-ordination of their efforts with those of other resources in the achievement of desired results.

Business conditions. State or level of business activity measured in various ways with recognition given to total output, employment, incomes, industrial production, and other indicators.

Business environment. The "climate" or set of conditions, economic, social, political, or institutional in which business operations are conducted.

Business firm. An establishment providing goods and/or services in the hope of profit—normally an individual proprietorship, partnership, or corporation.

Business operations. The process of utilizing resources in the production and marketing of goods and services.

Buyers' market. Conditions favorable to purchasers, such as large supplies, limited demand, many sellers, few buyers.

Capacity. Total possible output within a given period of time as determined

Capacity—*cont.*

by physical plant, raw materials, labor, or some other limiting factor. (This term is sometimes used to refer to the output possible during a given period without unit costs exceeding a specified figure and with a specified degree of maintenance being sustained.)

Capital. Productive power of savings, either free for investment or embodied in productive agents, in which case usually designated as *capital goods;* money, goods, equipment or land which is to be used to produce other goods or services.

Capital budgeting. The allocation of available funds among the various long-term investment opportunities available to the firm.

Capital spending. Expenditures for plant and equipment.

Capitalism. A social order based on private property, contract, and competition; the enterprise system.

Capitalization. The process of reflecting anticipated future earnings in present value.

Casualty insurance. A risk-pooling arrangement to protect against economic loss resulting from legal liability claims, dishonesty, explosion of boilers and machinery, glass breakage, personal accidents and illness, and certain other contingencies.

Central planning. The allocation of resources in an economy by decisions of one or more government officials rather than by decisions of buyers and sellers registered in the market.

Chain store. One of a number of retail outlets under the same ownership following uniform policies and practices.

Charter. A grant or guarantee of rights or privileges by governmental authority, as in the case of a charter of incorporation; the written evidence of such a grant.

Chattel mortgage. A transaction whereby the owner of personal property (chattels) transfers the title to such

Chattel mortgage—*cont.*

property to another as security for the performance of an obligation subject to being defeated on the performance of the obligation.

Civil action. Action by an individual or firm against another or others to secure remedy for wrongs alleged to have been committed.

Coercive regulations. Regulations or programs which require performance of certain actions or restraint from actions in order to avoid penalties; e.g., fines.

Collateral loans. A loan secured by the pledge of personal property, usually securities.

Collective bargaining. Negotiations between an employer or employers and an organized group of workers; typically, such things as wages, hours, working conditions, benefits, and the like are covered.

Commercial paper. Short-term obligations such as notes, bills, and acceptances sold by firms in the financial markets to raise funds.

Commission. Compensation based on a percentage of the value of goods sold or handled; often used as a means of determining earnings of salesmen.

Commission, regulatory. An official body appointed under appropriate authority to administer a program of regulation.

Common law. Rules based on usage; judge-made law in contrast to legislation or constitutions.

Common stock. Residual ownership of a corporation evidenced by certificates and normally characterized by voting rights and participation in earnings.

Communication. Transmission of thoughts and ideas.

Communism. Revolutionary socialism based on the concept of the class struggle with elimination of private ownership of income-producing property through violence; theoretically, agreement on main objectives and alternatives in life with the state

Communism—*cont.*
"withering away"; practically, a dictatorship of a party.

Community orientation. Concern with and emphasis on community objectives and programs.

Compensation. Payment, recompense, remuneration.

Compensatory damages. Awards for infringements of rights in the amounts necessary to compensate for the wrongs suffered.

Competition. The existence and general availability of alternate opportunities and the right to choose between them; a state of rivalry among persons or business firms striving for the same or similar goals.

Complementary product. A product which completes or supplements another; for example, tires are a complementary product for automobiles.

Conditional sales contract. A sale made on the basis of fulfilling an agreement such as payment at a later date.

Consumer goods. Those intended for direct consumption such as food or clothing as opposed to producers' goods such as machines intended for use in production.

Contract. An agreement between two or more persons that is legally enforceable; a written evidence of such an agreement.

Contractual savings. Stated and agreed upon amounts paid at regular intervals to a financial institution as in the case of insurance or annuities.

Controller. The chief accounting officer of a business firm, generally responsible for maintenance of the records; preparation of statements, forecasts, and budgets; and for giving advice on matters pertaining to accounting; the term "comptroller" is also used in this sense.

Controlling. The process of co-ordinating and regulating activities to assure performance in accordance with standards and plans designed to achieve objectives.

Convertible currency. Money that is unrestricted as to its use in interna-

Convertible currency—*cont.*
tional transactions and readily acceptable in payment for imports or readily exchangeable into other currencies and/or gold.

Copyright. The exclusive right to control the publication or reproduction of a literary or artistic work.

Corporation. A legal entity created by governmental charter (federal or state) for the purpose of carrying on approved activities as stated in its charter; owners (stockholders) enjoy limitation of liability beyond the amount of their investments; corporations may be organized for profit or not for profit.

Correlation. Relationship that is mutual or reciprocal; as a correlation between prices and quantity demanded; in statistics, a mathematical relationship between groups of data; the extent to which variations in one given phenomenon accompany directly or inversely variations in another given phenomenon.

Cost accounting. The determination of charges against income incurred in the production and distribution of goods and services and the allocation of such charges among departments, products, or other cost-accumulation units.

Cost of goods sold. The composite of the cost of material, labor, overhead, and other expenses involved in producing goods for sale; does not include costs of selling or general management.

Cost-plus pricing. Establishment of prices on the basis of a percentage advance over costs.

Costs. Outlays; input factors relative to output; that which is given up to secure what is wanted.

Council of Economic Advisors. A three-man board of experts and a staff established by the Employment Act of 1946 to provide information and advice on economic conditions and trends for the President of the United States.

Creative thinking. The process of getting and developing new ideas, concepts, and relationships.

Creditor. One who has extended credit, i.e., provided goods or services prior to receiving payments.

Crime. A positive or negative act in violation of a law that constitutes an offense against the state; wrongs that are injuries to the public.

Criminal action. Action by the state against an individual, firm, or agency to punish alleged infraction of laws.

Current assets. Cash or resources which will be converted into cash through normal operations of the business within an operating cycle, i.e., the time usually required from inception of the productive or merchandising process until cash is received for the goods or services sold; this cycle normally thought of as one year.

Current liabilities. Any amount owed or coming due for payment to a creditor within a year.

Current ratio. Current assets divided by current liabilities; the current ratio indicates the ability of the firm to operate without being dependent on short-term creditors; the "rule-of-thumb" acceptable ratio is two to one (2:1).

Cycle. A series of movements through time of more or less regular sequence such as a cycle of business activity, for example, expansion, recession, and recovery.

Debt-to-net-worth ratio. Total liabilities divided by net worth; this ratio indicates the extent to which borrowed funds from creditors are being used in the business as compared to the invested funds of the owners.

Decentralization of industry. Movement of operations from one or a few to many installations; sometimes involves movement from industrial centers to smaller cities.

Decentralization of management. Division and assignment of authority and responsibility to lower echelons of management.

Decision making. The process of selecting among alternatives; may be based on orderly, logical processes or on intuition or "hunches."

Deduction. Reasoning from general principles to specific cases.

Demand. The set of conditions indicating how much of a good or service will be bought at various prices.

Democracy. See *Political democracy*.

Depletion. Using up of a resource such as an oil pool or a mine by gradually exhausting the resource itself rather than by wear and tear. See *Depreciation*.

Depreciation. Loss of economic value through the physical wearing out of a fixed asset such as a building, machine or other equipment; sometimes used broadly to cover loss of value over time from being outmoded as well as from physical causes, but more frequently related to physical causes of loss of value over time. See *Obsolescence*. See also *Depletion*.

Direct labor. The human effort involved directly in the creation of a product or service.

Direct material. Things used in manufacturing a product which become a part of that product.

Diversification. Distribution as between products, plant location, sales outlets, etc.; reducing risks by distributing some thing or things, as in diversifying securities.

Dividend. The amount paid to shareholders or stockholders, usually stated as a percentage of the investment or in dollars per share.

Division of labor. Specialization of activities; dividing a job into parts to permit concentrated and specialized work.

Double taxation. Levying taxes on the same property twice while the ownership of the right to the income or the ownership of the property remains with the same taxpayer; sometimes applied to the levying of the taxes on the same stream or flow of income without regard to ownership in the hands of different taxpayers, as where

Double taxation—*cont.*
a tax is imposed on the income of a corporation and again on the dividends received by the shareholders from the residual corporate income remaining after paying the corporate tax.

Durable good. A good that renders service (i.e., is not fully consumed) in the current accounting or income period; there are both consumer durables (refrigerator) and business durables (drill press).

Economic growth. Rising levels of income, output, and employment relative to cost; sometimes used to refer to an expansion of gross national product or income.

Economics. The study of the social organization of want-satisfying activity; the study of the social organization for the use of resources in the attainment of desired objectives in an efficient manner.

Efficiency. Relationship between input and output factors such as energy, time, or money.

Eminent domain. The right of government to take private property for public use with just compensation being paid.

Entrepreneur. One who undertakes business risks and responsibilities.

Equity. The ownership interest in assets; in the case of a business firm this interest is usually represented by the capital stock and surplus.

Equity capital. See *Equity*.

Ethics. Moral principles or values; the study of moral principles or values.

Exchange economy. An economic system based largely on competitive and open markets with general freedom of exchange and the public enforcement of conditions necessary for private enterprise.

Executive development and training programs. Educational courses designed for the improvement and extension of managerial knowledge and methodology; may be sponsored by universities or by business firms or trade associations.

Fair-trade laws. Regulations permitting fixing of prices of trade-marked goods by manufacturer and distributor based on the Miller-Tydings Act and Amendments or upon acts of individual states in intrastate commerce.

Featherbedding rules. Rules that preserve outmoded and inefficient work methods or which require employment of persons even though they have been displaced by machines.

Financial institutions. Organizations specializing in finance such as commercial banks, savings banks, savings and loan associations, and insurance companies.

Fixed asset. Any asset used in the operation of a business which is of a permanent nature and which is normally *used* in the processes rather than being held for resale; generally includes land, buildings, machinery, furniture, autos, trucks, and other equipment.

Fixed liability. Amounts owed to creditors which will not be due for payment for at least a year.

Fixture. Anything permanently attached to land or buildings, as a furnace or an installation for ventilating or lighting a building.

Flow chart. A diagram depicting the relationships between the parts of an operation to assure that the entire process will be integrated; usually refers to production but may relate to other operations as well.

Franchise. A specific privilege conferred by government or, in the case of an exclusive dealership, conferred by a business firm.

Fraud. Deception; cheating; intended perversion of truth to gain an advantage.

Fringe benefits. Compensation above wages or salaries, such as insurance, pension, and/or profit-sharing benefits or nonquantifiable benefits such as pleasant working conditions.

Game theory. A theory of decision making in situations in which the results are jointly determined by two or more decision makers who have op-

Game theory—*cont.*
posing interests but no one of whom has complete control over the outcomes.

"G. I. Bill." Provisions of special benefits by Congressional action for veterans of World War II and the Korean War including educational benefits, mortgage guarantees, and others.

Goodwill. In business, the value of reputation, trade-marks, or position; value beyond that of physical assets; sometimes considered as the value of the business attributable to ability to earn an above-normal profit.

Gross national product (GNP). The sum of all goods and services produced in an economic system in any given period, usually a year, in terms of current prices.

Gross profit. The difference between sales and cost of goods sold; the difference between the selling price of a product and the cost of the product; computed for accounting purposes prior to assigning selling and administrative expenses.

Hedge. To counterbalance a contract for sale or purchase of commodities or securities by entering into an opposite contract, i.e., a contract to sell against a contract to buy and a contract to buy against a contract to sell.

Horizontal integration. Merging, consolidation, or amalgamation of business organizations operating at the same general level of production or marketing processes.

Human relations. The complex of responses arising out of the association of two or more people; the purpose of human relations programs in business is the integration of people into a work situation in a way that motivates them to work together productively, that is satisfactory to those involved; the work situation includes relationships between people outside as well as within an organization.

Hypothesis. A preliminary or tentative explanation of facts or observations or relationships.

Incentive. Spur, motive, special reward, such as extra payment for reaching or exceeding a standard of performance.

Income. Receipts, earnings, revenues; a flow of income from operations or investment.

Income and expense statement. A statement of incomes received and expenses incurred for a given period with the resulting difference representing the profit or loss from operations.

Individual proprietorship. An unincorporated business owned and often, although not necessarily, operated by one person.

Inducive regulations. Regulations or programs which hold out promise of rewards for compliance with desired lines of action.

Induction. Reasoning from specific observations to a general conclusion.

Industrial goods. See *Producers goods.*

Industrial relations. Activities pertaining to bargaining, contracts, and related matters involving firms, unions, and independent employees.

Industrial Revolution. The changes resulting from the introduction of power-driven machinery around the middle of the 18th century.

Inflation. Increases in prices due to declines in the value of money.

Injunction. A writ or order issued by a court to prohibit specified action or actions by a person or his agents; a mandatory injunction requires the performance of a specified act or actions.

Innovation. The introduction of something new—an idea, program, or process.

Institutional advertising. Advertising which stresses the company or line of business rather than particular products; it is usually intended to gain prestige and goodwill.

Institutional arrangements. Accepted ways and established practices developed through custom or usage, e.g., language.

Insurance. The pooling of risks to provide participants protection against certain economic losses in return for a premium payment.

Insurance companies. Organizations whose function is to pay specified or determinable sums to designated persons upon the happening of certain contingencies (such as death, fire, legal claim, and others) in consideration for payments (premiums) received by the organization from or on behalf of the beneficiary.

Interest rate. The percentage of a loan or investment paid for the use of funds customarily stated as an annual rate.

International business administration. Management of the foreign operations of a business firm.

Interurbia. Metropolitan strips connecting a number of cities; continuous urban and suburban areas which include at least several cities.

Inventory. The amount of raw materials, partially finished products, or finished products that a firm has on hand at any given time, awaiting either further processing or sale.

Investment banker. A banker who underwrites or guarantees the sale of long-term securities.

Isolationist. A person or position opposed to internationalism.

Job analysis. A study of particular work assignments to determine duties, responsibilities, qualifications, and other factors needed to differentiate between jobs and their relative values.

Job classification. An indication of the relationships between work assignments, usually as to skill, knowledge, or responsibility.

Job description specifications. A statement, based on a job analysis, of the abilities necessary to perform a work assignment and the duties and responsibilities involved in it.

Joint venture. See also *Syndicate*. An undertaking participated in by two or more persons or firms typically for a single project or purpose.

Labor market. Supply, demand, and price relationships for services of workers.

Labor productivity. Output per man-hour worked.

Labor union. See *Union (labor union)*.

Laissez fare. A French term literally meaning "let people do (or make) what they choose." The term also refers to an economic system which relies chiefly on competition as a method of control; it does not mean, as often suggested, a system of no government regulation.

Law. A generalization from experience that applies almost universally. A demonstrated relationship between cause and effect; in a legal sense, an established standard or rule of conduct or action.

"The law." A composite of customs, constitutions, legislation, court decisions, rulings of administrative boards, and institutional factors which govern relationships among persons, organizations, and society at large.

Leadership. The vital motivating force that inspires and directs an organization toward the achievement of its objectives.

Lease. Transfer of the use of property for a period of time in return for a rental payment.

Legal risks. Uncertainties arising from interpretation of laws, legal relationships, or documents pertaining to them.

Legally competent. Able to enter into binding legal agreements; often used in reference to legal age and sanity.

Liability. Any amount which is owed to a creditor by an individual, business firm, or other organization.

Liability insurance. An arrangement for pooling of risk to protect against economic loss because of legal obligations to pay claims to others for personal injury or property damage.

License. Authority or permission to do or to refrain from doing something; in business, formal permission from a government agency to carry on a busi-

License—*cont.*
ness activity; also, the written evidence of such permission.

Liens. A claim against real or personal property, for example, a mechanic's lien, a right to cause the property to be sold in satisfaction of the debt of the property owner to satisfy the claim.

Life insurance. A risk-pooling arrangement to provide for payments of specified amounts to beneficiaries in the event of death of the insured or at the maturity of the policy; term insurance has no maturity benefits.

Line (organization). An organizational arrangement in which supervisors have direct control over and responsibility for those supervised.

Linear programming. A method of allocating limited resources in order to optimize a measurable objective; both the restrictions on the resources and the objective must be expressed by linear relationships.

Litigation. Legal action or suit.

Lobbying. Attempting to influence legislation through organized effort.

Macroeconomics. Economic analysis applied to larger units such as activities outside a business firm, particularly to the economic system as a whole.

Management. The efficient utilization of resources in the achievement of desired results; effective use of means, human effort, and material to accomplish ends.

Management theory. Generalizations from experience explaining management processes and methods; often principles are included as well as theories.

Manager. One who makes and implements decisions; one who uses resources to pursue given ends and who accomplishes desired results through others.

Manufacturing. The process of adding value by changing the form of goods; creation of form utility.

Marine insurance. A risk-pooling arrangement to protect against economic loss of (1) water-borne imports

Marine insurance—*cont.*
and exports, (2) domestic shipments, (3) instrumentalities of transportation, and (4) certain other properties covered by "floaters"; category 1 is referred to as *ocean marine* and others as *inland marine.*

Market research. Collection and analysis of information pertaining to supply, demand, and price factors, usually for a particular commodity or service.

Marketing. The processes of distributing or transmitting economic values; the over-all selling efforts of a business firm.

Marketing channel. The route taken by goods in moving from producers to final users.

Markets. Areas over which forces affecting price operate effectively enough to bring about a tendency to uniform price; markets are people who have money or ability to command credit; markets may be thought of as centers of the interrelationships between the forces of demand, supply, and price.

Markup. A percentage advance; for example, the percentage by which a cost is adjusted to arrive at an asking price; markup percentages are most commonly expressed in terms of the selling price, but may also be expressed in terms of cost.

Mass marketing. Sale to the general public through large-scale outlets.

Mass production. Large-scale output intended for a general market as opposed to custom production or making goods to order.

Mean (arithmetic average). An average computed by dividing the total of a series of observations or items by the number of observations or items; for example, the mean of 9, 8, 7, 6, 5 is 7, obtained by dividing the sum of 9, 8, 7, 6, and 5 (or 35) by the number of items, 5, to get 7.

Mechanics liens. A claim by those who have furnished labor or materials for construction purposes; the claim ap-

Mechanics liens—*cont.*
plies to the land as well as to improvements on it.

Mechanization. A process of replacing human or animal effort with machines.

Median. In statistics an average based on the midpoint of a series of observations or numbers in an array from highest to lowest; for example, in this array 9, 8, 8, 6, 4, 1, 1, the median is 6; it is the middle number.

Mergers. Absorption of one business firm by another; uniting of two or more business firms into a new firm; (literally the latter process is "combination").

Microeconomics. Economic analysis or study of small units such as the internal operations of a business firm or firms.

Minimum wage law. Regulations placing a floor on wages that may be paid by an employer.

Mining. The activity of separating basic materials from the earth.

Misrepresentation. Giving a false impression; failing to represent adequately as in the case of an agent.

Mode. An average showing the most frequent observations in an array of data; for example, in this array, 9, 8, 7, 6, 6, 6, 2, 2, 1, the mode is 6.

Models. Theoretical situations often expressed mathematically or experimental plants set up or built according to various assumptions or specifications to test given hypotheses.

Monetary and credit policies. The programs of central monetary authorities relative to the money and capital markets, usually Federal Reserve and Treasury policies.

Monetary damages. Legal awards payable in money to redress wrongs.

Money. Anything that is generally accepted in business transactions as a medium of exchange including credit instruments as well as currency, bills, and coins.

Money markets. Supply, demand, and price relationships for money and credit; various money markets may be

Money markets—*cont.*
distinguished as long or short term, mortgage, government bond, and other markets.

Monopoly. Ability to control supply and hence to set prices.

Morale. Prevailing mood, spirit, or attitude of an individual or organization.

Mortgage. A pledge of property to assure the payment of a debt; real estate mortgages involve the pledge of real property; chattel mortgages of personal property.

Mortgage bonds. Bonds or promises to pay secured by a lien on real property.

Motivating. Developing and maintaining the desire of persons in an organization to achieve desired results; as an adjective, inspiring, stimulating.

Motivation research. Research intended to gain insights into human behavior, to find out why some products and some advertisements appeal to buyers and others do not, and to determine why some appeal more strongly than others.

Multinational firms. Firms whose operations are conducted in two or more nations.

Nationalism. Emphasis on national interests in contrasts to international or local and sectional interests.

Negative leadership. Direction and motivation by means of penalties or threats of penalty; the use of fear in contrast to the offering of rewards or hope, which is positive leadership.

Negotiable instruments. Documents that are transferable by endorsement and delivery or by delivery in the course of business, and that have special property characteristics which protect a holder in due course.

Net foreign investment, net sales abroad. The difference between sales abroad and purchases from other countries plus some other international balance-of-payment items.

Net worth. The difference between assets and liabilities; the ownership interest in a business.

Objective. A goal, target, end, or desired result.

Obsolescence. Loss of value through displacement by improved equipment or processes or by style or design changes. See *Depreciation*.

Operating profit. The profit resulting from the normal operations of the business for a given period; for accounting purposes it is computed by deducting the cost of goods sold, selling expenses, and administrative expenses from sales.

Operations research. The use of the scientific method and advanced mathematical and statistical techniques in the solution of management decision problems.

Opportunity costs. See *Principle of opportunity costs*.

Optimum. Best or most favorable condition for a given purpose.

Organization. Arrangements for putting resources together into an effective relationship; channeling authority and responsibility so that people will work together effectively.

Organization chart. A pattern showing relationships between positions and the people who occupy them as to authority, responsibility, and accountability.

Organizing. The process of establishing the proper relationships among work, people, and other resources; arranging for channeling authority and responsibility.

Output per man per hour. The average amount of production for each hour of labor time in a specified period.

Partnership. An association of two or more persons to carry on, as co-owners, a business for profit.

Patent. Authorization issued by government for an invention giving the holder exclusive right to make or sell goods based on the invention for a term of years.

Payout period. The length of time required for the present value of the earnings realized through the use of capital equipment to equal the cost of such equipment.

Per capita income. Average income per person during a given period.

Performance bonds. Deposit of funds or evidence of availability of funds as a pledge for carrying out a contract or agreement.

Personal property. All private property other than real estate.

Personnel. The persons in an organization.

Philosophy. Literally, love of wisdom; study of principles of reality, human nature, and conduct; a body of principles underlying a branch of knowledge; for example, the philosophy of management.

Plan. A guide to action; a program for achieving objectives or desired results.

Planning. Process of formulating a program in advance to achieve desired results.

Plowed-back earnings. Earnings not paid out as dividends but retained for use in the business.

Police power. The limitation of private property rights in which government has the power to regulate when necessary to safeguard the public health, morals, and safety and to promote the general welfare; e.g., zoning laws.

Policy. A guide to action; general rules of action that serve as guides to decisions and operations. (Also used to describe the written evidence of an insurance contract.)

Political democracy. Government by discussion and vote with majority rule but with basic protections for minorities; not a system of plebiscites or nose counting.

Positive leadership. Direction and motivation by means of reward or promise of reward; holding out hope in contrast to fear or threats of penalty, which is negative leadership.

Postulate. Estimate of potential developments on the basis of various assumptions.

Predict. To forecast; foretell, prophesy.

Preferred stock. Ownership of part of a corporation which ownership confers upon its owners a stated priority

Preferred stock—*cont.*
as to dividends or to assets in liquidation of the firm.

Present value. The current equivalent (worth) of an investment or stream of payments to be received in the future.

Pressure groups. Organizations of business, labor, farm, reform or other interests for the purpose of securing favorable action on legislation or other programs.

Prices. Values stated in terms of money.

Principal. From a legal standpoint, one who has another act for him; a principal as in contrast to an agent who acts for him.

Principle. A generalization that has widespread application but not to the extent of a law (see *Law*); a general proposition sufficiently applicable to a series of phenomena under consideration to provide a guide to action.

Principle of opportunity costs. Recognition that the real cost of a thing is that which is given up in place of it; for example, the cost of purchasing a pencil is the lost opportunity of buying something else.

Private property. The exclusive right to control economic goods in individual or business firm ownership. It is subject to limitations such as taxes, eminent domain, and the police power.

Processing. See also *Production*. The activity of changing the state or form of goods in such a way as to prepare them for later processing or distribution; the manufacturing stage of production.

Producers goods. Those used in the production process such as machinery or equipment in contrast to consumers goods which are ready for direct consumption by final users.

Product differentiation. Modification of a particular product through design or special identification through advertising or related programs made in an effort to cause it to stand out from others with which it competes.

Product mix. The combination of goods and/or services being turned out by a given firm at a given time; the "optimum" mix is the one which renders the maximum contribution to profit or to another objective of the firm.

Production. The process of creating economic values. Such values are things, goods, or services that people want and are willing to pay for.

Productivity. Relative efficiency in the creation of economic values; favorable or unfavorable output relative to cost indicates high or low productivity.

Profit. The residual return to the entrepreneur; the amount remaining after contractual obligations have been met. (May be positive or negative.)

Profit and loss statement. See *Income and expense statement.*

Profit and loss system. The enterprise system of risk assumption in the hope of profits but with the possibility of loss.

Profit-sharing plan. A program in which a share of a company's profits is set aside for distribution to employees.

Progress. Advancement toward accomplishment of objectives; not satisfactions alone but better wants: "pursuit of nobler things in a nobler way."

Property. Control of economic goods; ownership; a valuable right or interest in an economic good.

Property insurance. An arrangement for pooling of risks to protect against loss resulting from damage to or destruction of property; in a broad sense refers to all insurance other than life, accident, or sickness coverage.

Proxy. Authority to act for another as in voting stock; a written evidence of such authorization.

Public liability insurance. See *Liability insurance.*

Public relations. Programs designed to place a business firm in a favorable light and advance its general public interests; programs providing for ef-

Public relations—*cont.*
fective communication between a business firm and the public at large and vice versa.

Purchasing. Obtaining, acquiring for a price; buying.

Range. Extent of things encompassed as in space or time; extent from highest to lowest as in a range of figures.

Real estate. Land and buildings and the property rights in them.

Real estate market. Supply, demand, and price relationships for real properties and property services; several markets are included—those for residential, industrial, commercial, and farm properties, and others.

Real estate mortgage. Pledge of real property to secure a debt; the written evidence of such a pledge.

Recession. The declining phase of a business cycle; a decline in the volume of business activity.

Reciprocity. Mutuality; return in equal measure by two sides or parties as in the case of a reciprocal trade agreement.

Remedy. The legal means for gaining redress for wrong or for preventing a wrong or for recovering a right.

Renaissance. The revival period in history following the medieval period; the 14th–16th centuries; any revival or new birth.

Resources. Sources of power; economically land, labor, and capital with management also included.

Retailing. Selling to final users usually in small quantities; the final stage in the distribution process.

Retirement programs. Arrangements for systematic accumulation of funds for annuities payable to retired employees; often require joint contributions of employer and employee.

Revenue. Income, return from business operations or investments; also, income to government.

Risk. Exposure to loss; uncertainty; hazard.

Rule of law as against rule of men. The concept that relationships among members of society and as between a

Rule of law as against rule of men—*cont.*
member of society and society is based upon uniformly applicable principles, hence, impartiality, as opposed to the arbitrary reign of an authority based upon whim, caprice, or favoritism.

Sales promotion. Programs designed to expand volume of sales.

Sample surveys. Observations of some of the units in a group in the hope that the units observed are representative of all of the units in the group; the sample may or may not be selected at random.

Seasonal fluctuations. Changes in business conditions that take place from one season to another.

Securities. Evidences of ownership (stock) or debt (bonds) and other related documents.

Sellers' market. Conditions favorable to the seller, such as strong demand or limited supply; many buyers, few sellers.

Seniority rules. Provisions which give preference to those who have worked longest as to promotion, increased incomes, and the like.

Simulation. Use of an artificial situation in studying the characteristics and/or behavior of or instructing others in the characteristics and/or behavior of an organization, process, or other phenomenon; for example, simulated flight in a training device.

Social Security. A program established in 1935 and extended since that time providing for old-age and survivors' insurance, parental and child welfare, and assistance to disabled and blind persons.

Socialism. A theory or system of social organization based on government ownership and operation of the principal means of production and distribution of goods and services with the system achieved by gradual and peaceful processes.

Society. The social order, an enduring social group.

Specific performance. A legal principle under which the terms of an agree-

Specific performance—*cont.*
ment may be ordered by a court to be carried out exactly; not applicable in the case of contracts for personal services.

Speculative buying. Taking heavy risks in purchases; for example, buying for inventory in anticipation of price increase.

Splintered ownership. Widespread holding of small interests in a company with little concentration of control.

Staff (organization). An organizational arrangement which provides for technical or advisory services to the line or operating functions.

Standard. A guide or basis for measurement; a model; something to measure against.

Standard deviation. A measure of the extent to which data of a given type are dispersed about some specified average; technically, the square root of the mean of the sum of the squares of the deviations from the arithmetic mean in an array of data.

Statistics. The study or science of collecting, classifying, and analyzing facts based on number of occurrences or observations; or in popular terms, the study of ways to handle masses of data.

Stock option. An opportunity offered to managers, employees, or others to purchase the stock of a firm at specified prices.

Stock option and purchase plans. Provision for the purchase of the stock of a company at an established price usually given to key executives as an inducement for joining a firm.

Stockholder. An owner or partial owner of a company, usually a corporation.

Straight-line depreciation. Recovery of the cost of a fixed asset by charging off against income an equal amount per year over the estimated useful life of the asset. The annual charge-off is determined by dividing the cost of the asset by its estimated number of productive years.

Strategy. The use of available resources (of the firm or other organization) in

Strategy—*cont.*
such a way under current conditions and those of competitors or adversaries that optimum results will be achieved.

Subsidy. Payment by direct transfer, rebate, discount, or other means from one person or organization to another to induce, assist, or otherwise encourage that other person or organization to undertake some action; term is normally used to refer to a payment by a governmental agency to an individual or private organization.

Suits to quiet title. Court procedures to clear up uncertainties in titles to real property.

Supply. Amount available for sale.

Syndicate. An organization usually of two or more individuals or firms formed for the purpose of carrying out one or more transactions.

System of private property and contract. A term often used as a synonym for the enterprise system; a social organization based on widespread decision making as to the ownership of property or the entering of legally enforceable agreements.

Taxation. The legal assessment and collection of a payment from citizens by a government on a predetermined basis as in income taxes, property taxes, sales taxes, and the like.

Technology. Applied science; knowledge pertaining to industrial arts.

Title insurance. Agreement for pooling of risks to protect against loss resulting from unknown defects in the title of real property.

Tort. A wrongful act against another (other than a breach of contract) that may result in legal action.

Trade association. A voluntary organization of business firms and their owners and managers in a specific line of business activity for mutual assistance, education, information, representation, lobbying, and related activities.

Trade barrier. Any factor or condition which hampers or impedes the move-

Trade barrier—*cont.*
ment of commodities or services from one country or region to another and which exists as a consequence of governmental policy rather than economic conditions.

Trade-union. See *Union (labor union).*

Trade-mark. A designation for a line of goods, usually copyrighted and protected under copyright laws.

Trading on the equity. A terms used to designate the process of borrowing funds to augment invested capital in the hope of earning a higher return through use in the business than is paid in interest to borrow the funds.

Traffic management. Direction and coordination of the movement of people and things; usually in business the function of supervising shipping of goods to or from an installation.

Trend. A prevailing tendency, such as a sustained upward movement in prices.

Trust. A combination of business firms under trust agreement which is managed and operated by trustees for the benefit of members; device for holding property interest by one person for the benefit of another.

Underdeveloped countries. Nonindustrialized countries; countries having relatively large ratios of population to capital equipment.

Union (labor union). An organization of workers in a craft, trade, industry, or company attempting to safeguard and advance the interests of affiliated employees in economic, political, or social activities.

United Nations. An international organization arising out of the nations allied against the Axis powers in World War II; resulting from declaration of 26 nations, January 1, 1942, and under charter adopted January 1, 1945, and later ratified.

Universe (population). All units in a group of persons, places, or things which group is the subject of statistical treatment.

Urban plant. The entire complex of physical assets, such as streets, sewers, buildings, transportation facilities, and others that serve public and private real property.

Valuation. An estimate of value; the assignment of a value to a good or service; typically used in relation to real property, fixed assets, capital goods, and the like.

Value. Comparative importance of things that people consider essential for their purposes but that do not exist in sufficient quantities to meet demands for them; how much of one thing that may be secured in exchange for another.

Value judgments. Estimates of relative desirability based on predetermined standards.

Vertical integration. Merging, consolidation, or amalgamation of business organizations operating at different stages or levels of the production or marketing processes.

Warehouse receipts. Evidences of the deposit of goods in a warehouse.

Wholesaling. An intermediate stage in the production and distribution process; usually involves buying from manufacturers and selling to retailers.

Withholding tax. A deduction from income at the source as in the case of employers withholding the taxable portion of salaries or wages.

Working capital. The amount of money invested in the business to meet day-to-day operations; usually measured by deducting current liabilities from current assets; often referred to as net working capital.

Workmen's compensation insurance. Pooling of risks to cover an employer's statutory obligation to pay benefits to employees injured in the course of employment; in some cases applies to occupational diseases.

Zoning ordinance. A regulation of land use by areas.

TABLES

TABLE 1. COMPOUND INTEREST: $(1 + r)_n$

Amount of One Dollar Principal at Compound Interest after n Years

n	2%	2½%	3%	3½%	4%	4½%	5%	6%	7%
1	1.0200	1.0250	1.0300	1.0350	1.0400	1.0450	1.0500	1.0600	1.0700
2	1.0404	1.0506	1.0609	1.0712	1.0816	1.0920	1.1025	1.1236	1.1449
3	1.0612	1.0769	1.0927	1.1087	1.1249	1.1412	1.1576	1.1910	1.2250
4	1.0824	1.1038	1.1255	1.1475	1.1699	1.1925	1.2155	1.2625	1.3108
5	1.1041	1.1314	1.1593	1.1877	1.2167	1.2462	1.2763	1.3382	1.4026
6	1.1262	1.1597	1.1941	1.2293	1.2653	1.3023	1.3401	1.4185	1.5007
7	1.1487	1.1887	1.2299	1.2723	1.3159	1.3609	1.4071	1.5036	1.6058
8	1.1717	1.2184	1.2668	1.3168	1.3686	1.4221	1.4775	1.5938	1.7182
9	1.1951	1.2489	1.3048	1.3629	1.4233	1.4861	1.5513	1.6895	1.8385
10	1.2190	1.2801	1.3439	1.4106	1.4802	1.5530	1.6289	1.7908	1.9672
11	1.2434	1.3121	1.3842	1.4600	1.5395	1.6229	1.7103	1.8983	2.1049
12	1.2682	1.3449	1.4258	1.5111	1.6010	1.6959	1.7959	2.0122	2.2522
13	1.2936	1.3785	1.4685	1.5640	1.6651	1.7722	1.8856	2.1329	2.4098
14	1.3195	1.4130	1.5126	1.6187	1.7317	1.8519	1.9799	2.2609	2.5785
15	1.3459	1.4483	1.5580	1.6753	1.8009	1.9353	2.0789	2.3966	2.7590
16	1.3728	1.4845	1.6047	1.7340	1.8730	2.0224	2.1829	2.5404	2.9522
17	1.4002	1.5216	1.6528	1.7947	1.9479	2.1134	2.2920	2.6928	3.1588
18	1.4282	1.5597	1.7024	1.8575	2.0258	2.2085	2.4066	2.8543	3.3799
19	1.4568	1.5987	1.7535	1.9225	2.1068	2.3079	2.5270	3.0256	3.6165
20	1.4859	1.6386	1.8061	1.9898	2.1911	2.4117	2.6533	3.2071	3.8697
21	1.5157	1.6796	1.8603	2.0594	2.2788	2.5202	2.7860	3.3996	4.1406
22	1.5460	1.7216	1.9161	2.1315	2.3699	2.6337	2.9253	3.6035	4.4304
23	1.5769	1.7646	1.9736	2.2061	2.4647	2.7522	3.0715	3.8197	4.7405
24	1.6084	1.8087	2.0328	2.2833	2.5633	2.8760	3.2251	4.0489	5.0724
25	1.6406	1.8539	2.0938	2.3632	2.6658	3.0054	3.3864	4.2919	5.4274
26	1.6734	1.9003	2.1566	2.4460	2.7725	3.1407	3.5557	4.5494	5.8074
27	1.7069	1.9478	2.2213	2.5316	2.8834	3.2820	3.7335	4.8223	6.2139
28	1.7410	1.9965	2.2879	2.6202	2.9987	3.4297	3.9201	5.1117	6.6488
29	1.7758	2.0464	2.3566	2.7119	3.1187	3.5840	4.1161	5.4184	7.1143
30	1.8114	2.0976	2.4273	2.8068	3.2434	3.7453	4.3219	5.7435	7.6123
31	1.8476	2.1500	2.5001	2.9050	3.3731	3.9139	4.5380	6.0881	8.1451
32	1.8845	2.2038	2.5751	3.0067	3.5081	4.0900	4.7649	6.4534	8.7153
33	1.9222	2.2589	2.6523	3.1119	3.6484	4.2740	5.0032	6.8406	9.3253
34	1.9607	2.3153	2.7319	3.2209	3.7943	4.4664	5.2533	7.2510	9.9781
35	1.9999	2.3732	2.8139	3.3336	3.9461	4.6673	5.5160	7.6861	10.6766
36	2.0399	2.4325	2.8983	3.4503	4.1039	4.8774	5.7918	8.1473	11.4239
37	2.0807	2.4933	2.9852	3.5710	4.2681	5.0969	6.0814	8.6361	12.2236
38	2.1223	2.5557	3.0748	3.6960	4.4388	5.3262	6.3855	9.1543	13.0793
39	2.1647	2.6196	3.1670	3.8254	4.6164	5.5659	6.7048	9.7035	13.9948
40	2.2080	2.6851	3.2620	3.9593	4.8010	5.8164	7.0400	10.2857	14.9745
41	2.2522	2.7522	3.3599	4.0978	4.9931	6.0781	7.3920	10.9029	16.0227
42	2.2972	2.8210	3.4607	4.2413	5.1928	6.3516	7.7616	11.5570	17.1443
43	2.3432	2.8915	3.5645	4.3897	5.4005	6.6374	8.1497	12.2505	18.3444
44	2.3901	2.9638	3.6715	4.5433	5.6165	6.9361	8.5572	12.9855	19.6285
45	2.4379	3.0379	3.7816	4.7024	5.8412	7.2482	8.9850	13.7646	21.0025
46	2.4866	3.1139	3.8950	4.8669	6.0748	7.5744	9.4343	14.5905	22.4726
47	2.5363	3.1917	4.0119	5.0373	6.3178	7.9153	9.9060	15.4659	24.0457
48	2.5871	3.2715	4.1323	5.2136	6.5705	8.2715	10.4013	16.3939	25.7289
49	2.6388	3.3533	4.2562	5.3961	6.8333	8.6437	10.9213	17.3775	27.5299
50	2.6916	3.4371	4.3839	5.5849	7.1067	9.0326	11.4674	18.4202	29.4570

Note: Table 1 is reprinted from Table XIX of Richard Stevens Burington, *Handbook of Mathematical Tables and Formulas* (Sandusky, Ohio: Handbook Publishers, Inc., 1953) by permission of the author and the publishers.

TABLE 2. COMPOUND DISCOUNT: $1 / (1 + r)_n$

Present Value of One Dollar Due at the End of n Years

n	2%	2½%	3%	3½%	4%	4½%	5%	6%	7%
1	.98039	.97561	.97087	.96618	.96154	.95694	.95238	.94340	.93458
2	.96117	.95181	.94260	.93351	.92456	.91573	.90703	.89000	.87344
3	.94232	.92860	.91514	.90194	.88900	.87630	.86384	.83962	.81630
4	.92385	.90595	.88849	.87144	.85480	.83856	.82270	.79209	.76290
5	.90573	.88385	.86261	.84197	.82193	.80245	.78353	.74726	.71299
6	.88797	.86230	.83748	.81350	.79031	.76790	.74622	.70496	.66634
7	.87056	.84127	.81309	.78599	.75992	.73483	.71068	.66506	.62275
8	.85349	.82075	.78941	.75941	.73069	.70319	.67684	.62741	.58201
9	.83676	.80073	.76642	.73373	.70259	.67290	.64461	.59190	.54393
10	.82035	.78120	.74409	.70892	.67556	.64393	.61391	.55839	.50835
11	.80426	.76214	.72242	.68495	.64958	.61620	.58468	.52679	.47509
12	.78849	.74356	.70138	.66178	.62460	.58966	.55684	.49697	.44401
13	.77303	.72542	.68095	.63940	.60057	.56427	.53032	.46884	.41496
14	.75788	.70773	.66112	.61778	.57748	.53997	.50507	.44230	.38782
15	.74301	.69047	.64186	.59689	.55526	.51672	.48102	.41727	.36245
16	.72845	.67362	.62317	.57671	.53391	.49447	.45811	.39365	.33873
17	.71416	.65720	.60502	.55720	.51337	.47318	.43630	.37136	.31657
18	.70016	.64117	.58739	.53836	.49363	.45280	.41552	.35034	.29586
19	.68643	.62553	.57029	.52016	.47464	.43330	.39573	.33051	.27651
20	.67297	.61027	.55368	.50257	.45639	.41464	.37689	.31180	.25842
21	.65978	.59539	.53755	.48557	.43883	.39679	.35894	.29416	.24151
22	.64684	.58086	.52189	.46915	.42196	.37970	.34185	.27751	.22571
23	.63416	.56670	.50669	.45329	.40573	.36335	.32557	.26180	.21095
24	.62172	.55288	.49193	.43796	.39012	.34770	.31007	.24698	.19715
25	.60953	.53939	.47761	.42315	.37512	.33273	.29530	.23300	.18425
26	.59758	.52623	.46369	.40884	.36069	.31840	.28124	.21981	.17220
27	.58586	.51340	.45019	.39501	.34682	.30469	.26785	.20737	.16093
28	.57437	.50088	.43708	.38165	.33348	.29157	.25509	.19563	.15040
29	.56311	.48866	.42435	.36875	.32065	.27902	.24295	.18456	.14056
30	.55207	.47674	.41199	.35628	.30832	.26700	.23138	.17411	.13137
31	.54125	.46511	.39999	.34423	.29646	.25550	.22036	.16425	.12277
32	.53063	.45377	.38834	.33259	.28506	.24450	.20987	.15496	.11474
33	.52023	.44270	.37703	.32134	.27409	.23397	.19987	.14619	.10723
34	.51003	.43191	.36604	.31048	.26355	.22390	.19035	.13791	.10022
35	.50003	.42137	.35538	.29998	.25342	.21425	.18129	.13011	.09366
36	.49022	.41109	.34503	.28983	.24367	.20503	.17266	.12274	.08754
37	.48061	.40107	.33498	.28003	.23430	.19620	.16444	.11580	.08181
38	.47119	.39128	.32523	.27056	.22529	.18775	.15661	.10924	.07646
39	.46195	.38174	.31575	.26141	.21662	.17967	.14915	.10306	.07146
40	.45289	.37243	.30656	.25257	.20829	.17193	.14205	.09722	.06678
41	.44401	.36335	.29763	.24403	.20028	.16453	.13528	.09172	.06241
42	.43530	.35448	.28896	.23578	.19257	.15744	.12884	.08653	.05833
43	.42677	.34584	.28054	.22781	.18517	.15066	.12270	.08163	.05451
44	.41840	.33740	.27237	.22010	.17805	.14417	.11686	.07701	.05095
45	.41020	.32917	.26444	.21266	.17120	.13796	.11130	.07265	.04761
46	.40215	.32115	.25674	.20547	.16461	.13202	.10600	.06854	.04450
47	.39427	.31331	.24926	.19852	.15828	.12634	.10095	.06466	.04159
48	.38654	.30567	.24200	.19181	.15219	.12090	.09614	.06100	.03887
49	.37896	.29822	.23495	.18532	.14634	.11569	.09156	.05755	.03632
50	.37153	.29094	.22811	.17905	.14071	.11071	.08720	.05429	.03395

Note: Table 2 is reprinted from Table XX of Richard Stevens Burington, *Handbook of Mathematical Tables and Formulas* (Sandusky, Ohio: Handbook Publishers, Inc., 1953) by permission of the author and the publishers.

TABLE 3. AMOUNT OF AN ANNUITY

Amount of an Annuity of One Dollar per Year after n Years

n	2%	2½%	3%	3½%	4%	4½%	5%	6%	7%
1	1.0000	1.0000	1.0000	1.0000	1.0000	1.0000	1.0000	1.0000	1.0000
2	2.0200	2.0250	2.0300	2.0350	2.0400	2.0450	2.0500	2.0600	2.0700
3	3.0604	3.0756	3.0909	3.1062	3.1216	3.1370	3.1525	3.1836	3.2149
4	4.1216	4.1525	4.1836	4.2149	4.2465	4.2782	4.3101	4.3746	4.4399
5	5.2040	5.2563	5.3091	5.3625	5.4163	5.4707	5.5256	5.6371	5.7507
6	6.3081	6.3877	6.4684	6.5502	6.6330	6.7169	6.8019	6.9753	7.1533
7	7.4343	7.5474	7.6625	7.7794	7.8983	8.0192	8.1420	8.3938	8.6540
8	8.5830	8.7361	8.8923	9.0517	9.2142	9.3800	9.5491	9.8975	10.2598
9	9.7546	9.9545	10.1591	10.3685	10.5828	10.8021	11.0266	11.4913	11.9780
10	10.9497	11.2034	11.4639	11.7314	12.0061	12.2882	12.5779	13.1808	13.8164
11	12.1687	12.4835	12.8078	13.1420	13.4864	13.8412	14.2068	14.9716	15.7836
12	13.4121	13.7956	14.1920	14.6020	15.0258	15.4640	15.9171	16.8699	17.8885
13	14.6803	15.1404	15.6178	16.1130	16.6268	17.1599	17.7130	18.8821	20.1406
14	15.9739	16.5190	17.0863	17.6770	18.2919	18.9321	19.5986	21.0151	22.5505
15	17.2934	17.9319	18.5989	19.2957	20.0236	20.7841	21.5786	23.2760	25.1290
16	18.6393	19.3802	20.1569	20.9710	21.8245	22.7193	23.6575	25.6725	27.8881
17	20.0121	20.8647	21.7616	22.7050	23.6975	24.7417	25.8404	28.2129	30.8402
18	21.4123	22.3863	23.4144	24.4997	25.6454	26.8551	28.1324	30.9057	33.9990
19	22.8406	23.9460	25.1169	26.3572	27.6712	29.0636	30.5390	33.7600	37.3790
20	24.2974	25.5447	26.8704	28.2797	29.7781	31.3714	33.0660	36.7856	40.9955
21	25.7833	27.1833	28.6765	30.2695	31.9692	33.7831	35.7193	39.9927	44.8652
22	27.2990	28.8629	30.5368	32.3289	34.2480	36.3034	38.5052	43.3923	49.0057
23	28.8450	30.5844	32.4529	34.4604	36.6179	38.9370	41.4305	46.9958	53.4361
24	30.4219	32.3490	34.4265	36.6665	39.0826	41.6892	44.5020	50.8156	58.1767
25	32.0303	34.1578	36.4593	38.9499	41.6459	44.5652	47.7271	54.8645	63.2490
26	33.6709	36.0117	38.5530	41.3131	44.3117	47.5706	51.1135	59.1564	68.6765
27	35.3443	37.9120	40.7096	43.7591	47.0842	50.7113	54.6691	63.7058	74.4838
28	37.0512	39.8598	42.9309	46.2906	49.9676	53.9933	58.4026	68.5281	80.6977
29	38.7922	41.8563	45.2189	48.9108	52.9663	57.4230	62.3227	73.6398	87.3465
30	40.5681	43.9027	47.5754	51.6227	56.0849	61.0071	66.4388	79.0582	94.4608
31	42.3794	46.0003	50.0027	54.4295	59.3283	64.7524	70.7608	84.8017	102.0730
32	44.2270	48.1503	52.5028	57.3345	62.7015	68.6662	75.2988	90.8898	110.2182
33	46.1116	50.3540	55.0778	60.3412	66.2095	72.7562	80.0638	97.3432	118.9334
34	48.0338	52.6129	57.7302	63.4532	69.8579	77.0303	85.0670	104.1838	128.2588
35	49.9945	54.9282	60.4621	66.6740	73.6522	81.4966	90.3203	111.4348	138.2369
36	51.9944	57.3014	63.2759	70.0076	77.5983	86.1640	95.8363	119.1209	148.9135
37	54.0343	59.7339	66.1742	73.4579	81.7022	91.0413	101.6281	127.2681	160.3374
38	56.1149	62.2273	69.1594	77.0289	85.9703	96.1382	107.7095	135.9042	172.5610
39	58.2372	64.7830	72.2342	80.7249	90.4091	101.4644	114.0950	145.0585	185.6403
40	60.4020	67.4026	75.4013	84.5503	95.0255	107.0303	120.7998	154.7620	199.6351
41	62.6100	70.0876	78.6633	88.5095	99.8265	112.8467	127.8398	165.0477	214.6096
42	64.8622	72.8398	82.0232	92.6074	104.8196	118.9248	135.2318	175.9505	230.6322
43	67.1595	75.6608	85.4839	96.8486	110.0124	125.2764	142.9933	187.5076	247.7765
44	69.5027	78.5523	89.0484	101.2383	115.4129	131.9138	151.1430	199.7580	266.1209
45	71.8927	81.5161	92.7199	105.7817	121.0294	138.8500	159.7002	212.7435	285.7493
46	74.3306	84.5540	96.5015	110.4840	126.8706	146.0982	168.6852	226.5081	306.7518
47	76.8172	87.6679	100.3965	115.3510	132.9454	153.6726	178.1194	241.0986	329.2244
48	79.3535	90.8596	104.4084	120.3883	139.2632	161.5879	188.0254	256.5645	353.2701
49	81.9406	94.1311	108.5406	125.6018	145.8337	169.8594	198.4267	272.9584	378.9990
50	84.5794	97.4843	112.7969	130.9979	152.6671	178.5030	209.3480	290.3359	406.5289

Note: Table 3 is reprinted from Table XXI of Richard Stevens Burington, *Handbook of Mathematical Tables and Formulas* (Sandusky, Ohio: Handbook Publishers, Inc., 1953) by permission of the author and the publishers.

TABLE 4. PRESENT VALUE OF AN ANNUITY

Present Value of One Dollar per Year for *n* Years

n	2%	2½%	3%	3½%	4%	4½%	5%	6%	7%
1	.9804	.9756	.9709	.9662	.9615	.9569	.9524	.9434	.9346
2	1.9416	1.9274	1.9135	1.8997	1.8861	1.8727	1.8594	1.8334	1.8080
3	2.8839	2.8560	2.8286	2.8016	2.7751	2.7490	2.7232	2.6730	2.6243
4	3.8077	3.7620	3.7171	3.6731	3.6299	3.5875	3.5460	3.4651	3.3872
5	4.7135	4.6458	4.5797	4.5151	4.4518	4.3900	4.3295	4.2124	4.1002
6	5.6014	5.5081	5.4172	5.3286	5.2421	5.1579	5.0757	4.9173	4.7665
7	6.4720	6.3494	6.2303	6.1145	6.0021	5.8927	5.7864	5.5824	5.3893
8	7.3255	7.1701	7.0197	6.8740	6.7327	6.5959	6.4632	6.2098	5.9713
9	8.1622	7.9709	7.7861	7.6077	7.4353	7.2688	7.1078	6.8017	6.5152
10	8.9826	8.7521	8.5302	8.3166	8.1109	7.9127	7.7217	7.3601	7.0236
11	9.7868	9.5142	9.2526	9.0016	8.7605	8.5289	8.3064	7.8869	7.4987
12	10.5753	10.2578	9.9540	9.6633	9.3851	9.1186	8.8633	8.3838	7.9427
13	11.3484	10.9832	10.6350	10.3027	9.9856	9.6829	9.3936	8.8527	8.3577
14	12.1062	11.6909	11.2961	10.9205	10.5631	10.2228	9.8986	9.2950	8.7455
15	12.8493	12.3814	11.9379	11.5174	11.1184	10.7395	10.3797	9.7122	9.1079
16	13.5777	13.0550	12.5611	12.0941	11.6523	11.2340	10.8378	10.1059	9.4466
17	14.2919	13.7122	13.1661	12.6513	12.1657	11.7072	11.2741	10.4773	9.7632
18	14.9920	14.3534	13.7535	13.1897	12.6593	12.1600	11.6896	10.8276	10.0591
19	15.6785	14.9789	14.3238	13.7098	13.1339	12.5933	12.0853	11.1581	10.3356
20	16.3514	15.5892	14.8775	14.2124	13.5903	13.0079	12.4622	11.4699	10.5940
21	17.0112	16.1845	15.4150	14.6980	14.0292	13.4047	12.8212	11.7641	10.8355
22	17.6580	16.7654	15.9369	15.1671	14.4511	13.7844	13.1630	12.0416	11.0612
23	18.2922	17.3321	16.4436	15.6204	14.8568	14.1478	13.4880	12.3034	11.2722
24	18.9139	17.8850	16.9355	16.0584	15.2470	14.4955	13.7986	12.5504	11.4693
25	19.5235	18.4244	17.4131	16.4815	15.6221	14.8282	14.0939	12.7834	11.6536
26	20.1210	18.9506	17.8768	16.8904	15.9828	15.1466	14.3752	13.0032	11.8258
27	20.7069	19.4640	18.3270	17.2854	16.3296	15.4513	14.6430	13.2105	11.9867
28	21.2813	19.9649	18.7641	17.6670	16.6631	15.7429	14.8981	13.4062	12.1371
29	21.8444	20.4535	19.1885	18.0358	16.9837	16.0219	15.1411	13.5907	12.2777
30	22.3965	20.9303	19.6004	18.3920	17.2920	16.2889	15.3725	13.7648	12.4090
31	22.9377	21.3954	20.0004	18.7363	17.5885	16.5444	15.5928	13.9291	12.5318
32	23.4683	21.8492	20.3888	19.0689	17.8736	16.7889	15.8027	14.0840	12.6466
33	23.9886	22.2919	20.7658	19.3902	18.1476	17.0229	16.0025	14.2302	12.7538
34	24.4986	22.7238	21.1318	19.7007	18.4112	17.2468	16.1929	14.3681	12.8540
35	24.9986	23.1452	21.4872	20.0007	18.6646	17.4610	16.3742	14.4982	12.9477
36	25.4888	23.5563	21.8323	20.2905	18.9083	17.6660	16.5469	14.6210	13.0352
37	25.9695	23.9573	22.1672	20.5705	19.1426	17.8622	16.7113	14.7368	13.1170
38	26.4406	24.3486	22.4925	20.8411	19.3679	18.0500	16.8679	14.8460	13.1935
39	26.9026	24.7303	22.8082	21.1025	19.5845	18.2297	17.0170	14.9491	13.2649
40	27.3555	25.1028	23.1148	21.3551	19.7928	18.4016	17.1591	15.0463	13.3317
41	27.7995	25.4661	23.4124	21.5991	19.9931	18.5661	17.2944	15.1380	13.3941
42	28.2348	25.8206	23.7014	21.8349	20.1856	18.7236	17.4232	15.2245	13.4524
43	28.6616	26.1664	23.9819	22.0627	20.3708	18.8742	17.5459	15.3062	13.5070
44	29.0800	26.5038	24.2543	22.2828	20.5488	19.0184	17.6628	15.3832	13.5579
45	29.4902	26.8330	24.5187	22.4955	20.7200	19.1563	17.7741	15.4558	13.6055
46	29.8923	27.1542	24.7754	22.7009	20.8847	19.2884	17.8801	15.5244	13.6500
47	30.2866	27.4675	25.0247	22.8994	21.0429	19.4147	17.9810	15.5890	13.6910
48	30.6731	27.7732	25.2667	23.0912	21.1951	19.5356	18.0772	15.6500	13.7305
49	31.0521	28.0714	25.5017	23.2766	21.3415	19.6513	18.1687	15.7076	13.7668
50	31.4236	28.3623	25.7298	23.4556	21.4822	19.7620	18.2559	15.7619	13.8007

Note: Table 4 is reprinted from Table XXII of Richard Stevens Burington, *Handbook of Mathematical Tables and Formulas* (Sandusky, Ohio: Handbook Publishers, Inc., 1953) by permission of the author and the publishers.

TABLE 5. MEASURES AND WEIGHTS

(Based on National Bureau of Standards)

LINEAR MEASURE

1 foot	=	12 inches	1 furlong	=	40 rods
1 yard	=	3 feet	1 statute mile	=	8 furlongs
1 fathom	=	6 feet	1 statute mile	=	5280 feet
1 rod	=	5½ yards	1 nautical mile	=	6080¼ feet
		1 league	=	3 miles	

SQUARE MEASURE

1 sq. foot	=	144 sq. inches	1 acre	=	160 sq. rods
1 sq. yard	=	9 sq. feet	1 acre	=	43,560 sq. feet
1 sq. rd	=	30¼ sq. yards	1 sq. mile	=	640 acres

LIQUID MEASURE

1 pint	=	4 gills	1 barrel	=	31½ gallons
1 quart	=	2 pints	1 hogshead	=	2 bbl. (63 gal.)
1 gallon	=	4 quarts	1 tun	=	252 gallons
		1 barrel (petroleum)	=	42 gallons	

TABLE 6. METRIC EQUIVALENTS

(Based on National Bureau of Standards)

LENGTH

Cm.	=	0.3937 in.	In.	=	2.5400 cm.
Meter	=	3.2808 ft.	Ft.	=	0.3048 m.
Meter	=	1.0936 yd.	Yd.	=	0.9144 m.
Km.	=	0.6214 mile	Mile	=	1.6093 km.

AREA

Sq. cm.	=	0.1550 sq. in.	Sq. in.	=	6.4516 sq. cm.
Sq. m.	=	10.7639 sq. ft.	Sq. ft.	=	0.0929 sq. m.
Sq. m.	=	1.1960 sq. yd.	Sq. yd.	=	0.8361 sq. m.
Hectare	=	2.4710 acres	Acre	=	0.4047 hectare
Sq. km.	=	0.3861 sq. mile	Sq. mile	=	2.5900 sq. km.

VOLUME

Cu. cm.	=	0.0610 cu. in.	Cu. in.	=	16.3872 cu. cm.
Cu. m.	=	35.3145 cu. ft.	Cu. ft.	=	0.0283 cu. m.
Cu. m.	=	1.3079 cu. yd.	Cu. yd.	=	0.7646 cu. m.

CAPACITY

Liter	=	61.0250 cu. in.	Cu. in.	=	0.0164 liter
Liter	=	0.0353 cu. ft.	Cu. ft.	=	28.3162 liters
Liter	=	0.2642 gal. (U.S.)	Gal.	=	3.7853 liters
Liter	=	0.0284 bu. (U.S.)	Bu.	=	35.2383 liters

		1000.027 cu. cm.
Liter	=	1.0567 qt. (liquid) or 0.9081 qt. (dry)
		2.2046 lb. of pure water at 4 C. = 1 kg.

WEIGHT

Gram	=	15.4324 grains	Grain	=	0.0648 gm.
Gram	=	0.0353 oz. avdp.	Oz. avdp.	=	28.3495 gm.
Kg.	=	2.2046 lb. avdp.	Lb. avdp.	=	0.4536 kg.
Kg.	=	0.0011 ton (short)	Ton (short)	=	907.1848 kg.
Ton (met.)	=	1.1023 ton (short)	Ton (short)	=	0.9072 ton (met.)
Ton (met.)	=	0.9842 ton (long)	Ton (long)	=	1.0160 ton (met.)

Indexes

INDEX OF TERMS

INDEX OF NAMES

W

Y